THERE ONCE WAS A GORILLA FROM MANILA
WHO DECIDED TO RAISE A CHINCHILLA . . .

MY BABY WENT AND LEFT ME FOR ANOTHER
SHE DIDN'T EVEN SEND ME BACK MY RING . . .

Stuck for a rhyme when you're in the middle of a great idea?
Looking for a better word to end a love song? Tired of clichés or
the same old tired refrains? *The Complete Rhyming Dictionary*
allows you to express yourself with accuracy and originality.

And don't miss these extras:
- Rhyming first names of boys and girls, men and women
- Easily rhymable geographic names
- Common family names or last names
- Archaic, unusual, technical, and slang words

THE COMPLETE RHYMING DICTIONARY

An essential, affordable work
for every home, school, and office library

CLEMENT WOOD was a highly acclaimed American poet, critic,
and poetry teacher. His work "The Glory Road" was made famous
in song by Lawrence Tibbett. His other writing includes *The Craft
of Poetry* and *The Hunters of Heaven*.

THE COMPLETE RHYMING DICTIONARY REVISED

■

INCLUDING

THE POET'S CRAFT BOOK

Edited by
CLEMENT WOOD

Revised by
RONALD J. BOGUS

Published by
Dell Publishing
a division of
Random House, Inc.
New York, New York

Book Design by Diane Stevenson/SNAP-HAUS GRAPHICS

The trademark Laurel® is registered in the U.S. Patent and Trademark Office.

ISBN: 978-0-440-21205-8

Reprinted by arrangement with Doubleday

Printed in the United States of America

Published simultaneously in Canada

April 1992

38   37   36

OPM

ACKNOWLEDGMENTS

Acknowledgment is gratefully made to the following publishers and poets for the portions of their work used as illustrations herein:

Publisher	Author	Poem Source
Boni & Liveright	Samuel Hoffenstein	Poems in Praise of Practically Nothing
The Century Company	Brander Matthews	En Route
Dodd Mead & Company	Austin Dobson	July; The Ballade of Prose and Rhyme
Dodd Mead & Company	Carolyn Wells	Four Limericks
Doubleday, Doran & Company	Rudyard Kipling	The Sons of Martha
Henry Holt & Company	Walter de la Mare	The Listeners
Henry Holt & Company	Robert Frost	The Death of the Hired Man; The Black Cottage; "Out, Out—"
Henry Holt & Company	Carl Sandburg	Cahoots; Cool Tombs; Fog
Houghton, Mifflin & Company	Guy Wetmore Carryll	How the Helpmate of Bluebeard Made Free with a Door
Alfred A. Knopf, Inc.	John V. A. Weaver	Sonnet
The Macmillan Company	Edwin Arlington Robinson	Merlin; Roman Bartholow
Manas Press	Adelaide Crapsey	Triad

FOREWORD

The desire to write poetry, or at least acceptable verse, is almost universal. The achievement of this desire may be gained by anyone, without excessive effort. Almost everyone, at some stage of his or her life, has yielded to the seductive siren, and has done his or her best to write poetry. An adequate craftbook on versification is a necessity, when the urge becomes unconquerable.

When the versifier's problem is narrowed down to rhyme, the need for a convenient and logically arranged rhyming dictionary soon becomes self-evident. Rhyme is exclusively a matter of sound: what the scientists call phonetics. The logically arranged rhyming dictionary must be arranged scientifically by sound; arranged phonetically, to use the scientific word. The arrangement of rhyming sounds in the present volume is wholly phonetic.

The introductory study of versification is so complete, that the book will answer almost every question on technique that any would-be poet or versifier desires to have answered. Moreover, it provides models for the most intricate forms of poetry and versification that English-speaking poets use. Following a model is at best finger exercise. But finger exercise must precede mastery of the keyboard.

The phonetic devices in the volume are simplified from the leading standard dictionaries, by eliminating in general all phonetic signs except those placed above the accented or rhyming syllable. Once these simple phonetic devices are understood and absorbed, poets and versifiers will begin to think accurately, scientifically and phonetically about rhymes and rhyming. The technique of rhyming will become as automatic as the technique of walking: and the poetic energy will be proportionately released for the more effective creation of poetry.

CLEMENT WOOD.
Bozenkill.

CONTENTS

The Consonant Sounds, 114
Sound Does Not Depend on Spelling, 115
This Dictionary Makes Consonance Accurate, 116

THE DICTIONARY OF RHYMING WORDS

THE POET'S CRAFT BOOK

POETRY AND VERSIFICATION

Poetry and Verse

THE WORD *POETRY* is often used loosely to mean whatever embodies the products of imagination and fancy, the finer emotions and the sense of ideal beauty. In this lax usage, men speak of "the poetry of motion," the poetry of Rodin or Wagner, the poetry of dahlia-raising. In accurate usage, poetry is a specific fine art, defined as follows:

Poetry is the expression of thoughts which awake the higher and nobler emotions or their opposites, in words arranged according to some accepted convention.

This definition includes, for instance, Oriental forms of poetry, where the sole convention is the number of syllables to the line. Limiting it to usual Occidental poetry the following definition applies:

Occidental poetry, in its usual form, is the expression of thoughts which awake the higher and nobler emotions or their opposites, in words whose rhythm tends toward uniformity or regularity, rather than toward variety.

Both prose and poetry have rhythm. But the rhythm of prose tends toward variety; and that of poetry toward regularity. There is no definite dividing line; each poet, each reader and appreciator of poetry, must arrive at his or her own dividing line. To some, the borderline of poetry includes only the strict regularity of Pope or Dryden, or—

Baby in the caldron fell,—
   See the grief on mother's brow!
Mother loved her darling well.
   Darling's quite hard-boiled by now.
      Baby, Harry Graham.

No one can quarrel with this, if it is an honest boundary. To others, the magnificent wilder rhythms of Walt Whitman and Lincoln's *Gettysburg Address* are definitely poetry. No one can quarrel with this either.

The test as to subject matter is subjective: does the alleged poem awake in the reader the higher and nobler emotions or their opposites? Each reader, appreciator or poet is final arbiter in this test, as in the test of technique. The expression of thoughts which fail to register emotionally with a reader as poetry is called *verse*. Thus, divided by technique, there are the two classifications, poetry and prose; divided by subject matter and its emotional effect, there are the two classifications, poetry and verse.

Poetry in Human Affairs

Poetry preceded prose, as a persisting form of literary expression. Writing was unknown to early man; and poetry was far better adapted to be retained in the mind than its more plodding relative, prose. The conventions of poetry formed memory devices which prose lacked. In the beginning, lyric cries, folk wisdom, tales of tribal heroes, formal odes of jubilation or lamentation, religious teachings, philosophies, pseudo-sciences, histories of men, demigods, gods and peoples, developed first in the form of poetry.

Insofar as the conventions of poetry were artificial and unnatural, poetry tended constantly to rigidify and petrify. It became artificial and unnatural, whereas prose continued to be natural. Man learned to write, and to preserve his writing in stone, papyrus, sheepskin and paper. At first it was the poetry which was so preserved; at length the art patterns were broken, and humbler and more natural prose began to replace poetry. Today, we look to prose for folk wisdom, actual and fictional narratives, religious teachings, philosophies, scientific writings, and histories. Poetry, as the most concentrated and emotional expression of the soul of man, still should have its place in the lyric outbursts, the songs, of man. But poets, bound by fossilized conventions, have become a tepid social group, their words largely unimportant; and in the large prose tends today to have replaced poetry entirely. Many of the poets today and tomorrow seek to restore poetry to something of its original wide popularity, as a natural and unartificial expression of concentrated emotional speech.

Kings, rulers, statesmen, generals, philosophers, scientists were

once of necessity poets: it was their sole socially acceptable form of expression. This is so no longer. Poets were once doers; they are now at best sayers, increasingly unheard. This is one price of man's extreme specialization. The price paid may be more than the human gain, in this particular.

The Poet's Equipment

The poet, like all artists, is one of the race's sensitives: one of those more finely attuned to phrase the past and the present acceptably, and sense and phrase the future. The first necessary equipment is sincerity. This demands that commonplace phrasings must be avoided, in favor of fresh original expression of individual or group concentrated emotions. If the race recognizes these as its own, to that extent the poet will be hailed as poetically great.

Another essential is technical mastery; adeptness in the craft of poetry, skill in handling all the tools of the trade. Familiarity with all the conventions will enable you to break them and make new ones when your fresh subject matter demands it. Technical mastery is as easy, and no easier, than learning how to raise better peas than your neighbor, or how to build better bridges and skyscrapers than anyone else. Having learned the craft, anyone with an ear for word-music can improvise flawless heroic blank verse or any other form of blank verse by the hour, or improvise elaborately rhymed sonnets with no appreciable hesitation. This is not poetry. But the familiarity with the craft makes the coming of poetry easier, in the rare hours when the poet has a concentrated word that must be said.

Poetic Greatness

One can become great poetically, either in his own sight alone or in the opinions of others, without knowledge of the craft. Homer, Sappho, Villon, Burns, made their own patterns, or poured their burning emotional beauty into ready-made patterns followed without being comprehended. The definitions of patterns were made afterward, from a scholastic study of poetry widely recognized as great. Such greatness may be achieved by anyone today—the entirely satisfactory expression of one's soul's yearnings. But the recognition of

such greatness today will ordinarily be limited to the poet and his immediate circle of admirers within or without his family.

With a complete technical mastery of the craft of poetry, any poet today can achieve complete greatness in his own sight. Whether he is hailed by others as great, and especially whether or not his name is hailed by his own and subsequent generations as great, depends largely on the extent to which his own concentrated heart-utterances express the desires of the race, in a new, fresh and original form. Given such recognition by the race, an enduring poetic greatness has been achieved. The poet can no more control this than Cnut could act as dictator over the tide.

How Poems Come

Verse upon any theme, and in treatment ranging from the most ponderously serious to the most frivolously flippant, can be manufactured at any time. Its technique is comparatively simple. Its devices, meter, rhyme, alliteration, assonance, consonance, stanza arrangement may be mastered as easily as multiplication tables.

Poetry comes differently. It is primarily the intellect that manufactures verse; but the intellect plays only a secondary part in creating poetry. The desire that seeks expression, which it finds in the poem, springs from a deeper basic source than thinking. Man, indeed all forms of life, are compact of desires. The fulfillment of one desire causes others to spring hydra-like from its invisible corpse. Psychologists tell us that dreams are likewise expressions of desire, in the form of desires fulfilled; that is, wish fulfillments. Much thinking is likewise wish fulfillment; there is truth in Wordsworth's dictum, "The wish is father to the thought." There must be, also, an obstacle to the immediate fulfillment of the wish; otherwise the poet would proceed to achieve his wish and have no need for a poem to express it. As one poet has it:

> Singing is sweet; but be sure of this,
> Lips only sing when they cannot kiss.
> *Art*, James Thomson.

Because of the obstacle, a tremendous inner compulsion comes upon the sensitive poet to seek relief by creating his wish-fulfillment in words: and so it is that poems are born. This inner compulsion has, as

one of its names, inspiration. Inspiration blows from no outer sky, but from the universe of desires within. The woman's insistent inner compulsion to deliver her child at the appointed hour is hardly more shatteringly imperative than the true poet's insistent inner commandment to write.

At times the whole poem forms itself within the mind, before the first word is written down. At times a couplet, a single line—perhaps the first, but more often the last—or even a phrase or a mood comes first, with the dominant insistence that it be given the intermittent immortality of writing. The wise procedure for the poet is to write down what comes, as it comes, even if only a single line or less is the result. As far as possible, write out the poem without delay, to prevent another visitor from Porlock's silencing part of your poem forever, as Coleridge's *Kubla Khan* was silenced forever.

When the poem or poetic fragment is written down, the critical intellect comes into play. If technical mastery has become habitual, the intellect may have no changes to suggest. The poet who fails to be a critic as well is usually his own self-slayer. More extended poems, of course, require more preparation and slower writing and criticism. In all cases the danger is more in the overuse of the intellect than in the use of inspiration.

Originality in Poetry

The easiest way, in poetry, is to rephrase your own emotional reactions in the words and phrases created by the favorite poets of the past: so that a thing is "white as the driven snow," or "red as a June rose." When these similes were first invented, they were creations; their repetition, unless in slightly altered form, is plagiarism or borrowing. Second-rate poets distrust their own vision, which differs in every case from that of every other person in the world; and hence sag into such uncreative repetitions. It is wisest to be true to your own differing vision and seek to expand the boundaries of poetry by stating your own desires in your own terms.

The weakness of much verse and some poetry of the past is partly traceable to unoriginal teachers of English or versification, who advised their pupils to saturate themselves in this or that poet, and then write. Keats, saturated in Spenser, took a long time to overcome this echoey quality and emerge into the glorious highland of his *Hyperion*. Many lesser souls never emerge. It is valuable to know the

poetry of the past and love it. But the critical brain should carefully root out every echo, every imitation—unless some alteration in phrasing or meaning makes the altered phrase your own creation.

The present double decade has splendidly altered the technique of versification in poetry, by the addition of freer rhythms, consonance, and other devices in the direction of natural speech. It has altered the themes and subjects of poetry as much, until the *Verboten* sign is unknown to the present generations of poets, as far as themes are concerned. If the speech is natural and conversational; the treatment sincere and original; the craftsmanship matured—there is no reason in the poet's effort to withhold him from a seat among the immortals.

■ II ■

THE TECHNIQUE OF
VERSIFICATION: RHYTHM

Accent and Rhythm

RHYTHM IS THE emphasis structure of successive sounds. It is easy to understand and not easy to define. In prose and poetry it means the flow of accented and unaccented syllables. It may be defined as:

The successive rise and fall of sounds, in pitch, stress, or speed; when used of words, depending on accents, pauses, or durational quantities.

In classical Greek and Latin poetry, rhythm was not based on accent, but on the conventionalized time it took to pronounce syllables. Syllables were not accented or unaccented, as in modern poetry, from a standpoint of versification; but were long or short. Since two consonants occurring together made a syllable long, and a short vowel made a syllable short when followed by one consonant, the word *honest* was scanned as short-long: the rhythmic stress occurring on the second syllable, not on the first, as with us. *Honest,* pronounced in the classical Greek or Roman way, would be ta-TUM; with us, it is pronounced rhythmically TUM-ta, the accent falling on the first syllable.

This one example will show why verse written in English according to classical rules of scansion, based upon long and short syllables instead of accent, is unnatural and only slightly pleasing to the ear. It is no more at home among modern poets writing in English than Greek clothing or the Greek language would be.

Modern poetry written in English must be in words whose rhythm, based upon accent, tends toward uniformity rather than toward variety. Both prose and poetry have rhythm, the stream or flow of accented and unaccented syllables; in prose the pattern constantly varies, while in poetry it approaches some sort of regularity. This is clearly poetry:

> Music, when soft voices die,
> Vibrates in the memory—
> Odours, when sweet violets sicken,
> Live within the sense they quicken.
>
> Rose leaves, when the rose is dead,
> Are heap'd for the beloved's bed;
> And so thy thoughts, when Thou art gone,
> Love itself shall slumber on.
> > *"Music, When Soft Voices Die,"*
> > Percy Bysshe Shelley.

It would be no less poetry if it were set up:

> *Music, when soft voices die, vibrates in the memory.*
> *Odours, when sweet violets sicken, live within the sense*
> *they quicken. Rose leaves, when the rose is dead, are*
> *heap'd for the beloved's bed.*
> *And so thy thoughts, when Thou art gone, Love itself*
> *shall slumber on.*

It did not take the line division to make this poetry. Technically, the tendency toward regularity in the rhythm made it definitely verse and not prose, while its emotional appeal, to most people, makes it poetry. It is equally poetic in either typographic form. Set up the opening of the first chapter of this book in the same line division:

> The word poetry is often used
> Loosely to mean whatever embodies
> The products of imagination
> And fancy, the finer emotions
>
> And the sense of ideal beauty.
> In this lax usage, men speak of
> "The poetry of motion," the poetry
> Of Rodin or Wagner, the poetry

This is prose. No magic worked by the line division can bring it any closer to poetry. Only a comparative regularity in the alternation of accented and unaccented syllables can make it acceptable verse; this, plus the proper emotional appeal, alone can make it poetry.

Meter and Metric Feet

Meter is a comparatively regular rhythm in verse or poetry. There are four common metric feet used in English verse. Their names are taken over from classic durational or quantity meters. In the examples below, the accented syllable is marked thus (/), and the unaccented syllables thus (⌣). These feet are:

Name of Foot	Scansion	Description	Example	Example Scanned	Accent pronunciation
Iamb	⌣ /	Unaccent—accent	Delight	De-light	ta-TUM
Trochee	/ ⌣	Accent—unaccent	Going	Go-ing	TUM-ta
Anapest	⌣ ⌣ /	Unaccent—unaccent—accent	Appertain	Ap-per-tain	ta-ta-TUM
Dactyl	/ ⌣ ⌣	Accent—unaccent—unaccent	Merrily	Mer-ri-ly	TUM-ta-ta

The first two feet listed below are occasionally encountered in English verse, the third rarely or never.

Spondee	/ /	Accent—accent	Headlong	Head-long	TUM-TUM
Amphibrach	⌣ / ⌣	Unaccent—accent—unaccent	Believing	Be-liev-ing	ta-TUM-ta
Pyrrhic	⌣ ⌣	Unaccent—unaccent	with a	with a	ta-ta

In practice, the spondee may be used as an iamb or as a trochee; in combination, we may have—

$$\text{In head} \mid \text{-long flight}$$

in which the word is used as a trochee;

$$\text{He plunged} \mid \text{head-long}$$

in which the word is used as an iamb.

In actual verse and poetry, never forget that the actual rhythm of the words, as normally uttered in a conversational tone, differs from the artificial scansion pattern adopted. Take one of the most regular five-foot iambic lines in the language:

> The curfew tolls the knell of parting day.
> *Elegy Written in a Country Churchyard*,
> Thomas Gray.

Scanned normally, as this would be spoken, we have the following natural scansion:

> The curfew | tolls | the knell | of parting | day.

Here we have one iamb, two feet consisting of mere accented syllables for which we have no name, and two feet of three syllables each (unaccent—accent—unaccent, or amphibrachs). Yet this is described as an ideal iambic line, because the pattern indubitably is:

> ta TUM   ta TUM   ta TUM   ta TUM   ta TUM

To make the actual line fit the planned iambic pattern, we have to divide words as follows:

> The cur- | few tolls | the knell | of part- | ing day.

Absolutely natural iambic lines are rare:

> And dwell | upon | your grave | when you | are dead.
> *The Comedy of Errors*, William Shakespeare.

A repetition of such lines would be monotonous, unnatural and intrinsically unpoetic.

To show a still further group of variations, the opening of Hamlet's most famous soliloquy, commencing "To be or not to be," is theoretically in the same iambic five-foot pattern: three lines, each consisting theoretically of five ta-TUM's. The actual scansion brings in strange and unusual feet, or groups of unaccents with one accent, and shows that these three lines have only four actual feet apiece (a foot being, in

English, normally grouped around one accent), where the pattern called for five in each line:

> Tŏ bé | ŏr nót tŏ bé. | Thăt | ĭs thē quéstion.
> Whéther | 'tĭs nóblĕr | ĭn thē mínd | tŏ súffer
> Thē slíngs | ănd árrŏws | ŏf ŏutrágĕoŭs | fórtŭne . . .
>
> *Hamlet,* William Shakespeare.

Here are four feet of two syllables each (two iambs and two trochees); four of three syllables each (three amphibrachs and one anapest); one of one syllable; and three of four syllables each (two of one type, one of another). And only four natural feet to each line.

This is acceptable five-foot iambic verse, in the hands of the world's greatest master. In later plays, his variations became more extreme, until at times his rhythms were less regular than Whitman's typical free verse or polyrhythmic poetry.

What is desired, in metric poetry, is a regular pattern, with restrained freedom and variety in its use. The poet should learn to scan his poetry—that is, to mark the accented and unaccented syllables as above, and then to divide it both into the natural speech rhythm and into the artificial pattern rhythm. There is no need for pride, if the poetry is excessively regular. As a rule, that means that it is strained and unnatural in phrasing, and to that extent falls below true greatness in technique.

In reading poetry aloud or to oneself, avoid most of all an unnatural singsong. Never read the lines from *Hamlet* as if they had been printed:

> to *BE* or *NOT* to *BE* that *IS* the *QUES*tion.
> whe*THER* 'tis *NO*bler *IN* the *MIND* to *SUF*fer
> the *SLINGS* and *AR*rows *OF* out*RA*geous *FOR*tune . . .

Instead, read this and all other poetry as naturally as if it were unpatterned prose. The pattern is there and will make itself felt. Excellence in reading depends upon naturalness in expression.

Iambic Verse

The commonest line pattern in English verse is based upon the iamb ($\smile$ /). Many more words in English are trochees than iambs.

Iambic is the preferred pattern because such trochaic words are normally introduced by a one-syllabled unaccented article, preposition, or the like. Normally lines do not open with the trochee *hoping*, but rather with such a phrase as *in hoping, for hoping, and hoping, this hoping, if hoping,* and so on.

Lines name the metric pattern and are described by the type of foot and the number of feet to the line. Thus a one-foot iambic line could be written:

> All hail!

A two-foot iambic line would be:

> All hail to you!

A three-foot iambic line would be:

> All hail to you, my friends!

A four-foot iambic line would be:

> All hail to you, my worthy friends!

A five-foot iambic line would be:

> All hail to you, my wholly worthy friends!

Note how naturally trochaic words like *wholly* and *worthy* fit into this iambic pattern. This line might have been:

> In hailing friendship's wholly worthy sons,

in which case four words (*hailing, friendship's, wholly, worthy*) are complete trochees in themselves, yet are transformed into word-split units in the iambic pattern, by the introductory unaccented word *in* and the concluding accented word *sons*. This is an entirely legitimate following of the iambic pattern, which can be most easily remembered as:

ta TUM   ta TUM   ta TUM   ta TUM   ta TUM.

A word ending on an accented syllable is said to have a *masculine* ending; one ending on an unaccented syllable, a *feminine* ending. The iambic pattern may be used with a feminine ending: that is, with the addition of an unaccented syllable to the last foot. A stanza of five lines, successively one-, two-, three-, four-, and five-foot iambic lines with feminine endings, could be manufactured easily:

> Good morning,
> Benignant April,
> With all your rainbow blossoms,
> With birds all carolling their rapture,
> With love alive within the hearts of maidens.

The scansion for this would be:

> Good morn- | ing,
> Benig- | nant A- | pril,
> With all | your rain- | bow blos- | soms,
> With birds | all car- | olling | their rap- |ture,
> With love | alive | within | the hearts | of maid- | ens.

This is often described as if the first line, for instance, were a two-foot line, with one syllable missing, and is called catalectic verse. The reality is that of an iambic foot followed by a loose or unattached, unaccented syllable.

Writing iambic verse is as easy as writing any form of verse. Get the metrical pattern firmly in mind:

>   ta TUM   ta TUM   ta TUM   ta TUM

and then proceed to let the words flow into this pattern.

Iambic verse may be altered into trochaic at any time, by *adding* an accented syllable to each line's beginning or by *removing* the opening unaccented syllable. The process may be reversed as easily, thus changing trochaic verse into iambic. Start with this iambic version:

> And then the little Hiawatha
> Remarked unto the old Nokomis,
> I know that hills are edged with valleys.

By adding an accented syllable at the beginning of each line, this becomes trochaic:

> Now and then the little Hiawatha
> Said aloud unto the old Nokomis,
> Well I know that hills are edged with valleys.

By removing the opening unaccented syllable in each iambic line above, the lines are four-foot trochaic:

> Then the little Hiawatha
> Said unto the old Nokomis,
> All the hills are edged with valleys.

This is the regular meter of Longfellow's *Hiawatha* and is as easy to write as iambic verse.

Trochaic Verse

Trochaic verse is less usual in English than iambic, because the custom of the language is to introduce most remarks with an unaccented syllable or word. Based upon the trochee ($/\smile$), the pattern is, in the case of four-foot trochees,

> TUM-ta   TUM-ta   TUM-ta   TUM-ta

Hiawatha opens upon this pattern:

> Should you ask me, whence these stories,
> Whence these legends and traditions,
> With the odours of the forest,
> With the dew and damp of meadows.
>   *Hiawatha,* Henry Wadsworth Longfellow.

In natural accent the first three of the lines quoted have only two accents apiece, and not four: so that the natural scansion, as of the third line, is

> With the odours | of the forest.

Shakespeare commences a witches' incantation with the abrupt staccato natural accent:

> Round about the cauldron go;
> In the poisoned entrails throw.
> Toad, that under cold stone
> Days and nights has thirty-one
> Sweltered venom sleeping got,
> Boil thou first i' the charmed pot.
>> *Macbeth*, William Shakespeare.

An interesting variation here is the use of *cold* as a dissyllable, as if it were pronounced *có-ŏld*. It may be regarded as the one-syllabled *cold*, followed by a pause consuming the length of time it would take to pronounce an unaccented syllable. In any case, it is an effective variant device.

Trochaic verse might certainly be described with propriety as iambic verse, with the introductory unaccented syllable omitted in each line. The description is unimportant; the important thing is to choose, understand, and use adequately the pattern, whatever it is called.

Again, in the sixth line quoted above from *Macbeth*, there is an extra unaccented syllable, a sort of grace note, added: making the second foot in reality a dactyl:

$$\text{Bóil thŏu} \mid \text{fírst ĭ' thĕ} \mid \text{chármĕd} \mid \text{pót.}$$

If preferred, though it is less usual, this could be scanned slightly differently:

$$\text{Bóil thŏu} \mid \text{fírst ĭ'} \mid \text{thĕ chármĕd} \mid \text{pót,}$$

in which case there is an amphibrach in the third foot; or it might be scanned:

$$\text{Bóil thŏu} \mid \text{fírst ĭ'} \mid \text{thĕ chár-} \mid \text{mĕd pót,}$$

regarding it as two trochees followed by two iambs. But the accepted pattern is trochaic four-foot, and the custom is to prefer the first scansion given. At any time, within reason dictated by the poet's own

inner ear and sense of music, the substitution of an anapest or a dactyl for an iamb or a trochee is permitted. Or the substitution of a spondee (//), and any of the other feet (iamb, trochee, dactyl or spondee, as well as amphibrach, etc.) may be substituted for a foot in anapestic verse. Similar substitutions may take place in dactylic verse. The best poetry contains variety within uniformity.

Notice that in the trochaic lines from *Macbeth* the last unaccented syllable is omitted in every line. This again gives an example of catalectic verse. The name is unimportant: a trochaic line may end on a masculine ending as easily as an iambic line ends on a feminine ending. A dactylic line may end on a trochee or an accented syllable; an anapestic line may have its extra unaccented syllable, or even two of them, without losing its anapestic character. Variety in uniformity ...

Anapestic Verse

The anapest (⌣⌣/) is a foot of three syllables, the first two unaccented, the last accented. It may be described as an iamb with an extra unaccented syllable added before it. It may be indicated ta ta TUM, so that a three-foot anapestic pattern would be:

ta ta TUM   ta ta TUM   ta ta TUM.

A typical line following this pattern would be:

To the end of the world in the dawn.

The English language has more accented syllables than many others, and a succession of two unaccented syllables is comparatively infrequent. Constantly the anapestic pattern is broken by a foot called the *amphimacer* (/⌣/), accent—unaccent—accent, giving us a result such as:

Let me go anywhere I can find,

scanned as anapestic thus:

⌣ ⌣ ´ | ⌣ ⌣ ´ | ⌣ ⌣ ´
Let me go | anywhere | I can find,

but having a natural scansion consisting of three amphimacers:

$$\text{Let me go} \mid \text{anywhere} \mid \text{I can find.}$$

There are so few natural anapests in the language that this is usual and permitted. The same thing applies to dactylic verse. Even more unusual three-syllabled feet appear, each with two accents: the antibacchius (//⌣), the bacchius (⌣//), the tribrach (⌣⌣⌣), the molossus (///). In anapestic and dactylic verse, a fourth syllable, usually unaccented, again like a grace note, may appear in any foot. So long as such variations please the inner ear, the inner sense of word music, they are aids.

The natural poet will always make his own patterns, knowing that poetry is self-created and not devised by rigid rules.

Dactylic Verse

The dactyl (/⌣⌣) is a foot of three syllables, the first accented, the next two unaccented. It may be described as a trochee with an extra unaccented syllable added after it. Here is an illustration:

> Cannon to right of them,
> Cannon to left of them,
> Cannon in front of them
>   Volleyed and thundered;
> Stormed at with shot and shell,
> Boldly they fought, and well. . . .
> *The Charge of the Light Brigade*, Alfred Tennyson.

Scanned as dactylic verse, this would appear:

> Cannon to | right of them,
> Cannon to | left of them,
> Cannon in | front of them
>   Volleyed and | thundered;
> Stormed at with | shot and shell,
> Boldly they | fought, and well.

As a matter of fact, these last two lines would have a different natural scansion, including amphimacers:

Stormed at with | shot and shell,
Boldly they | fought, and well.

Once the technique of scansion is mastered, the poet must be his own court of last appeal upon it.

Dactylic verse is not wholly at home in English; and amphibrachic verse (using as its norm the amphibrach, ‿/‿) is as much of an alien. These feet become excessively monotonous in long poems, though they may be used with advantage in brief lyrics.

Variations in Metric Verse

The use of variations in metric verse is widespread. The development of every poet of importance, whose technique did not begin and remain rigid and crystallized, has been in the direction of more and more variety. This is displayed impressively by the development of Shakespeare and of Keats. Little such development is shown in the technique of more rigid minor poets. A few examples must suffice. Shakespeare in his final peak period wrote lines whose natural scansion was as loose as:

A malady

Most in- | cident | to maids; | bold oxlips and
The crown imperial; lilies of all kinds,

The flow- | er-de-luce | being one! O, these | I lack. . . .

The Winter's Tale, William Shakespeare.

The most unusual usage is the ending of the second line in the extraordinary foot which seems a spondee followed by a pyrrhic, (//‿‿). The reverse foot opens a line in one of his sonnets,

Of the wide world | dreaming | on things | to come.

Sonnet CVII, William Shakespeare.

One of the most praised lines in Keats is:

Robs not | one light | seed from | the feath- | er'd grass.
>   *Hyperion*, John Keats.

Here two spondees introduce the rest of the line, the scansion being as if his pattern were—

TUM TUM   TUM TUM   TUM ta   ta TUM   ta TUM

Keats has at least one line, in the same pattern, consisting of five trochees:

Thea! | Thea! | Thea! | Where is | Saturn?
>   *Hyperion*, John Keats.

Robert Frost has such masterly lines as the following, in the same five-foot iambic pattern:

> And spread her apron to it. She put out her hand. . . .
>   *The Death of the Hired Man*, Robert Frost.

> Strange how such innocence gets its own way.
>   *The Black Cottage*, Robert Frost.

> And the saw snarled and rattled, snarled and rattled.
>   *"Out, Out—"*, Robert Frost.

> So. But the hand was gone already.
>   *"Out, Out—"*, Robert Frost.

In this last line the monosyllable *So* is followed by a pause that takes the place of a foot and a half. One of Frost's most triumphant variations is:

> Little—less—nothing! And that ended it.
>   *"Out, Out—"*, Robert Frost.

In natural scansion, this would be:

Little— | less— | nothing! | And that ended it

A common variation is an alternation of iamb and anapest, as in this old English ballad:

> Ŏ Al- | ĭsŏn Gróss, | thăt lives | ĭn yŏn tówer.
> *Alison Gross*, Old English Ballad.

We find the reverse of this order in a Browning lyric,

> Whĕre thĕ chaf- | fĭnch sings | ŏn thĕ or- | chărd bough. . . .
> *Home-Thoughts, from Abroad*, Robert Browning.

So numerous are the variations to which the metric pattern in English can be adapted, to the greater naturalness of the poetry.

Accent Pattern Instead of Metric

Coleridge, in one poem, abandoned the formal metric foot altogether, in favor of a rediscovered Old English method of letting the line pattern consist of a definite number of accents, with any number of unaccented syllables, occurring in any order. Here are the opening lines:

> 'Tĭs thĕ mid- | dlĕ ŏf night | bў thĕ cas- | tlĕ clock,
> Ănd thĕ owls | hăve awak- | enĕd thĕ crow- | ĭng cock.
> Tu- | whit! | Tu- | whoo!
> Ănd hark, | agáin; | thĕ crow- | ĭng cock
> Hŏw drow- | sĭly | ĭt crew.
> *Christabel*, Samuel Taylor Coleridge.

Thomas Hood uses lines consisting of only three accented syllables,

> Stitch! | Stitch! | Stitch!
> Ĭn pov- | ertў, hung- | er ănd dirt. . . .
> *The Song of the Shirt*, Thomas Hood.

This follows the same method of accent versification. Walter de la Mare's most famous poem is built around a pattern of three accents to the line, as the second and fourth line below indicate; he uses unaccented syllables where he pleases:

> But on- | ly a host | of phantom listeners
> That dwelt | in the lone | house then,
> Stood lis- | tening in the qui- | et of the moonlight |
> To that voice | from the world | of men.
>
> *The Listeners,* Walter de la Mare.

Other modern poets have done as much, or more. Variety within uniformity . . .

Blank Verse and Free Verse

Blank verse means simply unrhymed verse. Any line pattern, if unrhymed, is blank verse. *Heroic blank verse* is unrhymed five-foot iambic poetry or verse. Most of Shakespeare is written in heroic blank verse. *Heroic couplets,* beloved of Dryden and Pope, are pairs of five-foot iambic lines rhymed with each other.

Free verse may be rhymed or unrhymed, although it is usually unrhymed, since rhyming is an even more unnatural convention of poetry than meter; and the poet who has abandoned formal meter will hardly, as a rule, still use the device of rhyming. Free verse is verse without a metric pattern, but with a wider pattern than meter allows. It still tends toward regularity, rather than variety, and the final court of appeals as to whether any example should be classified as poetry or prose from a standpoint of content, or as verse or prose from a standpoint of technique, is the individual poet or reader himself. To many readers, the following are all poetry:

> Lord, thou hast been our dwelling-place in all generations. Before the mountains were brought forth, or ever thou hadst formed the earth and the world, even from everlasting to everlasting, thou art God. Thou turnest man to destruction; and sayest, return, ye children of men. . . .
>
> *The Ninetieth Psalm.*

But, in a larger sense, we cannot dedicate—we cannot conse-crate—we cannot hallow—this ground. The brave men, living and dead, who struggled here, have consecrated it far above our poor power to add or to detract. The world will little note, nor long remember, what we say here; but it can never forget what they did here. . . .

The Gettysburg Address, Abraham Lincoln.

Out of the cradle endlessly rocking, out of the mockingbird's throat, the musical shuttle, out of the Ninth-month midnight, over the sterile sands, and the fields beyond, where the child leaving his bed wandered alone, bareheaded, barefoot, down from the show-ered halo, up from the mystic play of shadows twining and twisting as if they were alive. . . .

Out of the Cradle, Endlessly Rocking,
Walt Whitman.

Walt Whitman used the artificial line division of poetry to pre-sent the third of these selections; the King James version of the Bible and Lincoln used the natural line division so familiar in the printing of prose. Little or nothing is added by the artificial line division:

Out of the cradle endlessly rocking,
Out of the mocking-bird's throat, the musical shuttle,
Out of the Ninth-month midnight,
Over the sterile sands, and the fields beyond, where the
  child leaving his bed wandered alone, bareheaded,
  barefoot,
Down from the showered halo,
Up from the mystic play of shadows twining and
  twisting as if they were alive. . . .

It is poetry, to many, in either form; and the first form is the more natural and readable. Scan the Whitman selection, or any of the oth-ers, and the tendency toward regularity of rhythm becomes apparent: a wider regularity, perhaps only an up rhythm or a down rhythm, but still inevitably there. This distinguishes free verse from prose, from the technical point of view.

At times writers of free verse let their lines reach surprising lengths, no matter how lovely the music is: thus Sandburg,

Pocahontas' body, lovely as a poplar, sweet as a red haw in Novem-
ber or a pawpaw in May, did she wonder? does she remember?
in the dust, in the cool tombs. . . .

Cool Tombs, Carl Sandburg.

Again the lines can be extremely brief:

> It sits looking
> over harbor and city
> on silent haunches
> and then moves on.
> *Fog,* Carl Sandburg.

The free verse writer devises his own line-division pattern. This
form, eliminating the devices of meter and rhyme, calls on the poet to
avoid the inconsequential and the trivial, and to write down only his
important utterances. If rhyme is a shelter for mediocrity, as Shelley
wrote in his preface to *The Revolt of Islam,* free verse is a test of the
best that the poet has in him.

Line Length in Verse

Oliver Wendell Holmes, himself a doctor, advanced the theory that
line length in verse marked physiologically the normal breathing of
the poet. In other words, a breath should be taken at the end of each
line; and the line should be no longer than the poet's ability to hold
his breath. No artificial line division is used in prose, to indicate
where a breath should be taken. There is no greater reason for artificial line division in poetry. It still remains true that the long Greek
lines, each consisting of six feet, called for huge-breasted warrior-
bards to chant them; that the norm of English verse, the five-foot
iambic line, indicates a lesser chest expansion in the typical English
poet; and that the briefer modern tendency shows a further deterioration in the chest expansion of poets.

Where poetry consists in *end-stopped* lines—lines with a natural
pause at the end of each line—there is more reason for an artificial
line division. Shakespeare began so; many poets never get beyond
this, in the main. But when we come to poetry like—

> We are such stuff
> As dreams are made on, and our little life

> Is rounded with a sleep,
> > *The Tempest*, William Shakespeare.

the break comes after *on*, and not after *stuff* or *life;* and the last reason for the artificial line division has vanished.

A sonnet set up in this manner appears:

> *O bitter moon, O cold and bitter moon, climbing your midnight hillside of bleak sky, the earth, as you, once knew a blazing noon. Night brings the silver hour when she will die. We shall be cold as you are, and as bitter, icily circling toward a tepid fire, playing at life with our deceitful glitter, past joy, past hope, forever past desire.*
> *Yet still the forest lifts its leafy wings to flutter for a while before the chill. And still the careless heart is gay, and sings in the green temple on the dusty hill. And the gulls tumble, and the homing ships peer for the harbor. . . .*
> *And the sand drips.*
> > *The Flight of the Eagle*, v, Clement Wood.

In an earlier volume, this had appeared with the usual line division of poetry as ordinarily printed. Rhyme can occur of course in ordinary prose, although this usage is extremely rare. Where the rhythm of verse is used, as in the sonnet quoted, it is possible for poets to use the line and paragraph division usual to prose, if this is desired.

IMPORTANT CLASSICAL TERMS FOR POETIC DEVICES

VERSES AND GROUPS OF VERSES

Classical Name	*Common Name, or Explanation*
Monometer	A verse containing one metrical foot.
Dimeter	A verse containing two metrical feet.
Dipody	A measure consisting of two metrical feet; a ditrochee.
Trimeter	A verse containing three metrical feet.
Tetrameter	A verse containing four metrical feet.
Pentameter	A verse containing five metrical feet.
Hexameter	A verse containing six metrical feet.

Heptameter	A verse containing seven metrical feet.
Octometer	A verse containing eight metrical feet.
Distich	A strophic verse of two lines, usually called a couplet today.

UNUSUAL METRIC FEET

Tribrach	Three unaccented syllables	˘ ˘ ˘
Molossus	Three accented syllables	/ / /
Amphimacer	Accent, unaccent, accent	/ ˘ /
Bacchius	Unaccent, accent, accent	˘ / /
Antibacchius	Accent, accent, unaccent	/ / ˘
Ditrochee	Two trochees regarded as a compound foot	/ ˘ / ˘
Paeon	Accent, unaccent, unaccent, unaccent	/ ˘ ˘ ˘
Choriamb	Accent, unaccent, unaccent, accent	/ ˘ ˘ /
Epitrite	Three accents and one unaccent: of the first, second, third or fourth class, depending on the location of the unaccented syllable	/ / / ˘

OTHER TERMS

Classical Name	*Explanation*
Acatalectic Verse	Verse not defective in the last foot; verse complete in its number of syllables.
Arsis	The lighter or unstressed part of a foot, especially in quantitative verse; later, the accented syllable of a foot.
Caesura	A break in a verse caused by the ending of a word within a foot. A *masculine caesura* follows the thesis or stressed part of a foot. A *feminine caesura* follows the arsis or *caesura* comes after the third half foot, which means in the second foot; a *penthemimeral caesura*, after the fifth half foot; a *hepthemimeral caesura*, after the seventh half foot; and so on. A *bucolic caesura*, in dactylic hexameter, is a caesura occurring in the fourth foot, especially in pastoral poetry.

Catalectic Verse	Verse lacking a syllable at the beginning, or terminating in an imperfect foot.
Diaeresis, Dieresis	The break caused by the coincidence of the end of a foot with the end of a word. *Bucolic diaeresis,* a diaeresis occurring in the fourth foot, especially in pastoral poetry.
Enjambement	The extension of the sentence beyond the limitations of the distich.
Ictus	Metrical stress.
Thesis	The heavier or stressed part of a foot in classical prosody, especially in quantitative verse; later, the unaccented syllable or syllables of a verse.

THE TECHNIQUE OF VERSIFICATION: RHYME

Correct and Incorrect Rhyme

RHYME IS AS simple to define as rhythm is difficult.

Rhyme is the identity in sound of an accented vowel in a word, usually the last one accented, and of all consonantal and vowel sounds following it; with a difference in the sound of the consonant immediately preceding the accented vowel.

Rhyme deals exclusively with sounds and has nothing to do with spelling. The rhyming dictionary terminating this book is strictly phonetic and therefore logical and useful.

Correct rhymes may be spelled alike:

ate, plate, mate, abate, syncopate.

They may be spelled differently:

ate, bait, straight, freight.

In this case the spelling is immaterial.

So called "eye rhymes"—that is, words spelled alike that look alike but are pronounced differently—are not rhymes at all; they slip into versification, if at all, as *consonance,* which will be discussed later. That is, the incorrect rhyme

earth, hearth

so popular among English versifiers, is no more a rhyme than the following sets of words identically spelled, but pronounced differently:

cow, blow
climber, timber
finger, ginger, singer
cough, enough, plough, though, through.

Identities do not rhyme, no matter what the spelling is; since the preceding consonantal sounds must differ. The following are identities, and not rhymes:

bay, obey
bare, bear, forbear
laying, overlaying
ability, possibility, probability.

Sounds *almost* alike, after the identical accented vowel sounds, do not rhyme. These are properly called assonance and have not succeeded as a versification device in English. Examples are:

main, game, reins, lamed
hate, shape, played
feed, sleet, creep
sandwich, orange, lozenge
childhood, wildwood
Norfolk, war talk
anguish, Flatbush
silver, deliver

You can find examples of incorrect rhymes in poems by many accepted poets, and in a much higher percentage of popular songs and newspaper versification. Two of the above examples were taken directly out of songs nationally popular. Slovenly rhyming is one of the sure signs of mediocrity in versification. Learn correct rhyming first; then, if you wish to break the rule you understand, that is your privilege.

The language's poverty in rhyming has caused the following almost-rhymes to become widely accepted:

given, Heaven; bosom, blossom; shadow, meadow;
God, road; war, more; bliss, is; was, grass.

Among widely used "eye rhymes," which are not rhymes at all, but mere identities in spelling, are:

earth, hearth; bare, are; north, forth; real, steal.

Bosom-blossom, was-grass are combinations of consonance and assonance; *bliss-is* is assonance; the others in the first list are consonance. The first three pairs in the second set are acceptable consonance; *real, steal* is an attempt to rhyme a two-syllabled word with a one-syllabled one and has no justification from any standpoint. Use consonance or assonance purposely, if desired; but always know that this is not correct rhyming.

If the poet is tone-deaf as to sounds, it is best to rely upon the phonetic symbols above each group of rhyming words in the rhyming dictionary that terminates this book, or upon dictionary markings. Many people cannot distinguish the obvious difference in sounds between this pair of words, which do not rhyme:

north, forth.

Take away the *th* sound, and many people still hear no difference between this pair of words, which do not rhyme:

nor, fore.

Take away the *r* sound, and some people still hear no difference between this pair of words, which do not rhyme:

gnaw, foe.

Gnaw plus *r* plus *th* cannot rhyme with *foe* plus *r* plus *th*. If in doubt as to such off-rhymes, follow the phonetic markings.

A third common error in rhyming comes from such mispronunciations as dropping a terminal *-g.* These do not rhyme:

martin, parting.
herding, burden.

They may be rhymed colloquially, that is, in quoted words, as follows:

martin, partin',
herdin', burden,

the latter being not quite a rhyme at that. But unless writing colloquially, do not use such incorrect rhymes as those given first above. A
similar error comes from ignoring the *r* sounds, which causes such
off-rhymes as:

> court (pronounced *cou't*, like *coat*), boat
> Lord (pronounced *Lawd*), gaud.

Rhymes can be made of two or more words. Here are examples of
perfect rhymes:

> satin, flat in.
> Quentin, went in.
> pray tin, hate in.

Such couplings are more appropriate to light and humorous verse
than to serious poetry. Rhyming must always give the effect of unobtrusive *naturalness*, or it fails of its proper effect.

Robert Browning is in a class by himself in fantastic many-word
rhymings and near-rhymings, often in serious verse:

> The wolf, fox, bear and monkey
> By piping advice in one key. . . .
> *Pacchiarotto, and How He Worked*
> *in Distemper, et cetera,*
> > Robert Browning.

This is not a rhyme, because *monkey* is, phonetically, a rhyme sound
for *ŭngki*, or at best *ŭngke;* and *one key* is, phonetically, a rhyme
sound for *ŭnkē*, the unguessed *g* sound in the first spoiling it as a
rhyme. Again, in the same poem, he uses this fantastic coupling:

> While, treading down rose and ranunculus,
> You *Tommy-make-room-for-your-uncle-us!*

Ranunculus has its rhyme sound *ungk'-ū-lus;* the next line, *ŭngk'-
ōōl-us:* a minor difference, but enough to spoil the rhyme. Much
closer is Byron's celebrated couplet:

> O ye lords of ladies intel*lectual,*
> Inform us truly, have they not hen*pecked you all?*
> > *Don Juan*, I, xxii, Lord Byron.

The unaccented last syllable of the first line differs from the unaccented last syllable of the second with the difference of *ă* and *ô*. Barham furnishes many perfect many-worded rhymes, such as:

> Should it even set fire to one's castle and *burn it, you're*
> Amply insured for both building and *furniture*. . . .
> > *Sir Rupert the Fearless,*
> > Richard Harris Barham (Thomas Ingoldsby).

Samuel Hoffenstein furnishes a splendid example:

> You haven't the nerve to take bi*chloride;*
> You lie up nights till you're gaunt and *sore-eyed,*
> > *Poems in Praise of Practically Nothing,*
> > Samuel Hoffenstein.

In using such rhyme combinations, it is wise to put the combination with the inevitable sound first; *bichloride;* following this with the combination of words to rhyme with it. Thus W. S. Gilbert, a master rhymester, uses in this order:

> monotony, got any.
> cerebellum too, tell 'em to.

In light and humorous verse, such rhyming cleverness is a crown; in serious verse, if used sparingly, it is permitted.

Function and Types of Rhyme

In serious verse, since obvious cleverness defeats the appeal to the serious emotions, rhyming should be unobtrusive. To have your rhyme words merely conveniences demanded by your rhyming pattern is one of the chief faults of rhymed verse.

Rhyme is a potent shaper. Once you have written down a line of verse or poetry, and intend to have the next line or the next line but one rhyme with it, your choice of terminal words for the rhyming line is limited by the limited rhyming resources of the language. If a poet commences,

> October is the wildest month,

he has estopped himself from any rhyme, since *month* has no rhyme in English.

Assuming that the first line's rhyming word has certain rhyming mates, the choice of terminal rhyme words for the rhyming line is limited to these; and the direction of the poet's thought and its expression must be deflected into some natural use of one of these rhyming mate words. Rhyming is a brain stimulant and may even spur on the poetic imagination. The meaning of the planned poem may have been clear in the mind; but its expression, if rhyme is used, must work in limited fields, and only the master achieves in these that finality of natural utterance which is one of the charms of great poetry.

To the authentic poet, especially the living poet, there is no such thing as *poetic license:* the right to warp and twist the language out of its natural order or grammar, to suit the exigencies of rhyme. Mr. Browning continued his *Tommy-make-room-for-your-uncle-us* couplet with this:

> Quick march! for Xanthippe, my housemaid,
> If once on your pates she a souse made. . . .
> I would not for worlds be your place in,
> Recipient of slops from the basin!

What Browning meant, in the direct natural order, was:

> Quick march! for Xanthippe, my housemaid,
> If once she made a souse on your pates,
> I would not for worlds be in your place,
> Recipient of slops from the basin!

Even this is unnatural; the real order would be "Quick march! for if once Xanthippe, my housemaid, made . . ." etc. Let us suppose that inspiration worked with him in the erratic fashion quoted above. Then would be the time for the critical sense to come in, and rigorously to eliminate all such evidences of poetic license—inversions, ungrammatical constructions, and the like. Not one has a place in poetry, more than in speech.

This is a rigid rule to lay down. It is not any individual's rule. It is the rule that Shakespeare followed when he wrote:

> Tomorrow, and tomorrow, and tomorrow,
> Creeps in this petty pace from day to day

> To the last syllable of recorded time,
> And all our yesterdays have lighted fools
> The way to dusty death. Out, out, brief candle!
> Life's but a walking shadow, a poor player
> That struts and frets his hour upon the stage
> And then is heard no more; it is a tale
> Told by an idiot, full of sound and fury,
> Signifying nothing.
>
> *Macbeth*, William Shakespeare.

This was written some three hundred years ago. There is not an obsolete or even archaic word in it, not a strained construction, not an inversion or instance of ungrammatical poetic license. The quotation given in fragmentary form from Browning, which includes *ranunculus, homunculus, skoramis,* and countless inversions, was outdated long ago: the words of Shakespeare live. The best of Burns, of Shelley, of the Keats of *Hyperion*, of the best among the modern poets, always follows this rule: no inversions, no archaisms, no poetic license. This is the price of a chance for wide poetic greatness.

To return to the strict technique of rhyming, one-syllabled rhymes are called single or masculine rhymes. Examples are:

> we, flee, sea, apostrophe, harmony.
> disk, tamarisk, odalisque.
> fling, sing, carolling.

In the last pair of the first grouping, and the third rhymes in the others, note that only a secondary accent falls on the rhyming syllable. This is enough. A rhyme may be more smothered, if read naturally—a modern variation in which it may be said that an accented syllable is rhymed with an unaccented one: such as *anguish, wish; ring, wedding.* Used sparingly, this is effective.

Two-syllabled rhymes are called double or feminine rhymes. Examples are:

> ocean, motion, devotion.
> traded, aided, play did.
> see us, flee us.

Three-syllabled rhymes are called triple rhymes. Examples:

saleable, mailable.
lyrical, miracle, empirical, satirical.
going now, blowing now.
rest of it, best of it, palimpsest of it.

There may be rhymes, especially in light verse, of four or even more syllables. A rhyme like the one last given shows little cleverness, since it is merely "rest, best, palimpsest" with the phrase "of it" added. The lack of cleverness makes it more suitable for serious poetry than for light verse.

End rhyme is used at the end of the lines. Here is an example, the rhyming words being italicized, and the rhyme scheme indicated by the corresponding numerals:

> Gather ye rose-buds while ye *may*,   1
>   Old Time is still *a-flying;*   2
> And this same flower that smiles *today*,   1
>   Tomorrow will be *dying.*   2
>   *Counsel to Girls*, Robert Herrick.

Rhyme 1 is a single or masculine rhyme; rhyme 2 is a double or feminine rhyme.

Internal rhyme is rhyme used within the line, to give added effectiveness by a closer repetition of the rhyming sounds.

> "Each day, all day," these poor folk say,
> "In the same old *year-long, drear-long* way,
> We *weave* in the *mills* and *heave* in the *kilns*,
> We *sieve* mine-meshes under the hills,
> And *thieve* much gold from the Devil's bank tills,
> To *relieve*, O God, what manner of ills?"
>   *The Symphony*, Sidney Lanier.

Here *year-long* rhymes internally with *drear-long; weave, heave, sieve, thieve* and *relieve* are further internal rhymes; and *mills* is an internal rhyme to *kilns* and the three next end rhymes.

Undesirable Rhymes

Incorrect rhymes, or rhymes constructed by straining the natural expression into inversions and grammatical perversions, excused on

the outworn plea of poetic license, are always undesirable. Quite as undesirable are rhymes which are hackneyed and overworked, such as:

>kiss, bliss.
>yearn, burn; yearning, burning.
>love, dove, above.
>fire, desire.
>trees, breeze.

These are unobjectionable technically. But they have been so used and overused by other poets that the only excuse for them today is use in an entirely new manner.

It is the fact that most rhymes have been comparatively overworked that has caused the tendency toward consonance, which is such a marked feature of modern poetry, from Emily Dickinson onward.

Alliteration

Alliteration, like rhyme, is a repetition of sounds. But the sound repeated is only the initial consonant of syllables or words. This was one of the major devices of Anglo-Saxon poetry, which did not use rhyme. Langland's *Piers Plowman* opens:

>In a *s*ummer *s*eason, when *s*oft was the *s*un,
>I *sh*ope me in *sh*roudes, as I a *sh*eep were
>*The Vision of Piers Plowman*, William Langland.

Alliteration is used effectively by later poets in connection with rhyme, as this example illustrates:

>Whether *t*empter sent, or whether *t*empest *t*ossed thee here ashore,
>*D*esolate yet all un*d*aunted, on this *d*esert land enchanted,
>In this *h*ome by *H*orror *h*aunted, tell me truly, I implore.
>>>*The Raven*, Edgar Allan Poe.

If not overused, this is highly effective. Swinburne was one of the masters of alliteration, tending to overuse it, as in—

>The *l*ilies and *l*anguors of *v*irtue
> For the *r*oses and *r*apture of *v*ice.
>*Dolores*, Algernon Charles Swinburne.

Where there is no sense of unnaturalness in the repetition of alliterative sounds, it may be successfully employed.

Assonance

Assonance, called also *vowel rhyme*, consists in the identity of the final accented vowel sound, with dissimilarity in the subsequent consonantal and vowel sounds. It was used in Provençal and Old French poetry, and is still used in Spanish. George Eliot tried unsuccessfully to introduce it into English, the assonances being italicized:

> Maiden crowned with glossy *blackness,*
> Lithe as panther forest-*roaming,*
> Long-armed naead, when she *dances,*
> On the stream of ether *floating,*
> Bright, O bright Fedalma!
> *Song of Joan,* in *The Spanish Gipsy,*
> George Eliot.

The repetition here is not sufficiently marked to make this device popular in English versification. Typical groups of assonantal masculine or single-rhymed endings are:

> grab, crack, had, tan, sham, hang, fat
> face, shade, hate, pain, claim, male
> led, wreck, hem, then, set, step
> bide, kine, fight, pipe, wise, advice

In feminine endings, we would have:

> aiming, faded, scraping, hailing, painter, lateness
> roaming, floated, coping, goader, golden
> coming, dumbness, stubborn, rustle

Unpopular so far, at any time assonance may achieve a popularity in English versification.

Consonance

Consonance, also loosely called *off rhymes, sour rhymes* and *analyzed rhymes,* consists in an identity of all consonantal and vowel

sounds after the accented vowel; and a difference in the accented vowels. An improvised model would be:

> There's a golden willow
> > Underneath a hill,
>
> By a babbling shallow
> > Brook and waterfall;
>
> And a mill-wheel turning
> > Under moon and sun,
>
> As if gently scorning
> > Time and tide and man.

There can be any combination of end and internal consonance with end or internal rhyme in the same poem, according to the best modern practice: the poet himself being the judge of what form is most pleasing to his inner sense of music, and that of his prospective readers.

Edna St. Vincent Millay, in *The Poet and His Book*, uses these pairs of words in consonance:

> *worry, bury; withered, gathered; cluttered, spattered; quarrel, laurel; hunters, winter's; valleys, bellies.*

She also twice uses assonance:

> cupboard, upward; only, homely.

Elinor Wylie uses such instances of consonance as:

> *bloody, body; people, ripple; mourner, corner; primer, dreamer; standard, pondered; noble, trouble; music, physic; Circe, hearsay; Vulcan, falcon; languish, distinguish; lost, ghost; sword, lord; suns, bronze;*

and many more. Emily Dickinson is more lavish in her use of consonance than any of these.

The reason has been hinted before: the limited field of rhymes in the language, in spite of the impressive length of any rhyming dictionary. One advantage of a phonetic rhyming dictionary is that it makes the use of precise and accurate consonance possible. Words are arranged by rhyme and not by consonance; and yet the phonetic arrangement gives a start toward arriving at accurate consonance. If

the following method is used, consonance can be achieved by little more effort than is required for rhyme.

There are five *a* sounds that occur in accented syllables; three *e'*s; two *i*'s; six *o*'s; and three *u*'s, or a total of nineteen vowel sounds appearing in accented syllables. Most of these sets are grouped together: most of the *a*'s; two of the *e*'s (omitting the *e* followed by *r*, which appears only when *er* is reached); both of the *i*'s, and so on. Thus $\bar{A}D$ is followed by $\check{A}D$ and this by $\ddot{A}D$, so that we may proceed directly from rhyming sounds like *aid* to *sad* and then to *charade*. In double rhymes, $\bar{O}'l\bar{e}$, $\hat{O}L'\bar{e}$ and $\check{O}L'\bar{e}$ follow in regular sequence; thus *holy*, *Macaulay* and *folly* are near neighbors.

Suppose it is desired to locate all the consonance sounds possible for a line ending with *holy*. Turn under the *a*'s to all the phonetic symbols similar to $\bar{O}'l\bar{e}$—$\bar{A}'l\bar{e}$ (as, *daily*), $\check{A}L'\bar{e}$ (as, *alley*); under *e*, to $\bar{E}'l\bar{e}$ (as, *freely*), $\check{E}L'\bar{e}$ (as, *jelly*); under *i*, to $\bar{I}'l\bar{e}$ (as, *dryly*) and $\check{I}L'\bar{e}$ (as, *hilly*); also under *o* to $\overline{OO}L'\bar{e}$ (as, *woolly*), $OIL'\bar{e}$ (as, *oily*); under *u*, to $\bar{U}'l\bar{e}$ (as *truly*) and $\check{U}L'\bar{e}$ (as, *dully*). Look up also $OUL'\bar{e}$ and other possible vowel combinations, to make sure there are no rhyme sounds under them. And now the poet has an accurate test to see which words are in precise consonance with *holy*, and which are not.

Thus this most modern of all sound-repetition devices in English versification can be achieved most perfectly through the use of a phonetic rhyming dictionary. The phonetic symbols, of course, must be in precise alphabetical order. Turn, under each of the five vowels (not forgetting the vowel sounds OI, $\overline{OO}$, and OU come alphabetically also), to the vowel followed by the identical consonant and vowel sounds following the accented vowel in the rhymed syllable you wish consonances for; and all consonances that the lists of words afford will be found.

There is small adventure in rhyming, except in the made rhymes of two or more words more common to light verse. Compilers of rhyming dictionaries have completed the adventure long ago. There is great adventure in the use of consonance, which expands the sound-repetition resources of the language. It is possible to write a poem where not one of the consonance couplets has been used before. The adventurous will not overlook this.

Your Mental Rhyming Dictionary

As times it is inconvenient or impossible to have a rhyming dictionary available. Especially where the poet desires to write such a

Single (Vowel)	Double	Triple	Rare
B	BL		BW
	BR		
—	CH		
D	DR		DW
F	FL		
	FR		
G	GL		GW
	GR		
H			
J			
K (C)	KL (CL)		
	KR (CR)		
L			
M			
N			
P	PL		PW
	PR		
Q (KW)			
R			
S	SH	SHR	
	SK (SC)	SKR (SCR)	
	SL		
	SM		
	SN		
	SP	SPL	
		SPR	
	SQ (SKW)		
	ST	STR	
	SV		
	SW		
T	TH		
	th	thR	
	TR		
	TW		
V			VL
W			
Y			
Z			ZH
			ZL

piece of formal verse as a ballade, requiring fourteen rhymes on one sound, no two of which could be identical, it is advisable to be able to improvise your own temporary rhyming dictionary.

The method is simple. First write down all the single, double and triple consonantal sounds you can remember. It is not necessary to write down all of them, although for your convenience the list on page 41 is approximately complete.

Having jotted down as many of these as you remember, test the rhyme sound desired against this table, and write out the results. Thus, if the rhymes to *aye*, the long *Ā* sound, are desired, the poet would get, to begin with, of the single consonantal sounds:

> *aye, bay, day, fay, gay, hay, jay, kay or cay, lay, may, nay or neigh, pay, ray, say, decolleté for the* t *sound, survey for the* v *sound, way, yea.*

Be careful, when a one-syllabled rhyme in such an instance is missing, to use ingenuity to find longer words with the desired rhyme, as *decolleté, survey.*

Then, for the double consonantal sound rhymes, the following could be added:

> *redoublé for the* bl *sound, bray, dray, flay, fray, gray, clay, McCrae for the* cr *sound, play, pray or prey, shay, risqué for the* sk *sound, slay, dismay perhaps for the* sm *sound, stay, sway, they, tray, tway.*

In addition, the triple consonantal sounds would give:

> *splay, spray, stray.*

Altogether this has furnished thirty-nine rhymes for *aye:* and this is more than enough to satisfy the requirements of any formal verse.

Suppose only four rhymes for the purposes of the rhyming pattern are needed, and the poet decides to use *huge* as one of them. Using the above rhyming dictionary, only a group of *f* rhymes are discovered— *febrifuge, subterfuge, vermifuge* and so on; and perhaps, if the poet is expert in pronunciation, *gamboge,* which also rhymes with it. But no fourth rhyming sound. The *huge* rhyme sound would then have to be discarded and some other sound tried.

Try a double rhyme, *ended.* Using this mental rhyming dictionary, the poet discovers:

ended, bended, fended or defended, Jen did, Len did, mended or amended, depended, rended, tended or attended, vended, wended,

and, using double and triple consonantal initial sounds,

blended, friended and befriended, expended for sp, *extended for* st, *trended, then did, splendid,*

and this can be supplemented with *men did* and many other two-word rhymes. Here are at least eighteen rhyming mates, which can be used as the 2 rhyme in a ballade, which requires fourteen rhyming mates.

So even if the rhyming dictionary is left behind, a mental rhyming dictionary can always be improvised, once the mechanism is learned.

▪ IV ▪

STANZA PATTERNS

The Couplet

A SINGLE LINE of poetry is called, technically, a *verse* of poetry. A series of lines arranged formally as a part of a poem is called a *stanza*. Stanza forms may be rigid, with a fixed order of sequence as to line length, meter, or rhyme; or they may be mere divisions of a poem, corresponding to the paragraphs of prose.

The simplest stanza is one of two lines, called a couplet. The word *couplet* is used to mean either a two-line poem, or a two-line stanza— that is, a part of a poem; and this is equally true of triplets or tercets, quatrains and so on. It may be rhymed:

> "Where are you going, my pretty maid?" 1
> "I'm going a milking, sir," she said. 1
> *Mother Goose's Nursery Rhymes.*

Naturally, if our stanza has only two lines, it can be rhymed in only one way: each line followed immediately by its rhyming mate. This is called rhyming in couplets, and is indicated by 1, 1. The second rhyme sound used in the poem would be designated by 2, the third by 3, and so on. Thus a series of couplet stanzas, if rhymed, would be rhymed 1, 1; 2; 3, 3; and so on. This is called *couplet rhyming,* a term used of any lines rhymed in this fashion, even when not divided into separate couplet stanzas.

Five-foot iambic lines rhymed couplet fashion are called *heroic couplets.* This was the favorite measure employed by Dryden and Pope, who enriched the language with many polished quotations:

> Vice is a monster of so frightful mien 1
> As, to be hated, needs but to be seen; 1
> Yet seen too oft, familiar with her face, 2
> We first endure, then pity, then embrace. 2
> *An Essay on Man*, Alexander Pope.

These pairs of lines are not stanzas, much less complete two-line poems. Thus *couplet* is used with the third meaning of a method of rhyming—the 1, 1; 2, 2 method.

A couplet need not be rhymed: it may be an unrhymed two-line poem, or two-line stanza. It may be in any rhythm or combination of rhythms.

The Triplet or Tercet

A group of three lines, whether a complete poem or a stanza, is called a triplet, or tercet. This is not as common a form as the couplet or the four-line form, the quatrain. An example is:

> A still small voice spake unto me,   1
> "Life is so full of misery,   1
> Were it not better not to be?"   1
> *The Two Voices,* Alfred Tennyson.

It is clear that with three lines to work from, the lines in such a group might be rhymed 1, 1, 2, in which the third line rhymes with nothing in the triplet; or 1, 2, 2; or 1, 2, 1. In the case of groups of triplet stanzas, the rhymes may be interlocked:

> Make me thy lyre, even as the forest is: 1
> What if my leaves are falling like its own!   2
> The tumult of thy mighty harmonies   1
>
> Will take from both a deep autumnal tone,   2
> Sweet though in sadness. Be thou, Spirit fierce,   3
> My spirit! Be thou me, impetuous one!   2
>
> Drive my dead thoughts over the universe   3
> Like withered leaves to quicken a new birth!   4
> And, by the incantation of this verse,   3
>
> Scatter, as from an unextinguished hearth   4
> Ashes and sparks, my words among mankind!   5
> Be through my lips to unawakened earth   4
>
> The trumpet of a prophecy! O wind,   5
> If Winter comes, can Spring be far behind?   5
> *Ode to the West Wind,* Percy Bysshe Shelley.

This interlocked rhyming, where the unrhymed middle line of one triplet becomes the rhymed first and third lines of the next, the whole ending with a thirteenth and fourteenth line rhyming with the unrhymed central line of the preceding triplet, is a special Italian verse stanza form, called *terza rima*. As Shelley used it, it might be regarded as an apt variation of the Shakespearean sonnet. It may be constituted of less or more triplets, always followed by such a concluding couplet.

Notice, in the hands of this master, the rhyming devices. *Is-harmonies* illustrates rhyming a primary accent with a secondary one: and the secondary one is an indeterminate sound, more often rhymed with *seas* than with *is*, which gives it the effect of partial consonance. *Fierce-universe* is consonance, not rhyme, as is *birth-hearth-earth*, long defended as an "eye rhyme," but admissible as consonance. The same is true of *mankind-wind-behind*. It is incorrect to pronounce the noun *wind* as if it were the verb *to wind; wind* here rhymed with *thinned*, and is in consonance with *behind*.

Triplets may be in any rhythm, including free verse or polyrhythm. And they may be unrhymed:

> I have had playmates, I have had companions,
> In my days of childhood, in my joyful school-days;
> All, all are gone, the old familiar faces.
>
> I have been laughing, I have been carousing,
> Drinking late, sitting late, with my bosom cronies;
> All, all are gone, the old familiar faces.
> > *The Old Familiar Faces,* Charles Lamb.

In this poem Lamb invented his own pattern—unrhymed six-foot trochaic in the main, with seven feet in the fifth line; and with the terminal line of each triplet a refrain, repeated without alteration. Any poet may make his own pattern for any poem he wishes; and, if it finds favor, it may become a standard pattern.

The Quatrain

A quatrain is a stanza or poem of four lines. This is the most popular brief stanza in English versification, and has a variety of familiar rhyme schemes. Ordinary *ballad meter* was originally seven-foot iambic rhymed couplets:

> As Robin Hood in the forest strayed, all under the greenwood
>   tree,   1
> He was aware of a brave young man, as fine as fine might be.   1
> > > *Old English Ballad.*

As normally printed today, this becomes a quatrain, with the first and
third lines unrhymed, and only the second and fourth rhyming—a
rhyme scheme that may be used with other meters as well, and with
any number of feet to each line:

> > As Robin Hood in the forest strayed,   1
> > > All under the greenwood tree,   2
> > He was aware of a brave young man,   3
> > > As fine as fine might be.   2

Almost as popular is the quatrain rhymed on alternate lines:

> > A violet by a mossy stone   1
> > > Half-hidden from the eye!   2
> > —Fair as a star, when only one   1
> > > Is shining in the sky.   2
> > *The Lost Love,* William Wordsworth.

Quatrains may be rhymed couplet-wise:

> > Tiger, tiger, burning bright   1
> > In the forests of the night,   1
> > What immortal hand or eye   2
> > Could frame thy fearful symmetry?   2
> > > *The Tiger,* William Blake.

Note that this is not indented: that is, that line two is set directly
under line one. The purpose of *indentation* is primarily to show the
rhyme scheme: lines rhyming with each other may be normally set
beneath each other, as in the two previous examples. Indentation is
used either to show identities of rhyme, or to center briefer lines in a
stanza or poem.

    The *In Memoriam* stanza is built upon a four-foot iambic pattern,
rhymed as follows:

> > Ring out old shapes of foul disease;   1
> > > Ring out the narrowing lust of gold;   2

> Ring out the thousand wars of old,   2
> Ring in the thousand years of peace.   1
> > *In Memoriam,* Alfred Tennyson.

Edward Fitzgerald's translation or recreation of the quatrains or *Rubáiyát* of Omar Khayyám has one of the most famous quatrain rhyme patterns in the language, using five-foot iambic lines:

> The Moving Finger writes; and, having writ,   1
> Moves on: nor all your Piety nor Wit   1
> > Shall lure it back to cancel half a Line   2
> Nor all your Tears wash out a Word of it.   1
> > *The Rubáiyát of Omar Khayyám,*
> > translated by Edward Fitzgerald.

Other possible quatrain rhyme arrangements are: 1, 1, 1, 1; 1, 1, 1, 2; 2, 2, 2, 2; 1, 2, 1, 1; 1, 2, 3, 1; 1, 1, 2, 3; 1, 2, 3, 3; 1, 2, 2, 3; and no doubt others. Hereafter, no additional rhyming patterns will be listed, since by now it should be understood that none is forbidden.

As for the number of feet to the line in these quatrains, the number for the better-known patterns is as follows:

Ballad Meter, 4, 3, 4, 3. Called also Long Meter in hymns.
In Memoriam, 4, 4, 4, 4.
Rubáiyát, 5, 5, 5, 5.
Short Meter (in hymns), 3, 3, 4, 3.

This last was popular in the sixteenth century as *Poulter's measure.* These four are all in iambic lines. Of course, any metric foot or combination of feet may be employed. It need not be repeated again that the quatrain, as any other stanza, may be unrhymed or may be in polyrhythm.

Stanzas of More Than Four Lines

A five-line stanza or poem is called a cinquain. Adelaide Crapsey invented one containing 1, 2, 3, 4 and 1 iambic feet respectively in the lines:

These be
Three silent things:
The falling snow . . . the hour
Before the dawn . . . the mouth of one
Just dead.

Triad, Adelaide Crapsey.

A rhymed cinquain is used in one of Shelley's best-known odes:

Hail to thee, blithe Spirit!	1
Bird thou never wert,	2
That from heaven, or near it,	1
Pourest thy full heart	2
In profuse strains of unpremeditated art.	2

To a Skylark, Percy Bysshe Shelley.

Notice how the indentation centers the briefer lines, as well as indicating, in the first four, rhyming mates. The number of feet here is 3, 3, 3, 3, 6. A terminal six-foot iambic line is called an *Alexandrine;* this was constantly used with iambic five-foot lines as a terminal.

Shelley uses this pattern throughout his poem *To a Skylark*. Poe, another master craftsman, altered his rhyme and meter pattern from stanza to stanza in his greatest lyrics. The familiar love song *To Helen* ("Helen, thy beauty is to me—") has, in his three cinquains or five-line stanzas, these three different rhyme arrangements; 1, 2, 1, 2, 2; 3, 4, 3, 4, 3; 5, 6, 6, 5, 6. To his inner musical ear, these changes were more musical than regularity could have been.

A six-line stanza is called a sextet or sestet. Here is an example:

Fear no more the heat o' the sun	1
Nor the furious winter's rages;	2
Thou thy worldly task hast done,	1
Home art gone and ta'en thy wages:	2
Golden lads and girls all must,	3
As chimney-sweepers, come to dust.	3

Dirge from *Cymbeline*, William Shakespeare.

The trochaic pattern here is four-foot lines. One of the favorite stanzas of Robert Burns has the iambic pattern of 4, 4, 4, 2, 4, 2; as in his *To a Field-Mouse:*

Wee, sleekit, cow'rin', tim'rous beastie,   1
O what a panic's in thy breastie!   1
Thou need na start awa sae hasty,   1
    Wi' bickering brattle!   2
I wad be laith to rin and chase thee   1
    Wi' murd'ring pattle!   2
           To a Field-Mouse, Robert Burns.

The consonance *beastie, breastie, hasty, chase thee* was to be expected in the hands of a master. A popular pattern (using an unusual trochaic 4, 4, 2, 4, 4, 2 measure) was used by Whittier:

And if I should live to be   1
The last leaf upon the tree   1
    In the spring,   2
Let them laugh, as I do now,   3
At the old, forsaken bough   3
    Where I cling.   2
    The Last Leaf, Oliver Wendell Holmes.

This may be used in longer stanzas, with a scheme such as 1, 1, 1, 2, 3, 3, 3, 2, a variant of this being popularized by Tennyson:

Willows whiten, aspens quiver,   1
Little breezes dusk and shiver   1
Through the wave that runs for ever   1
By the island in the river   1
    Flowing down to Camelot.   2
Four gray walls, and four gray towers,   3
Overlook a space of flowers,   3
And the silent isle embowers   3
    The Lady of Shalott.   2
       The Lady of Shalott, Alfred Tennyson.

This stanza is called a *tail rhyme* stanza and is a mere elaboration of the pattern of *The Last Leaf.*

Certain Other Stanzas

It may seem like profanation to some, to subject to the critical scalpel such a masterpiece as Keats's *Ode to a Grecian Urn.* But the

poem suffers no loss from the process, for the reader returns to it to
find it all uninjured in the end; and no other method will permit an
understanding of the technical achievement involved in such lasting
beauty. Here are five ten-line stanzas. Each opens with a 1, 2, 1, 2
sequence. Thereafter there are differences. The first and last have the
next six lines 3, 4, 5, 4, 3, 5; the fourth and fifth use instead 3, 4, 5,
3, 4, 5; while the second has 3, 4, 5, 3, 5, 4.

A famous seven-lined stanza is called *Rhyme Royal*. This was used
by James I of Scotland in his *The Kinges Quhair*, and repeatedly by
Chaucer and others. Here is a typical use by Chaucer:

> To you, my purse, and to none other wight   1
> Complain I, for ye be my lady dear.   2
> I am full sorry, now that ye be light,   1
> For, certes, ye now make be heavy cheer.   2
> Me were as lief-y laid upon my bier   2
> For which unto your mercy thus I cry,   3
> Be heavy again, or elles mote I die.   3
> *The Complaint to His Empty Purse*, Geoffrey Chaucer.

This has a terminal couplet rhyming 3, 3, which breaks the flow of
the narrative somewhat. To avoid this, the *Canopus* stanza points a
way out:

The night's mysterious wings pulsed thru the dark,   1
The night's mysterious noises cracked and shivered,   2
And where their fingers met a visible spark   1
Seemed to leap forth at them, and pulsed and quivered   2
Throughout them both. Their thickened tongues were dumb,   3
The pretty words of star-lore undelivered,   2
The pretty words that found no breath would come.   3
                                         Canopus, Clement Wood.

Note here also that the use of some feminine or double rhymes with
single or masculine rhymes is effective. This is especially effective in
a Shakespearean sonnet.

Ottava rima is an Italian stanza adopted in English by many poets.
It is an eight-line stanza, composed of a sestet rhymed alternately, followed by a terminal rhyming couplet. The Italians use their heroic
meter, eleven syllables to the line, in it; the English prefer iambic
five-foot measure. Spenser, Milton, and Keats used it, and Byron preferred it, as in his *Don Juan*:

But "why then publish?"—There are no rewards   1
   Of fame or profit when the world grows weary.   2
I ask in turn,—Why do you play at cards?   1
   Why drink? Why read?—To make some hour
     less dreary.   2
It occupies me to turn back regards   1
   On what I've seen or pondered, sad or cheery;   2
And what I write I cast upon the stream   3
To sink or swim—I have had at least my dream.   3

           Don Juan, Lord Byron.

Again note the use of double and single rhymes in the same stanza, quite often effective.

The *Spenserian stanza* was invented by Edmund Spenser, and has long been used in serious dignified verse. The eight opening five-foot iambic lines are terminated by an Alexandrine, or six-foot iambic line; the pattern may be seen in this opening of Keats's poem, which uses the stanza throughout:

St. Agnes' Eve—ah, bitter chill it was!   1
   The owl, for all his feathers, was acold.   2
The hare limped trembling through the frozen grass,   1
   And silent was the flock in woolly fold.   2
   Numb was the Beadsman's fingers while he told   2
His rosary, and while his frosted breath   3
   Like pious incense from a censer old,   2
Seemed taking flight for heaven without a death.   3
Past the sweet Virgin's picture, while his prayer he saith.   3

           The Eve of St. Agnes, John Keats.

Terza rima is an iambic rhythm, usually of five feet to the line. It is usually written continuously, and not in stanzas. It consists of groups of three lines, rhymed 1, 2, 1; but the rhyming sound of the middle line, 2, becomes the first and third line of the next group; and so on. The end of the canto or poem is a couplet, tying up the rhyme sound left loose as the central line terminal sound in the preceding triplet. Thus it is a sort of chain verse, its rhyme scheme proceeding: 1, 2, 1; 2, 3, 2; 3, 4, 3; 4, 5, 4; . . . . . . n-1, n, n-1; n, n. Shelley, in his *Ode to the West Wind,* used this in fourteen-line groups, separating the triplets and concluding couplet as if they were separate stanzas.

It is advisable for the poet or versifier to spend some time in the

pleasant chore of analyzing the favorite poems of the great poets—the odes of Keats, the sonnets of Shakespeare, the greater lyrics of Poe, and so on. Scansion will indicate the meter employed; and the numeral system 1, 1, 2, 2 will mark for you the rhyming pattern. Let your attention be directed especially to ingenious devices for securing variety within a formal pattern.

The sonnet, which will be reached in the study of lyric poetry, has been used often and successfully as a stanza.

In polyrhythmic or free verse, the stanza division follows the poet's inner mandate of where each group of lines should end, as if it were a paragraph in prose.

Sapphics and Other Classic Forms

Elegiac verse, according to the classical models, consists of lines alternately dactylic hexameter and dactylic pentameter; and then this difference is explained away by saying that the shorter lines have six accents, but omit the unaccented syllables in the third and sixth feet. Coleridge indicates the method:

> In the hexameter rises the fountain's all-silvery radiance;
> In the pentameter aye falling in melody back.
> > *Translation from Schiller,* Samuel Taylor Coleridge.

It is significant that none of the five greatest examples of elegiac poetry—that based upon death, or reflections upon death—in the English language, use this form. These five poems are Milton's *Lycidas,* Shelley's *Adonais,* Tennyson's *In Memoriam,* Gray's famous elegy, and Whitman's *When Lilacs Last in the Dooryard Bloomed,* a tribute to Lincoln.

The Greek *dactylic hexameter,* the classic model as the iambic five-foot line is in English, is far more complicated, according to the prosodists, than it sounds. There are six feet. The first four are dactyls or spondees. The fifth must be a dactyl; otherwise, if a spondee appears here, the verse is called spondaic. The last is a spondee or a trochee. A diagram makes this clearer.

/ ⌣ ⌣	/ ⌣ ⌣	/ ⌣ ⌣	/ ⌣ ⌣	/ ⌣ ⌣	/ /
or	or	or	or		or
/ /	/ /	/ /	/ /		/ ⌣

This may be written in English, with an accent basis instead of a quantity basis (that is, long and short syllables).

Hendecasyllabics were eleven-syllabled lines composed of a spondee, a dactyl, and trochees. Thus:

//|/‿‿|/‿|/‿|/‿

This meter has never been successfully naturalized into English.

Alcaics, named from the lyric poet Alcaeus, a contemporary of Sappho, are of several kinds. The first variety has a five-foot line, consisting of a spondee or iamb, an iamb, a long syllable, and two dactyls. Here is the pattern:

//
or |‿/|/|/‿‿|/‿‿
‿/

The second variety has two dactyls and two trochees to the line:

/‿‿|/‿‿|/‿|/‿

And, for the third, the line is composed:

(I) ‿///			
or			
(II) /‿//			
or	/‿‿/	/‿‿/	
(III) //‿/	(stress on	(stress on	‿//
or	1st or 4th	1st or 4th	(Stress on first
(IV) ///‿	syllable)	syllable)	long syllable)

What are the names of these feet? The first is an epitrite (first, second, third or fourth epitrite, depending upon the location of the short syllable); two choriambi or choriambs as above; and a bacchius. This technique does not often produce poetry in English; more often, it produces prosody or verse.

For an *Alcaic ode,* each strophe consists of four lines. The first two are eleven-syllabled Alcaics of the first kind; the third an especial form of iambic two-foot of nine syllables, described as hypercatalectic; and the fourth a ten-syllabled Alcaic of the second kind. Tennyson tried to catch it in:

> O mighty-mouthed inventor of harmonies,
> O skilled to sing of time or eternity,

God-gifted organ-voice of England,
Milton, a name to resound for ages.
> *Milton*, Alfred Tennyson.

Sapphics are named after the poet Sappho, who is said to have used the form with high skill. A sapphic line consists of five equal beats, its central one of three syllables, and the rest of two each. The original Greek sapphic stanza consisted of three of these lines, followed by a shorter line called an *adonic*, the whole following this pattern:

/ ⌣	/ / or / ⌣	/ ⌣ ⌣	/ ⌣	/ / or / ⌣̃
/ ⌣	/ / or / ⌣	/ ⌣ ⌣	/ ⌣	/ / or / ⌣
/ ⌣	/ ⌣	/ ⌣ ⌣	/ ⌣	/ / or / ⌣
	/ ⌣	/ ⌣		

Certain English poets have essayed this meter. In the examples given, the accent sign ( ) means a syllable described as long; the other symbol ( ) means one described as short. Here is Swinburne's use of the form:

Saw the | white im- | placable | Aphro- | dite,

Saw the | hair un- | bound and the | feet un- | sandalled

Shine as | fire of | sunset on | western | waters;

Saw the re- | luctant

Feet, the straining plumes of the doves that drew her,
Looking, always looking with necks reverted,
Back to Lesbos, back to the hills whereunder
Shone Mitylene
> *Sapphics*, Algernon Charles Swinburne.

and so on to the end. A *choriambic line* consists of a spondee, three choriambi and an iamb. A *galliambic line* is composed of iambs, one of which drops its final syllable, the next foot to the last being an anapest.

Indentation

The purpose of indentation is primarily to indicate the rhyme scheme. Indenting a line means sinking it inward by an increased blank space in the left-hand margin. Every paragraph in prose is indented at its beginning. An early indentation of poetry was similar to this, and consisted in indenting only the first line of each stanza. Where the poet desires to impress the reader with his rhyme scheme, indenting of lines rhymed is proper:

> Yet this inconstancy is such
>   As you too shall adore:
> I could not love thee, Dear, so much,
>   Loved I not Honour more.
> *To Lucasta, on Going to the Wars,* Richard Lovelace.

The following indentation is improper and essentially illiterate:

> That which her slender waist confined
>   Shall now my joyful temples bind:
> No monarch but would give his crown
>   His arms might do what this has done.
>   *On a Girdle,* Edmund Waller.

Needless to say, the poet set this up without indentation. The motive for such misindentation seems to be the following foggy thinking on the part of the versifier:

(a) Some poems by great poets are indented.
(b) Therefore I must indent my poem, to make sure it is
     regarded as great.

Once the motive for indentation is learned—to show the similarity of rhyme sounds terminating lines indented to the same point—this error will be avoided.

A second purpose of indentation is to center short lines in the

central portion of the poem, instead of leaving them dangling off to
the left. One of Guy Wetmore Carryll's eight verse poems proceeds:

> A maiden from the Bosphorus,
> With eyes as bright as phosphorus,
> Once wed the wealthy bailiff
> Of the caliph
> Of Kelat.
> Though diligent and zealous, he
> Became a slave to jealousy.
> (Considering her beauty,
> 'Twas his duty
> To be that!)
>
> *How the Helpmate of Bluebeard Made Free with a Door,*
> Guy Wetmore.

Here the first, third, fourth and sixth indentations indicate rhyming
changes; the second and fifth are to center briefer rhyming lines. The
object is to make the poem appear as presentable as possible, consid-
ering the rhyme scheme and length of line. Recall the indentation of
Shelley's *To a Skylark,* already given.

As to sonnets, there are only two proper ways to present them:
indenting for rhyme and omitting indentation. The Italian and Shakespearean form would then have the following indentation, if this is
used to indicate the rhyme scheme:

Italian Sonnet	*Shakespearean Sonnet*
1	1
2	2
2	1
1	2
1	3
2	4
2	3
1	4
3	5
4	6
5	5
3	6
4	7
5	7

It is more usual to set up sonnets without indentation. The original method of indenting the Shakespearean sonnet consisted of twelve lines without indentation and an identation for the concluding couplet.

All this assumes that the poet wishes to impress on the reader the rhyming scheme and the poet's fidelity in following it. But this is initiating the reader into the irrelevant laboratory work of the poet, and has its many disadvantages, since the reader primarily wishes to know what the poet has to say, not the devices by which he increases his effectiveness. The modern tendency is to eliminate the indentation in all poems. If poems are printed similarly to prose, the indentation will be the same as prose, to indicate paragraph openings, or to insert a quotation.

DIVISIONS OF POETRY

Narrative Poetry

POETRY IS COMMONLY divided, from the point of view of the poet's presentation of his material, into narrative, dramatic, and lyric poetry. The distinction is simple:

- In *narrative poetry*, the poet tells us a story as if he had been a spectator, but not a participant, in the events.
- In *dramatic poetry*, the poet lets the characters of the story speak their own words.
- In *lyric poetry*, the poet speaks his own moods, thoughts and aspirations.

These, like all definitions, define from the centers, not from the boundaries. A long-winded narrative in the first person, telling the poet's own adventures, might be classed with reason as any of the three: narrative poetry because it tells a story; dramatic, like a long dramatic monologue; and lyric, because the poet himself is speaking. This attitude classification is not of primary importance.

A fourth division, *didactic poetry*, that which teaches or points a moral, was once popular and is still encountered. It is regarded at best as a low flight of poetry.

Epic, Metrical Romance, Tale

An *epic* is a long narrative poem, dealing with heroic events, usually with supernatural guidance and participation in the action. Epics are divided into natural or folk epics, and literary epics. There is a suggested theory that folk epics are preceded by and composed of folk ballads. The earliest known epics exhibit little or no trace of any welding or amalgamating process.

The earliest literary remains in Greece are of the epic type, of three varieties. Epics of personal romance and war center around the semimythical blind bard Homer, with his *Iliad*—the story of the flight of Helen of Sparta with her Trojan lover, Paris; the war of Greeks against Trojans to avenge this; the anger of Greek Achilles and its effects; the defeat of Troy—and the *Odyssey,* telling the world wanderings of Grecian Odysseus after the sack of Troy, and of his return to his native Ithaca. Parts of these long poems are essentially prosy; but they have never been equalled for long poetic flight in narrative form. Epics dealing with the mysteries of religion center around the mythical singer Orpheus. Epics of a didactic nature center around the name of Hesiod. Scholars state that many lost epics in all three fields preceded the epics now remaining.

The *Mahabharata* and the *Ramayana* in Sanskrit, the *Shahnameh* in Persian, the *Niebelungenlied* in Middle German, *Beowulf* in Anglo-Saxon, the fragmentary *Elder Edda* from Iceland, the *Poem of the Cid* from Spain, the *Song of Roland* in medieval France, the *Kalevala* from Finland are all folk epics. They originated before the invention of writing and were transmitted orally, with inevitable changes and additions from time to time. Literary epics are a later attempt to catch the charm of the ancient epics; and as a rule they are a lower flight. Virgil's *Aeneid,* Tasso's *Jerusalem Delivered,* Ariosto's *Orlando Furioso,* Dante's didactic *Commedia* are the most outstanding among these. The *Lusiads* of Camoëns gave form to the Portuguese language, much as Dante did to modern Italian, Chaucer to English and Luther to German. Spenser's *Faerie Queene* has lost most of its charm for many modern English readers; even Milton's *Paradise Lost,* which sought to express English Puritanism as Dante had sought to express medieval Catholicism, is largely dull to modern readers.

Stories in verse preceded stories in prose. Chaucer's *Canterbury Tales,* the narrative metrical romances and tales of Scott, Byron and others, preceded the novel and the short story in English. But prose has become the popular medium, as it is the more natural one, and the long poetic narrative today usually seems artificial.

Ballad

The ballad, the brief story in verse, alone retains some general popularity. The name meant first a folk song-and-dance, like the

surviving *London Bridge Is Falling Down* or *Oats, Peas, Beans and Barley Grow.* It came to mean the folksong that tells a brief story—at first to be sung, later to be said or read. The Germanic bards or scalds, the gleemen, harpers, minstrels, troubadours, and minnesingersrs were a distinguished lot—the oral literature (and music) of races in the pre-bookish age. The chief figures in the ballads at first were noble, since nobles were the patrons of the singers. Later on, the lower classes became vocal—the oppressed Saxons in the Robin Hood ballads, and many early ballads in which a commoner ends by marrying one of noble lineage. The technique at first was simple, often with a simple refrain that the hearers might chorus. In English, the first *ballad meter* was seven-foot iambic lines, rhymed in couplets. A variant of this is the Scottish ballad *Edward, Edward,* with a pause between the invoked names taking the place of a foot in alternate lines:

> "Quhy does zour brand sae drop wi' bluid, Edward, Edward?
> Quhy does zour brand sae drop wi' bluid, and quhy sae sad
>   gang zee, O?"
> "Oh, I hae kill-ed my hauke sae guid, Mither, Mither,
> O, I hae kill-ed my hauke sae guid; and I had nae mair but
>   he, O."

Like the majority of the older ballads, this is a gory thing, full of blood and stark universal passions. If modern poetry gave us more of such red meat instead of caviar canapés, it would hold a wider popularity than it now has.

The rhythm is much freer than centuries of later iambic versification. The modern versifier can learn much of the way to sprinkle anapests in an iambic pattern, and of more important devices in versification, from old English folk ballads, as from that other depository of English folk verse, *Mother Goose.* Folk ballads originate among people largely pre-bookish; certain American mountaineers and certain Negroes still commemorate thrilling events with folk ballads, like the one within our memory on *The Sinking of the Titantic.*

Literary ballads are more successful than literary epics. Ballads by Heine and Housman, or Coleridge's *Rime of the Ancient Mariner,* have been taken to the heart of the race. The stanza form is almost invariably simple. Yet it is worthwhile to study the slight elaborations of the ballad meter that Coleridge employed—with stanzas ranging from four to nine ballad half-lines. There are many more successful literary ballads.

Dramatic Poetry

Like storytelling, drama is largely a lost field to poetry, purely because of the unnaturalness of poetic drama as usually written. There is a field for drama in natural free verse, which may yet be widely used. Classic drama was divided into *tragedy,* a play ending in death, and *comedy,* a play not ending in death. This division was unworkable and has been abandoned today.

Thespis, reputed father of Grecian drama, never permitted more than one actor on the stage at one time, with a chorus to interpret the action to the audience. This rigid convention was shattered by Aeschylus, who added a second actor. Sophocles added a third; but classic Greek drama never permitted a fourth. The typical Shakespearean play had five acts, the climax occurring during the third act, the solution at the end. This usually meant a dragging fourth act, which only *Othello* among the great tragedies avoided. Shakespeare and most other English verse dramatists used a five-foot iambic line, most often in blank or unrhymed verse. None of these conventions are more sacred than the one-actor convention of Thespis.

The *dramatic monologue,* or *dramatic lyric,* sprung from the speeches of Thespis's actor and the unnatural soliloquy of classic and English drama, is the one form of drama in verse which preserves considerable popularity. Robert Browning made this field peculiarly his own, with such magnificent dramatic vignettes as *My Last Duchess, Andrea del Sarto, Caliban upon Setebos* and so many more. His tremendous *The Ring and the Book* is, within a brief framework, ten immense dramatic monologues: the same group of facts, as seen through the eyes of ten differing personalities. Such dramatic monologues may be in any rhythm, any line length, and with or without rhyme. Success comes in proportion to the naturalness of the speech, the universality and depth of the emotion displayed, and the accuracy in character drawing.

Lyric Poetry: Ode, Elegy, Pastoral

Perhaps the earliest, and certainly the most enduringly popular type of poetry, is the lyric. As the name indicates, it meant originally poetry to be sung to the lyre—a dance at first accompanying this.

The *ode,* the most exalted form of lyric poetry, had strict rules

in classic times. The Greek Pindaric ode had three movements: a strophe, in which the chorus moved from a given spot toward the right;
the antistrophe, following the same versification pattern, and to the
same tune, in which the chorus moved correspondingly to the left;
and the concluding epode, different in structure, sung to a different
tune, and with the chorus standing still. Efforts to revive this form in
English have not succeeded. In English, the ode is a dignified lyric on
some high theme, with constant progress in its stanzas toward its conclusion. Familiar odes in English include Wordsworth's:

> Our birth is but a sleep and a forgetting;
> The Soul that rises with us, our life's Star,
>   Hath elsewhere its setting
>   And cometh from afar;
>   Not in entire forgetfulness,
>   And not in utter nakedness,
> But trailing clouds of glory do we come
>   From God, who is our home.
> Heaven lies about us in our infancy!
>   *Ode on the Intimations of Immortality from Recollections of*
>   *Early Childhood*

and also the great odes by Shelley and Keats already referred to.

An *elegy* is a formal expression of the poet's grief at death, whether
general or centered about the death of an individual. It has no more
definite a pattern in English than the ode: Milton, in *Lycidas*, uses an
iambic measure, with lines of differing lengths, and a fluidic rhyme
scheme. Shelley, in *Adonais*, chose the Spenserian stanza. Tennyson,
in *In Memoriam*, selected the quatrain pattern already encountered.
Whitman, in his major Lincoln threnody, *When Lilacs Last in the
Dooryard Bloomed*, wrote in magnificent polyrhythmic verse. Gray's
familiar *Elegy Written in a Country Churchyard*, alone among these a
meditation upon death in general, used alternate-rhymed five-foot
iambic lines. There are many familiar short elegies in the language.

The *pastoral* is a reflective lyric upon some aspect of nature, formerly concerned with shepherd life, whence its name. Milton's
shapely *L'Allegro* and *Il Penseroso*, and Whittier's *Snowbound*, are
examples in this genre. As city living increasingly replaces country
living, some form of city lyric may supplant the pastoral, if it does not
die without offspring.

The Simple Lyric: The Song

The word *song* is loosely used for any simple lyric, on the theory that it may always be set to music. It is best to reserve the word for a lyric intended to be set to music. This calls for a knowledge, on the part of the poet, of the human voice in music, and the ease or difficulty with which the various sounds are produced. Certain consonants and combinations of consonants are singable only with great difficulty. A line like:

> The gross-sized much-touched scratch will itch

is not easily singable. The terminal consonants *m, n, l, r* are sung with ease; *s, z, ch, sh,* as terminals, with difficulty. Of the vowels, broad *a,* long *o,* long *a, ou* are easiest to sing, though no vowel is really difficult. The words chosen should always end, and as far as possible include, only sounds which open the mouth, instead of closing it. Simple words are to be preferred to complicated ones; definite precise words to indefinite abstract ones; emotion-evoking words to intellectualized ones.

The lyric canon in English is one of the glories of its literature. After the dawn-hour lyrics before the Elizabethan age, the golden song of Campion—

> Shall I come, sweet Love, to thee,
>   When the evening beams are set?
> Shall I not excluded be,
>   Will you find no feigned let?
> Let me not, for pity, more
> Tell the long hours at your door
> *Shall I Come, Sweet Love?* Thomas Campion.

the equally melodious singable lyrics of Shakespeare and his contemporaries, the lyrics of Shelley, Keats, Byron, Burns, Housman and so many more in England, and of Poe, Emily Dickinson, Sidney Lanier and a few later singers, together make up a body of song that the race continues to treasure.

The themes and treatments of the lyric may vary as widely as the desires and visions of the poets. A lyric may have any chosen form of rhythm, with or without rhyme. It is often natural and effective in free verse or polyrhythmic poetry, since in this form the precise emotion-

moving thoughts and images may be written down, without the warping often demanded by such devices of versification as rhyme, assonance, consonance, and formal meter and stanza arrangement. Here is an example from the chief American user of the form, in a lyric called *Reconciliation:*

> Word over all, beautiful as the sky,
> Beautiful that war and all its deeds of carnage
>   must in time be utterly lost,
> That the hands of the sisters Death and Night
>   incessantly softly wash again, and ever again,
>   this soil'd world;
> For my enemy is dead, a man divine as myself is dead,
> I look where he lies white-faced and still in the
>   coffin—I draw near,
> Bend down and touch lightly with my lips the white
>   face in the coffin.

> *Reconciliation*, Walt Whitman.

Modern users of polyrhythmic poetry as a rule use less eloquence than Whitman and less of the expansive cosmic note, and tend instead toward the tense and gripping emotional appeal usual in rhymed and metric lyrics. Much shorter line division is also common.

The Sonnet

The sonnet is the most popular fixed form in English. It is a lyric of fourteen iambic five-foot lines, with a defined and definite rhyme scheme. There are two forms of it widely used in English, the Italian or Petrarchan sonnet, and the Shakespearean sonnet.

The rhyme scheme of the Italian sonnet appears from the following example:

> The world is too much with us; late and soon;   1
> Getting and spending, we lay waste our powers: 2
> Little we see in Nature that is ours;   2
> We have given our hearts away, a sordid boon!   1
> This sea that bares her bosom to the moon,   1
> The winds that will be howling at all hours,   2
> And are up-gathered now like sleeping flowers;   2

> For this, for everything, we are out of tune;   1
> It moves us not.—Great God! I'd rather be   3
> A Pagan suckled in a creed outworn;   4
> So might I, standing on this pleasant lea,   3
> Have glimpses that would make me less forlorn;   4
> Have sight of Proteus rising from the sea;   3
> Or hear old Triton blow his wreathéd horn.   4
>
> *Sonnet,* William Wordsworth.

The first eight lines of any sonnet are called the *octave.* In the Italian sonnet, the rhyme scheme is rigid and may not be departed from. The octave consists of two quatrains rhymed 1, 2, 2, 1, the *In Memoriam* rhyming pattern made familiar by Tennyson's use of it. The entire octave then rhymes 1, 2, 2, 1; 1, 2, 2, 1. It is not permitted to vary the rhymes in the second half of the octave, by using 1, 2, 2, 1; 3, 2, 2, 3, or a form too commonly encountered, 1, 2, 2, 1; 3, 4, 4, 3.

The concluding six lines of any sonnet are called the sestet. The two permissible rhyme schemes for the sestet of an Italian sonnet are 3, 4, 3, 4, 3, 4, and 3, 4, 5, 3, 4, 5. It will be noted that the sonnet by Wordsworth, quoted above, uses the proper octave rhyme scheme and the first of these two sestet arrangements.

As to treatment, the octave must be end-stopped—that is, the eighth line must mark the termination of a sentence. Even the halves of the octave should be end-stopped. The first quatrain should introduce the theme and develop it in a certain direction; the second should continue this development in the same direction. The sestet introduces a new development in a different direction, with the first tercet carrying this new direction to a definite point; and the final tercet bringing the theme to a conclusion. The actual movement of the strict Italian sonnet may be expressed as a flow in the octave and an ebb in the sestet—so Theodore Watts-Dunton phrased it in his sonnet *The Sonnet's Voice.* This does not mean, of course, that the inspiration or the emotional effect should ebb.

Wordsworth's sonnet, emotionally effective as it is, violates several of these strict rules. The octave movement does not end with the eighth line, but trespasses into the ninth. There is no break in thought between the two tercets that together comprise the sestet. We will find constantly among the masters violations of the rules, at times in the nature of experiments; none of these has as yet established its popularity in English poetry. In his sonnet *On the Extinction of the*

Venetian Republic, Wordsworth's octave rhymes 1, 2, 2, 1; 1, 3, 3, 1—another variation.

One authority examined 6,283 Italian sonnets in English and found these variations for the terminal sestet rhymes:

3, 4, 5, 3, 4, 5	3, 3, 4, 5, 5, 4
3, 4, 3, 4, 5, 5	3, 4, 5, 5, 3, 4
3, 4, 4, 3, 5, 5	3, 4, 5, 5, 4, 3
3, 4, 5, 4, 3, 5	3, 4, 4, 5, 3, 5
3, 4, 3, 5, 4, 5	3, 4, 5, 4, 5, 3
3, 4, 5, 3, 5, 4	3, 4, 3, 5, 5, 4

Two of these have terminal couplets, the most regrettable variation of the Italian sonnet. Six others include a couplet somewhere within the sestet. In addition to the above, the following two-rhyme variants are found:

3, 4, 3, 4, 3, 4	3, 4, 3, 4, 4, 3
3, 4, 4, 3, 3, 4	3, 4, 3, 3, 4, 4
3, 4, 4, 3, 4, 3	3, 4, 3, 3, 4, 3

Only the first excludes any couplet rhyming. Shelley's poem *Ozymandias* had the rhyme scheme 1, 2, 1, 2; 1, 3, 4, 3; 5, 4, 5, 6, 5, 6. Milton led the way in failing to separate clearly the octave and sestet, so much so that his type of sonnet is sometimes called the Miltonic-Italian in rhyme pattern, but without the characteristic Italian flow and ebb of theme, broken after the eighth line.

The Shakespearean sonnet is simpler and more natural in rhyming, and is in wider favor among English-using poets. An example is:

When, in disgrace with fortune and men's eyes,	1
I all alone beweep my outcast state,	2
And trouble deaf heaven with my bootless cries,	1
And look upon myself and curse my fate,	2
Wishing me like to one more rich in hope,	3
Featur'd like him, like him with friends possess'd,	4
Desiring this man's art and that man's scope,	3
With what I most enjoy contented least;	4
Yet in these thoughts myself almost despising,	5
Haply I think on thee, and then my state,	6
Like to the lark at break of day arising	5

From sullen earth, sings hymns at heaven's gate;   6
  For thy sweet love remember'd such wealth brings   7
  That then I scorn to change my state with kings.   7
                        Sonnet XXIX, William Shakespeare.

This is the accepted Shakespearean indentation for this form: though it may be indented to show rhyming mates, as the Italian also may be. Both types of the sonnet at times are printed with octave and sestet separated, making a poem of two stanzas; or an octave divided into two quatrains, and at times the sestet similarly divided.

The rhyming scheme of the Shakespearean sonnet is three quatrains—1, 2, 1, 2; 3, 4, 3, 4; 5, 6, 5, 6—with a concluding couplet, 7, 7. A shrewd interspersing of double or feminine rhymes aids. Many variations have been tried on this simple rhyming basis. Sir Philip Sidney repeated the rhymes of the first quatrain in the second, giving him a pattern of 1, 2, 1, 2; 1, 2, 1, 2; 3, 4, 3, 4; 5, 5. Spenser, in his 120 sonnets, used a chain-verse device of interlocking rhymes throughout each sonnet, so that his pattern was: 1, 2, 1, 2; 2, 3, 2, 3; 3, 4, 3, 4; 5, 5. Keats, in his second sonnet on *Fame*, wedded the Shakespearean octave to the Italian sestet, with his rhyme scheme 1, 2, 1, 2; 3, 4, 3, 4; 5, 6, 5, 7, 7, 6. Rupert Brooke, in the first and fifth of his soldier sonnets, used the Shakespearean octave and a straight Italian sestet: 5, 6, 7, 5, 6, 7. The third and fourth of the same series also wander from any strict pattern.

The sonnet was invented in Italy in the 13th century, probably by Pier delle Vigne, Secretary of State in the Sicilian court of Frederick. His sonnet *Però ch' amore* is the earliest known. His rhyme form—1, 2, 1, 2; 1, 2, 1, 2; 3, 4, 5, 3, 4, 5—has never become popular in English. The French sonnet prefers the strict Italian octave, with a sestet of three rhymes commencing with a couplet. This also has not become naturalized in English. There are occasional variations in English poetry, such as 1, 2, 1, 2; 2, 1, 2, 1; 3, 4, 3, 4, 5, 5; Italian sonnets with sestet 3, 4, 3, 4, 5, 5; and so on. Watts-Dunton points out, in his article on the sonnet in the eleventh edition of the *Encyclopaedia Britannica*, that the charm of this and other fixed forms comes from familiarity in advance with the rhyme scheme to be followed; and that this charm is dissipated when any break in the expected rhyme scheme occurs. We feel somewhat as if we listened to a limerick with an extra foot or an extra line: a sense of surprise, its pleasure being doubtful. In spite of this, poets continue to vary the rigid forms from time to time and will continue to do so.

The sonnet, of either form, is used by many poets as a fourteen-line stanza. Many of the Elizabethan sonnet sequences illustrate this; and there are many more recent examples. In writing the sonnet, it will aid to write down the rhyme scheme to the right of the space where your lines are to be written, and thereafter to mark across from each numbered rhyme the initial consonantal sounds used: giving a check against repeating a rhyming sound (that is, identity), which is inexcusable false rhyming. We would then have a notebook page like:

		Rhyme Sounds			
		OLD	ĒN	ĪZ	ĔN
Much have I travell'd in the realms of gold	1	G			
And many goodly states and kingdoms seen;	2		S		
Round many western islands have I been	2		B		
Which bards in fealty to Apollo hold.	1	H			
Oft of one wide expanse had I been told	1	T			
That deep-browed Homer ruled as his demesne:	2		M		
Yet never did I breathe its pure serene	2		R		
Till I heard Chapman speak out loud and bold.	1	B			
—Then felt I like some watcher of the skies	3			SK	
When a new planet swims into his ken;	4				K
Or like stout Cortez—when with eagle eyes	3			Vowel	
He stared at the Pacific—and all his men	4				M
Look'd at each other with a wild surmise—	3			M	
Silent, upon a peak in Darien.	4				Vowel

On First Looking into Chapman's Homer, John Keats.

Thus, by this check, it appears that the poet used, for rhyme 1, OLD, these consonantal sounds: g, h, t, b; for rhyme 2, ĒN, s, b, m, r; for rhyme 3, ĪZ, sk, the unconsonanted vowel sound, and m; for rhyme 4, ĔN, k, m, and the unconsonanted vowel sound. No identities; rhyme throughout. The sonnet, from a technical rhyming standpoint, has no flaws. When this method is followed during the writing of the sonnet—the first group of columns, that containing the numerals, properly indented, being written down first—this gives a check as the writing of the sonnet proceeds and saves much rewriting.

▪ VI ▪

THE FRENCH FORMS, LIGHT AND HUMOROUS VERSE

Formal and Light Verse

ANY POETIC FORM may be used either to arouse the great serious emotions or the lighter and more frivolous ones. Nor is there any reason for holding the serious poet higher than the comic poet. Surely Aristophanes, the great Athenian comic dramatist, ranked as high and was doubtless more popular and influential than any of the great serious triad, Aeschylus, Sophocles and Euripides. Shakespeare the comic dramatist, the author of *Merry Wives of Windsor, Midsummer Night's Dream, The Taming of the Shrew,* is as impressive a figure as the Shakespeare who let the melancholy Dane live and die in Elsinore, the Shakespeare who was the chronicler of Othello's jealousy and Lear's senility. Cervantes, who jeered knighthood to death, is greater as a writer than any other Spaniard; Racine, Molière, Voltaire, Anatole France were greatest as satirists; and so the roll continues. Serious writers and poets are more popular and are taken more seriously; but this may be because it is more civilized and difficult to laugh than to weep. Animals can suffer agonies; but they cannot chuckle. And yet the race would not willingly exchange Robert Burns's *Tam o' Shanter* and W. S. Gilbert's *The Bab Ballards* for any number of closet dramas, ponderous versified essays and odes, or a whole trainload of lyrics to spring and young love.

Fixed forms of poetry tend to become outgrown, like a child's shirt too small to close over a man's heart. They then become relegated to minor versifiers, to light verse writers, and to college and high school exercises. Prose ages more quickly than poetry: witness such masterpieces, written for adults, as the world's great fairy stories, Aesop's fables, the *Arabian Nights, Robinson Crusoe, Gulliver's Travels* in the nursery; and the essays and novels of yesterday encountered in school or college. Poetry itself ages: Shakespeare, Milton, Virgil, Horace are more used in the classroom than in the living room today, and so of the rest of them. In spite of constant insistence that nothing changes

under the sun, the nature of man is stretched outward by his expanding environment, and coiled more tensely into molecules and atoms and complexes and other inner things; and the poetry, the concentrated heart's expression, of yesterday cannot forever be the poetry of today. Prose, in the large, must be rephrased every fifty years or less to be enjoyable to living men; poetry survives longer, but the hour will come when the most enduring poem of a Shakespeare or a Sappho will seem ancient, and must be restated or recreated by a living poet, to speak again for the maturing soul of man. If this is true of the poetry itself, it is truer of the patterns in which poetry has been uttered, and especially of the fixed forms.

The sonnet, an emigrant from Italy that became naturalized in English literature, still holds its own as a major method of expressing serious poetry, in the eyes of many poets and readers. Even at that, it is now regarded as puerile by the extreme advocates of free verse or polyrhythmic poetry, especially since Whitman and the Imagist movement. Numerous other alien verse forms did not fare so well and have established themselves primarily as mediums for light and humorous verse. These include the ballade, the rondeau, the villanelle, the triolet, and so on. This may be because of their rigid rules and formal repetitions, which were not acceptable to the living poet. And yet they started as seriously as Sapphics, heroic blank verse, or polyrhythms. . . .

Of all the forms of verse originating in medieval Provence, among those that failed to acclimatize themselves in English are the *vers, canzo, sirvente, tenso, alba, serena, pastorella, breu-doble,* and the *retroensa.* Only the most elaborate of the lot, the intricate *sestina,* has survived in English. When religious crusades wiped out this culture, the germs of formalized verse took root in northern France, especially under Charles d'Orleans and François Villon. The *ballade* appeared. Spenser used 3,848 of his nine-line Spenserian stanzas in one poem: across the Channel, Eustache Deschamps, a friend of Chaucer's, left no less than 1, 175 complete ballades. Froissart the chronicler wrote many. Charles d'Orleans is hailed as the early master of the roundel, as Villon is lauded as the prince of ballade-makers. Jean Passerat gave the villanelle its present form in the sixteenth century; Voiture, a century later, perfected the rondeau. In the seventeenth century, after the forms had been known for two hundred years in English, Patrick Carey published a series of dignified religious triolets; and the overartificialized forms have repeatedly been revived since.

Rules of the Fixed Verse Forms

In English verse, the rules for the fixed forms are stricter than in French:

I. No syllable once used as a rhyme can be used again in the same poem as a rhyme—not even if it is spelled differently or if the whole word is altered by a prefix.

This bars such identities as *Ruth*, a girl's name, and *ruth*, pity; *bear*, an animal, *bear*, to support, *bare*, *forbear*, and so on; *sale* and *sail; claim*, *reclaim*, and *disclaim; facility*, *imbecility;* and, if this is taken as a single rhyme, not a triple one, it forbids the use of more than one from this group: *tea*, *manatee*, *imbecility*, *impossibility*, *lenity*, and so on.

As to the *refrain*, an important element in many of these forms:

II. The refrain must not be a meaningless repetition of sounds as in many English ballads; it must aid in the progress of the thought; come in naturally; and be repeated in all its sounds, without any change of sound.

Slipshod versifiers alter the refrain by changing the introductory word, as by using an *and* for a *but*, a *then* for an *if*. This is unforgiveable. But the requirement goes no further than the repetition of all *sounds*. Punctuation may be changed, spelling may be changed, meaning may be changed: permitting the following—

It's meet, this sale; Its meat, this sale.
Gray day; Grade aye; Grade A.

The Ballade Family

There are two standard forms of the *ballade*. The more usual one consists of three stanzas of eight lines each; followed by a concluding quatrain, known as the *envoy*. It is thus a poem of twenty-eight lines, or twice the length of a sonnet. Each stanza, and the envoy, terminate with a line repeated sound by sound, and called the *refrain*. The rhyme scheme is 1, 2, 1, 2, 2, 3, 2, 3R for each stanza, 3R being the

refrain; and 2, 3, 2, 3R for the envoy. The rules of the ballade may be stated as follows:

I. The same set of rhyme sounds used in the first stanza, in the same order, must be used in each stanza; and the last half of this scheme must be used in the envoy.
II. No rhyme sound, once used as a rhyme, may be used again for that purpose anywhere else in the poem.
III. Each stanza and the envoy must close with the refrain line, repeated without any alteration of sound; though its punctuation, meaning and spelling may be altered.
IV. The sense of the refrain must be supreme throughout the ballade, the culminating refrain line being always brought in without strain or effort as the natural close of the stanza or envoy.

Formerly the length of the refrain governed the length of the stanza. Thus an eight-syllabled refrain dictated an eight-line stanza, and a ten-syllabled refrain a ten-line stanza. This rule is followed no longer.

V. The stanza should carry an unbroken sense throughout, and not be split in meaning into two quatrains, or any other division. The needful pauses for punctuation are allowed, but the sense is not to be finished midway of the stanza.
VI. The envoy, as used in ballades and the chant royal, was at first addressed to the patron of the poet. It is thus usual to commence it with some such invocation as *Prince! Princess! Sire!* or by some mythical or symbolic persons so introduced. This is at times omitted. The envoy is both a dedication and a culmination, and should be richer in wording and meaning and more stately in imagery than the preceding lines.

Here is a well-wrought ballade, in four-foot iambic verse. The rhyme scheme is indicated by the numerals 1, 2, and 3, the refrain line being designated 3R. To the right appear the checking columns for the three rhyming sounds, to make sure that there are no repetitions—unforgiveable, in strict formal verse of this type.

		Rhyme Sounds		
		ĀD	Ō	ŌL
Where are the passions they essayed,	1	S		

And where the tears they made to flow?	2	FL	
Where the wild humours they portrayed	1	TR	
For laughing worlds to see and know?	2	N	
Othello's wrath and Juliet's woe?	2	W	
Sir Peter's whims and Timon's gall?	3	G	
And Millamant and Romeo?	2	Vowel	
Into the night go one and all.	3R		Vowel

Where are the braveries, fresh or frayed?	1	FR	
The plumes, the armours—friend and foe?	2	F	
The cloth of gold, the rare brocade,	1	K	
The mantles glittering to and fro?	2	FR	
The pomp, the pride, the royal show?	2	SH	
The cries of youth and festival?	3	V	
The youth, the grace, the charm, the glow?	2	GL	
Into the night go one and all.	3R		Vowel

The curtain falls, the play is played:	1	PL	
The Beggar packs beside the Beau;	2	B	
The Monarch troops, and troops the Maid;	1	M	
The Thunder huddles with the Snow.	2	SN	
Where are the revellers high and low?	2	L	
The clashing swords? The lover's call?	3	K	
The dancers gleaming row on row?	2	R	
Into the night go one and all.	3R		Vowel

Envoy.

Prince, in one common overthrow	2	THR	
The Hero tumbles with the Thrall;	3	THR	
As dust that drives, as straws that blow,	2	BL	
Into the night go one and all.	3R		Vowel

Ballade of Dead Actors, William Ernest Henley.

As to the two requirements about rhyming, a ballade requires six 1 rhymes. Here the six consonantal sounds, as the checking column establishes, are *s, tr, fr, k, pl,* and *m.*

A ballade requires fourteen 2 rhymes. Here the fourteen consonantal sounds, as the checking column establishes, are *fl, n, w,* the unconsonanted vowel, *f, fr, sh, gl, b, sn, l, r, thr,* and *bl.*

A ballade requires five 3 rhymes, one of which reappears three

times as the refrain. The five sounds used here are *g*, the unconsonanted vowel, *v*, *k*, and *thr*. The rhyming is correct throughout.

The refrain line is used without any alteration of any kind throughout, satisfying the third requirement. It is used throughout as a natural climax of each stanza. Each stanza has its own climactic rise to the
refrain. The envoy meets the requirements wholly.

This ballade then may be used as a model.

The meter of a ballade need not be four-foot iambic, as in this
example. Andrew Lang's *Ballade of Primitive Man* has a three-foot
anapestic movement with the refrain, " 'Twas the manner of Primitive
Man." Dactyls may be used or anapests. A recent newspaper ballade
had only two trochees to the line, its refrain being "Life is gay."
Another had merely one iambic foot to each line, with the refrain "I
love." No doubt someone has written a ballade with only one syllable
to each line.

The most famous of all ballades is François Villon's ballade *Des
Dames du Temps Jadis (Ballade of Bygone Ladies)*. There are many
familiar translations of this: Dante Gabriel Rossetti's with the refrain
"But where are the snows of yester-year?", John Payne's with "But
what is become of last year's snow?", and others. None of these are
authentic recreations in living poetry; not even of the refrain *Mais où
sont les neiges d'antan?* (But where are the last year's snows?) In
technique, Rossetti has entirely different rhyming sounds in each
stanza and another in the envoy. Payne is accurate though he repeats
some rhyme sounds, and uses words as unliving as *vade* (that is, *go*,),
marish, *whilere*, *dole;* and surely "Virgin debonair" is an unfortunate
mistranslation of Villon's stately *Vierge souvraine*. At least, none of
this is as archaic as two words in this line of Rossetti's version:

(From love he won such dule and teen!)

Examining the Villon original, we find that he uses the terminal
sounds *-maine* seven times, and rhymes it with *moyne* and other
apparent consonances; rhymes *lis* and *Allis;* and otherwise is as lax as
French rules allow, rather than following the strict and at that time
unpromulgated English rules. An acceptable version in English may
take advantage of the practices in the original, although it will have to
be an authentic poetic recreation.

The second standard form of the ballade consists of stanzas of ten
lines, usually of ten syllables each, as in the five-foot iambic pattern;
followed by an envoy of five lines. The regular rhyme scheme for each

stanza is 1, 2, 1, 2, 2, 3, 3, 4, 3, 4R, 4R being the refrain line. For the envoy, the rhyme scheme is 3, 3, 4, 3, 4R. This is much rarer in English than the foregoing.

The *ballade with double refrain* uses two refrains, one occurring at the fourth line of every stanza, and one at the eighth; while, in the envoy, the refrains are the second and fourth lines respectively, the envoy being rhymed couplet-wise. The rhyme scheme for each stanza is 1, 2, 1, 2R; 2, 3, 2, 3R, 2R being the first refrain line, and 3R the second. The rhyme scheme for the envoy is 2, 2R, 3, 3R. The best technique selects two antithetical refrains, and develops each stanza upon the refrain used to close it. Here is an excellent example:

When the roads are heavy with mire and rut,	1
In November fogs, in December snows,	2
When the North Wind howls, and the doors are shut,	1
There is place and enough for the pains of prose;—	2R
But whenever a scent from the whitehorn blows,	2
And the jasmine-stars to the casement climb,	3
And a Rosalind-face at the lattic shows,	2
Then hey!—for the ripple of laughing rhyme!	3R

When the brain gets dry as an empty nut,	
When the reason stands on its squarest toes,	
When the mind (like a beard) has a "formal cut,"	
There is place and enough for the pains of prose;—	2R
But whenever the May-blood stirs and glows,	
And the young year draws to the "golden prime,"—	
And Sir Romeo sticks in his ears a rose,	
Then hey!—for the ripple of laughing rhyme!	3R

In a theme where the thoughts have a pedant strut,	
In a changing quarrel of "Ayes" and "Noes,"	
In a starched procession of "If" and "But",	
There is place and enough for the pains of prose;—	2R
But whenever a soft glance softer glows,	
And the light hours dance to the trysting-time,	
And the secret is told "that no one knows,"	
Then hey!—for the ripple of laughing rhyme!	3R

Envoy

In a work-a-day world,—for its needs and woes,	2
There is place and enough for the pains of prose;	2R
But whenever the May-bells clash and chime, . . .	3

Then hey!—for the ripple of laughing rhyme!'   3R
       The Ballade of Prose and Rhyme, Austin Dobson.

The position of the two refrains is indicated throughout by 2R and 3R; and the couplet rhyming of the envoy is also indicated.

The *double ballade* consists of six stanzas of eight or ten lines each, rhymed as in the ballades already given. Thus this may be six stanzas rhymed 1, 2, 1, 2, 2, 3, 2, 3R; or 1, 2, 1, 2, 2, 3, 3, 4, 3, 4R. Usually the envoy is omitted. Henley, who liked the form, always used an envoy. His *Double Ballade of the Nothingness of Things* goes beyond these schemes, and has eleven lines to each stanza, rhymed 1, 2, 1, 2, 2, 3, 3, 4, 5, 4, 5R; with an envoy rhymed 3, 3, 4, 5, 4, 5R. And he has stranger varieties. Swinburne's *Ballade of Swimming* has ten lines to the stanza, and seven anapests to each line—a long interval between rhymes.

The *chant royal* is the longest and most dignified offspring of the ballade. It has five stanzas of eleven lines each, usually rhymed 1, 2, 1, 2, 3, 3, 4, 4, 5, 4, 5R. The envoy has five lines, rhymed 4, 4, 5, 4, 5R. Sixty lines, in all. . . . Seven (5) rhymes, ten each of (1), (2), and (3), and eighteen separate rhymes for (4). . . .

Here is an amusing example:

    I would that all men my hard case might know;
        How grievously I suffer for no sin;
    I, Adolphe Culpepper Ferguson, for lo!
        I, of my landlady am locked in,
            For being short on this sad Saturday, ·
            Nor having shekels of silver wherewith to pay;
    She has turned and is departed with my key;
    Wherefore, not even as other boarders free,
        I sing (as prisoners to their dungeon stones
    When for ten days they expiate a spree):
        Behold the deeds that are done of Mrs. Jones!

    One night and one day I have wept my woe;
        Nor wot I when the morrow doth begin,
    If I shall have to write to Briggs & Co.,
        To pray them to advance the requisite tin
            For ransom of their salesman, that he may
            Go forth as other boarders go alway—
    As those I hear now flocking from their tea,

Led by the daughter of my landlady
 Piano-ward. This day, for all my moans,
Dry bread and water have been servéd me.
 Behold the deeds that are done of Mrs. Jones!

Miss Amabel Jones is musical, and so
 The heart of the young he-boardér doth win,
Playing "The Maiden's Prayer," *adagio*—
 That fetcheth him, as fetcheth the banco skin
  The innocent rustic. For my part, I pray:
  That Badarjewska maid may wait for aye
Ere she sits with a lover, as did we
Once sit together, Amabel! Can it be
 That all that arduous wooing not atones
For Saturday shortness of trade dollars three?
 Behold the deeds that are done of Mrs. Jones!

Yea! she forgets the arm was wont to go
 Around her waist. She wears a buckle whose pin
Galleth the crook of the young man's elbów;
 I forget not, for I that youth have been.
  Smith was aforetime the Lothario gay.
  Yet once, I mind me, Smith was forced to stay
Close in his room. Not calm, as I, was he:
But his noise brought no pleasaunce, verily.
 Small ease he gat of playing on the bones,
Or hammering on the stove-pipe, that I see.
 Behold the deeds that are done of Mrs. Jones!

Thou, for whose fear the figurative crow
 I eat, accursed be thou and all thy kin!
Thee will I shew up—yea, up will I shew
 Thy too thick buckwheats, and thy tea too thin.
  Ay! here I dare thee, ready for the fray!
  Thou dost *not* "keep a first-class house," I say!
It does not with the advertisements agree.
Thou lodgest a Briton with a puggaree,
 And thou hast harboured Jacobses and Cohns,
Also a Mulligan. Thus denounce I thee!
 Behold the deeds that are done of Mrs. Jones!
     Envoy
Boarders; the worst I have not told to ye:
She hath stolen my trousers, that I may not flee

Privily by the window. Hence these groans,
There is no fleeing in a *robe de nuit*.
Behold the deeds that are done of Mrs. Jones!
Behold the Deeds! (Being the Plaint of Adolphe
Culpepper Ferguson, Salesman of Fancy Notions,
held in durance of his Landlady for a failure to
connect on Saturday night), Henry Cuyler Bunner.

The stanza rhyme scheme is 1, 2, 1, 2, 3, 3, 4, 4, 5, 4, 5R, 5R being
the refrain; with the envoy 4, 4, 5, 3, 5R. The rhyming throughout is
accurate, and the result is a perfect chant royal. The form is intricate,
and the method of checking the various rhyme sounds as they are put
down should be followed, to be sure that no rhyming sound is
repeated. A great deal of reworking is often necessary to perfect such
a form as this. In order to make the envoy the culmination of the
verses, it is often necessary to shift the strongest and most vigorous
rhyming sounds to it and substitute other words in the earlier stanzas.

It is wise, for rhyme 4, which must be repeated eighteen times, and
similar others repeated constantly in the fixed forms, to choose a
comparatively simple rhyming sound, such as the Ē here, to prevent a
lack of rhyming words.

Chain Verse

We have already noted that form of chain verse used in *terza rima*,
where the triplets rhyme 1, 2, 1; 2, 3, 2; 3, 4, 3; 4, 5, 4; and so on.
Any repetition of a rhyme, word, phrase, line or group of lines, to tie
up a section of the poem with the succeeding section, constitutes
chain verse. John Byrom lets line four of each quatrain become line
one of the next:

My spirit longeth for thee
Within my troubled breast,
Although I be unworthy
Of so divine a Guest.

Of so divine a Guest
Unworthy though I be,
Yet has my heart no rest,
Unless it comes from thee.

> Unless it comes from thee,
> In vain I look around,
> > *The Desponding Soul's Wish*, John Byrom.

and so on. Chain verse can rise to the elaborateness of a chain of sonnets or more, with the final line in each repeated as the opening line of the next, or even the final word or rhyme sound so used.

The Kyrielle

The kyrielle, strictly described, consists of quatrains with eight syllables to the line, each stanza terminating with the same line—a simple use of the refrain. Here is an example from a poem by John Payne:

> A little pain, a little pleasure,
> A little heaping up of treasure,
> Then no more gazing upon the sun.
> All things must end that have begun.
>
> Where is the time for hope or doubt?
> A puff of the wind, and life is out;
> A turn of the wheel, and the rest is won.
> All things must end that have begun.
>
> Golden morning and purple night,
> Life that fails with the failing light;
> Death is the only deathless one.
> All things must end that have begun.
> > *Kyrielle,* John Payne.

Here the eight-syllabled pattern is intermittently broken. There is of course no sacredness in any pattern. Such a simple form must compensate by climactic development from stanza to stanza, to justify itself in poetry.

The Pantoum

Ernest Fouinet introduced the Malayan pantoum into French versification, and Victor Hugo popularized it in the *Orientales*. It is written

in four-line stanzas; and the second and fourth line of each stanza
become the first and third of the succeeding stanza. In the last stanza
the second and fourth lines are the third and first of the first stanza;
so that the opening and closing lines of the pantoum are identical.
The rhyme scheme would then be: 1, 2, 1, 2; 2, 3, 2, 3; 3, 4, 3, 4;
. . . n, 1, n, 1.

Brander Matthews gives an example of one in English:

> Here we are riding the rail,
>   Gliding from out of the station;
> Man though I am, I am pale,
>   Certain of heat and vexation.
>
> Gliding from out of the station,
>   Out from the city we thrust;
> Certain of heat and vexation,
>   Sure to be covered with dust.
>
> Out from the city we thrust:
>   Rattling we run o'er the bridges:
> Sure to be covered with dust,
>   Stung by a thousand of midges. . . .
>   *En Route*, Brander Matthews.

to the final stanza, ending as the verses began:

> Ears are on edge at the rattle,
>   Man though I am, I am pale,
> Sounds like the noise of a battle,
>   Here we are riding the rail.

The Triolet

The triolet was the first of the rondeau family to appear. The first
ones known appeared in the *Cléomadés* of Adenéz-le-Roi, who wrote
in the latter part of the thirteenth century. At first, with ten syllables
to each line, the triolet dealt with serious subjects. Today the form is
usually eight syllables to the line or even six; and the themes have
grown appreciably and constantly lighter. It has eight lines, with only
two rhymes. The first line is repeated as the fourth line; the first two
lines reappear as the seventh and eighth. The rhyme scheme is 1R,

2R, 1, 1R, 1, 2, 1R, 2R, the repeated lines appearing as 1R and 2R.

Suppose you decide to write a brief triolet, opening with the couplet:

> Drink deep—the glass
> Is full—and near!

You can at once fill out your fourth, seventh and eighth lines from this, making your pattern now appear as:

Drink deep—the glass	1R
Is full—and near!	2R
_____	1
Drink deep! The glass	1R
_____	1
_____	2
Drink deep—the glass	1R
Is full—and near!	2R

Only three lines, then, remain to be filled in. Once this is done, you have the triolet complete:

> Drink deep—the glass
> Is full—and near!
> Come, lad and lass,
> Drink deep! The glass
> Too soon will pass
> And disappear.
> Drink deep—the glass
> Is full—and near!

At times a more serious mood rules the use of the form. Thus H. C. Bunner wrote:

> A pitcher of mignonette
>   In a tenement's highest casement;
> Queer sort of a flower-pot—yet
> That pitcher of mignonette
> Is a garden of heaven set
>   To the little sick child in the basement,
> The pitcher of mignonette

> In the tenement's highest casement.
> > *Triolet*, Henry Cyler Bunner.

Here we have no progress in thought in the use of the reiterated refrain or repetend. Worse than that, the refrain line alters from *A pitcher* to *That pitcher* and *The pitcher*, a vital fault in the use of refrains in the French forms.

A transition to the rondeau form is furnished by this eight-line verse by Leigh Hunt:

> Jenny kissed me when we met,
> > Running to the chair I sat in.
> Time, you thief, who love to get
> > Sweets upon your list, put *that* in!
> Say I'm weary, say I'm sad,
> > Say that health and wealth have missed me;
> Say I'm growing old, but add—
> > > Jenny kissed me.
> > > *Jenny Kissed Me*, Leigh Hunt.

The opening half of line one, reappearing as the refrain in line eight, prophesies the rondeau and similar forms. This brilliant little pattern has never become accepted and named.

The Rondel, Rondeau and Roundel Family

The triolet is the seed of the rondeau family. The *rondel* (the word is an old form of the later word *rondeau*) arose in all probability in Provence and appeared later in the fourteenth century writings of north France, in the verse of Froissart, Deschamps and others. It began as a lyric of two stanzas, each stanza having four or five lines only, and rhyming triolet-wise upon two sounds . . . either a triolet or a ten-line variant of the triolet.

With Charles d'Orleans, the rondel took the distinct form now assigned to it, of fourteen lines on two rhymes. The first two lines reappear as the seventh and eighth, and as the final couplet—a mere variation of the triolet. This double repetition of the two-lined refrain made the form unwieldy. Later French poets shortened the form to thirteen lines, omitting the second line of the original refrain at the end.

The form as Charles d'Orleans used it appears in this rondel:

Paper, inviolate, white,	1R
Shall it be joy or pain?	2R
Shall I of fate complain,	2
Or shall I laugh tonight?	1
Shall it be hopes that are bright?	1
Shall it be hopes that are vain?	2
Paper, inviolate, white	1R
Shall it be joy or pain?	2R
A dear little hand so light,	1
A moment in mine hath lain;	2
Kind was its pressure again—	2
Ah, but it was so slight!	1
Paper, inviolate, white,	1R
Shall it be joy or pain?	2R

To a Blank Sheet of Paper, Cosmo Monkhouse.

The following rondel, by Samuel Minturn Peck, is in the preferred modern pattern:

Before the dawn begins to glow,	1R
A ghostly company I keep;	2R
Across the silent room they creep,	2
The buried forms of friend and foe.	1
Amid the throng that come and go,	1
There are two eyes that make me weep;	2
Before the dawn begins to glow,	1R
A ghostly company I keep.	2R
Two dear dead eyes. I love them so!	1
They shine like starlight on the deep,	2
And often when I am asleep	2
They stoop and kiss me, being low,	1
Before the dawn begins to glow.	1R

Before the Dawn, Samuel Minturn Peck.

The *rondeau* is, next to the ballade, the French form most popular in English. It is written, like the triolet and rondel, on two rhymes throughout: thirteen full-length lines and two briefer unrhymed

refrains. The refrain may consist of the first half of the first line, but may consist merely of the first word. The fifteen lines are grouped in three stanzas, the first of five lines, the second of three lines and refrain, the third of five lines and refrain. The rhyme scheme then is: 1, 1, 2, 2, 1; 1, 1, 2, R; 1, 1, 2, 2, 1, R. Here is a rondeau that is a poem as well:

A man must live. We justify	1
Low shift and trick to treason high,	1
A little vote for a little gold	2
To a whole senate bought and sold	2
By that self-evident reply.	1
But is it so? Pray tell me why	1
Life at such cost you have to buy?	1
In what religion were you told	2
A man must live?	R
There are times when a man must die.	1
Imagine, for a battle-cry,	1
From soldiers, with a sword to hold,—	2
From soldiers, with the flag unrolled,	2
This coward's whine, this liar's lie,—	1
A man must live!	R

A Man Must Live, Charlotte Perkins Gilman.

The *roundel,* based upon occasional early French variants, is today associated with the name of Swinburne, because of his volume *A Century of Roundels.* As used by Swinburne, the roundel was eleven lines long, two of which were the brief refrain lines. The refrain either consisted of the opening word of line one, or of a portion or a half of that line. If it consisted of more than one word, it usually rhymed with the (2) sound rhyme. The rhyming pattern then would be 1, 2, 1, R; 2, 1, 2; 1, 2, 1, R; or 1, 2, 1, 2R; 2, 1, 2; 1, 2, 1, 2R. Here is an example:

A Roundel is wrought as a ring or a starbright sphere,
With craft of delight and with cunning of sound unsought,
That the heart of the hearer may smile if to pleasure his ear
    A roundel is wrought.

Its jewel of music is carven of all or of aught—
Love, laughter, or mourning—remembrance of rapture or
    fear—
That fancy may fashion to hang in the ear of thought.

As a bird's quick song runs round, and the hearts in us
    hear—
Pause answers to pause, and again the same strain caught,
So moves the device whence, round as a pearl or tear,
    A roundel is wrought,
           The Roundel, Algernon Charles Swinburne.

The *rondelet* is a seven-line fixed form, normally of four eight-syllabled lines, and three, the refrain lines, with four syllables each. The
rhyme and rhythm scheme is: 1R, 2, 1R, 1, 2, 2, 1R—1R standing for
the refrain line, and 1 for the line rhyming with it. Here is an example
by May Probyn:

"Which way he went?"	1R
I know not—how should I go spy	2
Which way he went?	1R
I only know him gone. "Relent?"	1
He never will—unless I die!	2
And then, what will it signify	2
Which way he went?	1R

                    Rondelet, May Probyn.

The *rondeau redoublé,* a remote relative of the rondeau, is in reality a formalized theme-with-variations treatment. It starts with a quatrain as a theme. This is followed by four additional quatrains, in each
of which successively lines one, two, three, and four of the theme quatrain appear as the terminal lines. A concluding stanza has four lines
of regular length and a refrain (the first half of line one of the theme)
to terminate.

An example will make this clearer:

My soul is sick of nightingale and rose,	1-a
The perfume and the darkness of the grove;	2-b
I weary of the fevers and the throes,	1-c
And all the enervating dreams of love.	2-d
At morn I love to hear the lark, and rove	2
The meadows, where the simple daisy shows	1
Her guiltless bosom to the skies above—	2
My soul is sick of nightingale and rose.	1-a

The afternoon is sweet, and sweet repose,   1
   But let me lie where breeze-blown branches move.   2
I hate the stillness where the sunbeams doze,   1
   The perfume and the darkness of the grove.   2-b
   I love to hear at eve the gentle dove   2
Contented coo the day's delightful close.   1
   She sings of love and all the calm thereof,—   2
I weary of the fevers and the throes.   1-c

I love the night, who like a mother throws   1
   Her arms round hearts that throbbed and limbs that strove, 2
As kind as Death, that puts an end to woes   1
   And all the enervating dreams of love.   2-d
   Because my soul is sick of fancies wove   2
Of fervid ecstasies and crimson glows;   1
   Because the taste of cinnamon and clove   2
Palls on my palate—let no man suppose   1
     My soul is sick.   R

Rondeau Redoublé, Cosmo Monkhouse.

As far as strict rhyming goes, *repose—suppose* and *throes—throws* are
identities, and not rhymes.

The *glose*, which is superficially a freer variant of the foregoing
pattern, derives apparently from a different source, and is found more
often in Spanish and Portuguese verse than in French. It begins, like
the rondeau redoublé, with a quatrain, here called the *texte*, which
may be a quotation. This texte the glose proceeds to develop, in four
stanzas of ten lines each, closing each stanza, as in the rondeau redoublé, with the successive four lines of the texte. The concluding stanza
and refrain of the preceding form are omitted here. In the rhyme
scheme, lines six, nine and the tenth or texte line in each stanza
rhyme; the rest of the rhyme scheme differs with different users of the
form.

Gleeson White, author of a definitive book on the French forms,
was unable to discover at the time he wrote any example of the form
in English. There are not many examples available. The texte in the
following is from Graham R. Tomson's *Ballade of Asphodel*.

   "Queen Prosperine, at whose white feet   1-a
     In life my love I may not tell,   2-b
   Wilt give me welcome when we meet   1-c

Along the mead of Asphodel?   2-d
Your Majesty, permit me to   3
   Indite, as one would say, this bit   4
Of verse respectfully to you;   3
Of course admitting *entre nous*   3
   You may not really fancy it;   4
Although it will be rather neat.   1
   And yet the dedication's fit;   4
   I want assistance from your wit: 4
I should permit my heart to beat,   1
Queen Proserpine, at *whose* white feet?   1-a

Remember, Proserpine, I know   5
   That quite discriminatingly   6
You made your mind up long ago;   5
You did not like your Stygian beau;   5
   He smacked a bit of deviltry,—   6
And you were not designed for hell,   2
   This shows you're quite a clever she;   6
   Ergo, you ought to counsel me.   6
I *must* make up my mind, or,—well,   2
In life my love I may not tell.   2

Should I ask Venus, she would vote
   (That surely is a goddess' right)
For some dame with "a quivering throat
And bosom of desire"—I quote
   From memory the line tonight.
Minerva would choose some discreet
   Young woman, staid and erudite;
   But only she could give delight
Who would, though life's young roses sweet
Wilt, give me welcome when we meet.   1-c

Come, choose her for me! Let her be
   Stately or dumpy, brown or fair,
If only she'll agree that we
Should learn to dwell in harmony,
   Giving a gay good-bye to care,—
A beatific way to dwell!
   Come, Queen, be gracious to my prayer!
   But, no! Such maidens here are rare;

You'd scarce find such a demoiselle
Along the mead of Asphodel!   2-d

The Quest, Clement Wood.

Naturally, the rhyming scheme of the texte (which is 1, 2, 1, 2 here), dictates the rhyming of the sixth, ninth and tenth lines of each main stanza. In other examples, the quatrain that forms the texte may have any quatrain rhyming, and so a similar extent dictates similar rhymes in each stanza. It is permissible to use the same rhymes in each stanza, except where the rhyme sound of the texte line ordains differently. In other words the four stanzas might be:

        1-a, 2-b, 1-c, 2-d
        3, 4, 3, 3, 4, 1, 3, 3, 1, 1-a
        3, 4, 3, 3, 4, 2, 3, 3, 2, 2-b
        3, 4, 3, 3, 4, 1, 3, 3, 1, 1-c
        3, 4, 3, 3, 4, 2, 3, 3, 2, 2-d

This is not required by the strict rules.

The Sestina

Arnaut Daniel, a Provençal troubadour, invented the sestina at the end of the thirteenth century. In France it has been slightly popular. Dante and Petrarch liked to use it. Here are the rules, as drawn up by Daniel and his followers in Italy, Spain and Portugal:

1. The sestina has six stanzas—each of six lines, of the same length—and a concluding three-line stanza.
2. The lines of the six stanzas end with the same six words, not rhyming with each other; these end words are chosen exclusively from two-syllabled nouns.
3. The arrangement of these six terminal words follows a regular law, very complex in ancient times, and altered toward simplicity later, as appears hereafter.
4. The closing three-line stanza uses the six terminal words, three at the centers of the lines, three at their ends.

Modern usage permits the variation of allowing the terminating words to rhyme, either on two rhyming sounds, as Swinburne uses it,

or on three. In every case, the six terminal words must be repeated, with no change in sound or spelling, through each succeeding stanza. The order for the six terminal words in the six successive stanzas is as follows:

1st	stanza	1, 2, 3, 4, 5, 6
2nd	stanza	6, 1, 5, 2, 4, 3
3rd	stanza	3, 6, 4, 1, 2, 5
4th	stanza	5, 3, 2, 6, 1, 4
5th	stanza	4, 5, 1, 3, 6, 2
6th	stanza	2, 4, 6, 5, 3, 1

The concluding half stanza ends with 2, 4 and 6; and uses 1, 3 and 5 at the beginning—not necessarily as the first word—of the lines; or at the half line, in rhymes that permit their introduction there.

Here is an example: The numerals refer to terminal words, not rhyme sounds.

We are the smiling comfortable homes,	1
With happy families enthroned therein,	2
Where baby souls are brought to meet the world,	3
Where women end their duties and desires,	4
For which men labor as the goal of life,	5
That people worship now instead of God.	6

Do we not teach the child to worship God?—	6
Whose soul's young range is bounded by the homes	1
Of those he loves, and where he learns that life	5
Is all constrained to serve the wants therein,	2
Domestic needs and personal desires,—	4
These are the early limits of his world.	3

And are we not the woman's perfect world,	3
Prescribed by nature and ordained of God,	6
Beyond which she can have no right desires,	4
No need for service other than in homes?	1
For doth she not bring up her young therein?	2
And is not rearing young the end of life?	5

And man? What other need hath he in life	5
Than to go forth and labor in the world,	3
And struggle sore with other men therein?	2

Not to serve other men, nor yet his God,   6
But to maintain these comfortable homes,—   1
The end of all a normal man's desires.   4

Shall not the soul's most measureless desires   4
Learn that the very flower and fruit of life   5
Lies all attained in comfortable homes,   1
With which life's purpose is to dot the world   3
And consummate the utmost will of God,   6
By sitting down to eat and drink therein.   2

Yea, in the processes that work therein—   2
Fulfilment of our natural desires—   4
Surely man finds the proof that mighty God   6
For to maintain and reproduce his life   5
Created him and set him in the world;   3
And this high is best attained in homes.   1

Are we not homes? And is not all therein?   1, 2
Wring dry the world to meet our wide desires!   3, 4
We crown all life! We are the aim of God!   5, 6

Homes, Charlotte Perkins Gilman.

Here the lines end on accented syllables, and by no means on two-syllabled nouns exclusively. There is no sestina in any of the collections in English which follows this convention; it may be dismissed, with the reflection that the French, Spanish and Italian languages have more double rhymes than English.

The movements of each terminal word follow a definite pattern, as a graph of the numbered terminal words will show. The order of position is successively 1, 2, 4, 5, 3, 6, 1, 2, 4, 5, 3, etc. By this means the last word of one stanza terminates the first line of the next; and meanwhile the last line of next has been shifted from third position to last, to terminate line one of the ensuing stanza.

Swinburne uses, as terminal words in one of his rhymed sestinas, *day, night, way, light, may, delight,* as 1, 2, 3, 4, 5, 6; and thereafter achieves alternate rhymes throughout, by creating his own sequence pattern, as follows: 6, 1, 4, 3, 2, 5; 5, 6, 1, 4, 3, 2; 2, 5, 6, 1, 4, 3; 3, 2, 1, 6, 5, 4; 4, 3, 2, 5, 6, 1, with the terminals of the concluding triplet *light, way, delight* (4, 3, 6), and the internal rhymes here *day, night, may* (1, 2, 5). He has worked out even more intricately his rhymed double sestina, *The Complaint of Lisa*—twelve stanzas of

twelve lines each, with a concluding sestet, of 150 lines in all. Charles W. Coleman, in his sestina *Love's Going*, used three rhyme sounds, *sing, rose, heart, thing, goes, apart;* but he retains the unrhymed sequence formula, and thus has rhyming couplets in four of his stanzas. Swinburne's variation is to be preferred to this.

Clearly, in writing the sestina, after the first stanza has been completed, the next task is to write down the terminals for all the lines of the next five stanzas, and the terminals and center words of the brief concluding stanza. Then proceed to write. . . .The form is more suitable to clever light verse than to poetry.

The Villanelle

The villanelle lends itself to seriousness, as well as to frivolity. It consists of nineteen lines: five three-lined stanzas, concluding with a quatrain. The refrain couplet, which terminates the form, consists of lines one and three of the first triplet. Moreover, line one (the first half of the refrain) terminates stanzas two and four and line three (the other half of the refrain), stanzas three and five. Only two rhyming sounds are used. The following villanelle follows the pattern strictly:

> O Singer of Persephone!   1-a
>   In the dim meadows desolate,   2
> Dost thou remember Sicily?   1-b
>
> Still through the ivy flits the bee   1
>   Where Amaryllis lies in state,   2
> O Singer of Persephone!   1-a
>
> Simaetha calls on Hecate,   1
>   And hears the wild dogs at the gate;   2
> Dost thou remember Sicily?   1-b
>
> Still by the light and laughing sea   1
>   Poor Polypheme bemoans his fate,   2
> O Singer of Persephone!   1-a
>
> And still in boyish rivalry   1
>   Young Daphnis challenges his mate: 2
> Dost thou remember Sicily?   1-b
>
> Slim Lacon keeps a goat for thee;   1
>   For thee the jocund shepherds wait,   2

O Singer of Persephone!   1-a
Dost thou remember Sicily?   1-b

Theocritus, Oscar Wilde.

Edwin Arlington Robinson pours poetry into the form, in a villanelle concluding:

There is ruin and decay
    In the House on the Hill:
They are all gone away,
There is nothing more to say.

The House on the Hill, Edwin Arlington Robinson.

The Lai and the Virelai

The ancient French *lai* was composed of couplets of five-syllabled lines, all on the same rhyme, separated by single lines of two syllables each, which rhymed with one another. The number of lines in each stanza was not fixed, nor the number of stanzas in the complete poem. An improvised example would be:

Summer heat today   1
In its torrid way,   1
I see,   2
With its awful ray   1
Sears till it must slay   1
Poor me,   2
Tree and grass and clay.   1
It's the bay—the spray   1
And glee!   2

A curious old tradition connected with the form is that the indentation of the shorter lines is forbidden. This detail was called *arbre fourchu,* a forked tree, from the fancied resemblance of the poem on paper to a tree with branches projecting. Where lais have more than one stanza, the two rhymes in each stanza have no reference to the rhymes in any other.

The *virelai* or *virelai ancien* grew out of this, with a sequence of rhymes throughout. Thus, in a twelve-line stanza, the rhymes would be 1, 1, 2, 1, 1, 2, 1, 1, 2, 1, 1, 2. The next stanza would be 2, 2, 3,

2, 2, 3, 2, 2, 3, 2, 2, 3; and so on, until the last stanza appeared as n, n, 1, n, n, 1, n, n, 1, n, n, 1. Thus each rhyme sound would appear once in the longer lines, and once in the shorter. The form is too simple to need illustration.

The *virelai nouveau* is written throughout on two rhymes. Its initial rhymed couplet serves as a refrain for the later stanzas; and the two lines close each stanza alternately until the last, when they both appear together, but in inverse order. Here is an example which begins with the couplet as its first stanza.

> Good-bye to the Town!—good-bye!   1a
> Hurrah for the sea and the sky!   1-b
> > *July,* Austin Dobson.

The second stanza is rhymed, 1, 1, 1, 2, 1, 1-a. Its third stanza is 1, 2, 1, 2, 1, 2, 2, 1, 1-b. The succeeding stanzas are as irregular, but each is confined to the two rhymed sounds, and the refrains occur in the prescribed order. And here is the concluding stanza, showing the refrain reversed:

> So Phyllis, the fawn-footed, hie   1
> For a hansom! Ere close of the day   2
> Between us a "world" must lie,—   1
> Hurrah! for the sea and the sky!   1-b
> Good-bye to the Town! GOOD-BYE!   1-a

The *Sicilian octave* at times is used as a fixed form. It consists of eight iambic five-foot lines, rhymed 1, 2, 1, 2, 1, 2, 1, 2. No difficulty will be found in writing in this pattern.

The *rispetto* is an Italian form, with interrhyming lines ranging from six to ten in number, though not usually exceeding eight. Used rarely in English, it is usually divided into two stanzas, rhymed 1, 2, 1, 2; 3, 3, 4, 4.

A brief American fixed form, called the *sonnette,* was originated by Sherman Ripley and had a vogue for a time. It consisted of seven five-foot iambic lines, rhymed: 1, 2, 2, 1; 3, 2, 3. It differed only slightly from the *Canopus* stanza, already described, which also used seven five-foot iambic lines, but rhymed them 1, 2, 1, 2, 3, 2, 3. Both avoid the terminal couplet, and hence have an uninterrupted flow for narrative verse.

Another recent form is the *Douzet,* its origin unknown. It consists of twelve five-foot iambic lines, rhymed as follows: 1, 2, 2, 1; 3, 4, 4, 3; 1, 2, 3, 4. This introduces a novelty in the repetition of rhyme not encountered so far elsewhere: the concluding quatrain's rhyme scheme amounting to a summary of the rhyme sounds gone before.

There is no limit to the patterns that ingenuity in versification can produce. Only the rare few among these achieve enduring popularity.

The Japanese form, the *hokku,* follows Japanese poetry (*tanka* or *uta*) in having alternate verses of 5 and 7 syllables. The hokku or *haikai* consists of only three lines, 5, 7, and 5 syllables, or 17 in all. An improvised example is:

> More fleeting than the
> Flash of withered windblown leaf,
> This thing men call life.

The Japanese *tanka* ordinarily has 31 syllables, consisting of five lines, with respectively 5, 7, 5, 7, and 7 syllables. An improvised example is:

> The rippling sea-swell,
> Curling upon the gold sand,
> And, curving over,
> A bough of cherry blossoms,—
> Youth shielding eternal age.

Longer Japanese poems may be constructed in the tanka form, with the invariable alternation of 5 and 7 syllables to the line, and the addition of a terminal 7-syllabled line. The rhythm in Japanese poetry is not regarded. The only convention is the number of syllables to the line.

The Limerick

The limerick is the only fixed form indigenous to the English language. It first appeared in *Songs for the Nursery, or, Mother Goose's Melodies for Children,* published by Elizabeth Goose, (formerly Vertigoose, married to Thomas Fleet, a Boston printer) in 1719. Moreover, in this collection it appeared in all three of its successive forms. The first stage opened and closed the five-line form with a nonsense line:

> Hickory, dickory, dock!
> The mouse ran up the clock.
>> The clock struck one—
>> The mouse ran down,
> Hickory, dickory, dock!
> *Nursery Rhymes,* Mother Goose.

The second form, the one used by Edward Lear throughout, ended the first and fifth line with a geographical name, at times these lines being identical:

> As I was going to Bonner,
> Upon my word of honor,
>> I met a pig
>> Without a wig,
> As I was going to Bonner.
> *Nursery Rhymes,* Mother Goose.

The third and culminating form has a new rhyme sound in the fifth line—as in this example:

> There was an old soldier of Bister
> Went walking one day with his sister,
>> When a cow at one poke
>> Tossed her into an oak,
> Before the old gentleman missed her.
> *Nursery Rhymes,* Mother Goose.

A classic model to follow is the famous limerick—

> There was a young lady from Niger,
> Who smiled as she rode on a tiger.
>> They came back from the ride
>> With the lady inside,
> And the smile on the face of the tiger.
> *More Limericks,* Cosmo Monkhouse.

The identity instead of rhyme in lines 2 and 5 cannot spoil the charm of this, although the pure pattern would avoid it. This would be—

remembering that an extra unaccented syllable can be added either
to the 1, 2, 5 rhyme group, or to the 3, 4 group, or to both:

                 a TUM—ta ta TUM—ta ta TUM
                 ta TUM—ta ta TUM—ta ta TUM,
                  ta ta TUM—ta ta TUM
                  ta ta TUM—ta ta TUM
                 ta ta TUM—ta ta TUM—ta ta TUM.

In other words, an anapestic pattern, 5, 5, 3, 3, 5 feet to the lines
respectively, rhymed 1, 1, 2, 2, 1, usually with an iamb opening lines
1 and 2. Any trick rhyming device is permissible, as:

                 An amorous M. A.
                 Says that Cupid, that C. D.,
                  Doesn't cast for his health,
                  But is rolling in wealth—
                 He's the John Jaco-B. H.
                                             Anonymous.

This must be read by pronouncing *M. A.* as "master of arts," and by
rhyming lines two and five properly to it—"caster of darts" and
"Jacob Astor of hearts." Here is one of the tongue-twister variety:

                 A tutor who tooted the flute
                 Tried to teach two young tooters to toot.
                  Said the two to the tutor,
                  "Is it harder to toot, or
                 To tutor two tooters to toot?"
                             Four Limericks, Carolyn Wells.

Among other possible variations is:

                 There was a young lady of Diss,
                 Who said, "Now I think skating bliss!"
                  This no more will she state,
                  For a wheel off her skate
                 Made her finish up something like this!
                                             Anonymous.

The writing of limericks at times becomes extremely popular.

Little Willies

Any form may become, almost overnight, a favorite with poets and especially light verse writers. Some college student wrote and published in his college paper a rhyme proceeding approximately like this:

> Tobacco is a filthy weed.
>> I like it.
> It satisfies no normal need.
>> I like it.
> It makes you thin, it makes you lean,
> It takes the hair right off your bean;
> It's the worst darned stuff I've ever seen.
>> I like it.
>>>> Anonymous.

At once this form was copied by newspaper and other light versifiers the breadth and length of the land, and is still intermittently alive.

Another form assumed wide popularity, arising from one of Col. D. Streamer's (Harry Graham's) *Ruthless Rhymes for Heartless Homes:*

> Billy, in one of his nice new sashes,
> Fell in the fire and was burned to ashes.
> Now, although the room grows chilly,
> I haven't the heart to poke poor Billy.
>> *Tender-Heartedness,* Harry Graham.

The quatrain here consists of two couplets, rhymed 1, 1, 2, 2. The meter combines trochees and dactyls; it might be iambs and anapests, of course, or any of the four. Somehow Billy became rechristened Willie, and at least one anonymous volume has appeared since, dealing in this or other simple quatrains with the adventures of Willie and his family. Among famous ones are:

> Willie and two other brats
> Licked up all the Rough-on-Rats.
> Father said, when mother cried,
> "Never mind, they'll die outside."
>> Anonymous.

Father heard his children scream,
So he threw them in the stream,
Saying, as he drowned the third,
"Children should be seen, *not* heard!"
                              The Stern Parent, Harry Graham.

Late last night I slew my wife
Stretched her on the parquet flooring.
I was loath to take her life,
But I *had* to stop her snoring.
                              Necessity, Harry Graham.

Willie poisoned father's tea;
Father died in agony.
Mother looked extremely vexed:
"Really, Will," she said, "what next!"
                              Anonymous.

The model for a Little Willie, with its trick last line and its sadistic
content, can be taken from any of these.

Light Verse in English

   Light verse, including its elegant form called *vers de société,*
demands a technical dexterity greater than that of poetry; for the
obviousness and cleverness of the rhyme are a charm here, where they
usually interfere with the emotional effect of poetry. The student of
versification will benefit by studying Tom Hood, for the use of puns
in light verse; *Mother Goose,* for inspired use of rhythm; Edward Lear
and Lewis Carroll, for shapely nonsense verse; Charles Stuart
Calverly for mastery of every trick of rhyming, and great dexterity in
stanza-devising; W. S. Gilbert, for mastery of the whole field. The
long finale of his *Iolanthe* is his peak in rhyming, and almost the peak
of light verse in English. Split words are a constant device: as in
Carroll's—

              Who would not give all else for two p-
              Ennyworth of beautiful soup?
                              Soup of the Evening, Lewis Carroll.

or another surprise rhyming sung by Canning:

> Sun, moon, and thou vain world, adieu,
>   That kings and priests are plotting in;
> Here doomed to starve on water-gru-
> -El, never shall I see the U-
>   -Niversity of Gottingen,
>   -Niversity of Gottingen!
> > *Song by Rogero,* George Canning.

Humorous verse need not be clever. A poem like Ernest Lawrence Thayer's *Casey at the Bat* is a perpetual favorite because the theme invokes deep laughter, not because it is trickily versified. Dialect verse is in a class by itself. In writing dialect verse, be careful

(1) To use dialect spelling only where required.
(2) Not to overuse it or the reader will not understand it.

Such an improvised quatrain as—

> Sum peoples iz peculyer,
> I reitteratez agen,
> They mus' come f'um Atlanta
> An' not from Bummin'ham

is full of bad writing. *Sum* is the correct pronunciation of *some,* not a dialect pronunciation; the same is true of *iz, reitteratez,* and *agen.* The same is probably true of *peculyer.* And why *f'um* and *from* in the same poem? This is as inept as using *you* and *thou* (in any form) in the same poem, to refer to the same person. *F'um, mus'* and *an'* are accurate dialect speech.

Among other forms of light verse are *parody,* aping the versifying mannerisms of another; *nonsense verse; whimsical verse* of many kinds; *mosaic* or *composite verse,* each line taken from some other poet; *macaronic verse,* where two or more languages are hashed together; *shaped whimsies,* where the typography pictures the theme, as in the *Song of the Decanter,* on page 102.

Various forms of *typographical oddities* may be devised, in which certain of the lines (as the terminals of each quatrain) represent the way a person walks, sober, or intoxicated, or the way he falls down.

Acrostics are verses where the opening letters of the lines, or the closing letters, or letters arrived at by some other system, name a person, or convey a special message. Here is an example:

> *F*rom your bright sparkling Eyes I was undone;
> *R*ays, you have; more transparent than the Sun,

*A*midst its glory in the rising Day
*N*one can you equal in your bright array;
*C*onstant in your calm and unspotted mind,
*E*qual to all, but will to none Prove kind,
*S*o knowing, seldome one so Young, you'll Find,
*A*h! woe's me, that I should Love and conceal
*L*ong have I wished, but never dared reveal,
*E*ven though severely Love's Pains I feel;
*X*erxes that great, wasn't free from Cupid's Dart,
*A*nd all the great Heroes, felt the smart.

       Acrostic, George Washington.

The words conveyed by the acrostic are revealed by reading downward the first or italicized letters of each line.

The actual writing of light verse calls upon the versifier for every resource and device within the technique of versification. The rhymes should be natural and not rhyme-induced, and the entire treatment natural and adapted to please and amuse.

There was an old decanter and its
mouth was gaping wide; the
rosy wine had ebbed away
and left its crystal side;
and the wind went
humming—humming
up and down: the
wind it flew, and
through the reed-like
hollow neck the wildest
notes it blew. I placed it in
the window, where the blast
was blowing free, and fancied
that its pale mouth sang the queerest strains to me. "They tell me—puny
conquerors! the Plaque has slain his ten,
and war his hundred thousand of the very best
of men; but I"—'twas thus the Bottle spake—"but
I have conquered more than all your famous conquerors,
so feared and famed of yore, Then come, ye youths and
maidens all, come drink from out my cup, the beverage that
dulls the brain, and burns the spirits up; that puts to shame
your conquerors that slay their scores below; for this
has deluged millions with the lava tide of woe. Tho'
in the path of battle darkest streams of blood may
roll, yet while I killed the body, I have damned
the very soul. The cholera, the plague, the
sword such ruin never wrought, as I
in mirth or malice on the innocent have brought. And still I
breathe upon them, and they shrink
before my breath, while year by year my
thousands go my dusty way of death."

Song of the Decanter, Warfield Creath Richardson.

▪ VII ▪

POETRY AND TECHNIQUE

The Vocabulary of Poetry

THE VOCABULARY USED by a poet in his poetry should be the vocabulary that he uses in his living speech. Prose uses this, or else it becomes stilted and affected. If an orator commences,

> *O Mississippi, Father of Waters, thou wast engendered in the hills of Minnehaha; thou hast meandered through meadows green and valleys dappled for more miles than man computeth,*

his hearers feel that there is something strained and unnatural in his words. The same thought occurs, when poetry, especially modern poetry, contain words no longer in the living vocabulary of man, because they have become archaic; or else unknown to the living vocabulary, because they are artificially constructed to meet the exigencies of rhyme or meter: such words as—

Thou, thee, thy, ye, mineself.
Art (verb form), *wast, wert, dost, wilt* (verb form), *hast, hadst,
    wouldst, shouldst, shalt,* and all verb forms ending in *-est, -st*
    and the like.
'Tis, 'gainst, 'gin, 'tween, 'neath, e'er, and other contractions not
    in living speech; as opposed to *it's* and other contractions used
    in living speech.
*Wroth, bethink, reft, reaving, athwart, welkin, rathe, fardel, bur-
    then, murther, nave, chaps, gins, sooth, Norweyan, proof* (for
    armor), *composition* (for *terms of peace*), *ronyon,* and all other
    archaic, obsolescent or obsolete words.
Except for "unless," *memorize* for "make memorable," and other
    outworn usages of words.

All unnatural and elliptical expressions, improper in living speech,

such as *as to* for "as if to," *bethink me* for "recall," *for to that* for "for to that end" and the like.

All inversions and strained expressions improper in living speech, such as *the soldier brave, have I seen, I battles fought,* and the like. These are common, because they are rhyme-induced.

Poetry that speaks a dead language is dead from its birth; poetry that speaks a warped and distorted language is warped and distorted from its birth. For when real poetry from real poets is encountered, its speech is as direct, forthright and living as:

> Our revels now are ended. These our actors,
> As I foretold you, were all spirits, and
> Are melted into air, into thin air;
> And, like the baseless fabric of this vision,
> The cloud-capp'd towers, the gorgeous palaces,
> The solemn temples, the great globe itself,
> Yea, all of which it *inherit,* shall dissolve,
> And, like this insubstantial pageant *faded,*
> Leave not a *rack* behind. We are such stuff
> As dreams are made *on,* and our little life
> Is rounded with a sleep.
>
> *The Tempest,* William Shakespeare.

The captious might suggest *inherits* for *inherit;* might point out that *faded* is out of place; that "made *of* " is preferable to "made *on*"; we might query the *rack.* At that, *rack* is still used in "rack and ruin," a "cloud-rack," "the rack of a storm"; and *rack,* used here in the sense of a vestige, is intelligible and may be regarded as living. And this poetry was written more than three hundred years ago, by William Shakespeare, who knew too much, even then, to stud his verse with *thee's* and *thou's* and their outmoded verb forms, *welkin, athwart, amaranthine,* and so on.

The test for the phrasing of poetry is: could you have said the same thing, or its equivalent, to your maid or your butcher, and not been regarded as eccentric? If your poetry speaks your own living language, its vocabulary is acceptable. If it is marred with word fossils no longer acceptable in living speech, to that extent it falls below its possible flight.

No word acceptable in acceptable prose is out of place in poetry. Any word may be so ineptly or awkwardly used in poetry that it becomes a blemish. When Shakespeare wrote:

> It is a tale
> Told by an idiot, full of sound and fury,
> Signifying nothing,
> > *Macbeth,* William Shakespeare.

he used *idiot* magnificently and poetically; when Wordsworth wrote:

> Why bustle thus about your door?
> What means this bustle, Betty Foy?
> Why are you in this mighty fret?
> And why on horseback have you set
> Him whom you love, your Idiot Boy?
> > *The Idiot Boy,* William Wordsworth.

the word *idiot* is as unpoetic as the rest of the passage. The living speech, the colloquial, can be magical, poetic, as in this sonnet sestet:

> It is some lie that under a windswept tree,
> > Touching your lips, I touched my vanished youth,
> And found again a young, new ecstasy.
> > It is a lie, I say. This—this is Truth!
> Now—I shall rest. For youth and you are gone.
> Tomorrow I shall put my flannels on.
> > *Sonnet,* John V. A. Weaver

Edwin Arlington Robinson will be remembered for lines as colloquially magical as:

> The man who had made other men
> As ordinary as arithmetic . . .

> I'll have to tell you, Brother Bedivere,
> That crowns and orders, and high palaces, . . .
> Will not go rolling down to hell just yet
> Because a pretty woman is a fool.
> > *Merlin,* Edwin Arlington Robinson.

He will have to be forgiven for verse as bookish as:

> Born with a face
> That on a bullfrog would ensure for life
> The lucubrations of a celibate . . .

> Less to remembering an obscure monition
> Than to confessing an assured renascence—
> *Roman Barthalow,* Edwin Arlington Robinson.

though both of these are not so much archaic as morbidly pedantic. Frost rarely departs from living speech; he has enriched the language by phrases immortally and colloquially true, including the familiar:

> The trial by market everything must come to.

Even slang has its place: did not Shakespeare have Hamlet say this?

> So I do still, by these pickers and stealers . . .
> *Hamlet,* William Shakespeare.

Nor is Sandburg more unpoetic, when he writes:

> Play it across the table.
> What if we steal this city blind?
> If they want anything let 'em nail it down.
> *Cahoots,* Carl Sandburg.

John Livingston Lowes, in *Convention and Revolt in Poetry,* phrases words of gold for poets to remember:

> *The very greatest effects of poetry are often produced without the use of a single word which might not be employed in ordinary speech.*

Thomas Gray wrote in one of his letters:

> *The language of the age is never the language of poetry. . . . Our poetry . . . has a language peculiar to itself.*

This attitude explains the common idea permitting dead speech in verse; it cannot resurrect poets following it from the graves their practice of this dug. Such poets live only insofar as they violate this statement.

Wordsworth followed this, when he preluded his *The Force of Prayer* with the double archaism:

> What is good for a bootless bene?

Witty Mary Lamb flashed back, when her brother Charles read this to her, "A shoeless pea," and punned this absurd line into immortality. And there is Rossetti's phrase from his rendition of the Villon ballade,

> From Love he won such dule and teen!

Poetry does not gain by using such mummified speech.

Kipling was more successful than any previous poet so far in using the language of the machine age in poetry:

> It is their care, in all the ages, to take the buffet and cushion the
>   shock;
> It is their care that the gear engages; it is their care that the
>   switches lock;
> It is their care that the wheels run truly; it is their care to
>   embark and entrain,
> Tally, transport, and deliver duly the sons of Mary by land and
>   main.
>   *The Sons of Martha*, Rudyard Kipling.

In a memorandum dealing with the writing of *Leaves of Grass*, Walt Whitman wrote:

> I had great trouble in leaving out the stock
> "poetical" touches, but succeeded at last.

Even this great plain-speaking master slipped back, as he aged, into stock poeticisms such as:

> 'mid, unrecked, know I, yield we, ye valleys grand.

But in the main he avoided this blemish. And he has made the task easier for those who followed him.

Sidney Lanier lays stress upon *phonetic syzygy*, that extension of alliteration which includes all related consonants, as *t, d, th*, and *TH*; *g, k, ch*, and other gutturals; and so on. Other authorities deal extensively with *onomatopoeia*, the language device in which words reproduce the sounds they are intended to convey, as in—

> With lisp of leaves and ripple of rain.
> *Chorus from Atalanta in Calydon*, Algernon Charles Swinburne.

With any inner sense of music, we will avoid lines as awkward, inept and unsingable as Browning's familiar:

Irks care the crop-full bird, frets double the maw-crammed beast?
                                         Rabbi Ben Ezra, Robert Browning.

Let your poetic speech be your own living speech at its best, dictated by an innate sense of music, and the result will satisfy.

On Translating Poetry

Poetry cannot be translated; it can only be recreated in the new language. We are dealing with the ingredients of verse, not of poetry, in this book: a study of the essence of poetry would not deal with iambs and cinquains and sestinas, it would deal with the stimuli that most deeply affect the human emotions. The emotion-arousing quality in words cannot be stated otherwise even in the same language, much less in another one. There is no translation in English for emotion-arousing words such as *home, mother, love,* and so on; not *house* or *domicile,* not *mamma* or *maternal ancestor* or *Moms* or *ma,* not *affection,* or *devotion* or *lust* or *rut.* How can *night* be expressed in another word, or *moon* or *sun,* or *May,* or *December?* Each of these words—to some extent each word in the language—has a tone color, a history, a personality, an effectiveness of its own. With many of the words in the language, each person has strange and personal associations, naturally untranslatable. There are emotions which are not translatable from country to country, but which can only be recreated by some remote equivalent. When Noyes climaxes a poem with the glorious invocation,

Englande!—Englande!—Englande!—Englande!
                                         Marchant Adventurers, Alfred Noyes.

he utters a battle cry that only an Englishman could thrill to. Its word music is lost the moment it reappears as *Angleterre! Angleterre! Angleterre! Angleterre!* "Finland! Finland! Finland! Finland!" would not thrill similarly, though the rhythm and word tune are the same. A fourfold repetition of *Switzerland,* or *Czechoslovakia,* or, queerly enough, even of *United States* would not evoke a similar thrill. Moreover, Shelley could have used the same repetition of *England,* in a

poem in the bitter mood of *The Masque of Anarchy,* and it would have
evoked utter detestation: so intangible are the elements in sounds that
uplift or break the heart, that send a Cardigan or a Pickett with a
whole brigade of men to death at the monosyllable "Charge!"—that
spell heaven in a girl's whispered "Yes," and a lifetime's dearth in her
even briefer "No."

In Keat's *Ode to a Nightingale* we have two lines of peak magic:

> Charmed magic casements, opening on the foam
> Of perilous seas, in faery lands forlorn.

These two lines cannot be said differently in English without wrecking the magic. Accurately paraphrased, they would give:

> Enchanted supernatural windows, unclosing on the bubbles
> Of dangerous oceans, in unreal romantic countries dejected.

There is no poetry here now. Translate it with absolute fidelity into
another language, and the poetry is as dead. It must be recreated by a
poet of like emotional power in the other language, if it is to survive
there as poetry.

Fitzgerald did such magic, when he took a literal translation of
the poetic *Rubáiyát of Omar Khayyám,* such as these two groups of
lines:

> Everywhere that there has been a rose or tulip-bed,
> It has come from the redness of the blood of a king;
> Every violet shoot that grows from the earth
> Is a mole that was once on the cheek of a beauty.
> > *Quatrains,* Omar Khayyám.

This is inaccurate botanically and only whimsically effective as an
idea. It is certainly not poetry. Nor is:

> Hell is a spark from my useless worries,
> Paradise is a moment of time when I am tranquil.
> > *Quatrains,* Omar Khayyám.

But out of this material Fitzgerald wrought—created, recreated—
what thousands hail as poetry:

I sometimes think that never blows so red
The Rose, as where some buried Caesar bled;
    That every Hyacinth the Garden wears
Dropt in her Lap from some once lovely Head. . . .

Heav'n but the Vision of fulfilled Desire,
And Hell the Shadow from a Soul on fire,
    Cast on the Darkness into which Ourselves,
So late emerged from, shall so soon expire.
    Rubáiyát of Omar Khayyám, Edward Fitzgerald.

This is no longer Omar Khayyám; it is far more Fitzgerald, inspired by Omar Khayyám. The reflection about the rose is acceptable now; the whimsy about the hyacinth is more pleasing to us than the more fleshly Oriental passion of the mole on the cheek of a beauty. The definitions of heaven and hell no longer resemble the original at all. Oriental impassivity and superiority to things earthly have been replaced by a viewpoint accurate enough to have come out of Freud, and acceptable as concentrated truth to many of us. All of this is expressed with the most effective devices of versification, a language in which poetry must speak, if it speaks at all.

Something like this must be done, each time you seek to make a translation. A literal translation can give the idea, but never the poetry.

For a last example, here is an accurate translation of the first five verses of the first chapter of *Genesis* by Fagnani:

At the beginning of Elohim's forming the heavens and the earth, when darkness was upon the face of the abyss, Elohim said, "Let there be light," and there was light.
Elohim saw that the light was excellent.
And Elohim separated the light from the darkness and he called the light Day and the darkness he called Night.
Evening came, and Morning came.
    The Beginning of History, According to the Jews,
    Charles Prosper Fagnani.

This is near to poetry, so magnificent is the primitive conception. But it is not mere familiarity that makes us recognize, from the hands of greater poets writing in English, the magnificent poetry of the same verses, as they appear in the King James Bible:

> *In the beginning God created the heavens and the earth.*
> *And the earth was without form, and void; and darkness was upon the face of the deep. And the Spirit of God moved upon the face of the waters.*
> *And God said, Let there be light; and there was light.*
> *And God saw the light, that it was good; and God divided the light from the darkness.*
> *And God called the light Day, and the darkness he called Night. And the evening and the morning were the first day.*
>
> *Genesis,* King James's Translation.

The most accurate translation of a poem is no more than rude notes for a poem to be built upon. There is always need for accurate renditions of the poetry of other lands and tongues. But, unless the English versifier reissues the product as his own re-creation, it remains mere verse, a museum curiosity rather than impassioned song.

Exercises in Versification

To give the book its greatest value, the reader, having reached this point, should start over again, and write exercises in each poetic device treated. Practice iambic lines, each number of feet to the line, rhymed and unrhymed. The same with trochaic, anapestic, and dactylic lines. At times seek to pour poetry into these molds; at times find the relief of light verse in them.

Essay the stanzas, from the couplet up to such involved arrangements as the Spenserian stanza and *terza rima.* Work on sonnets of both kinds: aiming at technical mastery, rather than poetic excellence, at first. Get the patterns etched on your mind, and then you can write in them accurately without consciously remembering them. Try the solace of concentrated and poetic free verse. And then, if you care to, go to the fixed forms one after another, preferably in light verse, and among all these attempts you will startle yourself by achieving at times a veritable poem or gem of light verse when you merely intended finger exercises.

And at all times, when the poetic mood comes, write what comes, from a phrase, a line, a couplet, to an epic fragment: and preserve it, on the chance that, sooner or later, the rest of the poem will come.

THE COMPLETE RHYMING DICTIONARY

What Rhyme Is

RHYME IS THE identity in sound of an accented vowel in a word, usu-ally the last one accented, and of all consonantal and vowel sounds following it, with a difference in the sound of the consonant immedi-ately preceding the accented vowel.

Rhyme thus deals exclusively with sound. Sound is indicated in all dictionaries by phonetic markings. In this rhyming dictionary, each group of words that rhyme is preceded by a heading consisting of the accented vowel, marked phonetically, and followed by all the con-sonantal and vowel sounds following it. The unaccented syllables are not marked phonetically as thoroughly, since they are rela-tively unimportant: except to distinguish between rhyme sounds like *pasture* (ĂS′tūr) and *faster* (ĂS′tŭr), and to identify certain long vowels.

The one-syllabled rhymes are given first, with the rhyme-sound headings arranged alphabetically, from the first A sound to the last U sound. Then follow the two-syllabled rhymes, similarly arranged; and, last of all, the three-syllabled rhymes.

The Vowel Sounds

In this phonetic arrangement, the vowel sounds used are indicated as follows. After each is given the various ways in which the sound appears in spelling in English

A

Ā   as in *ale;* heard also in *pain, day, break, veil, obey, gaol, gauge, eh.*

Â   as in *care;* heard also in *there, pear, air, heir, prayer, e'er.*
Ă   as in *add;* heard also in *plaid, bade.*
Ȧ   as in *arm,* father; heard also in *hearth, sergeant, memoir.*
A   as in *ask.* Strictly, authorities say that A should be so
       pronounced (midway between the A in *father* and the A in
       add) when followed by *s, th, f,* or *m* or *n* plus a consonant. In
       practice, this sound is usually pronounced like the A in *add.*
       The rule becomes absurd when we try to pronounce *pan* with
       the A sound in *add,* and *pans* with a different A sound.

E

Ē   as in *me;* heard also in *eve, feet, beam, deceive, people, key,*
       Caesar, machine, field, quay, phoebe.
Ḝ   as in *here;* heard also in *fear, dreary, weird.*
Ĕ   as in *end;* heard also in *heifer, leopard, friends, Aetna, feather,*
       asafoetida, bury, any, Thames, said, says.

I

Ī   as in *ice;* heard also in *vie, rye, height, eye, aisle, aye* (meaning
       yes), *sky, buy, choir.*
Ĭ   as in *ill;* heard also in *sieve, English, pretty, been, breeches,*
       women, busy, build, nymph, hymnal.

O

Ō   as in *old;* heard also in *note, oh, roam, foe, shoulder, grow, owe,*
       sew, yeoman, beau, hautboy, brooch.
Ô   as in *or;* heard also in *all, talk, swarm, haul, caught, law,*
       fought, broad, memoir.
Ŏ   as in *odd;* heard also in *want, wash, shone.*
OI   as in *oil;* heard also in *boy.*
O͞O   as in *foot;* heard also in *full, wolf, could.*
OU   as in *out;* heard also in *cow, sauerkraut.*

U

Ū   as in *use;* heard also in *beauty, feud, pew, queue, lieu, view, cue,*
       suit, yule, you, do, rule, true, food, group, drew, fruit, canoe,
       rheum, maneuver, blue. (The difference in sound between
       dew and *do* is that *dew* is properly dyŪ, with a consonantal *y*
       sound preceding the long U. This difference does not affect

rhyming, except as it concerns preceding consonants. For the sake of convenience, the yŪ group ordinarily precedes the Ū group.)

Û   as in *urn;* heard also in *fern, err, heard, sir, word, journal, myrrh, colonel.*

Ŭ   as in *up;* heard also in *won, one, does, flood, double.*

The Consonant Sounds

The consonant sounds used in English, and in most instances spelled phonetically in the headings preceding all groups of words rhyming together, are as follows:

B   as in *baby.*

CH   as in *chair;* heard also in, *match, question, righteous.*

D   as in *did;* heard also in *robbed.*

F   as in *fill;* heard also in *philosophy, laugh.*

G   as in *go, anger;* heard also in *guard, plague, ghost.*

GZ   as the sound represented by *x* in *exist.*

H   as in *hat.*

HW   as the sound represented by *wh* in *what.*

J   as in *joke;* heard also in *gem, religion, pigeon, soldier, edge.*

K   as in *keep;* heard also in *chorus, epoch, cube, pack, conquer, pique.*

KS   as the sound represented by *x* in *vex.*

KW   as the sound represented by *qu* in *queen.*

L   as in *late.*

M   as in *man.*

N   as in *no.*

N   The French nasal sound, not natural in English.

NG   as in *sing;* heard also in *tongue, bank, junction, linger, canker.*

P   as in *papa.*

R   as in *red;* heard also in *rhombus.*

S   as in *so, this;* heard also in *cell, scene, hiss.*

SH   as in *she;* heard also in *machine, ocean, social, conscious, sure, nauseous, pension, issue, passion, nation.*

T   as in *time.*

TH   as in *then.*

th   as in *thin.*

TU   as in *nature.* This sound is more accurately TY consonantal.

V   as in *van.*
W   as in *want;* heard also in *persuade, choir.*
Y   as in *yet;* heard also in *union.*
Z   as in *zone;* heard also in *is, lives, Xenophon.*
ZH   as the sound represented by *z* in *azure;* heard in *glazier, pleasure, vision, abscission, rouge, genre.*

A few warnings are important:

C is not a separate sound. Words spelled with *c* appear under K or S.

Q is not a separate sound. Words spelled with *qu* or *q* appear under KW.

X is not a separate sound. Words spelled with *x* appear under GZ or KS; initial *x* appears as Z.

NK, in words like *rank,* is properly NGK and so appears.

To form plurals and other inflections, F, K, P and T are followed by the sound S; the plain vowel, G, D, B, M, N, S, V, J, CH, L, R, KS (X) and Z are followed by the sound Z.

To form past tenses and other inflections, CH, S, F, K, and P are followed by the sound T; the plain vowel, G, D, B, M, N, S, V, J, L, R and Z are followed by the sound D.

Sound Does Not Depend on Spelling

Sound does not depend on spelling. "Eye-rhymes," or words matched as rhymes only because they are spelled alike, need not be rhymes at all. For instance, here are five different sounds spelled alike, *ough:*

cough, enough, plough, though, through.

It is as logical to rhyme these together as to rhyme earth-hearth, bare-are, north-forth, real-steal.

Again note that *timber* and *climber* are spelled alike; but the first rhymes with limber (ĬM'bur) and the second with rhymer (ĪM'ur). Three more words spelled alike but rhymed very differently are *ginger* (ĬNJ'ur); *singer* (ĬNG'ur); and *finger* (ĬNG'ur). Until *cow* rhymes with *blow* it is well to avoid all these words spelled alike but pronounced differently.

This Dictionary Makes Consonance Accurate

Consonance consists in the identity of all consonantal and vowel sounds after the accented vowel; and a difference in the accented vowel. This dictionary, classified according to strict phonetic pronunciation, for the first time makes consonance easy and accurate. Alphabetically arranged by the headings preceding each group of rhyme words, the following three rhyme sounds appear together: Ō′lē (wholly), Ô′lē (Raleigh), ŎL′ē (folly). Naturally these three groups are in consonance with each other.

To get the other groups of rhyming words which may be used in consonance with these three, look up successively Ā′lē, ĂL′ē, Ē′lē, Ĕ′lē, OIL′ē, ŌŌL′ē, OUL′ē, ŪL′ē; and you have all the possible sounds in consonance with the three sounds given. You may stretch a point and add ÂR′lē, ĂR′lē, ÊR′lē, and ÛR′lē if you wish, and now nothing conceivable is omitted.

Consonance, always used by the best poets, is growing so increasingly in favor that this use of the present *Complete Rhyming Dictionary* may become very important.

* * *

This volume contains hundreds of rhyming words omitted from other collections: words recently added to the vocabulary, especially in the fields of general science, pure and applied; inventions and popular applications of them; and the vivid field of recent generally acceptable slang words. The effort has been to include all words that are a proper part of the living vocabulary of man, for it is in this language that living poetry must speak.

Archaic and obsolete words, words used in an artificial or solemn style, and words whose pronunciation in poetry may vary from their pronunciation in prose have also been included. They are available to the seeker who wishes to use them, each in its proper niche, usually identified by being in italics.

In addition to this, the present volume contains more proper names than were ever listed in a rhyming dictionary before. This includes especially:

The familiar first names of boys and girls, men and women.

The familiar and easily rhymable geographical names.

The more familiar surnames, family names, or last names.

In listing proper names, the name is often not repeated when it differs only from a common word by the use of a capital. Thus, since *wood* is included, *Wood* is not. Where the spelling differs, the rhyming proper name is usually added. Thus to *main* is added *Maine*. Moreover, unnecessary duplication of words is generally avoided throughout the book. A large number of words ending in -*y* is given as rhymes for the long E sound; but at the end of this large list, the reader is referred to other words ending in -*y*, to be found in such three-syllabled rhyme groups as the words rhyming with *ability*, which are to be consulted, if the seeker desires more rhymes for long *E*. Moreover, at the end of the rhyming words listed to rhyme with *fade*, the reader is referred to the list of words rhyming on the long A sound, to which -*ed* is to be added, to make further rhymes for *fade*; and this is to be consulted, if the seeker desires more rhymes for *fade*. There is as little such cross-reference as possible, and it is never perplexing.

The dictionary is not wholly complete, and probably none will ever be. Rare and unusual scientific and geographic terms and names, for instance, as a rule have been omitted. It will add to the value of your copy of the book if you add, at the appropriate place, all omitted words that you discover.

In the lists of words rhyming on the last syllable and on the syllable before the last, certain words are included which have no rhyming mates. The monosyllables or words accented on the last syllable which appear to be rhymeless are:

aitch, H	bourne	culm
avenge, revenge	bourse	cusp
avenged, revenged	bulb	doth
bilge	coif	film
forge	peart	sylph
fugue	porch	torsk
gulf, engulf	pork	twelfth
lounge	poulp	plagued, unplagued
mauve	prestige	warmth
month	puss	wasp
morgue	recumb	wharves
mourned, bemourned,	rouge	wolf
unmourned	sauce	wolves
mouthe	scarce	

| of, hereof, thereof, whereof | spoilt |
| | swoln |

In addition to these forty-three rhymeless sounds, there is a group which has no rhyme in the living vocabulary:

amongst	forth, fourth
breadth	ninth
depth	sixth
eighth	tenth
fifth	width

These can all be rhymed by using permissible contractions of archaic or obsolete forms, such as: *clung'st, shed'th, step'th, hate'th, sniff'th, pour'th, pine'th, mix'th, pen'th,* and *skid'th.* There is a limited group of words which find their rhyming mates only in proper names, including:

alb (De Kalb)   hemp (Kemp) oblige (Lije)

There are other words which have no proper rhyming mates, but have words so close in sound that they are used as rhyming mates by many poets:

blague (vague)	en masse (class)
raj (dodge)	basque (mask, masque)
wand (pond)	else (belts)
melange (blanc mange)	grilse (wilts)
swap (top)	Welsh (belch)

THE
DICTIONARY
OF
RHYMING
WORDS

■ Section I ■

MONOSYLLABLES, AND WORDS ACCENTED ON THE LAST SYLLABLE: MASCULINE RHYMES; SINGLE RHYMES

In compound words—words consisting of two or more words united—the parts of the words may be joined without a hyphen, may be joined with a hyphen, or may be written separately. In some words usage is fixed; in others it varies. No standard rule is followed; though the hyphen today is less used than formerly. In this book, the usual practice of the best prose writers and poets is followed, modified in instances by the editor's own preference. In general, poets and versifiers make such decisions for themselves in each instance.

A

These words include the following accented vowel sounds:

Ā as in *ale;* heard also in *pain, day, break, veil, obey, gaol, gauge, eh.*

Â as in *care;* heard also in *there, pear, air, heir, prayer, e'er.*

Ă as in *add;* heard also in *plaid, bade.*

Ä as in *arm, father;* heard also in *hearth, sergeant, memoir.*

A as in *ask.* In practice, this is usually pronounced like the A sound in *add.*

For the vowel sound heard in *all, talk, swarm, haul, caught, law,* see under Ô.

For the vowel sound heard in *want* and *wash,* see under Ŏ.

Ā	airway	archway	ashtray
affray	*alackaday*	array	assagai
agley	allay	Ascension Day	assay

astay	buffet	dapple-bay	entryway
astray	byplay	dapple-gray	épée
atelier	byway	day	espalier
attaché	cableway	dead-pay	espavé
au fait	cabriolet	decay	essay
auto-da-fé	cachet	déclassé	estaminet
away	café	deejay	estray
aweigh	Calais	defray	everyday
aye	caraway	dejeuner	exposé
backstay	castaway	delay	expressway
bay	Cathay	démodé	fair play
Beaujolais	causeway	dey	fairway
belay	cay	disarray	fay
beltway	Chevalier	dismay	feather-spray
bepray	chevet	disobey	fey
beret	Chevrolet	display	fiancé
betray	Christmas Day	distingué	fiancée
bewray	cinéma vérité	distrait	fireclay
bey	clay	divorcé	first-day
bidet	clearway	divorcée	flambé
birthday	cliché	DNA	flay
Biscay	Cloisonné	doomsday	foldaway
blasé	cogway	doorway	footway
bobsleigh	communiqué	Doré	foray
bobstay	consommé	dossier	forelay
bomb bay	convey	downplay	foreplay
Bombay	corvée	dragonné	foresay
bombé	coryphée	dray	forestay
Bordelais	couché	driveway	forlay
bouchée	coulé	Dubonnet	foul play
bouclé	coupé	Dupré	frae
boulevardier	couturier	Easter day	fray
bouquet	criblé	eh	freeway
brae	crochet	émigré	Friday
bray	croquet	employe	gainsay
breakaway	crossway	employee	gala day
bridle way	cruiseway	endplay	galloway
Broadway	cutaway	entrée	Galway
broché	D day	entremets	Gamay

āle, câre, ădd, ärm, ăsk; mē, hĕre, ĕnd; īce, ĭll;

gangway	judgment day	Monterrey	Passion play
Gaspé	Kay	Montpellier	paté
gateway	Labor Day	Montrachet	pathway
gay	lack-a-day	moray	pavé
getaway	Lady Day	motorway	pay
glacé	lai	nae	payday
gley	lamé	nay	Pelé
good day	lay	naysay	Pelée
gourmet	leaden-gray	née	per se
gray	leeway	negligee	photoplay
Green Beret	Leigh	neigh	pipe clay
grey	Lord's day	névé	piquet
guideway	lycée	noonday	pis aller
habitué	macramé	Norway	play
hae	mainstay	nosegay	playday
Haigh	Malay	O'Day	plié
half-day	Mandalay	O'Shay	plissé
halfway	manqué	ŏbey	plumassier
haole	margay	ofay	popinjay
hay	market day	okay	portray
hearsay	Massenet	Olivier	pourparler
hey	matelassé	outlay	pousse-café
heyday	matinee	outré	pray
hideaway	May	outstay	prepay
highday	May Day	outweigh	prey
highway	mayday	overlay	protegé
hodden-gray	melee	overpay	protegée
hogmanay	métayer	overplay	purvey
holiday	métier	overstay	qua
Honoré	midday	overweigh	quarter day
hooray	midway	papier mâché	Rabelais
horseplay	Midway	parfait	railway
inlay	Milky Way	parlay	raisonné
interlay	mislay	Parmentier	ray
interplay	misplay	parquet	Récamier
intraday	missay	pase	rechauffé
inveigh	moiré	passageway	recherché
iron gray	Monday	passé	relay
jay	Monterey	passepied	repay

replay	slipway	Thursday	weekday
respray	sobriquet	tideway	weigh
résumé	soigneé	today	welladay
resurvey	soiree	Tokay	*wellaway*
retroussé	someday	Torbay	wey
reveillé	someway	touché	whey
ricochet	sommelier	toupée	windlestrae
risqué	soothsay	toupet	wordplay
rissolé	sorbet	tourniquet	workaday
roadway	soufflé	towaway	workday
Roget	spay	tramway	working day
rokelay	speedway	tray	Wray
role-play	spillway	trey	X ray
rollaway	splay	trysting day	yea
roman à clef	spray	Tuesday	yesterday
roquet	stageplay	*tway*	
roturier	stairway	underlay	Ä
roué	stay	underpay	aa
roundelay	steerage way	underplay	abaca
runaway	sternway	undersay	acara
runway	stingray	underway	Aceldama
sachet	stowaway	under weigh	aga
Salomé	straightaway	unlay	ah
San Jose	strathspey	unpray	aha
Sante Fe	stray	unsay	Al Fatah
saskay	subway	uplay	algebra
Saturday	sundae	upstay	Allah
say	Sunday	velouté	alumina
scray	survey	vérite	alumna
screenplay	sway	video vérité	amah
seaway	Taipei	videoplay	amphibia
settling day	takeaway	virelay	anathema
seventh day	tay	visé	Andromeda
shay	Tay	walkway	anglophobia
silver-gray	teleplay	waterway	animalcula
skidway	thereaway	way	Apocrypha
slay	they	waylay	Aquila
sleigh	throwaway	wedding day	automata
sley	thruway	Wednesday	ayah

āle,   câre,   ădd,   ärm,   ăsk;   mē,   hĕre,   ĕnd;   īce,   ĭll;

ba
baa
baccarat
bacteria
bah
baklava
basilica
blah
bourgeois
bra
budgereegah
cabala
camera
carnivora
casbah
cha-cha
cha-cha-cha
chapeau bras
cholera
cinema
clepsydra
Contra
coup d'etat
cupola
da
dada
Dégas
diaspora
éclat
Egeria
ephemera
et cetera
fa
faux-pas
foie gras
formula
gaga
genera
Golgotha

gondola
grandmamma
guarana
ha
hah
ha-ha
Hegira
holla
howdah
hurrah
huzza
hydrophobia
hypochondria
incognita
insomnia
Jah
jataka
joie
ka
la
ma
maa
Mafia
majolica
mama
mamma
mandragora
Mensa
na
nah
nebula
oolala
oompah
opera
orchestra
pa
padishah
pah
palama

Panama
papa
parabola
pariah
pas
pasha
paté de foie
  gras
patois
peau de soie
peninsula
petit pois
phantasmago-
  ria
phenomena
pizza
plethora
pooh-bah
prolegomena
Pthah
purdah
pya
pyrola
qabbala
qua
quadrigesima
quadrumana
quinquagesima
rah
rah-rah
ranula
replica
retina
Sandinista
schwa
septuagesima
sexagesima
Shah
Shia

silica
spa
spatula
ta
taffeta
taha
taiaha
tanka
tarantula
tarentola
ta-ta
tonic sol-fa
tra-la
tra-la-la
Utopia
uvula
verglas
vertebra
viola
wa
wa'
wah
wah-wah
yah

ĀB

Abe
astrolabe
babe
cosmolabe
foster babe

ĂB

Abb
Ahab
bab
Babb
baffle-gab
baobab

ōld, ôr, ŏdd, oil, fŏŏt, out; ūse, ûrn; ŭp; THis, thin

bedab
blab
cab
Cantab
confab
crab
dab
drab
fab
frab
gab
grab
jab
Joab
knab
lab
mab
McNabb
Moab
nab
pedicab
prefab
rab
scab
shab
Skylab
slab
stab
tab
taxicab

ĀB

jawab
jelab
squab
swab
(See also ŌB.)

ĂCH

aitch
H

ĂCH

attach
bach
batch
brach
catch
coffee klatsch
cratch
crosshatch
crosspatch
detach
dispatch
hatch
kaffee klatsch
latch
match
mismatch
natch
nuthatch
overmatch
patch
percussion
    match
potlatch
rach
ratch
rematch
Satch
scatch
scratch
shooting match
slatch
smatch
snatch
tache
thatch

unlatch

ĂCH

deathwatch
dogwatch
overwatch
stopwatch
watch
wristwatch
(See also
OCH.)

ĂCHT

attached
hatched
semidetached
(See also
ĂCH; add -ed
where appro-
priate.)

ĀD

abrade
abraid
accolade
Ade
Adelaide
afraid
aid
alcaide
ambassade
ambuscade
arcade
bade
balustrade
barricade
bastinade
bejade
Belgrade

blade
blockade
braid
brigade
brocade
cade
camerade
camisade
cannonade
carronade
cascade
cassonade
cavalcade
centigrade
charade
co-aid
cockade
colonnade
corrade
croupade
crusade
dade
dairymaid
Damascus
    blade
decade
deep-laid
defilade
degrade
dissuade
dragonnade
enfilade
escalade
escapade
esplanade
estacade
estrapade
evade
fade

falcade
fanfaronade
fire brigade
flanconnade
free trade
fusillade
gabionnade
gallopade
gambade
gasconade
glade
glissade
grade
grass blade
grenade
grillade
háde
handmaid
harlequinade
harquebusade
inlaid
interlaid
invade
jade
lade
laid
lancepesade
lemonade
made
maid
make the grade
marinade
marmalade
masquerade
McDade
Medicaid
mermaid
milkmaid
new-made

nightshade
old maid
orangeade
overlaid
overpaid
overpersuade
overshade
overstayed
paid
palisade
panade
parade
pasquinade
passade
persuade
pervade
pesade
pistolade
plaid
plantigrade
pomade
postpaid
prepaid
promenade
raid
rayed
ready-made
renegade
retrograde
rodomontade
saccade
scalade
sea maid
self-made
serenade
serving maid
shade
slade
spade

stade
staid
stockade
storm-stayed
suade
suede
tirade
trade
unafraid
unarrayed
unassayed
unbraid
underaid
underlaid
undismayed
unessayed
unlade
unlaid
unmade
unmaid
unpaid
unprayed
unrepaid
unstaid
unweighed
upbraid
wade
(See also
Ā; add
-ed where
appropriate.)

ĂD

ad
add
bad
bedad
begad
bade

brad
cad
Chad
chiliad
clad
dad
egad
englad
fad
footpad
forbade
gad
glad
grad
had
heath-clad
hebdomad
iron-clad
ivy-clad
kilorad
krad
lad
launchpad
Leningrad
mad
moss-clad
myriad
Olympiad
pad
Petrograd
pine-clad
plaid
rad
sad
scad
shad
superadd
tongue-pad
Trinidad

ōld, ôr, ŏdd, oil, fŏŏt, out; ūse, ûrn, ŭp; THis, thin

unclad
undergrad
unforbade
unsad
winter-clad
yclad

ĂD
aubade
baaed
ballade
chamade
charade
couvade
death squad
estrade
façade
gallopade
glissade
ha-ha'd
hurrahed
hussa'd
jihad
kamerad
lancepesade
metad
noyade
oeillade
pomade
promenade
psha'd
quad
remoulade
rodomontade
roulade
squad
wad
(See also ŎD.)

ĂDZ
ads
adze
scads
(See also ĂD;
add -s where
appropriate.)

ĀF
chafe
enchafe
fail-safe
safe
strafe
unsafe
vouchsafe
waif

ĂF
actinograph
agrafe
anagraph
autograph
behalf
belly laugh
better half
calf
calligraph
carafe
cenotaph
chaff
choreograph
chronograph
cinematograph
cross-staff
cryptograph
diagraph
dictagraph
distaff

draff
eidograph
electrocardio-
graph
epigraph
epitaph
flagstaff
gaff
giraffe
graff
graph
hagiograph
half
half-and-half
halfstaff
heliograph
holograph
ideograph
idiograph
laugh
lithograph
monograph
mooncalf
paleograph
pantograph
paragraph
penny gaff
phonograph
photograph
polygraph
quaff
quarter-staff
raff
riff-raff
seismograph
shandy-gaff
staff
stenograph
stereograph

telegraph
tipstaff
whipstaff

ĂF
behalf
belly laugh
better half
calf
graf
haaf
half
half-and-half
laugh
mooncalf
strafe

ĂFT
abaft
aft
aircraft
allograft
antiaircraft
craft
daft
draft
draught
engraft
fellow craft
folkcraft
graft
haft
handicraft
hovercraft
ingraft
life raft
metalcraft
needlecraft
overdraft

priestcraft
raft
river craft
sea craft
shaft
stagecraft
waft
witchcraft
woodcraft

ĀG
fainaigue
Hague
plague
stravage
vague

ȦG
bag
barf bag
battle flag
brag
Bragg
bullyrag
cag
chew the rag
crag
drag
fag
fag hag
fishfag
flag
gag
hag
jag
jet lag
knag
lag
mag

nag
nighthag
quag
rag
ragtag
saddle bag
sag
scalawag
scrag
shag
shrag
slag
snag
sprag
stag
swag
tag
wag
Wragg
zigzag

ÄG
blague
Bundestag
gulag
Laoag
Prague
Reichstag

ĀGD
unplagued

ȦGD
bagged
betagged
tagged
untagged
(See also ȦG;
add -ed where

appropriate.)

ĀJ
acreage
age
alienage
anchorage
appanage
arbitrage
armitage
assuage
atomic age
average
backstage
baronage
beverage
brigandage
brokerage
cage
cartilage
chaperonage
compage
concubinage
cooperage
discage
disengage
downstage
encage
engage
enrage
equipage
espionage
flowerage
foliage
foot-page
fortilage
gage
gauge
hajj

harborage
hemorrhage
heritage
hermitage
hospitage
leverage
lineage
mage
matronage
middle age
mucilage
offstage
old age
outrage
overage
page
parentage
parsonage
pastorage
pasturage
patronage
peonage
personage
pilgrimage
pilotage
plunderage
porterage
preengage
presage
pupilage
quarterage
rage
ramguage
rampage
sage
saxifrage
seignorage
stage
surplusage

swage
tutelage
tutorage
uncage
underage
unsage
upstage
vassalage
verbiage
vicarage
villanage
villenage
wage
weather gauge

ĂJ
badge
cadge
fadge
hadj

ĀK
ache
after-rake
angel food
  cake
aslake
awake
backache
bake
barley brake
beefcake
bellyache
betake
blacksnake
Blake
brake
break
cake

coffee break
coffeecake
cornflake
crake
cupcake
daybreak
devil's food
  cake
double take
drake
earache
earthquake
fake
flake
foresake
forespake
fruitcake
garter snake
griddle cake
hake
hand brake
handshake
hard-bake
heartache
heartbreak
jailbreak
jake
johnnycake
lake
make
mandrake
milk shake
milk snake
mistake
moonquake
muckrake
namesake
opaque
outbreak

overtake
pancake
partake
piece of cake
quake
rake
rattlesnake
robin-wake
sake
seaquake
seedcake
shake
sheik
sheldrake
shortcake
slake
snake
snowflake
spake
stake
steak
stomachache
strake
sweepstake
take
toothache
undertake
unmake
upbreak
uptake
wake
wapentake
water break
water snake
water-crake
wedding cake

ĂK
aback

ack-ack
alack
almanac
ammoniac
amnesiac
aphrodisiac
applejack
attack
bac
back
backpack
bareback
biofeedback
bivouac
black
blackjack
bootblack
bootjack
brach
bric-a-brac
callback
cardiac
chack
clack
claque
comeback
crack
crackerjack
cul-de-sac
demoniac
dipsomaniac
drawback
Dyak
egomaniac
elegiac
fallback
feedback
flapjack
flashback

Fond du Lac
fullback
good-lack
gopak
greenback
gripsack
hack
Hackensack
hackmatack
halfback
hardback
hatchback
haversack
haystack
hemophiliac
hijack
horseback
huckaback
humpback
hunchback
hypochondriac
insomniac
jack
jimcrack
kayak
kickback
kleptomaniac
knack
knicknack
kodak
kodiak
lac
lack
ladybrach
laid-back
lakh
lampblack
leatherback
leather jack

lumberjack
macaque
maniac
megalomaniac
monomaniac
natterjack
nymphomaniac
offtrack
outback
pack
paperback
Pasternak
pickaback
piggyback
plack
Pontiac
pyromaniac
quack
rack
ransack
razorback
rucksack
sac
sack
sacque
sacroiliac
sal ammoniac
sea wrack
shack
skipjack
skyjack
slack
slapjack
Slovak
smack
snack
stack
stickleback
symposiac

tack
tamarack
tarmac
thrack
throwback
thunder crack
thwack
ticktack
track
umiak
Union Jack
unpack
WAAC
Wac
wetback
whack
wisecrack
woolpack
woolsack
wrack
yak
yashmak
yellow jack
zodiac
zwieback

ĂK
plaque
Sarawak

ĀKS
Great Lakes
jakes
(See also ĀK;
add -*s* where
appropriate.)

ĂKS
Analax

anthrax
anticlimax
Astyanax
ax
battle ax
beeswax
climax
earwax
excise tax
fax
flax
Halifax
income tax
lax
overtax
parallax
pax
relax
Sachs
sales tax
sax
Saxe
sealing wax
slacks
surtax
syntax
tax
Tay-Sachs
value-added tax
wax
zax
(See also ĂK;
add -*s* where
appropriate.)

ĂKT
abstract
act
attacked

attract	Airedale	exhale	paravail
backed	ale	fail	pass-fail
bract	all-hail	fairy tale	pigtail
cataract	assail	farthingale	prevail
compact	avail	fingernail	quail
contract	aventail	flail	rail
counteract	bail	foresail	regale
detract	bale	frail	retail
diffract	bepale	Gael	sail
distract	betail	Gail	sale
enact	bewail	gale	scale
entr'acte	blackmail	gaol	shale
exact	Bloomingdale	ginger ale	sliding scale
extract	bobtail	grail	snail
fact	brail	greenmail	spale
impact	Braille	grisaille	stale
infract	camail	hail	swale
intact	canaille	hale	tael
matter-of-fact	Chippendale	handrail	tail
overact	cocktail	hangnail	tale
pact	countervail	hobnail	telltale
protract	curtail	Holy Grail	tenaille
react	dale	impale	they'll
redact	dead-pale	inhale	trail
re-enact	death-pale	*interpale*	travail
refract	derail	inveil	*trundle-tail*
retract	detail	jail	unveil
retroact	disentail	kail	upscale
saddle-backed	dovetail	kale	vail
subtract	downscale	mail	vale
tact	draggle-tail	male	veil
tract	dwale	martingale	wail
transact	empale	monorail	wale
underact	engaol	nail	whale
untracked	engrail	nightingale	wholesale
	enjail	outsail	
ĀL	enscale	overveil	**ȦL**
Abigail	entail	pail	aboriginal
ail	*entrail*	pale	academical

āle,   câre,   ădd,   ärm,   ăsk;   mē,   hẽre,   ĕnd;   īce,   ĭll;

accentual
acritical
adhesional
admiral
aerial
aesthetical
affectional
agal
agricultural
Al
alchemical
alchemistical
alexipharmical
alexiterical
algebraical
alkalimetrical
allegorical
allodial
alluvial
alphabetical
amatorial
ambrosial
analogical
analytical
anarchical
anatomical
angelical
animal
annual
antediluvial
anthological
antiphonal
antipodal
antithetical
apical
apochryphal
apologetical
apostolical
arboreal

arboricultural
archeological
architectural
arithmetical.
arsenal
arsenical
ascetical
asexual
asthmatical
astrological
atmospherical
atypical
audiovisual
Babylonical
bacchanal
bacchical
bacteriological
bal
balsamical
banal
barometrical
baronial
basilical
beatifical
bestial
biblical
bibliographical
bibliomaniacal
bibliopolical
biographical
biological
bisexual
boreal
botanical
Brahmanical
bureaucratical
cabal
cacophonical
Cal

Calvinistical
canal
cannibal
canonical
capital
caracal
cardinal
carnival
carnivoral
cartographical
casual
casuistical
categorical
catholical
centrical
cerebral
cervical
chaparral
characteristical
chemical
cherubical
chimerical
chorale
chronological
circumlocu-
tional
classical
clerical
climactical
climatical
climatological
clinical
codical
collateral
collegial
colloquial
comical
communal
complexional

conclusional
conditional
confessional
congressional
conical
conjectural
conjugal
conjugial
connubial
consanguineal
consistorial
constitutional
continual
contradictional
conventical
conventional
conventual
conversational
corporal
corral
cortical
cosmetical
cosmical
coxcombical
criminal
critical
cryptical
cubical
cyclical
cylindrical
cynical
dal
decanal
decennial
decimal
deistical
democratical
demoniacal
demonological

---

denominational
descensional
despotical
destinal
devotional
diabolical
diaconal
diacritical
diagonal
diagraphical
dialectical
dialogical
dialogistical
diametrical
diaphonical
dictatorial
didactical
dietetical
digital
digressional
diluvial
diplomatical
dipsomaniacal
discretional
display termi-
nal
divisional
doctoral
doctrinal
dogmatical
dolorifical
dominical
dramatical
dropsical
Druidical
duodecennial
duodecimal
dynamical
eccentrical

ecclesiastical
echinal
economical
ecstatical
ecumenical
educational
effectual
egoistical
egotistical
electrical
elegiacal
elimactical
elliptical
emblematical
emotional
emphatical
empirical
empyreal
encomiastical
encyclical
encyclopedical
endemical
energetical
energical
engimatical
enthusiastical
ephemeral
epical
epidemical
epigrammatical
Episcopal
episodical
epithetical
equivocal
erotical
esoterical
ethereal
ethical
ethnical

ethnological
etymological
Eucharistical
eulogistical
euphemistical
euphonical
evangelical
eventual
evolutional
exceptional
exegetical
exoterical
exotical
expansional
expurgatorial
extemporal
extrinsical
falderal
fanatical
fantastical
farcical
federal
femoral
ferial
festival
fictional
fiducial
finial
finical
forensical
fractional
functional
funeral
funereal
gal
galvanical
geminal
genealogical
general

generical
genial
geographical
geological
geometrical
germinal
gerundial
gestural
geyseral
gradual
grammatical
graphical
guttural
habitual
Hal
Hannibal
harmonical
Hebraical
heliacal
hemispherical
heptagonal
herbal
heretical
hermetical
heroical
hexadecimal
hexagonal
hierarchical
historical
horticultural
hospital
hygienical
hymeneal
hyperbolical
hypercritical
hypochondria-
cal
hypocritical
hysterical

---

identical	lachrymal	metaphorical	optical
idiotical	lackadaisical	metaphysical	optional
illogical	laical	methodical	oratorical
imaginal	latitudinal	Methodistical	orbital
imitational	lethargical	metical	óriginal
immaterial	Levitical	metrical	pal
immechanical	liberal	microbal	palatal
immemorial	literal	microbial	parabolical
imperial	littoral	microscopical	paradisaical
impersonal	liturgical	millesimal	parasitical
inaugural	locale	mineral	parenthetical
incorporeal	logical	minimal	participial
individual	longitudinal	ministerial	partitional
industrial	lyrical	misanthropical	passional
ineffectual	machinal	missional	pastoral
infinitesimal	madrigal	monarchical	pastorale
infusorial	magical	morale	pastural
inguinal	magistral	municipal	pathetical
inimical	magnifical	musical	pathological
initial	majestical	mutual	patrimonial
inquisitorial	mall	mystical	patronal
inspirational	maniacal	mythical	patronymical
institutional	mareschal	mythological	pedagogical
instructional	marginal	national	pedantical
insurrectional	marital	natural	pedestal
integral	marsupial	nautical	pedestrial
intellectual	mathematical	nectareal	penological
intentional	matinal	neoliberal	pentagonal
intercessional	matronal	nepotal	perennial
interjectional	matutinal	nominal	periodical
international	mayoral	nonclassical	peripheral
interval	mechanical	nonsensical	periphrastical
intestinal	medical	notional	perpetual
iridal	medicinal	novercal	personal
ironical	memorial	numerical	phantasmago-
jesuitical	menstrual	nymphal	rial
jovial	mensural	occasional	Pharisaical
juridical	mercurial	octagonal	pharmaceutical
La Salle	meridional	oneirocritical	phenomenal

philanthropical
philological
philosophical
photographical
phrenological
phthisical
physical
physiological
pictorial
pictural
pietistical
piratical
pivotal
platonical
pneumatological
poetical
polemical
political
polygonal
pontifical
Portugal
postprandial
postural
practical
pragmatical
precautional
preceptoral
preceptorial
preternatural
primordial
principal
probational
problematical
processional
prodigal
professional
professorial
progressional

prophetical
proportional
Provençale
proverbial
provisional
psychiatrical
psychical
psychological
punctual
puritanical
purpureal
pyramidal
pyramidical
pyrotechnical
quadrennial
quadrigesimal
quadrilateral
quadrupedal
quetzal
quizzical
radical
rational
rationale
recessional
reciprocal
regional
remedial
residual
retinal
rhapsodical
rhetorical
rheumatical
rhythmical
ritual
root canal
sabbatical
sal
salle
sartorial

satanical
satirical
scenical
schismatical
scholastical
scriptural
sculptural
seasonal
seigneurial
seigniorial
Senegal
seneschal
sensational
sensual
seraphical
serial
several
sexual
shall
sideral
sidereal
skeletal
skeptical
sociological
Socratical
sophistical
soritical
spasmodical
spherical
splenial
sporadical
staminal
stoical
strategical
supernatural
sutural
sybaritical
symbolical
symmetrical

synchronal
synchronical
synodical
synonymal
synonymical
synoptical
synthetical
systematical
tactical
technical
technicological
technological
temporal
terminal
terrestrial
territorial
tertial
testimonial
textual
textural
theatrical
theological
theoretical
theosophical
topical
topographical
torsional
traditional
tragical
transsexual
trigonal
trivial
tropical
tympanal
typical
typographical
tyrannical
umbilical
uncanonical

āle,　câre,　ădd,　ärm,　ăsk;　mē,　hĕre,　ĕnd;　īce,　ĭll;

unethical
unusual
urinal
usual
uxorial
vaginal
vatical
vegetal
ventriloquial
veridical
vertebral
vertical
vesical
vesperal
vestigial
vicarial
victorial
video display
  terminal
viminal
virginal
virtual
visceral
visional
visual
volitional
vortical
whimsical
zodiacal
zoological

ĀL
kraal
Lasalle
morale
shamal

ĂLB
alb

De Kalb

ĀLD
aild
ailed
bobtailed
unassailed
unbewailed
unhaled
(See also ĀL;
add -ed where
appropriate.)

ĂLD
caballed
corralled
emerald
palled

ĂLF
Alf
Ralph

ĂLK
catafalque
talc

ĂLKS
calx
catafalques

ĂLP
alp
palp
scalp

ĂLPS
Alps
palps

(See also ĂLP;
add -s where
appropriate.)

ĂLT
alt
shalt

ĂLV
bivalve
priming valve
safety valve
salve
valve

ĀLZ
Marseilles
Wales
(See also ĀL;
add -s where
appropriate.)

ĀM
acclaim
aflame
aim
ashame
became
blame
brand name
came
claim
counterclaim
crème de la
  crème
dame
declaim
defame
disclaim

disfame
electronic game
endgame
entame
exclaim
fame
flame
frame
game
hame
inflame
lame
maim
Mame
melodrame
misname
name
nickname
overcame
proclaim
quitclaim
reclaim
same
self-same
shame
surname
tame
video game
war game

ĂM
Abraham
ad nauseam
am
Amsterdam
anagram
battering ram
Birmingham
cablegram

cam
Candygram
centrigram
Cham
clam
cofferdam
cram
cryptogam
cryptogram
Cunningham
dam
damn
decigram
dekagram
diagram
diaphragm
dithyramb
drachm
dram
echocardio-
   gram
electrocardio-
   gram
electroen-
   cephalogram
encephalogram
epigram
flimflam
gam
gram
ham
hectogram
hologram
ideogram
jam
jamb
kilogram
lam
lamb

ma'am
madame
Mam
mammogram
marjoram
McAdam
milligram
monogram
Nizam
Nottingham
oriflamme
parallelogram
Petersham
phonogram
photogram
phraseogram
pram
ram
roentgenogram
Rotterdam
salaam
Schiedam
scram
sham
shram
Siam
slam
sonogram
stereogram
swam
telegram
tram
Vietnam
whim-wham
yam

ĀM
balm
becalm

calm
embalm
Guam
imam
impalm
Islam
ma'am
malm
palm
psalm
qualm
salaam

ĂMB
dithyramb
gamb

ĀMD
acclaimed
unblamed
unclaimed
unframed
unnamed
unreclaimed
unshamed
untamed
(See also ĀM;
add -d or
-ed where
appropriate.)

ĂMP
afterdamp
amp
camp
champ
clamp
cramp
damp

Davy lamp
death damp
decamp
encamp
enstamp
firedamp
gamp
guimpe
lamp
minedamp
ramp
revamp
safety lamp
samp
scamp
signal lamp
stamp
tamp
tramp
vamp

ĂMP
swamp
(See also
ŎMP.)

ĂMPT
undamped
(See also ĂMP;
add -ed where
appropriate.)

ĀMZ
Ames
James
(See also ĀM;
add -s where
appropriate.)

āle, câre, ădd, ärm, ăsk; mē, hĕre, ĕnd; īce, ĭll;

ÄMZ

alms
balms
Brahms
Psalms
(See also ÄM;
add -s where
appropriate.)

ĀN

abstain
acid rain
aerophane
aeroplane
again
airplane
Aisne
allophane
amain
appertain
aquaplane
arraign
ascertain
attain
atwain
Bahrain
bane
battering train
Bayne
bearing rein
bestain
betweenbrain
blain
boatswain
bower thane
brain
braindrain
bridle rein
Cain

Caine
campaign
campane
cane
chain
chamberlain
champagne
champaign
Champlain
Charles's Wain
chatelaine
chicane
chilblain
chow mein
cocaine
Cockaigne
complain
constrain
contain
co-ordain
counterpane
coxswain
crane
Dane
deign
delaine
demesne
demimon-
　daine
deraign
detain
detrain
diaphane
disdain
distrain
domain
drain
Duchesne
Duquesne

elecampane
enchain
engrain
entertain
entrain
explain
fain
fane
featherbrain
feign
fleabane
forebrain
foreordain
frangipane
gain
germane
grain
henbane
hindbrain
humane
hurricane
hydrophane
hydroplane
immane
inane
ingrain
insane
interchain
interreign
inurbane
jain
Jane
Jayne
jean
lain
lamebrain
lane
legerdemain
lithophane

Lorraine
main
Maine
maintain
mane
Mayne
McLain
McLean
mediterrane
membrane
midbrain
misfeign
moraine
mortmain
obtain
ordain
pain
Paine
pane
Payne
pertain
plain
plane
pleasure train
porcelain
preordain
profane
pursuit plane
quatrain
rain
refrain
regain
reign
rein
remain
restrain
retain
role strain
sane

ōld, ôr, ŏdd, oil, fŏŏt, out; ūse, ûrn, ŭp; THis, thin

scatterbrain
Seine
sextain
Sinn Fein
skein
slain
soutane
Spain
sprain
stain
strain
subterrane
sugarcane
sustain
suzerain
swain
ta'en
tain
terrain
thane
thegn
train
twain
Ukraine
unchain
unrein
uptrain
urbane
vain
vane
vein
vervain
wain
wane
water crane
weather vane

ĂN
Acadian

adman
Afghan
Afghanistan
African
alabastrian
Alcoran
Aldebaran
alderman
Alexandrian
Algerian
also-ran
amatorian
Amazonian
American
amphibian
an
anchorman
Anglican
Ann
Anne
antediluvian
artisan
Baconian
bagman
ban
Barbadian
barbarian
barbican
barracan
bartizan
basilican
Bataan
Batavian
Bavarian
bedpan
began
best man
Bezonian
Bohemian

bran
Briarean
Bulgarian
caducean
Caledonian
Cambrian
can
Canadian
caravan
castellan
CAT scan
Catalan
catamaran
charlatan
Cimmerian
clan
clergyman
Columbian
comedian
Copernican
corban
Corinthian
cosmopolitan
countryman
courtesan
cran
custodian
Cyprian
Dan
Delphian
diluvian
dirty old man
divan
Dominican
Dutchman
echinidan
Englishman
equestrian
Ethiopian

fan
firman
fisherman
flan
foo yong dan
foremast man
foreran
Frenchman
frying pan
fugleman
Gallican
gamelan
gargantuan
gentleman
hardpan
harridan
Hesperian
historian
Hunan
husbandman
Indian
inspan
Iran
Irishman
Isfahan
Isle of Man
Japan
journeyman
juryman
khan
Klan
Klansman
Koran
Ku Klux Klan
latitudinarian
legman
librarian
lighterman
liveryman

āle, câre, ădd, ärm, ăsk; mē, hĕre, ĕnd; īce, ĭll;

longshoreman
luggage van
Lutheran
madman
madwoman
man
Marianne
Matapan
medicine man
Mensan
merchantman
meridian
merman
metropolitan
Mexican
Michigan
midshipman
Milan
minuteman
Mohammedan
Mussulman
Neapolitan
nectarean
nobleman
oat bran
octogenarian
Olympian
oppidan
orangutan
ortolan
ottoman
outran
outspan
overman
overran
Pakistan
pan
partisan
pavane

pecan
pedestrian
pelican
pemmican
Peruvian
plan
platitudinarian
postmeridan
Powhatan
praetorian
predestinarian
Presbyterian
prison van
procrustean
proletarian
Promethean
publican
puritan
quarry man
quotidian
Ramadhan
ran
rattan
Reagan
redan
Republican
Sabbatarian
Sacramentar-
  ian
sacristan
salesman
saleswoman
Samaritan
scan
Scotchman
Scotsman
Sedan
serving man
shandrydan

signalman
South
  American
span
spick-and-span
Stygian
subterranean
suffragan
superman
taipan
talisman
tallyman
tan
Teheran
than
Thespian
tragedian
trencherman
trepan
Turkestan
unman
utilitarian
Utopian
valerian
valetudinarian
Valkyrian
van
Vatican
vegetarian
Vesuvian
veteran
veterinarian
vulgarian
Walkman
warming pan
waterman
wherryman
Yucatan
Zoroastrian

ĂN
autobahn
corban
Genghis Khan
khan
Parmesan
swan
wan
Wotan
(See also ŎN.)

ĂNCH
avalanche
blanch
branch
carte-blanche
flanch
ganch
ranch
scranch
stanch

ÄNCH
Blanche
carte blanche
haunch
launch
manche
paunch
stanch
staunch

ÄNCHD
launched
unstanched
(See also
ÄNCH; add
-ed where
appropriate.)

ōld, ôr, ŏdd, oil, fŏŏt, out; ūse, ûrn, ŭp; THis, thin

ĀND
abstained
birdbrained
bloodstained
constrained
diaphaned
disdained
featherbrained
harebrained
hot-brained
interveined
maned
muddy-brained
rattlebrained
scatterbrained
self-restrained
shallow-brained
shatter-brained
travel-stained
unascertained
unconstrained
unplained
unprofaned
unreined
unrestrained
unstained
unstrained
unsustained
untrained
(See also ĀN;
add -ed where
appropriate.)

ĀND
aband
abbey-land
ampersand
analysand
and

backhand
band
bandstand
bland
brand
bridle hand
command
contraband
countermand
demand
deodand
disband
Disneyland
expand
fairyland
fatherland
firebrand
firsthand
four-in-hand
full-manned
gland
grand
grandstand
Greenland
hand
handstand
headband
hired hand
Holy Land
homeland
hotband
Iceland
ill-manned
imband
inland
land
Lapland
lotusland
mainland

manned
master hand
minute hand
motherland
multiplicand
name brand
newsstand
no-man's-land
offhand
overhand
overland
quicksand
rand
remand
reprimand
Rio Grande
Samarkand
sand
saraband
second hand
self-command
stagehand
stand
strand
sweatband
underhand
understand
unhand
unland
unmanned
unscanned
upper hand
waistband
washstand
wasteland
withstand
wonderland
(See also ĂN;
add -ed where

appropriate.)

ĀND
gourmand
wand
(See also ŌND.)

ĂNG
bang
bhang
big bang
boomerang
clang
fang
gang
gangbang
gobang
hang
harangue
meringue
Mont Blanc
mustang
orangoutang
overhang
pang
Penang
rang
sang
seatang
serang
shebang
slang
slap-bang
spang
sprang
stang
swang
tang
trepang

āle, câre, ădd, ärm, ăsk; mē, hĕre, ĕnd; īce, ĭll;

twang
uphang
vang
whang

ĂNGD
banged
langued
unpanged
(See also ĂNG;
add -ed where
appropriate.)

ĂNGK
bank
blank
brank
Cape Blanc
chank
clank
crank
dank
data bank
drank
embank
enrank
flank
franc
frank
hank
lank
mountebank
outflank
outrank
plank
point-blank
prank
rank
sank

savings bank
shank
shrank
slank
spank
stank
tank
thank
twank
watertank
West Bank
yank
Yank

ĂNGKS
branks
Fairbanks
lanx
longshanks
Manx
phalanx
spindleshanks
thanks
(See also
ĂNGK; add
-s where
appropriate.)

ĂNGKT
sacrosanct
spindle-
  shanked
unspanked
(See also
ĂNGK; add
-ed where
appropriate.)

ĂNJ
arrange

change
counterchange
derange
disarrange
enrange
estrange
exchange
grange
interchange
mange
prearrange
range
rearrange
sea change
shortchange
strange

ĂNJ
flange
phalange

ÁNS
advance
ambulance
appurtenance
arrogance
askance
bechance
break dance
chance
circumstance
clairvoyance
complaisance
concomitance
consonance
continuance
conversance
countenance

country dance
dance
death dance
deliverance
demilance
discountenance
dissonance
dominance
elance
elegance
enhance
entrance
expanse
extravagance
exuberance
finance
France
furtherance
glance
heritance
ignorance
impuissance
incogitance
incognizance
inconsonance
inhabitance
inheritance
insouciance
intemperance
intolerance
irrelevance
lance
luxuriance
manse
mischance
Nance
ordinance
penetrance
perchance

petulance
prance
precipitance
predominance
preponderance
protuberance
puissance
radiance
recognizance
reconnaissance
relevance
resonance
romance
séance
sibilance
significance
stance
sufferance
suppliance
tolerance
trance
utterance
variance
vigilance
(See also ĂNT;
add -s where
appropriate.)

ĂNS
fer-de-lance
insouciance

ĀNT
acquaint
ain't
attaint
bepaint
besaint
complaint

constraint
daint
depaint
distraint
faint
feint
Geraint
liver complaint
mayn't
paint
plaint
quaint
restraint
saint
self-restraint
straint
taint
'taint
teint
unconstraint
unsaint

ĂNT or ĄNT
abdicant
adamant
adjutant
adulterant
agglutinant
altitonant
altivolant
ambulant
annuitant
ant
anticipant
applicant
appurtenant
arrogant
askant
aslant

aunt
brant
cant
can't
chant
combatant
commandant
communicant
complaisant
concomitant
confidant
confidante
congratulant
consonant
conversant
cormorant
corposant
corroborant
Corybant
courant
covenant
decant
deodorant
deplant
descant
determinant
disenchant
disputant
dissonant
dominant
elegant
elephant
emigrant
enchant
enceinte
excommunicant
executant
exorbitant
extant

extravagant
exuberant
fabricant
figurant
figurante
flagellant
fulminant
gallant
gallivant
Gant
germinant
grant
gratulant
habitant
hesitant
hierophant
ignorant
illuminant
imaginant
immigrant
implant
impuissant
incogitant
incognizant
inconsonant
inhabitant
insignificant
intolerant
intoxicant
irradiant
irrelevant
irritant
itinerant
jubilant
Kant
Levant
litigant
luminant
luxuriant

mendicant
militant
miscreant
occupant
odorant
pant
penetrant
petulant
plant
pollutant
postulant
precipitant
predominant
preponderant
procreant
Protestant
protuberant
puissant
pursuivant
quant
rant
recalcitrant
recant
recreant
recusant
refrigerant
reiterant
relevant
Rembrandt
resonant
resuscitant
reverberant
ruminant
sacrificant
scant
scintillant
sensitive plant
shan't
sibilant

significant
slant
stimulant
supplant
suppliant
supplicant
sycophant
tant
termagant
tintinnabulant
tolerant
toxicant
transplant
undulant
variant
vigilant
visitant
vociferant

ĂNT
aunt
can't
debutante
detente
dilettante
nonchalant
shan't

ĂNth
amaranth
amianth
tragacanth

ĂNTS
fancy pants
Hant's
pants
underpants

(See also ĂNT;
add -*s* where
appropriate.)

ĀNZ
Great Plains
Plains
Raines
Raynes
(See also ĀN;
add -*s* where
appropriate.)

ĂNZ
banns
(See also ĂN;
add -*s* where
appropriate.)

ĀNZH
melange

ĀP
agape
ape
audiotape
cape
chape
crape
crepe
drape
escape
fire escape
gape
grape
jape
landscape
Lape
nape

pape
rape
red tape
scape
scrape
seascape
shape
shipshape
tape
transshape
trape
uncape
unshape
videotape

ĂP
afterclap
agape
ASCAP
bestrap
cap
chap
clap
claptrap
dap
entrap
enwrap
flap
flip-flap
foolscap
forage cap
frap
gap
gape
genapp
genappe
handicap
hap
heel-tap

ōld, ôr, ŏdd, oil, fŏŏt, out; ūse, ûrn, ŭp; THis, thin

Jap	**ĀPS**	rapt	compare
JAP	apes	snow-capped	concessionnaire
knap	jackanapes	wrapped	dare
lagniappe	Mapes	(See also ĂP;	debonair
lap	traipse	add -d, -ed, or	declare
Lapp	(See also ĀP;	-ped where	Delaware
map	add -s where	appropriate.)	despair
mayhap	appropriate.)		devil-may-care
mishap		**ÂR**	disrepair
nap	**ĂPS**	Adair	doctrinaire
nightcap	apse	affair	earthenware
overlap	collapse	affaire	éclair
pap	craps	air	e'er
percussion cap	elapse	aire	elsewhere
rap	illapse	anywhere	ensnare
rattletrap	interlapse	armchair	ere
sap	lapse	arrière	etagère
scrap	perhaps	au pair	everywhere
shoulder strap	prolapse	aware	eyre
slap	relapse	Ayr	fair
snap	schnapps	ayre	fare
stopgap	synapse	backstair	flair
strap		bare	flare
tap	**ĀPT**	bear	forbear
thunder clap	aped	bêche-de-mer	forswear
trap	shaped	bedare	gare
unlap	unshaped	beglare	glair
unwrap	V-shaped	beware	glare
wapp	(See also ĀP;	billionaire	Gruyère
water tap	add -ed where	blare	hair
wishing cap	appropriate.)	capillaire	hare
wrap		care	heir
yap	**ĂPT**	chair	howe'er
	adapt	chare	impair
	apt	chargé d'affaires	jardinière
ĀP	bestrapped	claire	lair
gape	enrapt	clare	laissez-faire
swap	inapt	cockle-stair	maidenhair
(See also ŎP.)	moss-capped	commissionaire	mal de mer

āle, câre, ădd, ärm, ăsk; mē, hēre, ĕnd; īce, ĭll;

mare
McNair
McNare
midair
millionaire
misfare
mohair
ne'er
otherwhere
outdare
outstare
outswear
outwear
overbear
pair
pare
parterre
pear
Pierre
portiere
prayer
prepare
prickly pear
proletaire
quair
rare
repair
scare
sedan chair
share
Sinclair
snare
solitaire
somewhere
spare
square
stair
stare
stere

sware
swear
tare
tear
their
there
thoroughfare
threadbare
trouvère
tuyère
unaware
unbeware
underbear
underwear
unfair
unswear
unware
upbear
upstare
uptear
vair
vare
vin-ordinaire
vivandière
Voltaire
ware
wear
whate'er
whatsoe'er
whene'er
where
where'er
wheresoe'er
yare
zillionaire

ÄR
Aar
abattoir

acetabular
afar
aide-mémoire
ajar
angular
animalcular
annular
antiar
are
armoire
au revoir
autocar
avatar
axillar
axle bar
bar
bazaar
bête noire
binocular
bizarre
bolivar
Bolívar
boudoir
boulevard
boxcar
boyar
budgerigar
calendar
canard
capsular
car
catarrh
caviar
centikar
char
chukkar
cigar
cinnabar
circular

columnar
commissar
consular
couloir
crepuscular
crossbar
crowbar
cultivar
cymar
czar
dar
daystar
debar
deodar
devoir
dinar
disbar
dissimilar
drawbar
durbar
earthstar
embar
escolar
escritoire
evening star
Excalibar
fabular
falling star
far
Farr
feldspar
flagellar
foliar
funicular
gangliar
gar
glandular
globular
gnar

ōld, ôr, ŏdd, oil, fŏŏt, out; ūse, ûrn, ŭp; THis, thin

guitar
gyrocar
handlebar
havildar
hospodar
hussar
incunabular
insofar
instar
insular
irregular
isallobar
isobar
jacamar
jaguar
jar
jaunting car
jemadar
jocular
jugular
kantar
kbar
kilobar
knar
lamellar
laminar
Lascar
lodestar
Loire
lonestar
louvar
maar
Malabar
mar
memoir
millibar
modular
moire
molecular

monocular
morning star
motorcar
narr
Navarre
nebular
night jar
north star
objet d'art
ocular
ovular
Palomar
par
parr
particular
peignoir
peninsular
perpendicular
pilot star
popular
pourboire
pulsar
quadrangular
Qatar
radar
railcar
railroad car
registrar
regular
Renoir
repertoire
reservoir
roll bar
rouge et noir
saddle bar
samovar
scapular
scar
schedular

scimitar
sea star
secular
segar
seminar
shackle bar
shikar
shofar
shooting star
sidecar
sillar
similar
simular
singular
sircar
sirdar
sitar
somnambular
sonar
spar
spatular
spectacular
spherular
star
stellular
streetcar
subahdar
sun star
tabernacular
tabular
tahr
tahsildar
tar
Telstar
tessellar
thenar
tintamarre
tintinnabular
titular

tonsillar
torcular
tow bar
Trafalgar
triangular
trocar
trolley car
tsar
tubular
turbocar
tutelar
unbar
unspar
upbar
uvular
valvular
vascular
vehicular
vermicular
vernacular
versicular
vinegar
Wanderjahr
zamindar
Zanzibar

ÄRB
barb
garb
yarb

ÄRCH
arch
countermarch
dead march
inarch
larch
march
outmarch

āle, câre, ădd, ärm, ăsk; mē, hĕre, ĕnd; īce, ĭll;

overarch
overmarch
parch
starch

ÂRD
aired
Baird
golden-haired
laird
silver-haired
uncared
unheired
unimpaired
unpaired
unprepared
unshared
unspared
(See also ÂR;
add -d or -ed
where
appropriate.)

ÄRD
after-guard
avant-garde
bard
Bernard
blackguard
blowhard
bodyguard
bombard
boulevard
camelopard
canard
card
chard
closebarred
diehard

discard
disregard
dynamitard
enguard
evil-starred
fard
foulard
Girard
guard
hard
interlard
Kierkegaard
lard
lifeguard
milliard
nard
pard
petard
placard
poultry yard
regard
retard
sard
shard
spikenard
starred
undersparred
unguard
unmarred
vanguard
Vanguard
wedding card
yard
(See also ÄR;
add -ed where
appropriate.)

ÄRF
'arf and 'arf

larf
scarf

ÄRJ
barge
charge
discharge
embarge
encharge
enlarge
Farge
La Farge
large
litharge
marge
overcharge
sea marge
sparge
surcharge
targe
uncharge
undercharge

ÄRJD
barged
charged
enlarged
undischarged
(See also ÄRJ;
add -ed where
appropriate.)

ÄRK
aardvark
arc
ark
Asiarch
bark
barque

bedark
cark
Clark
Clarke
clerk
dark
debark
Denmark
disembark
dispark
easy mark
ecclesiarch
embark
endark
floodmark
footmark
hark
hierarch
impark
iremarch
knark
lark
marc
mark
marque
meadowlark
narc
oligarch
park
patriarch
quark
remark
sark
sea lark
shark
skylark
snark
spark
stark

Starke
watermark

ÄRKS
Marx
Ozarks
(See also ÄRK;
add -s where
appropriate.)

ÄRKT
barked
unmarked
(See also ÄRK;
add -ed where
appropriate.)

ÄRL
Albemarle
carl
ensnarl
gnarl
harl
imparl
jarl
Karl
marl
snarl

ÄRLZ
Charles
(See also ÄRL;
add -s where
appropriate.)

ÄRM
alarm
arm
axle arm

barm
becharm
charm
countercharm
decharm
disarm
disencharm
farm
fire alarm
firearm
forearm
gendarme
harm
love charm
unarm
uncharm
unharm

ÄRMD
alarmed
forearmed
unalarmed
(See also
ÄRM; add
-ed where
appropriate.)

ÄRMZ
alarms
Armes
assault-at-arms
gentleman-
  at-arms
king-at-arms
man-at-arms
(See also
ÄRM; add
-s where
appropriate.)

ÂRN
bairn
cairn
tairn

ÄRN
barn
darn
imbarn
incarn
Marne
tarn
yarn

ÄRNZ
Barnes
(See ÄRN; add
-s where
appropriate.)

ÄRP
carp
epicarp
escarp
harp
monocarp
pericarp
scarp
sharp

ÂRS
scarce

ÄRS
farce
parse
sarse
sparse

ÄRSH
harsh
marsh

ÄRT
apart
art
cart
carte
chart
counterpart
dart
depart
Descartes
dispart
fart
flintheart
hart
heart
impart
indart
lionheart
mart
Mozart
old fart
op art
part
pop art
quart
sart
shopping cart
smart
start
state-of-the-art
sweetheart
tart
uncart
unheart
upstart

āle, câre, ădd, ärm, ăsk; mē, hĕre, ĕnd; īce, ĭll;

video art	abase	hiding place	aftergrass
water cart	ace	horse race	alas
	aerospace	idocrase	allhallowmas
ÄRTH	aface	inner space	amass
Applegarth	anelace	interface	ass
garth	apace	interlace	bass
hearth	attaché case	interspace	*bonnilass*
swarth	base	lace	brass
	basket case	Mace	Candlemas
ÄRV	bass	mace	class
carve	begrace	misplace	crass
larve	belace	outer space	crevasse
starve	birthplace	outface	cuirass
	boniface	outpace	declass
ÄRTS	brace	pace	demitasse
darts	breathing space	place	en masse
Harz	carapace	plaice	Eurailpass
martial arts	case	populace	fiberglass
(See ÄRT; add	chariot race	race	first-class
-s where	chase	rat race	flint glass
appropriate.)	commonplace	replace	galloglass
	dace	resting place	gas
ÂRZ	data base	retrace	glass
airs	debase	scapegrace	grass
backstairs	deface	space	Hallowmass
stairs	disgrace	steeplechase	hippocras
theirs	displace	test case	hourglass
unawares	efface	thoroughbass	isinglass
unbewares	embrace	Thrace	kavass
unwares	encase	trace	Khyber Pass
	enchase	trysting place	kvass
ÄRZ	enlace	ukase	landmass
Mars	erase	unbrace	lass
memoirs	face	uncase	looking glass
(See also ÄR;	footpace	underbrace	lower-class
add -s where	footrace	unlace	mass
appropriate.)	freebase	vase	Michaelmas
	grace		middle-class
ÀS	grimace	**ÀS**	minute glass

morass
object glass
outclass
overpass
paillasse
pass
paterfamilias
rubasse
sassafras
second-class
sparrow grass
strass
surpass
tarantass
tass
Tass
third-class
underclass
upper-class
weather glass
working-class

ÄS
coup de grâce
en masse
kvass
springhass
volte-face

ĀSH
crèche

ĂSH
abash
ash
backlash
balderdash
bash
bedash

brache
brash
cache
calabash
calash
calipash
cash
clash
crash
dash
Eurotrash
fash
flash
gash
gnash
hash
hot flash
interdash
lâche
lash
mash
mishmash
mountain ash
moustache
Nash
pash
patache
photoflash
plash
rash
rehash
sabretache
sash
slapdash
slash
smash
splash
splatter-dash
squabash

thrash
trash
unlash
weeping ash
whiplash

ÄSH
quash
wash
(See also
ÖSH.)

ĂSHT
abashed
undashed
unlashed
unthrashed
(See also ĂSH;
add -ed where
appropriate.)

ẠSK
antimask
ask
bask
basque
bemask
Bergamask
cask
casque
flask
immask
mask
masque
overtask
Pasch
powder flask
task
unmask

water cask

ẠSKT
basked
unasked
unmasked
(See also ẠSK;
add -ed where
appropriate.)

ĂSP
asp
clasp
enclasp
engrasp
gasp
grasp
hasp
rasp
unclasp

ÄSP
wasp

ĀST
abased
after-taste
apple-faced
barefaced
baste
brazen-faced
chaste
distaste
double-faced
dough-faced
fair-faced
foretaste
freckle-faced
furrow-faced

āle, câre, ădd, ärm, ăsk; mē, hĕre, ĕnd; īce, ĭll;

hard-faced
haste
hatchet-faced
horse-faced
impaste
Janus-faced
laced
lambaste
leaden-paced
lean-faced
lily-faced
mottle-faced
pale-faced
paper-faced
paste
pippin-faced
platter-faced
plump-faced
posthaste
pudding-faced
pug-faced
retraced
sad-faced
self-abased
shamefaced
sheep-faced
slow-paced
smock-faced
smooth-faced
smug-faced
snail-paced
straitlaced
tallow-faced
taste
thorough-paced
two-faced
traced
unbraced
unchaste

undefaced
undisgraced
ungraced
unshamefaced
untraced
waist
waste
weasel-faced
well-graced
whey-faced
wizen-faced
(See also ĀS;
add -d or -ed
where
appropriate.)

ĀST

aghast
avast
bast
blast
bombast
cablecast
cast
caste
cinéast
colorfast
contrast
devast
downcast
ecclesiast
ecdysiast
elegiast
ember-fast
encomiast
enthusiast
fast
flabbergast
forecast

ghast
gymnast
half-assed
handfast
hast
high caste
iconoclast
idoloclast
jury mast
last
mast
metaphrast
metaplast
miscast
newscast
outcast
outclassed
outlast
overcast
paraphrast
past
protoplast
recast
repast
scholiast
simulcast
sportscast
steadfast
storm-blast
symposiast
telecast
tight-assed
unfast
unsurpassed
vast
videocast
wast
(See also under
ĀS; add -ed

where
appropriate.)

ĀT

abacinate
abalienate
abate
abbreviate
abdicate
ablegate
ablocate
abnegate
abnodate
abominate
abrogate
absinthiate
absquatulate
accelerate
accentuate
acclamate
acclimate
accommodate
acculturate
accumulate
accurate
acerate
acerbate
acetate
acidulate
activate
actuate
aculeate
acuminate
adequate
adipate
adjudicate
administrate
adulate
adulterate

advocate
aerate
affectionate
affiliate
affreight
agglomerate
agglutinate
aggravate
aggregate
agitate
ait
alienate
alleviate
alliterate
allocate
altercate
alternate
aluminate
alveolate
amalgamate
ambulate
ameliorate
ammonate
ammoniate
ampliate
amputate
angulate
animate
annihilate
annotate
annulate
annumerate
annunciate
antedate
antepenultimate
anticipate
antiquate
apartheid
apostate

apostolate
applicate
appreciate
approbate
appropriate
approximate
arbitrate
armor plate
arrogate
arsenate
articulate
asphyxiate
aspirate
assassinate
asseverate
assibilate
assimilate
assimulate
associate
assonate
ate
attenuate
augurate
aureate
auscultate
auspicate
authenticate
automate
aviate
await
baccalaureate
bait
bantamweight
barbellate
bate
belate
benzoate
berate
bicarbonate

bidentate
bifoliate
biforate
bifurcate
Billingsgate
bilobate
bimaculate
binoculate
bipinnate
birthrate
blind date
brachiate
breastplate
bunkmate
cachinnate
calcarate
calculate
caliphate
calumniate
campanulate
camphorate
cancellate
candidate
cannulate
cantillate
capacitate
capitate
capitulate
capsulate
captivate
carbonate
carboxylate
cardinalate
carinate
caseate
casemate
castigate
cate
catenate

celebrate
celibate
cerebrate
certificate
chalybeate
cheapskate
checkmate
chelicerate
chlamydate
chlorinate
chocolate
cicurate
circinate
circulate
circumambu-
  late
circumnavigate
circumstan-
  tiate
citrate
classmate
coacervate
coadunate
coagulate
cochleate
coelenterate
cogitate
cohobate
collaborate
collate
collegiate
colligate
collimate
collocate
commemorate
commensurate
commentate
comminate
commiserate

communicate
compassionate
compensate
complicate
concatenate
concelebrate
concentrate
conciliate
condensate
conditionate
confabulate
confederate
confiscate
conflate
conglobate
conglomerate
conglutinate
congratulate
congregate
conjugate
consecrate
considerate
consociate
consolidate
constellate
consternate
constipate
constuprate
consulate
consummate
contaminate
contemplate
contriturate
cooperate
coordinate
copper plate
copulate
coronate
corporate

correlate
corroborate
corrugate
corticate
coruscate
costate
counterweight
crate
create
cremate
crenellate
crenulate
crepitate
criminate
cucullate
culminate
cultivate
cumulate
cupulate
cuspidate
cutrate
cyclamate
date
deactivate
deadweight
deaminate
death rate
debate
debilitate
decaffeinate
decapitate
decarbonate
decelerate
decerebrate
decimate
declinate
decollate
decolorate
deconsecrate

decontaminate
decorate
decorticate
decrepitate
·decudate
decurtate
decussate
dedicate
deescalate
defecate
deflocculate
deflorate
defoliate
degenerate
deglutinate
degustate
dehydrate
delaminate
delate
delectate
delegate
deliberate
delicate
delineate
demarcate
demonstrate
denigrate
denominate
dentate
denudate
denunciate
deodate
depilate
depopulate
deprecate
depreciate
depredate
depucelate
deracinate

derivate
derogate
desalinate
desecrate
desegregate
desiccate
desiderate
designate
desolate
desperate
despumate
desquamate
destinate
desublimate
deteriorate
determinate
detonate
detoxicate
devastate
deviate
devirginate
diaconate
diagnosticate
dial plate
dichromate
dictate
differentiate
digitate
dilapidate
dilate
dimidiate
diplomate
directorate
disaffiliate
disarticulate
discombobulate
disconsolate
discriminate
disgregate

disintegrate
dislocate
disorientate
disseminate
dissertate
dissimilate
dissimulate
dissipate
dissociate
distrait
divagate
divaricate
doctorate
domesticate
dominate
donate
double date
downstate
dunderpate
duplicate
ecalcarate
edentate
educate
edulcorate
effectuate
effeminate
efflate
eight
ejaculate
elaborate
elate
electorate
electroplate
elevate
eliminate
elucidate
elucubrate
emaciate
emanate

emancipate
emasculate
embrocate
emigrate
emolliate
emulate
enate
encapsulate
enervate
enucleate
enumerate
enunciate
episcopate
equate
equilibrate
equiponderate
equivocate
eradicate
eructate
escalate
estate
estimate
estivate
ethylate
etiolate
evacuate
evaginate
evaluate
evaporate
eventuate
eviscerate
exacerbate
exacinate
exaggerate
exasperate
exauctorate
excalcarate
excavate
excogitate

excommunicate
excoriate
excruciate
exculpate
execrate
exenterate
exfoliate
exhalate
exheridate
exhilarate
exonerate
exorbitate
expatiate
expatriate
expectorate
expiate
expiscate
explanate
explicate
expostulate
expurgate
exsanguinate
exsiccate
extenuate
exterminate
extirpate
extortionate
extrapolate
extravagate
extravasate
extricate
exuviate
fabricate
facilitate
falcate
fasciate
fascinate
fashionplate
fate

faveolate
featherweight
federate
felicitate
fenestrate
fête
figurate
figure eight
filiate
fimbriate
fimbrillate
first-mate
first-rate
flagellate
flocculate
floodgate
floriate
fluctuate
fluoridate
fluorinate
foliate
foliolate
foreordinate
formulate
fornicate
fortunate
fractionate
free-associate
freight
fructuate
frustrate
fulminate
fumigate
funambulate
functionate
fustigate
gait
gate
gelatinate

geminate	*immateriate*	indeterminate	insulate
generate	immediate	indevirginate	integrate
germinate	*immensurate*	indicate	intemperate
gesticulate	immigrate	indiscriminate	intenerate
gestate	immoderate	individuate	*intercessionate*
glaciate	immolate	indoctrinate	interdigitate
gladiate	impassionate	indurate	interlaminate
glutamate	impenetrate	inebriate	intermediate
gradate	imperforate	infatuate	interminate
graduate	impersonate	infibulate	interpolate
granulate	impetrate	infiltrate	interrelate
grate	implicate	inflate	interrogate
gratulate	importunate	infumate	interstate
gravitate	imprecate	infuriate	intestate
great	impregnate	infuscate	intimate
guesstimate	impropriate	ingeminate	intimidate
habilitate	improvisate	ingerminate	intonate
habituate	inaccurate	*ingrate*	intoxicate
hallucinate	inactivate	ingratiate	intricate
hate	inadequate	ingravidate	inundate
heavyweight	inanimate	ingurgitate	inusitate
hebetate	inappropriate	initiate	invaginate
helpmate	inarticulate	innate	invalidate
hesitate	inaugurate	innervate	invertebrate
hibernate	incapacitate	innovate	investigate
homologate	incarcerate	inoculate	inveterate
humiliate	*incastellate*	inordinate	invigilate
hundredweight	inchoate	inornate	invigorate
hydrogenate	incinerate	inquinnate	inviolate
hyphenate	incommensurate	insalivate	invocate
hypothecate	incompassionate	insatiate	irate
ideate	inconsiderate	inseminate	irradiate
illiterate	incorporate	insinuate	irradicate
illuminate	increate	insolate	irrigate
illustrate	incriminate	inspissate	irritate
imbricate	incubate	instantiate	irrogate
imitate	inculcate	instate	irrorate
immaculate	incurvate	instigate	isolate
immarginate	indelicate	insubordinate	iterate

itinerate	magnate	narrate	orate
jubilate	makebate	Nate	orchestrate
jugulate	mammillate	navigate	ordinate
Kate	mancipate	necessitate	orientate
labiate	manganate	negotiate	originate
lacerate	manipulate	neonate	ornate
laciniate	marginate	nervate	oscillate
lamellate	marinate	nickle plate	osculate
laminate	marquisate	nictitate	ostentate
lanceolate	masticate	nidificate	outdate
lancinate	masturbate	nodulate	overrate
lapidate	mate	nominate ·	overstate
late	matriculate	notate	overweight
Latinate	mediate	novitiate	ovulate
laureate	medicate	nucleate	oxalate
legislate	meditate	nucleolate	oxygenate
legitimate	mendicate	numerate	paginate
levigate	menstruate	obambulate	palamate
levirate	messmate	obdurate	palliate
levitate	methylate	obfuscate	palmate
liberate	micturate	objurgate	palpebrate
licentiate	middleweight	oblate	palpitate
lightweight	migrate	obligate	paperweight
lingulate	militate	obliterate	participate
liquate	miscalculate	obnubilate	passionate
liquidate	miscreate	obrogate	pastorate
literate	misdate	obsecrate	pate
litigate	mismate	obstinate	patinate
lixiviate	misstate	obturate	patronate
locate	mistranslate	obvallate	pectinate
loricate	mitigate	obviate	peculate
lubricate	moderate	ocellate	pendulate
lucubrate	modulate	oculate	penetrate
lunulate	mokebate	officiate	peninsulate
luxuriate	motivate	oleate	pennyweight
macerate	multiplicate	operate	perambulate
machicolate	muriate	opiate	percolate
machinate	muricate	oppignorate	peregrinate
magistrate	mutilate	oppilate	perennate ·

perforate
permanganate
permeate
permutate
perorate
perpetrate
perpetuate
personate
phenolate
phytate
picrate
pignorate
placate
plait
plate
playmate
poet laureate
pollinate
pontificate
populate
portrait
postdate
postulate
potentate
prate
precipitate
predate
predesignate
predestinate
predicate
predominate
prefabricate
premeditate
preponderate
presbyterate
prevaricate
prorate
probate
procrastinate

procreate
professoriate
profligate
prognosticate
proliferate
promulgate
propagate
propitiate
proportionate
prostate
prostrate
protectorate
protuberate
provinciate
proximate
pullulate
pulsate
pulvinate
punctuate
purpurate
pustulate
quadruplicate
quantitate
quaternate
quintuplicate
radiate
radicate
radioactivate
raffinate
rate
ratiocinate
rattlepate
reactivate
rebate
recalcitrate
recapitulate
reciprocate
reclinate
reconcentrate

reconciliate
reconfiscate
reconsecrate
recrate
recreate
recriminate
rectorate
recuperate
recurvate
redate
redecorate
rededicate
redintegrate
reduplicate
reescalate
refrigerate
regenerate
registrate
regrate
regulate
regurgitate
rehabilitate
reinstate
reiterate
rejuvenate
relate
relegate
relocate
remediate
remonstrate
remunerate
renegotiate
renovate
repatriate
repopulate
reprobate
repudiate
repullulate
resinate

resonate
restate
resuscitate
retaliate
reticulate
revegetate
reverberate
rhipidate
rollerskate
roseate
rotate
rubricate
ruminate
runagate
rusticate
saccharate
sagaciate
saginate
sagittate
salicylate
salivate
sanitate
sate
satiate
saturate
scholasticate
schoolmate
scintillate
Sea Gate
second mate
second-rate
secretariate
sedate
segmentate
segregate
self-hate
sensate
separate
septennate

sequestrate
seriate
shipmate
sibilate
silicate
silver plate
simulate
sinuate
situate
skate
slate
solid-state
somnambulate
sophisticate
spate
speculate
sphacelate
spifflicate
spinate
spoliate
sporulate
stalemate
state
steady state
stearate
stellulate
stereobate
stimulate
stipulate
straight
strait
strangulate
stridulate
stylobate
subacetate
subjugate
sublate
sublimate
subordinate

subrogate
substantiate
succinate
sufflate
suffocate
suffumigate
sulcate
sulfurate
sulphurate
sultanate
superannuate
supererogate
supinate
supplicate
suppurate
suricate
syllabicate
syncopate
syndicate
tabulate
Tait
tailgate
tellurate
temperate
tentmate
tergiversate
terminate
testate
tête-à-tête
third mate
third-rate
thwaite
titillate
titivate
tolerate
toluate
torquate
trait
translate

transliterate
translocate
transmigrate
transubstantiate
triangulate
tridentate
tridigitate
triturate
triumvirate
truncate
ulcerate
ultimate
ululate
uncrate
uncreate
underestimate
underrate
understate
underweight
undulate
unfortunate
unplait
unstate
upstate
urinate
urticate
vacate
vaccinate
vacillate
vacuate
validate
vallate
vanodate
variate
variegate
vassalate
vaticinate
vegetate
vellicate

venerate
ventilate
verberate
vermiculate
vertebrate
vertiginate
vesicate
vicariate
vindicate
violate
viscerate
vitiate
vituperate
vizierate
vociferate
vulgate
wait
Watergate
water rate
weight
welterweight
whitebait

ĂT
acrobat
aegrotat
aerostat
aflat
anastigmat
Arafat
Ararat
arhat
aristocrat
assignat
astigmat
at
autocrat
automat
baby-sat

āle, câre, ădd, ärm, ăsk; mē, hĕre, ĕnd; īce, ĭll;

backchat	Fermat	mud cat	stonechat
barostat	fiat	muscat	sun hat
bat	firebrat	muskrat	Surat
bear cat	flat	nougat	tabby cat
begat	*forgat*	numbat	tat
bepat	format	ochlocrat	technocrat
blat	frat	pat	that
bobcat	fruit bat	photostat	theocrat
brat	furzechat	physiocrat	thereat
brickbat	gat	pitapat	thermostat
bullbat	gerontocrat	plat	tipcat
bureaucrat	gnat	Platt	tit for tat
butterfat	grasschat	Platte	tomcat
carat	gynecocrat	plutocrat	top hat
cat	habitat	polecat	unhat
caveat	hardhat	pornocrat	vampire-bat
cervelat	hat	prat	vat
chat	heliostat	proletariat	water rat
chemostat	hellcat	pussycat	waterchat
chitchat	hepcat	pyrostat	whereat
civet cat	hereat	rabat	whinchat
clinostat	high hat	rat	wildcat
combat	humidistat	rat-a-tat	wombat
commissariat	hurlbat	rat-a-tat-tat	woodchat
Comsat	hydrostat	requiescat	xat
concordat	Intelsat	rheocrat	yellow-breasted
cow pat	isocrat	rheostat	chat
cravat	kat	sabbat	ziggurat
cryostat	kittycat	salariat	
dandiprat	lariat	sat	**ĀT**
democrat	lat	savate	gigawatt
dingbat	Laundromat	scat	Kalat
diplomat	Magnificat	secretariat	Khelat
doormat	marrow fat	shat	kilowatt
drat	mat	skat	megawatt
esbat	matte	slat	squat
fallow chat	meerkat	spat	terawatt
fat	meritocrat	splat	watt
fat cat	monocrat	sprat	what

yacht
(See also ŎT.)

ĀTH
bathe
lathe
scathe
snathe
spathe
swathe
unswathe

Āth
faith
i'faith
misfaith
rathe
Snaith
unfaith
water wraith
wraith

ĀTth
eighth
hate'th

Ăth
aftermath
allopath
Gath
hath
homeopath
math
osteopath
philomath
physiopath
polymath
psychopath

snath

Ăth
bath
bridle path
footpath
lath
path
rath
wrath

ĀTS
annates
Bates
Cates
Fates
othergates
Yates
Yeats
(See ĀT; add
-s where
appropriate.)

ĀV
angusticlave
architrave
autoclave
behave
belave
beslave
brave
cave
concave
crave
Dave
deprave
drave
élève
encave

enclave
engrave
enslave
forgave
galley slave
gave
glaive
grave
impave
knave
lave
microwave
misbehave
misgave
nave
new wave
outbrave
pave
rave
save
shave
shortwave
slave
stave
suave
they've
thrave
tidal wave
trave
ungrave
waive
wave

ĂV
calve
halve
have
lav
salve

Slav

ÄV
calve
enclave
halve
salve
Slav
suave
Yugoslav
Zouave

ĀZ
ablaze
adays
adaze
amaze
appraise
baize
Blaise
beacon-blaze
bepraise
blaze
braise
braze
chaise
chrysoprase
craze
daze
dispraise
emblaze
faze
fraise
gaze
glaze
graze
Haas
Hayes
haze

---

laze
maize
malaise
Marseillaise
Mays
Mayes
mayonnaise
maze
metaphrase
naze
nowadays
outblaze
outgaze
paraphrase
phase
phrase
polonaise
praise
raise
rase
raze
rephrase
self-praise
then-a-days
underpraise
unpraise
upblaze
upgaze
upraise
vase

wonder-maze
(See Ā; add
-*s* where
appropriate.)

ĂZ
as
has
jazz
pizzazz
razz
whereas

ÄZ
Shiraz
vase
(See Ä; add
-*s* where
appropriate.)

ĀZD
adazed
amazed
bemazed
crazed
dazed
glazed
unamazed
unappraised
undazed

unfazed
unglazed
ungrazed
unhazed
unphrased
unpraised
unraised
unrazed

ĂZD
jazzed
rázzed

ĀZH
cortege

ÄZH
arbitrage
badinage
barrage
camouflage
corsage
counterespi-
   onage
décolletage
découpage
entourage
espionage
garage
maquillage

massage
menage
mirage
montage
persiflage
photomontage
plage
raj
reportage
sabotage
triage

ĂZ'M
bioplasm
cataplasm
chasm
demoniasm
ectoplasm
enthusiasm
iconoclasm
metaplasm
miasm
phantasm
phasm
plasm
pleonasm
protoplasm
sarcasm
spasm

ōld, ôr, ŏdd, oil, fŏŏt, out; ūse, ûrn, ŭp; THis, thin

E

These words include the following accented vowel sounds:

Ē as in *me;* heard also in *eve, feet, beam, deceive, people, key, Caesar, machine, field, quay, phoebe.*
Ę as in *here;* heard also in *fear, dreary, weird.*
Ĕ as in *end;* heard also in *heifer, leopard, friend, Aetna, feather, asafetida, bury, any, Thames, said, says.*

Ē	bee	coatee	E-T
A.B.	bel-esprit	C.O.D.	eau-de-vie
abandonee	belee	consignee	employee
absentee	Benedicite	corroboree	endorsee
acne	biographee	coryphée	enfree
addressee	*blea*	CRT	ennui
advowee	bohea	Cybele	epopee
agape	bonhomie	D.D.	esprit
Agapemone	bootee	DAT	etui
agree	bouilli	DDT	Eugénie
alee	bourgeoisie	debauchee	Eulalie
allottee	Brie	debris	examinee
amicus curiae	bumblebee	decree	extempore
anemone	burgee	dedicatee	facetiae
Anglice	Burgundy	dee	facsimile
antistrophe	B.V.D.	degree	faerie
apogee	calipee	devisee	fairy
apostrophe	Calliope	devotee	fancy-free
appellee	calorie	diablerie	fee
appointee	cap-a-pie	disagree	felo-de-se
assignee	catastrophe	divorcee	fiddle-de-dee
avowee	CD	dominie	filigree
axletree	Chaldee	donee	flea
AZT	chariotee	drawee	flee
bailee	Cherokee	dree	fleur-de-lis
bain-marie	chickadee	druggie	foodie
banshee	chickeree	Dundee	foresee
bargee	chimpanzee	dungaree	free
bawbee	Chinee	Dupree	fricassee
be	Christmas tree	duty-free	Frisbee

āle, câre, ădd, ärm, ăsk; mē, hĕre, ĕnd; īce, ĭll;

fusee	manatee	perigee	selvagee
Galilee	Manichee	permittee	sesame
gallows tree	Marie	petitionee	settee
garnishee	marquee	Ph.D.	she
gee	Marshalsea	Pharisee	sí
geegee	master key	picotee	simile
Gethsemane	McFee	plea	skilligalee
ghee	McGee	pledgee	snee
glee	McKee	point-d'appui	snickersnee
goatee	me	poison tree	spree
grandee	Melpomene	pongee	stingaree
grantee	mestee	pontee	suttee
guarantee	Moonie	potpourri	sycee
he	mortgagee	presentee	synecdoche
heart-free	mustee	promisee	systole
honeybee	N.G.	pugaree	tax-free
humblebee	nebulae	Q.T.	tea
hyperbole	Niobe	quay	tee
interrogatee	nominee	raki	tehee
jamboree	nudgy	rani	Tennessee
Japanee	O.G.	rapparee	Terpsichore
jeu d'esprit	obligee	rappee	the
jinnee	ogee	razee	*thee*
jubilee	on dit	recipe	third degree
Kennedy	oversea	referee	three
key	oversee	refugee	topee
killdee	Parsee	releasee	toupee
knee	Parsi	remittee	transferee
langue d'oui	parti pris	repartee	tree
lea	*passaree*	rhe	trustee
lee	patentee	Rosalie	Tweedledee
legatee	Pawnee	rupee	unforesee
lessee	payee	Sadducee	unfree
levee	PC	sangaree	VDT
ley	PCB	Sault St. Marie	vendee
li	PCP	scarabee	vertebrae
licensee	pea	scree	vis-à-vis
litchi	pedigree	sea	vouchee
M.D.	Penelope	see	warrantee

ōld, ôr, ŏdd, oil, fŏŏt, out; ūse, ûrn, ŭp; THis, thin

we
wee
weeping tree
whiffletree
whippletree
ye
Zuyder Zee

abbacy
ability
absurdity
academy
acclivity
accompany
acerbity
acidity
acridity
activity
actuality
adaptability
adultery
adversity
advisability
affability
affinity
agency
agility
agony
alacrity
alchemy
allopathy
ambiguity
amenability
amenity
amicability
amity
amnesty
analogy

anarchy
anatomy
ancestry
animosity
anniversary
annuity
anomaly
anonymity
antipathy
antiphony
antiquity
anxiety
apathy
apology
apostasy
applicability
archery
argosy
aridity
aristocracy
armory
arrowy
artillery
artistry
ascendancy
asperity
assiduity
astrology
astronomy
atomic energy
atrocity
atrophy
audacity
augury
austerity
authenticity
authority
autonomy
avidity

bakery
balcony
barbarity
barony
barratry
bastardy
battery
beggary
benignity
bigamy
bigotry
billowy
biography
biology
blasphemy
blossomy
botany
bravery
brevity
bribery
brilliancy
brutality
bryony
burglary
cadency
calamity
calumny
Calvary
canopy
capability
capacity
captivity
casualty
catholicity
causticity
cavalry
cavity
celebrity
celerity

century
certainty
changeability
chancery
charity
chastity
chivalry
Christianity
chronology
civility
clemency
cogency
colloquy
colony
combustibility
comedy
comity
commodity
community
company
compatibility
complacency
complexity
complicity
complimentary
comprehensibil-
   ity
compulsory
conformity
connubiality
consanguinity
consistency
conspiracy
constancy
contiguity
contingency
contradictory
contrariety
conveniency

āle, câre, ădd, ärm, ăsk; mē, hĕre, ĕnd; īce, ĭll;

conventionality	discrepancy	equality	fluency
convexity	dishonesty	equanimity	flummery
coquetry	disparity	equity	foppery
courtesy	dissatisfactory	errantry	forestry
Coventry	dissimilarity	eternity	forgery
credulity	dissuasory	eulogy	formality
criminality	diversity	euphony	fortuity
crotchety	divinity	expectancy	fragility
crudity	docility	expediency	fragrancy
cruelty	domesticity	extended	fraternity
cupidity	doxology	family	frequency
curacy	drapery	extremity	frigidity
curiosity	drudgery	facility	frivolity
custody	dubiety	factory	frugality
debauchery	duplicity	faculty	futility
debility	dynasty	fallacy	futurity
decency	ebony	falsity	gaiety
declivity	eccentricity	familiarity	galaxy
deformity	economy	family	gallantry
deity	ecstasy	fantasy	gallery
delivery	efficiency	fatality	garrulity
democracy	effigy	fatuity	genealogy
demonry	effrontery	feathery	generosity
density	elasticity	fecundity	geniality
dependency	electricity	felicity	gentility
depravity	elegy	felony	geography
deputy	elementary	fernery	geology
destiny	elusory	ferocity	geometry
devilry	embassy	fertility	Germany
deviltry	emergency	fervency	gluttony
dexterity	enemy	festivity	gratuity
diary	energy	fidelity	gravity
dignity	enginery	fidgety	harmony
dimity	enmity	fiery	harvestry
diplomacy	enormity	finery	heathery
directory	entity	fixity	heraldry
discordancy	entropy	flagrancy	heredity
discourtesy	Epiphany	flattery	heresy
discovery	epitome	flippancy	hilarity

ōld, ôr, ŏdd, oil, fŏŏt, out; ūse, ûrn, ŭp; THis, thin

history
homeopathy
homily
honesty
hospitality
hostelry
hostility
humanity
humility
husbandry
hypocrisy
identity
idiocy
idiosyncrasy
idolatry
illiteracy
illusory
imagery
imbecility
immaturity
immensity
immodesty
immorality
immortality
immunity
imparity
impassivity
inpecuniosity
impetuosity
impiety
importunity
impropriety
impunity
impurity
inability
inadvertency
incapacity
inclemency
incompatibility

incomprehen-
  sibility
incongruity
inconsistency
inconstancy
incredulity
indignity
individuality
industry
inebriety
infallibility
infamy
infancy
infantry
infelicity
inferiority
infertility
infidelity
infinity
infirmary
infirmity
ingenuity
inhumanity
iniquity
injury
innumeracy
insincerity
insipidity
insufficiency
insularity
insurgency
integrity
intensity
intestacy
intrepidity
irony
Italy
ivory
jealousy

jeopardy
jewelry
jocundity
jollity
joviality
jugglery
juvenility
knavery
knight-errantry
laity
larceny
laxity
legacy
legality
leniency
lenity
lethargy
levity
liberality
liberty
limpidity
litany
liturgy
livery
Lombardy
longevity
loquacity
lottery
loyalty
lubricity
lucidity
lunacy
luxuriancy
luxury
machinery
magnanimity
mahogany
majesty
majority

malady
malignancy
malignity
masonry
mastery
maternity
maturity
mediocrity
melody
memory
mendacity
mendicity
merchantry
mercury
mimicry
ministry
minority
misanthropy
misery
mobility
mockery
modesty
monarchy
monody
monopoly
monotony
monstrosity
morality
mortality
multiplicity
mummery
municipality
mutability
mutiny
mystery
mythology
nationality
nativity
necessity

neutrality	perjury	probity	rarity
nobility	perpetuity	proclivity	rascality
nonconformity	perplexity	prodigality	reality
normalcy	personality	prodigy	reciprocity
Normandy	perspicuity	profanity	recovery
notary	pertinacity	professory	rectory
notoriety	perversity	proficiency	refractory
novelty	philanthropy	profundity	regency
nuclear family	philosophy	progeny	regeneracy
nudity	phylactery	prolixity	remedy
nullity	physiognomy	promiscuity	revelry
nursery	Picardy	propensity	rhapsody
obeisancy	piety	property	ribaldry
obesity	pillory	prophecy	rickety
obliquity	pillowy	propinquity	rigidity
obloquy	piracy	propriety	rivalry
obscurity	pleasantry	prosperity	robbery
oddity	pliancy	provinciality	rockery
Odyssey	poesy	proximity	roguery
opportunity	poetry	prudery	Romany
originality	poignancy	psalmistry	rosary
pageantry	policy	psalmody	rosemary
palmary	polity	psychiatry	rotundity
panoply	polygamy	publicity	royalty
papacy	pomposity	puerility	rubicundity
parity	ponderosity	pugnacity	rudimentary
parliamentary	popery	punctuality	rusticity
parody	popularity	pungency	sagacity
partiality	pornography	purity	salary
particularity	posterity	pusillanimity	salinity
paternity	potency	putridity	salubrity
peculiarity	poverty	quackery	sanctity
pedantry	precocity	quality	sanity
penalty	precursory	quandry	satiety
penury	prelacy	quantity	satisfactory
peppery	priority	quiescency	savagery
perfidy	priory	raillery	scarcity
perfumery	privacy	rapacity	scenery
perfunctory	privity	rapidity	scrutiny

ōld, ôr, ŏdd, oil, fŏŏt, out; ūse, ûrn, ŭp; THis, thin

secrecy	sublimity	travesty	villainy
security	subsidy	treachery	virginity
seigniory	subtlety	treasury	viridity
senility	sufficiency	trickery	virility
sensibility	sugary	trilogy	virtuality
sensuality	summary	trinity	virtuosity
sentimentality	superficiality	triviality	viscidity
serenity	superfluity	truancy	viscosity
servility	superiority	trumpery	vivacity
severity	supremacy	tyranny	volatility
shadowy	symmetry	ubiquity	voracity
shivery	sympathy	unanimity	votary
silvery	symphony	uniformity	vulgarity
similarity	taciturnity	unity	waggery
simony	tapestry	university	watery
simplicity	technicality	unsavory	whimsicality
sincerity	telegraphy	urbanity	willowy
sinewy	temerity	urgency	wintery
singularity	tenacity	usury	witchery
slavery	tenancy	utility	yeomanry
slippery	tenantry	vacancy	zoology
snuggery	tendency	vacuity	
sobriety	tenuity	vagrancy	
society	testamentary	valedictory	(See Section
solemnity	theocracy	valiancy	III, for many
solidity	theology	validity	more words
soliloquy	theory	vanity	ending in -y.)
solvency	theosophy	vapidity	absorbingly
sophistry	thievery	vapory	abusively
sorcery	threnody	variety	accordingly
spontaneity	thundery	velocity	accurately
stability	timidity	velvety	acidly
stagnancy	tonicity	venality	affectedly
sterility	topography	verbosity	aimlessly
stolidity	torpidity	verdancy	airily
strategy	totality	verity	alluringly
stupidity	tracery	versatility	allusively
suavity	tragedy	vicinity	ambitiously
subjectivity	tranquillity	victory	amusingly

āle, câre, ădd, ärm, ăsk; mē, hĕre, ĕnd; īce, ĭll;

anciently
appealingly
ardently
assertively
atrociously
auspiciously
awfully
banefully
becomingly
befittingly
beggarly
bespottedly
bewailingly
bitterly
bloodlessly
bloomingly
bloomlessly
blushingly
blushlessly
bodily
bootlessly
boundlessly
boyishly
brainlessly
breathlessly
broodingly
brotherly
brutally
bumptiously
carefully
carelessly
changelessly
chirpingly
chokingly
churlishly
civilly
clownishly
complainingly
concludingly

condescend-
  ingly
conducively
confoundedly
confusedly
consummately
convivially
countlessly
cousinly
cowardly
cravingly
crouchingly
crownlessly
cruelly
crushingly
cumbrously
dastardly
daughterly
decorously
deductively
defenselessly
deliciously
delusively
devotedly
disapprovingly
discerningly
disorderly
distastefully
distrustfully
divergently
divertingly
doggedly
dolefully
doubtfully
doubtingly
dreamingly
dreamlessly
drippingly
droopingly

dustily
easterly
elusively
enduringly
engagingly
engrossingly
eternally
exclusively
expansively
exultantly
exultingly
fadelessly
fairily
faithlessly
fatherly
feelingly
ferociously
fervidly
feudally
flippantly
floridly
flurriedly
flushingly
foolishly
foppishly
forebodingly
foreknowingly
forgivingly
formerly
forsakenly
fruitfully
fruitlessly
fulsomely
giddily
girlishly
gloomily
gloriously
gorgeously
gropingly

groundlessly
grudgingly
gruesomely
grumblingly
grumpily
guiltily
guiltlessly
gushingly
gustily
happily
harmfully
harmlessly
heartbrokenly
heartrendingly
heavenly
hereditarily
homelessly
hopefully
hopelessly
horridly
humanly
hungrily
hurriedly
illusively
immorally
immortally
imploringly
inclusively
indignantly
indulgently
infernally
inhumanly
insensately
instantly
instructively
insultingly
intermittently
inwardly
irksomely

ōld, ôr, ŏdd, oil, fŏŏt, out; ūse, ûrn, ŭp; THis, thin

iridescently	mournfully	prayerfully	secretly
jokingly	mournsomely	precociously	seducingly
joyfully	musingly	prepossessingly	seductively
joyously	nakedly	pretendingly	seemingly
judiciously	namelessly	productively	self-accusingly
juicily	necessarily	properly	self-consciously
laughingly	neighborly	propitiously	shamefully
lavishly	niggardly	provokingly	shamelessly
legendarily	noiselessly	publicly	shapelessly
lightfootedly	normally	pungently	sharp-wittedly
loathingly	northerly	pursuantly	shiftlessly
locally	northwardly	quarterly	shrewishly
lonesomely	obnoxiously	quiescently	silently
loungingly	obstructively	rapidly	sisterly
lovelessly	obtrusively	readily	sleepily
loverly	officiously	ready-wittedly	sleeplessly
lovingly	onwardly	recklessly	slouchingly
loyally	opposingly	recurrently	slovenly
lucidly	oppressively	refulgently	sluggishly
luckily	orderly	rejoicingly	smilingly
lucklessly	outrageously	relentlessly	smokily
luridly	overtoppingly	reluctantly	soakingly
luringly	owlishly	remorsefully	soberly
lustrously	painfully	remorselessly	solemnly
maidenly	painlessly	responsively	solidly
maliciously	pallidly	revengefully	somberly
mannerly	pathetically	rippingly	sordidly
masterly	peculiarly	ripplingly	sorrily
maternally	peerlessly	roaringly	sorrowfully
matronly	peevishly	rovingly	soulfully
meltingly	pellucidly	royally	soullessly
merrily	pervertedly	ruefully	soundlessly
misgivingly	piquantly	ruffianly	spirally
mistrustingly	*plaintfully*	ruggedly	splendidly
modestly	*plaintlessly*	savagely	spoonily
morally	playfully	scholarly	sportfully
morbidly	pluckily	scornfully	sportively
mortally	poetically	scowlingly	spotlessly
motherly	portentously	secretively	stirringly

āle, câre, ădd, ärm, ăsk; mē, hĕre, ĕnd; īce, ĭll;

stolenly
stormfully
stormily
stormlessly
straight-
  forwardly
stubbornly
studiedly
stupendously
stupidly
sturdily
stylishly
suddenly
sultrily
sunnily
superhumanly
superstitiously
surefootedly
suspiciously
swimmingly
swollenly
sylvanly
tauntingly
tediously
thanklessly
thornily
thoroughly
thumpingly
tonelessly
tranquilly
tremendously
trippingly
triumphally
triumphantly
troublously
trustfully
trustily
trustingly
truthfully

truthlessly
tunefully
tunelessly
unbecomingly
unbendingly
unbiddenly
unblushingly
unboundingly
unceasingly
unchangingly
uncloudedly
unerringly
unfailingly
unfeelingly
unfeignedly
unflaggingly
unguardedly
unknowingly
unlovingly
unmaidenly
unmannerly
unmotherly
unneighborly
unresistingly
unswervingly
unweariedly
unwittingly
unwontedly
unyieldingly
urgently
usurpingly
utterly
verily
vividly
voluntarily
wantonly
warningly
wastefully
waywardly

wearily
wholesomely
wittingly
wontedly
worthily
worthlessly
yearningly
yeomanly

ĒB
glebe
grebe

ĔB
cobweb
deb
ebb
keb
neb
Seb
web
Webb

ĔBD
ebbed
webbed

ĒBZ
Thebes
(See Ē B; add
-s where
appropriate.)

ĔBZ
Debs
ebbs
plebs
webbs
(See also ĔB;

add -s where
appropriate.)

ĔCH
beach
beseech
beech
bleach
breach
breech
each
forereach
forespeech
foreteach
impeach
keech
leach
leech
overreach
peach
preach
queach
reach
screech
sea reach
sleech
speech
teach
unbreech
unpreach

ĔCH
etch
fetch
fletch
Jack-Ketch
ketch
kvetch
letch

outstretch
retch
sketch
stretch
vetch
wretch

ĒCHD
beached
unbleached
unimpeached
(See also ĒCH;
add -ed where
appropriate.)

ĔCHD
etched
far-fetched
(See also ĔCH;
add -ed where
appropriate.)

ĒD
accede
aniseed
antecede
bead
bleed
brede
breed
cede
centipede
concede
creed
deed
dispeed
Ead
exceed
feed

Ganymede
glede
gleed
Godspeed
greed
heed
impede
implead
inbreed
indeed
interbreed
intercede
interplead
invalid
jereed
knead
knock-kneed
lead
mead
Meade
Mede
meed
millipede
misdeed
mislead
misread
need
off his feed
outspeed
overfeed
plead
precede
proceed
read
Reade
recede
rede
reed
Reid

retrocede
Runnymede
screed
seaweed
secede
seed
speed
stampede
steed
succeed
supersede
Swede
teed
treed
Tweed
undecreed
unfeed
unpedigreed
upbreed
uplead
velocipede
weed
we'd
(See also Ē;
add -d or -ed
where
appropriate.)

ĔD
abed
acidhead
adread
ahead
airhead
arrowhead
bed
bedspread
bedstead
behead

bespread
bestead
billethead
bled
blunderhead
bonehead
bread
breviped
chucklehead
coed
copperhead
dead
deadhead
deathbed
death's-head
dread
dunderhead
Ed
egghead
embed
fathead
featherhead
fed
figurehead
fissiped
fled
foresaid
fountainhead
Fred
full-fed
gingerbread
go-ahead
head
highbred
homebred
hophead
hothead
inbred
instead

jolterhead
lead
led
letterhead
loggerhead
lowlihead
maidenhead
masthead
misled
Ned
negrohead
niggerhead
outspread
overfed
overhead
overspread
pilot bread
pinhead
pled
poppyhead
pothead
quadruped
read
red
redd
said
shed
shewbread
shred
skinhead
sled
sorehead
sped
spread
stead
surbed
ted
thoroughbred
thread

thunderhead
timberhead
tread
truckle bed
truebred
trundle bed
trundlehead
underbred
unhead
unread
unsaid
unsped
unthread
unwed
warhead
watershed
wed
well-sped
woolly head
Winifred
zed

accustomed
anchored
answered
astonished
attributed
balanced
banished
barren-spirited
base-spirited
bediamonded
bewildered
bigoted
blemished
blistered
bold-spirited
bonneted

brandished
breakfasted
burnished
carpeted
clustered
conquered
continued
contributed
covered
coveted
crescented
diamonded
diminished
discomforted
discredited
dispirited
disquieted
distributed
dowered
embarrassed
emblazoned
enamored
exhibited
faceted
famished
fine-spirited
flowered
forfeited
furnished
garlanded
gathered
gay-spirited
glimmered
glistened
hearkened
helmeted
heralded
high-spirited
hungered

imprisoned
inhabited
inherited
inspirited
jeoparded
languished
light-spirited
limited
lingered
low-spirited
marvelled
mean-spirited
measured
merited
murmured
overpowered
overtowered
pardoned
patented
perjured
pirated
poor-spirited
prohibited
public-spirited
punished
quieted
ravaged
recovered
relinquished
remembered
ringleted
rivalled
sanctioned
shepherded
shimmered
showered
shuddered
signeted
slumbered

ōld, ôr, ŏdd, oil, fŏŏt, out; ūse, ûrn, ŭp; THis, thin

soft-spirited
sorrowed
spirited
suffered
talented
tempered
tenanted
thundered
turreted
unballasted
unbonneted
uninhabited
unlimited
unmerited
unprofited
unrespited
untenanted
visited
wandered
weak-spirited
wearied
winnowed
witnessed
wondered
worshipped

ĔDST
bespread'st
dread'st
fed'st
fled'st
led'st
overspread'st
said'st
thread'st
tread'st
wed'st

ĔDTH

bespread'th
breadth
hairbreadth

ĒDZ
Eades
Leeds
(See ĒD; add
-s where
appropriate.)

ĒF
aperitif
bas-relief
beef
belief
brief
chief
disbelief
fief
grief
interleaf
leaf
leitmotif
lief
motif
reef
relief
sheaf
shereef
thief
unbelief

ĔF
Brezhnev
chef
clef
deaf
enfeoff

F
feoff
Gorbachev
Kiev
Prokofiev
UNICEF

ĔFT
aleft
bereft
cleft
deft
eft
enfeoffed
heft
left
reft
theft
unbereft
weft
wheft

ĒG
big league
blitzkrieg
colleague
enleague
fatigue
Grieg
intrigue
klieg
league
Little League
major league
minor league
renege
sitzkrieg

ĔG

beg
beglerbeg
egg
goose egg
keg
leg
Meg
peg
philabeg
skeg
teg
unpeg
Winnipeg
yegg

ĒGD
fatigued
overfatigued
(See also ĒG;
add -ed where
appropriate.)

ĔGD
begged
spindle-legged
(See also ĔG;
add -ed or
-ged where
appropriate.)

ĔGZ
begs
dregs
Meggs
sea legs
(See also ĔG;
add -s where
appropriate.)

ĒJ
besiege
liege
siege

ĔJ
allege
cledge
cutting edge
dredge
edge
enhedge
fledge
hedge
impledge
interpledge
kedge
ledge
pledge
privilege
sacrilege
sedge
tedge
unedge
wedge

ĔJD
double-edged
dredged
sedged
two-edged
unhedged
(See also ĔJ;
add -ed where
appropriate.)

ĒK
afterpeak
aleak

antique
apeak
areek
batik
beak
beek
Belleek
bespeak
bezique
bleak
boutique
bubble and
    squeak
cacique
caique
Cazique
cheek
Chesapeake
chic
cleek
clinique
clique
comique
creak
creek
critique
demipique
doublespeak
ecofreak
eke
feak
fenugreek
forepeak
forespeak
freak
geek
gleek
Greek
grosbeak

halfbeak
hide-and-seek
Holy Week
houseleak
Jesus freak
keek
leak
leek
Martinique
meak
meek
midweek
Mozambique
mystique
newspeak
oblique
Passion Week
peak
peek
peke
physique
pipsqueak
pique
plastique
politique
pratique
radical chic
realpolitik
reek
relique
repique
reseek
saic
screak
seek
sheik
shriek
Sikh
silique

sleek
sneak
speak
squeak
sticky beak
streak
teak
technique
triptych
tweak
unique
unsleek
unspeak
upseek
weak
week
widow's peak
wreak
yesterweek

ĔK
afterdeck
Aztec
beck
bedeck
bewreck
blackneck
blank check
body check
bottleneck
breakneck
breck
by heck
check
cheque
Chiang
    Kai-shek
cleck
counter check

---

countercheck
crew neck
crombec
cromlech
crookneck
cross-check
cusec
Czech
deck
discotheque
dreck
feck
fleck
flyspeck
foredeck
geck
hatcheck
heck
henpeck
home ec
Kennebec
kopek
leatherneck
lech
leck
lek
Mixtec
neck
neck-and-neck
OPEC
overcheck
parsec
peck
pinchbeck
quarterdeck
Quebec
rain check
rebec
recheck

reck
redneck
roughneck
rubber check
rubberneck
sandek
sapeque
sec
seck
shipwreck
sneck
spec
speck
swanneck
tec
tech
Techuantepec
tenrec
Toltec
trek
turtleneck
undeck
wreck
wryneck
xebec
yech

ĔKS
beaks
breeks
sneaks
(See also ĔK;
add -s where
appropriate.)

ĔKS
annex
becks
bedecks

Celotex
circumflex
complex
convex
duplex
ex
Exe
flex
googolplex
inflex
kex
Kleenex
latex
lex
Middlesex
multiplex
narthex
perplex
prex
Pyrex
reflex
rex
Rolodex
sex
Tex-Mex
triplex
unisex
unsex
vex
videotex
vortex
weaker sex
(See also ĔK;
add -s where
appropriate.)

ĔKST
annexed
next

pretext
sexed
sext
text
unperplexed
unsexed
unvexed
videotext
(See also ĔKS;
add -ed where
appropriate.)

ĔKT
beaked
cherry-cheeked
peaked
rosy-cheeked
unwreaked
(See also ĔK;
add -ed where
appropriate.)

ĔKT
abject
adject
affect
analect
annect
architect
arrect
bedecked
benign neglect
bisect
circumspect
collect
confect
conject
connect
correct

āle, câre, ădd, ärm, ăsk; mē, hĕre, ĕnd; īce, ĭll;

defect
deflect
deject
detect
dialect
direct
disaffect
disconnect
disinfect
disrespect
dissect
domino effect
effect
elect
erect
expect
exsect
genuflect
greenhouse
　effect
incorrect
indirect
infect
inflect
inject
inspect
intellect
interject
intersect
introspect
misdirect
neglect
non-elect
object
perfect
porrect
prefect
prelect
project

prospect
protect
recollect
refect
reflect
reject
respect
resurrect
retrospect
ripple effect
sect
select
self-respect
subject
suspect
traject
trisect
unchecked
undecked
unsuspect
(See also ĔK;
add -ed where
appropriate.)

ĒL

abele
aiguille
alguazil
all heal
allele
anele
anneal
appeal
automobile
balance wheel
barleymeal
bastille
beal

bidonville
big deal
big wheel
bonspiel
breast wheel
Camille
cartwheel
Castile
cebil
ceil
chamomile
chenille
clownheal
cochineal
cockatiel
cogwheel
commonweal
conceal
congeal
cornmeal
creel
cystocele
datil
deal
deil
deshabille
dial-wheel
difficile
dishabille
driving wheel
eel
endocoele
enseal
exocoele
feal
feel
feil
fistmele
flywheel

forefeel
freewheel
gear wheel
genteel
glockenspiel
goldenseal
havermeal
heal
heel
he'll
ideal
imbecile
inchmeal
infantile
interdeal
Israfil
jeel
jheel
keel
Kiel
kneel
kriegspiel
leal
Lille
locomobile
Lucille
machineel
manteel
meal
mill wheel
misdeal
mobile
Mobile
Neal
ne'er-do-weel
Neil
Neill
neurocoele
newsreel

O'Neal
O'Neill
O'Sheel
oatmeal
ordeal
paddle wheel
pastille
peal
peel
piecemeal
pimpmobile
pinwheel
privy seal
real
recongeal
redeal
reel
repeal
reveal
schlemiel
seal
seel
shabby-
  genteel
she'll
sheal
skeel
snowmobile
speel
spiel
squeal
steal
steel
surreal
sweal
Tarheel
teal
teel
teil

thunderpeal
toril
tuille
tweel
uncongeal
unreal
unreel
unséal
unseel
unsteel
urodele
vakil
veal
weal
weel
we'll
wheal
wheel
wholemeal
zeal

ĔL

Abarbanel
aerogel
aludel
aquarelle
artel
asphodel
Astrophel
A.W.O.L.
bagatelle
barbell
béchamel
befell
bel
bell
belle
bluebell
bombshell

bonnibel
bretelle
bridewell
brocatel
cadelle
calomel
Canterbury
  bell
caramel
caravel
Carmel
carousel
cartel
cell
chandelle
chanterelle
Chaumontel
citadel
claribel
clientele
cockerel
cockleshell
compel
cordelle
Cornell
coronel
cowbell
Crannell
crenel
crenelle
Cromwell
damoiselle
damoselle
deathbell
decibel
dell
demoiselle
dentelle
dinner bell

dispel
divel
divingbell
doggerel
doorbell
dumbbell
dwell
eggshell
El
ell
Emmanuel
excel
expel
farewell
fell
ficelle
filoselle
fontanel
foretell
Fresnel
fricandel
gabelle
gazelle
gel
groundswell
handbell
hard sell
hard-shell
harebell
HDL
heather bell
hell
hotel
hydrogel
hydromel
Immanuel
immortelle
impel
indwell

āle, câre, ădd, ärm, ăsk; mē, hĕre, ĕnd; īce, ĭll;

infidel
inkwell
inshell
intermell
involucel
Isabel
jargonelle
jell
Jezebel
jumelle
jurel
kell
knell
kvell
lapel
Lionel
love spell
mackerel
mademoiselle
maître d'hôtel
mangonel
marcel
materiel
mel
mell
minute bell
mirabelle
misspell
morel
moschatel
Moselle
motel
muscatel
nacelle
Nell
Nobel
Noel
nonpareil
nutshell

oenomel
organelle
outsell
oversell
pallmall
parallel
Parnell
passing bell
pedicel
pell
pell-mell
pennoncelle
personnel
petronel
Philomel
photocell
pickerel
pimpernel
pipistrel
plasma cell
plasmagel
propel
prunelle
pucellé
Purnell
quadrelle
quell
quenelle
rappel
Ravel
rebel
red cell
refel
rel
repel
resell
respell
retell
ritornelle

rondel
rondelle
ruelle
sacring bell
sanctus bell
sarcel
sarcelle
sardel
sardelle
scalpel
seashell
sell
sentinel
shell
sickle cell
smell
snell
soft sell
soft-shell
solar cell
speedwell
spell
spinel
spirituel
stairwell
swell
Tavel
tell
tortoiseshell
tourelle
undersell
unicell
unshell
unspell
unwell
upswell
vesper bell
vielle
villanelle

well
white cell
yell
zel
Zell
zinfandel

ĚLCH

belch
squelch
Welch
Welsh

ĒLD

afield
annealed
battlefield
Chesterfield
Dangerfield
Delafield
enshield
field
harvest field
shield
unaneled
unrepealed
weald
wield
yield
(See also ĒL;
add -*ed* where
appropriate.)

ĚLD

beheld
belled
eld
geld
held

ōld, ôr, ŏdd, oil, fŏŏt, out; ūse, ûrn, ŭp; THis, thin

jet-propelled
meld
seld
unbeheld
unknelled
unparalleled
unquelled
upheld
weld
withheld
(See also ĔL;
add -*ed* where
appropriate.)

ĔLF
delf
elf
Guelph
herself
himself
itself
mantel shelf
myself
oneself
ourself
pelf
self
shelf
thyself
yourself

ĔLFT
delft

ĔLFth
twelfth

ĔLK
elk

whelk
yelk

ĔLM
dishelm
elm
helm
overwhelm
realm
underwhelm
unhelm
weather helm
whelm

ĔLP
help
kelp
self-help
skelp
swelp
whelp
yelp

ĔLPS
Phelps
(See also ĔLP;
add -*s* where
appropriate.)

ĔLS
else
(See also ĔL;
add -*s* where
appropriate.)

ĔLSH
Welsh

ĔLT

belt
black belt
borscht belt
brown belt
celt
dealt
dwelt
felt
gelt
heartfelt
kelt
knelt
melt
misspelt
pelt
Roosevelt
smelt
spelt
Sunbelt
svelte
swelt
unbelt
unfelt
veld
veldt
welt
white belt

ĔLth
commonwealth
dwell'th
health
stealth
wealth
(See also ĔL;
add -*th* where
appropriate.)

ĔLV

delve
helve
shelve
twelve

ĔLVZ
delves
elves
ourselves
selves
themselves
yourselves

ĔLZ
Dardanelles
Elles
Lascelles
Seychelles
Welles
Wells
(See also ĔL;
add -*s* where
appropriate.)

ĒM
abeam
academe
anatheme
beam
beseem
blaspheme
bream
centime
cream
daydream
deem
disesteem
distream
dream

āle, câre, ădd, ärm, ăsk; mē, hĕre, ĕnd; īce, ĭll;

embeam
enseam
esteem
extreme
fleam
gleam
ice cream
leam
misdeem
moonbeam
ream
redeem
reem
regime
riem
scheme
scream
seam
seem
self-esteem
steam
stream
supreme
team
teem
theme
unbeseem
unseam
unteam
weathergleam

ĒM
ad hominem
ahem
anadem
apothegm
bediadem
begem
Bethlehem

Brummagem
clem
condemn
contemn
diadem
em
'em
gem
hem
mem
phlegm
pro tem
requiem
stem
strategem
them
theorem

ĒMD
beamed
undreamed
unredeemed
(See also ĒM;
add *-ed* where
appropriate.)

ĔMD
begemmed
uncondemned
undiademed
(See also ĔM;
add *-ed* where
appropriate.)

ĔMP
hemp
Kemp

ĔMS

temse

ĔMT
adreamt
attempt
contempt
dreamt
exempt
kempt
preempt
self-contempt
tax-exempt
tempt
undreamt
unkempt

ĒMZ
beams
meseems
(See also ĒM;
add *-s* where
appropriate.)

ĔMZ
gems
temse
Thames
(See also ĔM;
add *-s* where
appropriate.)

ĒN
Aberdeen
achene
advene
Algerine
almandine
alpeen
alpigene

. amidine
ammine
amphetamine
aniline
anserine
antihistamine
aqua green
aquamarine
argentine
arsine
arsphenamine
astatine
atropine
atween
aubergine
Augustine
aventurine
Balanchine
baleen
bandoline
barkentine
bean
been
Beguine
bellarmine
bemean
Benzedrine
benzene
benzine
bescreen
beta carotene
between
bismarine
blue green
bombazine
bottine
bowling green
brigandine
brigantine

brilliantine
bromine
buckbean
buckeen
Byzantine
caffeine
canteen
capeline
Capuchin
capuchine
careen
carotene
carrageen
chagrin
chevaline
chlorobenzene
choline
chopine
chorine
chryselephan-
tine
cismarine
clean
Clementine
closet queen
codeine
colleen
come clean
complex
  machine
Constantine
contravene
convene
costean
crapaudine
crinoline
cuckquean
cuisine
cyanine

cysteine
cystine
damascene
damaskeen
dasheen
dauphine
dean
demean
demesne
dene
dentine
dopamine
dourine
drag queen
dudeen
duvetyn
ean
e'en
eighteen
elephantine
Eocene
epicene
epigene
Ernestine
Essene
Eugene
Evangeline
evergreen
fairy queen
fascine
fava bean
fellaheen
fellahin
fifteen
figurine
fillipeen
Florentine
fluorine
foreseen

fourteen
gabardine
galantine
gamine
gangrene
gardeen
gasoline
gazogene
gean
gelatine
gene
Geraldine
Ghibelline
glassine
glean
gleen
go-between
gombeen
good-e'en
gradine
grass green
green
grenadine
guillotine
Halloween
haratin
harvest queen
Hellene
heterogene
Hippocrene
histamine
hygiene
hypogene
imine
impregn
incarnadine
indene
indigene
intervene

Irene
isoprene
Jean
jean
jellybean
Josephine
keen
kerosene
kidney bean
kitt ereen
lateen
latrine
lean
lene
libertine
lien
lima bean
limousine
lipoprotein
long green
machine
magazine
Magdalene
mangosteen
margarine
margravine
marine
matachin
mavourneen
May Queen
mazarine
meadow queen
mean
mesne
mezzanine
mien
Miocene
misdemean
moline

āle, câre, ădd, ärm, ăsk; mē, hĕre, ĕnd; īce, ĭll;

moreen
morphine
mousseline
Mr. Clean
muscarine
mytho green
nankeen
naphthalene
narceine
navy bean
Nazarene
nectarine
nervine
Nicene
nicotine
nineteen
nitrobenzene
obscene
oleomargarine
olivine
opaline
organzine
ornithine
overseen
overween
palanquin
Palmyrene
patine
Pauline
pea bean
pea green
pean
peen
pelerine
pentene
Peregrine
philhellene
Philippine
phosgene

phosphene
phosphine
photogene
phthalein
physostigmine
pinto bean
piperidine
piperazine
pistareen
Pleistocene
Pliocene
polygene
polythene
porphyrogene
poteen
potheen
praline
praying
   machine
preen
preteen
prevene
pristine
proline
protein
purine
putting green
pyrene
quadragene
quarantine
quarentene
quean
queen
quinine
Racine
ratine
ratteen
ravine
reen

rescreen
rosmarine
routine
sakeen
salmatine
sardine
sateen
scalene
scene
screen
sea green
seen
seine
seltzogene
serene
serpentine
seventeen
sewing
   machine
shagreen
Shean
shebeen
sheen
shoneen
simple machine
Sistine
sixteen
skean
Slovene
sourdine
soybean
spalpeen
sphene
spleen
split screen
spodumene
squalene
St. Augustine
stean

steen
stein
string bean
submarine
subteen
subterrene
subvene
supergene
superterrene
supervene
takin
tambourine
tangerine
teen
terebene
terpene
terrene
terrine
therebetween
thirteen
Tolkien
toluene
tontine
tourmaline
toxaphene
transmarine
travertine
treen
trephine
tureen
'tween
ultramarine
umpteen
unclean
undine
unforeseen
unqueen
unseen
unscreen

ōld,   ôr,   ŏdd,   oil,   fŏŏt,   out;   ūse,   ûrn,   ŭp;   THis,   thin

uplean
vaccine
valine
Vaseline
velveteen
visne
vitrine
voting machine
wean
ween
wheen
wide-screen
wintergreen
wolverine
yean
yellow green
yestreen

ĔN
again
aldermen
amen
ben
brevipen
cayenne
Cheyenne
citizen
cyclamen
Darien
den
denizen
equestrienne
fen
fountain pen
glen
halogen
hen
hydrogen
impen

ken
Magdalen
men
nitrogen
oxygen
Parisienne
pen
prairie hen
regimen
Saracen
sen
sen-sen
specimen
ten
then
tragedienne
unpen
Valenciennes
varsovienne
water hen
wen
when
wren
yen

ĔNCH
bedrench
bench
blench
clench
drench
flench
French
intrench
mensch
monkey
wrench
quench
retrench

squench
stench
tench
trench
unclench
wench
wrench

ĔNCHD
bedrenched
unblenched
(See also
ĔNCH; add
-ed where
appropriate.)

ĒND
advened
cleaned
fiend
piend
teind
(See also ĒN;
add -ed where
appropriate.)

ĔND
amend
an-end
append
apprehend
ascend
attend
befriend
bend
blend
commend
comprehend

condescend
contend
defend
depend
descend
distend
dividend
emend
end
expend
extend
fend
forefend
forfend
friend
gable end
godsend
hornblende
impend
intend
interblend
kenned
lend
mend
minuend
misapprehend
misspend
obtend
offend
ostend
penned
perpend
pitch blende
portend
prepend
pretend
recommend
rend
repetend

āle, câre, ădd, ärm, ăsk; mē, hĕre, ĕnd; īce, ĭll;

reprehend
reverend
send
South Bend
spend
subtend
subtrahend
superintend
suspend
tend
transcend
trend
unbend
unfriend
unkenned
unpenned
upend
upsend
vend
vilipend
wend
Zend

ĔNDZ
amends
ascends
(See also ĔND;
add -s where
appropriate.)

ĔNGK
Schenck

ĔNGKS
Jenkes
Jenks

ĔNGTH
full-length

length
strength

ĔNJ
avenge
revenge
Stonehenge

ĔNJD
unavenged

ĔNS
abstinence
accidence
affluence
beneficence
benevolence
blandiloquence
breviloquence
circumference
coincidence
commence
common sense
competence
concupiscence
condense
conference
confidence
confluence
consequence
continence
convenience
corpulence
defense
deference
dense
difference
diffidence

diligence
disobedience
dispense
dissidence
eloquence
eminence
equivalence
evidence
excellence
exigence
expedience
expense
experience
fence
flatulence
flocculence
frankincense
fraudulent
grandiloquence
hence
immanence
immense
imminence
impenitence
impertinence
impotence
imprevalence
improvidence
impudence
incense
incidence
incipience
incoincidence
incompetence
incongruence
inconsequence
incontinence
inconvenience
indifference

indigence
indolence
inexpedience
inexperience
inference
influence
innocence
insipience
insolence
intelligence
intense
irreverence
magnificence
magniloquence
maleficence
malevolence
mellifluence
munificence
negligence
nescience
nonresidence
obedience
offense
omnipotence
omiscience
opulence
pence
penitence
percipience
permanence
pertinence
pestilence
plenipotence
preeminence
preference
prepense
prescience
pretense
prevalence

---

prominence
propense
providence
prurience
quantivalence
recompense
redolence
reference
residence
resilience
reticence
reverence
salience
sapience
self-confidence
self-defense
sense
somnolence
spence
subservience
subsidence
subtense
succulence
supereminence
suspense
tense
thence
truculence
turbulence
vehemence
videoconfer-
   ence
violence
virulence
whence
(See also
ĔNT; add
-*s* where
appropriate.)

ĔNST
against
anenst
commenced
condensed
dispensed
evidenced
experienced
fenced
fornenst
'gainst
incensed
inexperienced
influenced
reverenced
sensed

ĔNT
abandonment
abolishment
absent
abstinent
accent
accident
accipient
accompaniment
accomplishment
accoutrement
acknowledg-
   ment
admeasurement
admonishment
advertisement
affamishment
affluent
affranchisement
aggrandizement
aliment
ambient

anent
aperient
apportionment
acquent
arbitrament
argument
armament
ascent
assent
astonishment
attent
augment
babblement
banishment
battlement
bedevilment
bedizenment
belligerent
beneficent
benevolent
bent
besprent
betterment
bewilderment
blandishment
blazonment
blemishment
blent
botherment
brabblement
brent
cement
cent
chastisement
cherishment
circumambient
circumfluent
circumvent
coincident

comment
competent
complement
compliment
condiment
confident
confluent
congruent
consent
consequent
constituent
content
continent
convenient
corpulent
dazzlement
decipherment
decrement
deferent
dement
demolishment
dent
descent
detent
detriment
development
devilment
different
diffident
diffluent
diligent
diminishment
dimplement
disablement
disarmament
discontent
discourage-
   ment
disfigurement

āle, câre, ădd, ärm, ăsk; mē, hĕre, ĕnd; īce, ĭll;

disfranchise-ment	equivalent	immanent	Kent
disobedient	esculent	imminent	lament
disparagement	establishment	impediment	languishment
dispiritment	esurient	impenitent	lavishment
dissent	event	imperilment	leant
dissident	evident	impertinent	lenient
distinguish-ment	excellent	inplement	lent
divertisement	excrement	impotent	ligament
document	exigent	impoverishment	lineament
element	expedient	imprisonment	liniment
eloquent	experiment	improvident	luculent
embarrassment	extent	impudent	magnificent
embattlement	extinguishment	incident	magniloquent
embellishment	famishment	incipient	malcontent
embezzlement	fent	incoincident	maleficent
embitterment	ferment	incompetent	malevolent
emblazonment	filament	incongruent	management
embodiment	firmament	inconsequent	meant
eminent	flocculent	incontinent	measurement
emollient	foment	inconvenient	medicament
emolument	foremeant	increment	mellifluent
empannelment	*forespent*	indent	merriment
enablement	fornent	indifferent	miscontent
encompass-ment	fosterment	indigent	misrepresent
encouragement	franchisement	indolent	misspent
endangerment	fraudulent	inexpedient	monument
endeavorment	frequent	influent	munificent
enfeeblement	garnishment	ingredient	muniment
enfranchisement	gent	innocent	negligent
enlightenment	Ghent	insentient	nourishment
ennoblement	government	insipient	nutriment
enravishment	*gracilent*	insolent	obedient
entanglement	gradient	instrument	occident
envelopment	grandiloquent	integument	omnipotent
environment	habiliment	intelligent	opulent
envisagement	harassment	intent	orient
	hereditament	inveiglement	ornament
	ignipotent	invent	ostent
	ill-content	irreverent	overspent

ōld, ôr, ŏdd, oil, fŏŏt, out; ūse, ûrn, ŭp; THis, thin

parliament
pediment
penitent
pent
percipient
permanent
pertinent
pesterment
pestilent
plenipotent
portent
prattlement
precedent
predicament
preeminent
premonishment
prescient
present
presentiment
president
prevalent
prevent
prominent
provident
prurient
punishment
ravishment
recipient
redolent
refluent
regiment
relent
relinquishment
rent
repent
replenishment
represent
resent
resident

resilient
reticent
reverent
rudiment
sacrament
salient
sapient
scent
sediment
self-confident
sent
sentient
sentiment
settlement
somnolent
spent
sprent
stent
subsequent
subservient
succulent
supereminent
supplement
temperament
tenement
tent
testament
thereanent
torment
tournament
tremblement
Trent
truculent
turbulent
unbent
underwent
unkent
unmeant
unsent

unspent
untent
vanishment
vanquishment
vehement
vent
vinolent
violent
virulent
wanderment
well-content
well-meant
well-spent
went
wilderment
wonderment
worriment

ĔNth
fourteenth
greenth
lean'th
thirteenth
(See also ĒN;
add -*th* where
appropriate.)

ĔNth
pen'th
tenth
(See also ĔN;
add -*th* where
appropriate.)

ĔNTS
accoutrements
cents
contents
(See also ĔNS.)

ĒNZ
advenes
Essenes
greens
smithereens
teens
(See also ĒN;
add -*z* where
appropriate.)

ĔNZ
cleanse
ens
flense
gens
lens
Valenciennes
Vincennes
(See also ĔN;
add -*s* where
appropriate.)

ĒP
adeep
aheap
asleep
beauty sleep
beweep
bopeep
cheap
cheep
chepe
chimney sweep
clepe
creep
deep
ensweep
estrepe
forweep

heap
keep
leap
neap
outleap
outsleep
outweep
overleap
oversleep
peep
reap
seep
sheep
sleep
steep
sweep
swepe
threap
under-peep
unkeep
weep

ĔP
demirep
footstep
hep
overstep
pep
rep
schlep
skep
step
steppe

ĔPS
cheeps
creeps
(See also ĔP;
add -s where

appropriate.)

ĔPS
steps
(See also ĔP;
add -s where
appropriate.)

ĒPT
beneaped
heaped
neaped
unsteeped
upheaped
(See also ĒP;
add -ed where
appropriate.)

ĔPT
accept
adept
crept
except
inept
intercept
kept
leapt
outslept
overslept
overstepped
pepped
sept
slept
stepped
swept
unkept
unswept
unwept
wept

yclept

ĔPth
depth
stepp'th

ĒR
adhere
aerosphere
affeer
amir
ahear
appear
arrear
asmear
atmosphere
auctioneer
austere
bandoleer
bayadere
beer
belvedere
besmear
bevel gear
bier
blear
bombardier
brevier
brigadier
buccaneer
canceleer
cannoneer
caravaneer
carbineer
career
cashier
cavalier
cere
chandelier

chanticleer
charioteer
cheer
chevalier
chiffonier
chimere
circuiteer
clear
cohere
commandeer
compeer
congé d'élire
crotcheteer
cuirassier
dear
deer
disappear
domineer
drear
ear
electioneer
emir
endear
engineer
ensear
ensphere
fakir
fallow deer
fear
financier
fineer
fleer
friction gear
frontier
fusileer
garreteer
gaselier
gazeteer
gear

ginger beer	planisphere	upcheer	afterpiece
gondolier	privateer	uprear	ambergris
gonfalonier	pulpiteer	veer	apiece
grand vizier	queer	veneer	battlepiece
grenadier	racketeer	vizier	Berenice
halberdier	reappear	volunteer	Bernice
hear	rear	weir	cantatrice
Heer	reindeer	year	caprice
hemisphere	revere		cassis
here	scrutineer	**ĒRD**	cease
indear	sear	adhered	cerise
Indianeer	seer	beard	chimneypiece
inhere	sere	feared	Clarice
insincere	sermoneer	flap-eared	coulisse
insphere	severe	lop-eared	crease
interfere	shear	*uneared*	creese
jeer	sheer	unfeared	decease
killdeer	sincere	unpeered	decrease
lear	skeer	weird	degrease
leer	smear	(See also ĒR;	esquisse
madrier	sneer	add -ed where	Felice
meer	sonneteer	appropriate.)	fleece
mere	souvenir		fowling piece
mir	spear	**ĒRS**	frontispiece
mountaineer	specksioneer	fierce	geese
muffineer	sphere	pierce	grease
muleteer	steer	tierce	grece
musketeer	tabasheer	transpierce	Greece
mutineer	targeteer		increase
near	tear	**ĒRT**	lease
overhear	teer	peart	Lucrece
overseer	tier		mantelpiece
pamphleteer	*timberstere*	**ĒRZ**	masterpiece
peer	timoneer	adheres	Maurice
persevere	Tyr	Algiers	mouthpiece
petardeer	undersphere	shears	Nice
pier	ungear	sheers	niece
pioneer	*unnear*		obese
pistoleer	unsphere	**ĒS**	peace

āle, câre, ădd, ärm, ăsk; mē, hĕre, ĕnd; īce, ĭll;

pelisse
piece
pocket piece
police
popping crease
predecease
Reese
release
semese
sublease
surcease
Thais
Therese
timepiece
valise
verdigris

ĒS
access
accresce
acquiesce
address
aggress
ambassadress
ancestress
archeress
assess
baroness
Bess
blemishless
bless
bodiless
bottomless
bouillabaisse
canoness
caress
cess
chess
coalesce

colorless
comfortless
comfortress
compress
confess
conqueress
conscienceless
convalesce
cress
cultureless
cumberless
dauphiness
deaconess
deliquesce
demoness
depress
digress
dinnerless
dispossess
distress
diving dress
dress
duress
editress
effervesce
effloresce
effortless
egress
evanesce
excess
executress
express
fanciless
fatherless
fathomless
favorless
featureless
fess
fetterless

finesse
flavorless
flowerless
foreguess
fortuneless
frondesce
full-dress
gala dress
gentilesse
giantess
governess
guess
harborless
headdress
Hess
idolatress
impress
ingress
inheritress
intumesce
jess
Kress
largess
less
letterpress
limitless
marchioness
masterless
mayoress
meaningless
measureless
merciless
mess
ministress
moneyless
monitress
motherless
motionless
motiveless

nevertheless
noblesse
numberless
obsess
obsolesce
odorless
opalesce
oppress
overdress
pantheress
patroness
penniless
phosphoresce
pitiless
pleasureless
poetess
politesse
possess
powerless
power press
prepossess
press
prioress
procuress
profess
progress
phophetess
proprietress
purposeless
pythoness
Quakeress
quiesce
ransomless
recess
redress
regress
repress
respiteless
retrogress

rudderless
shadowless
shelterless
shepherdess
silverless
slumberless
S.O.S.
sorceress
spiritless
stewardess
stress
success
sultaness
suppress
tailoress
temptationless
Tess
Titaness
transgress
tress
turgesce
unbless
underdress
undress
unless
valueless
virtueless
votaress
watercress
weaponless
yes

abjectedness
abstractedness
abusiveness
accidentalness
adaptiveness
addictedness

adhesiveness
advantageous-
  ness
affectedness
affrontiveness
agedness
aggressiveness
agileness
agreeableness
airiness
alimentiveness
alliterativeness
allusiveness
almightiness
amazedness
ambitiousness
amiableness
amicableness
ampleness
ancientness
angelicalness
angriness
anonymousness
anticness
anxiousness
apishness
apparentness
appeasableness
appositeness
apprehensive-
  ness
approachable-
  ness
arbitrariness
ardentness
arduousness
aridness
artfulness
articulateness

artificialness
artlessness
assiduousness
atrociousness
attentiveness
attractiveness
auspiciousness
avariciousness
awfulness
awkwardness
backhanded-
  ness
backwardness
balefulness
banefulness
bareheadedness
barrenness
bashfulness
beastliness
beeriness
beseechingness
besottedness
bitterness
blamelessness
blessedness
blissfulness
blithesomeness
bloatedness
blockishness
bloodguiltiness
bloodiness
bloodthirsti-
  ness
bloomingness
bluntishness
boastfulness
boisterousness
bonniness
bookishness

boorishness
bootlessness
boundlessness
bounteousness
boyishness
brackishness
brassiness
brawniness
brazenness
breathlessness
brilliantness
brittleness
brokenness
brotherliness
brushiness
brutishness
bulkiness
bumptiousness
bunchiness
burliness
bushiness
buxomness
candidness
capaciousness
capriciousness
captiousness
carefulness
carelessness
cautiousness
ceaselessness
chalkiness
changefulness
chariness
charmingness
chattiness
cheerfulness
cheeriness
cheerlessness
childishness

āle, câre, ădd, ärm, ăsk; mē, hĕre, ĕnd; īce, ĭll;

childlessness
chilliness
chubbiness
churlishness
clandestineness
clannishness
cleanliness
clear-sighted-
  ness
cleverness
cliquishness
cloddishness
cloudiness
clownishness
clumsiness
coldhearted-
  ness
collectedness
collusiveness
comeliness
commonness
composedness
comprehensive-
  ness
compulsiveness
conceitedness
conclusiveness
conduciveness
confusedness
conjunctiveness
conscientious-
  ness
consciousness
consecutiveness
conspicuous-
  ness
constructiveness
contentedness
contentiousness

contradictious-
  ness
contrariness
contumacious-
  ness
copiousness
cordialness
corrosiveness
costliness
courageousness
courtliness
covertness
covetousness
crabbedness
craftiness
craggedness
cragginess
cravingness
craziness
creaminess
credulousness
crookedness
cruelness
crustiness
cumbrousness
curiousness
curliness
customariness
daintiness
dampishness
daringness
dauntlessness
deadliness
deathfulness
deathiness
debauchedness
deceitfulness
deceptiveness
decisiveness

decorativeness
defectiveness
defenselessness
defiantness
definiteness
deformedness
degenerateness
dejectedness
deliciousness
delightfulness
delightsome-
  ness
deliriousness
delusiveness
dementedness
depressiveness
derisiveness
desirousness
despitefulness
destructiveness
desultoriness
detersiveness
detractiveness
devotedness
dewiness
diffusedness
diffusiveness
dilatoriness
dilutedness
dinginess
direfulness
disastrousness
discontented-
  ness
discursiveness
disdainfulness
disinterested-
  ness
dismalness

disposedness
disputatious-
  ness
distastefulness
distinctiveness
dizziness
doggedness
dolefulness
doubtfulness
doughtiness
downiness
dreadfulness
dreaminess
dreariness
droughtiness
drowsiness
drunkenness
dumpishness
duskiness
dustiness
dwarfishness
eagerness
earliness
earnestness
earthiness
earthliness
earthly-mind-
  edness
easefulness
easiness
eeriness
effectiveness
efficaciousness
effusiveness
egregiousness
elatedness
emotiveness
emptiness
endearedness

endlessness
enduringness
engagingness
enormousness
entertainingness
equalness
essentialness
estrangedness
evasiveness
everlastingness
exaltedness
exceptiousness
excessiveness
exclusiveness
excursiveness
expansiveness
expeditiousness
expensiveness
explicitness
expressiveness
exquisiteness
extensiveness
facetiousness
factiousness
faithfulness
faithlessness
fallaciousness
false-hearted-
  ness
far-sightedness
fastidiousness
fatefulness
fatherliness
faultlessness
favoredness
fearfulness
fearlessness
feeble-minded-
  ness

feebleness
feignedness
ferociousness
fervidness
fickleness
fictiousness
fiendishness
fieriness
filminess
fishiness
fitfulness
fixedness
flabbiness
flaccidness
flakiness
flashiness
fleshiness
fleshliness
flexibleness
flightiness
flimsiness
flippantness
floridness
floweriness
fluentness
fogginess
foolhardiness
foolishness
foppishness
forcedness
foreignness
forgetfulness
formlessness
forwardness
fractiousness
fragileness
frankhearted-
  ness
franticness

fraudlessness
freakishness
freckledness
freeheartedness
fretfulness
friendlessness
friendliness
frightfulness
frigidness
friskiness
frivolousness
frostiness
frothiness
frowardness
frozenness
frugalness
fruitfulness
fruitlessness
frumpishness
fugaciousness
fulsomeness
fumishness
fundamental-
  ness
furiousness
fussiness
fustiness
gaddishness
gallantness
gamesomeness
garishness
garrulousness
gashliness
gaudiness
generousness
genialness
gentleness
ghastliness
ghostliness

giddiness
giftedness
girlishness
gladfulness
gladsomeness
glariness
glassiness
gloominess
gloriousness
glossiness
godlessness
godliness
goodliness
gorgeousness
gracefulness
gracelessness
graciousness
graphicness
grassiness
gratefulness
greasiness
greediness
greenishness
grievousness
griminess
grittiness
grogginess
groundlessness
guardedness
guidelessness
guilefulness
guiltiness
guiltlessness
gustfulness
hairiness
handiness
handsomeness
haplessness
happiness

āle, câre, ădd, ärm, ăsk; mē, hḙre, ĕnd; īce, ĭll;

hard-hearted-
ness
hardiness
harmfulness
harmlessness
harmonious-
ness
hastiness
hatefulness
haughtiness
haziness
headiness
healthfulness
healthiness
healthlessness
heartedness
heartiness
heartlessness
heathenness
heavenliness
heavenly-mind-
edness
heaviness
heedfulness
heedlessness
heinousness
hellishness
helpfulness
helplessness
heterogeneous-
ness
hiddenness
hideousness
highminded-
ness
hilliness
hoariness
hoggishness
holiness

hollowness
homelessness
homeliness
hopefulness
hopelessness
horridness
huffishness
humbleness
humidness
humorousness
hurtfulness
huskiness
iciness
idleness
ignobleness
illicitness
illiterateness
ill-naturedness
illusiveness
illustriousness
imaginative-
ness
imitativeness
immaculate-
ness
impartialness
impassiveness
imperfectness
imperiousness
imperviousness
impetuousness
impiousness
implicitness
imponderous-
ness
imposingness
impressiveness
impulsiveness
inattentiveness

inauspicious-
ness
incapacious-
ness
incautiousness
incidentalness
incoherentness
incomprehen-
siveness
inconclusive-
ness
incongruous-
ness
inconsistent-
ness
inconspicuous-
ness
indebtedness
indecisiveness
indecorousness
inefficacious-
ness
infectiousness
ingeniousness
ingenuousness
injuriousness
inkiness
innoxiousness
inobtrusiveness
inoffensiveness
insidiousness
insipidness
instructiveness
intensiveness
intrusiveness
inventiveness
invidiousness
invincibleness
involuntariness

inwardness
irefulness
irksomeness
jaggedness
jauntiness
jealousness
jettiness
Jewishness
jolliness
jovialness
joyfulness
joylessness
joyousness
judiciousness
juiciness
jumpiness
kind-hearted-
ness
kindliness
kingliness
knavishness
knightliness
knottiness
languidness
large-hearted-
ness
lasciviousness
lawfulness
lawlessness
laziness
leafiness
leaflessness
leaviness
lengthiness
licentiousness
lifelessness
light-hearted-
ness
lightsomeness

ōld, ôr, ŏdd, oil, fŏŏt, out; ūse, ûrn, ŭp; THis, thin

likableness
likeliness
limberness
limpidness
liquidness
lissomeness
listlessness
literalness
litigiousness
littleness
liveliness
lividness
livingness
loathliness
loathsomeness
loftiness
loneliness
lonesomeness
longsomeness
loquaciousness
lordliness
loutishness
love-in-idleness
loveliness
lovingness
lowliness
loyalness
lucidness
luckiness
lugubriousness
luminousness
lumpishness
lusciousness
lustfulness
lustiness
maidenliness
maliciousness
manfulness
manliness

mannerliness
mannishness
many-sidedness
marshiness
massiness
massiveness
matchlessness
mawkishness
maziness
meagerness
mealiness
meatiness
meditativeness
mellowness
meltingness
meritoriousness
meretricious-
    ness
merriness
mightiness
milkiness
mindfulness
miraculousness
miriness
mirthfulness
mirthlessness
miscellaneous-
    ness
mischievousness
misshapenness
missishness
mistiness
moderness
modishness
moldiness
momentousness
monkishness
monotonous-
    ness

monstrousness
moodiness
mopishness
morbidness
mortalness
mossiness
motherliness
mournfulness
mulishness
multifarious-
    ness
mumpishness
murkiness
muskiness
mustiness
mutinousness
mysteriousness
mysticalness
nakedness
namelessness
narrow-mind-
    edness
narrowness
nastiness
nationalness
nativeness
nattiness
naturalness
naughtiness
near-sighted-
    ness
nebulousness
necessariness
necessitious-
    ness
nectareousness
needfulness
neediness
needlessness

nefariousness
neglectedness
neglectfulness
neighborliness
nervousness
niggardliness
nimbleness
nobleness
noiselessness
noisiness
noisomeness
notableness
notedness
notelessness
nothingness
notoriousness
noxiousness
numerousness
nutritiousness
objectiveness
obligatoriness
obligingness
obliviousness
obsequiousness
observableness
obstreperous-
    ness
obstrusiveness
obviousness
odiousness
odoriferousness
odorousness
offensiveness
officiousness
oiliness
oleaginousness
openhandedness
openheartedness
openness

āle, câre, ădd, ärm, ăsk; mē, hĕre, ĕnd; īce, ĭll;

oppressiveness
opprobrious-
ness
orderliness
ostentatious-
ness
outlandishness
outrageousness
outwardness
painfulness
painlessness
pallidness
paltriness
parlousness
parsimonious-
ness
passiveness
pawkiness
peaceableness
peacefulness
pearliness
peerlessness
peevishness
pellucidness
penetrativeness
pennilessness
pensileness
pensiveness
penuriousness
peremptoriness
perfectness
perfidiousness
perfunctoriness
perilousness
perniciousness
perplexedness
perplexiveness
perspicacious-
ness

perspicuousness
persuasiveness
pertinacious-
ness
pervicacious-
ness
perviousness
pestilentialness
pettiness
pettishness
piercingness
pig-headedness
pitchiness
piteousness
pithiness
pitiableness
pitilessness
placableness
placidness
plaintiveness
playfulness
playsomeness
pleasantness
pleasingness
plenteousness
pliantness
poachiness
pointedness
pompousness
ponderousness
poorliness
porousness
portliness
positiveness
powerfulness
powerlessness
practicalness
praiseworthi-
ness

prayerfulness
prayerlessness
precariousness
preciousness
precipitousness
precociousness
prejudicialness
preposterous-
ness
presumptuous-
ness
pretentiousness
prettiness
previousness
prickliness
pridefulness
priestliness
priggishness
primitiveness
princeliness
prodigiousness
productiveness
progressiveness
properness
propitiousness
prosiness
prospectiveness
protectiveness
prudishness
public-minded-
ness
puffiness
pugnaciousness
pulpiness
pulpousness
pulselessness
punctiliousness
puniness
pursiness

pusillanimous-
ness
putridness
quakiness
qualmishness
quasiness
queenliness
quenchlessness
querulousness
quick-sighted-
ness
quick-witted-
ness
quietness
rabidness
raciness
raggedness
raininess
rakishness
rancidness
rapaciousness
rapidness
ravenousness
readiness
rebelliousness
recentness
receptiveness
recklessness
reddishness
reflectiveness
refractiveness
refractoriness
regardlessness
relativeness
relentlessness
remorsefulness
remorselessness
reproachfulness
repulsiveness

ōld, ôr, ŏdd, oil, fŏŏt, out; ūse, ûrn, ŭp; THis, thin

resistlessness
resoluteness
respectfulness
responsiveness
restfulness
restiveness
restlessness
restrictiveness
retentiveness
revengefulness
rightfulness
right-handed-
 ness
right-minded-
 ness
rigidness
rigorousness
riotousness
robustiousness
rockiness
roguishness
rompishness
roominess
ropiness
rosiness
rottenness
ruddiness
ruefulness
ruggedness
ruthlessness
sacredness
sacrilegiousness
sagaciousness
saintliness
salaciousness
sallowness
salutariness
sanctimonious-
 ness

sandiness
sanguineness
sappiness
satisfactoriness
sauciness
savageness
savingness
savoriness
scaliness
scantiness
scorchingness
scornfulness
scragginess
scruviness
seaworthiness
secondariness
secretiveness
secretness
sedentariness
seditiousness
seediness
seemingness
seemliness
seldomness
self-conceited-
 ness
self-conscious-
 ness
selfishness
self-righteous-
 ness
senselessness
sensitiveness
sensuousness
sententiousness
seriousness
shabbiness
shadiness
shadowiness

shagginess
shakiness
shallowness
shamefulness
shamelessness
shapelessness
shapeliness
sheepishness
shieldlessness
shiftiness
shiftlessness
shiningness
shoaliness
short-sighted-
 ness
showeriness
showiness
shrewishness
shrubbiness
sickliness
sightlessness
silentness
silkiness
silliness
simpleminded-
 ness
simpleness
simultaneous-
 ness
sinfulness
singleness
sinlessness
sketchiness
skillfulness
skittishness
slabbiness
slatiness
slavishness
sleaziness

sleepiness
sleeplessness
sleetiness
slenderness
sliminess
slipperiness
slothfulness
sluggishness
smilingness
smokiness
snappishness
sneakiness
snobbishness
sober-minded-
 ness
soberness
sociableness
soft-hearted-
 ness
solidness
solitariness
solubleness
somberness
sombrousness
sonorousness
sordidness
sorriness
sorrowfulness
sottishness
spaciousness
sparklingness
speciousness
speckledness
speculativeness
speechlessness
speediness
spiciness
spitefulness
splendidness

sponginess
spontaneous-
 ness
sportiveness
spotlessness
spottedness
spottiness
springiness
spriteliness
spuminess
spuriousness
squeamishness
starchiness
starriness
stateliness
steadfastness
steadiness
stealthfulness
stealthiness
steeliness
steepiness
stickiness
stinginess
stintedness
stolidness
stoniness
storminess
straightfor-
 wardness
strenuousness
stringentness
stringiness
stubbiness
stubbornness
studiousness
stuffiness
stuntedness
stupendousness
stupidness

sturdiness
stylishness
subjectiveness
submissiveness
subordinate-
 ness
substantialness
subtleness
successfulness
suddenness
sugariness
suggestiveness
suitableness
sulkiness
sullenness
sultriness
sumptuousness
sunniness
supercilious-
 ness
superstitious-
 ness
suppleness
suppliantness
surliness
surprisingness
susceptiveness
suspectedness
suspiciousness
swarthiness
sweatiness
sweetishness
talkativeness
tamelessness
tardiness
tastefulness
tastelessness
tawdriness
tawniness

tediousness
tempestuous-
 ness
temporariness
temptingness
tenaciousness
tender-hearted-
 ness
tepidness
testiness
thankfulness
thievishness
thirstiness
thoroughness
thoughtfulness
thoughtless-
 ness
threadiness
thriftiness
thriftlessness
thrivingness
ticklishness
tidiness
timeliness
timidness
timorousness
tipsiness
tiresomeness
toilsomeness
toothsomeness
torpidness
torridness
tortuousness
totalness
touchiness
toyishness
tracklessness
traitorousness
tranquilness

transcendent-
 ness
transientness
transitiveness
transitoriness
transparentness
trashiness
treacherousness
tremendousness
tremulousness
tributariness
trickiness
trickishness
tricksiness
true-hearted-
 ness
trustfulness
trustiness
trustlessness
trustworthiness
truthfulness
truthlessness
tunefulness
turfiness
turgidness
ugliness
umbrageous-
 ness
unanimousness
unbendingness
unblessedness
unboundedness
uncleanliness
uncloudedness
uncourtliness
undauntedness
uneasiness
unexpectedness
unfeignedness

ōld, ôr, ŏdd, oil, fŏŏt, out; ūse, ûrn, ŭp; THis, thin

unfriendliness
ungainliness
ungentleness
ungodliness
ungrounded-
 ness
unholiness
universalness
unkindliness
unlikeliness
unloveliness
unmanliness
unpreparedness
unquietness
unreadiness
unrighteous-
 ness
unruliness
unseaworthi-
 ness
unseemliness
unsightliness
unstableness
untowardness
untrustiness
unwieldiness
unwillingness
unwontedness
unworldliness
unworthiness
uppishness
usefulness
uselessness
uxoriousness
vacuousness
vagrantness
valetudinari-
 ness
valiantness

validness
vapidness
vexatiousness
viciousness
victoriousness
vigorousness
vindictiveness
viridness
virtuousness
viscousness
visionariness
vitreousness
vivaciousness
vividness
vociferousness
voluminous-
 ness
voluntariness
voluptuousness
voraciousness
vulgarness
waggishness
wakefulness
wantonness
warefulness
wariness
warm-hearted-
 ness
washiness
waspishness
wastefulness
watchfulness
waveringness
waviness
waxiness
waywardness
wealthiness
weariness
wearisomeness

weightiness
welcomeness
whimsicalness
whitishness
wholesomeness
wickedness
wilderness
willfulness
wiliness
willingness
winsomeness
wiriness
wishfulness
wistfulness
witheredness
witlessness
wittiness
woefulness
womanliness
wondrousness
wontedness
woodiness
woolliness
wordiness
wordishness
worldliness
worldly-
 mindedness
worshipfulness
worthiness
worthlessness
wrathfulness
wretchfulness
wretchedness
wretchlessness
wrongfulness
wrong
 headedness
yeastiness

yellowishness
yellowness
yieldingness
youthfulness
zealousness

ĚSH
affiche
fiche
leash
McLeish
McNeish
microfiche
nouveau riche
pastiche
quiche
scottische
ultrafiche
unleash

ĚSH
aresh
crèche
enmesh
flesh
fresh
mesh
nesh
refresh
secesh
thresh

ĚSK
arabesque
barbaresque
burlesque
chivalresque
Dantesque

āle, câre, ădd, ärm, ăsk; mē, hĕre, ĕnd; īce, ĭll;

desk
gardenesque
gigantesque
grotesque
humoresque
Moresque
naturalesque
picaresque
picturesque
plateresque
reading desk
Romanesque
sculpturesque
soldatesque
statuesque

ĔST
archpriest
arriviste
artiste
batiste
beast
ceased
deceased
east
Far East
feast
fleeced
harvest feast
least
Middle East
Mideast
modiste
Near East
northeast
pieced
priest
queest
southeast

triste
underpoliced
unpriest
wedding feast
yeast

ĔST
abreast
acquest
alkahest
anapest
arrest
attest
beau geste
behest
bequest
best
blest
breast
Brest
Bucharest
Budapest
cest
chest
congest
contest
crest
depressed
detest
devest
digest
distressed
divest
dressed
Everest
funest
gabfest
gest
golden-tressed

guest
hard-pressed
hest
imprest
incest
increst
infest
ingest
inquest
interest
invest
jessed
jest
Key West
lest
manifest
midwest
molest
nest
northwest
obsessed
obtest
overdressed
palimpsest
pest
predigest
protest
quest
recessed
request
rest
second-best
self-possessed
southwest
suggest
test
tressed
Trieste
unblest

unbreast
undercrest
underdressed
undressed
unexpressed
unguessed
unprepossessed
unpressed
unredressed
unrest
untressed
vest
west
wrest
yessed
zest
(See also ĔS;
add -*ed* where
appropriate.)

answerest
astonishest
attentivest
attributest
banishest
beamiest
beguilingest
bleariest
blestfullest
blisterest
blithefulest
blithesomest
blunderest
breeziest
brilliantest
briniest
burliest
cheerfullest

ōld,   ôr,   ŏdd,   oil,   fŏŏt,   out;   ūse,   ûrn,   ŭp;   THis,   thin

cheeriest	filmiest	hungriest	*murmurest*
cheerliest	filthiest	huskiest	muskiest
chilliest	fleeciest	iciest	mustiest
chokiest	flimsiest	*incumberest*	*narrowest*
cleanliest	flightiest	*inheritest*	noisiest
clusterest	flintiest	inkiest	*nourishest*
conquerest	*flowerest*	inliest	*offerest*
continuest	foamiest	*inspiritest*	*pardonest*
costliest	forcefulest	jolliest	patentest
courtliest	*forfeitest*	juiciest	pearliest
coverest	*freshenest*	kindliest	pensivest
coziest	friendliest	kingliest	pleasantest
creamiest	funniest	knightliest	*pleasurest*
creepiest	fussiest	*laborest*	portliest
cruelest	*gatherest*	*languishest*	preciousest
crustiest	genialest	*libelest*	*predestinest*
curliest	giddiest	likeliest	princeliest
daintiest	*glimmerest*	*lingerest*	prosiest
decisivest	*glistenest*	lissomest	*punishest*
derisivest	gloomiest	*listenest*	*quarrelest*
determinest	glossiest	lithesomest	*questionest*
dingiest	*glowerest*	liveliest	quietest
dizziest	goutiest	*livenest*	*recoverest*
doughtiest	grimiest	loftiest	*relinquishest*
dowdiest	guilefulest	loneliest	*rememberest*
dowerest	guiltiest	loveliest	*rescuest*
dreamiest	gustiest	*lowerest*	rightfulest
dreariest	happiest	lowliest	*rivalest*
drowsiest	haughtiest	loyalest	rosiest
dustiest	healthiest	*marvelest*	rowdiest
earliest	*hearkenest*	mellowest	royalest
easiest	heartiest	*meritest*	ruggedest
eeriest	heaviest	merriest	rustiest
effectedest	holiest	mightiest	sacredest
emblazonest	homeliest	moistiest	sedgiest
emptiest	hopefulest	moldiest	seemliest
enviest	horridest	morbidest	*severest*
evenest	huffiest	mossiest	*shimmerest*
exhibitest	*hungerest*	mournfulest	shiniest

āle, câre, ădd, ärm, ăsk; mē, hĕre, ĕnd; īce, ĭll;

shoddiest	thirstiest	cleet	Lafitte
showiest	thriftiest	compete	leat
shudderest	*thunderest*	complete	leet
slightliest	timidest	conceit	lorikeet
silentest	trustiest	concrete	maltreat
silliest	ugliest	countryseat	marguerite
sketchiest	unholiest	county seat	meadowsweet
skillfulest	unreadiest	Crete	meat
skinniest	veriest	deadbeat	meet
sleepiest	vindictivest	dead heat	mercy seat
slimiest	vulgarest	dead meat	mesquite
slumberest	*wanderest*	deceit	mete
smokiest	wealthiest	defeat	neat
snuffiest	weariest	delete	obsolete
soapiest	wheeziest	deplete	overeat
solidest	windiest	discreet	parakeet
sorrowest	wilfulest	downbeat	peat
spiciest	*winnowest*	Dutch treat	pleat
spikiest	winsomest	easy street	*preconceit*
spiritest	wintriest	eat	receipt
splendidest	*witnessest*	effete	repeat
spongiest	*wonderest*	elite	replete
spooniest	*worriest*	entreat	retreat
springiest	yeastiest	escheat	sea-beat
spriteliest		estreat	seat
steadiest	**ĒT**	*facete*	secrete
stealthiest	accrete	feat	self-conceit
stilliest	afreet	feet	self-deceit
stingiest	athlete	fleet	sheet
stormiest	balance sheet	gamete	skeet
stuffiest	beat	geat	sleet
stupidest	beet	greet	spirochete
sturdiest	bittersweet	heat	street
sufferest	bleat	helpmeet	suite
sunderest	carte-de-visite	honeysweet	sunny sweet
sunniest	catbird seat	ill-treat	sweet
surliest	cheat	incomplete	teat
tearfulest	cheet	indiscreet	terete
temperest	cleat	judgment seat	treat

unmeet	blanquette	facette	lorgnette
unseat	bobbinet	falconet	Lucette
unsweet	Brett	fan-jet	luncheonette
upbeat	brevet	farmerette	lunette
vegete	briquette	flageolet	Margaret
weet	brochette	flet	marionette
wheat	brunette	floweret	marmoset
winding-sheet	Burnett	forget	martinet
	cabinet	formeret	medalet
ĔT	cadet	fossette	met
abet	calumet	fourchette	microcassette
aigrette	canzonet	fret	mignonette
ailette	carcanet	frett	minaret
alette	cassette	fumette	minicassette
all wet	cassolette	gazette	*minionette*
allumette	castanet	genet	minuet
alphabet	cellaret	get	misbeget
amourette	chansonette	Gillette	motet
amulet	chemisette	globulet	musette
anchoret	cigarètte	grisette	Nanette
angelet	clarinet	Harriet	net
anisette	Colette	historiette	noisette
Annette	coquette	ill-set	novelette
Antoinette	coronet	inset	octet
audiocassette	corvette	interset	offset
backset	coverlet	Jeanette	Olivet
baguette	croquette	jet	omelet
banneret	crossette	Joliet	onset
banquette	crystal set	judgment debt	oubliette
barbette	curvet	Juliet	outlet
Barnett	dancette	Juliette	outset
baronet	dead set	jumbo jet	overset
bassinet	debt	Kismet	parapet
bayonet	diskette	landaulet	paroket
beget	duet	launderette	parquet
benet	epaulet	leaderette	pet
beset	epithet	let	pianette
bet	estafette	Lett	pillaret
bewet	etiquette	leveret	pipette

---

piquet
piquette
pirouette
planchette
poussette
quartet
quintet
regret
ret
revet
ricochet
rivulet
rosette
roulette
sarcenet
septet
serviette
sestet
set
sett
sextext
sharp-set
silhouette
smart set
somerset
soubrette
statuette
stet
subset
suffragette
sunset
sweat
tabaret
tabinet
taboret
tête-à-tête
Thibet
thickset
threat

Tibet
toilette
tournette
tourniquet
tret
triple threat
turbojet
underset
unfret
unget
upset
vedette
vet
videocassette
vignette
villanette
vinaigrette
violet
wagonette
well met
wet
whet
yet
zonulet

ETH
bequeath
breathe
ensheath
enwreathe
inbreathe
insheathe
interwreathe
inwreathe
seethe
sheathe
sneathe
teethe
unsheathe

unwreathe
upbreathe
wreathe

Ēth
beneath
heath
Keith
Leith
'neath
sheath
sneath
teeth
underneath
wreath

Ĕth
Ashtoreth
breath
death
Elizabeth
Macbeth
saith
'sdeath
Seth
shibboleth
thirtieth
twentieth

answereth
astonisheth
attributeth
banisheth
blemisheth
blistereth
blundereth
busieth
clustereth

conquereth
continueth
covereth
determineth
dowereth
emblazoneth
emspiriteth
envieth
exhĭbiteth
flowereth
forfeiteth
gathereth
glisteneth
glowereth
hearkeneth
hungereth
incumbereth
inheriteth
inspiriteth
laboreth
languisheth
libeleth
lingereth
listeneth
liveneth
lowereth
marveleth
measureth
meriteth
murmureth
nourisheth
offereth
overpowereth
overtowereth
pardoneth
pleasureth
predestineth
punisheth
quarrelleth

questioneth
quieteth
recovereth
relinquisheth
remembereth
rescueth
rivaleth
severeth
shimmereth
showereth
shuddereth
silvereth
slumbereth
sorroweth
spiriteth
suffereth
sundereth
tempereth
thundereth
ventureth
wandereth
wearieth
whispereth
winnoweth
witnesseth
wondereth
worrieth
worshippeth

ĒTHD
bequeathed
unbreathed
(See also ĒTH;
add -ed where
appropriate.)

ĒTZ
beats
Keats

(See also ĒT;
add -s where
appropriate.)

ĔTZ
bets
Metz
(See also ĔT;
add -s where
appropriate.)

ĒV
achieve
aggrieve
beeve
believe
bereave
breve
Christmas Eve
cleave
conceive
deceive
deev
disbelieve
eave
endive
engrieve
eve
greave
grieve
heave
interleave
interweave
inweave
keeve
khedive
leave
lieve
make believe

misconceive
naive
New Year's Eve
overachieve
perceive
preconceive
qui vive
reave
receive
recitative
reeve
relieve
reprieve
retrieve
seave
sheave
shire-reeve
shrieve
sleave
sleeve
steeve
Steve
thieve
undeceive
underachieve
unreave
unreeve
unweave
upheave
vive
weave
we've
yester-eve

ĒVD
achieved
self-deceived
unbelieved
unperceived

unrelieved
(See also ĒV;
add -ed where
appropriate.)

ĒVZ
achieves
eaves
(See also ĒV;
add -s where
appropriate.)

ĒZ
aborigines
academese
analyses
Annamese
antifreeze
antipodes
antitheses
appease
Aragonese
Arakanese
Assamese
bee's knees
Belize
Bengalese
big cheese
bise
Bolognese
boonies
breeze
Brooklynese
bureaucratese
Burmese
B.V.D.s
Cantonese
Carlylese
Caryatides

cerise	Hercules	Pentagonese	unfreeze
Ceylonese	Hesperides	periphrases	valise
cheese	hypotheses	Pierides	Veronese
chemise	imprese	please	Viennese
chersonese	indices	Pleiades	vortices
cheval-de-frise	isosceles	*Polonese*	wheeze
Chinese	Japanese	Portuguese	(See also Ē;
computerese	Javanese	Pyrenees	add -*s* where
congeries	Johnsonese	rabies	appropriate.)
D.T.'s	journalese	remise	
Diogenes	lees	sea breeze	**ĔZ**
disease	Leonese	seize	Cortés
displease	Louise	Senegalese	fez
ease	Maimonides	Siamese	Juárez
éminence grise	Maltese	Singhalese	says
enfreeze	mease	sleaze	Suez
Eumenides	Mephistophe-	sneeze	
feaze	les	Socrates	
federalese	Milanese	squeeze	**ĒZH**
freeze	Navarrese	syntheses	prestige
frieze	Nepaulese	tease	tige
Genevese	New Yorkese	these	
grease	obsequies	trapeze	**ĔZH**
Havanese	parentheses	tweeze	barege
heartsease	pease	Tyrolese	cortege
heeze	Pekingese	unease	manège

Ī

These words includes the following accented vowel sounds:

Ī as in *ice;* heard also in *vie, rye, height, eye, aisle, aye* meaning
      yes, sky, buy, choir.
Ĭ as in *ill;* heard also in *sieve, English, pretty, been, breeches,*
      women, busy, build, nymph, hymnal.

Ī	alibi	amplify	apply
acidify	alkali	angelify	awry
adry	alkalify	Anglify	ay
alacrify	ally	apple-pie	aye

ōld, ôr, ŏdd, oil, fo͝ot, out; ūse, ûrn, ŭp; THis, thin

beatify	deny	glorify	mollify
beautify	descry	go-by	mortify
bedye	die	good-bye	multiply
belie	dignify	gratify	my
bespy	disqualify	GRI	my eye
black eye	dissatisfy	guy	mystify
blue-sky	diversify	heigh	necktie
bow tie	dragonfly	hereby	nigh
brutify	drip-dry	hi-fi	notify
butterfly	dry	hie	nullify
buy	dye	high	nye
by	eagle eye	hog-tie	objectify
by the by	edify	horrify	occupy
by-and-by	electrify	humanify	ossify
bye	emulsify	humble pie	outcry
bye-bye	ensky	humidify	outfly
candify	espy	hushaby	outvie
cat's-eye	*eternify*	identify	overbuy
certify	evil eye	imply	overfly
citify	exemplify	incubi	oversimplify
clarify	eye	indemnify	pacify
classify	fall guy	*ineye*	Paraguay
cockneyfy	falsify	intensify	passerby
codify	fie	July	personify
comply	firefly	justify	petrify
counterspy	fish-eye	labefy	pi
countrify	fly	lazuli	pie
crucify	forby	lenify	pigsty
cry	fortify	lie	pinkeye
damnify	fossilify	lignify	ply
dandify	french fry	liquefy	porkpie
deadeye	Frenchify	lullaby	potpie
declassify	fructify	lye	preachify
decry	fry	magnify	preoccupy
defy	gadfly	magpie	prettify
deify	gasify	micrify	private eye
demi	Gemini	mince pie	prophesy
demy	genii	minify	pry
demystify	gentrify	modify	purify

putrefy
qualify
quantify
rabbi
ramify
rarefy
ratify
rectify
red-eye
reify
rely
reply
revivify
right to die
rye
saccharify
samurai
sanctify
satisfy
scarify
sci-fi
scorify
scye
sea pie
Shanghai
sheep's eye
shoofly
shoofly pie
shut-eye
shy
sigh
signify
simplify
Sinai
sky
Skye
sky-high
sly
small fry

sny
sockeye
solidify
specify
spry
spy
standby
stander-by
stellify
stultify
stupefy
sty
supply
syllabify
tabefy
termini
terrify
testify
Thai
thereby
thigh
thy
tie
tigereye
torpify
torrefy
transmogrify
try
typify
uglify
umble-pie
underbuy
underlie
unify
unshy
untie
Uruguay
verbify
verify

versify
vie
vilify
vitrify
vivify
walleye
weather eye
weather spy
well-nigh
whereby
why
wry
wye

ĪB

ascribe
bribe
circumscribe
describe
diatribe
gibe
imbibe
inscribe
interscribe
jibe
kibe
prescribe
proscribe
scribe
subscribe
superscribe
transcribe
tribe

ĬB

ad lib
bib
Bibb
crib

dib
drib
fib
gay lib
gib
Gibb
glib
jib
lib
nib
quib
rib
sib
squib
women's lib

ĬBD

ascribed
uninscribed
(See also ĪB;
add-*ed* where
appropriate.)

ĬBD

cribbed
rock-ribbed

ĪBZ

vibes
(See also ĪB;
add -*s* where
appropriate.)

ĬBZ

cribs
dibs
Gibbs
his nibs
(See also ĬB;

ōld, ôr, ŏdd, oil, fŏŏt, out; ūse, ûrn, ŭp; THis, thin

add -*s* where
appropriate.)

ĬCH
bewitch
bitch
Cesarewitch
chich
czarevitch
ditch
enrich
fitch
flitch
Gabrilowitsch
glitch
hitch
itch
kitsch
lich
miche
niche
pitch
quitch
rich
scritch
snitch
son of a bitch
stitch
switch
twitch
which
witch

ĬCHT
bewitched
unbewitched
unhitched
unwitched

(See also ĬCH;
add -*ed* where
appropriate.)

ĪD
abide
aborticide
acetaldehyde
aldehyde
Allhallowtide
allied
alongside
anhydride
applied
Argus-eyed
aside
astride
backslide
barmecide
Bartholomew
   tide
bedside
benzaldehyde
beside
bestride
betide
bide
bonafide
boride
bride
broadside
bromide
carbide
chide
chloride
Christmastide
Clyde
cockeyed
coincide

collide
confide
countrified
countryside
cowhide
cross-eyed
cyanamide
cyanide
decide
deicide
deride
dignified
dissatisfied
disulfide
diversified
divide
double-dyed
dove-eyed
dull-eyed
eagle-eyed
Eastertide
ebb tide
ecocide
elide
Ember tide
eventide
evil-eyed
excide
feticide
fireside
flip side
flood tide
fluoride
foreside
formaldehyde
fortified
fratricide
full-eyed
fungicide

genocide
germicide
glide
goggle-eyed
green-eyed
gride
guide
Hallow tide
hawk-eyed
herbicide
herpicide
hide
high tide
hillside
homicide
horsehide
Hyde
hydride
hydrochloride
I'd
infanticide
insecticide
inside
iodide
justified
Lammastide
landslide
lapicide
lee tide
liberticide
lynx-eyed
matricide
meek-eyed
misallied
misguide
morningtide
nationwide
nicotinamide
nide

āle, câre, ădd, ärm, ăsk; mē, hĕre, ĕnd; īce, ĭll;

noontide
nuclide
offside
onside
open-eyed
outride
outside
outstride
override
owl-eyed
ox-eyed
pale-eyed
parenticide
parricide
Passiontide
patricide
pesticide
pied
pie-eyed
pop-eyed
preoccupied
preside
pride
provide
purified
qualified
rawhide
refried
regicide
reside
ride
ringside
riverside
saccharide
seaside
self-pride
self-satisfied
Shrovetide
side

slide
snide
soft-eyed
sororicide
spring tide
squint-eyed
stateside
statewide
stillicide
stride
subdivide
subside
suicide
sulphide
telluride
tide
tie-dyed
tried
trisulfide
tyrannicide
unallied
unapplied
unbetide
underside
undertide
undescried
undignified
undried
unespied
ungratified
unoccupied
unpurified
unqualified
unsanctified
unsatisfied
unspied
untried
uxoricide
vaticide

vermicide
vitrified
vulpicide
wall-eyed
waterside
wayside
weather side
weather tide
Whitsuntide
wide
wide-eyed
worldwide
Yuletide
(See also Ī;
add -ed
where
appropriate.)

ĪD
amid
bid
chid
Cid
did
fid
forbid
fordid
gid
grid
hid
invalid
katydid
kid
lid
Madrid
mid
outbid
outdid
overbid

overdid
pyramid
quid
rid
skid
slid
squid
thrid
unbid
underbid
undid
unforbid

ĪDST
amidst
bid'st
chid'st
did'st
forbid'st
hid'st
kid'st
midst
rid'st
slid'st

ĪDTH
bid'th
width
(See also ĪD;
add -th where
appropriate.)

ĪDZ
abides
besides
ides
(See also ĪD;
add -s where
appropriate.)

ĬF
afterlife
bowie knife
fife
fishwife
goodwife
half-life
housewife
knife
life
pro-life
rife
right-to-life
still life
strife
wife

ĬF
biff
cliff
diff
glyph
griff
handkerchief
hieroglyph
hippogriff
if
jiff
miff
neckerchief
riff
skiff
sniff
stiff
Tenerife
Teneriffe
tiff
undercliff
whiff

wiff

ĬFT
adrift
drift
forelift
gift
lift
miffed
rift
shift
shrift
sift
snowdrift
spendthrift
spiffed
spindrift
swift
thrift
tift
topping lift
unthrift
uplift

ĬFth
fifth
miff'th

ĬG
big
brig
cig
dig
fig
gig
grig
guinea pig
infra dig
jig

nig
periwig
pig
prig
renege
rig
snig
sprig
swig
thimblerig
thingumajig
trig
twig
unrig
Whig
whirligig
wig

ĬGD
bewigged
digged
full-rigged
jury-rigged
square-rigged
(See also ĬG;
add -*ed* where
appropriate.)

ĬGZ
Biggs
Briggs
Higgs
Riggs
(See also ĬG;
add -*s* where
appropriate.)

ĬJ
Lije

oblige

ĬJ
abridge
bridge
enridge
midge
nidge
ridge
upridge
(See also ĂJ.)

ĬJD
abridged
unabridged
unbridged
(See also ĬJ;
add -*ed* where
appropriate.)

ĬK
Alibi Ike
alike
assassinlike
belike
bike
boarding pike
brotherlike
dike
dislike
dyke
fairylike
fyke
ghostlike
hike
kike
like
maidenlike
manlike

āle, câre, ădd, ärm, ăsk; mē, hĕre, ĕnd; īce, ĭll;

marlinspike
mike
minibike
mislike
motorbike
oblique
peasantlike
pike
psych
Reich
shrike
spike
starlike
strike
tyke
unlike
Vandyck
Vandyke
Van Wyck
womanlike
workmanlike
Wyke

ĬK
arithmetic
arsenic
bailiwick
beatnik
Benedick
bestick
bishopric
brick
candlestick
candlewick
Catholic
chick
chivalric
choleric
click

cowlick
crick
Dick
double-quick
fiddlestick
flick
geopolitic
heartsick
heretic
hick
impolitic
kick
kinnikinnick
lick
limerick
lovesick
lunatic
maverick
mick
nick
pick
plethoric
pogo stick
politic
prick
quick
realpolitik
rhetoric
rick
shtick
sic
sick
sidekick
singlestick
skin flick
slick
snick
stich
stick

Sufic
Tantric
thick
tic
tick
trick
turmeric
walking stick
water pick
wick

ĬKS
Dykes
Rikes
Sykes
(See also ĬK;
add -s where
appropriate.)

ĬKS
admix
affix
Beatrix
cicatrix
commix
crucifix
dirty tricks
Dix
eighty-six
executrix
fiddlesticks
fix
geopolitics
Hicks
Hix
immix
inheritrix
intermix
mix

nix
Pnyx
politics
prefix
prolix
pyx
quick-fix
Ricks
Rix
six
Styx
transfix
Trix
(See also ĬK;
add -s where
appropriate.)

ĬKST
admixed
atwixt
betwixt
click'st
kick'st
lick'st
pick'st
prick'st
stick'st
trick'st
'twixt
unfixed
unmixed
(See also
ĬKS; add
-ed where
appropriate.)

ĬKSth
mix'th
sixth

ōld, ôr, ŏdd, oil; fŏŏt, out; ūse, ûrn, ŭp; THis, thin

(See also ĬKS;
add -th where
appropriate.)

ĬKT
addict
afflict
astrict
benedict
bricked
conflict
constrict
contradict
convict
delict
depict
derelict
evict
inflict
interdict
Pict
predict
relict
restrict
strict
unlicked
unpicked
(See also ĬK;
add -ed where
appropriate.)

ĬL
aisle
Anglophile
audiophile
awhile
beguile
bibliophile
bile

chamomile
chyle
compile
crocodile
defile
diastyle
enisle
ensile
erewhile
erstwhile
file
Francophile
Germanophile
guile
homophile
infantile
isle
Japanophile
juvenile
Kabyle
lisle
Lyle
meanwhile
mercantile
mile
Negrophile
Nile
otherwhile
paper file
pentastyle
peristyle
pile
puerile
reconcile
resile
revile
rile
Russophile
Sinophile

smile
somewhile
spile
stile
style
therewhile
tile
up-pile
versatile
vibratile
videophile
vile
voltaic pile
while
wile

ĬL
Amityville
Anglophile
befrill
bestill
bibliophile
bill
Bozenkill
Brazil
brill
chill
chlorophyle
chrysophyll
Cobleskill
codicil
daffodil
dill
distil
domicile
downhill
drill
enthrill
Evansville

espadrille
fill
Francophile
free will
frill
fulfil
gill
goodwill
grill
grille
hill
ill
ill will
imbecile
infantile
instill
jill
juvenile
kill
landfill
Louisville
mercantile
mill
nil
pill
powder mill
prill
puerile
quadrille
quill
rill
self-will
Seville
shrill
sill
skill
spadille
spill
squill

āle, câre, ădd, ärm, ăsk; mē, hĕre, ĕnd; īce, ĭll;

still
stock-still
swill
thill
thrill
till
trill
twill
'twill
until
unwill
uphill
versatile
vibratile
vill
volatile
water mill
whippoorwill
will

ĬLCH
filch
milch
pilch
zilch

ĪLD
aisled
beguiled
child
childe
enfiled
foster child
love child
mild
self-styled
unbeguiled
unchild
unmild

unreconciled
unwild
wild
Wilde
(See also ĬL;
add -ed where
appropriate.)

ĬLD
befrilled
begild
build
chilled
gild
guild
rebuild
self-willed
unbuild
unchilled
unfulfilled
unskilled
untilled
unwilled
(See also ĬL;
add -ed where
appropriate.)

ĬLF
sylph

ĬLJ
bilge

ĬLK
bilk
ilk
milk
silk
spun silk

ĬLKS
Wilkes
(See also ĬLK;
add -s where
appropriate.)

ĬLM
film
microfilm
snuff film
splatter film

ĬLN
kiln
Milne

ĬLS
grilse
(See also
ĬLTS.)

ĬLST
beguil'st
defil'st
whilst
whils't
(See also ĬLS;
add -et where
appropriate.)

ĬLT
atilt
basket hilt
begilt
built
clinker-built
clipper-built
frigate-built
gilt

guilt
hilt
jilt
kilt
lilt
milt
quilt
rebuilt
silt
spilt
stilt
tilt
unbuilt
ungilt
Vanderbilt
wilt

ĬLTH
filth
spilth
till'th
tilth
(See also ĬL;
add -th where
appropriate.)

ĬLTS
basket hilts
kilts
(See also ĬLT;
add -s where
appropriate.)

ĪLZ
beguiles
Giles
Miles
otherwhiles
whiles

ōld, ôr, ŏdd, oil, fŏŏt, out; ūse, ûrn, ŭp; THis, thin

wiles
(See also ĪL;
add -s where
appropriate.)

ĪM

aftertime
bedtime
begrime
belime
berhyme
beslime
birdlime
breathing time
chime
chyme
climb
clime
crime
daytime
dime
dinnertime
downtime
enzyme
flextime
full-time
grime
Guggenheim
halftime
haying time
I'm
lifetime
lime
lunchtime
Lyme
maritime
meantime
mime
nickel and

dime
nighttime
overtime
pairing time
pantomime
paradigm
part-time
pastime
prime
prime time
quicklime
ragtime
real time
rhyme
rime
Rosenheim
seedtime
slime
sometime
springtime
sublime
summertime
suppertime
thyme
time
two-time
upclimb
uptime
weaning time
wintertime

ĬM

antonym
bedim
betrim
brim
cherubim
dim
enlimn

gim
glim
grim
gym
Hasidim
him
hymn
interim
Jim
Kim
Klim
limb
limn
maritime
Nym
prelim
prim
pseudonym
rim
Sanhedrim
seraphim
shim
skim
slim
swim
synonym
Tim
trim
vim
whim
zimb

ĪMD

begrimed
well-timed
(See also
ĪM; add
-ed where
appropriate.)

ĬMD

bedimmed
brimmed
untrimmed
(See also ĬM;
add -ed where
appropriate.)

ĬMF

lymph
nymph
sea nymph

ĬMP

blimp
chimp
crimp
gimp
imp
jimp
limp
pimp
primp
scrimp
shrimp
simp
skimp
tymp
wimp

ĬMPS

crimps
glimpse
(See also ĬMP;
add -s where
appropriate.)

ĪMZ

begrimes

---

betimes
oftentimes
oftimes
sometimes
(See also ĪM;
add -s where
appropriate.)

ĪMZ
Simms
(See also ĪM;
add -s where
appropriate.)

ĪN
Adaline
Adeline
adulterine
agatine
airline
align
alkaline
Alpine
aniline
anodyne
anserine
Apennine
apple wine
aquiline
Argentine
argentine
ashine
asinine
assign
auld lang syne
Beckstein
benign
Bernstein
beshine

bine
bottom line
brigantine
brine
Byzantine
caballine
caffeine
calcine
canine
Capitoline
carabine
Caroline
celandine
Celestine
chine
Clementine
Clyne
coastline
columbine
Columbine
combine
concubine
condign
confine
consign
Constantine
coraline
countermine
countersign
crystalline
dateline
deadline
decline
define
design
dine
disincline
divine
dyne

eglantine
Einstein
enshrine
ensign
entwine
Epstein
Esenwein
Esquiline
Evaline
Evangeline
eyne
Fescennine
fine
Florentine
fortified wine
Frankenstein
Ghibelline
gold mine
Goldstein
grapevine
guideline
headline
Hoffenstein
hyaline
incarnadine
incline
infantine
interline
intermine
intertwine
Jacqueline
Jain
kine
Klein
Kline
langsyne
leonine
libertine
Lichtenstein

lifeline
line
load line
Madeline
malign
matutine
May wine
mine
moonshine
nine
opaline
opine
outshine
overtwine
Palatine
Palestine
pavonine
peregrine
petaline
Philistine
pine
porcupine
powder mine
Proserpine
realign
recline
redline
red wine
refine
repine
resign
resupine
Rhine
Rubinstein
saline
sapphirine
saturnine
serpentine
shine

shrine
sibylline
sideline
sign
sine
skyline
snow line
sparkling wine
spine
spline
starshine
stein
streamline
strychnine
subdivine
subsign
sunshine
superfine
supine
swine
sycamine
syne
table wine
thine
tine
trephine
trine
Turn Verein
turpentine
twine
Tyne
unbenign
underline
undermine
undersign
unline
untwine
Ursuline
valentine

vespertine
vine
viperine
vulturine
waterline
Weinstein
whine
white wine
wine
Wittgenstein
wolverine
woodbíne
Zollverein

ĬN

absinthin
absinthine
adrenaline
adulterine
agatine
agglutinin
agrin
akin
alabastrine
Aladdin
albumin
Alexandrine
Algonquin
alizarin
alkaline
all in
almandine
alpestrine
alevin
amygdalin
Angevin
aniline
answerine
aquiline

argentine
asbestine
aspirin
atropine
backspin
bacterin
baldachin
bandoline
bearskin
Bedouin
been
begin
belaying pin
Benjamin
benzoin
Berlin
berlin
bin
blackfin
blood kin
bluefin
bodkin
Boleyn
botulin
bowfin
breastpin
buckskin
bulletin
buskin
Byzantine
caballine
caffeine
calfskin
calvecin
cannikin
capelin
Capuchin
carabine
carline

carotin
Catherine
catkin
Celestine
cephalin
chagrin
chamberlain
chaplain
characin
chin
chinquapin
chromaffin
chromatin
cipolin
clavecin
codeine
coffin
colin
colobin
coraline
corinne
coumarin
crankpin
crin
crinoline
crotalin
crystalline
culverin
dauphin
deerskin
din
discipline
doeskin
dolphin
drumlin
Dunedin
dunlin
dustbin
elaterin

āle,   câre,   ădd,   ärm,   ăsk;   mē,   hĕre,   ĕnd;   īce,   ĭll;

engine
ephedrine
Evangeline
feminine
Fescennine
fibrin
fibroin
fin
finikin
Finn
fiorin
Florentine
folliculin
foreskin
Formalin
francolin
gelatin
genuine
Ghibelline
gin
globin
globulin
glycerin
Glyn
Glynn
goatskin
Gobelin
gorgerin
grenadine
griffin
grimalkin
grin
gyn
hairpin
Harbin
Hardin
harlequin
has-been
hatpin

hemoglobin
heparin
herein
heroin
heroine
hin
hirudin
hirundine
Ho Chi Minh
hyaline
illumine
imagine
immunoglobu-
  lin
in
incarnadine
indiscipline
infantine
inn
insulin
intestine
intocostrin
Jacobin
jessamine
javelin
jinn
kaolin
Katherine
kerasin
keratin
kidskin
kilderkin
kin
kingpin
lambkin
lambrequin
lambskin
lanolin
lapin

larrikin
lecithin
Lenin
libertine
lin
linchpin
linn
Lohengrin
luciferin
lupulin
Lynn
mandarin
mandolin
manikin
mannequin
margarin
margarine
margin
masculine
melanin
mezzanine
Mickey Finn
Min
minikin
moccasin
moleskin
morindin
mortal sin
muscadin
muscardine
myoglobin
napkin
nectarine
niacin
nicotine
ninepin
nipperkin
nitroglycerin
noradrenaline

Odin
oilskin
olefin
oleomargarine
onionskin
opaline
origin
paladin
paraffin
pavonine
Pekin
pannikin
peregrine
petaline
Philistine
phytotoxin
pigskin
pin
pippin
porcelain
porphin
porphyrin
porphyrine
precipitin
provitamin
ptyalin
pushpin
quercetagetin
quercetagitrin
quercetin
quercimeritrin
quercitannin
quercitrin
quin
Quinn
ramekin
Rasputin
ravelin
redfin

ōld, ôr, ŏdd, oil, fŏŏt, out; ūse, ûrn, ŭp; THis, thin

redskin
rennin
respin
rosin
Rumpelstilt-
  skin
saccharine
safety pin
Sanhedrin
sapphirine
scarfskin
sculpin
sealskin
sharkskin
sheepskin
shin
sibylline
sidespin
sin
siskin
skin
snakeskin
sooterkin
sovereign
spillikin
spin
sporadin
stickpin
suberin
sycamine
sympathin
tailspin
take-in
tamarin
tambourin
tannin
tenpin
terrapin
therein

thiamine
thick and thin
thin
thoroughpin
threadfin
tiepin
tigerkin
tiger skin
tin
topspin
tourmaline
Turin
twin
underpin
unpin
unsin
Ursuline
Vaseline
venial sin
vespertine
Vietminh
violin
viperine
virgin
vitamin
vulterine
wankapin
warfarin
waringin
wherein
whin
whipper-in
win
wineskin
Wisconsin
within
yang-kin
yin
Yin

zein
Zeppelin

ĬNCH

bepinch
cinch
chinch
clinch
fallow finch
finch
flinch
inch
linch
lynch
pinch
unclinch
winch

ĬND

behind
bind
blind
color-blind
combined
crined
disinclined
find
gavelkind
grind
hind
humankind
inbind
interwind
intertwined
kind
mankind
mastermind
mind
nonaligned

overtwined
purblind
remind
rind
rynd
snow-blind
storm-wind
unbind
unblind
unconfined
undefined
underbind
undersigned
undesigned
unkind
unrefined
unshrined
unwind
upbind
upwind
vined
wind
womankind
(See also ĬN;
add -ed where
appropriate.)

ĪND

abscind
disciplined
exscind
grinned
lind
Lynd
rescind
Rosalind
storm wind
tamarind
thick-skinned

āle, câre, ădd, ärm, ăsk; mē, hĕre, ĕnd; īce, ĭll;

thin-skinned
undisciplined
wind
(See also ĬN;
add -*ed* where
appropriate.)

ĬNG
à la king
anything
atheling
besing
bewing
bing
bowstring
bring
bullring
chitterling
cling
daughterling
dayspring
ding
ding-a-ling
driving spring
easterling
enring
evening
everything
fairy king
fling
full swing
hairspring
handspring
headspring
heartstring
king
lifespring
ling
mainspring

Ming
Nanking
offspring
outwing
peiping
ping
plaything
ring
sea king
seal ring
sea wing
shufflewing
signet ring
sing
Sing Sing
sling
spring
starveling
sting
string
stripling
swing
Synge
thing
ting
underling
underwing
unking
unsling
unstring
watch spring
wedding ring
weeping spring
wing
wing ding
wring
abandoning
accomplishing
accrediting

accustoming
actioning
admonishing
afforesting
altering
angering
answering
appareling
arguing
armoring
astonishing
attributing
auctioning
auditing
auguring
awakening
badgering
balancing
ballasting
bandying
banishing
bantering
barbering
bargaining
barracking
barreling
bartering
battering
bedeviling
beflattering
beggaring
belaboring
beleaguering
belecturing
bellowing
bepattering
bepowdering
bepummeling
bescattering

beslabbering
bespattering
betokening
beveling
bewildering
bickering
blackening
blandishing
blanketing
blarneying
blathering
blazoning
blemishing
blistering
blossoming
blubbering
blundering
blustering
bolstering
bonneting
brandishing
breakfasting
broadening
buffeting
bullying
burdening
burnishing
burying
busying
butchering
buttressing
canceling
candying
cankering
cannoning
cantering
canvassing
capering
capturing

ōld, ôr, ŏdd, oil, fŏŏt, out; ūse, ûrn, ŭp; THis, thin

caroling	deciphering	entrammeling	gamboling
carpeting	destining	envisaging	gammoning
carrying	determining	envying	gardening
cautioning	deviling	establishing	garlanding
caviling	dickering	examining	garnishing
challenging	dieting	exhibiting	gathering
channeling	diminishing	faltering	gesturing
chartering	discouraging	famishing	gladdening
chastening	discrediting	fancying	glimmering
chattering	disestablishing	farrowing	glittering
chiseling	disfavoring	fashioning	glowering
christening	dishallowing	fathoming	graveling
Christmasing	dishonoring	favoring	groveling
ciphering	disparaging	feathering	hallowing
clambering	dispiriting	festering	hammering
clamoring	displeasuring	filtering	hampering
clattering	disquieting	fingering	hankering
clustering	dissevering	finicking	happening
cockering	distinguishing	finishing	harassing
coloring	distributing	flattering	harboring
comforting	doddering	flavoring	hardening
compassioning	dowering	flickering	harrowing
conditioning	driveling	flittering	harrying
conjecturing	duelling	flourishing	harvesting
conquering	embarrassing	flowering	hastening
considering	embellishing	flurrying	hazarding
continuing	emblazoning	flustering	hearkening
contributing	embodying	fluttering	heartening
conveyancing	emboldening	focusing	heralding
covering	embosoming	following	hovering
coveting	emptying	foregathering	humoring
cowering	enameling	foreshadowing	hungering
crediting	enamoring	foretokening	imagining
cudgeling	encouraging	forfeiting	imprisoning
cumbering	encumbering	forwarding	incumbering
dallying	enharboring	freshening	indenturing
damaging	enheartening	furnishing	inhabiting
darkening	enravishing	furthering	inheriting
deadening	entering	galloping	inspiriting

issuing	modeling	punishing	reckoning
jabbering	monkeying	purposing	recovering
jeopardizing	mothering	quarreling	remembering
jollying	motoring	quarreying	rendering
junketing	mouth-watering	quartering	rescuing
labeling	murdering	quavering	reveling
laboring	murmuring	querying	rivaling
lacquering	mustering	questioning	riveting
languishing	muttering	quieting	roistering
lathering	narrowing	quivering	rubbering
lavishing	neighboring	pandering	rubbishing
lazying	nourishing	paneling	saddening
lecturing	numbering	pardoning	sallying
lessening	offering	parrying	sanctioning
leveling	omening	passioning	sauntering
libeling	opening	patenting	savaging
limiting	ordering	pattering	savoring
lingering	outbalancing	pedaling	scaffolding
listening	outnumbering	penciling	scampering
littering	outrivaling	pensioning	scattering
livening	overbalancing	peppering	scavenging
lobbying	overburdening	perishing	seasoning
long-suffering	overmastering	perjuring	severing
lowering	overpowering	pestering	shadowing
lumbering	overshadowing	pilfering	shattering
maddening	overtowering	pillaging	shepherding
managing	paltering	placarding	shimmering
manufacturing	pampering	plastering	shivering
marketing	polishing	pleasuring	shouldering
marrying	pondering	plundering	showering
marshaling	pottering	racketing	shuddering
martyring	powdering	rallying	sickening
marveling	practicing	ransoming	silvering
meandering	predestining	rapturing	simmering
measuring	prohibiting	rationing	simpering
menacing	promising	ravaging	sistering
mentioning	prospering	ravening	slackening
meriting	publishing	ravishing	slandering
mirroring	pummeling	reasoning	slaughtering

slobbering
slumbering
smartening
smattering
smoldering
sniveling
sorrowing
spattering
spiraling
spiriting
spluttering
stammering
stationing
stenciling
stuttering
suffering
sugaring
summering
sundering
sweetening
sweltering
tallying
tampering
tapering
tarnishing
tarrying
tasseling
tempering
threatening
thundering
tinseling
tittering
toadying
tottering
toweling
towering
trafficking
traveling
tunneling

undervaluing
unfaltering
unflattering
unmeriting
unmurmuring
unperishing
unpitying
unpromising
unraveling
unreasoning
unremembering
unslumbering
unwandering
unwavering
upholstering
uttering
valuing
vanishing
vanquishing
vaporing
varnishing
velveting
venturing
video conferenc-
   ing
visioning
visiting
volleying
voyaging
wakening
walloping
wandering
wantoning
wassailing
watering
wavering
weakening
wearying
weathering

westering
whimpering
whinnying
whispering
winnowing
wintering
witnessing
wondering
worrying
worshiping

ĬNGD
bewinged
dinged
eagle-winged
ringed
stringed
winged
(See also ĬNG;
add *-ed* where
appropriate.)

ĬNGK
bethink
blink
bobolink
brink
chink
cinque
clink
countersink
doublethink
drink
enlink
Finck
Fink
forethink
gink
hoodwink

Humperdinck
ink
ınterlink
jink
kink
link
meadow pink
mink
outthink
pink
prink
rethink
rink
rinky-dink
shrink
sink
skink
slink
snowblink
stink
think
tiddlywink
tink
trink
twink
unlink
unthink
wink
zinc

ĬNGKS
clinks
jinx
lynx
methinks
minx
sphinx
tiddledywinks
tiddlywinks

(See also
ĬNGK; add -s
where
appropriate.)

ĬNGKT
blinked
clinked
distinct
extinct
indistinct
instinct
procinct
succinct
tinct
(See also
ĬNGK; add -ed
where
appropriate.)

ĬNGZ
awakenings
besings
leading strings
(See also ĬNG;
add -s where
appropriate.)

ĬNJ
befringe
binge
constringe
cringe
dinge
fringe
hinge
impinge
infringe
perstringe

scringe
singe
springe
swinge
tinge
twinge
unhinge

ĬNJD
befringed
unhinged
unsinged
(See also ĬNJ;
add -ed where
appropriate.)

ĬNS
blintz
convince
evince
merchant
    prince
mince
prince
quince
rinse
since
unprince
Vince
wince
(See also
ĬNTS.)

ĬNSK
Dvinsk
Minsk
Pinsk

ĬNT

ahint
behint
pint

ĬNT
asquint
calamint
dint
fingerprint
flint
footprint
glint
hint
hoofprint
imprint
lint
mezzotint
mint
misprint
newsprint
peppermint
print
quint
reprint
septuagint
skinflint
sodamint
spearmint
splint
sprint
squint
stint
thumbprint
tint
vint
voiceprint

ĬNth
ninth

pine'th

ĬNth
colocynth
hyacinth
labyrinth
plinth
terebinth

ĪNTS
Heintz
pints

ĬNTS
aquatints
chintz
flints
(See also ĬNS.)

ĪNZ
Appenines
dines
Tynes

ĬNZ
odsbodikins
winze
withershins
(See also ĬN;
add -s where
appropriate.)

ĪP
antitype
archetype
autotype
bagpipe
blowpipe
daguerreotype

ōld, ôr, ŏdd, oil, fŏŏt, out; ūse, ûrn, ŭp; THis, thin

dead ripe
electrotype
graphotype
gripe
guttersnipe
heliotype
hornpipe
hype
kipe
linotype
logotype
monotype
overripe
pipe
pitchpipe
prototype
ripe
snipe
stereotype
stipe
stripe
swipe
teletype
tintype
tripe
type
unripe
windpipe
wipe

ĬP
airstrip
apple pip
atrip
battleship
blip
blue chip
chip
clip

dip
drip
equip
flagship
flip
grip
grippe
gyp
head trip
hip
horsewhip
hyp
kip
landslip
lip
microchip
nip
outstrip
overtrip
pip
pleasure trip
quip
rip
rosehip
scrip
ship
sip
skip
slip
snip
spaceship
strip
tip
training ship
tranship
trip
underlip
unrip
unship

warship
weather strip
whip
zip

acquaintance-
    ship
administrator-
    ship
agentship
aldemanship
apprenticeship
archonship
babyship
bachelorship
cardinalship
censorship
chairmanship
championship
chancellorship
chaplainship
chieftainship
churchmanship
church mem-
    bership
citizenship
collectorship
commander-
    ship
companionship
consortship
consulship
controllership
copartnership
cousinship
craftsmanship
creatorship
deaconship

demonship
draftsmanship
eldership
electorship
emperorship
ensignship
farmership
fathership
fellowship
generalship
good-fellowship
governorship
guardianship
horsemanship
huntsmanship
impostorship
inspectorship
jockeyship
justiceship
leadership
lectureship
legislatorship
librarianship
lordship
marksmanship
marshalship
mastership
membership
Messiahship
neighborship
noviceship
one-upmanship
ownership
paintership
partnership
pastorship
penmanship
praetorship
preachership

prelateship
probationship
professorship
proprietorship
questorship
rajahship
rangership
readership
recordership
rectorship
regentship
relationship
scholarship
seamanship
secretaryship
senatorship
sextonship
sheriffship
sizarship
speakership
spectatorship
sponsorship
sportsmanship
statesmanship
stewardship
studentship
sultanship
suretyship
survivorship
swordsmanship
treasurership
umpireship
viceroyship
virtuosoship
wardenship
workmanship
wranglership

ĬPS

pipes
(See also ĬP;
  add -s where
  appropriate.)

ĬPS

acquaintance-
  ships
amidships
Apocalypse
buffalo chips
chips
cow chips
eclipse
ellipse
fish-and-chips
midships
Phipps
(See also ĬP;
  add -s where
  appropriate.)

ĬPST

chip'st
clip'st
dip'st
eclipsed
equip'st
grip'st
rip'st
ship'st
sip'st
skip'st
slip'st
strip'st
tip'st
trip'st
uneclipsed
whip'st

ĪPT

griped
hunger griped
prison striped
(See also ĪP;
  add -ed where
  appropriate.)

ĬPT

apocalypt
chipped
close-lipped
crypt
frost-nipped
hipped
manuscript
script
subscript
superscript
tight-lipped
tipt
transcript
(See also ĬP;
  add -ed where
  appropriate.)

ĪR

acquire
admire
afire
aspire
attire
beacon fire
bemire
byre
choir
conspire
death fire
desire

dire
enquire
entire
esquire
expire
fire
flat tire
galley fire
grandsire
gyre
hellfire
hire
inquire
inspire
ire
lyre
McIntyre
Meyer
mire
Molly Maguire
perspire
pyre
quire
require
respire
retire
shire
signal fire
sire
spire
spitfire
squire
suspire
swire
tire
transpire
Tyre
unsquire
Untermyer

ōld, ôr, ŏdd, oil, fŏŏt, out; ūse, ûrn, ŭp; THis, thin

vire
wildfire
wire
(See also Ĭur.)

ĪRD
acquired
overtired
spired
unacquired
undesired
unexpired
uninspired
(See also ĪR;
add -ed where
appropriate.)

ĪS
advice
bespice
bice
concise
device
dice
entice
gneiss
grice
ice
lice
mice
nice
overnice
paradise
precise
price
rice
sacrifice
self-sacrifice
sice

slice
spice
splice
suffice
syce
thrice
trice
twice
vice
vise
Weiss
Zeiss

ĬS
abiogenesis
abyss
acropolis
ambergris
amiss
anabasis
analysis
antithesis
apheresis
aphesis
armistice
artifice
avarice
Beatrice
benefice
biogenesis
bis
bliss
cannabis
chrysalis
cicatrice
clematis
cockatrice
cowardice
cuisse

dehisce
dentrifice
diaeresis
dialysis
diathesis
Dis
dismiss
ectogenesis
edifice
elephantiasis
emphasis
fortalice
French kiss
genesis
hiss
hypostasis
hypothesis
interstice
kiss
liquorice
Liss
metabasis
metamorphosis
metastasis
metathesis
metropolis
miss
Miss
M'liss
necropolis
nemesis
orifice
paralysis
parenthesis
periphrasis
precipice
prejudice
remiss
Salamis

sis
siss
soul kiss
sui generis
Swiss
synthesis
syphilis
this
verdigris
vis
wis
y-wis

ĬSH
death wish
dish
fish
gibberish
impoverish
McNish
pilot fish
pish
slish
squish
swish
Tish
unwish
wish

babyish
bitterish
cleverish
Cockneyish
devilish
dowdyish
feverish
heathenish

---

kittenish
knish
licorice
mammonish
ogreish
quakerish
tigerish
vaporish
viperish
vixenish
vulturish
waterish
willowish
womanish
yellowish

ĬSK
asterisk
basilisk
bisque
brisk
compact disc
disc
disk
fisc
Fiske
floppy disk
frisk
obelisk
odalisque
optical disc
risk
tamarisk
videodisc
whisk

ĬSP
crisp
encrisp

lisp
whisp
wisp

ĪST
Antichrist
bespiced
Christ
emparadised
enticed
poltergeist
tryst
zeitgeist
(See also ĪS;
add -ed where
appropriate.)

ĬST
agist
amethyst
assist
atwist
backlist
bekissed
bemist
beneficed
blacklist
checklist
cist
coexist
consist
cyclist
cyst
desist
dismissed
enlist
entwist
exist
fist

frist
gist
glist
grist
hissed
hist
insist
intertwist
kissed
list
Liszt
missed
mist
persist
pissed
preexist
prejudiced
resist
schist
sissed
sist
subsist
trist
tryst
twist
unkissed
unmissed
untwist
unwist
whist
white list
wist
wrist
xyst

abolitionist
abortionist
absolutist

academist
accompanist
activist
aerialist
aerologist
agamist
ageist
agonist
agricolist
agriculturalist
agriculturist
alchemist
alienist
allegorist
allopathist
altruist
amorist
anaesthetist
anagrammatist
analogist
analyst
anarchist
anatomist
animalculist
animist
annalist
annualist
antagonist
anthropologist
antinomist
antipathist
apathist
aphorist
apiarist
apologist
Arabist
arboriculturist
arborist
archaeologist

ōld, ôr, ŏdd, oil, fŏŏt, out; ūse, ûrn, ŭp; THis, thin

archivist
artillerist
atheist
atomist
augurist
Bahaist
balladist
behaviorist
biblicist
bibliophilist
bibliopolist
bicyclist
bigamist
bimetallist
biologist
Bolshevist
botanist
Bourbonist
Brahmanist
Buddhist
cabalist
Calvinist
campanologist
canonist
capitalist
casuist
catalyst
catechist
centralist
centrist
chauvinist
chirographist
chiropodist
choralist
chronologist
circumlocution-
ist
classicalist
classicist

coalitionist
collectivist
colloquist
colonist
colorist
communist
Communist
conchologist
Confucionist
congregational-
ist
constitutional-
ist
constitutionist
constructionist
contortionist
controversialist
conversationist
corruptionist
creationist
cremationist
culturist
dactylist
Dadaist
Darwinist
deconstruction-
ist
degenerationist
demonist
demonologist
despotist
destinist
destructionist
deuterogamist
devotionalist
devotionist
dialist
dialogist
diarist

diplomatist
dogmatist
dramatist
dualist
duelist
ecclesiologist
economist
educationalist
educationist
egoist
egotist
electrobiologist
elegist
elocutionist
empiricist
enamelist
enigmatist
entomologist
epigrammatist
epitomist
equilibrist
essayist
eternalist
ethicist
etymologist
Eucharist
eudemonist
eulogist
euphuist
Eurocommu-
nist
evangelist
evolutionist
excursionist
exorcist
expansionist
experimentalist
externalist
fabulist

Fascist
fascist
fatalist
federalist
feminist
fetishist
feudalist
fictionist
finalist
financialist
floriculturist
formalist
fossilist
fossilogist
funambulist
futilist
futurist
galvanist
genealogist
geologist
glacialist
gymnosophist
harmonist
Hebraist
hedonist
Hellenist
herbalist
horticulturist
humanist
humorist
hyperbolist
hypnotist
idealist
illusionist
imitationist
immaterialist
immersionist
immortalist
imperialist

industrialist
inspirationist
instrumentalist
insurrectionist
intellectualist
internationalist
Jainist
journalist
Judaist
Lamaist
Latinist
leftist
legitimist
Leninist
liberalist
literalist
lithologist
lobbyist
loyalist
lyricist
magnetist
malthusianist
mammonist
mannerist
Maoist
martyrologist
Marxist
masochist
materialist
mechanist
medalist
meliorist
melodist
melodramatist
memorialist
Mendelianist
Mendelist
Menshevist
mesmerist

metalist
meteorologist
methodist
Methodist
militarist
millenialist
mineralogist
minimalist
ministerialist
misanthropist
miscellanist
misogamist
misogynist
Mithraist
modernist
monogamist
monopolist
moralist
motorist
mythologist
Napoleonist
narcissist
nationalist
naturalist
naturist
necrologist
neoclassicist
neocolonialist
neo-Confucian-
    ist
neo-Darwinist
neofascist
neo-Fascist
neologist
neomercantilist
neoplasticist
Neoplatonist
neopopulist
nepotist

nihilist
nominalist
novelist
nudist
nutritionist
obstructionist
oculist
onanist
ontologist
opinionist
oppositionist
optimist
organist
Orientalist
ornithologist
Orphist
pacifist
passionist
pathologist
penologist
perfectionist
pessimist
petrologist
pharmacist
pharmacologist
phenomenist
philanthropist
philatelist
Philhellenist
philologist
philosophist
phlebotomist
photographist
phrenologist
physicist
physiognomist
physiologist
physiotherapist
pianist

pietist
plagiarist
platonist
pleasurist
pluralist
pneumatologist
pointillist
polygamist
Populist
positivist
postmillenialist
posturist
pragmatist
precisianist
prelatist
progressionist
prohibitionist
protagonist
protectionist
proverbialist
provincialist
psalmodist
psychiatrist
psychoanalyst
psychologist
psychothera-
    pist
publicist
pugilist
pythonist
quietist
rabbinist
racist
rapturist
rationalist
realist
receptionist
recidivist
religionist

repudiationist
resurrectionist
revisionist
revivalist
revolutionist
rhapsodist
rightist
rigorist
ritualist
Romanist
romanticist
royalist
ruralist
sadist
satanist
satirist
schematist
scientist
sciolist
scripturalist
scripturist
secessionist
secularist
segregationist
seismologist
sensationalist
sensualist
sentimentalist
separatist
sexualist
Shintoist
sibyllist
socialist
sociologist
solipsist
soloist
somnambulist
Sorbonist
specialist

spiritualist
steganographist
stenographist
strategist
subjectivist
suffragist
symbolist
sympathist
syncopist
syncretist
synodist
synonymist
synthesist
Tantrist
Taoist
tautologist
technicist
technologist
telegraphist
teleologist
telephonist
terrorist
textualist
theologist
theophilan-
  thropist
theorist
theosophist
therapist
threnodist
Titoist
tobacconist
topographist
toxicologist
trades unionist
traditionalist
traditionist
transcendental-
  ist

Trotskyist
unionist
universalist
vaccinist
vacuist
Vaticanist
ventriloquist
verbalist
violist
visionist
vitalist
vocabulist
vocalist
volumist
voluntarist
voluntaryist
votarist
zealotist
Zionist
zoologist
zoophilist
zootomist

ĪT
Aaronite
accite
achondrite
acolyte
aconite
actinolite
adamellite
Adamite
adamsite
Adullamite
aerolite
aerophyte
affright
airtight
albertite

albite
Albright
alexandrite
alight
all right
alstonite
aluminite
alunite
alurgite
alushtite
Amalekite
amazonite
ambatoarinite
amberlite
Ammonite
ampelite
amphibolite
anchorite
andersonite
andesinite
andesite
andradite
anhydrite
anight
annabergite
anorthite
anthoinite
anthophyllite
anthracite
anthropomor-
  phite
anthropopathite
anthro-
  pophagite
aplite
apophyllite
appetite
archimandrite
arenite

āle, câre, ădd, ärm, ăsk; mē, hĕre, ĕnd; īce, ĭll;

argentite	bryophyte	dendrite	felsite
argillite	bullfight	Denverite	fight
aright	byte	despite	finite
asaphite	calamite	*dight*	fistfight
attrite	calcite	dissight	Fite
austenite	Campbellite	disunite	flashlight
autunite	campsite	dite	fleabite
azurite	Canaanite	dogfight	flight
Baalite	candlelight	dolerite	flite
Babylonite	Carmelite	dolomite	floodlight
backbite	cartwright	downright	fluorite
Bakelite	catamite	droplight	footlight
barite	celestite	dynamite	foresight
bauxite	cellulite	Dyophysite	forthright
bedight	cenobite	Ebionite	fortnight
bedlamite	cheddite	ebonite	fright
behight	chiastolite	eclogite	frostbite
beknight	chrysolite	ectophyte	gadolinite
belemnite	cite	Edomite	garnierite
benight	cockfight	Elamite	gaslight
bentonite	columbite	electrolyte	geophyte
Bethlehemite	condite	endite	geyserite
bight	contrite	endophyte	ghostwrite
bipartite	coprolite	entomolite	goniatite
birthnight	copyright	enwrite	good night
birthright	corallite	epiphyte	Gothamite
bite	cordierite	eremite	granitite
blatherskite	cordite	erudite	granulite
blight	cosmopolite	erythrite	graphite
blite	crinite	erythrocyte	grapholite
bobwhite	crocidolite	essexite	graptolite
bombsight	cryolite	excite	green light
boracite	cryophyllite	expedite	gunfight
bornite	crystallite	extradite	half-light
box kite	cyanite	exurbanite	halite
bright	Dallasite	eyebright	Hamite
bromlite	daylight	eyesight	handwrite
Bronxite	deadlight	Fahrenheit	hanifite
Brooklynite	delight	fanlight	harbor light

Harlemite	kaolinite	Maronite	nephelinite
headlight	Karaite	martensite	Nephite
height	kilobyte	Masonite	New Hampshir-
hellgrammite	kimberlite	McCarthyite	ite
hellkite	kite	McKnight	New Jerseyite
hematite	knight	melanite	New Right
Hepplewhite	krait	Melchite	night
hermaphrodite	laborite	menilite	nightlight
heteroclite	labradorite	Mennonite	niobite
heulandite	lamplight	meropodite	nitrite
hight	laterite	metabolite	novaculite
hindsight	latite	meteorite	nummulite
Hollywoodite	lazulite	Michiganite	off-white
hoplite	lazurite	microcyte	omphalopsy-
Houstonite	lepidolite	microlite	chite
hydrophyte	leukocyte	Midianite	on-site
ichnite	Levite	midnight	oocyte
ichnolite	light	midshipmite	oolite
ichthyodorulite	lignite	might	oophyte
ichthyolite	limelight	millwright	ophite
ignite	limonite	Minorite	osteophyte
ilmenite	lintwhite	mite	out-a-sight
ilsemannite	lite	Moabite	outright
ilvaite	Lucite	moldavite	*overdight*
impolite	Luddite	molybdenite	overflight
incite	lyddite	Monophysite	overnight
indict	macrocyte	montroydite	overright
indite	magnetite	monzonite	oversight
insight	malachite	moonlight	overwrite
invite	mammonite	morganite	oxylophyte
Ishmaelite	manganite	Mormonite	ozokerite
Islamite	mange mite	multipartite	parasite
Israelite	Manhattanite	munite	pargasite
itacolumite	marcasite	Muscovite	partite
Jacobite	margarite	Mutazilite	pentlandite
jarosite	marlite	nadorite	peridotite
Jerseyite	marmatite	natrolite	phagocyte
kamacite	marmite	Nazarite	phosphorite
Kaneshite	marmolite	neophyte	playwright

āle, câre, ădd, ärm, ăsk; mē, hĕre, ĕnd; īce, ĭll;

plebiscite
plight
plowwright
podite
polite
pre-Adamite
pre-Raphaelite
prizefight
proselyte
Puseyite
pyrophyllite
pyrophyte
quadripartite
quartzite
quinquepartite
quite
radical right
Raphaelite
ratite
Rechabite
recite
recondite
red light
relight
renardite
requite
retinite
reunite
rhodizite
rhodonite
rhyolite
right
rite
Saint Paulite
Samnite
satellite
scapolite
sciophyte
scolecite

sea fight
sea light
searchlight
Seattleite
second sight
selenite
Semite
sennight
sexpartite
Shiite
shipwright
sidelight
siderite
siderolite
sight
signal light
site
skintight
skite
skylight
skywrite
sleight
slight
smite
smithsonite
snakebite
snite
snow-white
socialite
sodomite
somite
spermatocyte
spessartite
spherulite
spite
spotlight
sprite
stage fright
stalactite

stalagmite
starlight
sticktight
stoplight
streetlight
strombite
stylite
stylocerite
stylotypite
suburbanite
sulfite
sunlight
Sunnite
sybarite
syenite
sylvanite
sylvinite
sylvite
tachylyte
taconite
taillight
tantalite
tektite
tenorite
termite
theodolite
tight
Tokyoite
tonight
topazolite
toxophilite
traffic light
transvestite
trichite
trilobite
tripartite
trite
troglodyte
troostite

trothplight
Trotskyite
turfite
twilight
twite
typewrite
underwrite
undight
unite
unright
unsight
unwrite
upright
uptight
uralite
uraninite
uranospinite
urbanite
Vancouverite
variolite
variscite
ventriculite
vermiculite
vulcanite
wainwright
water sprite
watertight
wheelwright
white
white kite
white knight
widow's mite
wight
Wisconsinite
wite
wolframite
wright
write
wulfenite

ōld, ôr, ŏdd, oil, fŏŏt, out; ūse, ûrn, ŭp; THis, thin

Wyomingite
xerophyte
yesternight
yperite
zeolite
zoolite
zoophyte

ĬT
acquit
admit
afterwit
apposite
befit
beknit
benefit
bit
bitt
bullshit
chit
cit
commit
counterfeit
definite
demit
DeWitt
emit
exquisite
favorite
fit
flit
frit
grit
hit
horseshit
hypocrite
immit
indefinite
infinite

inknit
interknit
intermit
intromit
it
Jesuit
kit
knit
lit
manumit
mass transit
McNitt
misfit
mitt
moonlit
mother wit
nit
omit
opposite
outfit
outsit
outwit
permit
perquisite
pit
Pitt
plebiscite
prerequisite
preterite
pretermit
quit
recommit
refit
remit
requisite
rifle pit
Schmidt
shit
sit

slit
smit
spit
split
sprit
submit
tit
tomtit
to wit
transmit
twit
unbit
unfit
unknit
unwit
whit
wit
Witt
writ

ĪTH
blithe
lithe
scythe
Smythe
tithe
withe
writhe

Ĭth
myth
stythe

ĬTH
forthwith
herewith
therewith
wherewith
with

withe

Ĭth
acrolith
aerolith
Arrowsmith
forthwith
frith
herewith
kith
Ladysmith
lith
monolith
myth
paleolith
pith
sith
smith
therewith
wherewith
with
withe

ĪTS
acolytes
anights
footlights
tights
(See also ĪT;
add -*s* where
appropriate.)

ĬTS
acquits
blitz
Fritz
glitz
grits
quits

āle,   câre,   ădd,   ärm,   ăsk;   mē,   hẹre,   ĕnd;   īce,   ĭll;

Schlitz
(See also ĬT;
add -s where
appropriate.)

ĪV
alive
arrive
chive
Clive
connive
contrive
deprive
derive
dive
drive
endive
five
gyve
hive
I've
jive
live
power dive
revive
rive
shive
shrive
skive
stive
strive
survive
thrive
unhive
wive

ĬV
ablative
accusative

acquisitive
additive
admonitive
affirmative
alliterative
alternative
amative
appreciative
argumentative
causative
coercive
combative
commemora-
    tive
communicative
comparative
compellative
compensative
competitive
complimenta-
    tive
compulsative
confirmative
consecutive
conservative
contemplative
contributive
cooperative
correlative
curative
declarative
decorative
definitive
demonstrative
derivative
derogative
desiccative
diminutive
dispensative

disputative
distributive
evocative
exclamative
executive
expletive
figurative
forgive
formative
fugitive
genitive
give
illustrative
impeditive
imperative
imputative
incarnative
inchoative
incrassative
indicative
infinitive
informative
inoperative
inquisitive
insensitive
intensative
interrogative
intransitive
intuitive
irrelative
laudative
laxative
lenitive
live
lucrative
manipulative
misgive
narrative
negative

neoconserva-
    tive
nominative
nutritive
outlive
overlive
pejorative
photosensitive
positive
postoperative
premonitive
preparative
prerogative
preservative
primitive
prohibitive
provocative
pulsative
punitive
putative
quantitive
recitative
reformative
relative
remunerative
reparative
representative
restorative
retributive
sanative
sedative
semblative
sensitive
siccative
sieve
speculative
spiv
substantive
superlative

ōld, ôr, ŏdd, oil, fŏŏt, out; ūse, ûrn, ŭp; THis, thin

talkative
tentative
transitive
uncommunica-
   tive
undemonstra-
   tive
vibrative
vituperative
vocative

ĬVD
arrived
long-lived
short-lived
unshrived
unwived
(See also ĬV;
add -ed where
appropriate.)

ĬVD
long-lived
negatived
outlived
short-lived
unlived

ĬVZ
arrives
fives
Ives
knives
lives
(See also ĬV;
add -s where
appropriate.)

ĪZ

acclimatize
achromatize
actualize
adonize
advertise
advise
Africanize
afterwise
agatize
aggrandize
agonize
agrarianize
albumenize
alchemize
alcoholize
alkalize
allegorize
alphabetize
amalgamize
ambrosialize
Americanize
amortize
analyze
anathematize
anatomize
anesthetize
angelize
Anglicize
animalize
annalize
antagonize
anthologize
anthropomor-
   phize
anywise
aphorize
apologize
apostatize
apostrophize

apotheosize
appetize
apprise
arise
aromatize
artificialize
assize
astrologize
astronomize
atheize
atomize
atticize
attitudinize
augurize
authorize
balladize
baptize
barbarize
battologize
botanize
bowdlerize
brutalize
burglarize
cannibalize
canonize
capitalize
capsize
catechize
categorize
cauterize
centralize
characterize
chastise
chimerize
Christianize
circularize
circumcise
civilize
climatize

clockwise
cognize
collectivize
colonize
colorize
compartmental-
   ize
comprise
compromise
constitutional-
   ize
contrariwise
conventionalize
cornerwise
counterclock-
   wise
crescent-wise
criticize
crystallize
customize
dandyize
dastardize
decimalize
decolorize
dehumanize
demagnetize
demise
demobilize
democratize
demonetize
demoralize
denarcotize
denaturalize
deodorize
depressurize
deputize
desensitize
despise
detonize

devilize
devise
devitalize
diabolize
dialogize
dialyze
disguise
disillusionize
disorganize
dogmatize
doxologize
dramatize
ebonize
economize
ecstasize
Edenize
editorialize
effeminize
electrolyze
emblematicize
emblematize
emblemize
empathize
emphasize
emprize
energize
enigmatize
enterprise
epigrammatize
epitomize
equalize
eternalize
etherealize
etherize
etymologize
eulogize
euphemize
euphonize
euphuize

Europeanize
evangelize
excise
excursionize
exercise
exorcise
experimental-
  ize
extemporize
externalize
fabulize
familiarize
fanaticize
fantasize
federalize
fertilize
feudalize
fictionalize
finalize
fluidize
focalize
formalize
formulize
fossilize
fraternize
galvanize
gelatinize
genealogize
generalize
gentilize
geologize
geometrize
glamorize
gluttonize
gorgonize
gormandize
gospelize
guise
gutteralize

harmonize
heathenize
Hebraicize
Hebraize
Hellenize
Hibernicize
histrionize
hospitalize
humanize
hyperbolize
hypnotize
hypothesize
idealize
idiotize
idolatrize
idolize
immobilize
immortalize
immunize
impatronize
imperialize
improvise
incise
individualize
industrialize
internalize
international-
  ize
Italianize
italicize
itemize
jeopardize
journalize
Judaize
Latinize
legalize
legitimatize
lethargize
Levi's

liberalize
likewise
lionize
liquidize
literalize
Lize
lobotomize
localize
Londonize
macadamize
magnetize
Mahomeda-
  nize
mammonize
manumize
martialize
martyrize
materialize
matronize
maximize
mechanize
mediatize
memorialize
memorize
mercerize
merchandise
mesmerize
metastasize
metathesize
methodize
militarize
mineralize
miniaturize
minimize
misanthropize
misprize
mobilize
modelize
modernize

Mohammeda-
nize
moisturize
monetize
monopolize
moonrise
moralize
mythologize
narcotize
nasalize
nationalize
naturalize
neutralize
normalize
notarize
novelize
organize
ostracize
otherguise
otherwise
outsize
oversize
overwise
oxidize
oxygenize
paganize
panegyrize
parallelize
paralyze
particularize
pasteurize
patronize
pauperize
pavonize
peculiarize
pedestrianize
penalize
penny-wise
personalize

personize
pessimize
philologize
philosophize
physiognomize
pilgrimize
plagiarize
platitudinize
Platonize
plebeianize
pluralize
poetize
polarize
politicize
pollenize
polygamize
popularize
prelatize
pressurize
prize
proselytize
Protestantize
proverbialize
provincialize
psalmodize
publicize
pulverize
Puritanize
radicalize
rapturize
rationalize
realize
recognize
rejuvenize
remise
remonetize
reorganize
reprise
republicanize

resurrectionize
revise
revolutionize
rhapsodize
rhetorize
rise
Romanize
royalize
ruralize
saccharize
sacrifice
sanitize
satirize
scandalize
scepticize
schismatize
Scotticize
scrupulize
scrutinize
sectarianize
secularize
seigniorize
seniorize
sensualize
sentimentalize
sepulchralize
sermonize
sexualize
sice
signalize
silverize
singularize
size
soberize
socialize
Socinianize
solarize
solemnize
soliloquize

sonnetize
specialize
spiritualize
stabilize
standardize
sterilize
stigmatize
subsidize
subtilize
summarize
sunrise
supervise
surmise
surprise
syllogize
symbolize
sympathize
symphonize
synchronize
syncopize
synonymize
synthesize
synthetize
systematize
systemize
tabularize
tantalize
tautologize
temporize
tenderize
terrorize
Teutonize
theologize
theorize
theosophize
timonize
totalize
tranquilize
transistorize

traumatize
trivialize
tyrannize
underprize
universalize
unwise
uprise
urbanize
utilize
vagabondize
vaporize
ventriloquize
verbalize
victimize
villianize
visualize
vitalize
vocalize
volatilize
vulcanize
vulgarize
wantonize
weather-wise
weatherize
westernize
winterize
wise
womanize
(See also Ī;
add -s where
appropriate.)

ĬZ
Ariz.
befriz
biz
Cadiz
fizz
friz

his
is
Liz
ms.
phiz
quiz
riz
show biz
sizz
'tis
viz
whiz

ĪZD
acclimatized
ill-advised
unadvised
unapprised
unauthorized
unbaptized
uncanonized
uncivilized
undersized
undespised
undisguised
unprized
unsurmised
(See also ĪZ;
add -ed where
appropriate.)

ĬZ'M
abolitionism
absolutism
abysm
academism
accidentalism
achromatism
actinism

activism
aestheticism
Africanism
ageism
agnosticism
agonism
agrarianism
agriculturism
alcoholism
algorism
alienism
altruism
Americanism
anachronism
anarchism
anathematism
anatomism
aneurism
Anglicanism
Anglicism
Anglo-Saxonism
animalism
animism
anomalism
antagonism
anthropomor-
　phism
antiquarianism
anti-Semitism
aphorism
archaism
asceticism
Asiaticism
asteism
asterism
astigmatism
atavism
atheism
atomism

Baalism
babyism
bacchanalian-
　ism
bachelorism
Bahaism
barbarism
behaviorism
biblicism
bibliophilism
bibliopolism
bimetallism
bloomerism
blue-
　stockingism
bogeyism
Bohemianism
Bolshevism
boobyism
botulism
Bourbonism
braggardism
Brahmanism
brutalism
Buchmanism
Buddhism
cabalism
Calvinism
cannibalism
capitalism
careerism
cataclysm
catechism
Catholicism
centralism
centrism
characterism
Chauvinism
chloralism

ōld, ôr, ŏdd, oil, fŏŏt, out; ūse, ûrn, ŭp; THis, thin

chrism
classicalism
classicism
clericalism
Cockneyism
collectivism
colloquialism
colonialism
communalism
communism
Confucianism
congregational-
ism
conservatism
constitutional-
ism
consumerism
cosmopoli-
tanism
cretinism
criticism
cynicism
Dadaism
dandyism
Darwinism
deconstruction-
ism
demoniacism
demonianism
demonism
denomination-
alism
despotism
determinism
devilism
diabolism
dialogism
diamagnetism
diplomatism

dogmatism
dualism
dynamism
ecclesiasticism
eclecticism
egocentrism
egoism
egotism
electicism
embolism
emotionalism
empiricism
epicureanism
equestrianism
Erastianism
esotericism
etherealism
etherism
eudemonism
euphemism
euphonism
euphuism
Eurocommu-
nism
evangelism
exhibitionism
existentialism
exorcism
exoticism
expansionism
expressionism
exquisitism
fairyism
fanaticism
fantasticism
Fascism
fascism
fatalism
favoritism

federalism
feminism
Fenianism
fetishism
feudalism
flunkeyism
fogeyism
foreignism
formalism
fossilism
Fourierism
frivolism
Gallicism
galvanism
gentilism
Germanism
Ghandiism
heathenism
Hebraism
hedonism
Hellenism
heroism
Hibernianism
Hibernicism
Hinduism
histrionicism
histrionism
Hitlerism
homeroticism
humanism
hyperbolism
hypercriticism
hypnotism
hypochon-
driacism
Ibsenism
idealism
idiotism
immaterialism

imperialism
individualism
industrialism
intellectualism
international-
ism
Irishism
Islamism
ism
isolationism
Italianism
Italicism
Jainism
Jesuitism
jingoism
jism
jockeyism
journalism
Judaism
laconicism
laconism
ladyism
Lamaism
Lamarckism
Latinism
latitudinarian-
ism
leftism
legitimism
Leninism
lesbianism
liberalism
libertinism
literalism
localism
Lollardism
Londonism
loyalism
Lutheranism

---

lyricism
magnetism
Mahometanism
malapropism
mammonism
mannerism
Maoism
Marxianism
Marxism
masochism
materialism
Mazdaism
McCarthyism
mechanism
medievalism
meliorism
Mendelianism
Mendelism
Menshevism
mercantilism
mesmerism
metabolism
metacism
methodism
Methodism
microorganism
militarism
millenarianism
millennialism
minimalism
Mithraism
modernism
Mohammedan-
  ism
monarchism
monasticism
monkeyism
Montanism
moralism

Mormonism
Muslimism
mysticism
narcissism
nationalism
nativism
naturalism
naturism
Nazism
necessarianism
neoclassicism
neocolonialism
neo-Confucian-
  ism
neoconser-
  vatism
neo-Darwinism
neo-expression-
  ism
neo-Fascism
neofascism
neo-Hellenism
neo-impres-
  sionism
neoisolationism
neoliberalism
neologism
neo-Lutheran-
  ism
neomercantil-
  ism
neopaganism
neoplasticism
Neoplatonism
neopopulism
neorealism
neoromanti-
  cism
neo-scholasti-

cism
nepotism
nihilism
nominalism
nudism
occultism
ogreism
onanism
optimism
organism
Orientalism
Orphism
ostracism
pacifism
paganism
pantheism
parallelism
paroxysm
passivism
patricianism
patriotism
pauperism
peanism
pedantism
pedestrianism
peonism
peripateticism
personalism
pessimism
phalansterism
phenomenal-
  ism
phenomenism
philanthropism
Philhellenism
Philistinism
philosophism
physicism
pietism

plagiarism
plasticism
Platonism
plebeianism
pluralism
pointillism
Populism
positivism
postmillenial-
  ism
pragmatism
precisianism
predestinarian-
  ism
prelatism
pre-Raphaelism
Presbyterian-
  ism
priapism
prism
professionalism
proletarianism
protectionism
Protestantism
proverbialism
provincialism
pugilism
puppyism
Puritanism
Puseyism
pythonism
Quakerism
quietism
Quixotism
rabbinism
radicalism
rationalism
realism
recidivism

ōld, ôr, ŏdd, oil, fŏŏt, out; ūse, ûrn, ŭp; THis, thin

religionism
Republicanism
revisionism
revivalism
rheumatism
rightism
rigorism
ritualism
Romanism
romanticism
royalism
ruffianism
ruralism
sabbatarianism
sacerdotalism
sadism
sado-
    masochism
satanism
savagism
Saxonism
scepticism
schism
scholasticism
sciolism
Scotticism
scoundrelism
scripturalism

secessionism
sectarianism
secularism
Semitism
sensationalism
sensualism
sentimentalism
separatism
shamanism
Shavianism
Shiism
Shintoism
Shivaism
Sivaism
skepticism
socialism
Socinianism
solecism
solipsism
somnambulism
somnolism
sovietism
spiritualism
spoonerism
Stalinism
stoicism
subjectivism
subtilism

Sufism
Sunnism
supernatural-
    ism
syllogism
symbolism
synchronism
syncretism
Syrianism
Tantrism
Taoism
terrorism
Teutonicism
theosophism
tigerism
Titoism
tokenism
Toryism
totemism
trades-union-
    ism
traditionalism
transcendental-
    ism
tribalism
Trotskyism
truism
unionism

Unitarianism
universalism
utilitarianism
Utopianism
valetudinarian-
    ism
vampirism
vandalism
Vaticanism
vegetarianism
ventriloquism
verbalism
vitalism
vocalism
voluntarism
voluntaryism
volunteerism
vulgarism
vulpinism
vulturism
Wesleyanism
witticism
Yankeeism
zanyism
Zionism
Zoroastrianism

O

These words include the following accented vowel sounds:

Ō   as in *old;* heard also in *note, oh, roam, foe, shoulder, grow, owe, sew, yeoman, beau, hautboy, brooch.*

Ô   as in *or;* heard also in *all, talk, swarm, haul, caught, law, fought, broad, memoir.*

Ŏ   as in *odd;* heard also in *want, wash, shone.*

OI   as in *oil;* heard also in *boy.*

OŎ   as in *foot;* heard also in *full, wolf, could.*

OU   as in *out;* heard also in *cow, sauerkraut.*

For the vowel sound heard in *do,* see under Ū.

For the vowel sound heard in *one, flood,* see under Ŭ.

Ō	bravissimo	duodecimo	generalissimo
adagio	buffalo	eau	GIGO
aglow	bummalo	*embow*	gigolo
ago	bungalow	embroglio	glow
Alamo	bureau	embryo	go
alow	cachalot	entrepot	grow
although	calico	escargot	half a mo
apropos	cameo	escrow	haricot
Arapaho	chapeau	Eskimo	heigh-ho
archipelago	chateau	ex officio	ho
arow	Co.	fellatio	hoe
audio	comme il faut	Flo	honcho
banjo	crow	floe	howso
bateau	curaçoa	flow	hullo
beau	deathblow	foe	ice floe
below	death row	folio	Idaho
besnow	death throe	forego	imbroglio
bestow	depot	foreknow	impresario
blow	de trop	foreshow	in flagrante
bo	Diderot	fortissimo	delicto
bon mot	dildo	fro	in statu quo
Bordeaux	do	furbelow	incognito
Borneo	doe	gazabo	indigo
bow	domino	gazebo	inflow
braggadocio	dough	gazpacho	intaglio

ōld, ôr, ŏdd, oil, foŏt, out; ūse, ûrn, ŭp; THis, thin

jabot
Jim Crow
Jo
Joe
kayo
know
little go
lo
long-ago
longbow
Lothario
low
Lowe
magnifico
malapropos
manito
Mexico
Michelangelo
mistletoe
morceau
mot
mow
music video
mustachio
Navaho
no
nuncio
O
oboe
oh
olio
Ontario
oratorio
outflow
outgo
outgrow
overcrow
overflow
overgrow

overthrow
owe
Papilio
patio
pianissimo
pistachio
plateau
PLO
Po
Poe
politico
portfolio
portico
portmanteau
pro
proximo
punctilio
quid pro quo
radio
rainbow
raree-show
ratio
right to know
rodeo
roe
Romeo
rondeau
rouleau
Rousseau
row
Rowe
sabot
saddlebow
Sappho
scenario
schmo
Scorpio
seraglio
sew

shew
show
simpatico
skid row
sloe
slow
snow
so
so-and-so
so-ho
sow
status quo
stow
strow
studio
tableau
tallyho
though
throe
throw
timber toe
tiptoe
to-and-fro
toe
Tokyo
touch and go
tow
tremolo
trousseau
trow
ultimo
undergo
undertow
unknow
upgrow
upthrow
van Gogh
Velcro
vertigo

video
Westward ho
woe
yo-yo

Ô
Arkansas
awe
begnaw
braw
brother-in-law
caw
chaw
claw
craw
daughter-in-law
dauw
daw
dawe
draw
father-in-law
faugh
flaw
foresaw
gnaw
guffaw
haw
heehaw
jackdaw
jaw
landau
law
macaw
maw
McGraw
mother-in-law
overawe
overdraw
oversaw

āle,   câre,   ădd,   ärm,   ăsk;   mē,   hĕre,   ĕnd;   īce,   ĭll;

papaw
paw
pilau
pshaw
raw
saw
scaw
seesaw
Shaw
sister-in-law
slaw
son-in-law
spa
squaw
straw
tau
taw
thaw
thraw
underjaw
undraw
unlaw
usquebaugh
withdraw
yaw

ŌB
Anglophobe
conglobe
disrobe
enrobe
Francophobe
Germanophobe
globe
homophobe
Japanophobe
Job
lobe
Loeb

microbe
Negrophobe
probe
robe
Russophobe
Sinophobe
strobe
unrobe

ÔB
bedaub
daub
nawab

ŎB
athrob
blob
bob
cabob
cob
Cobb
corncob
fob
gob
hob
hob-and-nob
hobnob
job
kebab
knob
lob
mob
nob
quab
rob
shish kebab
slob
snob
sob

squab
stob
swab
thingamabob
throb

ŎBZ
blobs
Dobbs
Hobbes
Hobbs
ods-bobs
scobs
(See also ŎB;
add -s where
appropriate.)

ŌCH
abroach
approach
broach
brooch
coach
cockroach
croche
encoach
encroach
loach
poach
reproach
roach
self-reproach
slow coach

ÔCH
debauch
nautch

ŎCH

anchor watch
blotch
botch
crotch
deathwatch
gotch
harbor watch
hopscotch
hotch
hotch-potch
larboard watch
notch
outwatch
Scotch
splotch
swatch
watch

ŌCHD
approached
unapproached
unbroached
(See also ŌCH;
add -ed where
appropriate.)

ŌD
abode
à la mode
anode
antipode
area code
arrode
bestrode
bode
bridle road
Clode
code
commode

corrode
decode
discommode
encode
episode
erode
explode
forebode
freeload
genetic code
goad
implode
incommode
load
lode
lycopode
middle-of-the-
    road
mode
Morse code
node
ode
overload
payload
pigeon-toed
road
rode
spode
strode
toad
unbestowed
unload
unowed
woad
ZIP Code
(See also
Ō; add
-ed where
appropriate.)

ÔD
abroad
applaud
awed
bawd
belaud
broad
Claude
defraud
fraud
gaud
lantern-jawed
laud
maraud
maud
overawed
unawed
whopper-jawed
(See also
Ō; add
-ed where
appropriate.)

ŎD
Aaron's rod
begod
clod
cod
Codd
demigod
divining rod
Dodd
dry-shod
Eisteddfod
God
goldenrod
hod
hot rod
lycopod

nod
od
odd
piston rod
platypod
plod
pod
prod
quad
quod
river-god
rod
roughshod
sea-god
shod
slipshod
sod
squad
tightwad
tod
trod
ungod
unshod
untrod
wad

ŌDZ
Rhoades
Rhodes
(See also ŌD;
add -s where
appropriate.)

ŎDZ
clods
emerods
odds
(See also ŎD;
add -s where

appropriate.)

ŌF
goaf
loaf
oaf
quartern loaf

ÔF
bake-off
brush-off
beef Stroganoff
cast-off
cough
Gorbachev
Khrushchev
kickoff
lift-off
Molotov
Nabokov
off
Rachmaninoff
Rimsky-
    Korsakov
rip-off
Romanov
send-off
sign-off
Stroganoff
takeoff
trough
turnoff
wave-off
whooping
    cough

ŎF
cloff
doff

philosophe
prof
scoff
shroff
soph
toff

ŎFT
aloft
croft
doffed
loft
oft
soft
toft
undercroft
(See also ŎF;
add *-ed* where
appropriate.)

ŌG
apologue
astrologue
brogue
collogue
embogue
Hogue
pirogue
prorogue
rogue
togue
trogue
vogue

ŎG
agog
analog
apologue
befog

bog
bulldog
catalog
clog
cog
Dannebrog
decalogue
demagogue
dialogue
dog
eggnog
embog
epilogue
flog
fog
frog
Gog
grog
hedgehog
Herzog
hog
hot dog
incog
jog
log
monologue
mystagogue
nog
Patchogue
pedagogue
pettifog
philologue
Pokogue
polliwog
prairie dog
prog
prologue
Quogue
road hog

scrog
shog
slog
smog
synagogue
theologue
travelogue
unclog
underdog

ŎGÐ
befogged
frogged
waterlogged
(See also ŎG;
add *-ed* where
appropriate.)

ŎGZ
befogs
togs
(See also ŎG;
add *-s* where
appropriate.)

OI
ahoy
alloy
annoy
bok choy
boy
buoy
charity boy
chorus boy
cloy
convoy
corduroy
cowboy
coy

decoy
deploy
destroy
employ
enjoy
foy
good old boy
goy
Hanoi
hobbledehoy
hoi polloi
hoy
Illinois
joy
killjoy
loblolly boy
Loy
overjoy
paduasoy
playboy
Pomeroy
saveloy
Savoy
sepoy
soy
teapoy
Tolstoy
toy
troy
viceroy
yellow boy

OID
actinoid
albuminoid
alkaloid
alloyed
android
aneroid

anthropoid
asteroid
avoid
"boid"
celluloid
coralloid
crystalloid
deltoid
dendroid
devoid
fibroid
Freud
helicoid
hemorrhoid
hyaloid
metalloid
Mongoloid
Negroid
overjoyed
ovoid
pachydermatoid
paraboloid
petaloid
pyramidoid
steroid
tabloid
trapezoid
typhoid
unalloyed
unbuoyed
unemployed
varioloid
void
(See also OI;
add -ed where
appropriate.)

OIDZ
avoids

Lloyd's

OIF
coif

OIL
aboil
assoil
boil
Boyle
broil
coil
counterfoil
Coyle
despoil
disembroil
Doyle
embroil
entoil
estoile
foil
langue d'oil
moil
noil
oil
overtoil
parboil
quatrefoil
recoil
roil
soil
spoil
toil
turmoil
uncoil
upcoil

OILD
boiled

hard-boiled
unsoiled
unspoiled

OILT
spoilt

OILZ
boils
noils
(See also OIL;
add -s where
appropriate.)

OIN
adjoin
almoign
Boyne
coign
coin
conjoin
Des Moines
disjoin
eloign
enjoin
foin
frankalmoigne
groin
interjoin
join
loin
purloin
quoin
rejoin
sejoin
sirloin
subjoin
tenderloin

OIND
adjoined
dead poind
poind
uncoined

OINT
adjoint
anoint
appoint
aroint
checkpoint
conjoint
counterpoint
cover point
disappoint
disjoint
dowel joint
drypoint
gunpoint
joint
pinpoint
point
reappoint
repoint
viewpoint
West Point

OIS
Boyce
choice
Hobson's choice
invoice
Joyce
outvoice
pro-choice
rejoice
Rolls-Royce
voice

āle, câre, ădd, ärm, ăsk; mē, hĕre, ĕnd; īce, ĭll;

OIST
foist
hoist
joist
loud-voiced
moist
shrill-voiced
unrejoiced
unvoiced
voiced
(See also OIS;
add -ed where
appropriate.)

OIT
adroit
dacoit
Detroit
doit
droit
exploit
maladroit
quoit
Voight

OIZ
avoirdupois
counterpoise
equipoise
erminois
froise
noise
Noyes
poise
(See also OI;
add -s where
appropriate.)

ŌJ

doge
gamboge
horologe

ŎJ
dislodge
dodge
hodge
hodge-podge
horologe
lodge
splodge
stodge
unlodge

ŌK
artichoke
asoak
awoke
baroque
besmoke
bespoke
bloke
broke
choke
cloak
coak
coke
convoke
counterstroke
croak
death stroke
equivoque
evoke
folk
forespoke
forspoke
gentlefolk
invoke

joke
Larocque
loke
masterstroke
moke
oak
outbroke
poke
provoke
revoke
scrub oak
sloke
smoke
soak
spoke
stoke
stroke
toke
toque
unbroke
uncloak
understroke
unyoke
upbroke
woke
yoke
yolk

ŎK
auk
awk
baby talk
back talk
balk
boardwalk
cakewalk
calk
chalk
dawk

double-talk
Falk
gawk
hawk
jaywalk
mawk
Mohawk
outwalk
pawk
shoptalk
sidewalk
space walk
sparrow hawk
squawk
stalk
talk
tomahawk
walk

ŎK
acid rock
acock
ad hoc
alpenstock
amok
Antioch
Bach
Bangkok
baroque
bedrock
belock
bemock
billycock
biological clock
Bloch
block
bock
brock
chock

chockablock
clock
cock
crock
deadlock
dock
fetlock
firelock
flintlock
flock
folk-rock
forelock
frock
grok
half-cock
havelock
hoc
hock
hollyhock
interlock
jazz-rock
jock
knock
lady's-smock
langue d'oc
laughingstock
Little Rock
loch
lock
lovelock
Medoc
mock
Mohock
padlock
Painted Rock
peacock
penstock
percussion lock
plock

pock
poppycock
Ragnarock
roadblock
roc
rock
round-the-
  clock
schlock
shamrock
sherlock
shock
shuttlecock
shylock
smock
soc
sock
spatchcock
stock
stumbling
  block
turkey-cock
turncock
understock
undock
unfrock
unlock
Vladivostok
weathercock
weeping rock
woodcock
yock

ŌKS
artichokes
coax
hoax
Nokes
Oakes

Stokes
Vokes
(See also ŌK;
add -*s* where
appropriate.)

ŎKS
alpenstocks
ballot box
bandbox
boom box
boondocks
box
chatterbox
chickenpox
Christmas box
Cox
detox
Equinox
Fort Knox
fox
hard knocks
hatbox
heterodox
icebox
idiot box
jukebox
lox
mailbox
matchbox
orthodox
ox
paddlebox
paradox
phlox
pillar-box
power box
signal box
small pox

vox
Velox
Xerox

ŌKT
evoked
unprovoked
water-soaked

ŎKT
blocked
concoct
decoct
recoct
unfrocked
(See also ŎK;
add -*ed* where
appropriate.)

ŌL
amphibole
anisole
anole
apiole
armhole
arteriole
arvicole
augur hole
aureole
azarole
azole
banderole
bankroll
barcarolle
barge pole
bean pole
bedroll
bibliopole
black hole

blackpoll
blowhole
Bluebonnet
  Bowl
bole
boll
borecole
borehole
bowl
bricole
bronchiole
bunghole
buttonhole
cabriole
cajole
camisole
capriole
caracole
carambole
cariole
carmagnole
casserole
catchpole
centriole
charcoal
cholesterol
citole
clearcole
coal
cole
comptrol
condole
console
control
Cotton Bowl
Creole
creosol
croquignole
cubbyhole

curtain pole
dariole
de Gaulle
decontrol
dhole
dipole
dole
droll
enbowl
enroll
enscroll
ensoul
escarole
extol
eyehole
farandole
feme sole
Fiesta Bowl
fishbowl
fishing pole
flagpole
foal
foliole
foxhole
frijol
fumarole
furole
fusarole
Gator Bowl
girandole
girasole
gloriole
glory hole
goal
Grand Guignol
guignol
half sole
hawsehole
heart-whole

hellhole
hole
Independence
  Bowl
indole
inscroll
insole
Interpol
jelly roll
jobbernowl
jole
jowl
keyhole
kneehole
knoll
knothole
kohl
Liberty Bowl
lodgepole
logroll
loophole
manhole
Maypole
metropole
Mohole
mole
multirole
obole
Orange Bowl
oriole
ostiole
oversoul
parole
patrol
payroll
Peach Bowl
peephole
petiole
phytosterol

pigeonhole
pinhole
pinole
pistole
pole
Pole
poll
porthole
pothole
pratincole
profiterole
prole
punch bowl
pyrrole
quadrupole
rantipole
recontrol
remote control
reroll
resole
ridgepole
rigamarole
rigmarole
rissole
rocambole
rock and roll
rock 'n' roll
role
roll
Rose Bowl
safrole
scroll
scupper hole
segol
self-control
Seminole
Seoul
septimole
sestole

ōld, ôr, ŏdd, oil, fŏŏt, out; ūse, ûrn, ŭp; THis, thin

Sheol
shoal
shole
sinkhole
skatole
skoal
sol
sole
sotol
soul
squatarole
stole
stroll
sugar bowl
Sun Bowl
Super Bowl
swillbowl
swimming hole
tadpole
Tangerine
  Bowl
telephone pole
thiazole
thole
tole
toll
tophole
touchhole
troll
turnsole
unroll
unsoul
unwhole
uproll
vacuole
variole
virole
vole
Walpole

wassail bowl
whole
wormhole

ÔL

aerosol
all
all in all
appal
awl
ball
banquet hall
baseball
basketball
bawl
befall
bemawl
Bengal
Berlin Wall
bethrall
blackball
box stall
brawl
call
carryall
catchall
caterwaul
caul
Cornwall
crawl
disenthrall
downfall
drawl
dwal
enthrall
evenfall
eyeball
eyeball-to-eye-
  ball

fall
fireball
football
footfall
forestall
free-fall
free-for-all
gall
Gaul
hairball
hall
handball
haul
install
judgment hall
kraal
landfall
lowball
mall
maul
McCall
meatball
miscall
Montreal
mothball
Nepal
nightfall
oddball
off-the-wall
overfall
overhaul
pall
Paul
pawl
pitfall
pratfall
rainfall
recall
Saul

scall
scrawl
screwball
seawall
shawl
shortfall
small
snowball
spall
spawl
speedball
sprawl
spurgall
squall
stall
stonewall
tall
therewithal
thrall
trawl
trumpet call
urban sprawl
wall
waterfall
wherewithal
windfall
withal
yawl

ŎL

alcohol
atoll
baby doll
capitol
consol
doll
entresol
extol
folderol

girasol
gun moll
loll
moll
parasol
poll
protocol
Sol
vitriol

ÔLCH
Balch
Walch

ŌLD
acold
afterhold
ahold
anchor-hold
behold
blindfold
bold
bullet mold
cajoled
clay cold
coaled
cold
copyhold
enfold
fold
foothold
foretold
fourfold
freehold
gold
half-soled
high-souled
hold
household

ice-cold
infold
interfold
leafmold
leasehold
Leopold
manifold
marigold
mold
multifold
old
overbold
refold
retold
sable-stoled
scold
sold
spun gold
stone-cold
stronghold
thousandfold
told
twice-told
twofold, etc.
uncontrolled
unfold
unsold
untold
uphold
withhold
wold
(See also ŌL;
add -ed where
appropriate.)

ÔLD
appalled
Archibald
auld

bald
blackballed
scald
so-called
unappalled
uncalled
unenthralled
ungalled
unrecalled
(See also ÔL;
add -ed where
appropriate.)

ŎLF
golf
Randolf
rolf
Rolf
Rudolf

ŌLN
swoln

ÔLSH
Walsh

ŌLT
bolt
colt
demi-volt
dolt
holt
jolt
lavolt
molt
poult
revolt
shackle bolt
smolt

thunderbolt
unbolt
volt

ÔLT
assault
basalt
cobalt
default
envault
exalt
fault
gault
halt
malt
salt
sea-salt
smalt
somersault
spalt
vault

ÔLTS
assaults
false
salts
valse
waltz
(See also ÔL;
add -s where
appropriate.)

ŎLV
absolve
circumvolve
convolve
devolve
dissolve
evolve

exolve
intervolve
involve
resolve
revolve
solve

ŎLVD
absolved
undissolved
unresolved
unsolved
(See also ŎLV;
add -*ed* where
appropriate.)

ŌM
aerodrome
afoam
astrodome
Astrodome
befoam
brome
catacomb
chrome
chromosome
clomb
comb
currycomb
dome
endome
foam
Frome
gastronome
gloam
gnome
harvest home
heliochrome
hippodrome

holm
home
honeycomb
Jerome
loam
metallochrome
metronome
microsome
monochrome
motordrome
motor home
nobody home
no'm
Nome
ohm
palindrome
polychrome
pome
roam
Rome
Salome
sea-foam
sea-holm
sloam
Superdome
tome

ÔM
haum
imaum
maum
shawm

ŎM
A-bomb
aerosol bomb
aplomb
atom bomb
axiom

bomb
car bomb
dom
firebomb
from
Guam
H-bomb
hecatomb
hydrogen bomb
intercom
letter bomb
mail bomb
neutron bomb
om
pogrom
pompom
rhomb
sitcom
smoke bomb
swom
Syncom
the bomb
therefrom
volcanic bomb

ŎMP
comp
pomp
romp
swamp
trompe

ŎMPT
imprompt
prompt
romped
(See also ŎMP;
add -*ed* where
appropriate.)

ŌMZ
Holmes
(See also ŌM;
add -*s* where
appropriate.)

ŌN
accident-prone
acetone
air phone
aitchbone
aldosterone
allophone
alone
androsterone
Anglophone
anklebone
anticyclone
antiphone
Athlone
atone
audiphone
backbone
balaphon
barbitone
baritone
barytone
Beaune
begroan
bemoan
bestrown
bilestone
birthstone
bloodstone
blown
bolson
bone
Boulogne
breastbone

brimstone
brownstone
butanone
cabezone
Capone
capstone
car phone
cellular phone
chalone
chaperone
cheekbone
chon
chordophone
cicerone
clingstone
clone
cobblestone
cogon
collarbone
Cologne
cologne
colon
condone
cone
copestone
corn pone
cornerstone
cortisone
coumarone
crone
curbstone
cyclone
dependency
  prone
depone
dethrone
dial tone
dictaphone
disown

dispone
Dordogne
drone
duotone
earphone
eau de cologne
ecdysone
ecotone
electrophone
end stone
end zone
enterogastrone
enthrone
enzone
epigone
estrone
euphone
evzone
firestone
Firestone
flagstone
flavone
flown
flowstone
flyblown
foreknown
foreshown
foundation
  stone
Francophone
freestone
fresh-blown
frontal bone
full-blown
full-grown
funny bone
gallstone
gemstone
gladstone

gramophone
graphophone
grass-grown
gravestone
grindlestone
grindstone
groan
grown
hailstone
half-grown
halftone
headphone
headstone
hearthstone
heckelphone
herringbone
hexone
high-flown
hipbone
holy stone
homophone
hone
hormone
hydrophone
icebone
impone
imposing stone
ingrown
interphone
interpone
intone
Ionone
ironstone
isotone
jawbone
Joan
ketone
keystone
kidney stone

knee bone
known
knucklebone
lactone
ladrone
limestone
loadstone
loan
lodestone
lone
macrotone
marrowbone
megaphone
mellophone
methadone
microphone
milestone
millstone
moan
mobile phone
monotone
moonstone
moss-grown
mown
none
occipital bone
ochone
oilstone
outblown
outshone
overblown
overgrown
overthrown
overtone
own
ozone
parietal bone
peptone
phenobarbitone

ōld, ôr, ŏdd, oil, fŏŏt, out; ūse, ûrn, ŭp; THis, thin

pheromone
philosophers'
  stone
phone
phytohormone
Picturephone
pitchstone
polyphone
pone
postpone
prednisolone
prednisone
progesterone
prone
propone
pyrone
quarter tone
radiophone
radiotelephone
rail phone
reflown
reloan
repone
resewn
reshown
resown
rethrone
rhinestone
Rhone
rincon
roan
rone
rotenone
rottenstone
sacaton
Sacaton
sandstone
saxophone
scone

semitone
sewn
shewn
shinbone
shone
shoulder bone
shown
Sierra Leone
silicone
sine qua none
soapstone
sone
sousaphone
sown
speakerphone
spironolactone
stone
strown
sulfone
T-bone
telephone
testosterone
thighbone
throne
thrown
thunderstone
toadstone
tombstone
tone
touchstone
touch-tone
tritone
trombone
turnstone
two-tone
unbeknown
unblown
undergrown
undertone

unflown
unforeknown
ungrown
unknown
unmown
unsewn
unshown
unsown
unthrone
unthrown
vibraphone
videophone
vitaphone
weather-blown
whalebone
whetstone
whole-tone
windblown
wishbone
wristbone
xylophone
zone

ÔN
awn
"bawn"
brawn
"cawn"
dawn
drawn
faun
fawn
impawn
indrawn
lawn
pawn
prawn
sawn
spawn

undrawn
withdrawn
yawn

ŎN
Acheron
Agamemnon
agon
agone
aileron
Alençon
Amazon
amazon
anacoluthon
anon
antineutron
antinuclear
antiphon
antiproton
archon
argon
Argonne
asyndeton
Audubon
automaton
Avalon
Babylon
Balaton
baryton
baton
begone
Bellerophon
benison
Bion
blouson
bonbon
Bonn
bonne
Borazon

āle, câre, ădd, ärm, ăsk; mē, hĕre, ĕnd; īce, ĭll;

boson
boustrophedon
bygone
cabochon
Canton
carillon
carrying-on
carryon
catholicon
celadon
cephalon
Ceylon
chiffon
chignon
chronon
colophon
COMECON
con
conn
coupon
cretonne
cyclotron
Darvon
decagon
demijohn
dies non
dodecagon
doggone
Dogon
don
Donne
echelon
electron
elevon
elytron
encephalon
enchiridion
encomion
enteron

ephemeron
epimeron
epsilon
Esdraelon
estragon
etalon
etymologicon
etymon
Euroclydon
fanfaron
filet mignon
fleuron
foregone
glucagon
glyptodon
gnathion
gnomon
goings-on
gone
gonfalon
gonfanon
haematoxylon
hanger-on
hapteron
harmoniphon
helicon
Helicon
heptagon
hereon
hereupon
hexaemeron
hexagon
himation
hoot mon
Hyperion
hyperon
icon
iguanodon
interferon

irenicon
isogon
Jeanne
John
john
jupon
khan
kikumon
krypton
Laocoon
lepton
lexicon
liaison
limaçon
Little John
logion
long-field-on
Luzon
macédoine
Macedon
magneton
marathon
mascon
mastodon
megaron
mesencephalon
mesenteron
mesepimeron
Micklejohn
mon
mouflon
myrmidon
Neophron
nephron
neuron
neutron
ninon
Nippon
nonagon

noumenon
nuclear
   magneton
nucleon
nychthemeron
Oberon
octagon
olecranon
omicron
on
onomasticon
operon
opticon
Oregon
organon
Orlon
ornithon
orthicon
outshone
panopticon
pantechnicon
pantheon
papillon
paragon
parergon
parison
Parthenon
Pentagon
pentagon
Percheron
perigon
petalon
phaeton
phenomenon
phlogiston
phon
phyton
piton
polygon

ōld, ôr, ŏdd, oil, fŏŏt, out; ūse, ûrn, ŭp; THis, thin

polysyndeton
positron
pro-and-con
prolegomenon
protagon
proton
put upon
put-on
radon
Rubicon
Saigon
salon
Saskatchewan
Saticon
shone
silicon
sine qua non
Sphenodon
Stegodon
stereopticon
swan
synonymicon
tampon
tarragon
Teflon
telethon
tetragon
tetragrammaton
theologoumenon
thereon
thereupon
trianon
trilithon
trimetrogon
triskelion
trogon
Tucson
turn-on
tympanon

undecagon
undergone
upon
upsilon
vidicon
walk-on
wan
whereon
whereupon
woebegone
wonton
yon
Yukon
Ỳvonne
zircon
(See also ŬN.)

ÔNCH

craunch
haunch
launch
paunch
raunch

ŌND

atoned
high-toned
unatoned
unmoaned
unowned
unzoned
zoned
(See also ŌN;
add -*ed* where
appropriate.)

ÔND

beau monde
demimonde

Fronde
Gironde
monde

ŎND

abscond
beau monde
beyond
blond
bond
correspond
demimonde
despond
donned
fond
frond
junk bond
overfond
plafond
monde
pond
respond
unparagoned
vagabond
wand
yond

ŎNG

all along
along
battle song
belong
daylong
dingdong
drinking song
dugong
erelong
evensong
flong

gong
headlong
headstrong
Hong Kong
lifelong
livelong
long
mah-jongg
nightlong
overlong
Ping-Pong
prolong
prong
scuppernong
singsong
song
souchong
strong
thong
throng
tong
undersong
Viet Cong
wong
wrong

ŎNGD

belonged
unwronged
(See also
ŎNG; add
-*ed* where
appropriate.)

ŎNGK

conch
conk
honk
honky-tonk

āle,   câre,   ădd,   ärm,   ăsk;   mē,   hĕre,   ĕnd;   īce,   ĭll;

ŎNGKS
Bronx
conchs
(See also
ŎNGK; add
-s where
appropriate.)

ŎNGST
alongst
belong'st
long'st
prolong'st
throng'st
wrong'st

ŎNGZ
belongs
tongs
(See also
ŎNG; add
-s where
appropriate.)

ŎNS
ensconce
nonce
response
sconce

ŌNT
don't
won't

ÔNT
aflaunt
ataunt
avaunt

daunt
flaunt
gaunt
haunt
jaunt
romaunt
taunt
vaunt
want

ŎNT
Dupont
font
Hellespont
want

ŎNTS
fonts
wants
(See also
ŎNS.)

ŌNZ
atones
Davy Jones
Jones
nones
(See also ŌN;
add -s where
appropriate.)

ŎNZ
bonze
bronze
bygones
Johns
pons
(See also ŎN;
add -s where

appropriate.)

ŎŎD
could
deadwood
firewood
good
hood
misunderstood
plastic wood
purple wood
sandalwood
should
stood
understood
Underwood
unhood
wildwood
withstood
wood
would

angelhood
babyhood
brotherhood
deaconhood
fatherhood
foolhardihood
gentlemanhood
hardihood
kinglihood
kittenhood
ladyhood
likelihood
livelihood
lustihood
maidenhood
manhood

matronhood
monkshood
motherhood
neighborhood
orphanhood
parenthood
sisterhood
spinsterhood
unlikelihood
widowerhood
widowhood
womanhood

ŎŎK
betook
book
brook
Chinook
cook
crook
forsook
hook
inglenook
look
minute book
mistook
nook
outlook
overlook
overtook
partook
pastrycook
pocketbook
rook
shook
took
unhook
undertook
uplook

OŎKS
Crookes
crooks
snooks
tenterhooks
(See also OŎK;
add -s where
appropriate.)

OŎL
abb wool
bull
cock-and-bull
full
Kabul
lamb's wool
pull
wool

beautiful
bountiful
dutiful
fanciful
masterful
merciful
pitiful
plentiful
powerful
sorrowful
thimbleful
unmerciful
weariful
wonderful
worshipful

acceptable
accessible

accountable
adorable
affable
amenable
amiable
attainable
audible
available
avoidable
believable
capable
changeable
combustible
commendable
compatible
constable
contemptible
corruptible
crucible
culpable
damnable
delectable
deplorable
desirable
detestable
flexible
forcible
horrible
illegible
immovable
immutable
impalpable
impassable
impeccable
imperturbable
implacable
impossible
impregnable
improbable

improvable
inaccessible
inadmissible
inaudible
incapable
incomparable
incompatible
incomprehensi-
ble
inconceivable
incontestable
incontrovert-
ible
incorruptible
incredible
incurable
indelible
indescribable
indestructible
indispensable
ineffable
ineffaceable
inexcusable
inexhaustible
inexpressible
infallible
inflammable
inflexible
infrangible
inscrutable
insensible
insoluble
insupportable
insupposable
insuppressible
insurmount-
able
intangible
intelligible

interchangeable
intractible
invaluable
invincible
irascible
irrepressible
irreproachable
irresistible
irresponsible
irretrievable
justifiable
laudable
legible
Mehitable
mutable
notable
ostensible
palpable
passable
perceptible
permissible
placable
plausible
portable
possible
praisable
presentable
principle
probable
procurable
producible
pronounceable
ratable
redeemable
reliable
reprehensible
respectable
responsible
sensible

āle, câre, ădd, ärm, ăsk; mē, hĕre, ĕnd; īce, ĭll;

susceptible
syllable
tangible
tenable
terrible
tractable
unimpeachable
unmatchable
unquenchable
visible
voluble

OͦOLF
wolf

OͦOLVZ
wolves

OͦOS
puss

OͦOSH
bramble bush
bush
push

OͦOSK
brusque

OͦOT
afoot
foot
forefoot
pussyfoot
put
underfoot

OͦOTS
kibbutz

Schmutz
toots

ÔP
agrope
allotrope
amnioscope
antelope
antipope
apocope
aslope
astroscope
baroscope
bioscope
bronchoscope
cantaloupe
Cape of Good
   Hope
chronoscope
cope
diascope
dichroscope
dispope
dope
downslope
dragrope
electroscope
elope
endoscope
envelope
epidiascope
episcope
fluoroscope
footrope
galvanoscope
gastroscope
grope
gyroscope
helioscope

heliotrope
hope
horoscope
hydroscope
hygroscope
iconoscope
interlope
isotope
jump rope
kaleidoscope
kinescope
laparoscope
laryngoscope
lope
lycanthrope
manrope
metope
microscope
misanthrope
mope
myope
nope
ope
ophthalmo-
   scope
oscilloscope
otoscope
periscope
phalarope
pharyngoscope
philanthrope
polariscope
polemoscope
pope
proctoscope
protopope
pyrope
radarscope
radioisotope

rope
roup
sandsoap
scope
seismoscope
skiascope
skip rope
slope
sniperscope
snooperscope
soap
soft soap
soft-soap
spectroscope
statoscope
stauroscope
stereoscope
stethoscope
stope
stroboscope
tachistoscope
taupe
telescope
thermoscope
tightrope
tope
towrope
trope
unpope
upslope
urethroscope
zoetrope
zoopraxiscope

ÔP
gaup
scaup
whaup
yawp

ŎP

Aesop
aftercrop
agitprop
airdrop
atop
backdrop
backstop
barbershop
barhop
bebop
bedrop
bellhop
big top
blacktop
bookshop
bop
Boskop
carhop
carrottop
catch crop
chop
chop-chop
clip-clop
clippety-clop
clop
clop-clop
coffee shop
coin-op
co-op
cop
crop
desktop
dewdrop
doorstop
dop
drop
eardrop
eavesdrop

estop
flattop
flip-flop
flippity-flop
flip-top
flop
fop
foretop
full stop
galop
ginger pop
glop
grogshop
gumdrop
hardtop
hedgehop
hilltop
hippity-hop
hop
housetop
intercrop
joypop
karate chop
knop
kop
lollipop
lop
maintop
malaprop
milksop
mizzen top
mop
mountaintop
netop
nonstop
op
orlop
outcrop
overcrop

overtop
paradrop
pawnshop
plop
pop
pop-top
prop
pull-top
quop
raindrop
redtop
reprop
rest stop
riding crop
rollmop
rooftop
scop
sex shop
sharecrop
shop
short-stop
slipslop
slop
snowdrop
soda pop
sop
soursop
stonecrop
stop
strop
swap
sweatshop
sweetshop
sweetsop
table-hop
tabletop
teardrop
tea shop
tip-top

top
traffic cop
treetop
turboprop
underprop
unstop
whop
wineshop
wop
workshop

ŎPS

copse
drops
(See also ŎP;
add -s where
appropriate.)

ŌPT

eloped
unhoped
unsoaped
(See also ŌP;
add -ed where
appropriate.)

ŎPT

adopt
copped
Copt
dropped
outcropped
uncropped
unstopped
(See also ŎP;
add -ed where
appropriate.)

ŌR

adore
afore
albacore
ashore
backdoor
Baltimore
battledore
before
boar
Boer
bore
chore
commodore
core
corps
crore
death's door
deplore
door
encore
evermore
explore
first floor
floor
folklore
footsore
forbore
fore
foreshore
forswore
four
fourscore
frore
furthermore
galore
gore
heartsore
heretofore

hoar
ignore
implore
inshore
Lahore
lore
matador
mirador
more
nevermore
oar
o'er
ore
outpour
outroar
outsoar
Parramore
picador
pinafore
pore
pour
restore
roar
sagamore
score
seashore
semaphore
shore
Singapore
snore
soar
sophomore
sore
spore
stevedore
store
swore
sycamore
Theodore

tore
troubadour
underscore
uproar
upsoar
weather shore
whore
wore
yore

ÔR

abhor
ambassador
ancestor
anterior
apparitor
assignor
auditor
bachelor
chancellor
competitor
compositor
conquerer
conspirator
contributor
corridor
councillor
counselor
creditor
depositor
dinosaur
dor
Doukhobor
Ecuador
editor
emperor
excelsior
executor
expositor

exterior
for
governor
guarantor
ichthyosaur
inferior
inheritor
inquisitor
interior
interlocutor
janitor
Labrador
legator
lessor
lor
louis d'or
man-of-war
matador
metaphor
meteor
minotaur
mirador
monitor
mortgagor
nominor
nor
or
orator
posterior
primogenitor
progenitor
proprietor
Salvador
scaur
senator
senor
servitor
solicitor
superior

therefore
Thor
tor
toreador
troubadour
ulterior
verderor
vice-chancellor
visitor
war

ÔRB
absorb
corb
orb
reabsorb
resorb

ÔRBD
absorbed
full-orbed
(See also ÔRB;
add -ed where
appropriate.)

ÔRCH
porch

ÔRCH
bortsch
scorch
torch

ÔRD
aboard
adored
afford
beaverboard
board

broadsword
ford
gourd
hoard
horde
ironing board
oared
seaboard
shuffleboard
surfboard
sword
undeplored
unexplored
ungored
unhoard
unimplored
unrestored
weatherboard
(See also ÔR;
add -ed where
appropriate.)

ÔRD
abhorred
accord
award
belord
bord
chord
concord
cord
disaccord
fiord
fjord
Ford
harpsichord
landlord
lord
lyrichord

master chord
McCord
misericord
Orde
overlord
polychord
record
reward
sward
unlord
video record
ward

ÔRF
corf
dwarf
wharf

ÔRG
morgue

ÔRJ
forge

ÔRJ
disgorge
engorge
George
gorge
regorge

ÔRK
pork

ÔRK
cork
fork
New York
"orch"

stork
torque
uncork
weeding fork
York

ÔRKD
corked
storked

ÔRL
orle
schorl
whorl

ÔRM
aciform
acinaciform
aciniform
aeriform
aliform
anguiform
anguilliform
aquiform
aswarm
baculiform
barnstorm
bestorm
biform
bound form
brainstorm
bromoform
bursiform
cairngorm
calciform
cheliform
chloroform
Cominform
conform

āle, câre, ădd, ärm, ăsk; mē, hĕre, ĕnd; īce, ĭll;

cordiform
corm
cribriform
cruciform
cubiform
cuculiform
cuculliform
cumuliform
cuneiform
deform
deiform
dendriform
dentiform
digitiform
disinform
diversiform
dolabriform
dorm
electroform
ensiform
eruciform
falciform
fibrilliform
filiform
fire storm
floriform
form
forme
free form
free-form
fungiform
fusiform
gasiform
hailstorm
hamiform
harengiform
hippocrepiform
ice storm
inform

iodoform
landform
lentiform
ligniform
linguiform
linguistic form
lukewarm
misform
misinform
moniliform
multiform
napiform
nitrochloroform
nitroform
norm
oviform
panduriform
pectiniform
pediform
perform
piliform
pisiform
planform
platform
plexiform
poculiform
preform
pyriform
quadriform
rainstorm
ramiform
reconform
re-form
reform
reinform
remiform
reniform
reperform
retransform

rewarm
salverform
sandstorm
scobiform
scrotiform
scutiform
scyphiform
snowstorm
squaliform
stelliform
storm
strombiform
sunny-warm
swarm
tauriform
tectiform
thunderstorm
transform
triform
turdiform
unciform
unform
uniform
unwarm
upswarm
variform
vermiform
vitriform
vulviform
warm
waveform
windstorm

ÔRMD
bestormed
unformed
uninformed
unperformed
unreformed

unstormed
well-informed
(See also
ÔRM; add
-*ed* where
appropriate.)

ÔRMTH
storm'th
warmth
(See also
ÔRM; add
-*'th* where
appropriate.)

ŌRN
bemourn
betorn
borne
bourn
foot-worn
forborne
forsworn
mourn
outworn
overborne
seaworn
shorn
sworn
toilworn
torn
unshorn
unsworn
waterworn
wave-worn
wayworn
weatherworn
worn
(See also ŌRN.)

ÔRN

adorn
alpenhorn
barleycorn
bescorn
blackthorn
born
buckthorn
Cape Horn
Capricorn
cloud-born
corn
disadorn
dishorn
drinking horn
firstborn
foghorn
forewarn
forlorn
French horn
greenhorn
hard porn
hawthorn
heaven-born
highborn
horn
Horne
hunting horn
inborn
kiddie porn
Langhorne
longicorn
lorn
lovelorn
Matterhorn
morn
night born
Norn
peppercorn

popcorn
porn
powderhorn
priming horn
readorn
scorn
sea-born
self-scorn
skyborne
soft porn
stillborn
suborn
thorn
tricorn
trueborn
unborn
unicorn
video porn
warn
yestermorn

ÔRND

bemourned
mourned
unmourned

ÔRND

adorned
unadorned
unforewarned
(See also
ÔRN; add
-ed where
appropriate.)

ÔRP

dorp
gorp
thorp

time warp
warp

ÔRPS

corpse
warps
(See also ÔRP;
add *-s* where
appropriate.)

ÔRS

coarse
course
discourse
divorce
enforce
force
hoarse
intercourse
perforce
recourse
reinforce
resource
source
watercourse

ÔRS

corse
dead horse
dextrorse
dorse
endorse
gorse
hobbyhorse
horse
Morse
Norse
remorse
retrorse

sea horse
stalking-horse
torse
unhorse

ÔRSK

torsk

ÔRST

addorsed
endorsed
horsed
Horst
unhorsed

ÔRT

comport
county court
court
davenport
decourt
deport
disport
export
fort
forte
import
misreport
passport
port
Porte
rapport
report
sally port
seaport
sport
support
transport
(See also ÔRT.)

āle, câre, ădd, ärm, ăsk; mē, hĕre, ĕnd; īce, ĭll;

ÔRT	*abhorr'th*	actuose	coloss
abort	north	adipose	cross
amort	Orth	aggerose	doss
assort	swarth	albuminose	double-cross
athwart	(See also ÔR;	*animose*	dross
bort	add -'*th* where	annulose	emboss
cavort	appropriate.)	bellicose	fiery cross
consort		cellulose	floss
contort	**ÔRTS**	close	fosse
detort	aborts	comatose	gloss
distort	quartz	cose	joss
escort	Schwartz	diagnose	lacrosse
exhort	shorts	dose	loss
extort	Swarz	engross	moss
mort	(See also ÔRT;	floccose	recross
ort	add -*s* where	foliose	rhinoceros
quart	appropriate.)	gibbose	rosy cross
resort		globose	sea moss
retort	**ÔRVZ**	glucose	Setebos
short	wharves	grandiose	toss
snort		gross	weeping cross
sort	**ÔRZ**	jocose	
swart	adores	metempsychose	**ŌSH**
thwart	all fours	morose	brioche
tort	Azores	nodose	cloche
wart	indoors	otiose	Foch
	outdoors	overdose	gauche
ŌRth	(See also ŌR;	underdose	guilloche
forth	add -*s* where	verbose	
fourth	appropriate.)		**ŎSH**
henceforth		**ÔS**	awash
pour'th	**ÔRZ**	applesauce	belly wash
setter-forth	Louis Quatorze	sauce	bewash
thenceforth	quatorze		bigosh
(See also ŌR;	(See also ÔR;	**ŎS**	Boche
add -'*th* where	add -*s* where	across	Bosche
appropriate.)	appropriate.)	albatross	bosh
		Bos	brainwash
ÔRth	**ŌS**	boss	debosh

ōld, ôr, ŏdd, oil, fŏŏt, out; ūse, ûrn, ŭp; THis, thin

eyewash
frosh
galosh
gosh
goulash
hogwash
josh
kibosh
mackintosh
McIntosh
mouthwash
musquash
nosh
Oshkosh
quash
slosh
splosh
squash
swash
tosh
wash
whitewash

ŎSHT
caboshed
great unwashed
squashed
unwashed
(See also ŎSH;
add -ed where
appropriate.)

ŎSK
bosk
imbosk
kiosk
mosque

ŎSP

wasp

ŌST
aftermost
bettermost
boast
bottommost
coast
dosed
engrossed
fingerpost
foremost
furthermost
ghost
hindermost
hithermost
host
innermost
lowermost
most
nethermost
northernmost
oast
outermost
post
riposte
roast
seacoast
southernmost
toast
undermost
uppermost
uttermost
westernmost
whipping post

ÔST
exhaust
holocaust

ŎST
accost
adossed
betossed
cabossed
cost
crossed
double-crossed
embossed
enmossed
frost
geognost
glasnost
hoarfrost
Lacoste
lost
Pentecost
sea-tossed
tempest-tossed
uncrossed
unlost
wast
(See also ŎS;
add -ed where
appropriate.)

ŌT
afloat
anecdote
antidote
asymptote
bedote
bequote
billy goat
bloat
bluethroat
boat
capote
coat

commote
compote
connote
côte
cote
coyote
creosote
cuttthroat
demote
denote
devote
diptote
dote
dovecote
dreamboat
eighth note
emote
entrecote
epidote
epirote
ferryboat
float
folkmote
Fomalhaut
footnote
garrote
gemot
gloat
goat
gote
grace note
greatcoat
groat
gunboat
half note
haut
houseboat
housecoat
iceboat

keelboat
keynote
lepidote
lifeboat
longboat
lote
manbote
matelote
misquote
moat
mote
motorboat
mountain goat
nanny goat
note
oat
old goat
outvote
overcoat
overwrote
papillote
pardalote
petticoat
pilot boat
ploat
pote
powerboat
promote
quarter note
quote
raincoat
recoat
red coat
redcoat
redevote
redingote
refloat
remote
requote

revote
rewrote
riverboat
rote
rowboat
sailboat
scapegoat
scote
sea boat
sheepcote
shoat
shote
showboat
sixteenth note
sixty-fourth
    note
slote
smote
sore throat
speedboat
sproat
starthroat
steamboat
stoat
strep throat
surcoat
surfboat
swingboat
table d'hote
tailcoat
telephote
thirty-second
    note
throat
topcoat
tote
towboat
trench coat
triptote

troat
turncoat
undercoat
underquote
underwrote
unquote
unsmote
vote
waistcoat
whaleboat
whitethroat
whole note
Witenagemot
woodnote
wrote
wyliecoat
zygote

ŎT

aeronaut
afterthought
aquanaut
argonaut
astraught
astronaut
aught
besought
bestraught
bethought
bewrought
bought
brought
caught
cosmonaut
dear-bought
distraught
dreadnought
forethought
fought

fraught
free thought
ghat
hard-fought
hydronaut
inwrought
juggernaut
maut
merrythought
methought
naught
nought
onslaught
ought
overwrought
self-taught
sought
taught
taut
thought
unbesought
unbought
unfought
unfraught
untaught
unthought
unwrought
upbrought
upcaught
wrought

ŎT

abwatt
aliquot
allot
apricot
ascot
asquat
beauty spot

begot	dovecot	hotchpot	night spot
bergamot	dry rot	Hotnot	not
besot	earshot	hot pot	ocelot
big shot	ergot	hotshot	overhand knot
bloodshot	eschalot	hot spot	overplot
blot	eyeshot	Hottentot	overshot
bot	feedlot	Huguenot	paraquat
bott	fiery hot	ill-got	patriot
bowknot	figure-eight	ingot	pentaglot
bowshot	knot	inkblot	Pequot
boycott	firepot	inkpot	peridot
buckshot	first begot	ink spot	phot
cachalot	five-spot	jackpot	plague spot
calotte	fleshpot	jogtrot	plot
Camelot	flowerpot	jot	plumcot
Candiote	foreshot	kilowatt	polka dot
cannot	forget-me-not	knot	polyglot
capot	forgot	kumquat	pot
chamber pot	fox-trot	Lancelot	potshot
cheap shot	fusspot	long shot	prolonge knot
chimney pot	galipot	loop knot	quot
chip shot	gallipot	loquat	red-hot
clot	garrote	Lot	reef knot
cocotte	gavotte	lot	reknot
coffeepot	gigawatt	love knot	replot
compatriot	gluepot	mandelbrot	repot
complot	Gordian knot	marmot	robot
cot	got	mascot	rot
counterplot	granny knot	massicot	sansculotte
crackpot	grapeshot	megawatt	Sciot
culotte	grassplot	melilot	Scot
Cypriot	grot	microdot	Scott
dashpot	guillemot	misbegot	secondary
despot	gunshot	monkey pot	boycott
dicot	hard-got	monoglot	sexpot
diddly-squat	heptaglot	moon shot	shallot
diglot	hexaglot	mot	shot
dogtrot	hipshot	motmot	shoulder knot
dot	hot	motte	sighting shot

āle,   câre,   ădd,   ärm,   ăsk;   mē,   hĕre,   ĕnd;   īce,   ĭll;

slapshot
slide knot
slingshot
slip knot
slot
snapshot
snot
somewhat
sot
spot
square knot
squat
stevedore knot
stinkpot
stockpot
stot
Stott
subplot
sunspot
surgeon's knot
swat
swot
talipot
teapot
ten-spot
terawatt
tetraglot
tin pot
tommyrot
topknot
tosspot
tot
trot
truelove knot
true lover's
   knot
turkey trot
unbegot
underplot

undershot
unforgot
ungot
unknot
upshot
wainscot
wat
watt
what
whatnot
white-hot
witenagemot
wot
yacht

ŌTH
clothe
loathe

Ŏth
aftergrowth
behemoth
betroth
both
growth
loath
oath
overgrowth
quoth
sloth
Thoth
troth
undergrowth

Ôth
swath
wrath
wroth

Ŏth
Ashtaroth
barley broth
behemoth
broadcloth
broth
cloth
Coth
froth
Goth
moth
Ostrogoth
pilot cloth
saddlecloth
troth
Visigoth
wroth

ŌTS
boats
Coates
Oates
(See also ŌT;
add -s where
appropriate.)

ŎTS
Potts
(See also ŎT;
add -s where
appropriate.)

OU
allow
anyhow
avow
bough
bow

bowwow
brow
chow
cow
dhow
disallow
disavow
endow
enow
Foochow
frau
frow
Hankow
hoosegow
how
Howe
kowtow
Kwangchow
landau
mow
now
overbrow
plough
plow
powwow
prow
row
scow
slough
snowplow
somehow
Soochow
sow
Swatow
thou
upplow
vow
Wenchow
wow

ōld, ôr, ŏdd, oil, fŏŏt, out; ūse, ûrn, ŭp; THis, thin

OUCH
avouch
couch
crouch
grouch
ouch
pouch
scaramouch
slouch
vouch

OUD
allowed
aloud
becloud
beetle-browed
beshroud
cloud
crowd
disendowed
disenshroud
encloud
enshroud
intercloud
loud
overcloud
overcrowd
proud
shroud
thundercloud
unbowed
uncloud
unshroud
(See also OU;
add -ed where
appropriate.)

OUJ
gouge

scrouge

OUL
afoul
befoul
behowl
cowl
dowl
foul
fowl
growl
guinea fowl
howl
jowl
owl
peafowl
prowl
scowl
screech owl
seafowl
waterfowl

OULD
befouled
uncowled
(See also OUL;
add -ed where
appropriate.)

OUN
adown
breakdown
brown
Chinatown
clown
comedown
countdown
crosstown
crown

decrown
discrown
down
downtown
drown
eiderdown
embrown
evening gown
frown
godown
gown
hand-me-down
hoedown
lowdown
markdown
meltdown
midtown
Motown
nightgown
noun
nut-brown
Piltdown
pronoun
putdown
reach-me-down
renown
rubdown
shakedown
shantytown
showdown
shutdown
slowdown
splashdown
sundown
swansdown
touchdown
town
tumbledown
uncrown

ungown
upside-down
uptown

OUND
abound
aground
around
astound
background
bloodhound
bound
boozehound
browned
compound
confound
dumbfound
expound
flower-crowned
found
ground
hell bound
hidebound
homebound
hound
icebound
impound
inbound
ironbound
Mahound
merry-go-round
middle ground
mound
outbound
outward-bound
pine-crowned
pleasure
ground
pound

āle, câre, ădd, ärm, ăsk; mē, hĕre, ĕnd; īce, ĭll;

profound
propound
rebound
redound
renowned
resound
round
smut hound
sound
spellbound
superabound
surround
triple-crowned
ultrasound
unbound
underground
unground
unsound
vantage ground
wound
(See also
OUN; add -ed
where appro-
priate.)

OUNDZ
abounds
zounds
(See also
OUND; add
-s where
appropriate.)

OUNJ
lounge

OUNS
announce
bounce

denounce
enounce
flounce
frounce
ounce
pounce
pronounce
renounce
rounce
trounce
(See also
OUNT; add
-s where
appropriate.)

OUNT
account
amount
catamount
count
discount
dismount
fount
miscount
mount
paramount
recount
remount
surmount
tantamount

OUNTS
accounts
(See also
OUNT; add
-s where
appropriate.)

OUR

bescour
besour
deflour
devour
flour
hour
our
scour
sour
sustaining hour

OURD
bescoured
unsoured
(See also
OUR; add
-ed where
appropriate.)

OUS
alehouse
almshouse
backhouse
bakehouse
bathhouse
Bauhaus
bawdy house
birdhouse
black grouse
blockhouse
blouse
boardinghouse
boathouse
body louse
book louse
bughouse
bunkhouse
cathouse
chapter house

charnel house
charterhouse
chiaus
chophouse
chouse
clearinghouse
clothes louse
clubhouse
coach house
coffeehouse
cookhouse
countinghouse
courthouse
crab louse
crazy house
customhouse
deckhouse
deer mouse
degauss
delouse
doghouse
dollhouse
dormouse
doss house
douse
farmhouse
field mouse
firehouse
flindermouse
flittermouse
flophouse
fraternity
    house
full house
gashouse
gatehouse
gauss
glasshouse
Gnauss

ōld, ôr, ŏdd, oil, fŏŏt, out; ūse, ûrn, ŭp; THis, thin

grasshopper
  mouse
greenhouse
grouse
guardhouse
guesthouse
halfway house
harvest mouse
headhouse
head louse
henhouse
hothouse
house
house mouse
icehouse
jailhouse
jerboa mouse
jerboa pouched
  mouse
jumping mouse
kangaroo
  mouse
Kraus
lighthouse
lobscouse
longhouse
louse
madhouse
meadow mouse
meetinghouse
Mickey Mouse
mouse
nous
outhouse
penthouse
pilothouse
plant house
plant louse
playhouse

pleasure-house
pocket mouse
poorhouse
porterhouse
pothouse
powerhouse
prairie grouse
prison house
public house
red grouse
reremouse
roadhouse
roughhouse
roundhouse
row house
ruffed grouse
safe house
sage grouse
sand grouse
schoolhouse
scouse
shrewmouse
slaughterhouse
smokehouse
snow grouse
souse
sporting house
spouse
springhouse
statehouse
steakhouse
storehouse
Strauss
sugarhouse
summerhouse
sweathouse
teahouse
titmouse
tollhouse

town house
warehouse
water house
Westinghouse
wheelhouse
white-footed
  mouse
White House
whorehouse
Wodehouse
wood grouse
wood louse
workhouse

OUST
browst
choused
oust
roust
unhoused
(See also OUS;
add -ed where
appropriate.)

OUT
about
beshout
bespout
blackout
bout
boy scout
brownout
buyout
carryout
clout
cookout
cop-out
devout
diner-out

doubt
drinking bout
dropout
drought
dugout
fallout
flout
gadabout
girl scout
gout
grout
hangout
hereabout
hereout
holdout
holing out
in-and-out
knockabout
knockout
knout
kraut
lockout
lookout
lout
mahout
out
out-and-out
pig out
pout
put out
rain out
redoubt
right-about
roundabout
roustabout
rout
sauerkraut
scout
shout

shutout
snout
spaced-out
spout
sprout
stakeout
stirabout
stout
takeout
thereabout
thereout
throughout
tout
trout
tryout
turnout
umlaut
washout
waterspout
whereabout
whereout
without

OUTH
mouthe

OUth
allow'th
bemouth
drouth
mouth
south
(See also OU;
add -'th where
appropriate.)

OUTS
bouts
hereabouts

outs
thereabouts
whereabouts
(See also OUT;
add -s where
appropriate.)

OUZ
arouse
blouse
blowze
bouse
browse
carouse
drowse
espouse
house
rouse
souse
spouse
touse
unhouse
unprouse
(See also OU;
add -s where
appropriate.)

ŌV
clove
cove
dove
drove
grove
hove
interwove
inwove
Jove
mauve
rove

shrove
stove
strove
throve
treasure trove
wove

ŎV
hereof
of
thereof
whereof

ŌZ
arose
bramble rose
brose
chose
close
clothes
compose
couleur de rose
damask rose
decompose
depose
disclose
discompose
dispose
doze
enclose
expose
foreclose
froze
gloze
hose
impose
inclose
indispose
interclose

interpose
moss rose
nose
oppose
pose
predispose
presuppose
propose
prose
recompose
repose
rose
superpose
suppose
those
transpose
tuberose
unclose
unfroze
(See also Ō;
add -s where
appropriate.)

ÔZ
applause
because
cause
clause
Dawes
gauze
Hawes
hawse
lantern jaws
menopause
pause
taws
vase
yaws
(See also Ô;

ōld, ôr, ŏdd, oil, fŏŏt, out; ūse, ûrn, ŭp; THis, thin

add -*s* where | **ŌZD** | unopposed | eloge
appropriate.) | closed | well-disposed | loge
 | dozed | (See also ŌZ; |
ŎZ | ill-disposed | add -*ed* where | **ŎZ'M**
Boz | indisposed | appropriate.) | macrocosm
Oz | juxtaposed | | microcosm
was | predisposed | **ŌƵH** |

U

These words includes the following accented vowel sounds:

Ū as in *use;* heard also in *beauty, feud, pew, queue, lieu, view, cue, suit, yule, you, do, rule, true, food, group, drew, fruit, canoe, rheum, maneuver, blue.* The difference between *dew* and *do* is that *dew* is properly dyŪ, with a consonantal *y* sound preceding the long U, while *do* is merely dŪ.

Û as in *urn;* heard also in *fern, err, heard, sir, word, journal, myrrh, colonel.*

Ŭ as in *up;* heard also in *won, one, does, flood, double.*

For the vowel sound in *full,* see under ŎŎ.

Ū	argue	*beshrew*	cachou
acajou	askew	bestrew	calalu
accrue	Attu	bhikshu	canoe
adieu	avenue	bijou	cap screw
ado	baboo	billet-doux	caribou
Agnew	babu	blew	cashew
ague	baku	blue	catechu
ahu	ballyhoo	boo	chandoo
aircrew	bamboo	boo-boo	chew
airscrew	Bantu	boohoo	choochoo
aku	barbecue	brake shoe	chou
amadou	barley-broo	brew	clerihew
Andrew	Bartholomew	broo	clew
anew	battue	buckaroo	clue
aperçu	bayou	bugaboo	coach screw
Archimedes'	bazoo	bunraku	cock-a-doodle-
screw	bedew	burgoo	doo

āle, câre, ădd, ärm, ăsk; mē, hĕre, ĕnd; īce, ĭll;

cockapoo
cockatoo
conspue
construe
coo
cooboo
Corfu
corkscrew
coup
couru
coypu
crew
crewe
cru
cuckoo
cue
curfew
curlew
curlicue
cuscousou
Daibutsu
Daikoku
Danu
debut
Depew
derring-do
dew
didgeridoo
Dien Bien Phu
differential
   screw
do
doo-doo
drew
due
ecru
ejoo
elephant shrew
Elihu

emu
endew
endue
enew
ensue
entre nous
eschew
ewe
feu
feverfew
few
fichu
firenew
Fitzhugh
flew
flu
flue
fondue
fordo
foreknew
fou
froufrou
gardyloo
garoo
gayyou
Gentoo
genu
gillaroo
glue
gnu
golf shoe
goo
goo-goo
goût
Grand Cru
grew
grue
gugu
gumshoe

guru
gym shoe
hairdo
halloo
haut gout
Hebrew
hereinto
hereto
hereunto
hew
Hindley's
   screw
Hindu
hitherto
honeydew
Honolulu
Honshu
hoochinoo
hoodoo
hoopoe
horseshoe
how-do-you-do
hue
Hugh
hullabaloo
Hutu
igloo
imbrue
imbue
immew
impromptu
imu
indue
ingenue
interrupted
   screw
interview
into
in transitu

IOU
Irish stew
jabiru
jackeroo
jack screw
Jesu
Jew
Ju
jujitsu
juju
Kalamazoo
kangaroo
karroo
Katmandu
kazoo
kerchoo
Kew
Khufu
Kinabalu
kinkajou
knew
kudu
kung fu
kuru
kwazoku
Kyushu
lag screw
lasso
lean-to
lieu
long-tailed
   shrew
loo
loup-garou
lulliloo
lulu
machine screw
Machu Picchu
mafoo

ōld, ôr, ŏdd, oil, fŏŏt, out; ūse, ûrn, ûp; THis, thin

malentendu
Malibu
Manchu
Manitou
Manu
Matthew
meadow rue
mew
mildew
mirabile dictu
misconstrue
misdo
Mogadishu
Montague
moo
mountain dew
move
mu
Mu
muumuu
napoo
Nehru
nephew
new
night dew
non-U
nu
Nu
old-shoe
onto
ooh
ormolu
outdo
outgrew
overdo
overdrew
overdue
overflew
overgrew

overshoe
overstrew
overthrew
overview
pari passu
parlez-vous
parvenu
passe-partout
pâté à chou
peekaboo
perdu
Peru
pew
phew
phoo
plew
poilu
poo
pooh
pooh-pooh
Port Salut
potoroo
Premier Cru
preview
prie-dieu
pugh
Pugh
Purdue
purlicue
purlieu
pursue
purview
queue
ragout
reconstrue
redo
redrew
reglue
regrew

rendezvous
renew
Renfrew
reshoe
residue
resue
retinue
revenue
review
revue
right-handed
  screw
rompu
roo
roughhew
roux
rue
running shoe
sapajou
screw
sea mew
see-through
self-tapping
  screw
set-to
setscrew
shampoo
shapoo
Shih Tzu
shizoku
Shluh
shoe
shoo
short-tailed
  shrew
shrew
shu
Shu
Sioux

skew
skidoo
sky-blue
slew
sloo
slough
slue
smew
snowshoe
soft-shoe
sou
spew
spreeuw
sprue
stage screw
stew
strew
subdue
succès fou
sue
sundrew
surtout
surview
susu
switcheroo
taboo
tap shoe
tapping screw
tattoo
teju
teledu
tennis shoe
tew
thereinto
thereto
thereunto
thew
thitherto
threw

āle, câre, ădd, ärm, ăsk; mē, hĕre, ĕnd; īce, ĭll;

		ŬB	crutch
through	wahoo		cutch
thumbscrew	wallaroo	battle club	Dutch
Timaru	wanderoo	Beelzebub	forasmuch
Timbuktu	Waterloo	blub	hutch
tinamou	waterloo	.bub	inasmuch
Tippecanoe	water shrew	chub	insomuch
to	well-to-do	Chubb	master touch
to-do	Whangpoo	club	much
toe shoe	whereinto	Clubb	mutch
too	whereto	cub	overmuch
toodle-oo	whereunto	drub	retouch
to-whit-towhoo	whew	dub	scutch
tree shrew	who	fub	smutch
trou-de-loup	Who's Who	grub	such
true	widdifow	hub	touch
true-blue	witches' brew	hubbub	
tutu	withdrew	nub	**ŬCHD**
Tuvalu	woo	pub	clutched
twenty-three	wooden shoe	rub	untouched
skidoo	wood screw	rub-a-dub	(See also ŬCH;
two	worricow	scrub	add -ed where
unclew	Wu	shrub	appropriate.)
underdo	Wuhu	sillabub	
undo	Xanadu	slub	**ŪD**
undue	yahoo	snub	abrood
unglue	yew	stub	*abstrude*
unmew	ynambu	sub	*acerbitude*
unscrew	yoo-hoo	tub	*acritude*
unshoe	you		allude
unto	zebu	**ŬCH**	altitude
untrue	zoo	brooch	*amaritude*
Urdu	zoozoo	cooch	amplitude
vendue	Zulu	hooch	aptitude
view		hoochy-cooch	assuetude
view halloo	**ŪB**	mooch	attitude
virtu	boob	pooch	beatitude
virtue	cube		brood
Vishnu	Rube	**ŬCH**	certitude
voodoo	tube	clutch	

ōld, ôr, ŏdd, oil, fŏŏt, out; ūse, ûrn, ŭp; THis, thin

claritude
collude
conclude
consuetude
crassitude
crude
decrepitude
definitude
delude
denude
desuetude
detrude
disquietude
dude
elude
exactitude
exclude
extrude
exude
fast-food
feud
finitude
food
fortitude
gratitude
habitude
hebetude
home brewed
illude
inaptitude
incertitude
include
ineptitude
infinitude
ingratitude
inquietude
insuetude
interclude
interlude

intrude
Jude
lassitude
latitude
lenitude
lewd
longitude
lude
magnitude
mansuetude
mollitude
mood
multitude
necessitude
nude
obtrude
occlude
parvitude
platitude
plenitude
pood
preclude
prelude
promptitude
protrude
prude
pulchritude
Quaalude
quietude
rainbow hued
reclude
rectitude
retrude
rood
rude
seclude
senectitude
serenitude
servitude

shrewd
similitude
slewed
snood
solicitude
solitude
stude
subnude
subtrude
thewed
torpitude
transude
turpitude
unglued
unpursued
unrenewed
unrude
unrued
unstrewed
unsubdued
unwooed
vastitude
verisimilitude
vicissitude
you'd
(See also Ū;
add -*ed* where
appropriate.)

ŪD
bestud
blood
bud
Budd
cud
dud
flood
fud
HUD

Judd
lifeblood
lud
mud
rudd
'sblood
scud
spud
stud
thud

ŬDZ
buds
duds
suds
(See also ŬD;
add -*s* where
appropriate.)

ŪF
aloof
behoof
bulletproof
disproof
fireproof
foolproof
gable roof
goof
hoof
loof
opera-bouffe
proof
reproof
roof
shadoof
spoof
Tartuffe
unroof
virtue proof

waterproof
weatherproof
woof

ŬF
bepuff
besnuff
blindman's buff
bluff
breadstuff
buff
chough
chuff
clough
counterbuff
cuff
duff
enough
fluff
garden stuff
gruff
huff
luff
muff
off-the-cuff
on the cuff
powder puff
puff
rebuff
rough
ruff
scruff
scuff
slough
snuff
sough
stuff
tough
tuff

ŬFS
bepuffs
fisticuffs
(See also ŬF;
add -s where
appropriate.)

ŪFT
cloven-hoofed
hoofed
roofed
(See also ŪF;
add -ed where
appropriate.)

ŬFT
bepuffed
candytuft
tuft
(See also ŬF;
add -ed where
appropriate.)

ŪG
fugue

ŬG
bug
bunny hug
debug
doodlebug
drug
dug
fug
hug
jitterbug
jug
litterbug
lug

mug
plug
pug
rug
shrug
slug
smug
snug
thug
trug
tug

ŬGZ
drugs
go bugs
(See also ŬG;
add -s where
appropriate.)

ŪJ
demonifuge
febrifuge
gamboge
huge
insectifuge
Scrooge
scrouge
stooge
subterfuge
vermifuge

ŬJ
adjudge
begrudge
budge
drudge
forejudge
fudge
grudge

judge
misjudge
nudge
prejudge
rejudge
Rudge
sludge
smudge
trudge

ŬJD
adjudged
ill-judged
unjudged
(See also ŬJ;
add -ed where
appropriate.)

ŪK
archduke
bashi-bazouk
beduke
chibouk
Chinook
duke
fluke
Heptateuch
Hexateuch
juke
kook
Luke
mameluke
Marmaduke
nuke
Pentateuch
peruke
puke
rebuke
snook

spook
stook

ŬK
amuck
awestruck
beduck
beginner's luck
buck
Canuck
chuck
cluck
dead duck
Donald Duck
duck
dumb cluck
dumbstruck
fast buck
fuck
guck
high-muck-a-
  muck
horror-struck
ill luck
Kalmuck
Lady Luck
lame duck
laverock
luck
megabuck
misluck
moonstruck
muck
muckamuck
nip and tuck
pluck
potluck
puck
roebuck

ruck
rukh
sawbuck
schmuck
shuck
stagestruck
struck
stuck
suck
sunstruck
terror struck
thunderstruck
truck
tuck
waterbuck
wonder struck
woodchuck
yuk

ŬKS
big bucks
crux
dux
flux
lux
shucks
(See also ŬK;
add -s where
appropriate.)

ŬKT
abduct
aqueduct
beducked
conduct
construct
deduct
duct
educt

eruct
good-plucked
induct
instruct
misconduct
misconstruct
obstruct
oviduct
product
reduct
reluct
subduct
substruct
superstruct
unplucked
usufruct
viaduct
(See also ŬK;
add -ed where
appropriate.)

ŪL
April Fool
befool
buhl
carpool
charity school
cool
dirty pool
drool
ducking stool
fool
footstool
gene pool
ghoul
Istambul
Liverpool
mewl
misrule

molecule
mule
O'Toole
overrule
pool
pule
reticule
ridicule
rule
school
spool
stool
Sunday school
toadstool
tool
Toole
tulle
vermicule
vestibule
whirlpool
who'll
you'll
Yule

ŬL
ahull
annul
barnacle
chronicle
cull
disannul
dull
gull
hull
lull
miracle
Mogul
monocle
mull

numskull
obstacle
pinnacle
scull
seagull
skull
spectacle
stull
trull
vehicle
versicle

ŬLB
bulb

ŬLCH
gulch
mulch

ŪLD
unruled
unschooled
(See also ŪL;
add -d where
appropriate.)

ŬLD
annulled
mulled
thick-skulled
(See also ŬL;
add -ed where
appropriate.)

ŬLF
engulf
gulf

ŬLJ
bulge
divulge
effulge
indulge
promulge

ŬLK
bulk
hulk
skulk
sulk

ŬLKT
bulked
hulked
mulct
(See also ŬLK;
add -ed where
appropriate.)

ŬLM
culm

ŪLP
poulp

ŬLP
gulp
pulp
sculp

ŬLS
appulse
bulse
convulse
dulse
expulse

impulse
mulse
pulse
repulse
(See also ŬLT;
add -s where
appropriate.)

ŬLT
adult
catapult
consult
cult
difficult
exult
incult
indult
insult
occult
result

ŪLZ
gules
(See also ŪL;
add -s where
appropriate.)

ŪM
abloom
addoom
anteroom
assume
baby boom
begloom
beplume
bloom
boom
bridegroom
broom

brougham
brume
consume
coom
coomb
costume
disentomb
displume
doom
dining room
drawing room
dressing room
elbowroom
embloom
engloom
entomb
enwomb
exhume
flume
foredoom
fume
gloom
groom
grume
heirloom
illume
inhume
jibboom
khartoum
legume
living room
loom
lumber room
perfume
plume
power loom
predoom
presume
reading room

ōld, ôr, ŏdd, oil, fŏŏt, out; ūse, ûrn, ŭp; THis, thin

reassume
relume
resume
rheum
room
sea room
simoom
spoom
spume
subsume
tomb
unplume
untomb
whom
womb

ŬM

ad libitum
adventuresome
adytum
aquarium
auditorium
become
benumb
bum
bumbledom
burdensome
cardamom
christendom
chrysanthe-
  mum
chum
cockneydom
come
compendium
consortium
cranium
crematorium
crum

crumb
cumbersome
curriculum
delirium
drearisome
drum
dumb
emporium
encomium
epithalamium
equilibrium
exordium
fee-fi-fo-fum
flunkeydom
frolicsome
geranium
glum
grum
gum
gymnasium
halidom
heathendom
hum
humdrum
humorsome
intermeddle-
  some
kettledrum
laudanum
lum
martyrdom
maximum
meddlesome
medium
mettlesome
millennium
minimum
misbecome
modicum

moratorium
mum
natatorium
numb
odium
opium
opprobrium
overcome
pabulum
palladium
pandemonium
pelargonium
pendulum
pericardium
petroleum
platinum
plum
plumb
premium
prud'homme
psyllium
quarrelsome
quietsome
radium
rascaldom
rebeldom
recumb
residuum
rhumb
rum
sanatorium
saxondom
scrum
scum
sensorium
slum
some
speculum
strum

stum
succumb
sugarplum
sum
swum
symposium
tedium
thrum
thumb
troublesome
tum
tum-tum
tweedledum
tympanum
unplumb
vacuum
venturesome
viaticum
wearisome
worrisome
wranglesome

ŪMD

addoomed
assumed
full-bloomed
implumed
unfumed
ungloomed
unillumed
(See also ŪM;
add -*ed* where
appropriate.)

ŬMD

begummed
benumbed
bethumbed
unplumbed

āle, câre, ădd, ärm, ăsk; mē, hĕre, ĕnd; īce, ĭll;

ŬMD

(See also ŬM;
add -ed where
appropriate.)

ŬMP
bethump
bump
chump
clump
crump
dump
frump
hump
jump
lump
mugwump
mump
plump
pump
rump
slump
stump
sump
thump
trump
tump
ump

ŬMPS
bethumps
mumps
(See also ŬMP;
add -s where
appropriate.)

ŪN
afternoon
apolune
aswoon

attune
autoimmune
baboon
balloon
barracoon
bassoon
batoon
Behistun
bestrewn
boon
Boone
bridoon
Broun
buffoon
cacoon
Calhoun
Cameroon
cardoon
cartoon
cocoon
coffee spoon
cohune
Colquoun
commune
coon
coquetoon
croon
demilune
dessertspoon
detune
Doon
doubloon
dragoon
dune
eftsoon
entune
excommune
expugn
festoon

forenoon
frigatoon
full moon
gadroon
galloon
gambroon
gazon
goon
gossoon
Gudrun
Half Moon
half-moon
harpoon
harvest moon
hewn
high noon
honeymoon
immune
importune
impugn
inopportune
intercommune
jejune
June
Kowloon
kroon
lacune
lagoon
lampoon
loon
lune
macaroon
Mahoun
maroon
matzoon
midnoon
monsoon
moon
musketoon

Neptune
new moon
noon
octoroon
old moon
opportune
oppugn
oversoon
overstrewn
Pantaloon
pantaloon
patroon
perilune
picaroon
picayune
platoon
poltroon
pontoon
poon
prune
puccoon
quadroon
quintroon
raccoon
Rangoon
ratoon
repugn
retune
rigadoon
rockoon
roughhewn
runcible spoon
rune
saloon
sand dune
saskatoon
Saskatoon
scandaroon
Schroon

ōld, ôr, ŏdd, oil, fŏŏt, out; ūse, ûrn, ŭp; THis, thin

seroon
shalloon
shoon
silver spoon
simoon
soon
spadroon
spittoon
spontoon
spoon
strewn
swoon
tablespoon
teaspoon
testoon
toon
tribune
triune
tuchun
tune
Tycoon
typhoon
unhewn
untune
vinegarroon
waning moon
waxing moon
wooden spoon
woon
walloon

ŬN
A-1
accordion
Albion
amazon
begun
benison
bun

Bunn
cardamon
caparison
cinnamon
colophon
comparison
Chesterton
done
dun
Dunn
foredone
forerun
foster son
fun
galleon
Galveston
ganglion
garrison
gonfalon
gun
halcyon
hard run
hard won
Helicon
homespun
hon
Hun
jettison
Middleton
minute gun
mon
myrmidon
none
Number one
nun
Oberon
oblivion
octagon
one

outdone
outrun
overdone
overrun
pantechnicon
paragon
Parthenon
pentagon
percussion gun
phenomenon
polygon
prolegomenon
pun
quaternion
run
Sally Lunn
shun
simpleton
singleton
skeleton
son
spun
stun
sun
sunn
ton
tun
unbegun
underrun
undone
unison
unnun
venison
Whitsun
won

ŬNCH
box lunch
brunch

bunch
clunch
crunch
free lunch
hunch
lunch
munch
punch
scrunch

ŪND
attuned
crooned
disattuned
unattuned
untuned
wound
(See also ŪN;
add -ed where
appropriate.)

ŬND
bund
cummerbund
dunned
fund
immund
moribund
obrotund
orotund
punned
refund
retund
Rosamond
rotund
rubicund
shunned
stunned
unparagoned

āle,   câre,   ădd,   ärm,   ăsk;   mē,   hĕre,   ĕnd;   īce,   ĭll;

unsunned
verecund
(See also
ŬN; add
-*ed* where
appropriate.)

ŬNG

among
behung
betongue
bung
clung
dung
flung
high-strung
hung
lung
mother tongue
overhung
pung
rung
slung
sprung
strung
stung
sung
swung
tongue
underhung
Ung
unhung
unstrung
unsung
unwrung
upsprung
wither-wrung
wrung
young

ŬNGD

bunged
double-tongued
honey-tongued
leather-lunged
loud-lunged
pleasant-
    tongued
shrill-tongued
silver-tongued
tongued
trumpet-
    tongued

ŬNGK

bunk
chunk
debunk
drunk
flunk
funk
hunk
junk
monk
plunk
punk
quidnunc
shrunk
skunk
slunk
spunk
stunk
sunk
trunk
unk
wunk

ŬNGKT

bunked

compunct
conjunct
defunct
disjunct
funked
trunked

ŬNGST

amongst
clung'st
(See also
ŬNG; add
-*'st* where
appropriate.)

ŬNJ

allonge
blunge
dispunge
expunge
lunge
muskellunge
plunge
sponge

ŬNS

dunce
once
(See also ŬNT;
add -*s* where
appropriate.)

ŬNT

affront
afront
blunt
breakfront
brunt
bunt

confront
cunt
exeunt
forefront
front
grunt
hunt
Lunt
manhunt
punt
runt
seafront
shunt
sprunt
stunt
waterfront
witch-hunt
wont

ŬNth

month
run'th
(See also ŬN;
add -*'th* where
appropriate.)

ŬNZ

Cameroons
croons
eftsoons
(See also ŬN;
add -*s* where
appropriate.)

ŬP

adroop
aggroup
apple scoop
cantaloupe

cock-a-hoop
coop
croup
droop
drupe
dupe
Guadeloupe
group
hoop
jupe
liripoop
loop
nincompoop
poop
recoup
roup
scoop
scroop
sloop
soup
stoop
stoup
supe
swoop
troop
troupe
unhoop
whoop

ŬP
backup
blowing-up
blowup
breakup
buildup
buttercup
buy-up
catch-up
checkup

chin-up
cleanup
close-up
coverup
crup
cup
dial-up
fed up
Gallup
getup
grace cup
grown-up
gup
hangup
hard up
hiccup
holdup
hookup
ketchup
keyed up
larrup
letup
lineup
linkup
lockup
lookup
loving cup
makeup
markup
mock-up
pasteup
pickup
pinup
pull-up
punch-up
pup
push-up
roundup
scup

send-up
setter-up
setup
slap-up
smashup
speedup
stickup
stirrup cup
sunup
sup
teacup
tone-up
toss-up
tup
turnup
up
up-and-up
wake-up
warm-up
wassail cup
whup
windup
write-up

ŬPT
abrupt
corrupt
cupped
disrupt
erupt
incorrupt
interrupt
supped

ŪR
abature
abbreviature
abjure
adjure

allure
amateur
amour
aperture
armature
assure
blackamoor
boor
breviature
brochure
calenture
candidature
caricature
cocksure
colure
comfiture
conjure
connoisseur
contour
çoverture
cure
curvature
cynosure
demure
detour
discomfiture
divestiture
dure
endure
ensure
entablature
epicure
expenditure
forfeiture
furniture
garmenture
garniture
guipure
immature

āle,   câre,   ădd,   ärm,   ăsk;   mē,   hĕre,   ĕnd;   īce,   ĭll;

immure
impure
insecure
insure
intermure
inure
investiture
judicature
Kohinoor
ligature
liqueur
literature
lure
manicure
manure
mature
miniature
moor
obscure
Ostermoor
overture
paramour
pedicure
perdure
perendure
poor
portraiture
premature
primogeniture
procure
pure
quadrature
reassure
reinsure
secure
sepulture
signature
sinecure
spoor

sure
tablature
temperature
tour
troubadour
unmoor
unsure
vestiture
water cure
your
you're

ÛR
aberr
astir
aver
befur
bestir
blur
burr
chirr
concur
confer
cur
defer
demur
deter
disinter
err
fir
fur
her
incur
infer
inter
Kerr
knur
liqueur
myrrh

occur
per
prefer
purr
recur
refer
shirr
sir
slur
spur
stir
transfer
were
whir

accoucheur
amateur
chasseur
chauffeur
coeur
colporteur
connoisseur
farceur
franc-tireur
friseur
frondeur
hauteur
litterateur
mitrailleur
persifleur
restaurateur
trouveur
voltigeur
voyageur

administer
admonisher

adulterer
adventurer
affiancer
almoner
amphitheater
answerer
arbiter
arbitrageur
archiater
armiger
armorer
artificer
astrologer
astronomer
autobiographer
baluster
banisher
banister
banqueter
banterer
bargainer
barometer
barrister
barterer
batterer
bibliographer
bickerer
biographer
blandisher
blazoner
blunderer
blusterer
borrower
botherer
brandisher
broiderer
burdener
burnisher
calendar

ōld, ôr, ŏdd, oil, fŏŏt, out; ūse, ûrn, ŭp; THis, thin

caliper	endeavourer	lingerer	pilferer
canister	engenderer	lithographer	pillager
carpenter	enlightener	loiterer	pitier
caterer	enlivener	Londoner	plasterer
cellarer	establisher	Lowlander	plunderer
chafferer	examiner	Lucifer	polisher
challenger	Excalibur	malingerer	porringer
character	executioner	manager	posturer
chatterer	fashioner	manufacturer	poulterer
cherisher	favorer	mariner	practitioner
chorister	flatterer	marshaller	presbyter
chronicler	flutterer	massacre	prisoner
cofferer	forager	measurer	probationer
comforter	foreigner	messenger	profferer
commissioner	forester	milliner	provender
commoner	forfeiter	minister	publisher
confectioner	furtherer	miniver	punisher
conjurer	galloper	modeler	purchaser
coroner	gardener	murderer	quarreler
cottager	gatherer	murmurer	quaverer
coverer	gossamer	mutterer	questioner
cricketer	gossiper	nourisher	ransomer
customer	harbinger	officer	ravager
cylinder	harborer	palaverer	ravisher
decipherer	harvester	parishioner	reasoner
deliverer	hexameter	passenger	register
demolisher	idolater	pasturer	relinquisher
determiner	imprisoner	patterer	reveler
diameter	interpreter	pensioner	reversioner
diaper	islander	pentameter	rioter
discoverer	jabberer	pepperer	riveter
disparager	juniper	perjurer	roisterer
distributer	Jupiter	pesterer	saunterer
dowager	languisher	petitioner	scavenger
driveler	lavender	pewterer	scimiter
embellisher	lavisher	philologer	sepulcher
emblazoner	lecturer	philosopher	sinister
enameler	leveler	phonographer	skirmisher
encourager	libeler	photographer	slanderer

slaughterer	voyager	evener	lonesomer
slumberer	wagerer	filmier	lovelier
smatterer	wagoner	filthier	lowlier
sophister	wanderer	fleecier	loyaler
sorcerer	wassailer	flightier	merrier
splutterer	waverer	flimsier	mightier
squanderer	whimperer	foamier	moldier
stenographer	whisperer	friendlier	mossier
stutterer	widower	funnier	mournfuler
succorer	wonderer	fussier	muskier
sufferer	worshiper	giddier	mustier
swaggerer		gloomier	narrower
tamperer		glossier	noisier
TelePrompter	blearier	goutier	pearlier
terrier	breezier	grimier	pleasanter
tetrameter	brinier	guiltier	portlier
theater	burlier	happier	princelier
thermometer	cheerfuller	healthier	prosier
thunderer	cheerier	heavier	rosier
topographer	cheerlier	hillier	rowdier
torturer	chillier	holier	ruggeder
totterer	cleanlier	homelier	seemlier
traveler	costlier	horridor	shinier
treasurer	cozier	huffier	shoddier
trespasser	creamier	hungrier	showier
trumpeter	creepier	huskier	sightlier
typographer	crueler	icier	silenter
upholsterer	curlier	inkier	sillier
usurer	dingier	jollier	skilfuller
utterer	dizzier	juicier	skinnier
valuer	doughtier	kindlier	sleepier
vanquisher	dowdier	kinglier	slimier
vaporer	drearier	knightlier	soapier
venturer	drowsier	likelier	solider
verderer	dustier	lissomer	spicier
victualer	earlier	lithesomer	spikier
villager	easier	livelier	spongier
vintager	eerier	loftier	spoonier
visiter	emptier	lonelier	springier

spritelier
steadier
stealthier
stingier
stormier
stuffier
stupider
sturdier
sunnier
surlier
thirstier
thriftier
timider
trustier
vivider
wealthier
wearier
wheezier
windier
winsomer
wintrier
(See also ŎR.)

ÛRB
acerb
blurb
burb
curb
disturb
gerb
herb
perturb
Serb
suburb
superb
urb
verb

ÛRBD

curbed
imperturbed
uncurbed
undisturbed
unperturbed
(See also ÛRB;
add -ed where
appropriate.)

ÛRCH
besmirch
birch
church
lurch
perch
research
search
smirch
weeping birch

ÛRCHT
birched
unsmirched
(See also
ÛRCH;
add -ed where
appropriate.)

ÛRD
abjured
ensured
gourd
reassured
self-assured
unassured
uninsured
unmatured
(See also ŪR;
add -ed where

appropriate.)

ÛRD
absurd
adjutant bird
afterward
afterword
apostle bird
begird
bird
blackbird
bluebird
bowerbird
butcher-bird
buzzword
Byrd
byword
Cape Verde
cardinal bird
catbird
catchword
code word
cowbird
cowherd
crocodile bird
crossword
curd
deterred
dirty word
disinterred
dollar bird
engird
firebird
foreword
friarbird
frigate bird
furred
fyrd
gallows bird

game bird
gird
goatherd
guide word
halberd
half heard
headword
heard
hedge bird
herd
hummingbird
immerd
interred
inward
jailbird
jarbird
jaybird
key word
kingbird
Kurd
ladybird
lovebird
lyrebird
Mesa Verde
mockingbird
nerd
night bird
nonce word
outward
ovenbird
overheard
overword
password
pilot bird
potsherd
puffbird
railbird
rainbird
redbird

reheard
reinterred
reword
riflebird
seabird
secretary bird
sepulchered
sherd
shirred
shorebird
snakebird
snowbird
songbird
stormbird
sunbird
surd
swanherd
swearword
swineherd
tailorbird
third
thunderbird
turd
undergird
undeterred
ungird
unheard
unsepulchered
urd
verd
wading bird
watchword
wattlebird
weaverbird
whirlybird
word
yardbird
(See also ÛR;
add -ed where

appropriate.)

ÛRF

AstroTurf
scurf
serf
surf
turf

ÛRG

berg
burg
exergue
Goldberg
Heidelberg
iceberg

ÛRJ

converge
demiurge
deterge
dirge
diverge
dramaturge
emerge
gurge
immerge
merge
purge
scourge
serge
splurge
Spurge
submerge
surge
thaumaturge
urge
verge

ÛRJD

converged
unurged
(See also ÛRJ;
add -ed where
appropriate.)

ÛRK

O'Rourke

ÛRK

artwork
beadwork
berserk
breastwork
brushwork
Burke
casework
cirque
clerk
clockwork
dirk
Dunkirk
fancywork
firework
footwork
framework
frostwork
groundwork
guesswork
hackwork
handiwork
headwork
homework
housework
irk
jerk
jerque
kirk

legwork
lurk
make-work
masterwork
murk
network
openwork
overwork
paperwork
perk
piecework
quirk
right-to-work
roadwork
salesclerk
schoolwork
shirk
smirk
soda jerk
stirk
teamwork
Turk
underwork
waterwork
waxwork
wonderwork
woodwork
work
yerk

ÛRKT

irked
overworked
(See also ÛRK;
add -ed where
appropriate.)

ÛRL

becurl

bepearl
burl
call girl
charity girl
chorus girl
churl
cowgirl
curl
earl
furl
girl
hurl
impearl
knurl
merle
mother-of-
  pearl
pearl
pirl
playgirl
purl
querl
seed pearl
show girl
skirl
swirl
thurl
twirl
uncurl
unfurl
upcurl
upwhirl
whirl
whorl

ÛRLD
becurled
impearled
New World

Old World
pearled
Third World
uncurled
underworld
world
(See also ÛRL;
add -ed where
appropriate.)

ÛRM
affirm
berm
confirm
derm
disaffirm
firm
germ
infirm
isotherm
misterm
pachyderm
reaffirm
sperm
squirm
term
worm

ÛRMD
affirmed
unconfirmed
(See also
ÛRM; add
-ed where
appropriate.)

ÛRN
bourn

ÛRN
adjourn
astern
attorn
Berne
burn
Byrne
churn
concern
Dern
durn
discern
earn
erne
eterne
externe
fern
Hearn
Hearne
hern
intern
interne
inurn
kern
learn
lucern
lucerne
O'Byrne
overturn
pirn
quern
return
secern
sojourn
spurn
stern
subaltern
taciturn
tern

turn
unconcern
unlearn
upturn
urn
yearn

ÛRND
adjourned
hard-earned
unconcerned
undiscerned
unlearned
unturned
(See also ÛRN;
add -ed where
appropriate.)

ÛRNT
burnt
earnt
learnt
unburnt
unlearnt
weren't

ÛRNZ
Burns
Kearns
(See also ÛRN;
add -s where
appropriate.)

ÛRP
blurp
burp
chirp
discerp
extirp

---

twirp
usurp

ÛRPT
chirped
excerpt
unsurped

ÛRS
bourse

ÛRS
accurse
adverse
amerce
asperse
averse
becurse
birse
burse
coerce
converse
curse
cutpurse
disburse
disperse
diverse
Erse
excurse
foster nurse
hearse
herse
imburse
immerse
inhearse
intersperse
inverse
nurse
perverse

precurse
purse
rehearse
reimburse
reverse
sesterce
submerse
subverse
terce
terse
transverse
traverse
universe
verse
worse

ÛRST
accursed
accurst
athirst
becurst
burst
curst
double first
durst
erst
first
Hearst
Hurst
outburst
thirst
uncursed
unversed
versed
verst
worst
(See also ÛRS;
add -ed where
appropriate.)

ÛRT
Adelbert
advert
alert
animadvert
assert
avert
begirt
Bert
blurt
cert
chert
concert
controvert
convert
curt
desert
dessert
dirt
disconcert
divert
engirt
Englebert
Ethelbert
evert
exert
expert
exsert
extrovert
flirt
girt
gurt
hairshirt
hurt
indesert
inert
inexpert
insert

intersert
intervert
introvert
invert
liverwort
malapert
maxiskirt
midiskirt
miniskirt
obvert
pert
pervert
preconcert
retrovert
revert
seagirt
shirt
skirt
spirt
spurt
squirt
subvert
syrt
transvert
ungirt
unhurt
vert
wert
Wirt
wort

ÛRth
berth
birth
dearth
earth
firth
fuller's earth
girth

ōld, ôr, ŏdd, oil, foŏt, out; ūse, ûrn, ŭp; THis, thin

inearth
mirth
pennyworth
Perth
unearth
unworth
worth

ÛRTZ
Wurtz
(See also ÛRT;
add -s where
appropriate.)

ÛRV
conserve
curve
deserve
disserve
incurve
nerve
observe
outcurve
preserve
reserve
serve
subserve
swerve
unnerve
verve

ÛRVD
conserved
ill-deserved
undeserved
well-preserved
(See also ÛRV;
add -ed where
appropriate.)

ÛRVZ
conserves
turves
(See also ÛRV;
add -s where
appropriate.)

ÛRZ
amours
Tours
yours
(See also ÛR;
add -s where
appropriate.)

ÛRZ
furze
(See also ÛR;
add -s where
appropriate.)

ŪS
abstruse
abuse
adduce
Bruce
burnoose
caboose
calaboose
charlotte russe
conduce
cruse
deduce
deuce
diffuse
disuse
douce
Druce
educe

excuse
flower-de-luce
goose
hypotenuse
induce
introduce
juice
loose
luce
misuse
moose
noose
nous
papoose
obtuse
occluse
pertuse
produce
profuse
puce
recluse
reduce
reproduce
retuse
Roos
Russ
seduce
sluice
spruce
superinduce
Syracuse
Toulouse
traduce
transluce
truce
unloose
unsluice
use
vamoose

Zeus

ŬS
abaculus
abacus
acephalus
angelus
animus
blunderbuss
bus
buss
caduceus
Cerberus
convolvulus
cumulus
cunnilingus
cuss
denarius
discuss
Erebus
esophagus
excuss
fuss
harquebus
Hesperus
hippopotamus
humerus
hydrocephalus
ignis fatuus
impetus
incubus
incuss
Leviticus
minimus
muss
nautilus
nonplus
nucleus
octopus

omnibus
overplus
Pegasus
percuss
phosphorus
platypus
plus
polypus
pus
radius
ranunculus
repercuss
rhus
Russ
sarcophagus
Sirius
stimulus
succubus
syllabus
tantalus
Tartarus
terminus
thus
truss
untruss
us

abstemious
acclivitous
acephalous
acidulous
adulterous
adventurous
agricolous
albuminous
aliferous
aligerous
alimonious

alkalous
alluvious
aluminous
amatorious
ambiguous
Americus
amorous
amphibious
amphibolous
analogous
androgenous
androphagous
anemophilous
anfractuous
angulous
anomalous
anonymous
anserous
antipathous
aqueous
arborous
arduous
armigerous
assiduous
augurous
balsamiferous
barbarous
beauteous
bibulous
bicephalous
bigamous
bipetalous
bituminous
blasphemous
blusterous
boisterous
bounteous
bulbiferous
burdenous

burglarious
cadaverous
calamitous
calcareous
calumnious
cancerous
cankerous
cantankerous
carboniferous
carnivorous
cautelous
cavernous
censorious
ceremonious
chivalrous
cinereous
circuitous
clamorous
commodious
compendious
congruous
consan-
  guineous
conspicuous
contemporane-
  ous
contemptuous
conterminous
contiguous
continuous
contrarious
contumelious
copious
courteous
covetous
crapulous
credulous
crepusculous
Cretaceous

criminous
curious
dangerous
deciduous
deleterious
delirious
devious
dexterous
diaphanous
diatomous
discourteous
disingenuous
doloriferous
dolorous
dubious
dulcifluous
duteous
emulous
endogenous
envious
eponymous
equilibrious
erroneous
ethereous
exiduous
expurgatorious
extemporane-
  ous
extraneous
fabulous
farinaceous
fastidious
fatuitous
fatuous
felicitous
felonious
ferruginous
fluminous
fortitudinous

ōld, ôr, ŏdd, oil, fŏŏt, out; ūse, ûrn, ŭp; THis, thin

fortuitous
fossiliferous
frivolous
fuliginous
furious
garrulous
gelatinous
generous
globulous
glorious
glutenous
glutinous
gluttonous
graminivorous
gratuitous
gregarious
harmonious
hazardous
herbaceous
heterogeneous
hideous
hilarious
homogeneous
homologous
humorous
idolatrous
igneous
ignominious
illustrious
imaginous
immeritous
impecunious
imperious
impervious
impetuous
impious
imponderous
imposturous
incendious

incestuous
incommodious
incongruous
inconspicuous
incredulous
incurious
indecorous
indigenous
indubious
industrious
inebrious
infamous
infelicitous
ingenious
ingenuous
inglorious
inharmonious
iniquitous
injurious
innocuous
inodorous
inquisitorius
insensuous
insidious
instantaneous
invidious
jeopardous
laborious
languorous
lascivious
lecherous
leguminous
libelous
libidinous
ligneous
litigious
ludicrous
lugubrious
luminous

luxurious
magnanimous
marvelous
mellifluous
melodious
membranous
meritorious
metalliferous
meticulous
miraculous
miscellaneous
mischievous
monogamous
monotonous
mountainous
mucilaginous
multifarious
multitudinous
multivious
murderous
murmurous
mutinous
mysterious
nauseous
nebulous
necessitous
nectareous
nefarious
notorious
numerous
oblivious
obsequious
obstreperous
obvious
odious
odoriferous
odorous
oleaginous
ominous

omnivorous
onerous
opprobrious
oviparous
pachyderma-
  tous
parsimonious
pendulous
penurious
perfidious
periculous
perilous
perjurous
perspicuous
pervious
pesterous
pestiferous
petalous
piteous
platinous
platitudinous
plenteous
poisonous
polygamous
ponderous
populous
posthumous
precarious
precipitous
predaceous
preposterous
presumptuous
previous
promiscuous
prosperous
pseudonymous
punctilious
pusillanimous
quarrelous

querulous
rancorous
rapturous
ravenous
rebellious
resinous
ridiculous
rigorous
riotous
roisterous
ruinous
sacchariferous
salacious
salubrious
sanctimonious
sanguineous
saponaceous
savorous
scandalous
scintillous
scrofulous
scrupulous
scrutinous
scurrilous
sedulous
sensuous
serious
setaceous
sibilous
simultaneous
sinuous
slanderous
slumberous
solicitous
somniferous
spontaneous
spurious
stentorious
strenuous

stridulous
studious
subterraneous
sulphurous
sumptuous
supercilious
superfluous
synchronous
synonymous
tautologous
tedious
temerarious
tempestuous
tenebrous
tenuous
thunderous
timidous
timorous
tintinnabulous
tortuous
torturous
traitorous
treacherous
treasonous
tremulous
tuberculous
tumultuous
tyrannous
ubiquitous
unanimous
unchivalrous
undulous ·
ungenerous
unscrupulous
uproarious
usurious
uxorious
vacuous
vagarious

vainglorious
valetudinarious
valetudinous
valorous
vaporous
various
vegetous
velutinous
venomous
ventriculous
venturous
verdurous
verisimilous
verminous
vernaculous
vertiginous
vicarious
vicissitudinous
victorious
vigorous
villainous
viperous
virtuous
vitreous
viviparous
vociferous
voluminous
voluptuous
voraginous
vortiginous
vulturous
zoophagous

ŪSH
barouche
bonne bouche
bouche
cartouche
debouch

douche
gobemouche
Hindu Kush
Joosh
mouche
ruche ·
Scaramouch

ŬSH
blush
brush
crush
flush
gush
hush
lush
missel thrush
mush
outblush
outrush
plush
rush
slush
thrush
tush
underbrush
uprush

ŬSK
adusk
brusque
busk
dehusk
dusk
fusc
husk
Lusk
musk
rusk

---

subfusk
tusk

ŬSP
cusp

ŬST
adduced
deduced
unproduced
(See also ŬS;
add -ed where
appropriate.)

boost
browst
joust
loosed
noosed
roost
roust
spruced
unloosed
vamoosed

ŬST
adjust
adust
angel dust
angust
august
bedust
betrust
blind trust
bust
coadjust
combust
crust

disgust
distrust
dost
dust
encrust
entrust
fust
gust
just
lust
mistrust
must
nonplussed
robust
rust
sawdust
self-distrust
stardust
thrust
trust
unjust
untrussed
wanderlust
(See also ŬS;
add -ed where
appropriate.)

ŪT
absolute
acute
argute
arrowroot
astute
Asyût
attribute
baldicoot
bandicoot
bathing suit
beaut

beetroot
Beirut
birthday suit
birthroot
bitterroot
bloodroot
boot
breadfruit
breadroot
brierroot
bruit
brut
brute
bumbershoot
butte
Butte
cahoot
Canute
cheroot
chute
cloot
comminute
commute
compute
confute
consolute
constitute
convolute
coot
coralroot
cornute
crinkleroot
crowboot
cube root
cute
deaf-mute
depute
destitute
dilute

dispute
disrepute
dissolute
dress suit
electrocute
emeute
enroot
en route
evolute
execute
firstfruit
flagroot
flute
folie du doute
folkmoot
forbidden fruit
freeboot
fruit
galoot
grapefruit
gym suit
Hatshepsut
hirsute
hoot
imbrute
immute
impute
institute
involute
irresolute
jackboot
jackfruit
jute
Knut
lawsuit
loot
lute
malamute
marabout

meute
minute
moot
musquash root
mute
newt
obvolute
offshoot
orangeroot
orrisroot
outshoot
overboot
overshoot
pants suit
pantsuit
parachute
passion fruit
permute
persecute
Piute
playsuit
pollute
prosecute
prostitute
pursuit
puttyroot
Rajput
reconstitute
recruit
redroot
refute
repute
resolute
restitute
revolute
root
route
salute
Salyut

scoot
scute
seroot
shoot
slack suit
sluit
smoot
snakeroot
snoot
snowsuit
solute
soot
space suit
square root
squawroot
statute
subacute
substitute
suit
sunsuit
suppute
sweat suit
swimsuit
taproot
toot
tracksuit
transmute
trapshoot
troubleshoot
unboot
undershoot
union suit
unroot
uproot
upshoot
Ute
versute
volute
wet suit

zoot suit

ŬT
abut
astrut
besmut
betel nut
but
butt
catgut
clear-cut
coconut
crut
cut
glut
gut
halibut
hut
jut
Lilliput
McNutt
mutt
nut
occiput
outshut
peanut
putt
rebut
rut
scut
scuttlebutt
shut
slut
smut
strut
surrebut
tut
uncut
water butt

woodcut

ŪTH
besmooth
booth
polling booth
smooth
soothe

Ŭth
booth
Duluth
forsooth
insooth
ruth
sleuth
sooth
tooth
truth
uncouth
untooth
untruth
youth

Ŭth
doth

ŪTHD
smoothed
unsoothed
(See also ŪTH;
add -*ed* where
appropriate.)

ŪTS
boots
cahoots
(See also ŪT;
add -*s* where
appropriate.)

ōld, ôr, ŏdd, oil, fŏŏt, out; ūse, ûrn, ŭp; THis, thin

ŬTS

ifs, ands, or
    buts
klutz
nuts
putz
smuts
(See also ŬT;
add -s where
appropriate.)

ÛV

amove
approve
behoove
disapprove
disprove
groove
improve
ingroove
move
prove
remove
reprove
you've

ŬV

above
belove
dove
foxglove
glove
ladylove
light-o'-love
love

mourning dove
self-love
shove
truelove
turtledove
unglove

ÛVD

approved
unimproved
unmoved
unproved
unreproved
(See also ÛV;
add -ed where
appropriate.)

ŬVD

beloved
unbeloved
unloved
(See also ŬV;
add -ed where
appropriate.)

ÛZ

abuse
accuse
amuse
bemuse
Betelgeuse
blues
booze
bruise
choose

circumfuse
confuse
contuse
cruise
cruse
diffuse
disabuse
disuse
effuse
enthuse
excuse
fuse
guze
Hughes
incuse
infuse
interfuse
lose
mews
misuse
muse
news
noose
ooze
percussion fuse
perfuse
peruse
refuse
ruse
Santa Cruz
schmooze
sea ooze
snooze
suffuse
superinfuse

the blues
transfuse
trews
use
Vera Cruz
who's
whose
(See also Û;
add -s where
appropriate.)

ÛZ

Chartreuse

ŬZ

abuzz
buzz
coz
does
doz.
fuzz
Luz
Uz

ÛZD

abused
fused
ill-used
misused
self-accused

ÛZH

Bruges
rouge

▪ Section II ▪

WORDS ACCENTED ON THE SYLLABLE BEFORE THE LAST: PENULTS; FEMININE RHYMES; DOUBLE RHYMES

A

For a discussion of words included under the following accented vowels, see the beginning of A rhymes in Section I.

Ā′ad
naiad

Ā′al
Baal
betrayal
defrayal
portrayal
surveyal

Ā′an
Altaian
Biscayan
Malayan

Ā′ans
abeyance
conveyance
purveyance
surveyance

Ā′ant
abeyant

mayn't

Ā′ba
copaiba
Faba

Ä′ba
aba
Addis Ababa
Ali Baba
baba
casaba
indaba
Kaaba
piassaba

Ā′ban
Laban

ĂB′ard
(See also

ĂB′urd.)

ĂB′as
Barabbas

ĂB′ath
Sabbath

Ā′bē
Abey
Abie
baby
bush baby
crybaby
gaby
maybe

ĂB′ē
abbey
Abbie
babby

blabby
cabby
crabby
dabby
drabby
flabby
gabby
grabby
rabbi
scabby
shabby
slabby
tabby
yabbi
yabby

Ä′bē
kohlrabi
Punjabi
squabby
tabi

Wahabi

ĂB′er
(See also
ĂB′ur.)

ÂB′es
abbess

ĂB′est
blabbest
dabbest
drabbest
gabbest
grabbest
jabbest
stabbest

ĂB′eth
blabbeth
dabbeth
gabbeth
grabbeth
jabbeth
stabbeth

Ä′bez
babies
Jabez
rabies
scabies
tabes
(See also Ä′bē;
add -s where
appropriate.)

ĂB′id
crabbed
rabid

tabid

ĂB′ij
cabbage

ĂB′ik
asyllabic
bisyllabic
decasyllabic
dissyllabic
hendecasyl-
    labic
imparisyllabic
monosyllabic
multisyllabic
octosyllabic
parisyllabic
polysyllabic
quadrisyllabic
syllabic
trisyllabic

ĀB′īl
labile
(See also
ĂB′′l.)

Ä′bīn
Sabine

ĂB′ing
blabbing
cabbing
confabbing
dabbing
gabbing
grabbing
jabbing
nabbing

scabbing
slabbing
stabbing
taxicabbing

ĂB′it
babbitt
Babbitt
cohabit
grab it
habit
inhabit
rabbet
rabbit
riding habit

ĂB′jekt
abject

Ā′b′l
Abel
Abe′ll
able
Babel
cable
card table
disable
disenable
dwaible
enable
end table
fable
flabel
gable
label
labile
Mabel
Nabal
nabel

night table
retable
Round Table
sable
stable
table
timetable
turntable
unable
unstable
water table
worktable

ĂB′′l
babble
bedabble
bedrabble
brabble
cabble
dabble
drabble
gabble
gibble-gabble
grabble
habile
jabble
rabble
ribble-rabble
scabble
scrabble

ĀB′lē
ably
stably
unstably

ĂB′lē
babbly
dabbly

drably
scrabbly

Ā'blest
ablest
cablest
(See also
Ā'b'l; add
-*est* where
appropriate.)

ĂB'lest
babblest
bedabblest
brabblest
dabblest
drabblest
gabblest
scrabblest

ĂB'let
tablet

ĂB'leth
cableth
(See also
Ā'b'l; add
-*eth* where
appropriate.)

ĂB'leth
babbleth
bedabbleth
brabbleth
dabbleth
drabbleth
gabbleth
scrabbleth

ĂB'ling
babbling
bedabbling
bedrabbling
brabbling
cabbling
dabbling
drabbling
gabbling
grabbling
scrabbling

ĂB'lish
disestablish
establish
reestablish
stablish

Ā'blur
abler
disabler
enabler
fabler
stabler
tabler

ĂB'lur
babbler
bedrabbler
brabbler
cabbler
dabbler
drabbler
gabbler
grabbler
scabbler
scrabbler

Ā'bob
nabob

ĂB'ot
abbot
Abbott
Cabot
sabot

Ä'bra
candelabra

Ā'brāk
daybreak

ĂB'sens
absence

ĂB'sent
absent

Ā'bur
beggar-my-
   neighbor
belabor
caber
Gheber
good-neighbor
labor
neighbor
saber
tabor

ĂB'ur
beslabber
blabber
bonnyclabber
clabber
crabber

dabber
gabber
gibber-jabber
grabber
jabber
knabber
nabber
slabber
stabber
yabber

ĀB'urd
belabored
unlabored
(See also
Ā'bur; add
-*ed* where
appropriate.)

ĂB'urd
beslabbered
clapboard
gabbard
jabbered
scabbard
slabbered
tabard

ĂCH'ē
catchy
patchy
scratchy
seecatchie
snatchy

ĂCH'el
Rachel
Vachel

ĂCH'el
hatchel
satchel

ĂCH'est
attachest
catchest
detachest
dispatchest
hatchest
latchest
matchest
patchest
scratchest
snatchest
thatchest
unlatchest

ĂCH'et
Bob Cratchet
hatchet
latchet
ratchet

ĂCH'eth
attacheth
batcheth
catcheth
detacheth
dispatcheth
hatcheth
latcheth
matcheth
patcheth
scratcheth
snatcheth
thatcheth
unlatcheth

ĂCH'ez
attaches
batches
catches
detaches
dispatches
hatches
latches
matches
Natchez
patches
scratches
snatches
thatches
unlatches

ĂCH'ing
attaching
batching
catching
detaching
dispatching
hatching
latching
matching
patching
scratching
snatching
thatching
unlatching

ĂCH'les
matchless
patchless
scratchless
thatchless

ĂCH'ment
attachment

catchment
detachment
dispatchment
hatchment
ratchment

ĂCH'ō
macho
nacho

ĂCH'up
catchup

ĀCH'ur
denature
legislature
nature
nomenclature

ĂCH'ur
attacher
back scratcher
body snatcher
catcher
conycatcher
detacher
dispatcher
flycatcher
hatcher
matcher
patcher
scratcher
snatcher
Thatcher
thatcher
unlatcher

ĂCH'wā
hatchway

ĂCH'wurk
catchwork
patchwork

Ā'dā
heyday
lay day
Mayday
payday
playday

Ā'då
Ada
armada
cicada
digitigrada
Grenada
Maida
Veda
Zayda

ĂD'a
adda
dada

ÄD'a
armada
autostrada
cicada
colada
dada
Dada
empanada
enchilada
Granada
Haggadah
Intifada
Nevada
panada

āle,   câre,   ădd,   ärm,   ăsk;   mē,   hĕre,   ĕnd;   īce,   ĭll;

piña colada
posada
Sierra Nevada

ĂD'am
Adam
macadam
madam
McAdam

ĂD'ans,
ĂD'ens
aidance
cadence
decadence

ĂD'ant,
ĂD'ent
abradant
aidant
cadent
decadent

ĂD'kap
madcap

Ā'dē
bag lady
belady
Brady
braidy
cadi
cascady
charlady
cleaning lady
fady
forelady
glady
Grady

jady
lady
landlady
maidy
milady
O'Grady
shady

ĂD'ē
baddie
Big Daddy
caddie
caddy
daddy
faddy
finnan haddie
gladdy
haddie
laddie
paddy
plaidie
sugar daddy

Ā'dē
cadi
irade
Mahdi
qadi
wadi

ĀD'ed
abraded
aided
ambuscaded
barricaded
bejaded
blockaded
braided
brocaded

cannonaded
degraded
dissuaded
evaded
faded
graded
invaded
jaded
masqueraded
persuaded
pervaded
raided
serenaded
shaded
traded
unaided
unbraided
unfaded
unshaded
upbraided
waded

ĂD'ed
added
padded
plaided
superadded

ĀD'en
Aden
Aidenn
bowermaiden
dairymaiden
handmaiden
heavy-laden
laden
maiden
menhaden
mermaiden

milkmaiden
overladen
sea-maiden
serving maiden
underladen
unladen

ĂD'en
Abaddon
engladden
gladden
madden
Macfadden
McFadden
sadden

ĀD'en
Aden

ĀD'ens
cadence
(See also
ĂD'ans.)

ĀD'ent
cadent
(See also
ĂD'ant.)

ĀD'est
abradest
aidest
bejadest
braidest
degradest
dissuadest
evadest
fadest
invadest

madest
overpersuadest
persuadest
pervadest
staidest
tradest
upbraidest
wadest

ĂD′est
addest
baddest
gaddest
gladdest
maddest
paddest
saddest

ĀD′eth
aideth
bejadeth
braideth
degradeth
dissuadeth
evadeth
fadeth
invadeth
madeth
over-per-
　suadeth
pervadeth
raideth
serenadeth
spadeth
tradeth
upbraideth
wadeth

ĂD′eth

addeth
gladdeth
paddeth

ĀD′ēz
Hades
ladies

ĂD′ēz
caddies
(See also ĂD′ē;
drop the -y and
add -ies where
appropriate.)

ĂD′ful
gladful
madful
sadful
(See also ĂD;
add -ful where
appropriate.)

ĂD′ij
adage

ĂD′ik
Cycladic
decadic
dyadic
faradic
haggadic
Helladic
monadic
nomadic
octadic
Sotadic
sporadic
tetradic

triadic
vanadic

ĀD′ing
abrading
aiding
ambuscading
barricading
bejading
blockading
braiding
brocading
cascading
co-aiding
crusading
degrading
dissuading
enfilading
evading
fading
free trading
gasconading
grading
insider trading
invading
jading
lading
masquerading
overlading
overpersuading
parading
persuading
pervading
raiding
retrograding
serenading
shading
spading
trading

unbraiding
underaiding
unlading
upbraiding
wading

ĂD′ing
adding
gadding
gladding
madding
padding
superadding

ĂD′is
Addis
caddis

ĀD′ish
jadish
maidish
mermaidish
old-maidish
staidish

ĂD′ish
baddish
caddish
faddish
gladdish
horseradish
maddish
radish
saddish

ĂD′it
adit

ĂD′jet
gadget

āle, câre, ădd, ärm, ăsk; mē, hĕre, ĕnd; īce, ĭll;

Padgett

ĀD′′l
cradle
dreidel
encradle
hadal
ladle
tradal

ĂD′′l
addle
astraddle
bestraddle
daddle
dog paddle
faddle
fiddle-faddle
packsaddle
paddle
raddle
saddle
scaddle
sidesaddle
skedaddle
spraddle
staddle
straddle
unsaddle

ĀD′lē
gradely
retrogradely
staidly

ĂD′lē
badly
Bradley
gladly

madly
sadly

ĀD′les
aidless
barricadeless
bladeless
braidless
brigadeless
brocadeless
fadeless
gradeless
maidless
paradeless
serenadeless
shadeless
spadeless
tradeless

ĀD′ling
cradling
encradling
ladling

ĂD′ling
addling
daddling
faddling
fiddle-faddling
paddling
raddling
saddling
skedaddling
spraddling
straddling
unsaddling

ĂD′lok
padlock

ĂD′lur
addler
daddler
faddler
fiddle-faddler
paddler
raddler
saddler
skedaddler
straddler

ĂD′man
Cadman

ĂD′mus
Cadmus

ĂD′nē
Ariadne

ĀD′nes
staidness
unstaidness

ĂD′nes
badness
gladness
madness
plaidness
sadness

Ä′dō
ambuscado
barricado
bastinado
camisado
carbonado
crusado
dado
desperado

fumado
gambado
grenado
muscovado
renegado
scalado
stoccado
strappado
tornado

ĂD′ō
foreshadow
overshadow
shadow

Ä′dō
amontillado
amorado
avocado
bravado
Colorado
dado
desperado
El Dorado
imbrocado
Mikado
passado
pintado
stoccado
strappado
travado

ĂD′ōd
foreshadowed
overshadowed
shadowed
unshadowed

ĂD′ok
haddock

paddock
raddocke
shaddock

ĂD'on
Abaddon

ĀD'os
extrados
intrados

ĀD'pōl
tadpole

ĂD'som
gladsome
madsome

ĀD'ur
aider
barricader
blockader
braider
corporate
 raider
crusader
degrader
dissuader
evader
free trader
gasconader
grader
harquebusader
invader
nadir
overpersuader
parader
persuader
promenader

raider
serenader
trader
unbraider
upbraider
wader

ĂD'ur
adder
bladder
gadder
gladder
ladder
madder
padder
sadder
stepladder

Ä'dur
cadre

ĀD'us
gradus

ĂD'vent
advent

ĂD'vurb
adverb

Ā'ē
clayey
spayey
wheyey

Ä'ē
Baha'i
ruba'i
Tai

Ä'ēb
sahib

Ā'est
allayest
arrayest
assayest
bayest
betrayest
bewrayest
brayest
conveyest
defrayest
delayest
dismayest
disobeyest
displayest
essayest
flayest
frayest
gainsayest
gayest
grayest
greyest
inlayest
inveighest
layest
mislayest
missayest
obeyest
overpayest
overstayest
payest
playest
portrayest
prayest
preyest
purveyest
repayest

sayest
slayest
sprayest
stayest
surveyest
swayest
underpayest
uplayest
waylayest
weighest

Ā'eth
allayeth
arrayeth
assayeth
betrayeth
bewrayeth
brayeth
conveyeth
decayeth
defrayeth
delayeth
dismayeth
disobeyeth
displayeth
essayeth
frayeth
gainsayeth
inlayeth
inveigheth
layeth
mislayeth
missayeth
obeyeth
overpayeth
overstayeth
payeth
playeth
portrayeth

āle,   câre,   ădd,   ärm,   ăsk;   mē,   hĕre,   ĕnd;   īce,   ĭll;

▸rayeth
▸reyeth
▸urveyeth
▸epayeth
sayeth
slayeth
stayeth
strayeth
surveyeth
swayeth
underpayeth
uplayeth
waylayeth
weigheth

ĂF′ā
café

Ā′fâr
Mayfair
Playfair

ĂF′ē
baffy
chaffy
daffy
draffy
taffy

Ā′fēld
Mayfield
Rayfield

ĂF′est
chafest
safest
vouchsafest

ĂF′eth

chafeth
Japheth
vouchsafeth

ĂF′gan
Afghan

ĂF′ik
anaglypto-
   graphic
autobiographic
autographic
bibliographic
biographic
cacographic
calligraphic
cartographic
chirographic
choreographic
chorographic
chromographic
chronographic
cinemato-
   graphic
clinographic
cosmographic
cryptographic
crystallo-
   graphic
dactylographic
demographic
diagraphic
edaphic
epigraphic
epitaphic
ethnographic
galvanographic
geographic
glyptographic

graphic
heliographic
heterographic
hierographic
historiographic
holographic
homographic
homolographic
horologio-
   graphic
hydrographic
hyetographic
ichnographic
ideographic
idiographic
isographic
lexicographic
lexigraphic
lichenographic
lithographic
logographic
macrographic
maffick
micrographic
monographic
neurographic
oleographic
orographic
orthographic
paleographic
pantographic
paragraphic
pasigraphic
petrographic
phonographic
photographic
polygraphic
pornographic
pyrographic

Sapphic
scenographic
sciagraphic
seismographic
selenographic
seraphic
siderographic
sphenographic
stenographic
stereographic
stratigraphic
stratographic
stylographic
tachygraphic
telegraphic
topographic
traffic
typographic
uranographic
xylographic
zincographic
zoographic

ĂF′ing
chafing
enchafing
vouchsafing

ĂF′ing
chaffing
gaffing
graffing
heliographing
lithographing
paragraphing
photographing
stenographing
telegraphing

ōld, ôr, ŏdd, oil, fŏŏt, out; ūse, ûrn, ŭp; THis, thin

ĂF′ing
laughing
quaffing
strafing

ĂF′īr
sapphire

ĂF′ish
raffish

ĂF′′l
baffle
gaffle
haffle
raffle
scraffle
snaffle
yaffle

ĀF′lē
safely
unsafely

ĂF′ling
baffling
haffling
raffling
scraffling
snaffling

ĂF′lur
baffler
haffler
raffler
scraffler

ĂF′nē
Daphne

ĂF′old
Saffold
scaffold

ĂF′rāl
taffrail

ĂF′rik
Afric

ĂF′ron
saffron

ĂF′som
laughsome

ĀF′tē
safety

ĂF′tē
crafty
drafty
grafty

ĂF′ted
upwafted
wafted

ȦF′ted
drafted
engrafted
grafted
ingrafted
rafted
shafted
wafted

ȦF′test
daftest

draughtest
graftest
waftest

ȦF′teth
draughteth
grafteth
wafteth

ȦFT′hors
draft horse
shaft horse

ȦF′tij
waftage

ȦF′ting
engrafting
drafting
grafting
hafting
rafting
shafting
wafting

ȦFT′les
craftless
draftless
graftless
raftless
shaftless

ȦF′ton
Afton
Grafton

ȦFTS′man
craftsman
draftsman

handicraftsman
raftsman

ĂF′tūr
wafture

ĂF′tŭr
after
dafter
drafter
grafter
hafter
hereafter
hereinafter
laughter
rafter
thereafter
wafter

Ā′ful
playful
trayful

Ā′fur
chafer
cockchafer
safer
wafer

ĂF′ur
Kaffir
zaffer

ȦF′ur
chaffer
gaffer
graffer
laugher
quaffer

āle, câre, ădd, ärm, ăsk; mē, hĕre, ĕnd; īce, ĭll;

ĂF'urd
Safford
Stafford
Trafford

ĀG'a
plaga
rutabaga
saga

ĂG'a
aga
quagga

Ä'ga
aga
saga

ĂG'al
bagel
finagle
Hegel
inveigle
paigle
plagal
vagal

ĂG'an
Hagan
O'Hagan
pagan
Regan

ĂG'ard
haggard
laggard
staggard
staggered
swaggered

ĂG'art
braggart
Taggart

ĂG'at
agate
moss agate
(See also
ĂG'ot.)

ĂG'ē
Aggie
baggy
braggy
craggy
daggy
draggy
faggy
flaggy
gaggy
haggy
jaggy
knaggy
laggy
Maggie
naggy
quaggy
raggy
ragi
saggy
scraggy
shaggy
slaggy
snaggy
staggy
swaggy
taggy
waggy

ĂG'ed
cragged
jagged
ragged
scragged

ĂG'end
fag end
lagend

ĀG'est
plaguest
vaguest

ĂG'est
braggest
draggest
faggest
flaggest
gaggest
laggest
naggest
waggest

ĂG'eth
braggeth
draggeth
faggeth
flaggeth
gaggeth
laggeth
naggeth
raggeth
waggeth

ĂG'ij
baggage

ĂG'ing

bagging
bragging
dragging
fagging
flagging
gagging
lagging
magging
nagging
ragging
sagging
tagging
unflagging
wagging

ĂG'is
haggis

ĂG'ish
haggish
laggish
naggish
waggish

ĂG'l
bedaggle
bedraggle
daggle
draggle
gaggle
haggle
raggle
raggle-taggle
straggle
waggel
waggle

ĂG'ling
bedaggling

bedraggling
daggling
draggling
gaggling
haggling
raggling
straggling
waggling

ĂG'lur
bedraggler
daggler
draggler
haggler
straggler
waggler

ĂG'mag
cagmag

ĂG'man
bagman
dragman
flagman
ragman

ĂG'ment
fragment

ĂG'mīr
quagmire

ĂG'mīte
stalagmite

ĂG'nant
stagnant

ĂG'nāt

agnate
magnate
stagnate

ĂG'nes
Agnes

ĂG'net
magnet

ĂG'num
magnum

Ā'gō
cacafuego
farrago
galago
galapago
imago
lumbago
pichiciago
plumbago
sago
San Diego
sebago
suffrago
Tierra del Fuego
Tobago
virago
vorago

Ä'gō
Chicago
farrago
Iago
Santiago

ĂG'on
dragon

flagon
pendragon
snapdragon
wagon

ĂG'ot
fagot
maggot
magot
(See also
ĂG'at.)

ĂG'pī
magpie

ĂG'pīp
bagpipe

ĂG'rans
flagrance
fragrance
(See also
ĂG'rant; add -s
where appro-
priate.)

ĂG'rant
flagrant
fragrant
infragrant
vagrant

ĂG'rik
chiragric
podagric

Ā'gū
ague

ĂG'ur
maigre
plaguer
vaguer

ĂG'ur
bagger
bragger
carpetbagger
dagger
dragger
fagger
flagger
four-bagger
gagger
jagger
lagger
magger
nagger
one-bagger
ragger
sagger
stagger
swagger
tagger
three-bagger
two-bagger
wagger

Ā'gus
archimagus
choragus
magus

ĂGZ'man
cragsman
dragsman

Ä'hoo
wahoo

āle,   câre,   ădd,   ärm,   ăsk;   mē,   hĕre,   ĕnd;   īce,   ĭll;

yahoo
Ä'ij
drayage
weighage

Ä'ik
Alcaic
algebraic
Alhambraic
Altaic
ante-Mosaic
apotropaic
Aramaic
archaic
Brahmaic
Chaldaic
Cyrenaic
deltaic
Eddaic
formulaic
Hebraic
Jagataic
Judaic
laic
mosaic
Mosaic
paradisaic
pharisaic
prosaic
Ptolemaic
Passaic
Romaic
Sadduseaic
Sinaic
sodaic
spondaic
stanzaic
stenopaic

tesseraic
trochaic
voltaic

Ä'ing
allaying
amaying
arraying
assaying
baying
belaying
betraying
bewraying
braying
claying
conveying
decaying
defraying
delaying
disarraying
dismaying
disobeying
displaying
essaying
flaying
foresaying
fraying
gainsaying
haying
horseplaying
hurraying
inlaying
interlaying
interplaying
inveighing
laying
maying
mislaying
missaying

neighing
obeying
outlaying
outstaying
outweighing
overlaying
overpaying
overstaying
paying
playing
portraying
praying
prepaying
preying
purveying
relaying
repaying
saying
slaying
soothsaying
spraying
staying
surveying
swaying
undecaying
underpaying
underplaying
unsaying
unweighing
waylaying
weighing

Ä'is
dais
Lais

Ä'ish
clayish
gayish

grayish
greyish
silver-grayish

Ä'ist
algebraist
archaist
prosaist
Ptolemaist

Ä'iz'm
Chaldaism
Laism
Mosaism
prosaism

Ä'ja
maharaja
raja

ĂJ'ant
pageant

Ä'jē
cagey
ragy
sagy
stagy

ĂJ'ē
cadgy
hadji
howadji

ĂJ'ed
aged

Ä'jent
agent

double agent
reagent

ĀJ′est
agest
assuagest
engagest
enragest
gagest
gaugest
outragest
presagest
ragest
sagest
stagest
swagest
wagest

ĀJ′eth
ageth
assuageth
engageth
enrageth
gageth
gaugeth
outrageth
presageth
rageth
wageth

ĀJ′ez
ages
assuages
cages
disengages
encages
engages
enrages
gages

gauges
greengages
outrages
pages
pre-engages
presages
rages
sages
stages
wages
weather gauges

ĂJ′ik
archipelagic
ellagic
hemorrhagic
magic
omophagic
pelagic
tragic

ĂJ′il
agile
fragile

ĂJ′in
imagine

ĂJ′ind
imagined
unimagined

ĂJ′ing
aging
assuaging
caging
engaging
enraging
gaging

gauging
paging
presaging
raging
staging

ĂJ′ing
badging
cadging

ĀJ′lē
sagely

ĀJ′les
ageless
cageless
gageless
gaugeless
pageless
rageless
sageless
stageless
wageless

ĀJ′ling
cageling

ĀJ′ment
assuagement
encagement
engagement
enragement
pre-engage-
  ment
presagement

ĀJ′nes
sageness

ĀJ′ur
ager
assuager
cager
disengager
drum major
engager
enrager
gager
gauger
major
old stager
pager
presager
rager
sager
sergeant major
stager
swager
teenager
trumpet major
wager

ĂJ′ur
agger
badger
cadger

ĀJ′us
advantageous
ambagious
contagious
courageous
disadvanta-
  geous
oragious
outrageous
rampageous
umbrageous

āle, câre, ădd, ärm, ăsk; mē, hĕre, ĕnd; īce, ĭll;

Ā'ka
Jamaica
raca

ĂK'a
alpaca
Malacca
polacca

Ä'ka
jararaca

ĂK'al
jackal
pack-all

ĂK'ard
Packard
placard

ĂK'at
baccate
placate
saccate

ĂK'brānd
crack-brained
slack-brained

ĂK'but
hackbut
sackbut

ĂK'daw
jackdaw

ĂK'doun
breakdown
shakedown

ĂK'ē
achy
braky
caky
faky
flaky
headachy
laky
quaky
shaky
slaky
snaky

ĂK'ē
blackie
cracky
hackie
hacky
Iraqi
khaki
knacky
lackey
maki
Nagasaki
quacky
raki
tacky
ticky-tacky
wacky
whacky

Ä'kē, À'kē
cocky
Iraqi
kaki
khaki
Nagasaki
sake
saki

sukiyaki
teriyaki

ĀK'ed
naked
(See also ĀK;
add -ed where
appropriate.)

ĀK'en
awaken
bacon
forsaken
godforsaken
Jamaican
kraken
mistaken
overtaken
reawaken
rewaken
shaken
taken
undertaken
unforsaken
unmistaken
unshaken
untaken
uptaken
waken
wind-shaken

ĂK'en
blacken
bracken
slacken

Ä'ken
kraken

ĂK'end
awakened
unawakened
(See also
ĂK'en;
add -ed where
appropriate.)

ĀK'est
achest
awakest
bakest
betakest
breakest
fakest
forsakest
makest
mistakest
opaquest
overtakest
partakest
quakest
rakest
shakest
spakest
stakest
takest
undertakest
wakest

ĂK'est
attackest
backest
blackest
clackest
crackest
hackest
lackest
packest

quackest
rackest
ransackest
sackest
slackest
smackest
tackest
trackest
unpackest
whackest

ĂK′et
bluejacket
bracket
cracket
flacket
Hackett
jacket
leatherjacket
lumber jacket
nacket
packet
placket
racket
rackett
red jacket
sacket
sports jacket
straitjacket
tacket
yellow jacket

ĀK′eth
acheth
awaketh
baketh
betaketh
breaketh
faketh

forsaketh
maketh
mistaketh
overtaketh
partaketh
quaketh
raketh
shaketh
staketh
taketh
undertaketh
waketh

ĂK′eth
attacketh
backeth
blacketh
clacketh
cracketh
hacketh
lacketh
packeth
quacketh
racketh
ransacketh
sacketh
slacketh
smacketh
tacketh
tracketh
unpacketh
whacketh

ĀK′ful
wakeful

ĀK′ij
breakage

ĂK′ij
package
sackage
stackage
trackage
wrackage

ĂK′ik
Bacchic
stomachic

ĀK′ing
aching
awaking
backbreaking
baking
betaking
braking
breaking
breathtaking
caking
dressmaking
earthshaking
faking
flaking
forsaking
haymaking
heartbreaking
housebreaking
lovemaking
making
merrymaking
mistaking
overtaking
painstaking
partaking
quaking
raking
shaking

slaking
spaking
staking
stocktaking
taking
undertaking
unmaking
upbreaking
uptaking
waking

ĂK′ing
attacking
backing
bivouacking
blacking
clacking
cracking
hacking
knacking
lacking
packing
quacking
racking
ransacking
sacking
slacking
smacking
tacking
thwacking
tracking
unpacking

ĀK′ish
rakish
snakish

ĂK′ish
blackish
brackish

---

knackish	cackly	**ĂK'nes**	**Ā'korn**
quackish	crackly	blackness	acorn
	shackly	slackness	
ĂK'kloth	tackly		**ĂK'pot**
packcloth		**ĂK'nē**	crackpot
sackcloth	**ĂK'les**	acne	jackpot
	knackless	hackney	
ĂK''l	sackless		**ĀK'red**
cackle	trackless	**ĀK'ning**	sacred
crackle		wakening	
debacle	**ĀK'let**		**ĂK'rid**
grackle	lakelet	**Ā'kō**	acrid
hackle		Saco	
hibernacle		Waco	**ĀK'ring**
jackal	**ĂK'ling**		sacring
mackle	cackling	**ĂK'ō**	
macle	crackling	goracco	**ĀK'rist**
piacle	hackling	Sacco	sacrist
quackle	shackling	shako	
ramshackle	tackling	tobacco	**ĀK'rum**
retackle			sacrum
shackle	**ĂK'log**	**Ä'kō**	simulacrum
spackle	backlog	guaco	
Spackle	hacklog	guanaco	**ĂK'sē**
tabernacle		Gran Chaco	biotaxy
tackle	**ĂK'lur**		braxy
unshackle	cackler	**ĀK'of**	Cotopaxi
untackle	crackler	takeoff	flaxy
	hackler		heterotaxy
ĂK''ld	shackler	**Ā'kob**	homotaxy
cackled	tackler	Jacob	taxi
unshackled			waxy
(See also	**ĂK'man**	**ĀK'on**	
ĂK''l; add -ed	blackman	bacon	**ĂK'sēn**
where	jackman	Lacon	vaccine
appropriate.)	packman	Macon	
		(See also	**ĂK'sent**
ĂK'lē	**ĂK'mē**	ĀK'en.)	accent
blackly	acme		

ĂK'ses
access

ĂK'sēz
axes

ĂK'sez
axes
battle-axes
Maxie's
relaxes
taxes
waxes

ĂK'shun
abreaction
abstraction
action
arefaction
assuefaction
attraction
benefaction
calefaction
coaction
compaction
contaction
contraction
counteraction
counterattrac-
    tion
detraction
diffraction
dissatisfaction
distraction
exaction
extraction
faction
fraction
inaction

infraction
interaction
labefaction
liquefaction
lubrifaction
madefaction
malefaction
paction
petrifaction
protraction
putrefaction
rarefaction
reaction
redaction
refraction
retraction
retroaction
rubefaction
satisfaction
stupefaction
subaction
subtraction
tabefaction
taction
tepefaction
torrefaction
traction
transaction
tumefaction

ĂK'shus
factious
fractious

ĂK'sid
flaccid

ĂK'sim
maxim

ĂK'sis
axis
praxis
synaxis
taxis

ĂK's'l
axle

ĂKS'man
cracksman
tacksman

ĂK'son
Anglo-Saxon
caxon
flaxen
Jackson
klaxon
Saxon
waxen

ĂK'stā
backstay
jackstay

ĂK'ston
Braxton
Caxton
Claxton

ĂKS'wel
Maxwell

ĂK'tāt
ablactate
lactate
tractate

ĂK'ted
abstracted
acted
attracted
compacted
contracted
counteracted
detracted
distracted
enacted
exacted
extracted
overacted
protracted
reacted
refracted
retracted
subtracted
transacted
unacted
underacted

ĂK'test
abstractest
actest
attractest
contractest
counteractest
detractest
distractest
enactest
exactest
extractest
protractest
reactest
retractest
subtractest
transactest

ĂK′teth
abstracteth
acteth
attracteth
contracteth
counteracteth
detracteth
distracteth
enacteth
exacteth
extracteth
protracteth
reacteth
retracteth
subtracteth
transacteth

ĂKT′ful
tactful

ĂK′tik
catallactic
didactic
emphractic
eupractic
galactic
intergalactic
lactic
parallactic
prophylactic
protactic
stalactic
syntactic
tactic

ĂK′tiks
catallactics
tactics

ĂK′tĭl
attractile
contractile
dactyl
didactyl
heterodactyl
leptodactyl
pachydactyl
protractile
pterodactyl
retractile
tactile
tractile

ĂK′ting
abstracting
acting
attracting
contracting
counteracting
detracting
distracting
double-acting
enacting
exacting
infracting
overacting
protracting
reacting
refracting
retracting
retroacting
self-acting
subtracting
transacting
underacting

ĂK′tis
practice

ĂK′tīt
stalactite

ĂK′tiv
abstractive
active
attractive
calefactive
coactive
contractive
counteractive
counterattrac-
　tive
detractive
diffractive
distractive
enactive
extractive
inactive
liquefactive
olfactive
petrifactive
protractive
putrefactive
radioactive
rarefactive
reactive
refractive
retractive
retroactive
satisfactive
stupefactive
subtractive
tractive

ĂKT′lē
compactly
exactly
matter-of-factly

ĂKT′les
actless
bractless
factless
tactless
tractless

ĂKT′ment
enactment
extractment
reenactment

ĂKT′nes
compactness
exactness
intactness

ĂK′tō
de facto
ex post facto

ĂK′tres
actress
benefactress
contractress
detractress
exactress
factress
malefactress

ĂK′tūr
facture
fracture
manufacture
vitrifacture

ĂK′tŭr
abactor
abstracter

ōld, ôr, ŏdd, oil, fŏŏt, out; ūse, ûrn, ŭp; THis, thin

actor
attracter
attractor
benefactor
chiropractor
climacter
compacter
contactor
contractor
detractor
distracter
enactor
exacter
extractor
factor
infractor
malefactor
olfactor
phylacter
protractor
reactor
redactor
refractor
retractor
subcontractor
subtracter
tactor
tractor
transactor
varactor

ĂK'tus
cactus

ĀK'up
breakup
makeup
wake-up

ĀK'ur
acre
awaker
backbreaker
baker
ballad maker
boilermaker
boneshaker
bookmaker
braker
breaker
caretaker
clockmaker
dressmaker
faker
fakir
flaker
forsaker
God's acre
grubstaker
haymaker
heartbreaker
housebreaker
icebreaker
image breaker
image maker
jawbreaker
laker
Laker
lawbreaker
lawmaker
maker
matchmaker
merrymaker
mischief-maker
mistaker
money-maker
moonraker
nacre

naker
pacemaker
painstaker
partaker
peacemaker
Quaker
raker
Sabbath
    breaker
saker
shaker
Shaker
shoemaker
simulacre
staker
stavesacre
strikebreaker
taker
tiebreaker
troublemaker
truce breaker
undertaker
waker
watchmaker
wiseacre

ĂK'ur
attacker
backer
blacker
bushwacker
clacker
clamcracker
corncracker
cracker
firecracker
hacker
hijacker
knacker

lacker
lacquer
nutcracker
packer
quacker
racker
ransacker
sacker
slacker
smacker
snacker
stacker
tacker
thwacker
tracker
unpacker
whacker
yakker

ĀK'urz
awakers
breakers
(See also
ĀK'ur; add
-s where
appropriate.)

ĂK'us
Bacchus
Flaccus
jacchus

ĂK'wā
backway
packway
trackway

Ā'kwēn
fay queen

āle, câre, ădd, ärm, ăsk; mē, hĕre, ĕnd; īce, ĭll;

May queen

ĂK′woodz
backwoods

Ā′la
gala
shillalah

ĂL′a
Allah
calla
galla
mashallah
Valhalla

Ā′la
gala

ĂL′ad
ballad
salad

ĂL′ans
balance
counterbalance
outbalance
overbalance
valance

ĂL′anst
balanced
outbalanced
overbalanced
unbalanced

ĂL′ant
assailant
exhalant

inhalant
intranscalent
transcalent

Ā′lanks
phalanx

ĂL′ard
Allard
Ballard
Callard
mallard

ĂL′as
balas
Dallas
palace
Pallas
(See also
ĂL′is.)

ĂL′ast
ballast

ĂL′bum
album

ĂL′burd
jailbird

ĂL′burt
Albert

ĂL′dik
heraldic

ĂL′din
Aldine

Ā′lē
Bailey
bailie
Braley
capercaillie
daily
Daly
Disraeli
gaily
Haley
Israeli
kali
Mailly
Maley
Old Bailey
shaly
shillelagh
ukelele
vale

ĂL′ē
alley
Allie
Aunt Sally
bally
dally
dilly-dally
galley
Hallie
kali
Lallie
O'Malley
rally
Sallie
sally
Sally
shilly-shally
tally
tomalley

valley

Ä′lē
finale
kali
pastorale

Ā′leb
Caleb

ĂL′ek
Aleck
Halleck
smart aleck
Talleck

ĂL′en
Alan
Allen

ĂL′enj
challenge

ĂL′enjd
challenged
unchallenged

ĀL′ens
valence

ĂL′ent
gallant
talent
ungallant

Ā′les
clayless
dayless
hayless

ōld, ôr, ŏdd, oil, fŏŏt, out; ūse, ûrn, ŭp; THis, thin

payless
playless
preyless
rayless
sprayless
wayless

ĀL'est
ailest
assailest
availest
bailest
balest
bewailest
curtailest
derailest
detailest
engaolest
entailest
exhalest
failest
frailest
hailest
halest
impalest
inhalest
mailest
nailest
outsailest
palest
prevailest
quailest
railest
regalest
retailest
sailest
scalest
trailest
unveilest

wailest

ĂL'et
gallet
mallet
palate
palette
pallet
sallet
valet

ĀL'eth
aileth
assaileth
availeth
baileth
baleth
bewaileth
curtaileth
deraileth
detaileth
engaoleth
entaileth
exhaleth
haileth
impaleth
inhaleth
naileth
outsaileth
paleth
prevaileth
quaileth
raileth
regaleth
retaileth
saileth
scaleth
traileth
unveileth

veileth
waileth

Ā'lez or Ă'lez
or Ä'lez
Gonzales

ĂL'fa
alfalfa
alpha

ĂL'fred
Alfred

ĂL'ful
baleful
pailful
wailful

ĂL'gam
amalgam

ĂL'id
dallied
dilly-dallied
impallid
invalid
pallid
rallied
sallied
shilly-shallied
tallied
valid

ĂL'if
bailiff
Caliph

ĂL'ij

bailage
curtailage
retailage

ĂL'ik
Gaelic
malic
Salic

ĂL'ik
acrocephalic
bimetallic
brachisto-
  cephalic
brachycephalic
cephalic
dolichocephalic
encephalic
eurycephalic
Gallic
grallic
italic
macrencephalic
macrocephalic
malic
medallic
mesocephalic
metallic
microcephalic
monometallic
oxalic
phallic
platycephalic
salic
thallic
Uralic
Vandalic
vocalic

āle, câre, ădd, ärm, ăsk; mē, hĕre, ĕnd; īce, ĭll;

ĂL'ik
pashalic

ĂL'iks
calyx
Salix

ĂL'in or
ĂL'in
Stalin

ĂL'ing
ailing
assailing
availing
bailing
baling
bewailing
blackmailing
countervailing
curtailing
derailing
detailing
empaling
entailing
exhaling
grayling
Greyling
hailing
haling
impaling
inhaling
jailing
mailing
nailing
outsailing
paling
prevailing
quailing

railing
regaling
retailing
sailing
scaling
Schmeling
tailing
trailing
unveiling
veiling
wailing
whaling
wholesaling

ĂL'ing
caballing
palling

ĂL'is
Alice
allice
chalice
Challis
malice
(See also
ĂL'as.)

ĂL'is
Cornwallis

ĀL'ish
palish
shalish
stalish

ĂL'jē
algae
cephalalgy
neuralgy

nostalgy
odontalgy

ĂL'jik
antalgic
cephalalgic
neuralgic
nostalgic
odontalgic

ĀL'kar
mail car
railcar

ĂL'kat
defalcate
falcate

ĂL'ker
Valkyr

ĂL'kin
grimalkin

ĀL'lē
frailly
halely
palely
staley

ĂL'ma
Alma
Thalma

ĂL'mat
palmate

ĀL'ment
ailment
assailment

availment
bailment
bewailment
curtailment
derailment
entailment
impalement
inhalement
prevailment
regalement
retailment

ĂL'mud
Talmud

ĂL'muk
Kalmuck

ĀL'nes
frailness
haleness
paleness
staleness

Ā'lō
halo

ĂL'ō
Allhallow
aloe
callow
dishallow
fallow
hallow
mallow
marshmallow
sallow
shallow
summer-fallow

ōld, ôr, ŏdd, oil, fŏŏt, out; ūse, ûrn, ŭp; THis, thin

tallow	**ĂL'spin**	nailer	Calvin
unhallow	tailspin	paler	
		prevailer	**ĂL'vō**
ĂL'ō	**ĀL'tē**	quailer	salvo
swallow	frailty	railer	
wallow		regaler	**ĂL'vur**
(See also Ŏ'lo.)	**ĂL'tō**	retailer	quacksalver
	alto	sailer	salver
ĂL'on	contralto	sailor	salvor
gallon		Sayler	
talon	**ĀL'tō**	scaler	**ĂL'vurt**
	rialto	squalor	Calvert
ÀL'on		staler	
salon	**ĂL'ū**	tailor	**ĂL'win**
	undervalue	Taylor	Alwin
ĂL'op	value	trailer	
gallop		unveiler	**ĀL'ya**
jalap	**ĂL'um**	wailer	azalea
scallop	alum	whaler	Bacchanalia
shallop			castalia
	ĀL'ūr	**ĂL'ur**	dahlia
ĂL'ot	failure	caballer	mammalia
ballot		pallor	marginalia
	ĀL'ŭr	valor	paraphernalia
ĂL'ōz	assailer		penetralia
gallows	bailer	**ĂL'us**	regalia
hallows	baler	callous	saturnalia
(See also	bewailer	gallus	terminalia
ĂL'ō; add	curtailer		
-s where	derailer	**ĂL'va**	**ĂL'ya**
appropriate.)	detailer	Alva	dahlia
	entailer	Alvah	
ĂL'pin	failer	Halveh	**ĀL'ya**
Alpine	frailer		dahlia
cisalpine	gaoler	**ĂL'vij**	
transalpine	haler	salvage	**ĀL'yan**
	impaler		alien
ĂL'ping	inhaler	**ÀL'vin**	Australian
scalping	jailer	Alvin	bacchanalian

āle, câre, ădd, ärm, ăsk; mē, hĕre, ĕnd; īce, ĭll;

Daedalian
Episcopalian
Idalian
mammalian
marsupialian
Messalian
paralian
phantasmalian
Phigalian
Pygmalion
regalian
saturnalian
sesquipedalian
tenaillon
tobaccanalian
universalian

ĂL'yant
valiant

ĀL'yard
gaolyard
kailyard

ĂL'yō
intaglio
seraglio

ĂL'yon
battalion
Italian
medallion
rapscallion
rascallion
scallion
stallion

ĀLZ'man
dalesman

salesman
talesman
whalesman

ĀM'a
Bahama
krama

ĂM'a
Alabama
digamma
mamma

ÄM'a
Bahama
Brahma
Cinerama
cosmorama
cyclorama
Dalai Lama
diorama
docudrama
drama
duodrama
Fujiyama
georama
kaama
Kama
lama
llama
mamma
melodrama
monodrama
neorama
pajama
panorama
psychodrama
pyjama
Rama

teledrama
Teshu Lama
Vasco da Gama
video drama
Yama
Yokohama

Ā'man
cayman
dayman
drayman
highwayman
layman

ĀM'ant
claimant
(See also
Ā'ment.)

ĂM'ant
clamant

ĂM'as
Lammas

ĂM'ask
damask

Ā'māt
day mate
desquamate
hamate
playmate

ÄM'az
Brahmas
cat's pajamas
(See also ÄM'a;
add -s where

appropriate.)

ĂM'ba
gamba

ĂM'bē
Bambi
namby-pamby

ĂM'bent
lambent

ĂM'bik
choliambic
choriambic
dithyrambic
elegiambic
galliambic
iambic

ĂM'bist
cambist
gambist

ĂM'bit
ambit
gambit

ĂM'kin
lambkin

ĂM'b'l
amble
bramble
gamble
preamble
ramble
scamble
scramble

ōld, ôr, ŏdd, oil, fŏŏt, out; ūse, ûrn, ŭp; THis, thin

shamble
skimble-
  skamble

ĂM'blest
amblest
gamblest
ramblest
scramblest
shamblest

ĂM'bleth
ambleth
gambleth
rambleth
scrambleth
shambleth

ĂM'b'lz
ambles
gambles
rambles
scrambles
shambles

ĂM'bling
ambling
brambling
gambling
rambling
scambling
scrambling
shambling

ĂM'blur
ambler
gambler
rambler
scambler

scrambler
shambler

ĂM'bō
ambo
crambo
flambeau
sambo
zambo

ĂM'bol
gambol

ĀM'brik
cambric

ĀM'bur
antechamber
chamber

ĀM'būr
tambour

ĂM'bur
amber
camber
clamber

ĂM'bus
dithyrambus
iambus

ĂM'bush
ambush

ĀM'ē
Amy
flamy
gamy

Mamie

ĀM'ē
chamois
clammy
gammy
mammy
rammy
shammy
tammy

ĀM'ē
balmy
calmy
Miami
palmy
pastrami
qualmy
salmi
swami

ĂM'el
camel
Campbell
enamel
untrammel
Hamal
mammal
trammel

ĂM'eld
enameled
untrammeled

Ā'men
amen
Bremen
examen
flamen

foramen
gravaman
Haman
Lehmann
stamen

Ā'men
amen
ramen

Ā'ment
allayment
betrayment
defrayment
payment
prepayment
raiment
(See also
ĀM'ant.)

ĀM'est
acclaimest
aimest
blamest
claimest
declaimest
defamest
disclaimest
exclaimest
flamest
framest
gamest
inflamest
lamest
maimest
namest
proclaimest
reclaimest
shamest
tamest

ĂM'est
crammest
dammest
damnest
rammest
shammest
slammest

ĂM'est
calmest
embalmest
salaamest

ĂM'eth
acclaimeth
aimeth
blameth
claimeth
declaimeth
defameth
disclaimeth
exclaimeth
flameth
foreshameth
frameth
inflameth
lameth
maimeth
nameth
overcameth
proclaimeth
reclaimeth
shameth
tameth

ĂM'eth
crammeth
dammeth

damneth
rammeth
shammeth
slammeth

ĂM'eth
calmeth
embalmeth
salaameth

ĂM'fir
samphire

ĂM'flet
pamphlet

ĂM'for
camphor

ĂM'ful
blameful
flameful
shameful

ĂM'ij
damage

ĂM'ik
Abrahamic
Adamic
adynamic
agamic
autodynamic
balsamic
biodynamic
ceramic
cinnamic
cosmoramic
cryptogamic

cycloramic
dioramic
dynamic
electrodynamic
epithalamic
gamic
hydrodynamic
hyperdynamic
Islamic
isodynamic
keramic
monogamic
monogrammic
panoramic
parallelogram-
   mic
phanerogamic
polygamic
potamic
preadamic
telegrammic
trigrammic

ĂM'il
amyl
Tamil

ĂM'in
examine
famine
gamin

ĀM'ing
acclaiming
aiming
blaming
claiming
declaiming
defaming

disclaiming
exclaiming
flaming
framing
gaming
inflaming
laming
maiming
misnaming
naming
nicknaming
proclaiming
reclaiming
shaming
surnaming
taming

ĂM'ing
cramming
damming
damning
lambing
lamming
ramming
shamming
slamming
tramming

ĀM'ing
becalming
calming
embalming
qualming
salaaming

ĂM'is
amice
chlamys
tamis

ĀM'ish
lamish
tamish

ĂM'ish
affamish
enfamish
famish
Hamish
rammish

ĀM'ish
calmish
qualmish

ĂM'ist
embalmist
palmist
psalmist

ĂM'īt
samite

ĀM'lē
gamely
lamely
namely
tamely

ĂM'lē
calmly

ĀM'les
aimless
blameless
claimless
fameless
flameless

frameless
gameless
nameless
shameless
tameless

ĂM'les
balmless
palmless
psalmless
qualmless

ĂM'let
camlet
hamlet
samlet

ĂM'ling
lambling

ĂM'ment
becalmment
embalmment

ĂM'nes
gameness
lameness
sameness
tameness

ĂM'nes
calmness

ĂM'ok
hammock
mammock

ĂM'on
Ammon

backgammon
daman
gammon
mammon
salmon
shaman

Ā'mond
Raymond

ĂM'ond
Hammond

Ā'mos
Amos
Shaemas

ĂM'oth
mammoth

ĂM'pan
jampan
sampan
tampan

ĂM'part
rampart

ĂM'paz
pampas

ĂM'pē
crampy

ĂM'pen
dampen

ĂM'pēr
ampere

ĂM'pest
campest
crampest
dampest
decampest
encampest
rampest
scampest
stampest
trampest
vampest

ĂM'peth
campeth
crampeth
dampeth
decampeth
encampeth
rampeth
scampeth
stampeth
trampeth
vampeth

ĂM'ping
camping
clamping
cramping
damping
decamping
encamping
lamping
ramping
scamping
stamping
tamping
tramping
vamping

āle, câre, ădd, ärm, ăsk; mē, hĕre, ĕnd; īce, ĭll;

ĂM'pīr
vampire

ĂM'pish
dampish
scampish

ĂM'p'l
ample
ensample
example
sample
trample

ĂM'p'ld
sampled
untrampled
(See also
ĂM'p'l; add
-ed where
appropriate.)

ĂMP'lē
damply

ĂMP'ling
ensampling
sampling
trampling

ĂMP'lur
ampler
examplar
sampler
trampler

ĂMP'ment
decampment
encampment

ĂMP'nes
dampness

ĂM'prē
lamprey

ĂMP'son
Lampson
Sampson
(See also
Samson.)

ĂMP'ton
Crampton
Hampton

ĂM'pur
camper
champer
clamper
cramper
damper
hamper
pamper
scamper
stamper
tamper
tramper
vamper

ĂM'purd
hampered
pampered
tampered
unhampered

ĂM'pus
campus
grampus

ĂM'rod
ramrod

ĂM'rok
shamrock

ĀM'stur
gamester

ĂM'ond
almond
bitter almond

ĀM'ur
acclaimer
aimer
blamer
claimer
declaimer
defamer
disclaimer
disfamer
exclaimer
framer
gamer
inflamer
Kramer
lamer
lion tamer
maimer
misnamer
namer
nicknamer
proclaimer
reclaimer
shamer
tamer
testamur

ĂM'ur
air hammer
ball peen ham-
mer
clamor
claw hammer
crammer
dammer
damner
drop hammer
enamor
gammer
glamour
grammar
hammer
jackhammer
jammer
lamber
lammer
ninnyhammer
programmer
rammer
shammer
slammer
sledgehammer
stammer
windjammer
yammer
yellowhammer

ĂM'ur
Balmer
calmer
embalmer
palmer

ĂM'wā
tramway

ōld, ôr, ŏdd, oil, fŏŏt, out; ūse, ûrn, ŭp; THis, thin

ĂM'us
biramous
famous
hamous
ignoramus
mandamus
squamous

ĂM'ut
gamut

ĂM'zē
Malmsey

ĂM'zel
amsel
damsel

ĂM'zon
damson

Ā'na
Americana
ana
anana
arcana
campana
Cartagena
Curtana
fistiana
scena
vox humana

ĂN'a
Americana
ana
Anna
anna
banana

bandanna
canna
cassabanana
Christiana
damiana
Diana
dulciana
fistiana
Georgiana
goanna
Guiana
Guyana
Hanna
Hannah
Havana
hosanna
Indiana
ipecacuanha
Joanna
Juliana
liana
Louisiana
manna
Montana
nanna
nicotiana
poinciana
Pollyanna
Roxana
savanna
Savannah
Stephana
sultana
Susanna
Susquehanna
Texarkana
Tia Juana
Urbana
Victoriana

Än'a
acqua tofana
Americana
ana
anana
anna
apadana
bwana
Curtana
dhyana
Fata Morgana
Ghana
gymkhana
Hinayana
hiragana
iguana
kana
katakana
kerana
lantana
liana
Mahayana
mana
mañana
marijuana
Messana
nagana
Nirvana
piranha
pozzuolana
prana
purana
Rama
rana
Rosh Hashanah
sultana
Tana
thana
Tijuana

tramontana
Victoriana
vox humana
zenana

Ā'nal
anal

ĂN'al
annal
cannel
channel
empanel
flannel
impanel
panel
pannel
scrannel
stannel
unpanel

ĂN'alz
annals
flannels
(See also
ĂN'al; add
-s where
appropriate.)

ĂN'ant
complainant

ĂN'at
impanate
lanate

ĂN'at
khanate
pomegranate

āle,　câre,　ădd,　ärm,　ăsk;　mē,　hĕre,　ĕnd;　īce,　ĭll;

tannate

ĂN'at
khanate

ĂN'bō
rainbow

ĂN'chē
paunchy

ȦN'chē
branchy

ĂN'chest
launchest
stanchest

ȦN'chest
blanchest
scranchest

ȦN'chet
manchet
planchet

ĂN'cheth
launcheth
stancheth

ȦN'cheth
blancheth
scrancheth

ĂN'chez
launches
paunches
stanches

ȦN'chez
avalanches
blanches
branches
ranches

ĂN'ching
launching
stanching

ȦN'ching
blanching
branching
ranching

ĂN'chīz
affranchise
disfranchise
enfranchise
franchise

ÄNCH'les
launchless
paunchless

ȦNCH'les
branchless
ranchless
stanchless

ĂN'chur
launcher
stancher

ȦN'chur
brancher
rancher

ĂN'da

Amanda
jacaranda
Miranda
memoranda
propaganda
veranda

ĂN'dal
Randall
(See also
ĂN'd'l.)

ȦN'dant
commandant
demandant
mandant

ȦN'dāt
mandate

ĂND'bag
handbag
sandbag

ĂND'bal
handball
sandball

ĂND'boi
bandboy
sandboy

ĂND'boks
bandbox
sandbox

ĂND'child
grandchild

ĂN'dē
Andy
bandy
brandy
candy
dandy
handy
jaborandi
jackadandy
Jim Dandy
Mandy
pandy
randy
Rio Grande
sandy
sugar candy
unhandy

ÄN'dē
Rio Grande

ĂN'dēd
bandied
brandied
candid
candied
uncandid
(See also
ĂN'ded.)

ĂN'ded or
ĂN'ded
backhanded
banded
bare-handed
black-handed
branded
candid
clean-handed

ōld, ôr, ŏdd, oil, fŏŏt, out; ūse, ûrn, ŭp; THis, thin

close-handed
commanded
contrabanded
countermanded
demanded
deodanded
disbanded
empty-handed
evenhanded
expanded
first-handed
forehanded
four-handed
freehanded
full-handed
handed
hard-handed
heavy-handed
high-handed
landed
left-handed
light-handed
lily-handed
neat-handed
open-handed
overhanded
red-handed
remanded
reprimanded
right-handed
shorthanded
single-handed
stranded
swift-handed
two-handed
unbranded
underhanded
unhanded
unlanded

ĂN'dent
candent
scandent

ĀN'dẽr
reindeer

ĂN'dest or
ĄN'dest
bandest
brandest
commandest
demandest
disbandest
expandest
grandest
handest
landest
remandest
reprimandest
standest
withstandest

ĂN'deth or
ĄN'deth
bandeth
brandeth
commandeth
demandeth
disbandeth
expandeth
handeth
landeth
remandeth
reprimandeth
standeth
withstandeth

ĂN'dēz

Andes
Hernandez

ĂND'fast
handfast

ĂN'dij
bandage
glandage
standage

ĂN'ding or
ĄN'ding
ampersanding
banding
branding
commanding
countermand-
  ing
demanding
disbanding
expanding
freestanding
handing
landing
notwithstand-
  ing
outstanding
remanding
reprimanding
sanding
standing
stranding
understanding
withstanding

ĂN'dish
blandish
brandish

grandish
outlandish

ĂN'dist
contrabandist
propagandist

ĂN'dit
bandit

ĂN'd'l
candle
dandle
handle
Randle
sandal
scandal
vandal

ĂND'lē
blandly
grandly

ĂND'les
bandless
brandless
commandless
glandless
handless
landless
sandless
strandless

ĂND'ling
brandling
handling

ĂND'lur
Candler

āle, câre, ădd, ärm, ăsk; mē, hĕre, ĕnd; īce, ĭll;

...andler	**ĂND'out**	**ĂN'drus**	bystander
...ndler	handout	meandrous	candor
...ndler		polyandrous	commander
...llow chandler	**ĂN'dra** or		coriander
	ĀN'dra	**ĂND'sīr**	dander
...ND'lord	Alessandra	grandsire	demander
...ndlord	Alexandra		disbander
	Cassandra	**ĂND'skāp**	dittander
...ND'mād		landscape	expander
...andmade	**ĂNdrē** or		gander
...andmaid	**ĀN'drē**	**ĂND'son**	gerrymander
	chandry	grandson	glander
...ND'mark	commandry		goosey-gander
...andmark	meandry	**ĂND'stand**	grander
	polyandry	bandstand	hander
...ND'ment or	shandry	grandstand	lander
...ND'ment			Leander
...ommandment	**ĀN'drē**	**ĂN'dum**	meander
...isbandment	laundry	ad captandum	Menander
...emandment		avizandum	oleander
	ĂN'drel	mandom	pander
...ND'nes	spandrel	memorandum	philander
...olandness		random	Pomander
...randness	**ĂN'drēn**	tandem	remander
	Alexandrine		reprimander
...N'dō or	salamandrine	**ĀN'dur**	right-hander
...N'dō		attainder	salamander
...commando	**ĂN'dres**	remainder	sander
...Ferdinando	pandress		slander
...Fernando		**ĀN'dūr**	stander
...grando	**ĂN'dres**	grandeur	understander
...Hernando	laundress		withstander
...dentando		**ĂN'dur** or	
...Orlando	**ĂN'drik**	**ĀN'dur**	**ĂN'dur**
	polyandric	Africander	launder
ĂN'don	theandric	Alexander	
...abandon		backhander	**ĂN'durd** or
...Landon	**ĂN'dril**	blander	**ĀN'durd**
...Shandon	mandril	brander	meandered

pandered
philandered
slandered
standard

ĂN'durz
Sanders
Saunders

ĂNDZ'man
bandsman
landsman

Ā'nes
feyness
gayness
grayness

ĀN'est
abstainest
appertainest
arraignest
ascertainest
attainest
canest
chainest
complainest
constrainest
containest
cranest
deignest
detainest
disdainest
enchainest
entertainest
explainest
feignest
humanest
inanest

maintainest
obtainest
ordainest
painest
plainest
profanest
rainest
refrainest
regainest
reignest
remainest
restrainest
retainest
sanest
stainest
strainest
sustainest
trainest
unchainest
urbanest
vainest
wanest

ĀN'ē
Allegheny
brainy
Cheyney
Delaney
Eugenie
grainy
Rainey
rainy
veiny
zany

ĂN'ē
Annie
branny
canny

cranny
Fannie
granny
mannie
Nannie
uncanny

ĂN'ē
frangipani
Galvani
Hindustani
rani
soprani

ĂN'ēd
crannied

ĂN'est
bannest
fannest
mannest
plannest
scannest
spannest
tannest

ĂN'et
gannet
granite
Janet
planet
quannet
(See also
ĂN'at.)

ĀN'eth
abstaineth
appertaineth
arraigneth
ascertaineth

attaineth
caneth
chaineth
complaineth
constraineth
containeth
craneth
deigneth
detaineth
disdaineth
draineth
enchaineth
entertaineth
explaineth
feigneth
foreordaineth
gaineth
maintaineth
obtaineth
ordaineth
paineth
profaneth
raineth
refraineth
regaineth
reigneth
remaineth
restraineth
retaineth
staineth
straineth
sustaineth
traineth
unchaineth
waneth

ĂN'eth
banneth
fanneth

manneth
planneth
scanneth
spanneth
tanneth

ĂN'fâr
fanfare

ĂN'fēld
Canfield

ĀN'ful
baneful
complainful
disdainful
painful

ĀN'gang
chain gang
train gang

ĂNG'ē
clangy
fangy
slangy

ĂNG'gar
hangar

ĂNG'gôr
languor

ĂNG'gur
anger
angor
Bangor
clangor

ĂNG'gwid

languid

ĂNG'gwij
language

ĂNG'gwin
anguine
ensanguine
sanguine

ĂNG'gwish
anguish
languish

ĂNG'ing
banging
clanging
hanging
haranguing
overhanging
paperhanging
slanging
slang-whang-
   ing
twanging

ĂNG'kē
cranky
hanky
hanky-panky
lanky
planky
pranky
Yankee

ĂNG'kest
blankest
clankest
dankest

embankest
flankest
frankest
lankest
outflankest
rankest
sankest
spankest
thankest

ĂNG'ket
banket
blanket

ĂNG'keth
clanketh
embanketh
flanketh
franketh
outflanketh
ranketh
sanketh
thanketh

ĂNGK'ful
prankful
thankful

ĂNG'king
banking
clanking
embanking
flanking
franking
outflanking
outranking
planking
ranking
spanking

thanking
yanking

ĂNG'kish
dankish
frankish
lankish
prankish

ĂNGK''l
ankle
crankle
hankle
rankle

ĂNGK'lē
blankly
dankly
frankly
lankly
rankly

ĂNGK'les
bankless
clankless
crankless
flankless
plankless
prankless
rankless
shankless
spankless
thankless

ĂNGK'let
anklet

ĂNGK'ling
hankling
rankling

ōld, ôr, ŏdd, oil, f┌┐t, out; ūse, ûrn, ŭp; THis, thin

ĂNGK'ment
bankment
embankment
outflankment

ĂNGK'nes
blankness
crankness
dankness
frankness
lankness
rankness

ĂNG'kō
banco
calamanco

ĂNGK'shun
sanction

ĂNGK'shus
anxious

ĂNGK'tum
sanctum

ĂNGK'wet
banquet

ĂNGK'wil
tranquil

ĂNGK'wish
vanquish

ĂNG'kur
anchor
banker
blanker

canker
clanker
danker
encanker
flanker
franker
hanker
outflanker
planker
pranker
rancor
ranker
sheet anchor
spanker
tanker
thanker
unanchor

ĂNG'kurd
anchored
brancard
cankered
tankard
unanchored
(See also
ĂNG'kur; add
-ed where
appropriate.)

ĂNG''l
angle
bangle
bemangle
bespangle
brangle
dangle
disentangle
embrangle
entangle

interjangle
intertangle
jangle
mangle
mingle-mangle
pentangle
phalangal
quadrangle
rectangle
sea tangle
spangle
strangle
tangle
triangle
twangle
untangle
wangle
Wrangel
wrangle

ĂNG''ld
angled
newfangled
star-spangled
(See also
ĂNG''l; add
-ed where
appropriate.)

ĂNG'lē
spangly
tangly

ĂNG'les
fangless
pangless

ĂNG'ling
angling

dangling
(See also
ĂNG''l; add
-ing where
appropriate.)

ĂNG'lur
angler
dangler
(See also
ĂNG''l; add
-er where
appropriate.)

ĂNG'man
hangman

ĂNG'ō
contango
fandango
mango
Pago Pago
tango

ĂNG'grē
angry

ĂN'grōv
mangrove

ĂNG'stur
gangster

ĂNG'ur
banger
clangor
ganger
hangar
hanger

haranguer
paperhanger
slang-whanger
straphanger

ĂN′hoŏd

manhood

ĀN′ij

cranage
drainage

ĂN′ij

manage
pannage
tannage

ĂN′ik

Alcoranic
aldermanic
Alemannic
Aristophanic
auto mechanic
botanic
Brahmanic
Britannic
charlatanic
cyanic
diaphanic
ferricyanic
galvanic
Germanic
Hispanic
hydrocyanic
Indo-Germanic
inorganic
interoceanic
lexiphanic
Magellanic

manic
mechanic
Messianic
montanic
Mussulmanic
oceanic
organic
Ossianic
paganic
panic
Puranic
Puritanic
quercitannic
rhodanic
Romanic
satanic
stannic
sultanic
talismanic
tannic
tetanic
Theophanic
Titanic
titanic
transoceanic
tympanic
tyrannic
Uranic
valerianic
volcanic
vulcanic

ĂN′iks

humanics
mechanics
panics

ĂN′il

anil

ĂN′īl

anile

Ā′nim

paynim

ĀN′ing

abstaining
airplaning
appertaining
arraigning
ascertaining
attaining
bestaining
braining
campaigning
caning
chaining
complaining
constraining
containing
craning
deigning
deraigning
detaining
disdaining
draining
enchaining
entertaining
entraining
explaining
feigning
foreordaining
gaining
graining
hydroplaning
ingraining
maintaining
obtaining

ordaining
paining
pertaining
plaining
planing
preordaining
profaning
raining
refraining
regaining
reigning
reining
remaining
restraining
retaining
spraining
staining
straining
sustaining
training
unchaining
uncomplaining
unfeigning
uptraining
veining
waning

ĂN′ing

banning
canning
fanning
flanning
inspanning
japanning
manning
outspanning
panning
planning
scanning

ōld, ôr, ŏdd, oil; foŏt, out; ūse, ûrn, ŭp; THis, thin

spanning
tanning
trepanning
unmanning

ĂN'is
anise

ĂN'ish
Danish
sanish
urbanish
vainish

ĂN'ish
Alcoranish
banish
clannish
evanish
fannish
mannish
Mussulmanish
planish
Spanish
vanish

ĂN'ist
Alcoranist
pianist
tanist

ĀN'jē
mangy
rangy

ĀN'jel
angel
archangel

ĀN'jel
evangel

ĂN'jent
frangent
plangent
tangent

ĂN'jest
arrangest
changest
derangest
disarrangest
estrangest
exchangest
rangest
strangest

ĀN'jeth
arrangeth
changeth
derangeth
disarrangeth
estrangeth
exchangeth
interchangeth
rangeth

ĀN'jez
arranges
changes
deranges
disarranges
enranges
estranges
exchanges
granges
interchanges

ranges

ĂN'jēz
Ganges
phalanges

ĀN'jing
arranging
changing
counterchanging
deranging
disarranging
estranging
exchanging
interchanging
ranging
unchanging

ĀNJ'lē
strangely

ĀNJ'ling
changeling

ĀNJ'les
changeless
rangeless

ĀNJ'ment
arrangement
derangement
disarrangement
estrangement
exchangement
interchange-
ment

ĀNJ'nes
strangeness

ĂN'jur
arranger
bushranger
changer
danger
deranger
disarranger
endanger
estranger
exchanger
granger
interchanger
manger
money changer
ranger
stranger

ĂN'ka or
ĂN'ka
Bianca

ĂN'kin
Hankin
Rankin

ĂN'king
Nanking

ĂN'kinz
Hankins
Rankins

ĂN'kok
Hancock

ĀN'land
mainland

ĀN'lē
gainly

humanely
inanely
insanely
mainly
plainly
profanely
sanely
vainly

ĂN'lē
Danley
Manley
manly
spick-and-
spanly
Stanley
unmanly

ĀN'les
brainless
caneless
chainless
craneless
domainless
drainless
gainless
grainless
maneless
painless
rainless
stainless
swainless
vaneless

ĂN'les
banless
clanless
fanless
manless

planless
spanless
tanless

ĂN'ling
manling
tanling

ĀN'ment
arraignment
ascertainment
attainment
obtainment
ordainment

ĀN'nes
humaneness
inaneness
insaneness
plainness
profaneness
saneness

Ā'no
volcano

ĂN'ō
piano
Hanno
soprano

Ä'nō
guano
Montesano
piano
soprano

ĂN'ok
bannock

jannock

ĂN'on
Balleyshannon
cannon
canon
fanon
Shannon

ĀN'sā
gainsay

ĀN'sāl
mainsail

ĂN'sē
accordancy
accountancy
adjutancy
aeromancy
aldermancy
alectoromancy
alectryomancy
aleuromancy
alphitomancy
anthropo-
    mancy
antsy
arrogancy
astragalomancy
austromancy
axinomancy
belomancy
bibliomancy
botanomancy
buoyancy
capnomancy
captaincy
catoptromancy

ceromancy
chancy
chiromancy
cleromancy
concomitancy
consonancy
constancy
consultancy
conversancy
coscinomancy
crithomancy
crystallomancy
dactyliomancy
dancy
Delancey
diathermancy
discordancy
discrepancy
dissonancy
elegancy
enoptromancy
errancy
exorbitancy
expectancy
extravagancy
exuberancy
exultancy
fancy
gastromancy
geomancy
gyromancy
habitancy
halomancy
hesitancy
hieromancy
hydromancy
ichthyomancy
incognitancy
inconsonancy

ōld, ôr, ŏdd, oil, fŏŏt, out; ūse, ûrn, ŭp; THis, thin

inconstancy
incumbency
infancy
inhabitancy
insignificancy
intemperancy
intolerancy
irrelevancy
irritancy
lecanomancy
lieutenancy
lithomancy
luxuriancy
mendicancy
meteoromancy
militancy
mischancy
Miss Nancy
mordancy
myomancy
Nancy
necromancy
neuromancy
occupancy
oenomancy
oneiromancy
onomancy
onychomancy
oomancy
ophiomancy
ornithomancy
oscitancy
pedomancy
petulancy
phyllomancy
piquancy
poignancy
prancy
precipitancy

predominancy
pregnancy
preponderancy
protuberancy
psephomancy
psychomancy
pyromancy
radiancy
recalcitrancy
recreancy
redundancy
relevancy
rhabdomancy
sciomancy
sergeancy
sibilancy
sideromancy
significancy
spodomancy
stagnancy
stichomancy
supplicancy
sycophancy
tenancy
tephramancy
termagancy
theomancy
truancy
unchancy
unfancy
vacancy
verdancy
vigilancy

ĂN'sēd
fancied

ĂN'sel
cancel

chancel
handsel

ĂN'sest
advancest
chancest
dancest
enhancest
entrancest
glancest
prancest
romancest

ĂN'set
lancet

ĂN'seth
advanceth
chanceth
danceth
enhanceth
entranceth
glanceth
pranceth
romanceth

ĂN'sez
advances
chances
dances
enhances
entrances
expanses
finances
glances
lances
mischances
prances
romances

trances

ĂNS'fur
transfer

ĂN'shal
circumstantial
financial
substantial
supersubstan-
tial

ĂN'shē
banshee

ĀN'shent
ancient

ĂN'shent
transient

ĂN'shun
expansion
mansion
scansion
stanchion

ĂN'sing
advancing
chancing
dancing
enhancing
entrancing
financing
glancing
lancing
Lansing
necromancing
prancing
romancing

āle, câre, ădd, ärm, ăsk; mē, hĕre, ĕnd; īce, ĭll;

ĂN'sis
Frances
Francis

ĂN'sist
romancist

ĂN'siv
advancive
expansive

ĂNS'ment
advancement
enhancement
entrancement

ĂN'som
handsome
hansom
ransom
transom
unhandsome

ĂN'son
Anson
Hanson

ĂN'stā
mainstay

ĂN'sur
advancer
Anser
answer
cancer
chancer
chiromancer
dancer
enhancer

entrancer
geomancer
glancer
lancer
merganser
necromancer
prancer
romancer

ĂN'tā
infante

ĂN'ta
anta
Atalanta
Atlanta
infanta
Santa
Vedanta

ÄN'tä
andante
Dante

ÄN'ta
Vedanta

ÄN'tal
consonantal
gigantal
quadrantal

ĂN'tam
bantam
phantom

ÄN'tans
acquaintance

ĂN'taz'm
phantasm

ĀN'tē
dainty

ĂN'tē
bacchante
canty
panty
scanty
shanty

ȦN'tē
ante
chianti
Dante
dilettante
pococurante
Zante

ÄN'tē
aunty

ĀN'ted
acquainted
attainted
bepainted
besainted
depainted
fainted
feinted
painted
sainted
tainted
unacquainted
unattainted
unsainted

untainted

ȦN'ted,
ĂN'ted
canted
chanted
decanted
enchanted
granted
implanted
panted
planted
ranted
recanted
slanted
supplanted

ĀN'test
acquaintest
faintest
feintest
paintest
quaintest
taintest

ĂN'test,
ȦN'test
cantest
chantest
decantest
enchantest
grantest
implantest
pantest
plantest
rantest
recantest
scantest
supplantest

ĀN'teth
acquainteth
feinteth
painteth
tainteth

ĂN'teth,
ĂN'teth
canteth
chanteth
decanteth
enchanteth
granteth
implanteth
panteth
planteth
recanteth
supplanteth

ĂN'tēz
atlantes
corybantes
(See also
ĂN'tē; add
-s where
appropriate.)

ĂN'them
anthem

ĀNT'hood
sainthood

ĂN'thik
oenanthic
xanthic

ĂN'thin
acanthine
amaranthine
anthine
Rhadaman-
thine
tragacanthin
xanthin

ĂN'thur
anther
Black Panther
Gray Panther
panther

ĂN'thus
acanthous
acanthus
Agapanthus
ailanthus
amianthus
anacanthous
ananthous
canthus
Chimonanthus
dianthus
epanthous
Galanthus
Haemanthus
hysteranthous
polyanthus
synanthous

ĀN'tif
plaintiff

ĂN'tij
advantage
disadvantage
plantage
vantage

ĂN'tik
antic
Atlantic
chiromantic
consonantic
corybantic
frantic
geomantic
gigantic
hierophantic
hydromantic
mantic
necromantic
onomantic
pedantic
pyromantic
romantic
spodomantic
sycophantic
transatlantic

ĀN'tik
Vedantic

ĂN'tin
adamantine
Brabantine
Byzantine
chryselephan-
tine
Diophantine
elephantine
gigantine
Levantine

ĀN'ting
acquainting
attainting
fainting
feinting
painting
tainting
word-painting

ĂN'ting,
ĂN'ting
Banting
canting
chanting
decanting
descanting
disenchanting
enchanting
granting
hanting
implanting
panting
planting
ranting
recanting
slanting
supplanting
transplanting

ĂN'tist
ignorantist
Kantist

ĀN'tist
Vedantist

ĀN'tiv
constraintive
plaintive

ĂN'tiz'm
dilettantism
ignorantism
Kantism

āle, câre, ădd, ärm, ăsk; mē, hĕre, ĕnd; īce, ĭll;

obscurantism
pococurantism
rantism

ĂN't'l
cantle
dismantle
immantle
mantel
mantle
scantle

ĂN't'ld
dismantled
ivy-mantled
mantled

ĀNT'lē
quaintly
saintly
unsaintly

ĂNT'lē
aslantly
scantly

ĂNT'let
cantlet
mantelet
plantlet

ĀNT'let
gauntlet

ȦNT'let
gantlet

ĀNT'līk
saintlike

ĂNT'ling
bantling
mantling
scantling

ȦNT'lur
antler
dismantler
mantler
pantler

ȦNT'ment
disenchant-
  ment
enchantment

ĀNT'nes
faintness
quaintness

ĂNT'nes
scantness

ĂN'tō or
ȦN'tō
canto
coranto
portmanteau
pro tanto
quo warranto

ĂN'ton
Canton
Clanton
Danton
Scranton
Stanton

ĂN'tor

cantor
grantor

ĂN'trē
pantry

ȦN'trē
chantry

ȦN'tres
chantress
enchantress

ĂN'tu
Bantu

ĀN'tur
acquainter
fainter
painter
quainter
tainter
word-painter

ĂN'tur or
ȦN'tur
banter
canter
chanter
decanter
descanter
enchanter
granter
implanter
instanter
Levanter
panter
planter
ranter

recanter
supplanter
transplanter
trochanter

ȦN'tur
chanter
disenchanter
enchanter

ȦN'turn
lantern

ĀN'ur
abstainer
appertainer
arraigner
ascertainer
attainer
bestainer
campaigner
complainer
constrainer
container
cordwainer
detainer
disdainer
drainer
enchainer
entertainer
explainer
feigner
gainer
grainer
inaner
maintainer
nonabstainer
obtainer
ordainer

---

plainer
profaner
refrainer
regainer
restrainer
retainer
saner
stainer
strainer
sustainer
trainer
unchainer
uptrainer
vainer

ĂN′ur
banner
canner
fanner
japanner
lanner
manner
manor
planner
scanner
spanner
tanner
trepanner
vanner

ĂN′urd
bannered
ill-mannered
mannered
unmannered
well-mannered

ĀN′us
anus

heinous
incanous
Janus
Silvanus
veinous

ĂN′vas
canvas
canvass

ĂN′vil
anvil
Danville
Granville

ĀN′wurk
brainwork
chainwork
plain work

ĂN′yan
banyan
canyon
companion

ĂN′yard
lanyard
Spaniard

ĂN′yel
Daniel
Nathaniel
spaniel
staniel
water spaniel

ĂN′yur
pannier

ĂN′za
bonanza
extravaganza
ganza
stanza

ĂN′zē
chimpanzee
pansy
tansy

ĂNZ′fēld
Mansfield

ĂNZ′vil
Janesville
Zanesville

Ä′ō
cacao
tetrao

Ā′on
crayon
rayon

Ä′on
gaon

Ā′os
chaos

Ā′oth
Sabaoth

ĀP′ē
crapy
gapy
red-tapy

scrapy

ĂP′ē
chappy
gappy
gapy
happy
knappy
nappy
sappy
scrappy
snappy

ĂP′en
happen

ĀP′est
apest
drapest
escapest
gapest
rapest
scrapest
shapest

ĂP′est
clappest
enwrappest
flappest
lappest
mappest
nappest
rappest
sappest
slappest
snappest
trappest
wrappest

ĂP′et
lappet
tappet

ĀP′eth
apeth
drapeth
escapeth
gapeth
rapeth
scrapeth
shapeth

ĂP′eth
clappeth
enwrappeth
flappeth
lappeth
mappeth
nappeth
rappeth
sappeth
slappeth
snappeth
trappeth
wrappeth

ĀP′gōt
scapegoat

ĀP′grās
scapegrace

ĂP′id
rapid
sapid
vapid

ĂP′ik

jalapic
Lappic

ĀP′īn
rapine

ĀP′ing
aping
draping
escaping
gaping
raping
scraping
shaping

ĂP′ing
capping
clapping
Japping
entrapping
enwrapping
flapping
gapping
handicapping
lapping
mapping
napping
overlapping
rapping
sapping
scrapping
slapping
snapping
strapping
tapping
trapping
understrapping
unwrapping
wrapping

yapping

ĀP′is
apis
lapis
Serapis
tapis

ĂP′is
lapis
tapis

ĀP′ish
apish
papish

ĂP′ish
knappish
snappish

ĀP′ist
escapist
landscapist
Papist
rapist
red-tapist

ĀP′iz'm
escapism
papism
red-tapeism

ĀP′'l
antipapal
capel
maple
papal
staple
wool staple

ĂP′'l
antechapel
apple
chapel
dapple
grapple
knapple
love apple
rappel
scapple
scrapple
thrapple

ĀP′lē
shapely

ĂP′lē
haply

ĀP′les
apeless
capeless
crapeless
escapeless
grapeless
napeless
scrapeless
shapeless
tapeless

ĂP′les
capless
hapless
napless
sapless

ĂP′let
chaplet

ĂP′lin
chaplain
Chaplin

ĂP′ling
dappling
grappling
lapling
sapling

ĀP′'lz
Naples
Staples

ĂP′man
Capman
Chapman
Knapman

ĂP′nel
grapnel
shrapnel

ĀP′on
capon
misshapen
tapen
unshapen

ĀP′ril
April

ĂP′shun
caption
collapsion
contraption
elapsion
recaption

ĂP′shus
captious

ĂP′sing
collapsing
lapsing
relapsing

ĂP′stan
capstan

ĂP′stur
tapster

ĂP′ted
adapted

ĂP′test
adaptest
aptest
inaptest
raptest

ĂP′tin
captain

ĂP′tiv
adaptive
captive

ĂP′tiz'm
anabaptism
baptism

ĂPT′lē
aptly
inaptly
raptly

ĂPT′nes
aptness
inaptness
raptness
unaptness

ĂP′trap
claptrap

ĂP′tūr
capture
enrapture
rapture
recapture

ĂP′tŭr
adapter
apter
captor
chapter
rapter
recaptor

ĀP′ur
aper
caper
draper
escaper
gapper
landscaper
paper
raper
sapor
scraper
shaper
skyscraper
taper
tapir
undraper

ĂPT′nes
vapor

ĂP′ur
capper
clapper
dapper
entrapper
enwrapper
flapper
flyflapper
gapper
handicapper
lapper
mapper
napper
overlapper
rapper
sapper
slapper
snapper
snippersnapper
strapper
tapper
trapper
understrapper
unwrapper
whippersnapper
wrapper
yapper

ĀP′urz
capers
walking papers
(See also ĀP′ur;
add -s where
appropriate.)

ĂP′us
pappus

āle,   câre,   ădd,   ärm,   ăsk;   mē,   hĕre,   ĕnd;   īce,   ĭll;

crappous

ĂP'wing
lapwing

Ā'ra
cordillera
dulcamara
Marah
Sara
Sarah

ÂR'a
Sahara
tiara

Ă'ra
Bara
Clara

Ä'ra
caracara
Ferrara
Gemara
Sahara
solfatara
tiara

ĂR'ab
Arab
scarab

ĂR'ak
arrack
barrack
carrack

Â'rans
abearance

forbearance
(See also
ÄR'ens.)

Â'rant
declarant
forbearant
(See also
ÄR'ent.)

ĂR'ant
arrant

ÂR'ant
warrant
(See also
ŎR'ent.)

ĂR'as
arras
debarrass
disembarrass
embarrass
harass

ÄR'bē
Darby
Derby

ÂR'bel
harebell
prayer bell

ÄR'bij
garbage

ÄR'b'l
barbel

emmarble
garbel
garble
marble

ÄR'bling
garbling
marbling

ÄR'blur
garbler
marbler

ÄR'bôrd
larboard
starboard

ÄR'boil
parboil

ÄR'bon
carbon
charbon
chlorofluoro-
    carbon
fluorocarbon

ÄR'bur
arbor
barber
Barbor
enharbor
harbor
unharbor

ÄR'chē
archy
larchy
starchy

ÄR'chest
archest
enarchest
marchest
parchest
starchest

ÄR'cheth
archeth
enarcheth
marcheth
parcheth
starcheth

ÄR'chez
arches
countermarches
larches
marches
outmarches
overarches
parches
starches

ÄR'ching
arching
countermarch-
    ing
marching
outmarching
overarching
overmarching
parching
starching

ÄRCH'ment
archment
emparchment
parchment

ÄRCH'nes
archness

ÄR'chur
archer
clearstarcher
Larcher
marcher
starcher

ÄRCH'wā
archway

ÄR'dant
gardant
regardant
(See also
ÄR'dent.)

ÄRD'arm
yardarm

ÄR'dē
foolhardy
hardy
tardy

ÄR'ded
bombarded
carded
discarded
disregarded
guarded
larded
regarded
retarded
sharded
unguarded
unregarded
unretarded

ÄR'del
fardel

ÄR'dēn
nardine
sardine

**ÄR'den,
ÄR'don**
beer garden
bombardon
case harden
enharden
garden
harden
pardon

**ÄR'dend,
ÄR'dond**
case-hardened
hardened
pardoned
weather-
    hardened

ÄR'dent
ardent
(See also
ÄR'dant.)

ÄR'dest
bombardest
discardest
disregardest
guardest
hardest
lardest
regardest
retardest

ÄR'deth
discardeth
disregardeth
guardeth
lardeth
regardeth
retardeth

ÄRD'ful
disregardful
guardful
regardful

ÄRD'ik
anacardic
bardic
bezoardic
Lombardic
pericardic

ÄR'ding
bombarding
carding
discarding
disregarding
guarding
Harding
larding
placarding
regarding
retarding
unguarding
wool carding

ÄR'd'l
Bardle
McArdle

ÄRD'lē

hardly

ÄRD'les
cardless
guardless
regardless

ÄRD'ment
bombardment
retardment

ÄRD'nes
hardness

ÄRD'ning
gardening
hardening
pardoning

ÄRD'nur
gardener
hardener
pardner
pardoner

ÄR'dō
bocardo
bombardo

ÂR'dom
backstairdom
heirdom

ÄRD'ship
guardship
hardship

ÄR'dur
ardor

āle,   câre,   ădd,   ärm,   ăsk;   mē,   hĕre,   ĕnd;   īce,   ĭll;

bombarder
carder
discarder
disregarder
guarder
harder
larder
regarder
retarder

ÄRDZ′man
guardsman

ÂR′ē
ablutionary
abolitionary
accessary
accidentiary
accustomary
actuary
additionary
adminculary
adversary
aerie
airy
airy-fairy
ancillary
antiquary
apothecary
arbitrary
ary
Ave Mary
axillary
bacillary
beneficiary
bicentenary
calamary
canary
capillary

Carey
cassowary
cautionary
centenary
chary
circumplane-
    tary
clary
columbary
commentary
commissary
confectionary
confectionery
constabulary
consuetudinary
contemporary
contrary
contributary
coparcenary
corollary
coronary
costmary
culinary
customary
dairy
depositary
dictionary
dietary
dignitary
disciplinary
discretionary
distributary
divisionary
doctrinary
dromedary
eleemosynary
elocutionary
epistolary
estuary

evolutionary
extemporary
extraordinary
faerie
fairy
February
fiduciary
flary
formicary
formulary
fragmentary
functionary
ganglionary
glairy
glary
Guarneri
hairy
hebdomadary
hereditary
honorary
hypothecary
imaginary
incendiary
insurrectionary
intermediary
itinerary
janissary
January
lairy
lapidary
legendary
legionary
literary
luminary
mammillary
marry
Mary
maxillary
medullary

mercenary
military
millenary
missionary
momentary
monetary
mortuary
nary
necessary
noctuary
obituary
ordinary
ossuary
ostiary
parcenary
passionary
patibulary
pecuniary
pensionary
persicary
petitionary
planetary
prairie
prebendary
precautionary
preliminary
probationary
processionary
prolegomenary
proletary
proprietary
prothonotary
provisionary
pulmonary
quandary
questionary
questuary
reactionary
reliquary

residuary	tumulary	carbonari	Â'rans.)
retiary	tumultuary	charry	
reversionary	tutelary	scarry	**ĂR'ent**
revisionary	ubiquitary	sparry	apparent
revolutionary	unchary	starry	celarent
rosemary	unnecessary	tarry	parent
salivary	unwary		transparent
salutary	vagary	**ÂR'ēd**	(See also
sanctuary	vairy	varied	Â'rant;
sanguinary	valetudinary		ĂR'ant.)
sanitary	vary	**ĂR'el**	
scapulary	veterinary	apparel	**ÂR'es**
scary	vicenary	barrel	heiress
secondary	vicissitudinary	carol	
secretary	visionary	Carroll	**ÂR'est**
sedentary	vocabulary	disapparel	*airest*
seditionary	voluntary	Farrell	*barest*
seminary	voluptuary	Harrell	*bearest*
silentiary	vulnerary	parrel	*carest*
snary	wary	pork barrel	*comparest*
solitary	(See also ĔR'ē.)		*darest*
starey		**ĂR'eld**	*declarest*
stationary	**ĂR'ē**	appareled	*despairest*
stationery	Barrie	caroled	*ensnarest*
statuary	Carrie	double-	*fairest*
stipendiary	carry	barreled	*farest*
sublunary	charivari		*forbearest*
subsidiary	hari-kari	**ÂR'em**	*glarest*
sumptuary	harry	harem	*impairest*
supernumerary	intermarry		*outdarest*
syllabary	Larry	**ĂR'en**	*pairest*
temporary	marry	Karen	*parest*
tertiary	miscarry	McLaren	*preparest*
Tipperary	parry		*rarest*
titulary	tarry	**ĂR'ens**	*repairest*
topiary		apparence	*sharest*
traditionary	**ÄR'ē**	Clarence	*snarest*
tributary	araçari	transparence	*sparest*
tuitionary	barry	(See also	*squarest*

starest

swearest

tearest

unfairest

wearest

ÄR'est

barrest

debarrest

jarrest

marrest

scarrest

sparrest

starrest

tarrest

ĂR'et

carat

carrot

claret

garret

Garrett

parrot

ÂR'eth

aireth

bareth

beareth

careth

compareth

dareth

declareth

despaireth

ensnareth

fareth

flareth

forbeareth

forsweareth

glareth

impaireth

outdareth

paireth

pareth

prepareth

repaireth

shareth

snareth

spareth

squareth

stareth

sweareth

teareth

weareth

ÄR'eth

barreth

debarreth

marreth

scarreth

sparreth

starreth

tarreth

ÂR'ez

Benares

Buenos Aires

ÂR'fāsd

barefaced

fair-faced

ÄR'fish

garfish

starfish

ÂR'fôr

therefore

wherefore

ÂR'ful

careful

prayerful

uncareful

ÄR'gan

Dargan

ÄR'get

target

ÄR'gin

bargain

plea-bargain

ÄR'g'l

argle-bargle

gargle

ÄR'gō

Argo

argot

botargo

cargo

Dargo

embargo

Fargo

largo

Spargo

supercargo

ÄR'gon

argon

jargon

Sargon

ÄR'gū

argue

ĂR'id

arid

carried

harried

intermarried

married

miscarried

parried

tarried

ÂR'if, ĂR'if

hairif

ĂR'if

harif

tariff

ĂR'ij

carriage

disparage

intermarriage

marriage

miscarriage

railway car-

    riage

water carriage

ĂR'ik

agaric

Amharic

Balearic

barbaric

baric

Bulgaric

cinnabaric

Garrick

isobaric

Megaric

pimaric

Pindaric
polaric
saccharic
stearic
tartaric

ÄR'ik
Amharic

ÂR'ing
airing
baring
bearing
blaring
caring
chairing
charing
cheeseparing
comparing
daring
declaring
despairing
ensnaring
fairing
faring
flaring
forbearing
forswearing
glaring
impairing
outdaring
outstaring
outswearing
outwearing
overbearing
pairing
paring
preparing
repairing

scaring
seafaring
sharing
snaring
sparing
squaring
staring
swearing
tale-bearing
tearing
upbearing
underbearing
unsparing
upbearing
upstaring
uptearing
wayfaring
wearing

ÄR'ing
barring
charring
debarring
disbarring
jarring
marring
scarring
sparring
starring
tarring
unbarring

ÄR'ingks
larynx
pharynx

ÄR'is
Farris
Harris

Paris
phalaris
Polaris

ÂR'ish
bearish
debonairish
fairish
garish
marish
squarish
tarish

ĂR'ish
marish
parish

ÂR'iz'm
proletairism
Voltairism

ÄR'jent
argent
sergeant

ÄR'jest
chargest
dischargest
enlargest
largest
overchargest

ÄR'jet
garget
parget

ÄR'jeth
chargeth
dischargeth
enlargeth

overchargeth

ÄR'jez
barges
charges
discharges
enlarges
marges
targes

ÄR'jik
lethargic

ÄR'jin
margin

ÄR'jing
barging
charging
discharging
enlarging
overcharging

ÄRJ'lē
largely

ÄRJ'ment
enlargement

ÄRJ'ur
barger
charger
discharger
enlarger
larger
sparger
surcharger
undercharger

ÄR′kal	*marketh*	ÄR′k′l	darker
anarchal	*remarketh*	darkle	embarker
hierarchal		sparkle	harker
monarchal	**ÄR′kik**		larker
oligarchal	anarchic	**ÄRK′lē**	marcor
patriarchal	antianarchic	clarkly	marker
squirearchal	climatarchic	darkly	parker
	heptarchic	starkly	sharker
ÄR′kaz′m	hierarchic		sparker
sarcasm	monarchic	**ÄRK′let**	starker
	oligarchic	parklet	
ÄR′kē	patriarchic	sparklet	**ÄRK′wis**
barky			marquis
darky	**ÄR′kin**	**ÄRK′ling**	
heterarchy	Larkin	darkling	**ÄR′land**
hierarchy		sparkling	engarland
larky	**ÄR′king**		Farland
oligarchy	barking	**ÄRK′nes**	garland
patriarchy	carking	darkness	
	disembarking		**ÂR′lē**
ÄR′ken	embarking	**ÄRK′nur**	barely
bedarken	harking	darkener	fairly
darken	larking	hearkener	rarely
endarken	marking		unfairly
hearken	parking	**ÄR′kōl**	*yarely*
	remarking	charcoal	
ÄR′kest	skylarking		**ÄR′lē**
barkest		**ÄRK′som**	Arleigh
darkest	**ÄR′kish**	darksome	barley
embarkest	darkish		Charley
markest	larkish	**ÄRK′spur**	Farley
remarkest	sparkish	larkspur	gnarly
starkest			Harley
	ÄR′kist	**ÄRK′tik**	marli
ÄR′ket	heptarchist	Antarctic	McCarley
market	oligarchist	Arctic	parley
ÄR′keth	**ÄR′kīvs**	**ÄR′kur**	**ÂR′les**
barketh	archives	barker	airless
embarketh			

ōld, ôr, ŏdd, oil, fŏŏt, out; ūse, ûrn, ŭp; THis, thin

areless
nairless
heirless
pairless
prayerless
snareless
tareless

ÄR'les
scarless
starless
(See also ÄR;
add -less where
appropriate.)

ÄR'let
carlet
scarlet
starlet
varlet
(See also
ÄR'lot.)

ÄR'līk
starlike
(See also ÄR;
add -like where
appropriate.)

ÄR'lĭk
garlic
pilgarlic
sarlyk

ÂR'lĭn
airline
hairline

ÂR'līnd
carelined
hair-lined

ÄR'ling
darling
Harling
snarling
sparling
starling

ÄR'līt
starlight

ÄR'lit
far-lit
starlit

ÄR'lok
charlock
harlock
warlock

ÄR'lot
Charlotte
harlot
(See also
ÄR'let.)

ÂR'lūm
heirloom

ÄR'lur
gnarler
parlor
snarler

ÄR'lus
parlous

ÄR'mād
barmaid

ÂR'man
chairman

ÄR'men
carmen
larmen

ÄR'ment
debarment
disbarment
garment
sarment

ÄR'mest
alarmest
armest
charmest
disarmest
farmest
harmest

ÄR'met
armet

ÄR'meth
alarmeth
armeth
charmeth
disarmeth
farmeth
harmeth

ÄRM'ful
armful
charmful
harmful

unharmful

ÄR'mē
army
barmy

ÂR'mik
alexipharmic
lexipharmic
ptarmic

ÄR'min
carmine
harmine

ÄR'ming
alarming
arming
baby farming
charming
disarming
farming
forearming
harming
unalarming
unarming
uncharming
unharming

ÄRM'les
armless
charmless
harmless

ÄRM'let
armlet
charmlet

ÄR'mot
carmot

āle, câre, ădd, ärm, ăsk; mē, hĕre, ĕnd; īce, ĭll;

armot

R'mur
armer
mor
aby farmer
aarmer
sarmer
armer
armer
late armor
erpent
 charmer

R'nal
arnal
arnel
harnel
arnel
ncharnel

R'nard
Barnard

AR'nat
ncarnate

ÄR'nē
larney
arny
Killarney

ÄR'nes
aareness
lebonairness
fairness
areness
spareness
squareness

threadbareness
unfairness
whereness

ÄR'nes
farness
harness

ÄRN'ham
Farnham

ÄR'nij
carnage

ÄR'nish
garnish
tarnish
varnish

ÄR'nisht
garnished
tarnished
ungarnished
untarnished
unvarnished
varnished

ÄRN'lē
Darnley

ÄR'nold
Arnold

ÄR'nur
darner
garner
yarner

ÄR'ō
pharaoh

Rio de Janeiro

ÂR'ō
bolero
caballero
faro
llanero
sombrero
vaquero

ĂR'ō
arrow
barrow
farrow
harrow
marrow
narrow
sparrow
yarrow

ÄR'ō
carbonaro
claro
taro

ÄR'old
caroled
Harold

ÂR'on
Aaron
Charon

ĂR'on
baron
barren

ÄR'pest
carpest

harpest
sharpest

ÄR'pet
carpet

ÄR'peth
carpeth
harpeth

ÄR'pē
carpy
harpy

ÄR'ping
carping
harping
sharping

ÄR'pist
harpist

ÄRP'nes
sharpness

ÄR'pur
carper
harper
sharper

ÄR'sal
metatarsal
tarsal
varsal

ÄR'sel
parcel
sarcel

ÄR′sez
farces
parses
sarses

ÄR′shal
earl marshal
field marshal
immartial
impartial
marshal
Marshall
martial
partial
unmartial

ÂRS′lē
scarcely

ÂRS′ness
scarceness

ÄR′son
arson
Carson
Larsen
Larson
parson

ÄR′sur
parser
sparser

ÄR′tan
Spartan
tartan
(See also
ÄR′ten,
ÄR′ton.)

ÄR′tē
Astarte
charter party
ex parte
hearty
McCarty
party

ÄR′ted
broken-hearted
carted
charted
chicken-
  hearted
cold-hearted
darted
departed
double-hearted
down-hearted
faint-hearted
false-hearted
flint-hearted
frank-hearted
free-hearted
full-hearted
gentle-hearted
great-hearted
half-hearted
hard-hearted
hare-hearted
hearted
hen-hearted
high-hearted
imparted
iron-hearted
kind-hearted
large-hearted
leaden-hearted
light-hearted

lion-hearted
marble-hearted
open-hearted
pale-hearted
parted
pigeon-hearted
proud-hearted
public-hearted
right-hearted
sad-hearted
shallow-
  hearted
simple-hearted
single-hearted
smarted
soft-hearted
started
stony-hearted
stout-hearted
tender-hearted
traitor-hearted
triparted
truehearted
unhearted
unimparted
upstarted
warm-hearted
weak-hearted
wise-hearted

ÄR′ten,
ÄR′ton
barton
carton
dishearten
enhearten
hearten
kindergarten
marten

smarten

ÄR′test
cartest
dartest
departest
impartest
partest
smartest
startest
upstartest

ÄR′teth
carteth
darteth
departeth
imparteth
parteth
smarteth
starteth
upstarteth

ÄRT′ful
artful

ÄR′tha
Martha

ÄR′thē
McCarthy

ÄR′THest
farthest

ÄR′THing
farthing

ÄR′THur
farther

ÄR'thur
Arthur

ÄR'tin
martin

ÄR'ting
carting
darting
departing
hearting
imparting
smarting
starting
sweethearting
uncarting
upstarting

ÄR'tist
artist
Chartist

ÄR'tīt
bipartite

ÄR't'l
dartle
startle

ÄRT'lē
partly
smartly
tartly

ÄRT'les
artless
chartless
heartless

ÄRT'let
heartlet
martlet
tartlet

ÄRT'ling
startling

ÄRT'ment
apartment
compartment
department
impartment

ÄRT'nes
smartness
tartness

ÄRT'rij
cartridge
partridge

ÄRT'wā
cartway
partway

ÄR'tur
barter
bemartyr
carter
charter
darter
departer
garter
imparter
martyr
parter
protomartyr

smarter
starter
tartar
tarter
unmartyr
upstarter

ĂR'um
arum
carom
harum-scarum
larum
marum

ÄR'um
alarum

ÂR'ur
airer
armor-bearer
barer
bearer
blarer
comparer
darer
declarer
despairer
ensnarer
fairer
flarer
forbearer
forswearer
glarer
impairer
mace-bearer
outdarer
outstarer
overbearer
parer

preparer
rarer
repairer
seafarer
sharer
snarer
sparer
squarer
standard-bearer
starer
swearer
sword-bearer
talebearer
tankard bearer
tearer
trainbearer
upbearer
wayfarer
wearer

ÄR'ur
barrer
bizarrer
debarrer
marrer
sparrer
tarrer

ÄR'val
larval

ÄR'vē
Garvey
Harvey

ÄR'vel
carvel
marvel

ÄR'veld
marveled

ÄR'ven
carven

ÄR'vest
harvest
starvest

ÄR'ving
carving
starving

ÄRV'ling
marveling
starveling

ÄR'vur
carver
marver
starver

ÂR'wāvs
airwaves

ÂR'wel
farewell

ÂR'whīl
erewhile

ÂR'wôrn
careworn
prayer worn

ÄS'a
Amasa
Asa

ĂS'a
Hadasseh
Manasseh

Ā'sal
basal
casal

ĂS'āt
cassate
incrassate

ĂS'ē
Gracie
Lacey
lacy
précis
racy

ĂS'ē
brassie
brassy
classy
gassy
glassy
grassy
lassie
Malagasy
massy
morassy
sassy
Tallahassee

Ā'sens,
Ā'sans
abaisance
adjacence
complacence
connascence

interjacence
obeisance
renascence

Ā'sent,
Ā'sant
adjacent
circumjacent
complacent
connascent
"daycent"
enascent
indurascent
interjacent
jacent
naissant
nascent
"raycent"
renaissant
renascent
subjacent
superjacent

ĀS'est
abasest
basest
begracest
belacest
bracest
chasest
debasest
defacest
disgracest
displacest
effacest
embracest
enlacest
erasest
facest

gracest
interlacest
lacest
outpacest
pacest
placest
racest
replacest
retracest
spacest
tracest
unlacest

ĂS'est
amassest
classest
crassest
massest
passest
surpassest

ĂS'et
asset
basset
brasset
facet
fascet
placet
(See also
ĂS'it.)

ĂS'eth
abaseth
baseth
begraceth
belaceth
braceth
chaseth
debaseth

defaceth
disgraceth
displaceth
effaceth
embraceth
enlaceth
eraseth
faceth
graceth
interlaceth
laceth
outpaceth
paceth
placeth
raceth
replaceth
retraceth
spaceth
traceth
unlaceth

ĂS'eth
amasseth
classeth
masseth
passeth
surpasseth

ĀS'ez
aces
bases
begraces
belaces
braces
breathing
  spaces
cases
chariot traces
chases

commonplaces
debases
defaces
disgraces
displaces
effaces
embraces
enlaces
faces
footpaces
footraces
graces
grimaces
hiding places
horse races
interlaces
interspaces
laces
maces
misplaces
outfaces
outpaces
paces
places
races
replaces
resting-places
retraces
spaces
steeplechases
traces
trysting places
ukases
uncases
unlaces
vases

ĂS'ez
amasses

asses
brasses
classes
gases
glasses
grasses
lasses
masses
molasses
morasses
passes
surpasses

ĀS'ful
disgraceful
graceful
ungraceful

ĂSH'ā
attaché
cachet
sachet

Ā'shal
abbatial
craniofacial
facial
glacial
palatial
prelatial
racial
spatial
unifacial

ĂSH'bôrd
dashboard
splashboard

Ā'shens

patience

Ā'shent
impatient
patient

ĂSH'est
cashest
clashest
crashest
dashest
flashest
gashest
gnashest
lashest
mashest
slashest
smashest
splashest
thrashest

ĂSH'eth
casheth
clasheth
crasheth
dasheth
flasheth
gasheth
gnasheth
lasheth
masheth
slasheth
smasheth
splasheth
thrasheth

ĂSH'ez
abashes
ashes

caches
cashes
clashes
crashes
dashes
flashes
gashes
gnashes
hashes
lashes
mashes
mustaches
rashes
rehashes
sashes
slashes
smashes
splashes
unlashes

ĂSH′ful
bashful
gashful
rashful
unbashful

ĂSH′ē
ashy
flashy
hashy
mashie
mashy
plashy
slashy
splashy
trashy

ĂSH′ing
abashing

balderdashing
cashing
clashing
crashing
dashing
fashing
flashing
gashing
gnashing
hashing
lashing
mashing
plashing
slashing
smashing
splashing
thrashing
unlashing

ĂSH′lē
Ashley
flashly
gashly

ĂSH′man
ashman
flashman

Ā′shō
Horatio

Ā′shun
abacination
abalienation
abbreviation
abdication
aberration
abjudication
abjuration

ablactation
ablation
abnegation
abomination
abrogation
absentation
acceleration
acceptation
acclamation
acclimatation
acclimation
acclimatization
accommoda-
   tion
accreditation
accrimination
accubation
accumulation
accusation
acervation
acidification
activation
actualization
actuation
acumination
acupunctuation
adaptation
adequation
adhortation
adjudication
adjuration
administration
admiration
adoration
adornation
adulation
adulteration
adumbration
adversation

advocation
aeration
aerostation
affectation
affiliation
affirmation
afflation
afforestation
aggeration
agglomeration
agglutination
aggrandization
aggravation
aggregation
agitation
agnation
agnomination
alcoholization
alienation
alimentation
alkalization
allegation
allegorization
alleviation
alligation
alliteration
allocation
alteration
altercation
alternation
amalgamation
ambulation
amelioration
Americaniza-
   tion
ampliation
amplification
amputation
analyzation

āle, câre, ădd, ärm, ăsk; mē, hĕre, ĕnd; īce, ĭll;

anathematiza-
   tion
anglicization
Anglification
angulation
animalization
animation
annexation
annihilation
annomination
annotation
annulation
annumeration
annunciation
anticipation
antilibration
appellation
application
appreciation
approbation
appropriation
approximation
aration
arbitration
arcuation
argentation
argumentation
aromatization
arrestation
arrogation
articulation
Asian
asphyxiation
aspiration
assassination
assentation
asseveration
assignation
assimilation

assimulation
association
atomization
attenuation
attestation
attrectation
augmentation
auguration
auscultation
authentication
authorization
averruncation
aviation
avocation
backwardation
basification
beatification
beautification
bifurcation
blood relation
blusteration
bombilation
botheration
brutalization
brutification
cachinnation
calcification
calcination
calculation
calorification
calumniation
cameration
canalization
cancellation
canonization
cantillation
capitalization
capitation
capitulation

caprification
captivation
carbonization
carbunculation
carnation
cassation
castellation
castigation
castrametation
catechization
causation
cauterization
celebration
cementation
centralization
cerebration
certification
cessation
cetacean
chain station
characteriza-
   tion
chrismation
Christianiza-
   tion
cineration
circulation
circumgyration
circumnaviga-
   tion
circumnutation
circumvallation
circumvolation
citation
civilization
clarification
classification
coagulation
coaxation

codification
cogitation
cognation
cohabitation
collation
colligation
collocation
colonization
coloration
columniation
combination
commemora-
   tion
commendation
commensura-
   tion
commination
commiseration
communication
commutation
compellation
compensation
compilation
complication
compotation
compurgation
computation
concentration
concertation
conciliation
condemnation
condensation
condonation
confabulation
confederation
configuration
confirmation
confiscation
conflagration

---

conformation
confrontation
confutation
congelation
conglomeration
congratulation
congregation
conjugation
conjuration
connotation
consecration
conservation
consideration
consolation
consolidation
constellation
consternation
consubstantia-
   tion
consultation
consummation
contamination
contemplation
continuation
contravallation
conversation
convocation
cooperation
co-optation
coordination
copulation
cornification
coronation
corporation
correlation
corroboration
corrugation
coruscation
creation

cremation
crenellation
crepitation
crimination
crustacean
crustation
crystallization
cubation
culmination
cultivation
cupellation
curvation
Dalmatian
damnation
damnification
debarkation
debilitation
decalcification
decantation
decapitation
decentraliza-
   tion
decimation
declamation
declaration
declination
decollation
deconsecration
decoration
decortication
decrepitation
decubation
decussation
dedication
defalcation
defamation
defecation
deflagration
defloration

deformation
defraudation
degeneration
degradation
degustation
dehortation
deification
delation
delectation
delegation
deliberation
delimitation
delineation
deliration
deltafication
demarcation
dementation
demonetization
demonstration
demoralization
denationaliza-
   tion
denization
denomination
denotation
dentation
denticulation
dentilation
denudation
denunciation
deodorization
deoppilation
deosculation
deoxidation
deoxygenation
depilation
deploration
depopulation
deportation

depositation
depravation
deprecation
depreciation
depredation
deprivation
depuration
deputation
derivation
derogation
desecration
desiccation
desideration
designation
desolation
desperation
despoliation
desquamation
destination
deterioration
determination
deterration
detestation
detonization
detruncation
devastation
deviation
devirgination
dictation
diffarreation
differentiation
digitation
dilapidation
dilatation
dilation
dimidiation
disapprobation
discoloration
discontinuation

āle, câre, ădd, ärm, ăsk; mē, hĕre, ĕnd; īce, ĭll;

discrimination
disculpation
disfiguration
disinclination
disintegration
dislocation
dispensation
disputation
disqualification
dissemination
dissentation
dissertation
disseveration
dissimulation
dissipation
dissociation
distillation
divagation
divarication
diversification
divination
divulgation
documentation
domestication
domiciliation
domination
donation
dotation
dulcification
duplication
duration
economization
edification
education
edulcoration
effectuation
effemination
effeminization
efflation

effoliation
ejaculation
ejulation
elaboration
elation
electrification
electrization
electrolyzation
elevation
elimination
elixation
elucidation
emaciation
emanation
emancipation
emasculation
embrocation
emendation
emigration
emulation
endenization
enervation
enthronization
enucleation
enumeration
enunciation
equalization
equation
equilibration
equitation
equivocation
eradication
eructation
estimation
estivation
eternization
etherealization
etiolation
evacuation

evangelization
evaporation
eventuation
evisceration
evocation
evolation
exacerbation
exaggeration
exaltation
examination
exasperation
excavation
excitation
exclamation
excogitation
excommunica-
    tion
excoriation
excruciation
exculpation
execration
exemplification
exercitation
exfoliation
exhalation
exhilaration
exhortation
exhumation
exoneration
expatiation
expatriation
expectation
expectoration
experimenta-
    tion
expiation
expiration
explanation
explication

exploitation
exploration
expoliation
exportation
expostulation
expropriation
expugnation
expurgation
exsiccation
exsufflation
extemporiza-
    tion
extenuation
extermination
externalization
extirpation
extravasation
extrication
exudation
exultation
fabrication
facilitation
falcation
falsification
familiarization
fasciation
fascination
fecundation
federation
felicitation
feneration
fenestration
fermentation
ferrumination
fertilization
feudalization
fibrination
figuration
filiation

filtration
fissiparation
fixation
flagellation
flagitation
flirtation
floccillation
florification
flossification
flotation
fluctuation
flusteration
fluxation
foliation
fomentation
forcipation
foreordination
formation
formulization
fortification
fossilification
fossilization
foundation
fraternation
fraternization
frequentation
friation
frication
frondation
fructification
frumentation
frustration
fulguration
fulmination
fumigation
furcation
furfuration
galvanization
gasification

gelatination
gelatinization
gemination
gemmation
generalization
generation
generification
geniculation
germination
gestation
gesticulation
glaciation
glandulation
glomeration
gloriation
glorification
glutination
gradation
graduation
granitification
granulation
graticulation
gratification
gratulation
gravidation
gravitation
gunation
gustation
gyration
habilitation
habitation
habituation
hallucination
hariolation
harmonization
hebetation
Hellenization
hepatization
hesitation

hibernation
Hibernicization
homologation
horrification
hortation
humanization
humectation
humiliation
hybridization
hydration
hypothecation
idealization
ideation
identification
illaqueation
illation
illustration
imagination
imbrication
imitation
immaculation
immanation
immigration
immoderation
immolation
immortaliza-
    tion
impanation
impersonation
implication
imploration
importation
imprecation
impregnation
improvisation
impugnation
imputation
inadequation
inaffectation

inanimation
inapplication
inappreciation
inarticulation
inauguration
inauration •
incameration
incantation
incapacitation
incarceration
incarnation
incarnification
inchoation
incineration
incitation
incivilization
inclination
incommodation
inconsideration
incorporation
incrassation
incremation
incrustation
incubation
inculcation
inculpation
incultivation
incurvation
indemnification
indentation
indetermination
indication
indigitation
indignation
indiscrimina-
    tion
individualiza-
    tion
individuation

---

indoctrination
induration
inebriation
inequation
infatuation
infestation
infeudation
infiltration
inflammation
inflation
information
ingemination
ingratiation
ingravidation
ingurgitation
inhabitation
inhalation
inhumation
initiation
innervation
innovation
inoculation
inordination
inosculation
insinuation
inspiration
inspissation
installation
instauration
instigation
instillation
instrumenta-
   tion
insubordina-
   tion
insufflation
insulation
insultation
integration

integumenta-
   tion
inteneration
intensation
intensification
intercalation
intercolumnia-
   tion
intercommuni-
   cation
interdigitation
interlineation
interlocation
intermediation
intermigration
intermutation
interpellation
interpenetra-
   tion
interpolation
interpretation
interrelation
interrogation
interstratifica-
   tion
intimation
intimidation
intoleration
intonation
intoxication
intrication
inundation
invalidation
investigation
invigoration
invitation
invocation
irradiation
irrigation

irritation
isolation
iteration
jactitation
jaculation
jobation
jollification
jubilation
Judaization
justification
laceration
lachrymation
lactation
lallation
lamentation
lamination
lancination
laniation
lapidation
lapidification
Latinization
laudation
laureation
lavation
laxation
legalization
legation
legislation
legitimation
levation
levigation
levitation
libation
liberation
libration
licentiation
lignification
limitation
lineation

liquation
liquidation
literalization
litigation
lixiviation
localization
location
lubrication
lucubration
lunation
lustration
luxation
luxuriation
macadamiza-
   tion
maceration
machicolation
machination
maculation
magnetization
magnification
maladministra-
   tion
maleficiation
malformation
malleation
malversation
manifestation
manipulation
marmoration
martyrization
mastication
materialization
materiation
matriculation
maturation
maximization
mediation
mediatization

ōld, ôr, ŏdd, oil, fŏŏt, out; ūse, ûrn, ŭp; THis, thin

medication	negation	occupation	peculation
meditation	negotiation	oneration	penetration
melioration	neologization	operation	perambulation
mellification	nervation	oppugnation	percolation
mendication	neutralization	oration	peregrination
mensuration	nictation	orbiculation	perfectation
mesmerization	nictitation	orchestration	perfectionation
metallization	nidification	ordination	perforation
methodization	nidulation	organization	perlustration
migration	nigrification	orientation	permeation
ministration	nitrification	origination	permutation
miscegenation	*nobilitation*	ornamentation	pernoctation
mitigation	noctambulation	oscillation	peroration
mobilization	noctivagation	oscitation	perpetration
moderation	nodation	osculation	perpetuation
modernization	nomination	ossification	perscrutation
modification	normalization	ostentation	personation
modulation	notation	*otiation*	personification
molestation	notification	ovation	perspiration
mollification	Novatian	oxidation	perturbation
monetization	novation	oxygenation	pestillation
monstration	nudation	ozonation	petrification
moralization	nudification	ozonification	*philosophation*
mortification	*nugation*	ozonization	phonation
multiplication	nullification	pacation	phonetization
mummification	numeration	pacification	piscation
mundification	obfuscation	pagination	placation
murmuration	objurgation	palification	plantation
mutation	oblation	palliation	plebification
mutilation	*oblatration*	palpation	plication
mutuation	obligation	palpitation	pluralization
mystification	obliteration	pandiculation	polarization
narration	obnubilation	panification	police station
nasalization	obscuration	paralyzation	pollicitation
natation	obsecration	participation	pollination
nation	observation	patronization	polling station
naturalization	obstination	pauperization	population
navigation	obviation	pausation	porphyrization
necessitation	occultation	pectination	postillation

postulation
potation
precipitation
predacean
predation
predestination
predication
predomination
premeditation
preoccupation
preparation
preponderation
presensation
presentation
preservation
prestidigitation
prevarication
privation
probation
proclamation
procrastination
procreation
procuration
profanation
profligation
prognostication
prolation
prolification
prolongation
promulgation
pronation
pronunciation
propagation
propination
propitiation
propugnation
prorogation
prostration
protestation

protuberation
provocation
publication
pullulation
pulsation
pulverization
punctuation
purgation
purification
quadruplication
qualification
quantification
quartation
quassation
quotation
racemation
radiation
radication
ramification
ratification
ratiocination
ration
realization
recalcitration
recantation
recapitulation
recidivation
reciprocation
recitation
reclamation
recognization
recommenda-
tion
reconciliation
recordation
recreation
recrimination
rectification
recubation

recuperation
recurvation
recusation
redintegration
reformation
refrigeration
refutation
regelation
regeneration
registration
regulation
rehabilitation
reiteration
rejuvenation
relation
relaxation
relegation
relocation
remanation
remonetization
remonstration
remuneration
renegation
renovation
renunciation
reparation
repatriation
replication
representation
reprobation
reptation
repudiation
reputation
reservation
resignation
resinification
respiration
restoration
resupination

resuscitation
retaliation
retardation
reticulation
retractation
retrogradation
revelation
reverberation
revibration
revivification
revocation
rhetorication
roboration
rogation
rose carnation
rotation
rubification
ruination
rumination
rustication
saburration
sacrification
salification
salination
salivation
saltation
salutation
salvation
sanctification
sanguification
sanitation
saponification
satiation
sation
saturation
scarification
scintillation
sciscitation
scorification

ōld, ôr, ŏdd, oil, fŏŏt, out; ūse, ûrn, ŭp; THis, thin

scrutation
secularization
secundation
sedimentation
segmentation
segregation
self-centration
self-preserva-
tion
self-renuncia-
tion
semination
sensation
sensualization
separation
sequestration
serration
serrulation
sibilation
siccation
sideration
signation
signification
silicification
simplification
simulation
sinuation
situation
solarization
solemnization
solicitation
solidification
somnambula-
tion
sophistication
specialization
specification
speculation
speechification

spifflication
spiritualization
spoliation
sputation
stagnation
starvation
station
stellation
sternutation
stigmatization
stimulation
stipulation
strangulation
stratification
striation
stridulation
stultification
stupration
subarrhation
subjugation
sublation
sublevation
subligation
sublimation
sublimification
sublimitation
sublineation
subordination
subornation
subrogation
substantiation
subtilization
succussation
sudation
sufflation
suffocation
suggilation
sulcation
sulphuration

summation
superannuation
supererogation
supination
supplantation
supplementa-
tion
supplication
supportation
suppuration
surrogation
suspensation
suspiration
sustentation
susurration
syllabication
syllogization
symbolization
synchroniza-
tion
syncopation
systematization
tabularization
tabulation
tantalization
tarnation
tartarization
taxation
temeration
temporization
temptation
terebration
tergiversation
termination
tessellation
testacean
testamentation
testation
testification

theorization
Thracian
thurification
tintinnabulation
titillation
titration
titteration
titubation
toleration
trabeation
tractation
tractoration
tralation
tranquillization
transanimation
transcolation
transfiguration
transformation
translation
transliteration
translocation
transmigration
transmogrifica-
tion
transmutation
transpiration
transplantation
transportation
transubstantia-
tion
transudation
tremulation
trepidation
triangulation
tribulation
triplication
tripudiation
trituration
trucidation

---

trullization
truncation
tubulation
tumultuation
turbination
typification
ulceration
ultimation
ululation
undulation
unification
ustulation
usurpation
utilization
vacation
vaccination
vacillation
vacuolation
validation
valuation
vaporation
vaporization
vapulation
variation
variegation
vaticination
vegetation
vellication
venation
venenation
veneration
ventilation
verbalization
verberation
verification
vermiculation
vernation
versification
vesication

vexation
vexillation
vibration
vigesimation
vilification
vindemiation
vindication
violation
visitation
vitalization
vitiation
nitrification
vitriolation
vitriolization
vituperation
vivification
vocalization
vocation
vociferation
volatilization
volcanization
vulcanization
(See also
ĀSH'ē-an.)

**ĀSH'en,
ĀSH'un**
ashen
compassion
fashion
impassion
master passion
passion
(See also
ĀSH'ē-an.)

ĀSH'und
dispassioned
fashioned

impassioned
old-fashioned
passioned
unfashioned
unimpassioned
unpassioned

ĂSH'ur
Asher
baggage-
   smasher
Brasher
casher
clasher
crasher
dasher
flasher
gasher
haberdasher
lasher
masher
rasher
slasher
smasher
splasher
thrasher
unlasher

Ā'shus
audacious
bibacious
capacious
contumacious
disgracious
disputatious
edacious
efficacious
execratious
fallacious

feracious
flirtatious
fugacious
fumacious
gracious
incapacious
inefficacious
linguacious
loquacious
mendacious
minacious
misgracious
mordacious
ostentatious
palacious
perspicacious
pertinacious
pervicacious
predacious
procacious
pugnacious
rampacious
rapacious
sagacious
salacious
sequacious
spacious
tenacious
ungracious
veracious
vexatious
vivacious
voracious

acanaceous
acanthaceous
alliaceous
amylaceous
arenaceous

bulbaceous
cactaceous
camphoraceous
capillaceous
carbonaceous
cetaceous
corallaceous
coriaceous
cretaceous
crustaceous
cylindraceous
erinaceous
fabaceous
farinaceous
ferulaceous
filaceous
foliaceous
frumentaceous
fungaceous
furfuraceous
gallinaceous
gemmaceous
herbaceous
lappaceous
lardaceous
liliaceous
marlaceous
micaceous
olivaceous
orchidaceous
palmaceous
pectinaceous
perdaceous
perlaceous
piperaceous
pomaceous
porraceous
psittaceous
pulveraceous

ranunculaceous
resinaceous
rosaceous
rutaceous
sabaceous
salicaceous
saponaceous
sarmentaceous
saxifragaceous
schorlaceous
scoriaceous
sebaceous
setaceous
stercoraceous
testaceous
tophaceous
torfaceous
truttaceous
turbinaceous
vinaceous
violaceous

ĂSH'vil
Ashville
Nashville

Ā'sīd
bayside
braeside
wayside

ĂS'id
acid
placid

ĂS'ij
brassage
passage

ĂS'ik
aphasic
basic
bibasic
dibasic
quadribasic
tribasic

ĂS'ik
boracic
classic
Jurassic
Liassic
potassic
sebacic
thoracic
Triassic

ĂS'il
facile
gracile

ĂS'in
basin
(See also
ĂS''n.)

ĂS'in
assassin

ĂS'in
spadassin

ĂS'ing
abasing
basing
begracing
belacing
bracing

casing
chasing
debasing
defacing
disgracing
displacing
effacing
embracing
enlacing
erasing
facing
foot racing
gracing
horse racing
interlacing
interspacing
lacing
misplacing
outfacing
outpacing
pacing
placing
racing
replacing
retracing
self-abasing
spacing
steeplechasing
tight-lacing
tracing
uncasing
underbracing
unlacing

ĂS'ing
amassing
classing
gassing
massing

āle, câre, ădd, ärm, ăsk; mē, hĕre, ĕnd; īce, ĭll;

overpassing
passing
surpassing
underclassing

ĀS'is
basis
crasis
glacis
oasis
phasis

ĂS'is
chassis

ĂS'it
tacit
(See also
ĀS'et.)

ĀS'iv
assuasive
dissuasive
evasive
invasive
persuasive
pervasive
suasive

ĂS'iv
impassive
massive
passive

ĂS'ka
Alaska
Athabaska
Nebraska

ĂS'kal
mascle
paschal
rascal

ĂS'kar
Lascar
Madagascar

ȦS'kest
askest
baskest
bemaskest
maskest
taskest
unmaskest

ȦS'ket
basket
breadbasket
casket
flasket
gasket
lasket

ȦS'keth
asketh
basketh
bemasketh
masketh
tasketh
unmasketh

ȦS'king
asking
basking
bemasking
masking
overtasking

tasking
unmasking

ĀS'kō
Belasco
fiasco
tabasco
tasco

ȦS'kur
asker
basker
casquer
masker

ĂS'kus
Damascus

ĂSK'with
Asquith

ȦS''l
castle
entassel
envassal
tassel
vassal
wrastle

ĀS'lē
basely
commonplacely

ĀS'les
aceless
baseless
caseless
faceless
graceless

laceless
maceless
paceless
placeless
raceless
spaceless
traceless

ĀS'let
bracelet

ĂS'let
haslet
taslet

ĀS'man
baseman
first baseman
laceman
paceman
placeman
raceman
second base-
    man
third baseman

ȦS'man
classman
gasman
glassman

ĀS'ment
abasement
basement
begracement
belacement
casement
debasement
defacement

displacement
effacement
embracement
encasement
enlacement
erasement
interlacement
misplacement
placement
replacement
retracement
self-abasement

ĂS'ment
amassment

ĂS'min or
ĂZ'min
jasmine

ĀS''n
chasten
enchasten
hasten
(See also
ĀS'on.)

ĂS''n
fasten
(See also
ĂS'on.)

ĀS'nur
chastener
hastener

ĂS'nes
crassness

ĀS'ō, ĂS'ō
basso
lasso
Sargasso
Tasso

ĂS'ok
cassock
hassock

ĀS'on
caisson
Grayson
Jason
mason
(See also
ĀS'n.)

ĂS'on
casson
(See also
ĂS''n.)

ĂS'pen
aspen

ĂS'pest
claspest
enclaspest
gaspest
graspest
raspest
unclaspest

ĂS'peth
claspeth
enclaspeth
gaspeth
graspeth

ráspeth
unclaspeth

ĂS'pik
aspic

ĂS'ping
clasping
enclasping
engrasping
gasping
grasping
rasping
unclasping

ĂS'pur
asper
Caspar
Casper
clasper
gasper
grasper
jasper
rasper

ĂS'ta
Shasta

Ā'star
daystar

ĀS'tē
hasty
pasty
tasty

ĂS'tē
blasty
epinasty

genioplasty
masty
nasty
vasty

ĀS'ted
basted
hasted
long-waisted
pasted
short-waisted
tasted
untasted
unwasted
war-wasted
wasted

ĂS'ted
blasted
contrasted
fasted
flabbergasted
lasted
masted
outlasted
unblasted
undermasted

ĂS'tel
pastel

ĀST'est
bastest
chastest
foretastest
hastest
pastest
tastest
wastest

āle,   câre,   ădd,   ärm,   ăsk;   mē,   hĕre,   ĕnd;   īce,   ĭll;

ȦST'est
castest
contrastest
fastest
lastest
outlastest
vastest

ĀST'eth
basteth
foretasteth
hasteth
pasteth
tasteth
wasteth

ȦST'eth
casteth
contrasteth
fasteth
lasteth
outlasteth

ĀST'ful
distasteful
tasteful
wasteful

ȦS'tif
mastiff

ĀS'tij
wastage

ĂS'tik
amphiblastic
anaclastic
antiphrastic
antonomastic

bioplastic
bombastic
ceroplastic
chiliastic
clastic
deutoplastic
dichastic
docimastic
drastic
dynastic
ecclesiastic
elastic
emplastic
encomiastic
esemplastic
fantastic
galvanoplastic
gelastic
gymnastic
Hudibrastic
iconoclastic
inelastic
mastic
metaphrastic
monastic
neoplastic
onomastic
orgiastic
paraphrastic
parasceuastic
paronomastic
pierastic
periphrastic
phelloplastic
plagioclastic
plastic
pleonastic
proplastic

protoplastic
sarcastic
scholastic
scholiastic
spastic
tetrastich

ĂS'tiks
ecclesiastics
elastics
fantastics
gymnastics
phelloplastics

ȦS'tīm
pastime

ĀST'ing
basting
foretasting
hasting
pasting
tasting
unwasting
wasting

ȦST'ing
blasting
casting
contrasting
everlasting
fasting
flabbergasting
forecasting
lasting
recasting

ĀS'tingz
bastings

Hastings
(See also
ĀST'ing; add
-*s* where
appropriate.)

ȦST'lē
ghastly
lastly
steadfastly
vastly

ĀST'les
basteless
hasteless
pasteless
tasteless
waistless
wasteless

ȦST'ment
blastment
contrastment

ȦST'nes
fastness
vastness

ȦST'ning
fastening

ĂS'ton
Aston
Gaston

ĂS'tral
astral
cadastral
subastral

ōld, ôr, ŏdd, oil, fŏŏt, out; ūse, ûrn, ŭp; THis, thin

ĀS′trē
pastry

ĂS′trik
cacogastric
digastric
gastric
hypogastric
perigastric

ĂS′tron
apastron
plastron

ĀS′trus
disastrous

ĀS′tur
baster
chaster
foretaster
paster
taster
waster

ĀS′tūr
pasture

ĂS′tŭr,
ĂS′tur
alabaster
aster
Astor
bandmaster
barrack master
beplaster
blaster
broadcaster

burgomaster
bushmaster
cablecaster
cadastre
canaster
caster
castor
China aster
choirmaster
concertmaster
contraster
court plaster
criticaster
disaster
faster
flabbergaster
forecaster
ghetto blaster
Goniaster
grammaticaster
grand master
headmaster
housemaster
interpilaster
Latinitaster
master
medicaster
oleaster
overmaster
past master
pastor
paymaster
piaster
pilaster
plaster
poetaster
postmaster
quartermaster
ringmaster

schoolmaster
scoutmaster
shinplaster
stationmaster
sticking plaster
taskmaster
toastmaster
vaster
Zoroaster

ĀS′tur
shaster

ĂS′turd,
ĀS′turd
bastard
beplastered
dastard
mastered
overmastered
pilastered
plastered
unmastered

ĂS′tus
Erastus
Rastus

ĂS′tyun
bastion

ĀS′ur
abaser
ambulance
   chaser
baser
begracer
belacer
bracer

chaser
debaser
defacer
disgracer
displacer
effacer
embracer
encaser
eraser
facer
footracer
gracer
grimacer
horse racer
interlacer
lacer
macer
misplacer
outpacer
pacer
placer
racer
replacer
retracer
spacer
steeplechaser
tracer
unlacer

ĂS′ur
amasser
antimacassar
masser
passer
placer
surpasser

ĀS′ur
kirschwasser

āle, câre, ădd, ärm, ăsk; mē, hĕre, ĕnd; īce, ĭll;

Ā'ta	(See also	ĀT'ed	antiquated
albata	ĀT'on.)	abated	appreciated
data		abbreviated	approbated
dentata	**ĀT'ant**	abdicated	appropriated
errata	blatant	ablocated	approximated
Invertebrata	latent	abnegated	arbitrated
postulata	natant	abominated	armillated
pro rata	patent	abrogated	armor-plated
strata	statant	accelerated	arrogated
ultimata		accentuated	articulated
Vertebrata	**ĀT'ē**	accommodated	asphyxiated
	Ate	accumulated	aspirated
ĂT'a	eighty	acidulated	assassinated
matamata	ex necessitate	actuated	asseverated
regatta	Haiti	addle-pated	assimilated
strata	Jubilate	adjudicated	assimulated
	maty	adulterated	associated
Ä'ta	platy	advocated	asteriated
a ballata	slaty	aerated	attenuated
batata	weighty	affiliated	augurated
cantata		agglomerated	aurated
data	**ĂT'ē**	aggravated	authenticated
imbrocata	batty	aggregated	awaited
inamorata	catty	agitated	baited
Mahratta	chatty	alienated	bated
pro rata	Cincinnati	alleviated	belated
reata	fatty	allocated	berated
serenata	Hattie	alternated	bifurcated
sonata	Mattie	amalgamated	calculated
	matty	ameliorated	calumniated
ĀT'al	natty	ampliated	camphorated
fatal	Pattie	amputated	capacitated
natal	patty	annihilated	capitulated
postnatal	ratty	annotated	captivated
prenatàl		annulated	carbonated
Statal	**ȦT'ē**	*annumerated*	castellated
	antenati	annunciated	castigated
ĀT'an	illuminati	antedated	celebrated
Satan	literati	anticipated	certificated

ōld, ôr, ŏdd, oil, fŏŏt, out; ūse, ûrn, ŭp; THis, thin

circulated	culminated	dominated	expectorated
circumstanti-	cultivated	dunder-pated	expiated
ated	dated	duplicated	expostulated
coagulated	debated	educated	extenuated
cogitated	debilitated	effectuated	exterminated
collated	decapitated	efflated	extricated
collocated	decimated	ejaculated	fabricated
commemorated	decorated	elaborate	facilitated
comminated	dedicated	elated	fascinated
commiserated	degenerated	electroplated	fated
communicated	delegated	elevated	federated
compensated	deliberated	eliminated	felicitated
complicated	delineated	elucidated	feted
concentrated	demonstrated	emaciated	flagellated
conciliated	denominated	emanated	fluctuated
confabulated	depopulated	emancipated	foreordinated
confederated	deprecated	emasculated	formulated
confiscated	depreciated	emigrated	freighted
conglomerated	derogated	emulated	frustrated
congratulated	desecrated	enumerated	fulminated
congregated	desiderated	enunciated	fumigated
conjugated	designated	equivocated	gaited
consecrated	desolated	eradicated	gated
consolidated	deteriorated	estimated	generated
consummated	detonated	evacuated	germinated
contaminated	devastated	evaporated	gesticulated
contemplated	deviated	eventuated	graduated
cooperated	dictated	exaggerated	granulated
coordinated	differentiated	exasperated	grated
copper-plated	dilapidated	excavated	gratulated
copulated	dilated	excommuni-	gravitated
coronated	discriminated	cated	habituated
correlated	disintegrated	excoriated	hated
corroborated	dislocated	execrated	heavy-gaited
corrugated	disseminated	exhilarated	heavy-weighted
created	dissimulated	exonerated	hesitated
cremated	dissipated	exorbitated	humiliated
crenellated	dissociated	expatiated	idle-pated
crepitated	domesticated	expatriated	ill-fated

---

illuminated	investigated	obliterated	punctuated
illustrated	invigorated	obviated	radiated
imitated	invocated	officiated	rated
immigrated	irradiated	operated	rattle-pated
immolated	irrigated	opinionated	recapitulated
impersonated	irritated	originated	reciprocated
implicated	isolated	oscillated	recreated
imprecated	iterated	osculated	recriminated
impropriated	jasperated	overrated	recuperated
inaugurated	legislated	overstated	refrigerated
incapacitated	levigated	palliated	regenerated
incarcerated	liberated	palpitated	regulated
incastellated	liquidated	participated	rehabilitated
incinerated	located	penetrated	reinstated
incorporated	lubricated	perambulated	reiterated
incriminated	luxuriated	percolated	rejuvenated
incubated	macerated	peregrinated	related
indicated	manipulated	perforated	relegated
indoctrinated	marinated	permeated	remunerated
indurated	masticated	perpetrated	renovated
inebriated	mated	perpetuated	Reno-vated
infatuated	matriculated	personated	repatriated
inflated	medicated	placated	repudiated
infuriated	meditated	plaited	resuscitated
ingratiated	methylated	plated	retaliated
initiated	migrated	plicated	reverberated
innovated	militated	populated	ruminated
inoculated	mitigated	postulated	rusticated
insinuated	moderated	prated	salivated
instated	modulated	precipitated	sated
instigated	mutilated	predestinated	satiated
insulated	narrated	predicated	saturated
interpolated	navigated	predominated	scintillated
interrogated	necessitated	premeditated	segregated
intimated	negotiated	prevaricated	separated
intimidated	nickel-plated	procrastinated	shallow-pated
intoxicated	nominated	prognosticated	sibilated
inundated	nucleolated	propagated	silicated
invalidated	obligated	propitiated	silver-plated

ōld, ôr, ŏdd, oil, fŏŏt, out; ūse, ûrn, ŭp; THis, thin

simulated	unilluminated	ratten	*decoratest*
situated	unmitigated		*deprecatest*
skated	unpremeditated	**ĀT′ent,**	*devastatest*
slated	unrelated	**ĂT′ent**	*dictatest*
sophisticated	unsophisticated	patent	*dilatest*
speculated	unstated		*ejaculatest*
spifflicated	vacated	**ĀT′est**	*elevatest*
stated	vaccinated	*abatest*	*emulatest*
stimulated	vacillated	*abdicatest*	*exaggeratest*
stipulated	validated	*accommodatest*	*fascinatest*
subjugated	variated	*accumulatest*	*frustratest*
sublimated	variegated	*adulteratest*	*graduatest*
subordinated	vegetated	*advocatest*	*greatest*
substantiated	venerated	*aggravatest*	*hatest*
suffocated	ventilated	*agitatest*	*hesitatest*
superannuated	vindicated	*alleviatest*	*imitatest*
supplicated	violated	*animatest*	*indicatest*
syncopated	vitiated	*annihilatest*	*irritatest*
syndicated	vituperated	*anticipatest*	latest
tabulated	vociferated	*appreciatest*	*liberatest*
tergiversated	waited	*articulatest*	*matest*
terminated	weighted	*assimilatest*	*narratest*
tessellated		*associatest*	*necessitatest*
titillated	**ĂT′ed**	*awaitest*	*overratest*
titivated	batted	*baitest*	*plaitest*
tolerated	chatted	*beratest*	*pratest*
translated	dratted	*calculatest*	*radiatest*
triangulated	fatted	*captivatest*	*ratest*
triturated	hatted	*celebratest*	*regulatest*
ululated	matted	*cogitatest*	*relatest*
unabated	patted	*commemoratest*	*repudiatest*
unappropriated	plaited	*communicatest*	*skatest*
unauthenti-	platted	*conjugatest*	*slatest*
cated		*consecratest*	*statest*
uncreated	**ĂT′en**	*contaminatest*	*toleratest*
undecorated	batten	*contemplatest*	*translatest*
underrated	fatten	*createst*	*underratest*
understated	flatten	*cultivatest*	*vacatest*
undulated	paten	*debatest*	*violatest*

āle,   câre,   ădd,   ärm,   ăsk;   mē,   hĕre,   ĕnd;   īce,   ĭll;

waitest

ĀT′est
battest
chattest
fattest
flattest
pattest

ĀT′eth
abateth
abdicateth
accelerateth
accommo-
    dateth
accumulateth
adulterateth
advocateth
agitateth
alleviateth
ameliorateth
animateth
annihilateth
anticipateth
appropriateth
arbitrateth
articulateth
associateth
awaiteth
baiteth
calculateth
cancellateth
captivateth
celebrateth
circulateth
conciliateth
confiscateth
congratulateth
consecrateth

contaminateth
contemplateth
createth
createth
cremateth
cultivateth
debateth
decorateth
dedicateth
depopulateth
devastateth
dictateth
dilateth
dissipateth
dominateth
educateth
ejaculateth
elevateth
emulateth
estimateth
exaggerateth
excavateth
excommuni-
    cateth
exhilarateth
expiateth
extenuateth
extricateth
fabricateth
fascinateth
frustrateth
hateth
hesitateth
imitateth
indicateth
irritateth
liberateth
locateth
luxuriateth
mateth

meditateth
narrateth
operateth
overrateth
prateth
rateth
regulateth
relateth
separateth
skateth
stateth
suffocateth
underrateth
vaccinateth
violateth
waiteth

ĂT′eth
batteth
chatteth
fatteth
patteth

ĂT′ēz
penates

ĂT′fŏŏt
flatfoot

ĂT′fôrm
platform

ĀT′ful
fateful
grateful
hateful
ungrateful

ĂT′ha
Jagannatha

Ăth′an
Elnathan
Nathan

ĂT′hed
fathead
flathead

Ăth′en
lathen

Āth′ful
faithful

Ăth′ful,
Ăth′ful
wrathful

Ăth′ik
allopathic
antipathic
chrestomathic
electropathic
empathic
felspathic
heteropathic
homeopathic
hydropathic
idiopathic
neuropathic
orthognathic
osteopathic
philomathic
polymathic
prognathic
psychopathic
spathic
telempathic

ōld, ôr, ŏdd, oil, fŏŏt, out; ūse, ûrn, ŭp; THis, thin

telepathic
theopathic

ĀTH'ing
bathing
swathing
unswathing

Ā'thing
plaything

ATH'ing
bathing
lathing

Āth'les
faithless
scatheless

Ath'les
bathless
pathless
wrathless

ĂTH'om
fathom

ĂTH'omd
unfathomed

Āth'os
bathos
pathos

Ăth'ū
Matthew

ĀTH'ur
bather

swather

ĀTH'ur
blather
forgather
gather
lather
ungather
upgather

ĀTH'ur,
ATH'ur
father
rather
(See also
ŎTH'ur.)

ĀTH'urz
gathers
slathers
(See also
ĀTH'ur; add
-s where
appropriate.)

ĂT'īd
bat-eyed
cat-eyed

ĂT'īd
caryatid
(See also
ĂT'ed.)

ĂT'if
caitiff

ĂT'ik
achromatic

acousmatic
acroatic
acrobatic
acromono-
  grammatic
adiabatic
Adriatic
aerostatic
agnatic
aliphatic
anabatic
anagrammatic
anastatic
anathematic
antistatic
aphorismatic
aplanatic
apochromatic
apophtheg-
  matic
aposematic
apostatic
aquatic
aristocratic
arithmocratic
aromatic
Asiatic
astatic
asthmatic
astigmatic
asymptomatic
Attic
attic
autocratic
automatic
axiomatic
biquadratic
bureaucratic
caryatic

catastatic
categorematic
charismatic
chromatic
cinematic
climatic
commatic
creatic
cryptogram-
  matic
cuneatic
dalmatic
democratic
diagrammatic
diaphragmatic
diastatic
diastomatic
dichromatic
dilemmatic
diplomatic
dogmatic
dramatic
ecbatic
ecstatic
Eleatic
electrostatic
emblematic
emphatic
empyreumatic
enatic
endermatic
enigmatic
epigrammatic
episematic
erratic
eustatic
fanatic
fluviatic
geostatic

āle, câre, ădd, ärm, ăsk; mē, hĕre, ĕnd; īce, ĭll;

geratic
grammatic
gyrostatic
hallelujatic
Hanseatic
heliostatic
hematic
hemostatic
hepatic
hieratic
hierogram-
  matic
hydrostatic
hyperbatic
hypostatic
iconomatic
idiocratic
idiomatic
idiosyncratic
isochromatic
isodiabatic
judgmatic
kinematic
komatik
lavatic
lipogrammatic
lymphatic
magistratic
majestatic
mathematic
melanocratic
melismatic
melodramatic
mesocratic
metastatic
miasmatic
micromatic
mobocratic
monochromatic

monocratic
monogram-
  matic
morganatic
muriatic
mydriatic
noematic
numismatic
ochlocratic
operatic
opiatic
osmatic
palatic
pancratic
pancreatic
pantisocratic
paradigmatic
parallelogram-
  matic
pathematic
phantomatic
phatic
pherecratic
phlegmatic
phosphatic
photostatic
phreatic
physiocratic
piratic
plasmatic
platic
pleochromatic
plutocratic
pneumatic
poematic
polychromatic
pragmatic
prelatic
prismatic

problematic
proceleusmatic
programmatic
prostatic
protatic
psychosomatic
quadratic
rhematic
rheumatic
sabbatic
Sarmatic
schematic
schismatic
sciatic
sematic
sinalagmatic
smegmatic
Socratic
somatic
spermatic
static
stigmatic
stomatic
stromatic
subaquatic
sulphatic
sylvatic
symptomatic
systematic
technocratic
thematic
theocratic
theorematic
thermostatic
timocratic
traumatic
trichromatic
trigrammatic
truismatic

unsystematic
vatic
venatic
viatic
villatic
zeugmatic
zygomatic

ĂT′ik
aquatic
(See also
ŌT′ik.)

ĂT′iks
aerostatics
attics
electrostatics
hydrostatics
hygrostatics
mathematics
pneumatics
statics
(See also
ĂT′ik; add
-*s* where
appropriate.)

Ā′tīm
daytime
playtime

ĀT′im
literatim
seriatim
verbatim

ĂT′in
Latin
matin

ōld, ôr, ŏdd, oil, fŏŏt, out; ūse, ûrn, ŭp; THis, thin

patine
platen
satin

ĀT'ing
abating
abbreviating
abdicating
abnegating
abominating
accelerating
accentuating
accommodat-
ing
accumulating
adulterating
advocating
aerating
aggravating
aggregating
agitating
alienating
alleviating
alternating
amalgamating
ameliorating
amputating
animating
annihilating
annumerating
anticipating
appreciating
appropriating
approximating
arbitrating
armor-plating
articulating
assassinating
assimilating

associating
attenuating
augurating
authenticating
awaiting
baiting
bating
berating
calculating
calumniating
capitulating
castigating
celebrating
circulating
coagulating
cogitating
collocating
commemorat-
ing
commiserating
communicating
compensating
complicating
concentrating
conciliating
confabulating
confederating
confiscating
congratulating
congregating
conjugating
consecrating
consolidating
consummating
contaminating
contemplating
cooperating
corroborating
corrugating

creating
cremating
criminating
culminating
cultivating
dating
debating
debilitating
decapitating
decimating
decorating
dedicating
degenerating
delegating
deliberating
delineating
demonstrating
denominating
depopulating
deprecating
depreciating
derivating
derogating
desecrating
designating
deteriorating
determinating
detonating
devastating
deviating
dictating
differentiating
dilapidating
dilating
discriminating
disintegrating
dislocating
disseminating
dissimulating

dissipating
dissociating
dominating
duplicating
educating
ejaculating
elaborating
electroplating
elevating
eliminating
elucidating
emaciating
emanating
emancipating
emigrating
emulating
enumerating
equivocating
eradicating
estimating
evacuating
evaporating
exaggerating
exasperating
excavating
excommunicat-
ing
excruciating
execrating
exhilarating
exonerating
expatiating
expectorating
expiating
expostulating
extenuating
extricating
fabricating
facilitating

fascinating	inebriating	migrating	premeditating
federating	infanticipating	militating	prevaricating
felicitating	infatuating	mitigating	prognosticating
feting	inflating	moderating	promulgating
flagellating	infuriating	modulating	propagating
fluctuating	ingratiating	mutilating	propitiating
formulating	initiating	narrating	punctuating
fornicating	innovating	navigating	quadruplicating
freighting	inoculating	necessitating	radiating
frustrating	insinuating	negotiating	rating
fulminating	instigating	nickel-plating	rebating
fumigating	insulating	nominating	recapitulating
generating	interpolating	obliterating	reciprocating
germinating	interrogating	obviating	recreating
gesticulating	intimating	operating	recriminating
graduating	intimidating	originating	recuperating
granulating	intoxicating	oscillating	refrigerating
grating	inundating	osculating	regulating
gratulating	invalidating	overrating	reinstating
gravitating	investigating	overstating	reiterating
hating	invigorating	palliating	rejuvenating
hesitating	invocating	palpitating	relating
humiliating	irradiating	participating	relegating
illuminating	irrigating	penetrating	remunerating
illustrating	irritating	perambulating	renovating
imitating	isolating	percolating	repudiating
immigrating	iterating	peregrinating	resuscitating
immolating	legislating	perforating	retaliating
impersonating	liberating	permeating	reverberating
implicating	liquidating	perpetrating	ruminating
imprecating	locating	perpetuating	rusticating
inaugurating	lubricating	personating	satiating
incapacitating	luxuriating	plaiting	saturating
incarcerating	manipulating	plating	scintillating
incriminating	masticating	populating	separating
incubating	mating	postulating	simulating
indicating	matriculating	prating	skating
indiscriminat-	mediating	precipitating	slating
ing	meditating	predominating	sophisticating

---

speculating
stating
stimulating
stipulating
subjugating
suffocating
supplicating
syncopating
tabulating
terminating
titillating
titivating
tolerating
translating
unabating
unaccommo-
  dating
underrating
understating
undeviating
undiscriminat-
  ing
undulating
vacating
vaccinating
vacillating
validating
variegating
vegetating
venerating
ventilating
verberating
vindicating
violating
vitiating
vituperating
vociferating
waiting
weighting

ĀT′ing

batting
chatting
fatting
matting
patting
platting
ratting
tatting
vatting

ĀT′īr

satire

ĀT′is

gratis

ĀT′is

brattice
lattice

ĀT′ish

cattish
fattish
flattish

ĀT′iv

abnegative
abrogative
accelerative
accommodative
accumulative
adjudicative
administrative
agglomerative
agglutinative
aggregative
agitative
alleviative

alliterative
alterative
ameliorative
animative
anticipative
annunciative
appreciative
approbative
appropriative
approximative
assimilative
associative
authoritative
calculative
carminative
circulative
coagulative
cogitative
collative
combinative
commemora-
  tive
commiserative
communicative
complicative
concentrative
conciliative
confederative
congratulative
consecrative
consolidative
consultative
contaminative
contemplative
continuative
cooperative
coordinative
copulative
corporative

corroborative
creative
criminative
cumulative
dative
decorative
dedicative
degenerative
deliberative
denominative
denunciative
deprecative
depreciative
desiderative
designative
desiccative
deteriorative
determinative
dilative
discriminative
disseminative
dissociative
dominative
duplicative
educative
edulcorative
elaborative
elative
elucidative
emanative
emulative
enumerative
enunciative
eradicative
estimative
evaporative
exaggerative
excommunica-
  tive

āle,   câre,   ădd,   ärm,   ăsk;   mē,   hĕre,   ĕnd;   īce,   ĭll;

execrative
exhilarative
exonerative
explicative
expostulative
exsiccative
facultative
federative
figurative
frustrative
geminative
generative
germinative
gesticulative
glutinative
gravitative
hesitative
illative
illuminative
illustrative
imaginative
imbricative
imitative
impenetrative
implicative
inappreciative
incogitative
incommunica-
 tive
incorporative
incriminative
incubative
indiscrimina-
 tive
inhabitative
initiative
innovative
inoperative
insinuative

interpenetra-
 tive
interpretative
investigative
invigorative
invocative
irrigative
irritative
iterative
jaculative
judicative
justificative
lacerative
legislative
limitative
manipulative
medicative
meditative
ministrative
mitigative
modificative
modulative
multiplicative
native
nomenclative
nominative
noncooperative
nonnative
nonstative
operative
opinionative
originative
oscillative
palliative
participative
penetrative
perforative
pignorative
postoperative

predestinative
premeditative
procreative
prognosticative
prolative
pronunciative
propagative
punctuative
purificative
qualificative
qualitative
quantitative
radiative
ratiocinative
recapitulative
recreative
recriminative
recuperative
refrigerative
regenerative
regulative
reiterative
remunerative
renunciative
replicative
reprobative
resuscitative
retaliative
reverberative
ruminative
sative
segregative
separative
significative
simulative
speculative
stative
stimulative
subordinative

suffocative
supplicative
suppurative
terminative
translative
ulcerative
unappreciative
uncommunica-
 tive
uncreative
undulative
unimaginative
unremunerative
variative
vegetative
velicative
ventilative
verificative
vindicative
violative
vituperative
vivificative

ĂT′kins
Atkins
Batkins
(See also
ŎT′kins.)

ĂT″l
battel
battle
cattle
chattel
death rattle
embattle
prattle
rattle
Seattle

ōld, ôr, ŏdd, oil, fŏŏt, out; ūse, ûrn, ŭp; THis, thin

tattle
tittle-tattle

ĂT'las, ĂT'les
atlas
cravatless
hatless
(See also ĂT;
add -less where
appropriate.)

ĀT'lē (ĬT'lē)
accurately
adequately
affectionately
alternately
appropriately
approximately
compassion-
  ately
consummately
delicately
desolately
desperately
disconsolately
effeminately
elaborately
extortionately
fortunately
greatly
illiterately
immaculately
immoderately
inarticulately
inconsiderately
intemperately
intimately
irately
lately

legitimately
moderately
sedately
stately
straitly
ultimately

ĂT'lē
fatly
flatly
patly
rattly

ĂT'les
baitless
dateless
estateless
freightless
gaitless
gateless
grateless
hateless
mateless
rateless
stateless
weightless

ĂT'ling
battling
catling
fatling
gatling
prattling
rattling
tattling

ĂT'lur
battler
prattler

rattler
Statler
tattler

ĀT'ment
abatement
affreightment
instatement
overstatement
reinstatement
statement
understatement

ĂT'nes
appropriate-
  ness
considerateness
greatness
innateness
lateness
ornateness
sedateness
straightness

ĂT'nes
fatness
flatness
patness

ĀT'ō
Cato
couch potato
hot potato
literato
NATO
Plato
pomato
potato
tomato

ĂT'ō
chateau
mulatto
plateau

Ä'tō
annatto
chateau
enamorato
legato
obbligato
pizzicato
pomato
staccato
tomato

ĂT'om
atom

ĀT'on
Clayton
Dayton
Leighton
peyton
Satan

ĂT'on
baton
Hatton

ĂT'ra
Cleopatra

Ä'trē
bay tree
May tree

ĂT'red
hatred

ĀT′res
dictatress
imitatress
spectatress
traitress
waitress

ĂT′res
mattress
mulattress

ĂT′rik
hippiatric
iatric
kinesiatric
matric
Patrick
theatric

ĀT′riks
administratrix
aviatrix
cicatrix
generatrix
imitatrix
impropriatrix
matrix
mediatrix
spectatrix
testatrix

ĀT′ris, ĂT′ris
matrice

ĀT′ron
matron
natron
patron

ĀTS′man
statesman

ĂTS′man
batsman

ĂT′son
Batson
Matson

ĂT′ū
statue

ĂT′um
datum
desideratum
erratum
pomatum
postulatum
stratum
substratum
superstratum
ultimatum

ĀT′um
stratum

ĀT′um
datum
pomatum

ĀT′ūr
good nature
ill nature
legislature
nature
nomenclature
plicature
unnature

ĀT′ŭr
abator
abbreviator
abdicator
ablator
abnegator
abrogater
accelerator
accumulator
activator
adjudicator
administrator
adulator
affreighter
aggravator
agitator
alienator
alleviator
alligator
allocator
alma mater
alternator
amalgamator
ameliorator
annihilator
annotator
annunciator
applicator
appropriator
arbitrator
arch-traitor
articulator
aspirater
asseverator
assimilator
authenticator
aviator
awaiter
baiter

barrater
barrator
bater
berater
buccinator
calculator
calumniator
captivator
carburetor
castigator
cater
caveator
cinerator
classificator
cogitator
collaborator
commemorator
commentator
comminator
commiserator
commutator
compotator
compurgator
computator
concentrator
conciliator
confiscator
confrater
conjugator
consecrator
conservator
consolidator
contaminator
contemplator
cooperator
coordinator
corporator
corroborator
corrugator

ōld, ôr, ŏdd, oil, fŏŏt, out; ūse, ûrn, ŭp; THis, thin

crater
creator
cremator
criminator
cultivator
curator
dater
debater
decapitator
decorator
dedicator
delator
deliberator
delineator
demonstrator
denominator
denunciator
depopulator
depreciator
depredator
desiccator
designator
detonator
devastator
deviator
dictater
dictator
dilator
discriminator
disintegrator
disseminator
dissimulator
divaricator
dumbwaiter
duplicator
dura mater
educater
ejaculator
elaborator

elater
elevator
eliminator
elucidator
emanator
emancipator
emendator
emulator
enumerator
enunciator
equator
equivocator
eradicator
escalator
evaporator
exaggerator
excavator
execrator
exequatur
exhilarator
exonerator
expatiator
expectorator
expiator
extenuator
exterminator
extricator
fabricator
facilitator
fascinator
federator
felicitator
first-rater
flagellator
formulator
fornicator
frater
freighter
frustrator

fumigator
gaiter
gater
generator
germinator
gesticulator
gladiator
grater
greater
hater
hesitater
humiliater
hypothecator
illuminator
illustrator
imitator
imperator
impersonator
imprimatur
incarcerator
incinerator
incorporator
incriminator
incubator
indicator
inflater
inhalator
initiator
innovator
inoculator
insinuator
instigator
insulator
integrator
interpolator
interrogator
intimidator
investigator
invigilator

invigorator
invocator
irrigator
irritator
judicator
later
laudator
legislator
levator
liberator
liquidator
litigator
locater
lubricator
malaxator
man-hater
manipulator
masticator
mater
mediator
meditator
migrater
mitigator
moderator
modificator
modulator
multiplicator
mutator
mutilator
narrator
navigator
negator
negotiator
nomenclator
nominator
numerator
obliterator
officiator
operator

originator
oscillator
pacificator
palliator
palpitator
pater
perambulator
percolator
peregrinator
perforator
permeator
perpetrator
personator
philiater
pia mater
piscator
placater
plaiter
plater
pontificator
postulator
prater
precipitator
predominator
prestidigitator
prevaricator
procrastinator
procurator
prognosticator
promulgator
propagator
propitiator
propugnator
pulsator
purificator
qualificator
radiator
rater
rebater

reciprocator
recuperator
refrigerator
regenerator
regrater
regulator
reinstater
reiterator
relater
remonstrator
renovator
repudiator
respirator
resuscitator
retaliator
revelator
reverberator
rotator
ruminator
rusticator
satyr
scarificator
scintillator
scrutator
second-rater
sedater
separator
significator
simulator
skater
slater
sophisticator
spectator
speculator
Stabat Mater
stater
stimulator
stipulator
straighter

straiter
subjugator
supererogator
supinator
supplicator
tabulator
"tater"
tergiversator
terminator
testator
third-rater
titillator
titivator
trafficator
traitor
translator
vacater
vaccinator
vacillator
vaticinator
venerator
ventilator
versificator
viator
vibrator
vindicator
violator
vituperator
vociferator
waiter
woman hater

ĂT′ŭr
stature

ĂT′ŭr
attar
batter
beflatter

bepatter
bescatter
bespatter
blatter
chatter
clatter
clitter-clatter
fatter
flatter
hatter
latter
matter
patter
platter
ratter
satyr
scatter
shatter
smatter
spatter
splatter
subject matter
tatter

ĀT′ur
alma mater
mater
pater
Stabat Mater

ĂT′urn
pattern
Saturn
slattern
willow pattern

ĀT′us
afflatus
apparatus
hiatus

ōld, ôr, ŏdd, oil, fŏŏt, out; ūse, ûrn, ŭp; THis, thin

literatus
saleratus
senatus
status
stratous
stratus

ĂT′us
apparatus

ĂT′ūt
statute

ĀT′wā
gateway
straitway

Ā′ur
affrayer
allayer
arrayer
assayer
belayer
betrayer
brayer
conveyer
defrayer
delayer
disarrayer
dismayer
disobeyer
displayer
essayer
flayer
gainsayer
gayer
grayer
greyer
hoorayer

inlayer
interlayer
inveigher
layer
matineer
mayor
mislayer
missayer
neigher
obeyer
outlayer
outstayer
outweigher
overlayer
payer
player
portrayer
prayer
prepayer
preyer
purveyor
relayer
repayer
slayer
soothsayer
sprayer
stayer
strayer
surveyer
swayer
underpayer
underplayer
viséer
waylayer
weigher

Ä′vā
ave

Ä′va
brava
cassava
guava
Java
lava

ĂV′āl
travail

ĀV′ē
affidavy
cavy
Davie
Davy
gravy
navy
peccavi
ravy
slavey
wavy

ĀV′e
agave
ave

ĀV′el
gavel
naval
navel

ĂV′el
gavel
gravel
ravel
travel
unravel

ĂV′eld
graveled

raveled
traveled
untraveled

ĀV′en
craven
engraven
graven
haven
maven
shaven

ĀV′est
behavest
beslavest
bravest
cravest
depravest
engravest
enslavest
forgavest
gavest
gravest
lavest
pavest
ravest
savest
shavest
slavest
suavest
waivest
wavest

ĀV′eth
behaveth
beslaveth
braveth
craveth
depraveth
engraveth

āle, câre, ădd, ärm, ăsk; mē, hĕre, ĕnd; īce, ĭll;

enslaveth
forgaveth
gaveth
laveth
paveth
raveth
saveth
shaveth
slaveth
waiveth
waveth

ĀV′ēz
Davies

ĀV′id
Camp David
David
engraved
(See also ĀV; add *-ed* where appropriate.)

ĂV′id
avid
gravid
impavid
pavid

ĂV′ij
ravage
savage
scavage

ĂV′ik
gravic
Pan-Slavic
Slavic

ĂV′in
savin
spavin

ĀV′ing
behaving
belaving
beslaving
braving
caving
craving
depraving
engraving
enslaving
graving
labor saving
laving
misbehaving
outbraving
paving
raving
saving
shaving
slaving
staving
steel engraving
waiving
waving
wood engraving

ĂV′ing
having
salving

ÄV′ing
calving
halving
salving

ĀV′is
clavis
Davis
mavis
rara avis

ĀV′ish
bravish
knavish
slavish

ĂV′ish
enravish
lavish
McTavish
ravish

ĀV′it
affidavit
indicavit

ĂV′it
davit

ĀV′lē
bravely
gravely
knavely
suavely

ĀV′les
caveless
graveless
slaveless
staveless
waveless

ĂV′lin
javelin
ravelin

ĀV′ling
shaveling

ĀV′ment
depravement
engravement
enslavement
lavement
pavement

ĀV′nes
braveness
graveness
suaveness

ĀV′ō
bravo
octavo

ÄV′ō
bravo
octavo

ĂV′ok
havoc

ĀV′ur
braver
cadaver
claver
craver
demiquaver
depraver
disfavor
engraver
enslaver
favor
flavor
graver

laver	**ĀV′us**	**Ā′yard**	lazy
marriage favor	Gustavus	Bayard	mazy
Papaver			paraphrasey
paver	**ĀV′yur**	**Ā′yō**	phrasey
quaver	behavior	K.O.	
raver	havior	kayo	**ĂZ′ē**
saver	misbehavior	Mayo	Benghazi
savor	Pavier		ghawazi
semiquaver	pavior	**Ā′yū**	ghazi
shaver	savior	gayyou	kamikaze
slaver	Xavier	Vayu	
suaver			**ĀZ′est**
waiver	**Ā′ward**	**ĂZ′a**	*amazest*
waver	wayward	cazazza	*bepraisest*
wood engraver		piazza	*blazest*
	Ā′ward	plaza	*braisest*
	vaward		*dazest*
ĂV′ur		**ĂZ′a**	*gazest*
beslaver	**Ā′wīr**	Gaza	*glazest*
cadaver	haywire		*hazest*
palaver		**ĀZ′al**	*paraphrasest*
haver	**Ā′worn**	appraisal	*phrasest*
	spray worn	hazel	*praisest*
ĂV′ur	wayworn	nasal	*raisest*
palaver		witch hazel	*razest*
suaver	**Ā′ya**		*upraisest*
	Aglaia		
	ayah	**ĂZ′ard**	
ĀV′urd	calisaya	haphazard	**ĀZ′eth**
favored	Isaiah	hazard	*amazeth*
flavored	naia	*mazard*	*bepraiseth*
ill-favored		mazzard	*blazeth*
quavered	**Ā′yan**		*braiseth*
savored	Altaian	**ĀZ′ē**	*dazeth*
wavered	Cataian	blazy	*gazeth*
well-favored	Himalayan	crazy	*glazeth*
	Malayan	daisy	*hazeth*
ĂV′urn		hazy	*paraphraseth*
cavern	**Ā′yan**	jasey	*phraseth*
tavern	Himalayan	lackadaisy	*praiseth*

raiseth
razeth
upraiseth

ĀZ′ez
amazes
bemazes
blazes
braises
brazes
chaises
crazes
daisies
dazes
gazes
glazes
grazes
hazes
mayonnaises
mazes
paraphrases
phases
phrases
praises
raises
razes

Ā′zhun
abrasion
dissuasion
erasion
evasion
invasion
occasion
persuasion
suasion
(See also
Ā′zē-an.)

Ā′zhur
azure
brazier
embrasure
erasure
Frazier
glazier
grazier
razure

ĀZH′ur
azure

ĂZ′il
Basil
Fazil
(See also
ĂZ″l.)

ĀZ′in
raisin

ĀZ′ing
ablazing
amazing
bemazing
bepraising
blazing
braising
brazing
dazing
gazing
glazing
grazing
hazing
lazing
outblazing
outgazing
paraphrasing

phrasing
praising
raising
self-praising
stargazing
upblazing
upraising

ĂZ″l
Basil
bedazzle
dazzle
frazzle
razzle-dazzle

ĀZ′les
praiseless

ĀZ′ling
dazzling
frazzling

ĂZ′ma
asthma
miasma
phantasma
Phasma
plasma
protoplasma

ĂZ′mal
miasmal
phantasmal
protoplasmal

ĂZ′mē
chasmy

ĀZ′ment

amazement
appraisement
praisement

ĂZ′mik
bioplasmic
miasmic
protoplasmic

ĂZ′mus
Erasmus

ĂZ′on
blazon
brazen
diapason
emblazon
glazen
scazon

ĀZ′ur
appraiser
blazer
dispraiser
Eleazer
Fraser
gazer
geyser
lazar
paraphraser
phaser
phraser
praiser
raiser
razer
razor
self-praiser
stargazer
upgazer
upraiser

ōld, ôr, ŏdd, oil, fŏŏt, out; ūse, ûrn, ŭp; THis, thin

E

For a discussion of words included under the following accented vowels, see the beginning of E rhymes in Section I.

Ē'a
Althaea
Astraea
Ave Maria
Cassiopea
cavalleria
Crimea
Cypraea
dahabeah
Dorothea
dyspnea
Hosea
Hygeia
idea
Latakia
Lucia
Maria
Medea
melopoeia
obeah
onomatopoeia
panacea
pathopoeia
pharmaco-
    poeia
ratafia
Rhea
spiraea
Zea

Ē'al
Arctogaeal
beau ideal
empyreal

hymeneal
ideal
laryngeal
real
unideal
unreal

Ē'an
Achean
Achillean
adamantean
Adonean
Aeaean
Aegean
aeon
amoebean
amphigean
Andean
Anomoean
Antaean
Antillean
antipodean
apogean
Archimedean
Argean
Assidean
astraean
Atlantean
Augean
Behan
Berean
Cadmean
Caribbean
Chaldean

Circean
colossean
Crimean
cyclopean
Cytherean
ditrochean
empyrean
epicurean
epigean
Eritrean
Etnean
European
Galilean
gigantean
Hasmonaean
Hebridean
Herculean
Hyblaean
Hygeian
hymenean
Indo-European
Jacobean
Judean
Korean
Laodicean
laryngean
leguleian
lethean
Linnaean
lyncean
Maccabean
Manichaean
mausolean
Medicean

Melibean
Nemean
Niobean
nymphean
Odyssean
Orphean
paean
Palaeogaean
pampean
Pandean
Parthenopean
peon
perigean
phalangean
Pharisean
plebeian
Ponce de
    León
Priapean
protean
Pyrenean
Pythagorean
Sabaean
Sadducean
Shandean
Sisyphean
Sophoclean
spelaean
tempean
Tennesseean
terpsichorean
theodicean
Vendean
Zoilean

āle, câre, ădd, ärm, ăsk; mē, hĕre, ĕnd; īce, ĭll;

Ē'as
Aeneas
Zaccheus

Ē'ba
amoeba
Reba
Seba
Sheba
zareba

Ē'bē
BB
beebee
CB
Hebe
Phoebe
TB

ĒB'en
Eben

Ē'bēz
heebie-jeebies
(See also Ē'bē;
add -s where
appropriate.)

ĔB'ing
ebbing
unebbing
webbing

ĔB''l
enfeeble
feeble

ĔB''l
arch-rebel

djebel
pebble
rebel
treble

Ē'bō
gazebo
Nebo
placebo

ĔB'on
ebon

Ē'bord
freeboard
keyboard
seaboard

Ē'born
freeborn
sea-born

ĒB'ra
zebra

ĔB'rok
pibroch

ĔB'ru
Hebrew

ĒB'ur
Gheber

ĔB'ur
ebber
webber
Weber

Ē'bus

glebous
Phoebus
rebus

ĒCH'ē
beachy
Beatrice
beechy
bleachy
breachy
campeachy
peachy
preachy
queachy
reachy
reechy
screechy
speechy

ĔCH'ē
fetchy
sketchy
stretchy
tetchy
vetchy

ĔCH'ed
wretched
(See also ĔCH;
add -ed where
appropriate.)

ĒCH'est
beseechest
bleachest
forereachest
impeachest
overreachest
preachest

reachest
screechest
sea chest
tea chest
teachest

ĒCH'eth
beseecheth
bleacheth
forereacheth
impeacheth
overreacheth
preacheth
reacheth
screecheth
teacheth

ĒCH'ez
beaches
beeches
beseeches
bleaches
breaches
breeches
forereaches
impeaches
leeches
overreaches
peaches
preaches
reaches
screeches
sea reaches
speeches
teaches

ĒCH'ing
beaching
beseeching

bleaching	**ĒCH'ur**	**ĔD'ant**	eddy
breaching	Beecher	pedant	Freddie
breeching	beseecher		heady
forereaching	bleacher	**ĒD'bed**	leady
foreteaching	breacher	reedbed	ready
I Ching	breecher	seedbed	reddy
impeaching	forereacher	weed bed	shreddy
leaching	impeacher		steady
leeching	leacher	**ĔD'bēt**	thready
overreaching	leecher	deadbeat	unready
peaching	overreacher		unsteady
preaching	peacher	**ĔD'brest**	
reaching	preacher	redbreast	**ĒD'ed**
screeching	reacher		acceded
teaching	screecher	**ĔD'bug**	anteceded
	teacher	bedbug	beaded
ĔCH'ing	(See also Ē'tūr.)	red bug	ceded
etching			conceded
fetching	**ĔCH'ur**	**ĒD'ē**	deeded
sketching	etcher	beady	exceeded
stretching	fetcher	creedy	heeded
	fletcher	deedy	impeded
ĔCH'les	lecher	encyclopedy	interceded
beachless	retcher	greedy	kneaded
beechless	sketcher	heedy	needed
breachless	stretcher	indeedy	pleaded
peachless	*treacher*	Leedy	preceded
reachless		needy	proceeded
speechless	**Ē'da**	*predy*	receded
teachless	Leda	reedy	reeded
	olla podrida	seedy	retroceded
ĔCH'ment	Theda	speedy	seceded
beseechment	Veda	unheedy	seeded
impeachment	Vida	weedy	stampeded
preachment			succeeded
	ĔD'a		superseded
ĔCH'up	Edda	**ĔD'ē**	unheeded
catchup	Hedda	already	unweeded
ketchup	Nedda	Eddie	weeded

āle, câre, ădd, ärm, ăsk; mē, hĕre, ĕnd; īce, ĭll;

ĔD'ed
addle-headed
arrowheaded
bareheaded
bedded
beetleheaded
beheaded
blunderheaded
bullheaded
chuckleheaded
clearheaded
dreaded
dunderheaded
embedded
fatheaded
featherheaded
fiddleheaded
flatheaded
giddy-headed
gross-headed
headed
heavy-headed
hoary-headed
hotheaded
hydra-headed
idleheaded
Janus-headed
leaded
light-headed
longheaded
many-headed
muddleheaded
pigheaded
puddingheaded
puzzleheaded
rattleheaded
shock-headed
shredded
sleek-headed

softheaded
thickheaded
threaded
trundleheaded
unbedded
undreaded
unthreaded
unwedded
warm-headed
weak-headed
wedded
wrongheaded

ĔD'en
Eden
reeden
Sweden

ĔD'en
deaden
leaden
redden
threaden

ĔD'ens
antecedence
credence
intercedence
precedence

ĔD'ent
antecedent
credent
decedent
intercedent
needn't
precedent
retrocedent
sedent

Ē'dēp
knee-deep
sea-deep
three-deep

ĒD'est
accedest
bleedest
breedest
cedest
concedest
exceedest
feedest
heedest
impedest
intercedest
kneadest
leadest
misleadest
needest
overfeedest
pleadest
precedest
proceedest
readest
recedest
secedest
seedest
speedest
stampedest
succeedest
supersedest
weedest

ĔD'est
beheadest
dreadest
outspreadest
reddest

sheddest
spreadest
threadest
treadest
weddest

ĒD'eth
accedeth
bleedeth
breedeth
cedeth
concedeth
exceedeth
feedeth
heedeth
impedeth
intercedeth
kneadeth
leadeth
misleadeth
needeth
overfeedeth
pleadeth
precedeth
proceedeth
readeth
recedeth
secedeth
seedeth
speedeth
stampedeth
succeedeth
supersedeth
weedeth

ĔD'eth
beheadeth
dreadeth
headeth

ōld, ôr, ŏdd, oil, fŏŏt, out; ūse, ûrn, ŭp; THis, thin

outspreadeth
overspreadeth
sheddeth
shreddeth
spreadeth
threadeth
treadeth
weddeth

ĚD′ēz
teddies
(See also
ĚD′ē; add
-*s* where
appropriate.)

ĚD′fast
steadfast

ĒD′ful
deedful
heedful
meedful
needful
speedful
unheedful
unneedful

ĚD′ful
dreadful

ĒD′grōn
reed-grown
seed-grown
weed-grown

ĚD′hed
deadhead
redhead

ĚD′hēt
dead heat
red heat

ĒD′ik
comedic
cyclopedic
encyclopedic
Vedic

ĚD′ik
Eddic
Samoyedic

ĒD′ikt
edict

ĒD′ing
acceding
beading
bleeding
breeding
ceding
conceding
exceeding
feeding
Godspeeding
heeding
impeding
interbreeding
interceding
interpleading
kneading
leading
love-lies-
  bleeding
misleading
misreading
needing

outspeeding
overfeeding
pleading
preceding
proceeding
reading
receding
reeding
retroceding
seceding
seeding
speeding
stampeding
succeeding
superseding
unbleeding
underfeeding
unheeding
weeding

ĚD′ing
bedding
beheading
bespreading
dreading
embedding
heading
leading
outspreading
overspreading
redding
shedding
shredding
sledding
spreading
steading
tedding
threading
treading

wedding

ĚD′ish
deadish
eddish
reddish

ĚD′it
accredit
credit
discredit
edit
miscredit
subedit
you said it

ĚD′ith
Edith
(See also
ĒD′eth.)

ĒD′′l
beadle
bipedal
centipedal
daedal
needle
pedal
semipedal
tweedle
wheedle

ĚD′′l
bipedal
heddle
intermeddle
medal
meddle
pedal

āle,   câre,   ădd,   ärm,   ăsk;   mē,   hĕre,   ĕnd;   īce,   ĭll;

peddle
reddle
treadle
tripedal

ĔD'lam
Bedlam

ĔD'land
headland

ĔD'lē
chance medley
deadly
medley
redly

ĔD'les
breedless
creedless
deedless
heedless
needless
seedless
speedless
steedless
weedless

ĔD'les
bedless
breadless
dreadless
headless
leadless

ĔD'līn
breadline
deadline
headline

ĔD'ling
needling
reedling
seedling
wheedling

ĔD'ling
intermeddling
meddling
peddling

ĔD'līt
deadlight
red light

ĔD'lok
deadlock
wedlock

ĔD'lur
needler
wheedler

ĔD'lur
intermeddler
meddler
medlar
peddler
treadler

ĔD'man
Friedman

ĔD'man
deadman
Edman
headman
red man

ĔD'na
Edna

ĔD'nes
deadness
redness

Ē'dō
credo
ido
Lido
stampedo
teredo
Toledo
torpedo

ĔD'ō
meadow

ĔD'ra
ex cathedra
exedra

ĔD'ral
cathedral
decahedral
didecahedral
diedral
dihedral
procathedral

ĔD'rest
bed rest
headrest

ĔD'stōn
headstone

ĔD'tīm

feed time
seedtime

Ē'dum
freedom

ĔD'ūr
procedure
supersedure

ĔD'ŭr
acceder
anteceder
bandleader
bleeder
breeder
cattle breeder
cedar
ceder
cheerleader
conceder
exceeder
feeder
heeder
impeder
impleader
interceder
interpleader
kneader
leader
lip-reader
misleader
needer
overfeeder
pleader
preceder
proceeder
proofreader
reader

ōld, ôr, ŏdd, oil, fŏŏt, out; ūse, ûrn, ŭp; THis, thin

receder
retroceder
ringleader
scripture
  reader
seceder
seeder
speeder
stampeder
stockbreeder
succeeder
superseder
weeder

ĔD'ur
bedder
beheader
bespreader
Cheddar
deader
doubleheader
dreader
edder
embedder
header
homesteader
leader
redder
shedder
shredder
spreader
tedder
threader
treader
triple-header
unthreader

ĔD'wā
headway

ĔD'ward
bedward
Edward

ĔD'wood
deadwood
redwood

ĔDZ'man
beadsman
bedesman
seedsman

ĔDZ'man
headsman
leadsman

ĔD'zō
intermezzo
mezzo

Ē'est
agreest
feest
fleest
foreseest
freest
overseest
refereest
seest
weest

Ē'eth
agreeth
feeth
fleeth
foreseeth
freeth
overseeth

seeth

ĒF'as
Cephas

ĔF'dom
chiefdom
fiefdom

ĒF'ē
beefy
leafy
reefy
sheafy

ĔF'en
deafen

ĒF'ij
leafage

ĒF'ik
malefic
peristrephic

ĒF'les
briefless
chiefless
griefless
leafless
sheafless

ĔF'nes
deafness

Ē'fōm
seafoam

Ē'foul

peafowl
seafowl

ĔFT'nes
deftness

ĔF'rē
Geoffrey
Jeffrey

ĒF'stāk
beefsteak

ĒF'tin
chieftain

ĔF'uj
refuge

Ē'ful
gleeful

ĒF'ur
beefer
briefer
chiefer
liefer
reefer

ĔF'ur
deafer
feoffor
heifer
zephyr

Ē'ga
Amiga
Auriga
omega

āle, câre, ădd, ärm, ăsk; mē, hĕre, ĕnd; īce, ĭll;

Riga
Talladega
Vega

ĔG'ē
dreggy
eggy
leggy
Peggy

ĔG'ing
fatiguing
intriguing
leaguing

ĔG'ing
begging
egging
legging
pegging
unpegging

ĔG''l
bald eagle
beagle
eagle
gregal
illegal
inveigle
kleagle
legal
regal
viceregal

ĔG'lur
beagler
inveigler

ĔG'ment

segment

ĔG'nant
impregnant
pregnant
queen regnant
regnant

Ē'gō
ego
Oswego
Otsego

Ē'gren
pea green
sea green

ĔG'res
egress
Negress
regress

ĔG'rō
Negro

ĔG'ur
beleaguer
big-leaguer
bush leaguer
eager
eagre
fatiguer
intriguer
leaguer
Little Leaguer
major leaguer
meager
minor leaguer
overeager

ĔG'ur
beggar
booklegger
bootlegger
egger
legger
pegger
seggar

Ē'gurt
seagirt

Ē'ik
caffeic
mythopoeic
rheic
xanthoproteic

Ē'ing
agreeing
being
clear-seeing
decreeing
disagreeing
far-seeing
feeing
fleeing
foreseeing
freeing
guaranteeing
inbeing
nonbeing
overseeing
refereeing
seeing
sightseeing
spreeing
teeing
unforeseeing

unseeing
well-being

Ē'ist
antitheist
atheist
deist
hylotheist
Manicheist
monotheist
polytheist
theist

Ē'it
albeit
sobeit

Ē'iz'm
absenteeism
antitheism
autotheism
cosmotheism
deism
henotheism
hylotheism
Manicheism
monotheism
Parseeism
Phariseeism
polytheism
Sadduceeism
sciotheism
Sutteeism
theism
weism

Ē'jance
allegiance

ĔJ'burd
hedge bird
sedge bird

ĔJ'ē
cledgy
edgy
hedgy
ledgy
sedgy
wedgy

ĔJ'end
legend

ĔJ'ent
regent

ĔJ'est
allegest
dredgest
fledgest
hedgest
impledgest
pledgest
wedgest

ĔJ'eth
allegeth
dredgeth
fledgeth
hedgeth
impledgeth
pledgeth
wedgeth

ĔJ'ez
alleges
dredges

edges
hedges
kedges
ledges
pledges
sledges
wedges

ĔJ'ing
alleging
dredging
edging
enhedging
fledging
hedging
kedging
impledging
interpledging
pledging
sledging
wedging

ĔJ'ling
fledgling

ĔJ'man
liegeman

ĔJ'ment
besiegement

ĔJ'un
legion
region
under-region

ĔJ'ur
alleger
dredger

edger
hedger
ledger
leger
pledger
sledger

ĔJ'us
egregious
sacrilegious

ĔJ'wood
Edgewood
Wedgewood

Ē'ka
bibliotheca
chica
Costa Rica
Dominica
eureka
Frederica
Fredrika
glyptotheca
Meeka
Tanganyika
Topeka
Ulrica
zotheca

ĔK'a
Mecca
Rebecca
Tribeca

ĔK'ād
decade

ĔK'al
bibliothecal

caecal
faecal
thecal
treacle

ĒK'ant
cosecant
piquant
precant
secant

ĔK'ant
impeccant
peccant

ĒK'ē
bleaky
Bolsheviki
cheeky
cliquey
cockaleekie
creaky
leaky
Mensheviki
peeky
reeky
sheiky
sleeky
sneaky
squeaky
streaky

ĒK'en
weaken
(See also
ĒK'on.)

ĒK'est
bespeakest

āle,   câre,   ădd,   ärm,   ăsk;   mē,   hĕre,   ĕnd;   īce,   ĭll;

bleakest
meekest
leakest
reekest
seekest
shriekest
sneakest
speakest
squeakest
streakest
uniquest
weakest
wreakest

ĔK′est
bedeckest
checkest
deckest
reckest
wreckest

ĔK′eth
bespeaketh
leaketh
reeketh
seeketh
shrieketh
sneaketh
speaketh
squeaketh
streaketh
wreaketh

ĔK′eth
bedecketh
checketh
decketh
recketh
wrecketh

ĒK′īd
meek-eyed
oblique-eyed
weak-eyed

ĒK′ing
bespeaking
cheeking
creaking
eking
forespeaking
leaking
reeking
seeking
self-seeking
sheiking
shrieking
sneaking
speaking
squeaking
tweaking
wreaking

ĔK′ing
bedecking
bewrecking
checking
decking
flecking
henpecking
pecking
recking
trekking
wrecking

ĔK′ish
bleakish
cliquish
freakish

Greekish
meekish
peakish
sneakish
weakish

ĔK′ish
peckish

ĔK′′l
treacle
(See also
ĒK′al.)

ĔK′′l
befreckle
bespeckle
deckle
freckle
heckle
Jekyll
keckle
Seckel
shekel
speckle

ĔK′lē
bleakly
meekly
obliquely
sleekly
treacly
uniquely
weakly
weekly

ĔK′lē
freckly
speckly

ĔK′les
feckless
fleckless
necklace
reckless
speckless

ĔK′ling
weakling

ĔK′ling
freckling
heckling
keckling
speckling

ĔK′lur
freckler
heckler
(See also
ĔK′′l; add
-*er* where
appropriate.)

ĔK′māt
checkmate
deck mate

ĔK′nes
antiqueness
bleakness
meekness
obliqueness
Preakness
sleekness
uniqueness
weakness

ĔK′nik
philotechnic

polytechnic
pyrotechnic
technic
theotechnic

ĔK'ning
beckoning
reckoning
unreckoning

Ē'kō
beccafico
fico

ĔK'ō
echo
gecko
re-echo
secco

Ē'kok
Leacock
meacock
peacock

ĔK'on
archdeacon
beacon
deacon
meeken
weaken

ĔK'on
beckon
reckon

ĔK'ond
second
unreckoned

(See also
ĔK'on; add
-ed where
appropriate.)

Ē'krab
pea crab
sea crab
tree crab

ĔK'ret
secret

ĔK'sas
Texas

ĔK'sē
apoplexy
kexy
kyriolexy
prexy
pyrexy
sexy

ĔK'sest
annexest
flexest
perplexest
unsexest
vexest

ĔK'seth
annexeth
flexeth
perplexeth
unsexeth
vexeth

ĔK'shun

abjection
adjection
affection
bisection
by-election
circumspection
circumvection
collection
complexion
confection
connection
convection
correction
defection
deflection
dejection
detection
dilection
direction
disaffection
disinfection
dissection
effection
ejection
election
erection
evection
flection
genuflexion
imperfection
incorrection
indirection
infection
inflection
injection
insection
inspection
insubjection
insurrection

intellection
interjection
intersection
introjection
introspection
irreflection
lection
midsection
misdirection
objection
perfection
predilection
preelection
prelection
projection
prospection
protection
provection
recollection
rection
redirection
re-election
reflection
rejection
resurrection
retrospection
section
selection
subjection
trajection
trisection
venesection
vivisection

ĔK'shus
infectious

ĔK'sīl
exile

āle, câre, ădd, ärm, ăsk; mē, hĕre, ĕnd; īce, ĭll;

flexile

ĔK′sing
annexing
flexing
inflexing
perplexing
unsexing
vexing

ĔK′sis
Alexis

ĔK′sit
exit

ĔK′stant
extant
sextant

ĔK′stīl
bissextile
sextile
textile

ĔK′ston
sexton

ĔK′strin
dextrin
textrine

ĔK′strus
ambidextrous
ambisextrous
dextrous

ĔK′stūr
intertexture

texture

ĔK′stŭr
ambidexter
dexter

ĔK′sūr
deflexure
flexure
inflexure
plexure

ĔK′sŭr
annexer
flexor
perplexer
unsexer
vexer

ĔK′sus
nexus
plexus
(See also
ĔK′sas.)

ĔK′tant
amplectant
annectent
aspectant
disinfectant
expectant
humectant
inexpectant
reflectant
respectant
suspectant
unexpectant

ĔK′ted

affected
bisected
collected
complected
confected
connected
corrected
defected
deflected
dejected
detected
directed
disaffected
disconnected
disinfected
dissected
effected
ejected
elected
erected
expected
flected
ill-affected
infected
inflected
injected
inspected
interjected
intersected
invected
misdirected
neglected
objected
obtected
perfected
prelected
projected
protected
recollected

reflected
rejected
respected
resurrected
selected
subjected
suspected
unaffected
unconnected
unexpected
unprotected
unsuspected

ĔK′test
abjectest
affectest
bisectest
collectest
connectest
detectest
directest
disinfectest
dissectest
effectest
ejectest
electest
erectest
expectest
infectest
injectest
inspectest
interjectest
neglectest
objectest
projectest
protectest
recollectest
reflectest
rejectest

ōld, ôr, ŏdd, oil, fŏŏt, out; ūse, ûrn, ŭp; THis, thin

respectest
resurrectest
selectest
subjectest
suspectest

ĔK′teth
affecteth
bisecteth
collecteth
connecteth
detecteth
directeth
disinfecteth
dissecteth
effecteth
ejecteth
electeth
erecteth
expecteth
infecteth
injecteth
inspecteth
interjecteth
misdirecteth
neglecteth
objecteth
projecteth
protecteth
recollecteth
reflecteth
rejecteth
respecteth
resurrecteth
selecteth
subjecteth
suspecteth
trisecteth

ĔKT′ful
disrespectful
neglectful
respectful

ĔK′tik
acatalectic
analectic
apoplectic
brachycatalec-
    tic
cachectic
catalectic
dialectic
eclectic
hectic
hypercatalectic
pectic

ĔK′tiks
dialectics

ĔK′tĭl
insectile
projectile
sectile

ĔK′ting
affecting
bisecting
collecting
connecting
deflecting
detecting
directing
disconnecting
disinfecting
dissecting
effecting

ejecting
electing
erecting
expecting
infecting
injecting
inspecting
interjecting
misdirecting
neglecting
objecting
projecting
protecting
recollecting
reflecting
rejecting
respecting
resurrecting
selecting
self-respecting
subjecting
suspecting
trisecting
unsuspecting

ĔK′tiv
affective
circumspective
collective
connective
corrective
cost-effective
defective
deflective
detective
directive
effective
elective
erective

humective
ineffective
infective
inflective
injective
inspective
introspective
invective
irreflective
irrespective
neglective
objective
perfective
perspective
prospective
protective
recollective
refective
reflective
rejective
respective
retrospective
sective
selective
subjective

ĔK′tiz′m
eclectism
sectism

ĔKT′ment
ejectment
projectment
rejectment

ĔKT′nes
abjectness
correctness
directness

āle,   câre,   ădd,   ärm,   ăsk;   mē,   hĕre,   ĕnd;   īce,   ĭll;

erectness
incorrectness
indirectness
selectness

ĔK′tor
Hector
nectar
rector
sector
vector
vivisector
(See also
ĔK′tur.)

ĔK′tord
hectored
nectared
rectored

ĔK′tral
spectral

ĔK′tres
directress
electress
inspectress
protectress
rectress

ĔK′tric
anelectric
dielectric
electric
idioelectric

ĔK′tron
electron

ĔK′trum
electrum
plectrum
spectrum

ĔK′tūr
architecture
belecture
confecture
conjecture
lecture
projecture

ĔK′tur
bisector
collector
connector
convector
corrector
defector
deflector
detector
director
disrespector
dissector
ejector
elector
erecter
epecter
flector
Hector
hector
inflecter
injecter
inspector
interjecter
lector
misdirecter
nectar

neglecter
objector
prelector
projector
prospector
protector
recollecter
rector
reflector
rejecter
respecter
resurrecter
sector
selector
specter
spectre
subjecter
suspecter
trisecter
vector

ĔK′tus
conspectus
pectous
prospectus

ĒK′um
caecum
vade mecum

ĒK′und
fecund
infecund

ĒK′ur
beaker
bespeaker
bleaker
Bleecker

cheeker
creaker
meeker
peeker
reeker
seeker
self-seeker
shrieker
sleeker
sneaker
speaker
squeaker
stump speaker
tweaker
weaker

ĔK′ur
bedecker
brekker
checker
chequer
decker
exchequer
flecker
henpecker
pecker
three-decker
trekker
woodpecker
wrecker

ĔK′urd
checkered
off-the-record
record
video record

ĔK′urz
beakers

ōld, ôr, ŏdd, oil, fŏŏt, out; ūse, ûrn, ŭp; THis, thin

sneakers
(See also
ĒK'ur; add
-s where
appropriate.)

ĒK'urz
checkers
henpeckers
(See also
ĒK'ur; add
-s where
appropriate.)

ĒK'wal
coequal
equal
inequal
sequel

ĒK'wence
frequence
infrequence
sequence

ĒK'went
frequent
infrequent
sequent

Ē'la
gila
philomela
sequela
stele
seguidilla
Venezuela

ĔL'a

a cappella
Adela
Bella
canella
Capella
cella
chlorella
Cinderella
citronella
clarabella
columella
corella
Della
doncella
Ella
favella
fellah
fenestella
fustanella
gentianella
glabella
Isabella
justanella
lamella
lirella
Littorella
Marcella
micella
mozzarella
navicella
novella
paella
panatela
patella
Pella
Pimpinella
predella
prunella
Rosabella

rosella
rubella
salmonella
scutella
sella
sequela
Shigella
stella
tabella
tarantella
tiarella
umbella
umbrella
varicella
villanella
vorticella
Yiyella

ĔL'an
Atellan
Magellan
McClellan

ĔL'ant
appellant
divellent
impellent
interpellant
propellant
repellent
revellent

ĔL'arz
Sellars
(See also
ĔL'ur; add
-s where
appropriate.)

ĔL'at
appellate
constellate
debellate
flabellate
interpellate
ocellate
prelate
stellate

ĔL'ba
Elba
Melba

ĔL'bôrn
hell born
well-born

ĔL'bound
hell bound
spellbound

ĔL'burt
Elbert

ĔL'chest
belchest
(See also
ĔLCH; add
-est where
appropriate.)

ĔL'cheth
belcheth
(See also
ĔLCH; add
-eth where
appropriate.)

ĔL'ching
belching
squelching
welching

ĔL'chur
belcher
squelcher
welsher

ĔL'da
Griselda
Nelda
Zelda

ĒL'dans
yieldance

ĒL'dē
unwieldy

ĒL'ded
fielded
shielded
unshielded
wielded
yielded

ĔL'dest
eldest
heldest
weldest

ĔL'dur
elder
Gelder
Melder
Van Gelder
welder

ĒLD'fâr
fieldfare

ĒL'ding
enshielding
fielding
shielding
unshielding
unyielding
wielding
yielding

ĔL'ding
gelding
welding

ĔL'dom
seldom
swelldom

Ēl'ē
Ealey
freely
Healey
Keeley
mealy
seely
steely
wheely

Ĕl'ē
belly
cancelli
Donatelli
felly
helly
jelly
Kelly
O'Delly

rakehelly
Shelley
shelly
Skelly
·smelly
vermicelli

ĔL'ēd
bellied
gelid
jellied

ĔL'en
Ellen
Helen
Llewellyn
Mellen

ĒL'est
annealest
appealest
concealest
congealest
dealest
feelest
genteelest
healest
kneelest
lealest
pealest
peelest
reelest
repealest
revealest
sealest
squealest
stealest
steelest
wheelest

ĔL'est
compellest
dispellest
dwellest
excellest
expellest
fellest
foretellest
impellest
knellest
propellest
quellest
rebellest
repellest
sellest
shellest
smellest
spellest
swellest
tellest
undersellest
yellest

ĒL'eth
annealeth
appealeth
concealeth
congealeth
dealeth
feeleth
healeth
kneeleth
pealeth
peeleth
reeleth
repealeth
·*revealeth*
sealeth
squealeth

ōld, ôr, ŏdd, oil, fŏŏt, out; ūse, ûrn, ŭp; THis, thin

stealeth
steeleth
wheeleth

ĔL'eth
compelleth
dispelleth
dwelleth
excelleth
expelleth
felleth
foretelleth
impelleth
knelleth
propelleth
quelleth
rebelleth
repelleth
selleth
shelleth
smelleth
spelleth
swelleth
telleth
underselleth
yelleth

ĔL'fâr
welfare

ĔL'fik
Delphic
Guelphic

ĔL'fin
delphin
delphine
elfin

ĔL'fīr
hellfire

ĔL'fish
elfish
pelfish
selfish
shellfish
unselfish

ĔL'frē
belfry
pelfry

ĔL'ful
seelful
wealful
zealful

ĔL'ij
keelage
wheelage

ĔL'ij
pellage

ĔL'ik
parhelic

ĔL'ik
angelic
archangelic
Aristotelic
bellic
evangelic
melic
nickelic
parhelic
Pentelic
pimelic

relic
superangelic
telic

ĔL'iks
Felix
helix

Ē'līn
beeline
feline
sea line

ĔL'ing
annealing
appealing
automobiling
ceiling
concealing
congealing
dealing
double-dealing
feeling
fellow feeling
freewheeling
healing
heeling
interdealing
keeling
kneeling
misdealing
pealing
peeling
reeling
repealing
revealing
sealing
self-healing
shealing

squealing
stealing
steeling
uncongealing
underdealing
unfeeling
unsealing
wheeling

ĔL'ing
belling
cloud com-
   pelling
compelling
dispelling
dwelling
excelling
expelling
felling
foretelling
fortune-telling
impelling
knelling
misspelling
paralleling
propelling
quelling
rebelling
repelling
selling
sentineling
shelling
smelling
spelling
swelling
telling
underselling
welling
yelling

ĔL'is
Ellis
trellis

ĔL'ish
disrelish
embellish
hellish
relish
swellish

ĔL'kom
welcome

ĔL'ma
Elma
Selma
Thelma
Velma

ĔL'man
bellman
Elman
Wellman

ĔL'ment
concealment
congealment
repealment
revealment

ĔL'met
helmet

ĔL'ming
dishelming
helming
overwhelming
unhelming

whelming

ĔL'mur
Elmer

ĔL'nes
genteelness
lealness

ĔL'nes
fellness
wellness

ĔL'ō
bellow
brocatello
cobra de
  capello
cello
duello
felloe
fellow
good fellow
mellow
morello
niello
playfellow
prunello
punchinello
saltarello
scrivello
violoncello
yellow

ĔL'od
bellowed
unmellowed
(See also ĔL'o;
add -ed where

appropriate.)

ĔL'on
enfelon
felon
melon
watermelon

ĔL'op
develop
envelop

ĔL'ot
helot
zealot

ĔL'ōz
bellows
fellows
(See also ĔL'ō;
add -s where
appropriate.)

ĔLP'ful
helpful
self-helpful
unhelpful

ĔL'pē
kelpie

ĔL'ping
helping
yelping

ĔLP'les
helpless
whelpless
yelpless

ĔL'pur
helper
self-helper
yelper

ĔL'sa
Elsa

ĔL'skin
eel skin
sealskin

ĔL'son
kelson
Nelson

ĔL'ta
delta
pelta

ĔL'ted
belted
felted
melted
pelted
smelted
unbelted
welted

ĔL'test
beltest
(See ĔLT;
add -est where
appropriate.)

ĔL'teth
belteth
(See ĔLT; add
-eth where
appropriate.)

ōld, ôr, ŏdd, oil, fŏŏt, out; ūse, ûrn, ŭp; THis, thin

ĔL'thē
healthy
stealthy
wealthy

ĔL'tik
Celtic
Keltic

ĔL'ting
belting
felting
melting
pelting
smelting
unbelting
welting

ĔLT'les
beltless
Celtless
feltless
peltless
weltless

ĔL'trē
peltry
sweltry

ĔL'tur
belter
felter
helter-skelter
inshelter
kelter
melter
pelter
shelter
smelter

spelter
swelter
welter

ĔL'turd
sheltered
unsheltered
(See also
ĔL'tur; add
-ed where
appropriate.)

ĔL'ūd
prelude

ĔL'ūg
deluge

ĔL'um
cerebellum
flabellum
flagellum
vellum

ĔL'ur
annealer
appealer
concealer
congealer
dealer
double-dealer
feeler
four-wheeler
healer
heeler
interdealer
keeler
kneeler
misdealer

New Dealer
pealer
peeler
reeler
repealer
revealer
sealer
squealer
stealer
steeler
two-wheeler
velar
ward heeler
wheeler
wheeler-dealer

ĔL'ur
appellor
cave dweller
cellar
cloud com-
    peller
compeller
dispeller
dweller
exceller
expeller
feller
foreteller
fortune-teller
Geller
impeller
interstellar
Keller
lamellar
"meller"
nonstellar
propeller
queller

rebeller
repeller
salt cellar
screw propeller
Sellar
seller
sheller
smeller
speller
stellar
storyteller
sweller
tale-teller
teller
twin propeller
underseller
Weller
wine cellar
yeller

ĔL'us
apellous
entellus
jealous
overzealous
procellous
vitellus
zealous

ĔL'vet
velvet

ĔL'ving
delving
helving
shelving

ĔL'vish
elvish

ĔL'vur
delver
helver
shelver

ĔL'ya
Amelia
Aurelia
Bedelia
camellia
Cecelia
Celia
Cordelia
Cornelia
Delia
Lelia
lobelia

ĔL'yal
Belial

ĔL'yon
chameleon

ĔL'yon
rebellion

ĔL'yus
rebellious

ĔL'za
Elsa

ĔM'a
bema
blastema
eczema
edema
empyema

erythema
Fatima
Lima
myxedema
schema
seriema
terza rima

ĔM'a
analemma
dilemma
Emma
gemma
lemma
maremma
neurilemma
stemma
trilemma

Ē'māl
female
she-male

ĒM'ăl
blastemal
hemal

Ē'man
able seaman
beeman
freeman
gleeman
G-man
he-man
leman
merchant
   seaman
seaman
teaman

ĔM'b'l
assemble
dissemble
resemble
semble
tremble

ĔM'blans
assemblance
dissemblance
resemblance
semblance

ĔM'blant
resemblant
semblant

ĔM'b'ld
assembled
undissembled
(See also
ĔM'b'l; add
-ed where
appropriate.)

ĔM'blē
assembly
trembly

ĔM'blem
emblem

ĔM'blij
assemblage

ĔM'bling
assembling
dissembling
resembling
trembling

ĔM'blur
assembler
dissembler
resembler
trembler

ĔM'bral
bimembral
trimembral

ĔM'brans
remembrance

ĔM'bur
December
dismember
disremember
ember
member
November
remember
September

ĔM'burd
dismembered
unremembered
(See also
ĔM'bur; add
-ed where
appropriate.)

ĔM'ē
beamy
creamy
daydreamy
dreamy
gleamy
screamy
seamy

---

steamy
streamy
teemy

ĒM′ē
demi
gemmy
jemmy
semi

ĒM′ens
Clemens

Ē′ment
agreement
decreement
disagreement

ĒM′ent
clement
inclement

ĒM′est
beamest
blasphemest
deemest
dreamest
esteemest
extremest
gleamest
misdeemest
redeemest
schemest
screamest
seemest
steamest
streamest
supremest

ĔM′est
begemmest
condemnest
hemmest
stemmest

ĔM′et
Emmett

ĒM′eth
beameth
blasphemeth
deemeth
dreameth
esteemeth
gleameth
redeemeth
schemeth
screameth
seemeth
steameth
streameth

ĔM′eth
begemmeth
condemneth
contemneth
hemmeth
stemmeth

ĒM′ful
beamful
dreamful
schemeful
teemful

ĔM′ik
anemic
racemic

systemic

ĔM′ik
academic
alchemic
chemic
endemic
epidemic
pandemic
polemic
stratagemic
systemic
theoremic
totemic

ĒM′ing
beaming
beseeming
blaspheming
creaming
daydreaming
deeming
dreaming
esteeming
gleaming
overstreaming
redeeming
scheming
screaming
seeming
steaming
streaming
summer-
  seeming
teeming
unbeseeming

ĔM′ing
begemming

condemning
contemning
Fleming
gemming
hemming
lemming
self-condemn-
  ing
stemming

ĔM′ish
blemish
Flemish
unblemish

ĔM′isht
blemished
unblemished

ĔM′ist
extremist
schemist

ĔM′ist
chemist

ĒM′īt, ĔM′īt
Semite

ĒM′land
dreamland

ĒM′lē
extremely
seemly
supremely
unseemly

ĒM′less
beamless

āle,   câre,   ădd,   ärm,   ăsk;   mē,   hĕre,   ĕnd;   īce,   ĭll;

creamless
dreamless
schemeless
seamless
streamless

ĒM'let
streamlet

ĒM'non
Agamemnon
Memnon

ĒM'ō
a tempo primo
Cremo
primo

ĒM'ō
memo

ĒM'on
agathodaemon
cacodemon
demon
eudaemon

ĒM'on
lemon

ĒM'pest
tempest

ĒM'pīr
empire

ĒM'p'l
Semple
stemple

temple

ĔM'plar
exemplar
templar

ĔM'plāt
contemplate
template

ĔMP'shun
ademption
coemption
diremption
emption
exemption
preemption
redemption

ĔMP'stur
dempster
sempster

ĔMP'ted
attempted
exempted
preempted
tempted
unattempted
untempted

ĔMP'test
attemptest
exemptest
temptest

ĔMP'teth
attempteth
exempteth

tempteth

ĔMP'tē
empty

ĔMP'ting
attempting
exempting
preempting
tempting

ĔMP'tiv
preemptive
redemptive

ĔMP'tres
temptress

ĔMP'tur
attempter
exempter
preemptor
tempter
unkempter

ĔM'pur
attemper
distemper
Semper
temper
untemper

ĔM'purd
ill-tempered
tempered
untempered

ĔM'son
Clemson

Empson

ĒM'song
theme song

ĒM'stur
deemster
seamster
teamster

ĒM'ur
beamer
blasphemer
daydreamer
dreamer
femur
lemur
reamer
redeemer
schemer
screamer
seamer
seemer
steamer
streamer
teemer

ĔM'ur
begemmer
condemner
contemner
hemmer
stemmer

ĒM'us
Nicodemus
Remus

ĒM'yer
premier

ōld, ôr, ŏdd, oil, fŏŏt, out; ūse, ûrn, ŭp; THis, thin

ĒN′a
arena
Alexandrina
Argentina
Athena
catena
cavatina
Celestina
Christina
Clementina
concertina
czarina
farina
Faustina
galena
gena
Georgina
Helena
hyena
Justina
Lena
Magdalena
maizena
Medina
Messina
Modena
Paulina
philopena
scarlatina
scena
Selena
semolina
Serena
signorina
subpoena
Tsarina
verbena
Wilhelmina

ĔN′a
antenna
duenna
Gehenna
henna
Ravenna
senna
Sienna
Vienna

ĔN′al
machinal
penal
plenal
renal
venal
weanel

ĔN′al
antennal

ĔN′ant
lieutenant
pennant
sublieutenant
tenant

ĔN′ard
Leonard

Ē′nas
Enas
Zenas

ĔN′as
menace
tenace
(See also
ĔN′is.)

ĔN′āt
brevipennate
impennate
longipennate
pennate
tripennate

ĔN′chant
trenchant

ĔN′chest
bedrenchest
blenchest
clenchest
drenchest
flenchest
intrenchest
quenchest
retrenchest
trenchest
unclenchest
wrenchest

ĔN′cheth
bedrencheth
blencheth
clencheth
drencheth
flencheth
intrencheth
quencheth
retrencheth
trencheth
unclencheth
wrencheth

ĔN′ching
bedrenching
benching

blenching
clenching
drenching
flenching
intrenching
quenching
retrenching
trenching
unclenching
unquenching
wrenching

ĔNCH′les
quenchless
(See also
ĔNCH; add
-*less* where
appropriate.)

ĔNCH′man
Frenchman
henchman

ĔNCH′ment
intrenchment
retrenchment

ĔN′chur
bedrencher
bencher
blencher
clencher
drencher
intrencher
quencher
retrencher
trencher
unclencher

wrencher

ĔN'da
agenda
Benda
Brenda
corrigenda
delenda
hacienda
Zenda

ĔN'dal
prebendal
sendal
trendle

ĔN'dans
ascendance
attendance
condescen-
    dence
dependence
descendance
impendence
independence
interdepen-
    dence
pendence
resplendence
superinten-
    dence
tendance
transcendence
(See also
ĔN'dant,
ĔN'dent; add
-s where
appropriate.)

ĔN'dant,
ĔN'dent
appendant
ascendant
attendant
contendant
defendant
dependant
dependent
descendant
descendent
equipendent
impendent
independent
intendant
interdependent
pendant
pendent
resplendent
splendent
superintendent
transcendent
transplendent

ĔN'dē
bendy
Effendi
trendy
Wendy

ĔN'ded
amended
appended
apprehended
ascended
attended
befriended
bended
blended

commended
comprehended
condescended
contented
defended
depended
descended
distended
emended
ended
expended
extended
fended
friended
impended
inextended
intended
interblended
mended
misappre-
    hended
offended
portended
pretended
reascended
recommended
reprehended
subtended
superintended
suspended
tended
transcended
trended
unattended
unbefriended
unblended
undefended
unextended
unfriended

wended

ĔN'dest
amendest
appendest
apprehendest
ascendest
attendest
befriendest
bendest
blendest
commendest
comprehendest
condescendest
contendest
defendest
dependest
descendest
emendest
endest
expendest
extendest
fendest
intendest
interblendest
lendest
mendest
offendest
pretendest
recommendest
rendest
reprehendest
sendest
spendest
subtrendest
superintendest
suspendest
tendest
unbendest

ōld, ôr, ŏdd, oil, fŏŏt, out; ūse, ûrn, ŭp; THis, thin

vendest
wendest

ĔN′deth
amendeth
appendeth
apprehendeth
ascendeth
attendeth
befriendeth
bendeth
blendeth
commendeth
comprehendeth
condescendeth
contendeth
defendeth
dependeth
descendeth
emendeth
endeth
expendeth
extendeth
fendeth
impendeth
intendeth
interblendeth
lendeth
mendeth
misapprehend-
eth
offendeth
portendeth
pretendeth
reascendeth
recommendeth
rendeth
reprehendeth
sendeth

spendeth
subtendeth
suspendeth
tendeth
transcendeth
vendeth
wendeth

ĔN′dik
Wendic
zendik

ĔN′ding
amending
appending
apprehending
ascending
attending
befriending
bending
blending
commending
comprehending
condescending
contending
defending
depending
descending
distending
emending
ending
expending
extending
forelending
forespending
forfending
heartrending
impending
intending

interblending
lending
mending
misspending
offending
pending
perpending
portending
pretending
recommending
rending
reprehending
sending
spending
subtending
superintending
suspending
tending
transcending
trending
unattending
unbending
unending
unfriending
unoffending
unpretending
vending
wending

ĔN′dish
fiendish

ĔND′lē
friendly
unfriendly

ĔND′les
endless
friendless

ĔND′ment
amendment
befriendment
intendment

ĔN′dō
crescendo
decrescendo
diminuendo
innuendo

ĔN′dron
liriodendron
lithodendron
rhododendron

ĔND′ship
friendship

ĔN′dum
addendum
agendum
corrigendum
credendum
referendum

ĔN′dur
amender
apprehender
ascender
attender
bartender
befriender
bender
blender
commender
comprehender
contender
defender

āle, câre, ădd, ärm, ăsk; mē, hĕre, ĕnd; īce, ĭll;

depender
descender
emender
ender
engender
entender
expender
extender
fender
fender bender
gender
intender
interblender
lender
mender
mind-bender
moneylender
offender
perpender
pretender
recommender
render
reprehender
sender
slender
spender
splendor
surrender
suspender
tailender
tender
vendor
weekender
wender

ĔN′durd
tendered
unsurrendered
(See also

ĔN′dur; add
-ed where
appropriate.)

ĔN′dus
stupendous
tremendous

ĔN′ē
blini
Cheney
Cheyney
fantoccini
genie
greeny
Hippocrene
meany
rollatini
Selene
sheeny
spleeny
Sweeney
teeny
visne
weeny

ĔN′ē
any
Benny
fenny
Jenny
Kilkenny
many
Penney
penny
Rennie
spinning jenny
tenney
truepenney

wenny

ĔND′wāz
endways

ĔN′el
fennel
Fennell
kennel
unkennel

ĔN′elm
Kenelm

ĔN′est
bescreenest
cleanest
contravenest
convenest
demeanest
gleanest
greenest
intervenest
keenest
leanest
meanest
screenest
serenest
supervenest
weanest
weenest

ĔN′et
Bennett
jennet
rennet
senate
tenet

ĔN′eth
bescreeneth
cleaneth
contraveneth
conveneth
demeaneth
gleaneth
interveneth
keeneth
leaneth
meaneth
screeneth
superveneth
weaneth
weeneth

ĔN′eth
Kenneth
penneth
(See also ĔN;
add *-eth* where
appropriate.)

ĔN′ēz
bennies
pennies
spinning-
   jennies

ĔNG′then
lengthen
strengthen

ĔN′horn
greenhorn

ĔN′īd
green-eyed
keen-eyed

ĒN'ij
careenage
greenage
teenage

ĒN'ik
phenic
scenic

ĔN'ik
acrogenic
agnogenic
allergenic
allogenic
alphenic
androgenic
anthropogenic
asthenic
audiogenic
calisthenic
carcinogenic
cariogenic
chromogenic
cryogenic
cryptogenic
crystallogenic
Demosthenic
deuterogenic
Diogenic
diplogenic
dysgenic
ecumenic
Edenic
embryogenic
endogenic
erotogenic
estrogenic
eugenic
exogenic

extragenic
fennec
galenic
genic
geoselenic
glycogenic
hallucinogenic
Hellenic
heptagenic
hygienic
hysterogenic
iatrogenic
immunogenic
intragenic
irenic
lactogenic
lichenic
metagenic
monogenic
myogenic
neotenic
nephrogenic
neurasthenic
neurogenic
nitrogenic
oncogenic
organogenic
orthogenic
oxygenic
Panhellenic
paragenic
paraphrenic
parthenic
parthenogenic
pathogenic
phenic
Philhellenic
phosphoro-
  genic

photogenic
phrenic
phylogenic
phytogenic
polygenic
protogenic
Prutenic
pyrogenic
pythogenic
radiogenic
saprogenic
Saracenic
scenic
schizophrenic
selenic
sirenic
splenic
sthenic
telegenic
teratogenic
thermogenic
toxicogenic
tungstenic
typhogenic
videogenic
zoogenic

ĔN'im
denim

ĔN'in
Lenin

ĒN'ing
advening
bemeaning
cleaning
contravening
convening

demeaning
double meaning
eaning
gleaning
greening
intervening
keening
leaning
machining
meaning
overweening
preening
queening
screening
shebeening
subvening
supervening
unmeaning
upleaning
weaning
weening
well-meaning
yeaning

ĒN'ingz
cleanings
screenings
(See also
ĒN'ing;
add -*s* where
appropriate.)

ĔN'ingz
Jennings
pennings
(See also
ĔN'ing;
add -*s* where
appropriate.)

āle,   câre,   ădd,   ärm,   ăsk;   mē,   hĕre,   ĕnd;   īce,   ĭll;

ĔN′is
Dennis
tennis
(See also
ĔN′as.)

ĔN′ish
cleanish
greenish
keenish
leanish
meanish
queenish
spleenish

ĔN′ish
plenish
replenish
Rhenish
wennish

ĔN′ist
machinist
magazinist
plenist
routinist

ĔN′jans
vengeance

ĔN′jin
engine

ĔN′jing
avenging
revenging
venging

ĔN′jur

avenger

ĒN′lē
cleanly
greenly
keenly
leanly
meanly
obscenely
queenly
serenely

ĔN′lē
cleanly
Henley
Schenley
Senley
uncleanly

ĒN′ling
weanling
yeanling

ĔN′man
fenman
penman

ĔN′nes
cleanness
greenness
keenness
leanness
meanness
obsceneness
sereneness
uncleanness

ĒN′ō
andantino

Angeleno
baldachino
bambino
casino
festino
Filipino
keno
maraschino
merino
peacherino
peperino
pianino
Reno
rondino
San Marino
Sereno
sopranino
tondino
Valentino
vetturino

ĒN′ok
Enoch

ĒN′old
Reynold

ĒN′olz
Reynolds

ĔN′om
envenom
venom

ĔN′on
pennon
tenon

ĒN′os

Enos

ĔN′rē
Denry
Henry

ĔN′sal
bimensal
commensal
forensal
mensal

ĔN′sāt
compensate
condensate
insensate
intensate

ĔN′sē
agency
belligerency
competency
corpulency
diligency
eminency
excellency
exigency
expediency
fluency
immanency
imminency
impertinency
impotency
impudency
incompetency
incontinency
indigency
indolency
inexpediency

innocency
insolency
irreverency
negligency
nonresidency
obstinancy
omnipotency
omnisciency
opulency
penitency
percipiency
permanency
pertinency
potency
preeminency
presidency
prevalency
prominency
pruriency
regency
residency
reticency
saliency
somnolency
subserviency
subsidency
succulency
truculency
turbulency
vehemency
virulency

ĔN'sest
commencest
condensest
densest
dispensest
fencest
incensest

intensest
recompensest

ĔN'seth
commenceth
condenseth
dispenseth
fenceth
incenseth
recompenseth

ĔN'sēz
Albigenses
amanuenses
menses

ĔNS'forth
henceforth
thenceforth
whenceforth

ĔN'shal
agential
bigential
circumferential
coessential
componential
conferential
confidential
consequential
credential
deferential
differential
equipotential
essential
evidential
existential
expediential
experiential

exponential
inconsequen-
tial
indulgential
inessential
inferential
influential
intelligential
irreverential
jurisprudential
nonessential
obediential
omnipresential
penitential
pestilential
potential
precedential
preferential
presidential
Provencial
providential
prudential
querulential
quintessential
referential
reminiscential
residential
reverential
rodential
sapiential
sciential
sentential
sequential
subsequential
superessential
tangential
torrential
transferential
unessential

ĔN'ship
deanship
queenship

ĔN'shun
abstention
accension
apprehension
ascension
attention
circumvention
coextension
comprehension
condescension
consension
contention
contravention
convention
declension
deprehension
descension
detention
dimension
dissension
distention
extension
gentian
hortensian
hypertension
hypotension
inapprehension
inattention
incomprehen-
sion
indention
inextension
intension
intention
intervention

āle, câre, ădd, ärm, ăsk; mē, hĕre, ĕnd; īce, ĭll;

invention
Lawrentian
mention
misapprehen-
  sion
noncondescen-
  sion
nonintervention
obtention
obvention
ostension
pension
portention
preapprehen-
  sion
prehension
presention
pretension
prevention
propension
reascension
recension
reprehension
retention
subvention
supervention
suspension
tension
thermotension

ĚN'shund
unmentioned
unpensioned
well-inten-
  tioned

ĚN'shus
conscientious
contentious

dissentious
licentious
pestilentious
pretentious
sententious
silentious

ĚN'sil
extensile
pencil
pensile
prehensile
stencil
tensile
utensil

ĚN'sild
penciled
stenciled

ĚN'sing
commencing
condensing
dispensing
fencing
incensing
recompensing

ĚN'siv
apprehensive
ascensive
coextensive
comprehensive
condensive
condescensive
counteroffen-
  sive
defensive
descensive

distensive
expensive
extensive
inapprehensive
incensive
incomprehen-
  sive
indefensive
inexpensive
inextensive
influencive
inoffensive
intensive
offensive
ostensive
pensive
prehensive
protensive
recompensive
reprehensive
self-defensive
suspensive
tensive
unapprehensive

ĚNS'les
defenseless
expenseless
fenceless
offenseless
senseless

ĚNS'ment
commencement
incensement

ĚNS'nes
denseness
immenseness

intenseness
propenseness
tenseness

ĚN'son
Benson
Henson

ĚN'sūr
censure

ĚN'sŭr
censer
censor
commencer
condenser
denser
dispenser
extensor
fencer
incensor
intenser
prehensor
recompenser
spencer
Spenser
tensor

ĚN'sus
census

ĚN'ta
magenta
Pimenta
polenta

ĚN'tal
accidental
alimental

antecedental
argental
argumental
atramental
bidental
cental
coincidental
compartmental
complemental
complimental
continental
dental
dentil
dentile
departmental
detrimental
developmental
documental
elemental
environmental
experimental
falcon-gentle
firmamental
fragmental
fundamental
gentle
governmental
impedimental
incidental
instrumental
intercontinen-
    tal
kentle
labiodental
Lental
ligamental
linguadental
medicamental
mental

monumental
nutrimental
occidental
oriental
ornamental
parental
parliamental
pedimental
pigmental
placental
predicamental
recremental
regimental
rental
rudimental
sacramental
segmental
sentimental
supplemental
temperamental
tenemental
testamental
transcendental
transcontinen-
    tal
trental
tridental
ungentle
(See also
ĔN'til.)

ĔN'tans
repentance
sentence
unrepentance

ĔN'tant
repentant
representant

unrepentant

ĔN'tāt
bidentate
commentate
dementate
dentate
edentate
quadridentate
tridentate

ĔN'tē
dolce far niente
Henty
plenty
presidente
tormenty
twenty

ĔN'te
aguardiente
cognoscente
diapente

ĔN'ted
absented
accented
assented
augmented
battlemented
cemented
circumvented
commented
complimented
consented
contented
demented
dented
discontented

dissented
fermented
fomented
frequented
ill-contented
indented
invented
lamented
misrepresented
ornamented
presented
prevented
relented
rented
repented
represented
resented
scented
supplemented
sweet-scented
tented
tormented
unlamented
unornamented
unprecedented
unprevented
unrepented
untented
untormented
vented
well-contented

ĔN'test
absentest
accentest
assentest
augmentest
cementest
circumventest

commentest
complimentest
consentest
contentest
dissentest
fermentest
fomentest
frequentest
indentest
inventest
lamentest
misrepresentest
ornamentest
presentest
preventest
relentest
rentest
repentest
representest
resentest
scentest
sentest
supplementest
tormentest
ventest

ĔN′teth
absenteth
accenteth
assenteth
augmenteth
cementeth
circumventeth
commenteth
complimenteth
consenteth
contenteth
dissenteth
fermenteth

fomenteth
frequenteth
indenteth
inventeth
lamenteth
misrepresenteth
ornamenteth
presenteth
preventeth
relenteth
renteth
repenteth
representeth
resenteth
scenteth
supplementeth
tormenteth
venteth

ĔNT′ful
eventful
resentful
uneventful

ĔNT′hous
penthouse

ĔN′tij
percentage
ventage

ĔN′tik
argentic
authentic
identic

ĔN′til
Gentile

ĔN′til
lentil
(See also
ĔN′tal.)

ĔN′tin
dentin
Quentin
San Quentin
torrentine
tridentine

ĔN′ting
absenting
accenting
assenting
augmenting
cementing
circumventing
commenting
complimenting
consenting
contenting
dementing
denting
dissenting
fermenting
fomenting
frequenting
indenting
inventing
lamenting
misrepresent-
ing
ornamenting
presenting
preventing
relenting
renting

repenting
representing
resenting
scenting
self-tormenting
supplementing
tenting
tormenting
unconsenting
unrelenting
unrepenting
venting

ĔN′tis
appentice
apprentice
non compos
mentis
pentice
prentice

ĔN′tist
apprenticed
dentist
preventist

ĔN′tiv
adventive
assentive
attentive
circumventive
inattentive
incentive
inventive
irretentive
predentive
presentive
preventive
resentive

retentive

ĔNT'lē
eminently
evidently
gently
impotently
innocently
insolently
intently
(See also ĔNT;
add -ly where
appropriate.)

ĔNT'les
cementless
centless
dentless
lamentless
relentless
rentless
scentless
tentless
(See also ĔNT;
add -less where
appropriate.)

ĔNT'ment
contentment
discontentment
presentment
relentment
representment
resentment

ĔNT'nes
intentness

ĔN'tō

cento
cinquecento
divertimento
lento
memento
pimento
polento
portamento
pronuncia-
    mento
quattrocento
rifacimento
Sacramento

ĔN'ton
Benton
Denton
Fenton
Trenton

ĔN'tôr
bucentaur
centaur
mentor
stentor
succentor
(See also
ĔN'tur.)

ĔN'tral
central
ventral

ĔN'trans
entrance

ĔN'trāt
concentrate

ĔN'trē
entry
gentry
sentry

ĔNT'res
inventress
tormentress

ĔN'trik
acentric
androcentric
anthropocentric
barycentric
centric
concentric
eccentric
egocentric
ethnocentric
geocentric
gynecocentric
heliocentric
paracentric
selenocentric

ĔN'tum
momentum
sarmentum

ĔN'tūr
adventure
debenture
indenture
misadventure
peradventure
tenture
venture

ĔN'tŭr

assenter
augmenter
cementer
center
circumventor
commenter
concenter
consenter
contenter
dead center
denter
dissenter
enter
epicenter
experimenter
fermenter
fomenter
frequenter
indenter
inventor
lamenter
lentor
misrepresenter
ornamenter
precentor
presenter
preventer
reenter
relenter
renter
repenter
representer
resenter
supplementer
tenter
tormenter
venter
(See also
ĔN'tôr.)

āle,   câre,   ădd,   ärm,   ăsk;   mē,   hĕre,   ĕnd;   īce,   ĭll;

ĔN'turd
centered
entered
self-centered
(See also
ĔN'tŭr; add
-ed where
appropriate.)

ĔN'tus
immomentous
ligamentous
momentous
pedetentous
pigmentous
portentous
sarmentous
unguentous

ĔN'um
frenum
plenum

ĒN'ur
cleaner
contravener
convener
demeanor
gleaner
greener
intervener
keener
leaner
machiner
magaziner
meaner
misdemeanor
obscener
screener

seiner
serener
shebeener
supervener
weaner
wiener

ĔN'ur
Fenner
penner
tenner
tenor
Venner

ĒN'us
genus
Silenus
venous
Venus

ĔN'vē
envy

ĔN'vil
Bienville
Glenville
Grenville

ĔN'yal
congenial
(See also
Ē'nē-al.)

ĔN'yan
Armenian
(See also
ĔN'ē-an.)

ĔN'yens

lenience
(See also
ĔN'ē-ens.)

ĔN'yent
convenient
(See also
ĔN'ē-ent.)

ĒN'yôr
monsignor
seignior
senior
signor

ĒN'yus
genius
(See also
Ē'nē-us.)

ĔN'za
cadenza
influenza

ĔNZ'dā
Wednesday

ĔN'zes
cleanses
lenses

ĔN'zē
frenzy
McKenzie

ĔN'zō
Lorenzo

ĔN'zon

tenzon
venison

Ē'ō
brio
Cleo
Keogh
Leo
Rio
Theo
trio

Ē'on
aeon
Creon
eon
freon
Leon
neon
odeon
paeon
pantheon
peon
pheon
pleon

ĔP'ard
jeopard
leopard
peppered
shepherd

ĒP'ē
cheepy
creepy
heapy
kepi
seepy
sleepy

ōld, ôr, ŏdd, oil, fŏŏt, out; ūse, ûrn, ŭp; THis, thin

steepy
sweepy
tepee
weepy

ĔP'ē
peppy
preppy
tepee

ĒP'en
cheapen
deepen
steepen

ĒP'est
cheapest
cheepest
creepest
deepest
heapest
keepest
leapest
outsleepest
overleapest
oversleepest
peepest
reapest
sleepest
steepest
sweepest
weepest

ĒP'eth
cheepeth
creepeth
heapeth
keepeth
leapeth

outsleepeth
overleapeth
oversleepeth
peepeth
reapeth
sleepeth
sweepeth
weepeth

ĔP'id
intrepid
lepid
tepid
trepid

ĒP'ij
seepage
sweepage

ĒP'ik
epic
orthoepic

ĒP'ing
bookkeeping
cheeping
creeping
heaping
housekeeping
keeping
leaping
outsleeping
overleaping
oversleeping
peeping
reaping
safekeeping
sleeping
steeping

sweeping
unsleeping
unweeping
weeping

ĒP'ish
deepish
sheepish
steepish

ĒP''l
empeople
people
steeple
unpeople

ĒP'les
sleepless
weepless

ĒP'nes
cheapness
deepness
sleepness

ĔP'on
weapon

ĔP'sē
apepsy
catalepsy
dyspepsy
epilepsy
eupepsy

ĔP'shun
abreption
apperception
arreption

conception
contraception
deception
direption
ereption
exception
imperception
inception
interception
introsusception
intussusception
misconception
obreption
perception
preception
preconception
preperception
reception
self-deception
subreption
surreption
susception

ĔP'sis
asepsis
analepsis
epanalepsis
metalepsis
paralepsis
prolepsis
scepsis
syllepsis

ĒP'skin
sheepskin

ĔP'tans
acceptance

āle, câre, ădd, ärm, ăsk; mē, hĕre, ĕnd; īce, ĭll;

ĔP'tant
acceptant
exceptant
reptant

ĔP'ted
accepted
excepted
intercepted

ĔP'test
acceptest
adeptest
exceptest
interceptest

ĔP'teth
accepteth
excepteth
intercepteth

ĔP'tik
acataleptic
analeptic
antiseptic
aseptic
bradypeptic
cataleptic
dyspeptic
epileptic
eupeptic
metaleptic
nympholeptic
organoleptic
peptic
proleptic
sceptic
septic
sylleptic

ĔP'ting
accepting
excepting
incepting
intercepting

ĔP'tiv
acceptive
conceptive
deceptive
exceptive
imperceptive
inceptive
insusceptive
interceptive
intussusceptive
irreceptive
perceptive
preceptive
receptive
susceptive

ĔPT'nes
ineptness

ĔP'tūn
Neptune

ĔP'tur
accepter
adepter
excepter
inceptor
intercepter
preceptor
scepter
susceptor

ĔP'ur

cheaper
cheeper
creeper
deeper
heaper
hedge keeper
housekeeper
keeper
leaper
peeper
reaper
shopkeeper
sleeper
steeper
sweeper
wall creeper
weeper
wicketkeeper

ĔP'ur
hepper
high-stepper
leper
overstepper
pepper
stepper

ĔP'wäk
sheepwalk
sleepwalk

Ē'ra
Ça ira
chimera
era
gerah
Hera
lira
Madeira

Vera

ĔR'af
seraph
teraph

Ē̯R'al
feral
spheral

ĔR'ald
Gerald
herald
Herrold

ĔR'ans
aberrance

ĔR'ant
aberrant

ĔR'as
terrace
(See also
ĔR'is.)

ĔR'āt
serrate

Ē̯R'ded
bearded

Ē̯RD'lē
weirdly

Ē̯'rē, Ē'rē
aerie
aweary
beery

bleary
bokmakierie
cheery
deary
domino theory
dreary
eerie
Erie
forweary
hara-kiri
jeery
Kashmiri
kiri
kyrie
leary
leery
life weary
metatheory
overweary
peri
quaere
query
siri
smeary
sneery
speary
sphery
teary
theory
uncheery
Valkyrie
veery
weary
whigmaleery
world-weary

Ĕ̲R′ē
baneberry
barberry

bayberry
beriberi
berry
bilberry
blackberry
blueberry
brambleberry
burberry
bury
catberry
cemetery
checkerberry
cherry
chinaberry
chokeberry
chokecherry
Christmas-
   berry
coffeeberry
cranberry
crowberry
dangleberry
dayberry
deerberry
Derry
dewberry
dogberry
equerry
ferry
flos ferri
Gerry
gooseberry
guavaberry
hackberry
huckleberry
inkberry
intercalary
Jerry
jerry

Juneberry
Kerry
knobkerrie
knobkerry
lamasery
limeberry
locustberry
loganberry
Londonderry
mere
merry
mesentery
millinery
miserere
Miserere
monastery
mossberry
mulberry
naseberry
orangeberry
partridgeberry
perry
phrontistery
Pondicherry
presbytery
quatercente-
   nary
quaternary
raspberry
redberry
rowanberry
sedentary
serry
shadberry
sherry
skerry
snowberry
squawberry
stationary

stationery
strawberry
tangleberry
Terry
terry
thumbleberry
Tom and Jerry
unbury
very
wherry
whortleberry
wineberry
winterberry
youngberry
(See also
  ÂR′ē.)

Ē̲R′ēd
queried
unwearied
war-wearied
wearied
world-wearied

Ĕ̲R′ēd
berried
buried
cherried
ferried
serried
unburied

Ē̲R′ens
adherence
appearance
arrearance
clearance
coherence
disappearance

incoherence
inherence
interference
perseverance
reappearance

ĒR′ent
adherent
coherent
inadherent
incoherent
inherent
perseverant
querent
vicegerent

ĒR′est
adherest
appearest
austerest
besmearest
careerest
cheerest
clearest
coherest
dearest
disappearest
drearest
endearest
fearest
gearest
hearest
insincerest
interferest
jeerest
leerest
merest
nearest
overhearest

peerest
perseverest
queerest
reappearest
rearest
reverest
searest
serest
severest
shearest
sheerest
sincerest
smearest
sneerest
spearest
steerest
unrearest
uprearest
veerest

ĔR′et
ferret
terret

ĒR′eth
adhereth
appeareth
besmeareth
careereth
cheereth
cleareth
disappeareth
endeareth
feareth
geareth
heareth
interfereth
jeereth
leereth

overheareth
peereth
persevereth
reappeareth
reareth
revereth
seareth
sheareth
smeareth
sneereth
speareth
steereth
upreareth
veereth

ĒR′ēz
dearies
overwearies
queries
series
wearies

ĔR′ēz
berries
buries
cherries
ferries
sherries
wherries

ĒR′fōn
earphone

ĒR′ful
cheerful
earful
fearful
sneerful
tearful

uncheerful
unfearful

ĒR′īd
blear-eyed
clear-eyed
tear-eyed

ĔR′if
sans serif
serif
sheriff

ĒR′ij
arrearage
clearage
peerage
pierage
steerage

ĔR′ik
alexiteric
amphoteric
anisomeric
atmospheric
chimeric
chromospheric
cleric
climacteric
derrick
enteric
Eric
esoteric
exoteric
ferric
generic
helispheric
hemispheric
Herrick

ōld, ôr, ŏdd, oil, fŏŏt, out; ūse, ûrn, ŭp; THis, thin

Homeric
hysteric
icteric
isomeric
masseteric
mesmeric
neoteric
numeric
peripheric
perispheric
phylacteric
piperic
spheric
suberic
valeric

ĔR′iks
clerics
esoterics
hysterics
(See also
ĔR′ik; add -s
where appro-
priate.)

ĔR′il
beryl
Cheryl
chrysoberyl
peril
sterile

ĘR′in
Erin

ĘR′ing
adhering
appearing
auctioneering

Bering
besmearing
blearing
cannoneering
careering
cashiering
cheering
clearing
cohering
Dearing
disappearing
domineering
earing
electioneering
endearing
engineering
fearing
gearing
gondoliering
hearing
interfering
jeering
leering
mountaineer-
ing
nearing
overhearing
peering
persevering
pioneering
privateering
queering
reappearing
rearing
rehearing
revering
searing
shearing
skeering

sneering
spearing
steering
ungearing
upcheering
uprearing
veering
veneering
volunteering

ĔR′is
ferris
terrace
Terris

ĔR′ish
cherish
perish

ĔR′it
demerit
disherit
disinherit
immerit
inherit
merit

ĘR′lē
austerely
cavalierly
cheerly
clearly
dearly
merely
nearly
queerly
severely
sincerely
yearly

ĘR′les
cheerless
earless
fearless
gearless
peerless
spearless
tearless
yearless

ĘR′ling
shearling
steerling
yearling

ĘR′ment
cerement
endearment

ĘR′nes
austereness
clearness
dearness
nearness
queerness
severeness
sincereness

ĘR′ō, Ē′rō
hero
lillibullero
zero

ĔR′on
heron

Ē′rŏŏm
sea room
tearoom

ĔR′ôr
error
terror

ĔR′os, ĔR′os
Eros

ĔRS′nes
fierceness

ĔR′sur
fiercer
piercer

ĔR′sing
ear-piercing
piercing
transpiercing

ĔR′son
Grierson
Pearson

ĔR′ub
cherub

ĔR′ūl
ferrule
ferule
perule
spherule

ĔR′ur
adherer
appearer
austerer
besmearer
cheerer
clearer

dearer
disappearer
electioneerer
endearer
fearer
fleerer
hearer
interferer
jeerer
leerer
nearer
overhearer
peerer
perseverer
queerer
rearer
reverer
severer
shearer
sneerer
spearer
steerer
teerer
ungearer
veerer

ĔR′us
sclerous
serous

ĔR′us
ferrous

ĔRZ′man
privateersman
steersman

Ē′sa
Felica

mesa
Theresa

Ē′saj
presage

ĔS′chun
congestion
digestion
indigestion
ingestion
question
suggestion

ĔS′chund
questioned
unquestioned

ĔS′ē
creasy
fleecy

ĔS′ē
Bessie
Cressy
dressy
Jesse
Jessie
messy
Tessie
tressy

ĔS′ed
blessed
(See also ĔS;
add -ed where
appropriate.)

ĔS′el

Diesel

ĔS′en
lessen

ĔS′ens
indecence

ĔS′ens
accrescence
acquiescence
adolescence
arborescence
calescence
calorescence
candescence
coalescence
concrescence
contabescence
convalescence
defervescence
deliquescence
delitescence
effervescence
efflorescence
emollescence
erubescence
essence
evanescence
exacerbescence
excrescence
florescence
fluorescence
fremescence
frondescence
fructescence
frutescence
glaucescence
hyalescence

incalescence
incandescence
incoalescence
ineffervescence
inflorescence
intumescence
iridescence
juvenescence
lactescence
lapidescence
latescence
obsolescence
opalescence
petrescence
phosphores-
  cence
pubescence
putrescence
quiescence
quintessence
recrudescence
reflorescence
rejuvenescence
revalescence
revirescence
rubescence
senescence
spumescence
supercrescence
torpescence
tumescence
turgescence
viridescence
virilescence
vitrescence

ĔS′ent
decent
indecent

recent

ĔS′ent
accrescent
acescent
acquiescent
aculescent
adolescent
albescent
alkalescent
antidepressant
arborescent
calorescent
candescent
canescent
cessant
coalescent
confessant
congrescent
contabescent
convalescent
crescent
decalescent
decrescent
deflorescent
deliquescent
delitescent
depressant
detumescent
deturgescent
effervescent
efflorescent
erubescent
evanescent
excrescent
fervescent
flavescent
florescent
fluorescent

fremescent
frondescent
fructescent
frutescent
gangrenescent
glaucescent
herbescent
ignescent
incalescent
incandescent
incessant
increscent
ineffervescent
inflorescent
ingravescent
intumescent
iridescent
jessant
juvenescent
lactescent
languescent
lapidescent
latescent
liquescent
luminescent
lutescent
marcescent
maturescent
nigrescent
nonacquiescent
noncandescent
nondeliques-
  cent
nonefferves-
  cent
nonfluorescent
nonluminescent
nonputrescent
obmutescent

obsolescent
opalescent
petrecent
phosphores-
  cent
postpubescent
prepubescent
pubescent
putrescent
quiescent
rancescent
recrudescent
rejuvenescent
repressant
requiescent
revalescent
rubescent
rufescent
senescent
spinescent
spinulescent
spumescent
suffrutescent
sugescent
supercrescent
suppressant
tabescent
torpescent
tumescent
turgescent
uneffervescent
violescent
virescent
viridescent
virilescent
vitrescent

ĔS′ept
precept

āle, câre, ădd, ärm, ăsk; mē, hĕre, ĕnd; īce, ĭll;

ĒS'est
ceasest
creasest
decreaest
fleecest
greasest
increasest
leasest
releasest

ĔS'est
acquiescest
addressest
assessest
blessest
caressest
compressest
confessest
depressest
digressest
distressest
dressest
expressest
guessest
impressest
oppressest
possessest
pressest
professest
progressest
redressest
repressest
suppressest
transgressest
undressest

ĒS'eth
ceaseth
creaseth

decreaseth
fleeceth
greaseth
increaseth
leaseth
releaseth

ĔS'eth
acquiesceth
addresseth
assesseth
blesseth
caresseth
compresseth
confesseth
depresseth
digresseth
distresseth
dresseth
expresseth
guesseth
impresseth
oppresseth
possesseth
presseth
professeth
progresseth
redresseth
represseth
suppresseth
transgresseth
undresseth

ĒS'ez
battlepieces
caprices
ceases
creases
decreases

fleeces
greases
increases
leases
mantelpieces
masterpieces
nieces
peaces
pelisses
pieces
releases

ĔS'ez
dresses
presses
(See also ĔS;
add -es where
appropriate.)

ĒS'ful
capriceful
peaceful
unpeaceful

ĔS'ful
successful
(See also ĔS;
add -ful where
appropriate.)

ĔSH'al
especial
special

ĔSH'an
Grecian
(See also
ĔSH'un.)

ĔSH'ē
fleshy
meshy

ĔSH'est
enmeshest
freshest
immeshest
refreshest
threshest

ĔSH'eth
enmesheth
immesheth
mesheth
refresheth
thresheth

ĔSH'ēz
species

ĔSH'ing
meshing
refreshing
threshing

ĔSH'ingz
fleshings
meshings
(See also ĔSH;
add -ings where
appropriate.)

ĔSH'les
fleshless
meshless

ĔSH'lē
fleshly

ōld, ôr, ŏdd, oil, fŏŏt, out; ūse, ûrn, ŭp; THis, thin

freshly
unfleshly

ĔSH'man
freshman

ĔSH'ment
refreshment

ĔSH'nes
freshness

Ē'shôr
seashore

Ē'shun
accretion
completion
concretion
deletion
depletion
Grecian
impletion
incompletion
internection
repletion
secretion
(See also
Ē'shi-an.)

ĔSH'un
accession
aggression
cession
compression
concession
confession
depression
digression
discretion

dispossession
egression
expression
freshen
impression
indiscretion
ingression
insession
intercession
introgression
intropression
nonaggression
obsession
oppression
possession
precession
prepossession
procession
profession
progression
recession
regression
reimpression
repossession
repression
retrocession
retrogression
secession
self-possession
session
succession
supersession
suppression
transgression

ĔSH'unz
accessions
quarter ses-
   sions

(See also
ESH'un; add
-s where
appropriate.)

ĔSH'ur
flesher
fresher
mesher
pressure
refresher
thresher
tressure

Ē'shus
facetious
specious

ĔSH'us
precious

Ē'sīd
leeside
seaside

ĔS'ij
expressage
message
pesage
presage

ĔS'ik
eugenesic
geodesic

Ē'sil, ĔS'il,
or ĬS'il
Cecil

ĒS'ing
ceasing
creasing
decreasing
fleecing
greasing
increasing
leasing
piecing
policing
releasing
surceasing
unceasing

ĔS'ing
acquiescing
addressing
assessing
blessing
caressing
coalescing
compressing
confessing
convalescing
depressing
digressing
dispossessing
distressing
dressing
excessing
expressing
guessing
impressing
messing
oppressing
possessing
prepossessing
pressing
professing

āle,   câre,   ădd,   ärm,   ăsk;   mē,   hĕre,   ĕnd;   īce,   ĭll;

progressing
redressing
repressing
retrogressing
suppressing
undressing
unprepossess-
   ing
water dressing

ĒS'is
anamnesis
anesthesis
anthesis
aposiopesis
catachresis
deesis
diaphoresis
diesis
erotesis
exegesis
hyperesthesis
mathesis
mimesis
ochlesis
paracentesis
perichoresis
schesis
synteresis
telekinesis
thesis
tmesis

ĒS'iv
adhesive
cohesive

ĔS'iv
accessive

aggressive
compressive
concessive
concrescive
congressive
crescive
depressive
digressive
excessive
expressive
impressive
inexpressive
obsessive
oppressive
possessive
progressive
recessive
redressive
regressive
repressive
retrogressive
successive
suppressive
transgressive
unexpressive
unimpressive

ĔS'kē
de Reszke
pesky

ĔSK'nes
grotesquesness
picturesque-
   ness
statuesqueness

ĔS'kō
al fresco

fresco
tedesco

ĔS'kū
fescue
rescue

Ē'skwar
T square

ĔS''il
Cecil
chessel
nestle
pestle
redressal
trestle
unnestle
vessel
wrestle

ĒS'les
capriceless
ceaseless
creaseless
fleeceless
leaseless
peaceless

ĔS'ling
nestling
pestling
wrestling

ĔS'lur
nestler
wrestler

ĔS'man

policeman

ĔS'man
pressman
yes man

ĔS'māt
messmate

ĔS'mĕl
piecemeal

ĔS'ment
assessment
impressment
redressment

ĒS'nes
obeseness

ĒS'on
Gleason
Leisen

ĔS'on
lessen
lesson

ĔS'pit
respite

ĔS'pur
Hesper
vesper

ĔS'ta
Hesta
podesta
siesta

Vesta
Zend-Avesta

ĔS′tal
festal
vestal

ĔS′tan
Avestan
sebesten

ĔS′tant
contestant
gestant

ĔS′tāt
intestate
testate

ĔS′tē
beastie
bheesty
yeasty

ĔS′tē
chesty
cresty
resty
testy
yesty

ĔS′ted
arrested
attested
bested
breasted
castle-crested
chested
chicken-
  breasted

congested
contested
crested
detested
digested
disinterested
divested
double-
  breasted
foam-crested
indigested
infested
ingested
interested
invested
jested
manifested
marble-
  breasted
molested
nested
pigeon-breasted
predigested
protested
redigested
requested
rested
sable-vested
single-breasted
suggested
tested
unbreasted
undigested
unmolested
unrested
vested
wrested

ĔS′test

arrestest
attestest
bestest
breastest
contestest
crestest
detestest
digestest
divestest
infestest
interestest
investest
jestest
manifestest
molestest
protestest
requestest
restest
suggestest
testest
wrestest

ĔS′teth

arresteth
attesteth
breasteth
contesteth
cresteth
detesteth
digesteth
divesteth
infesteth
interesteth
investeth
jesteth
manifesteth
molesteth
nesteth
protesteth

requesteth
resteth
suggesteth
testeth
wresteth

ĔS′tēz
Estes
Orestes
ornitholestes
testes

ĔST′ful
blestful
jestful
restful
unrestful

ĔS′tik
agrestic
alkahestic
anamnestic
anapestic
asbestic
catachrestic
domestic
gestic
majestic
telestic
telestich

ĔS′tin
asbestine
clandestine
destine
intestine
predestine
sestine

āle,   câre,   ădd,   ärm,   ăsk;   mē,   hĕre,   ĕnd;   īce,   ĭll;

ĔS'tind
destined
predestined
undestined

ĔS'ting
easting
feasting
unpriesting
yeasting

ĔS'ting
arresting
attesting
besting
breasting
congesting
contesting
cresting
detesting
digesting
disinteresting
divesting
infesting
ingesting
interesting
investing
jesting
manifesting
molesting
nesting
protesting
questing
reinvesting
requesting
resting
suggesting
testing
uninteresting

unresting
vesting
westing
wresting

ĔS'tiv
attestive
congestive
digestive
festive
infestive
restive
suggestive
tempestive

ĒST'lē
beastly
priestly

ĔST'les
breastless
crestless
guestless
jestless
questless
restless

ĔST'ling
nestling
wrestling

ĔST'ment
arrestment
divestment
investment
vestment

ĔS'tō
manifesto

mesto
pesto
presto

Ē'stōn
freestone
keystone

ĔS'ton
Weston

ĔS'tral
ancestral
campestral
fenestral
kestrel
orchestral
trimestral

ĔS'trāt
fenestrate
orchestrate
sequestrate

ĔS'trik
orchestric
palaestric

ĔS'tūr
divesture
gesture
investure
purpresture
revesture
vesture

ĔS'tus
asbestos
cestus

ĒST'ward
eastward

ĒST'ward
westward

ĒS'ter
Dniester
down-easter
Easter
feaster
northeaster
southeaster

ĔS'tur
arrester
attester
Bester
Bestor
breaster
Chester
contester
digester
divester
Dnestr
Esther
fester
Hester
infester
investor
jester
Leicester
Lester
midsemester
molester
nester
nor'wester
pester
prester

ōld, ôr, ŏdd, oil, fŏŏt, out; ūse, ûrn, ŭp; THis, thin

protester
requester
rester
semester
sequester
sou'wester
suggester
Sylvester
tester
trimester
vester
wrester
yester

ĔS'turd
festered
sequestered
unsequestered
(See also
ĔS'tur; add
-ed where
appropriate.)

ĔS'turn
eastern

ĔS'turn
hestern
northwestern
southwestern
western
yestern

ĔS'ur
creaser
decreaser
fleecer
greaser
increaser

leaser
piecer
releaser

ĔS'ŭr
acquiescer
addresser
aggressor
antecessor
assessor
blesser
caresser
cesser
compressor
confessor
depressor
digresser
distresser
dresser
excesser
guesser
impresser
intercessor
lesser
messer
oppressor
possessor
predecessor
presser
professor
progressor
redresser
represser
successor
suppressor
transgressor

ĔT'a
amrita

Bhagavad Gita
cheetah
Chiquita
dolce vita
eta
excreta
granita
Juanita
keta
Lolita
manzanita
margarita
partita
pita
Rita
señorita
vita
zeta

ĔT'a
animetta
arietta
biretta
burletta
codetta
comedietta
Etta
Henrietta
lametta
mozetta
operetta
Retta
Rosetta
vendetta
Yetta

ĔT'ē
entreaty
meaty

peaty
sleety
spermaceti
sweetie
sweety
treaty

ĔT'ē
Alligretti
Bettie
betty
confetti
fretty
Hettie
Hetty
Irish confetti
jetty
Lettie
Letty
libretti
netty
Nettie
petit
petty
Rossetti
spaghetti
spermaceti
Vanizetti
sweaty

ĒT'ed
accreted
bleated
cheated
competed
completed
conceited
defeated
deleted

depleted
entreated
escheated
evil-treated
excreted
greeted
heated
ill-treated
incompleted
maltreated
meted
receipted
reheated
repeated
retreated
seated
secreted
self-conceited
sheeted
sleeted
treated
unmeeted
unseated
wine-heated

ĔT'ed
abetted
benetted
betted
brevetted
coquetted
coroneted
curvetted
fretted
gazetted
indebted
interfretted
jetted
netted

petted
pirouetted
regretted
sweated
unfretted
unnetted
wetted
whetted

ĔT'en
beaten
Cretan
eaten
moth-eaten
overeaten
storm-beaten
sweeten
tempest-beaten
unbeaten
weather-beaten
wheaten
worm-eaten
(See also
ĔT'on.)

ĔT'en
fretten
threaten
(See also
ĔT'on.)

ĔT'est
beatest
bleatest
cheatest
competest
completest
defeatest
deletest

depletest
discreetest
eatest
effetest
elitest
entreatest
fleetest
greetest
heatest
ill-treatest
incompletest
maltreatest
meetest
neatest
overeatest
pleatest
receiptest
repeatest
repletest
retreatest
seatest
sweetest
treatest

ĔT'est
abettest
backsettest
bayonettest
begettest
benettest
besettest
bettest
coquettest
forgettest
frettest
gettest
lettest
nettest
oversettest

pettest
regrettest
settest
upsettest
wettest
whettest

ĔT'eth
beateth
bleateth
cheateth
competeth
completeth
defeateth
deleteth
depleteth
eateth
entreateth
greeteth
heateth
maltreateth
meeteth
overeateth
pleateth
receipteth
repeateth
retreateth
seateth
treateth

ĔT'eth
abetteth
begetteth
benetteth
betteth
bewetteth
coquetteth
forgetteth
fretteth

getteth
letteth
netteth
petteth
regretteth
setteth
whetteth

ĒT′ēz
entreaties
sweeties
treaties

ĒT′ful
deceitful

ĔT′ful
forgetful
fretful
regretful

ĒTH′al
bequeathal

Ĕth′al
ethal
lethal

Ĕth′an
Ethan

Ĕth′el
Bethel
ethal
Ethel
(See also
Ĕth′il.)

ĔTH′en

heathen
wreathen

Ēth′ē
heathy
Lethe
lethy

Ĕth′ē
deathy

Ĕth′il
ethyl
methyl

ĒTH′ing
bequeathing
breathing
ensheathing
enwreathing
inbreathing
incense-
    breathing
interwreathing
inwreathing
seething
sheathing
teething
terror-breath-
    ing
unsheathing
wreathing

Ĕth′lē
deathly

Ĕth′les
sheathless
wreathless

Ĕth′les
breathless
deathless

ĒTH′ment
bequeathment
ensheathment
enwreathment

Ĕth′nik
ethnic
holethnic

Ĕth′od
method

ĒTH′ren
brethren

ĒTH′ur
bequeather
breather
either
enwreather
neither
seether
sheather
wreather

Ĕth′ur
ether

ĒTH′ur
altogether
aweather
blether
feather
heather
leather

nether
patent leather
pinfeather
tether
together
weather
wether
white feather
whitleather
whether

ĔTH′urd
feathered
unfeathered
weathered
(See also
ĔTH′ur; add
-ed where
appropriate.)

ĒT′id, ĔT′id
fetid
(See also
ĒT′ed, ĔT′ed.)

ĒT′ij
cheatage
cleatage
eatage
escheatage
metage

ĒT′ik
acetic
cetic
Cretic
Rhaetic

āle, câre, ădd, ärm, ásk; mē, hĕre, ĕnd; īce, ĭll;

ĚT'ik
abietic
abiogenetic
aesthetic
agamogenetic
alexipyretic
algetic
allopathic
aloetic
alphabetic
amuletic
analgetic
anchoretic
anesthetic
anoetic
anoretic
antimagnetic
antipathetic
antipyretic
antithetic
apatetic
apathetic
aphetic
apologetic
apyretic
arithmetic
ascetic
asynartetic
asyndetic
athletic
auletic
autokinetic
auxetic
balletic
Baphometic
bathetic
biogenetic
biomagnetic
catechetic

colletic
cometic
copacetic
cosmetic
cosmothetic
cybernetic
diabetic
diamagnetic
dianoetic
diaphoretic
diathetic
dietetic
diuretic
docetic
eidetic
electromag-
    netic
emetic
emporetic
energetic
enthetic
epenthetic
epexegetic
epigenetic
epithetic
erotetic
esthetic
eugenetic
exegetic
frenetic
galactopoietic
gametic
Gangetic
genetic
geodetic
goetic
gyromagnetic
hebetic
Helvetic

hermetic
heterogenetic
histogenetic
homiletic
homogenetic
hydrokinetic
hyperesthetic
hypnogenetic
hypothetic
idiopathetic
inergetic
isomagnetic
Japhetic
kinetic
Lettic
limnetic
logarithmetic
ludicropathetic
magnetic
Masoretic
mesothetic
metic
mimetic
monogenetic
morphogenetic
mythopoetic
noetic
nomothetic
ochletic
onomatopoetic
ontogenetic
oogenetic
Ossetic
paleogenetic
palingenetic
pangenetic
parasympa-
    thetic
parathetic

parenthetic
paretic
parthenogenetic
pathetic
pathogenetic
peripatetic
phenetic
phlogogenetic
phonetic
photosynthetic
phrenetic
phyletic
phylogenetic
plethoretic
poetic
polygenetic
polyphyletic
polysynthetic
prophetic
prosthetic
prothetic
psychogenetic
pyretic
pyrogenetic
quercetic
quodlibetic
seismetic
splenetic
strategetic
sympathetic
synartetic
syncretic
syndetic
synergetic
synthetic
syzygetic
tabetic
telekinetic
theopathetic

ōld, ôr, ŏdd, oil, fŏŏt, out; ūse, ûrn, ŭp; THis, thin

theoretic
thermogenetic
thermomag-
  netic
threnetic
tonetic
uletic
uretic
Venetic
zetetic
zoetic

ĔT'iks
aesthetics
apologetics
dietetics
esthetics
exegetics
homiletics
poetics
(See also
ĔT'ik; add
-s where
appropriate.)

ĔT'ing
beating
bittersweeting
bleating
cheating
competing
completing
concreting
defeating
eating
entreating
fleeting
flesh-eating
greeting

heating
ill-treating
maltreating
meeting
meting
overeating
receipting
repeating
retreating
seating
secreting
sheeting
sweeting
toad-eating
treating
unseating

ĔT'ing
abetting
backsetting
begetting
benetting
besetting
betting
brevetting
coquetting
curvetting
forgetting
fretting
gazetting
getting
intersetting
jetting
letting
minuetting
netting
oversetting
petting
regretting

retting
setting
somersetting
sweating
undersetting
upsetting
wetting
whetting

ĔT'is
Thetis

ĔT'is
lettuce

ĔT'ish
coquettish
fetish
Lettish
pettish
wettish

ĔT'ist
defeatist
(See also ĒT;
add -ist where
appropriate.)

ĔT'it
beat it

ĔT'iv
accretive
completive
concretive
decretive
depletive
discretive
repletive

secretive

ĔT' 'l
beetle
betel
decretal
fetal

ĔT' 'l
abettal
Babbitt metal
Chettle
fettle
kettle
metal
mettle
Monel metal
nettle
petal
Popocatapetl
resettle
settle
type metal
white metal

ĔT' 'ld
high-mettled
nettled
petalled
unsettled
mettled
(See also ĔT' 'l;
add -ed where
appropriate.)

ĒT'lē
completely
concretely
discreetly

āle, câre, ădd, ärm, ăsk; mē, hĕre, ĕnd; īce, ĭll;

discretely
featly
fleetly
indiscreetly
meetly
neatly
obsoletely
sweetly
unmeetly

ĔT'les
debtless
petless
threatless

ĔT'ling
nettling
settling
unsettling

ĒT'ment
entreatment
ill treatment
maltreatment
treatment

ĔT'ment
abetment
besetment
indebtment
revetment

ĒT'nes
completeness
concreteness
discreetness
discreteness
effeteness
featness

fleetness
incompleteness
meetness
neatness
obsoleteness
repleteness
sweetness

ĔT'nes
setness
wetness

ĒT'ō
bonito
mosquito
sanbenito
veto

ĔT'ō
allegretto
amaretto
amoretto
falsetto
ghetto
lazaretto
libretto
palmetto
stiletto
terzetto
zucchetto

ĒT'on
Beaton
Eaton
Eton
Keaton
Keyton
Seaton
Seyton

Zyzzogeton
(See also
ĒT'en.)

ĔT'on
Bretton

ĔT'ral,
ĔT'rel
diametral
petrel

ĒT'rē
Petrie

ĔT'rik
actinometric
aerometric
algometric
alkalimetric
allometric
anemometric
anisometric
anthropometric
astrometric
asymmetric
audiometric
barometric
bathometric
bathymetric
biometric
bisymmetric
bolometric
calorimetric
cephalometric
chlorometric
chronometric
clinometric
coulometric

craniometric
cryometric
cyclometric
densitometric
diametric
dimetric
dynamometric
econometric
electrometric
endosmometric
ergometric
eudiometric
fluorometric
galvanometric
gasometric
geometric
goniometric
gravimetric
hexametric
hydrometric
hygrometric
hypsometric
interferometric
iodometric
isobarometric
isometric
kilometric
logometric
magnetometric
manometric
metric
micrometric
monometric
nitrometric
obstetric
odometric
optometric
ozonometric
pedometric

ōld, ôr, ŏdd, oil, fŏŏt, out; ūse, ûrn, ŭp; THis, thin

phonometric
photometric
piezometric
planometric
plastometric
potentiometric
psychometric
pycnometric
pyrometric
radiometric
refractometric
rheometric
salinometric
sclerometric
sensitometric
sociometric
spectrometric
speedometric
spirometric
stereometric
stoichiometric
symmetric
tacheometric
tasimetric
tellurometric
thermometric
tonometric
trigonometric
trimetric
unsymmetric
viscometric
volumetric
zoometric

ĔT′rok
sheetrock

ĔT′rus,
ĔT′rus

petrous
saltpetrous
triquetrous

ĔT′sō
intermezzo
mezzo

ĔT′um
arboretum
fretum
pinetum
zibetum

ĔT′ūr
creature
feature
(See also
ĔCH′ur.)

ĔT′ur
beater
beefeater
bleater
cake-eater
cheater
centimeter
competer
completer
decaliter
defeater
Demeter
depleter
eater
entreater
escheater
fire-eater
fleeter
frog-eater

gas meter
goldbeater
greeter
heater
hectoliter
ill-treater
kilometer
liter
lotus-eater
meeter
meter
neater
overeater
Peter
praetor
receipter
repeater
retreater
saltpeter
seater
secreter
skeeter
smoke-eater
superheater
sweeter
teeter
toad-eater
treater
unseater
water meter

ĔT′ur
abettor
begetter
besetter
better
carburetor
coquetter
curvetter

dead-letter
debtor
enfetter
fetter
forgetter
fretter
getter
go-getter
jetter
letter
netter
petter
red-letter
regretter
resetter
setter
somersetter
sweater
typesetter
wetter
whetter

ĔT′urd
featured

ĔT′urd
bettered
fettered
unfettered
unlettered
(See also
ĔT′ur; add
-ed where
appropriate.)

ĔT′urz
Peters

ĔT′us
acetous

Cetus
fetus
quietus

ĔT′wurk
fretwork
network

Ē′um
amoebaeum
anthenaeum
bronteum
colosseum
lyceum
mausoleum
museum
peritoneum
prytaneum
Te Deum

Ē′ur
agreer
feer
fleer
freer
overseer
seer
sightseer

Ē′us
choreus
corypheus
gluteus
onomato-
  poeous
plumbeous
scarabaeus

Ē′va

diva
Eva
Geneva
Kamadeva
Kivah
Mahadeva
Shiva
Siva
viva
yeshiva

ĒV′al
coeval
longeval
medieval
primeval
retrieval
shrieval
upheaval
(See also
Ē′vil.)

ĔV′an
Evan
Devon
(See also
Ĕv′en.)

ĔV′ans
achievance
grievance
perceivance
retrievance

Ē′vē
Levy

ĔV′ē
bevy

chevy
clevy
heart-heavy
heavy
levee
levy
nevvy
top-heavy

ĔV′el, ĔV′l
bedevil
bevil
devil
dishevel
Greville
kevel
level
Neville
revel
sea level
spirit level
water level

ĒV′en
even
good-even
Hallow-even
Stephen
Steven
unbereaven
uneven
yester-even

ĔV′en
eleven
heaven
leaven
seven

ĔV′end
leavened
unleavened

ĔV′enth
eleventh
seventh

ĒV′enz
Stevens

ĒV′est
achievest
believest
bereavest
cleavest
conceivest
deceivest
disbelievest
grievest
heavest
inweavest
leavest
perceivest
receivest
relievest
reprievest
retrievest
thievest
upheavest
weavest

ĒV′eth
achieveth
believeth
bereaveth
cleaveth
conceiveth
deceiveth

disbelieveth
grieveth
heaveth
inweaveth
leaveth
perceiveth
receiveth
relieveth
reprieveth
retrieveth
thieveth
upheaveth
weaveth

Ē'vī
Levi

ĒV'ij
cleavage
leavage

ĒV'il
evil
king's evil
weevil

ĚV'il
devil
Neville
(See also
ĚV'el.)

ĚV'ilz
blue devils
devils
(See also
ĚV'el,
ĚV'il; add
-s where

appropriate.)

ĚV'in
levin
replevin

ĒV'ing
achieving
aggrieving
believing
bereaving
cleaving
conceiving
deceiving
disbelieving
grieving
heaving
interweaving
inweaving
leaving
misconceiving
perceiving
preconceiving
receiving
relieving
reprieving
retrieving
sheaving
steeving
thieving
unbelieving
undeceiving
unweaving
upheaving
weaving

ĒV'ingz
leavings
(See also

ĒV'ing;
add -s where
appropriate.)

ĒV'ish
peevish
thievish

ĒV'les
leaveless
sheaveless
sleeveless

ĒV'ment
achievement
bereavement
retrievement

ĒV'ning
evening

ĚV'rē
every

ĒV'ur
achiever
aggriever
ballast heaver
beaver
believer
bereaver
brever
cantilever
cleaver
coal heaver
conceiver
deceiver
Deever
disbeliever
enfever

fever
griever
Guadalquivir
hay fever
heaver
interleaver
interweaver
jungle fever
keever
leaver
lever
liever
livre
make-believer
misconceiver
naïver
overachiever
perceiver
preconceiver
reaver
receiver
reever
reiver
reliever
repriever
retriever
scarlet fever
sheaver
spring fever
unbeliever
undeceiver
underachiever
upheaver
weaver
weever
yellow fever

ĚV'ur
assever

cantilever
clever
dissever
endeavor
ever
forever
however
howsoever
lever
never
sever
unsever
whatever
whatsoever
whencever
whencesoever
whenever
whensoever
wheresoever
wherever
whichever
whichsoever
whithersoever
whoever
whomsoever
whosesoever
whosoever

ĔV'urd
dissevered
unsevered
(See also
ĔV'ur; add
-*ed* where
appropriate.)

ĔV'us
grievous

longevous
primevous

Ē'wā
leeway
seaway

Ē'ward
leeward
seaward

Ē'wit
peewit

Ē'ya
Cassiopeia
(See also Ē'a.)

Ē'yan
Tarpeian
(See also
Ē'an.)

ĔZ'a
Liza
Louisa
Pisa

ĔZ'ans
defeasance
easance
malfeasance
misfeasance

**ĔZ'ans,
ĔZ'ens**
omnipresence
peasants
pleasance

presence

**ĔZ'ant,
ĔZ'ent**
displeasant
omnipresent
peasant
pheasant
pleasant
present
unpleasant

ĔZ'dāl
Teasdale

ĔZ'dāl
Esdale

ĔZ'ē
breezy
cheesy
easy
free-and-easy
freezy
greasy
queasy
sleazy
sneezy
speakeasy
uneasy
wheezy
Zambezi

ĔZ'el
easel
teasel
Teazle
weasel

ĔZ'el
bezel
(See also ĔZ''l.)

ĔZ'els
easels
measles
(See also ĔZ''l;
add -*s* where
appropriate.)

Ē'zha
magnesia

Ē'zhan
Milesian

Ē'zhun
adhesion
cohesion
inadhesion
inhesion
lesion
Silesian
trapezian

Ē'zhur
leisure
seizure

ĔZH'ur
admeasure
displeasure
entreasure
leisure
measure
outmeasure
pleasure
treasure

Ē′zhurd
unleisured

Ĕ′zhurd
immeasured
measured
unleisured
unmeasured
untreasured
(See also
ĒZH′ur; add
-ed where
appropriate.)

ĒZ′iks
skeeziks

ĒZ′in
seizin

ĒZ′ing
appeasing

breezing
displeasing
easing
foreseizing
freezing
greasing
pleasing
seizing
self-pleasing
sneezing
squeezing
teasing
unpleasing
wheezing

ĒZ′it
cheese it

ĔZ′′l
embezzle
(See also
ĔZ′el.)

ĔZ′lur
embezzler

ĔZ′ment
appeasement
easement

ĒZ′on
reason
season
treason
unreason
unseason

ĒZ′ra
Ezra

ĒZ′ur
appeaser
Caesar
easer
Ebenezer
freezer

friezer
geezer
greaser
leaser
pleaser
sneezer
squeezer
teaser
tweezer
wheezer

ĔZ′urt
desert

ĒZ′urz
tweezers
(See also
ĒZ′ur; add
-s where
appropriate.)

ĒZ′us
Jesus

I

For a discussion of words included under the accented vowels following, see the beginning of I rhymes in Section I.

Ī′a
Amariah
asthenia
Azariah
Beniah
Beriah
Black Maria
gorgoneia
Hezekiah
Jedediah
Jeremiah

Josiah
Keziah
latria
messiah
Obadiah
Sophia
stria
Thalia
Tobiah
Uriah
via

Zachariah
Zebediah
Zedekiah
Zephaniah

Ī′ad
dryad
dyad
hamadryad
Jeremiad
Pleiad

triad

Ī′adz
dryads
Hyads
(See also Ī′ad;
add -s where
appropriate.)

Ī′ak
elegiac

guiac
kayak
phrenesiac

Ī'al, Ī'ol
basihyal
bass viol
decrial
denial
dial
espial
genial
phial
retrial
rial
self-denial
supplial
trial
vial
viol

Ī'am
Priam
Siam

Ī'amb
iamb

Ī'an
Altaian
Brian
Bryan
Chian
genian
Orion
O'Ryan
Paraguayan
Ryan
styan

thalian
Uruguayan

Ī'and
viand

Ī'andz
viands

Ī'ans
affiance
alliance
appliance
compliance
defiance
incompliance
misalliance
reliance
science
self-reliance
suppliance
(See also Ī'ant;
add -s where
appropriate.)

Ī'ant
affiant
alliant
calorifient
client
compliant
defiant
giant
pliant
reliant
scient
self-reliant

Ī'as

Ananias
bias
Elias
eyas
Jeremias
Josias
Lias
Matthias
Messìas
Tobias
unbias
(See also Ī'us.)

Ī'at
fiat

Ī'az'm
miasm

Ī'ba
capaiba
Ziba

ĬB'ald
ribald
Theobald

ĬB'dis
Charybdis

ĬB'ē
Kibbee
Libbey
Libby
Tibbie

ĬB'est
ascribest
bribest

circumscribest
describest
gibest
imbibest
inscribest
prescribest
proscribest
subscribest
superscribest
transcribest

ĬB'est
fibbest
glibbest
jibbest

ĬB'et
flibbertigibbet
gibbet
Tibbett
zibet

ĬB'eth
ascribeth
bribeth
circumscribeth
describeth
gibeth
imbibeth
inscribeth
prescribeth
proscribeth
subscribeth
superscribeth
transcribeth

ĬB'eth
fibbeth
jibbeth

ōld, ôr, ŏdd, oil, fŏŏt, out; ūse, ûrn, ŭp; THis, thin

ĬB'ing
ascribing
bribing
circumscribing
describing
gibing
imbibing
inscribing
prescribing
proscribing
subscribing
transcribing

ĬB'ing
fibbing
jibbing
ribbing
squibbing

ĬB'it
adhibit
cohibit
exhibit
inhibit
prohibit

Ī'b'l
Bible
libel
tribal

ĬB''l
cribble
dibble
dribble
fribble
gribble
ish ka bibble
kibble

nibble
quibble
scribble
sibyl
thribble

ĬB''ld
cribbled
dibbled
ribald
(See also ĬB''l;
add -d where
appropriate.)

ĬB'lē
dribbly
glibly
nibbly
quibbly
scribbly
thribbly
tribbly

ĬB'lest
dribblest
scribblest
(See also ĬB''l;
add -st where
appropriate.)

ĬB'let
driblet
giblet
triblet

ĬB'leth
dribbleth
scribbleth
(See also ĬB''l;

add -*th* where
appropriate.)

ĬB'lik
niblick

ĬB'ling
cribbling
dibbling
dribbling
fribbling
kibbling
nibbling
quibbling
scribbling
tribbling

Ī'blō
by-blow
flyblow

ĬB'lur
cribbler
dibbler
dribbler
fribbler
kibbler
nibbler
quibbler
scribbler
transcribbler

Ī'bäl
eyeball
highball
sky-ball

Ī'bôld
piebald

ĬB'on
gibbon
ribbon

ĬB'onz
Gibbons
ribbons

Ī'bôrn
highborn
skyborne

ĬB'rant
vibrant

ĬB'rāt
equilibrate
librate
vibrate

Ī'brou
eyebrow
highbrow

ĬB'sen
Ibsen

ĬB'son
Ibson
Gibson

ĬB'ūn
tribune

ĬB'ur
ascriber
briber
circumscriber
describer

fiber
giber
imbiber
inscriber
Leiber
liber
prescriber
proscriber
scriber
subscriber
Tiber
transcriber

ĬB'ur
bibber
cribber
dibber
fibber
flibbergibber
gibber
glibber
jibber
nibber
quibber
squibber
wine-bibber

ĬB'ūt
attribute
contribute
distribute
redistribute
retribute
tribute

ĬCH'ard
Pritchard
Richard

ĬCH'ē
bitchy
fitchy
itchy
pitchy
Richie
stitchy
witchy

ĬCH'el
Kitchell
Mitchell
switchel

ĬCH'en
kitchen
lichen

ĬCH'est
bewitchest
enrichest
hitchest
pitchest
richest
stitchest
switchest
twitchest

ĬCH'et
fitchet
Fitchett
Pritchett
Twichett
witchet

ĬCH'eth
bewitcheth
enricheth
hitcheth

pitcheth
stitcheth
switcheth
twitcheth

ĬCH'ez
bewitches
bitches
breeches
ditches
enriches
flitches
hitches
itches
niches
pitches
riches
scritches
stitches
switches
twitches
witches

ĬCH'ing
bewitching
bitching
ditching
enriching
hitching
itching
miching
pitching
stitching
switching
twitching
witching

ĬCH'les
bitchless

hitchless
itchless
stitchless
switchless
witchless

ĬCH'ment
bewitchment
enrichment

ĬCH'nes
richness

ĬCH'ur
bewitcher
ditcher
enricher
hitcher
itcher
pitcher
richer
stitcher
switcher
twitcher

ĬCH'us
righteous

Ī'da
Ida
Lida
Oneida

ĪD'ans
abidance
guidance
misguidance
subsidence

ĬD'ans
forbiddance
riddance

ĬD'ant
dividant
guidant

ĪD'ē
bonafide
Friday
sidy
tidy
untidy
vide

ĬD'ē
biddy
chickabiddy
giddy
kiddy
middy
stiddy
widdy

ĪD'ed
backslided
betided
bided
chided
coincided
collided
confided
decided
derided
divided
elided
glided

guided
lopsided
many-sided
misguided
one-sided
presided
prided
provided
resided
sided
slab-sided
subdivided
subsided
tided
undecided
undivided
unguided
unprovided
(See also
ĪD'ēd.)

ĪD'ēd
tidied
(See also
ĪD'ed.)

ĬD'ed
kidded
lidded
(See also ĬD;
add -ed or
-ded where
appropriate.)

ĪD'en
Dryden
widen
(See also
ĪD'on.)

ĬD'en
bidden
chidden
forbidden
hag-ridden
hidden
kitchen-
     midden
midden
overridden
priest-ridden
ridden
slidden
stridden
unbidden
unforbidden
wife-ridden

ĪD'ent
bident
rident
strident
trident

ĪD'est
abidest
backslidest
bidest
chidest
coincidest
collidest
confidest
decidest
deridest
dividest
elidest
glidest
guidest
hidest

overridest
presidest
pridest
providest
residest
ridest
sidest
slidest
stridest
subdividest
subsidest
tidest
widest

ĬD'est
biddest
forbiddest
(See also
ĬD; add
-*est* where
appropriate.)

ĪD'eth
abideth
betideth
bideth
chideth
coincideth
collideth
confideth
decideth
derideth
divideth
elideth
glideth
guideth
hideth
overrideth
presideth

āle, câre, ădd, ärm, ăsk; mē, hĕre, ĕnd; īce, ĭll;

prideth
provideth
resideth
rideth
sideth
slideth
strideth
subdivideth
subsideth
tideth

ĬD′eth
biddeth
forbiddeth
(See also ĬD;
add *-eth* where
appropriate.)

ĬD′ij
guidage
hidage

ĬD′ik
druidic
fatidic
juridic
pyramidic

ĬD′il or ĬD′il
idyll

ĬD′ing
abiding
backsliding
bestriding
betiding
biding
chiding

coinciding
colliding
confiding
deciding
deriding
dividing
eliding
gliding
guiding
hiding
law-abiding
misguiding
niding
outriding
outstriding
overriding
presiding
priding
providing
residing
riding
siding
sliding
striding
subsiding

ĬD′ing
bidding
forbidding
kidding
lidding
outbidding
overbidding
ridding
skidding
unforbidding

ĬD′ingz
backslidings

tidings
(See also
ĬD′ing; add
-s where
appropriate.)

ĬD′′l
bridal
bridle
fratricidal
homicidal
idle
idol
infanticidal
matricidal
parricidal
patricidal
regicidal
sidle
suicidal
tidal
tyrannicidal

ĬD′′l
Biddle
diddle
fiddle
flumadiddle
griddle
Liddle
middle
quiddle
riddle
rum-tum-tiddle
tiddle
twiddle
unriddle

ĬD′′ld

bridled
unbridled
(See also
ĬD′′l; add
-ed where
appropriate.)

ĬD′ld
fiddled
(See also ĬD′′l;
add *-ed* where
appropriate.)

ĬD′lē
bridely
widely

ĬD′lest
idlest
(See also ĬD′′l;
add *-est* where
appropriate.)

ĬD′lest
fiddlest
(See also ĬD′′l;
add *-est* where
appropriate.)

ĬD′leth
idleth
(See also ĬD′′l;
add *-eth* where
appropriate.)

ĬD′leth
fiddleth
(See also ĬD′′l;

ōld, ôr, ŏdd, oil, fŏŏt, out; ūse, ûrn, ŭp; THis, thin

add -*eth* where
appropriate.)

ĬD'ling
bridling
idling
sidling

ĬD'ling
diddling
fiddling
kidling
middling
riddling
twiddling

ĬD'lings
kidlings
middlings
(See also
ĬD'ling; add
-*s* where
appropriate.)

ĬD'līt
guide light
sidelight

ĬD'lur
bridler
idler

ĬD'lur
fiddler
quiddler
riddler
tiddler
twiddler

ĬD'nē
kidney
Sidney
Sydney

ĬD'nes
piedness
snideness
wideness

ĬD'ō
Dido
Fido

ĬD'ō
kiddo
widow

ĬD'on
guidon
Poseidon
Sidon
(See also
ĬD'en.)

ĬD'or
nidor
stridor
(See also
ĬD'ur.)

ĬD'rule
slide rule

ĬD'ur
backslider
bestrider
chider
cider

coincider
collider
confider
decider
derider
divider
eider
elider
glider
guider
hider
insider
misguider
night rider
one-sider
outrider
outsider
presider
provider
resider
rider
roughrider
Schneider
sider
slider
Snider
Snyder
spider
strider
subdivider
subsider
wider

ĬD'ur
bidder
consider
forbidder
kidder
outbidder

overbidder
ridder
skidder

ĬD'urd
considered
ill-considered
unconsidered

Ī'ens
science
(See also
Ī'ans.)

Ī'ent
calorifient
client
inscient
scient
(See also Ī'ant.)

Ī'est
alliest
amplifiest
appliest
awryest
beautifiest
bedyest
beliest
bespyest
brutifiest
buyest
certifiest
clarifiest
classifiest
compliest
criest
crucifiest
decriest

āle,   câre,   ădd,   ärm,   ăsk;   mē,   hĕre,   ĕnd;   īce,   ĭll;

defiest	pacifiest	piet	horrifieth
deifiest	personifiest	quiet	identifieth
deniest	pliest	(See also Ī′ot.)	implieth
descriest	prophesiest		justifieth
diest	pryest	**Ī′eth**	lieth
dignifiest	purifiest	allieth	liquefieth
diversifiest	qualifiest	amplifieth	magnifieth
driest	ratifiest	applieth	modifieth
dyest	rectifiest	bedyeth	mollifieth
edifiest	reliest	belieth	mortifieth
electrifiest	repliest	bespyeth	multiplieth
espiest	sanctifiest	buyeth	mystifieth
eyest	satisfiest	certifieth	notifieth
falsifiest	shyest	clarifieth	nullifieth
fliest	sighest	classifieth	occupieth
fortifiest	signifiest	complieth	outvieth
friest	simplifest	crieth	pacifieth
glorifiest	slyest	crucifieth	personifieth
gratifiest	specifiest	decrieth	plieth
hiest	spryest	defieth	prophesieth
highest	spyest	deifieth	purifieth
horrifiest	stupefiest	denieth	qualifieth
identifiest	suppliest	descrieth	ratifieth
impliest	terrifiest	dieth	rectifieth
justifiest	testifiest	dignifieth	relieth
liest	tiest	diversifieth	replieth
liquefiest	tryest	drieth	sanctifieth
magnifiest	typifiest	dyeth	satisfieth
modifiest	untiest	edifieth	sigheth
mollifiest	verifiest	electrifieth	signifieth
mortifiest	versifiest	espieth	simplifieth
multipliest	viest	eyeth	specifieth
mystifiest	vilifiest	falsifieth	spyeth
nighest	vitrifiest	flieth	stupefieth
notifiest	wryest	fortifieth	supplieth
nullifiest		frieth	terrifieth
occupiest	**Ī′et**	glorifieth	testifieth
ossifiest	diet	gratifieth	tieth
outviest	inquiet	hieth	trieth

ōld, ôr, ŏdd, oil, fŏŏt, out; ūse, ûrn, ŭp; THis, thin

typifieth
untieth
verifieth
versifieth
vieth
vilifieth
vitrifieth
vivifieth

ĬF'ē
cliffy
jiffy
sniffy
spiffy
squiffy

ĬF'en, ĬF'on
hyphen
siphon
Typhon

ĬF'en, ĬF'on
griffon
stiffen

ĬF'est
sniffest
stiffest
whiffest

ĬF'et
whiffet

ĬF'eth
sniffeth

ĬF'ik
acidific
algific

anaglyphic
aurific
beatific
calorific
classific
colorific
cornific
damnific
deific
diaglyphic
dolorific
finific
frigorific
glyphic
grandific
hieroglyphic
honorific
horrific
humorific
incoherentific
lactific
lapidific
lithoglyphic
lucific
magnific
mellific
mirific
morbific
mucific
omnific
ossific
pacific
Pacific
petrific
petroglyphic
photoglyphic
phytoglyphic
pontific
prolific

pulsific
rubific
sacrific
salvific
saporific
scientific
sensific
siccific
somnific
sonorific
soporific
specific
sudorific
tabific
tenebrific
terrific
torporific
transpacific
triglyphic
vaporific
vivific
vulnific

ĬF'in
biffin
griffin
tiffin
(See also
ĬF'en, ĬF'on.)

ĬF'ing
sniffing
tiffing
whiffing

ĬF'ish
miffish
sniffish
stiffish

tiffish

Ī' 'fl
Eiffel
rifle
strifle
trifle

ĬF''l
piffle
riffle
sniffle
whiffle

ĬF'lē
rifely
wifely

ĬF'les
fifeless
knifeless
lifeless
strifeless
wifeless

ĬF'līk
lifelike
wifelike

ĬF'ling
rifling
stifling
trifling

ĬF'ling
piffling
riffling
sniffling
whiffling

āle, câre, ădd, ärm, ăsk; mē, hĕre, ĕnd; īce, ĭll;

ĬF′lur
rifler
(See also ĬF″l;
add -r where
appropriate.)

ĬF′lur
piffler
riffler
sniffler
whiffler

ĬF′on, ĬF′en
hyphen
siphon
Typhon

ĬF′ted
drifted
gifted
lifted
rifted
shifted
sifted
ungifted
uplifted

ĬF′test
driftest
liftest
riftest
shiftest
siftest
swiftest
upliftest

ĬF′teth
drifteth
lifteth

rifteth
shifteth
sifteth
uplifteth

ĬF′tē
clifty
drifty
fifty
fifty-fifty
nifty
rifty
shifty
thrifty

ĬF′ting
drifting
lifting
rifting
shifting
shoplifting
sifting
uplifting

ĬFT′les
driftless
riftless
shiftless
thriftless

ĬFT′nes
swiftness

ĬF′ton
Clifton

ĬF′thong
diphthong
triphthong

ĬFT′ur
drifter
lifter
sceneshifter
shifter
shoplifter
sifter
swifter
uplifter

ĬF′ur
cipher
decipher
fifer
lifer
kniver
rifer

ĬF′ur
differ
sniffer
stiffer

Ī′ga
saiga

ĬG′and
brigand

ĬG′at
frigate

ĬG′bē
Digby
Rigby

ĬG′ē
biggy
piggy

piggy-wiggy
spriggy
twiggy

ĬG′est
biggest
diggest
riggest
triggest

ĬG′eth
diggeth

ĬG′ing
digging
gigging
jigging
rigging
sprigging
swigging
thimblerigging
trigging
twigging
unrigging
wigging

ĬG′inz
Dwiggins
Higgins
Wiggins

ĬG′ish
piggish
priggish
whiggish

ĬG″l
giggle
higgle

ōld, ôr, ŏdd, oil, fŏŏt, out; ūse, ûrn, ŭp; THis, thin

jiggle
niggle
sniggle
squiggle
wiggle
wriggle

Ī'glas
eyeglass
spyglass

ĬG''ld
giggled
(See also ĬG''l;
add -d where
appropriate.)

ĬG'lest
gigglest
(See also ĬG''l;
add -st where
appropriate.)

ĬG'leth
giggleth
(See also ĬG''l;
add -th where
appropriate.)

ĬG'lē
giggly
Piggly-Wiggly
wiggly
(See also ĬG''l;
change -e to
-y where
appropriate.)

ĬG'lif

diglyph
monotriglyph
triglyph

ĬG'ling
giggling
higgling
(See also ĬG''l;
change -e to
-ing where
appropriate.)

ĬG'lur
giggler
higgler
(See also ĬG''l;
add -r where
appropriate.)

ĬG'ma
engima
sigma
stigma

ĬG'ment
figment
pigment

ĬG'mē
pygmy

ĬG'nal
signal

ĬG'nans
malignance

ĬG'nant
benignant

indignant
malignant

ĬG'net
cygnet
signet

ĬG'nīt
lignite

ĬG'num
ecce signum
lignum

Ī'gō
caligo
fuligo
impetigo
Loligo
vertigo

Ī'gon
bygone
trigone

ĬG'on
big 'un
Ligon

Ī'gor
rigor
vigor
(See also
ĬG'ur.)

Ī'got
bigot
gigot
spigot

(See also
ĬG'at.)

ĬG'res
tigress

Ī'gur
tiger

ĬG'ūr
configure
disfigure
figure
ligure
prefigure
transfigure

ĬG'ur
bigger
chigger
digger
"figger"
gold digger
gravedigger
gigger
jigger
ligger
market rigger
nigger
outrigger
prigger
rigger
snigger
sprigger
swigger
thimblerigger
trigger
twigger
(See also Ī'gor.)

āle, câre, ădd, ärm, ăsk; mē, hĕre, ĕnd; īce, ĭll;

ĬG′urd
"figgered"
jiggered
niggard
sniggered
unniggard

Ī′ing
acidifying
adrying
alibing
allying
amplifying
applying
beatifying
beautifying
bedying
belying
bespying
brutifying
butterflying
buying
candifying
certifying
clarifying
classifying
codifying
complying
countrifying
crucifying
crying
damnifying
dandifying
decrying
defying
deifying
denying
descrying
dignifying

disqualifying
dissatisfying
diversifying
drying
dulcifying
dyeing
dying
edifying
electrifying
emulsifying
espying
exemplifying
eyeing
falsifying
fying
fortifying
Frenchifying
fructifying
frying
glorifying
gratifying
guying
hieing
horrifying
humanifying
hushabying
identifying
implying
indemnifying
intensifying
justifying
kite flying
labifying
liquefying
lying
magnifying
modifying
mollifying
mortifying

multiplying
mystifying
notifying
nullifying
occupying
ossifying
outcrying
outflying
outlying
outvying
overbuying
pacifying
personifying
petrifying
piing
plying
preachifying
preoccupying
prophesying
prying
purifying
putrefying
qualifying
ramifying
rarefying
ratifying
rectifying
relying
replying
revivifying
sanctifying
satisfying
scarifying
scorifying
self-denying
self-relying
self-satisfying
shying
sighing

signifying
simplifying
skying
solidifying
specifying
spying
stultifying
stupefying
supplying
terrifying
testifying
torpifying
torrefying
trying
typifying
uncomplying
underbuying
underlying
undying
unifying
unsatisfying
untying
verifying
versifying
vilifying
vitrifying
vivifying
vying

Ī′ja
Abijah
Elijah

Ī′jak
highjack
skyjack

ĪJ′est
digest

disobligest
obligest

ĬJ'id
frigid
rigid

ĬJ'il
sigil
strigil
vigil

ĬJ'ing
disobliging
obliging

ĬJ'ing
abridging
bridging
ridging

ĬJ'it
Bridget
Brigit
digit
fidget
Gidget
"ijjit"
midget
widget

ĬJ'on
irreligion
pigeon
religion
widgeon

ĬJ'ur
Niger

ĬJ'ur
abridger
bridger

ĬJ'us
irreligious
litigious
prodigious
religious
sacrilegious

ĪK'a
balalaika
lorica
mica
Micah
pica
pika

Ī'kal
Michael

ĬK'ard
Pickard
Rickard

ĬK'at
exsiccate
siccate

ĪK'ē
spiky

ĬK'ē
bricky
dickey
do-hickey
Ficke
gin rickey

mickey
quickie
rickey
sticky
tricky

ĬK'ed
wicked
(See also ĬK;
add -ed where
appropriate.)

ĬK'en
lichen
liken
unliken

ĬK'en
chicken
horror-stricken
quicken
sicken
stricken
terror-stricken
thicken
wicken
wonder-
    stricken

ĬK'enz
chickens
slickens
the dickens
(See also
ĬK'en; add
-s where
appropriate.)

ĪK'est

dislikest
likest
obliquest
spikest
strikest

ĬK'est
clickest
flickest
kickest
lickest
pickest
prickest
slickest
stickest
thickest
tickest
trickest

ĬK'et
clicket
cricket
midwicket
picket
Pickett
pricket
Prickett
Rickett
thicket
ticket
walking ticket
wicket

ĪK'eth
disliketh
liketh
spiketh
striketh

ĬK'eth
clicketh
flicketh
kicketh
licketh
picketh
pricketh
sticketh
ticketh
tricketh

ĬK'ets
crickets
rickets
(See also
ĬK'et; add
-*s* where
appropriate.)

ĬK'ik
psychic

ĬK'iks
psychics

ĬK'ing
biking
disliking
dyking
liking
misliking
piking
spiking
striking
viking
well-liking

ĬK'ing
besticking

bricking
clicking
cricking
flicking
kicking
licking
nicking
picking
pocket-picking
pricking
snicking
sticking
thicking
ticking
tricking
wicking

ĬK'ish
brickish
sickish
slickish
thickish

ĪK''l
cycle
epicycle
Michael
psychal

ĬK''l
fickle
mickle
nickel
pickle
prickle
sickle
stickle
strickle
tickle

trickle

ĪK'lē
belikely
likely
unlikely

ĬK'lē
prickly
quickly
sickly
slickly
stickly
thickly
trickly

ĬK'lest
ficklest
picklest
ticklest
tricklest

ĬK'leth
pickleth
prickleth
tickleth
trickleth

ĬK'lik
bicyclic
cyclic
encyclic
epicyclic
geocyclic

ĪK'ling
cycling

ĬK'ling

chickling
pickling
prickling
tickling
trickling

ĬK'lish
pricklish
ticklish

ĬK'list
cyclist

ĪK'lōn
cyclone

ĬK'lur
fickler
prickler
stickler
strickler
tickler

ĪK'nes
likeness
unlikeness

ĬK'nes
lovesickness
quickness
sickness
slickness
thickness

ĬK'nik
picnic
strychnic

ōld, ôr, ŏdd, oil, fŏŏt, out; ūse, ûrn, ŭp; THis, thin

ĬK'nīn
strychnine

ĬK'ning
quickening
sickening
thickening

ĬK'on
icon

ĬK'or
ichor

Ĭ'kount
viscount

ĬK'sē
Dixey
Dixie
nixie
pixie
tricksy
Trixie
water nixie

ĬK'sen
mixen
vixen

ĬK'sest
affixest
fixest
intermixest
mixest
prefixest
transfixest

ĬK'set

quickset
thickset

ĬK'seth
affixeth
fixeth
intermixeth
mixeth
prefixeth
transfixeth

ĬK'shun
abstriction
addiction
affixion
affliction
affriction
benediction
confliction
constriction
contradiction
conviction
crucifixtion
depiction
dereliction
diction
eviction
fiction
friction
indiction
infliction
interdiction
jurisdiction
malediction
obstriction
prediction
prefixion
reliction
restriction

suffixion
transfixion
valediction

ĬK'shus
contradictious
fictious

ĬK'sing
admixing
affixing
fixing
intermixing
mixing
prefixing
transfixing

ĬK'son
Dickson
Dixon
Hickson
Hixon
Nixon

ĬK'stē
sixty

ĬK'stŭr
admixture
affixture
fixture
immixture
incommixture
intermixture
mixture

ĬK'stŭr
trickster

ĬK'sur
affixer
elixir
fixer
intermixer
mixer
prefixer
transfixer

ĬK'tāt
dictate
nictate

ĬK'ted
addicted
afflicted
conflicted
constricted
contradicted
convicted
depicted
evicted
inflicted
interdicted
predicted
relicted
restricted
self-inflicted
unrestricted

ĬK'test
addictest
afflictest
conflictest
contradictest
convictest
depictest
evictest
inflictest

āle, câre, ădd, ärm, ăsk; mē, hĕre, ĕnd; īce, ĭll;

predictest   ĬK'tiv   ĬK'tŭr   kicker
restrictest   addictive   afflicter   knicker
strictest   afflictive   boa constrictor   licker
                benedictive   conflicter   liquor
ĬK'teth   conflictive   constrictor   nicker
addicteth   constrictive   contradicter   picker
afflicteth   contradictive   depicter   pricker
conflicteth   convictive   *fictor*   quicker
contradicteth depictive   inflicter   sicker
convicteth   fictive   lictor   slicker
depicteth   indictive   Pictor   snicker
evicteth   inflictive   predicter   sticker
inflicteth   interdictive   restricter   thicker
predicteth   jurisdictive   stricter   ticker
restricteth   predictive   victor   tricker
                restrictive   vicar
ĬK'tik   vindictive   **ĬK'tus**   wicker
apodictic   acronyctous
deictic   **ĬKT'lē**   Benedictus   **ĬK'urz**
endeictic   derelictly   ictus   bickers
epideictic   strictly   knickers
ictic   **ĪK'ur**   (See also
                ĬKT'nes   biker   ĬK'ur; add
ĬK'tim   strictness   Diker   *-s* where
victim   hiker   appropriate.)
                ĬK'tor   liker
ĬK'ting   victor   obliquer   **ĬK'us**
addicting   (See also   piker   Picus
afflicting   ĬK'tŭr.)   Riker   spicous
conflicting   spiker
constricting   **ĬK'tum**   striker   **ĬK'wid**
contradicting   dictum   liquid
convicting   **ĬK'ur**
depicting   **ĬK'tŭr**   bicker   **ĪL'a**
evicting   depicture   bootlicker   Hyla
inflicting   impicture   bumper sticker   Lila
interdicting   picture   clicker
predicting   stricture   dicker   **ĬL'a**
restricting   word picture   flicker   anilla

ōld, ôr, ŏdd, oil, fŏŏt, out; ūse, ûrn, ŭp; THis, thin

armilla
barilla
bismillah
camarilla
Camilla
cascarilla
cedilla
chinchilla
codilla
Drusilla
flotilla
gorilla
granadilla
granilla
guerrilla
Lilla
Manila
manilla
mantilla
maxilla
Priscilla
sabadilla
sapodilla
sarsaparilla
seguidilla
Sybilla
vanilla
villa

ĬL'ak
lilac

ĬL'aks
lilacs
smilax

ĬL'an
arch-villain
villain

villein

Ī'land
highland
island
Rhode Island

Ī'lark
phylarch
skylark

ĬL'as
Silas
Vilas

Ī'lash
eyelash

ĬL'āt
distillate
penicillate

ĬL'burt
filbert
Gilbert
Wilbert

ĬL'da
Gilda
Hilda
Mathilda
Matilda

ĬL'ded
begilded
builded
gilded
ungilded

ĬL'dest
mildest
wildest

ĬL'dest
begildest
buildest
gildest

ĬL'deth
begildeth
buildeth
gildeth

ĬLD'hood
childhood

ĬL'ding
childing
wilding

ĬL'ding
begilding
building
castle building
gilding
rebuilding
unbuilding
ungilding

ĬL'dish
childish
mildish
wildish

ĬLD'les
childless
mildless

ĬLD'lē
childly
mildly
wildly

ĬLD'līk
childlike

ĬLD'nes
mildness
riledness
unmildness
wildness

ĬL'dred
Mildred

ĬLD'ren
children

ĬL'dur
milder
wilder

ĬL'dur
begilder
bewilder
builder
castle builder
gilder
guilder
rebuilder
wilder

ĬLD'wood
wildwood

Ī'lē
ancile

āle,   câre,   ădd,   ärm,   ăsk;   mē,   hĕre,   ĕnd;   īce,   ĭll;

dryly
highly
O'Reilly
Reilly
Riley
shyly
slyly
wily
wryly

ĬL'ē
Billee
Billie
billy
Billy
Chile
chili
chilly
daffy-down-
  dilly
filly
frilly
gillie
grilly
hillbilly
hilly
illy
lily
Millie
Milly
Piccadilly
piccalilli
rockabilly
silly
shrilly
skilly
stilly
tiger lily
Tillie

Tilly
water lily
Willie
Willy
willy-nilly

ĬL'ēd
lilied

ĬL'ens
silence

ĬL'ent
silent

ĬL'est
beguilest
compilest
defilest
filest
pilest
reconcilest
revilest
rilest
smilest
stylest
vilest
whilest
wilest

ĬL'est
befrillest
chillest
distillest
drillest
enthrillest
fillest
frillest

fulfillest
grillest
illest
instillest
killest
millest
shrillest
spillest
stillest
swillest
thrillest
tillest
trillest
willest

Ī'let, Ī'lot
eyelet
islet
pilot
sky-pilot
stylet

ĬL'et
billet
fillet
millet
rillet
skillet
willet

ĬL'eth
beguileth
compileth
defileth
fileth
pileth
reconcileth
revileth
rileth

smileth
styleth
tileth
up-pileth
whileth
wileth

ĬL'eth
chilleth
distilleth
drilleth
enthrilleth
filleth
fulfilleth
instilleth
killeth
milleth
spilleth
stilleth
thrilleth
tilleth
trilleth
willeth

ĬL'ēz
chilies
fillies
gillies
lilies
sillies
the Willies

ĬL'ful
guileful
smileful
wileful

ĬL'ful
skillful

ōld, ôr, ŏdd, oil, fŏŏt, out; ūse, ûrn, ŭp; THis, thin

willful
unskillful

ĬL'fur
pilfer

ĬL'grim
pilgrim

Ī'lid
eyelid

ĬL'ij
grillage
pillage
tillage
thrillage
village

ĬL'ik
amylic
basilic
Cyrillic
dactylic
idyllic
macrodactylic
methylic
odylic
salicylic
zygodactylic

Ī'līn
skyline
styline

ĬL'in
MacMillin
McQuillin

ĬL'ing
beguiling
compiling
defiling
filing
piling
reconciling
reviling
riling
smiling
styling
tiling
time-beguiling
up-piling
whiling
wiling

ĬL'ing
befrilling
billing
chilling
distilling
drilling
enthrilling
filling
frilling
fulfilling
grilling
instilling
killing
milling
shilling
shrilling
skilling
spilling
stilling
swilling
thrilling
tilling

trilling
unwilling
upfilling
willing

ĬL'ingz
Billings
drillings
(See also
ĬL'ing; add
-s where
appropriate.)

ĬL'ip
fillip
Philip

ĬL'ips
fillips
Philips

ĬL'is
Amaryllis
Myrtillis
Phyllis
Willis
Wyllis

ĬL'ish
stylish

Ī'līt
dry-light
highlight
skylight
stylite
twilight
xylite

ĬL'iz'm
Carlylism
hylism

ĬL'joi
killjoy

ĬL'kē
milky
silky

ĬL'ken
milken
silken

ĬL'king
bilking
filking
milking

ĬL'koks
Philcox
Silcox
Wilcox

ĬL'les
guileless
smileless
wileless

ĬL'man
billman
Gilman
grillman
hillman
millman
Stillman

ĬL'mē
filmy

āle, câre, ădd, ärm, ăsk; mē, hĕre, ĕnd; īce, ĭll;

ĬL'ment
beguilement
defilement
exilement
irreconcile-
    ment
reconcilement
revilement

ĬL'ment
distillment
fulfillment
instillment

ĬL'mor
Filmore
Gilmore

ĬL'nes
juvenileness
vileness

ĬL'nes
chillness
illness
shrillness
stillness

ĬL'nur
Milner

ĬL'ō
high-low
milo
silo

ĬL'ō
armadillo
billow

Brillo
cigarillo
embillow
grenadillo
killow
kilo
lapillo
Murillo
negrillo
peccadillo
pillow
pulvillo
weeping wil-
    low
willow

ĬL'od
billowed
unpillowed

ĬL'oid
styloid
xyloid

Ī'lok
Shylock

ĬL'ok
hillock

ĬL'om
whilom

ĬL'on
Dillon

ĬL'ot
pilot
sky pilot

(See also Ī'let,
Ī'lot.)

ĬL'pin
Gilpin

ĬL'room
grillroom
stillroom

ĬL'sīd
hillside
rillside

ĬL'son
Gilson
Stillson
Wilson

ĬL'tē
guilty
silty
stilty

ĬL'ted
hilted
jilted
kilted
lilted
overtilted
quilted
silted
stilted
tilted
tip-tilted
wilted

ĬL'test
jiltest

kiltest
liltest
quiltest
tiltest
wiltest

ĬL'teth
jilteth
kilteth
lilteth
quilteth
tilteth
wilteth

ĬL'thē
filthy

ĬL'ting
jilting
kilting
lilting
quilting
silting
tilting
wilting

ĬL'ton
Chilton
Hilton
Milton
Stilton
Tilton

ĬL'tur
filter
infilter
jilter
kilter
philter

ōld, ôr, ŏdd, oil, fŏŏt, out; ūse, ûrn, ŭp; THis, thin

quilter
tilter
wilter

ĬL'um
asylum
phylum
Wylam

ĬL'ur
beguiler
bifilar
compiler
defiler
filar
filer
Huyler
piler
reconciler
reviler
riler
Schuyler
smiler
stylar
tiler
Tyler
up-piler
viler
wiler
Zuyler

ĬL'ur
befriller
biller
caterpillar
chiller
distiller
driller
filler

friller
fulfiller
griller
iller
ill-willer
instiller
Joe Miller
killer
lady-killer
man-killer
maxillar
miller
pillar
Schiller
shriller
siller
spiller
stiller
swiller
thiller
thriller
tiller
willer

ĬL'us
aspergillus
bacillus
favillous
fibrillous
orgillous
villus

ĬL'van
sylvan

ĬL'vur
silver

ĬL'yam

Gilliam
William

ĬL'yans
brilliance

ĬL'yant
brilliant

ĬL'yar
atrabiliar
auxiliar
conciliar
domiciliar
familiar

ĬL'yardz
billiards
milliards

ĬL'yun
billion
cotillion
decillion
mandillon
million
modillion
nonillion
octillion
pavilion
pillion
postillion
quadrillion
quintillion
sextillion
stillion
trillion
tourbillion
vermilion

ĬL'yunth
billionth
millionth
trillionth

ĬM'a
cyma
Jemima
Lima

ĬM'aks
anticlimax
climax

ĬM'al
isocheimal
isocrymal
primal

Ī'man
hymen
Hymen
pieman
Simon
Wyman

ĬM'at
acclimate
climate
primate

ĬM'bal
cymbal
fimble
gimbal
nimble
symbol
thimble
tymbal

āle, câre, ădd, ärm, ăsk; mē, hĕre, ĕnd; īce, ĭll;

wimble

ĬM′bō
akimbo
bimbo
kimbo
limbo

ĬM′brel
timbrel
whimbrel

ĬM′bur
imber
limber
timber
unlimber

ĬM′burd
limbered
untimbered
(See also
ĬM′bur; add
-ed where
appropriate.)

ĬM′bus
cumulonimbus
limbus
nimbus

ĬM′ē
beslimy
blimy
grimy
limy
rimy
rhymy
slimy
stymie

thymy

ĬM′ē
gimme
jimmy
shimmy
whimmy

ĬM′el
Friml
gimmal
Grimmell
Himmel
kümmel

Ī′men
hymen
Hymen
(See also
Ī′man.)

ĬM′en
women
(See also
ĬM′on.)

ĬM′est
begrimest
berhymest
beslimest
chimest
climbest
primest
rhymest
sublimest

ĬM′est
brimmest
dimmest

grimmest
primmest
skimmest
slimmest
swimmest
trimmest

ĬM′eth
begrimeth
berhymeth
beslimeth
chimeth
climbeth
rhymeth

ĬM′eth
brimmeth
dimmeth
skimmeth
swimmeth
trimmeth

ĬM′flam
flimflam

ĬM′id
timid

ĬM′ij
image
scrimmage

ĬM′ik
alchimic
cacochymic
cherubimic
eponymic
etymic
homonymic

lipothymic
metonymic
metronymic
mimic
pantomimic
patronymic
synonymic
zymic

ĬM′ing
begriming
beliming
berhyming
besliming
chiming
climbing
griming
liming
priming
rhyming
sliming
timing

ĬM′ing
bedimming
betrimming
brimming
dimming
grimming
skimming
slimming
swimming
trimming

ĬM′ist
rhymist
timist

ĬM′it
limit

ĬM'jams
jimjams

ĬM'krak
gimcrack

ĬM'lē
primely
sublimely
timely
untimely

ĬM'lē
dimly
grimly
primly
slimly
trimly

ĬM'les
chimeless
crimeless
grimeless
limeless
overtimeless
rhymeless
rimeless
slimeless
thymeless
timeless

ĬM'les
brimless
gymless
hymnless
limbless
rimless
scrimless
swimless

trimless
vimless
whimless

**ĬM'nal,
ĬM'nel**
hymnal
simnel

ĬM'nē
chimney

ĬM'nes
primeness
sublimeness

ĬM'nes
dimness
grimness
primness
slimness
trimness

Ī'mon
Kimon
Simon
Timon
(See also
Ī'man.)

ĬM'on
persimmon
Rimmon
(See also
ĬM'en.)

ĬM'onz
persimmons
Simmons

ĬM'pē
crimpy
impi
impy
skimpy
wimpy

ĬM'pet
limpet

ĬM'ping
blimping
crimping
imping
limping
primping
scrimping
shrimping
skimping

ĬM'pish
impish
pimpish

ĬM'pit
lime pit
slime pit

ĬM'p'l
bewimple
crimple
dimple
pimple
rimple
simple
wimple

ĬM'plē
crimply

dimply
limply
pimply
simply

ĬM'plest
crimplest
dimplest
pimplest
rimplest
simplest
wimplest

ĬM'pleth
crimpleth
(See also
ĬM'p'l; add
-eth where
appropriate.)

ĬM'pling
crimpling
dimpling
impling
pimpling
rimpling
shrimpling
wimpling

ĬM'plur
crimpler
dimpler
rimpler
simpler
wimpler

ĬM'pur
crimper
limper

āle, câre, ădd, ärm, ăsk; mē, hĕre, ĕnd; īce, ĭll;

scrimper
shrimper
simper
skimper
whimper

ĬM'rōz
primrose

ĬM'shē
imshi

ĬM'son
jimson

ĬM'stur
rhymester

ĬM'ur
begrimer
chimer
climber
Hergesheimer
old-timer
primer
rhymer
timer
sublimer

ĬM'ur
brimmer
dimmer
gimmer
glimmer
grimmer
primer
primmer
shimmer
simmer

skimmer
slimmer
swimmer
trimmer
Zimmer

ĬM'us
primus
rimous
simous
timeous
untimeous

ĬM'zē
flimsy
mimsy
slimsy
whimsy

ĬM'zon
crimson
encrimson

Ī'na
Adelina
Angelina
Carolina
Catalina
China
Dinah
Evelina
farina
Indochina
Jaina
Lucina
Meleagrina
Messalina
mynah
Platyrhina

Regina
Sabina
Sabrina
salina
semolina
Shekinah
trichina

Ĭn'a
Corinna
Erinna
Minna

ĬN'al
acclinal
anticlinal
binal
caninal
cerebrospinal
crinal
declinal
doctrinal
endocrinal
equinal
final
isoclinal
matutinal
officinal
periclinal
piscinal
rhinal
spinal
synclinal
trinal
Vinal
vinyl

ĬN'as
pinnace

ĬN'āt
binate
quinate

ĬN'chest
clinchest
flinchest
lynchest
pinchest

ĬN'cheth
clincheth
flincheth
lyncheth
pincheth

ĬN'ching
clinching
flinching
lynching
pinching
unflinching

ĬN'chur
clincher
flincher
lyncher
pincher

ĬN'churz
pinchers
(See also
ĬN'chur; add
-s where
appropriate.)

ĬN'da
Belinda
Chlorinda

Dorinda
Ethelinda
Linda
Lucinda

ĬN'dē
Cindy
Indy
Lindy
Lucindy
shindy
windy

ĬN'ded
alike-minded
blinded
bloody-minded
carnal-minded
double-minded
even-minded
earthly minded
evil-minded
fair-minded
feebleminded
fleshly minded
free-minded
high-minded
light-minded
like-minded
low-minded
minded
narrow-minded
open-minded
public-minded
reminded
rinded
self-blinded
simpleminded
single-minded

small-minded
snow-blinded
soberminded
strong-minded
weak-minded
winded
worldly
   minded

ĬN'ded
abscinded
brinded
broken-winded
exscinded
interscinded
long-winded
rescinded
short-winded
winded

ĬN'den
linden
Lindon
Minden

ĬN'dest
bindest
blindest
findest
grindest
kindest
remindest
windest

ĬN'deth
bindeth
blindeth
findeth
grindeth

mindeth
remindeth
windeth

ĬND'ful
mindful
remindful
unmindful

ĬN'dig
shindig

ĬN'dik
indic
syndic

ĬN'ding
binding
blinding
finding
grinding
inbinding
minding
reminding
unbinding
unwinding
upbinding
upwinding
winding

ĬN'd'l
brindle
dwindle
enkindle
kindle
rekindle
spindle
swindle

ĬN'd'ld
brindled
(See also
ĬN'd'l; add -d
where appro-
priate.)

ĬND'lē
blindly
kindly
unkindly

ĬND'lē
Hindley
spindly

ĬN'dlest
brindlest
(See also
ĬN'd'l; add
-st where
appropriate.)

ĬN'dleth
brindleth
(See also
ĬN'd'l; add -th
where appro-
priate.)

ĬND'ling
brindling
dwindling
enkindling
kindling
rekindling
swindling

ĬND'lur
dwindler

āle, câre, ădd, ärm, ăsk; mē, hĕre, ĕnd; īce, ĭll;

kindler
swindler
(See also
ĬN′d′l; add
-r where
appropriate.)

ĬND′nes
blindness
color-blindness
kindness
loving kindness

ĬN′dō
window

ĬN′drans
hindrance

ĬN′dred
kindred

ĬN′dur
binder
blinder
faultfinder
finder
grinder
hinder
kinder
minder
pathfinder
reminder
spellbinder
stem-winder
water finder
winder

ĬN′dur

cinder
flinder
hinder
pinder
rescinder
tinder

ĬN′ē
briny
Heine
liney
miny
moonshiny
outliney
piney
shiny
spiny
sunshiny
tiny
twiney
viny
whiney
winy

ĬN′ē
finny
guinea
hinny
ignominy
jinny
Minnie
ninny
pickaninny
pinny
Pliny
shinney
skinny
spinney
squinny

tinny
vinny
whinny

ĬN′en
linen

Ī′nes
dryness
highness
nighness
shyness
slyness
spryness
wryness

ĬN′es
Inness
Guinness
(See also
ĬN′as.)

ĬN′est
assignest
benignest
combinest
condignest
confinest
consignest
countersignest
declinest
definest
designest
dinest
divinest
enshrinest
entwinest
finest
inclinest

intertwinest
malignest
minest
outlinest
outshinest
overtwinest
pinest
reassignest
reclinest
refinest
resignest
shinest
signest
superfinest
supinest
twinest
underlinest
underminest
undersignest
untwinest
whinest
winest

ĬN′est
beginnest
dinnest
grinnest
pinnest
sinnest
skinnest
spinnest
thinnest
winnest

ĬN′et
linnet
minute
spinet

ĬN'eth
assigneth
combineth
confineth
consigneth
countersigneth
declineth
defineth
designeth
dineth
divineth
enshrineth
entwineth
inclineth
intertwineth
maligneth
mineth
outlineth
outshineth
overtwineth
pineth
reassigneth
reclineth
refineth
resigneth
shineth
signeth
twineth
underlineth
undermineth
undersigneth
untwineth
whineth
wineth

ĬN'eth
beginneth
dinneth
ginneth

grinneth
pinneth
sinneth
skinneth
spinneth
winneth

ĬN'fant
infant

ĬN'ful
sinful

ĬNG'am
Bingham

ĬNG'bolt
king-bolt
ring-bolt
wring-bolt

ĬNG'dom
kingdom

ĬNG'duv
ring-dove

ĬNG'ē
clingy
springy
stingy
stringy
swingy
wingy

ĬNG'ed
winged
(See also ĬNG;
add -ed where
appropriate.)

ĬNG'est
bringest
clingest
flingest
outwingest
ringest
singest
slingest
springest
stingest
stringest
swingest
wingest
wringest

ĬNG'eth
bringeth
clingeth
flingeth
outwingeth
ringeth
singeth
slingeth
springeth
stingeth
stringeth
swingeth
unslingeth
wingeth
wringeth

ĬNG'ga
anhinga

ĬNG'gē
dinghy

ĬNG'g'l
commingle

cringle
dingle
immingle
intermingle
jingal
jingle
Kris Kringle
mingle
shingle
single
springal
surcingle
swingle
tingle
tringle

ĬNG'g'ld
commingled
unmingled
(See also
ĬNG'g'l; add
-d where
appropriate.)

ĬNG'glē
jingly
mingly
shingly
singly
tingly

ĬNG'glest
jinglest
minglest
tinglest

ĬNG'gleth
jingleth
mingleth

tingleth

ĬNG'gling
intermingling
jingling
kingling
mingling
singling
tingling
wingling

ĬNG'glish
English
tinglish

ĬNG'glur
intermingler
jingler
mingler
shingler
tingler

ĬNG'gō
dingo
flamingo
gringo
jingo
lingo
stingo

ĬNG'gur
finger
forefinger
index-finger
linger
malinger

ĬNG'gurd
fingered

light-fingered
rosy-fingered
web-fingered
(See also
ING'gur; add
-ed where
appropriate.)

ĬNG'gus
dingus

ĬNG'gwal
bilingual
lingual

ĬNG'gwish
contradistin-
  guish
distinguish
extinguish

ĬNG'ing
bringing
clinging
dinging
enringing
flinging
outwinging
plainsinging
ringing
singing
slinging
springing
stinging
stringing
swinging
unslinging
unstringing
upbringing

upstringing
winging
wringing

ĬNGK'ē
blinky
inky
kinky
pinky
zincky

ĬNGK'est
bethinkest
blinkest
chinkest
clinkest
drinkest
hoodwinkest
inkest
linkest
pinkest
shrinkest
sinkest
slinkest
stinkest
thinkest
winkest

ĬNGK'et
trinket

ĬNGK'eth
bethinketh
blinketh
chinketh
clinketh
drinketh

hoodwinketh
inketh
linketh
pinketh
shrinketh
sinketh
slinketh
stinketh
thinketh
winketh

ĬNGK'gō
ginkgo

ĬNGK'īd
blink-eyed
pink-eyed

ĬNGK'ing
bethinking
blinking
chinking
clinking
drinking
enlinking
free-thinking
hoodwinking
inking
interlinking
linking
pinking
rinking
shrinking
sinking
slinking
stinking
thinking
unblinking
unlinking

unshrinking
unthinking
unwinking
winking

crinkleth
sprinkleth
tinkleth
twinkleth
wrinkleth

contradistinc-
tive
distinctive
instinctive

tiddledewinker
tinker
winker

ĬNGK''l
besprinkle
crinkle
inkle
periwinkle
sprinkle
tinkle
twinkle
winkle
wrinkle

ĬNGK'ling
besprinkling
crinkling
inkling
sprinkling
tinkling
twinkling
wrinkling

ĬNGKT'nes
distinctness
indistinctness
succinctness

ĬNGK'us
ornithorhynchus
oxyrhynchus
rhampho-
rhynchus
scincus
zincous

ĬNGK''ld
besprinkled
unwrinkled
(See also
ĬNGK''l; add
-*d* where
appropriate.)

ĬNGK'lur
sprinkler
tinkler
twinkler
wrinkler

ĬNGK'tur
cincture
encincture
tincture

ĬNGK'turd
cinctured
encinctured
uncinctured
untinctured

ĬNG'les
kingless
ringless
springless
stingless
wingless

ĬNGK'lē
crinkly
pinkly
tinkly
twinkly
wrinkly

ĬNGK'ō
gingko
pinko
stinko

ĬNGK'ur
bethinker
blinker
clinker
drinker
enlinker
free-thinker
hoodwinker
inker
linker
pinker
prinker
rinker
shrinker
sinker
slinker
stinker
thinker

ĬNG'let
kinglet
ringlet
springlet
winglet

ĬNGK'on
Lincoln
pink 'un

ĬNG'līk
kinglike
springlike
winglike

ĬNGK'lest
crinklest
sprinklest
tinklest
twinklest
wrinklest

ĬNGK'shun
contradistinc-
tion
distinction
extinction
indistinction
intinction

ĬN'gram
Ingram

ĬNG'song
singsong
spring song

ĬNGK'leth

ĬNGK'tiv

ĬNG'tīm
ring-time

āle, câre, ădd, ärm, ăsk; mē, hĕre, ĕnd; īce, ĭll;

spring time

ĬNG'ur
ballad singer
bringer
clinger
dinger
flinger
humdinger
mastersinger
Meistersinger
minnesinger
ringer
singer
slinger
springer
stinger
stringer
swinger
unslinger
unstringer
whinger
winger
wringer

ĬN'ik
kinic
pinic
vinic

ĬN'ik
aclinic
actinic
adiactinic
Brahminic
clinic
cynic
delphinic
diactinic

finic
Franklinic
fulminic
isoclinic
Jacobinic
mandarinic
monoclinic
narcotinic
Odinic
pinic
platinic
polygynic
quinic
rabbinic
vinic

ĬN'im
minim

ĬN'ing
aligning
assigning
beshining
combining
confining
consigning
countermining
countersigning
declining
defining
designing
dining
divining
enshrining
entwining
fining
inclining
interlining
intermining

intertwining
lining
maligning
mining
moonshining
opining
outlining
outshining
overtwining
pining
reclining
refining
repining
resigning
shining
signing
subsigning
trephining
twining
underlining
undermining
untwining
whining
wining

ĬN'ing
beginning
chinning
dinning
grinning
inning
pinning
shinning
sinning
skinning
spinning
thinning
tinning

underpinning
unpinning
unsinning
winning

ĬN'ingz
beginnings
innings
winnings

ĬN'ish
diminish
finish
Finnish
thinnish
tinnish

ĬN'ist
violinist

ĪN'it
crinite
finite

ĬN'jē
cringy
dingy
fringy
stingy
swingy
twingy

ĬN'jens
contingence

ĬN'jent
astringent
constringent
contingent

fingent
impingent
refringent
restringent
ringent
stringent
tingent

ĬN'jest
befringest
cringest
fringest
hingest
imfringest
infringest
singest
swingest
tingest
twingest
unhingest

ĬN'jeth
befringeth
cringeth
fringeth
hingeth
impingeth
infringeth
singeth
swingeth
tingeth
twingeth
unhingeth

ĬN'jez
befringes
constringes
cringes
fringes

hinges
impinges
infringes
perstringes
scringes
singes
springes
swinges
tinges
twinges
unhinges

ĬN'jing
cringing
fringing
hinging
infringing
singeing
swingeing
tingeing
twinging

ĬNJ'les
fringeless
hingeless
swingeless
tingeless
twingeless

ĬNJ'ment
impingement
infringement
unhingement

ĬNJ'ur
cringer
fringer
ginger
hinger

infringer
injure
singer
swinger
twinger

ĪN'ka
Inca
Katinka

ĪN'klad
pine-clad
vine-clad

ĬN'kom
income

ĬN'krēs
increase

ĪN'kround
pine-crowned
vine-crowned

ĬN'kwent
delinquent
relinquent

ĬN'kwish
relinquish
vinquish

ĪN'lē
aquilinely
benignly
caninely
condignly
divinely
finely

malignly
saturninely
superfinely
supinely

ĬN'lē
Finley
inly
McGinley
McKinley
thinly

ĬN'les
dinless
finless
ginless
kinless
pinless
sinless
skinless
tinless
winless

ĪN'ment
alignment
assignment
confinement
consignment
designment
entwinement
inclinement
interlinement
refinement
resignment

ĬN'nes
condignness
divineness
fineness

salineness
superfineness
supineness

ĬN'nes
thinness
(See also
ĬN'es.)

ĬN'ō
Aino
albino
jure divino
rhino
wino

ĬN'ō
minnow
winnow

ĬN'of
sign-off

ĬN'sē
Quincy
rinsey

ĬN'sel
tinsel

ĬN'sens
incense

ĬN'sent
St. Vincent
vincent

ĬN'ses
princess

ĬN'sest
convincest
evincest
mincest
rinsest
wincest

ĬN'seth
convinceth
evinceth
minceth
rinseth
winceth

ĬN'shal
provincial

ĬN'sing
convincing
evincing
mincing
rinsing
unconvincing
wincing

ĬN'siv
evincive

ĬNS'lē
princely

ĬNS'ment
convincement
evincement

ĬN'som
winsome

ĬN'strel

minstrel

ĬN'stur
minster
spinster

ĬN'sur
convincer
mincer
pincer
rinser
wincer

ĬN'surz
convincers
pincers
(See also
ĬN'sur; add
-s where
appropriate.)

ĬN'tē
ninety

ĬN'tē
Dinty
flinty
glinty
linty
McGinty
squinty

ĬN'ted
dinted
glinted
hinted
imprinted
minted
misprinted

printed
rainbow-tinted
rosy-tinted
sprinted
squinted
stinted
tinted
vinted

ĬN'test
glintest
hintest
imprintest
mintest
printest
sprintest
squintest
stintest
tintest

ĬN'teth
glinteth
hinteth
imprinteth
minteth
printeth
sprinteth
squinteth
stinteth
tinteth

ĬNT'īd
flint-eyed
squint-eyed

ĬN'tij
mintage
vintage

ōld, ôr, ŏdd, oil, fŏŏt, out; ūse, ûrn, ŭp; THis, thin

ĬN'thik	self-interest	combiner	Steiner
absinthic	*winterest*	confiner	streamliner
labyrinthic		consignor	supiner
	ĬN'tur	cosigner	twiner
ĬN'thin	aquatinter	countersigner	underliner
hyacinthine	dinter	decliner	underminer
labyrinthine	hinter	decliner	undersigner
terebinthine	imprinter	definer	viner
	minter	designer	whiner
ĬN'ting	nuclear winter	diner	winer
aquatinting	printer	diviner	
dinting	splinter	enshriner	**ĬN'ur**
glinting	sprinter	entwiner	after-dinner
hinting	squinter	eyeliner	antiforeigner
imprinting	stinter	finer	beginner
minting	tinter	forty-niner	breadwinner
misprinting	winter	freightliner	Bynner
printing		headliner	dinner
sprinting	**ĬN'ū**	incliner	finner
squinting	continue	intertwiner	foreigner
stinting	discontinue	jetliner	ginner
tinting	*retinue*	liner	grinner
	sinew	maligner	inner
ĬN't'l	unsinew	miner	mariner
lintel		minor	milliner
pintle	**ĬN'ud**	moonshiner	muleskinner
quintal	continued	one-liner	pinner
	discontinued	opiner	predinner
ĬN'tō	sinewed	outliner	shinner
mezzotinto	unsinewed	penny-a-liner	sinner
Shinto		piner	skinner
	ĬN'ur	pulvinar	spinner
ĬN'trē	aerliner	recliner	thinner
splintry	aligner	refiner	tinner
vintry	aquiliner	repiner	twinner
wintry	arch-designer	resigner	winner
	assigner	shiner	
ĬN'trest	benigner	Shriner	**ĬN'us**
interest	calciner	signer	binous

āle,   câre,   ădd,   ärm,   ăsk;   mē,   hĕre,   ĕnd;   īce,   ĭll;

echinus
linous
Linus
Lupinus
minus
Pinus
salinous
sinus
spinous
vinous

ĬN′ward
inward

ĬN′yon
dominion
minion
opinion
pinion
(See also
ĬN′ē-an.)

ĬN′yond
dominioned
opinioned
pinioned
self-opinioned

ĬN′zē
Lindsay
Lindsey
linsey
quinsey
thinsey

ĬN′zik
extrinsic
intrinsic

ĬN′zman
kinsman

ĬN′zor
Windsor

Ī′ō
bio
Io

Ī′ol
bass-viol
(See also Ī′al.)

Ī′on
dandelion
ion
Ixion
lion
Orion
scion
sea-lion
Zion

Ī′ôr
prior
(See also Ī′ur.)

Ī′ot
eyot
piot
riot
Sciot
(See also Ī′et.)

ĬP′a
Philippa

Ī′pal, Ī′p'l

disciple
ectypal

ĬP′ant
flippant
trippant

ĪP′ē
pipy
swipey

ĬP′ē
chippy
dippy
grippy
hippy
Lippo Lippi
lippy
Mississippi
nippy
shippy
snippy
zippy

ĪP′en
enripen
ripen

ĪP′end
ripened
stipend

ĪP′est
pipest
ripest
typest
wipest
(See also Īp;
add -est where

appropriate.)

ĬP′est
chippest
clippest
dippest
drippest
equippest
flippest
grippest
gyppest
horsewhippest
nippest
outstrippest
rippest
shippest
sippest
skippest
slippest
snippest
strippest
tippest
trippest
whippest

ĬP′et
sippet
skippet
snippet
tippet

ĪP′eth
gripeth
pipeth
typeth
wipeth

ĬP′eth
chippeth

---

clippeth
dippeth
drippeth
equippeth
flippeth
grippeth
gyppeth
horsewhippeth
nippeth
outstrippeth
rippeth
shippeth
sippeth
skippeth
slippeth
snippeth
strippeth
tippeth
trippeth
whippeth

ĬP′id
insipid

ĬP′ij
kippage
scrippage
strippage

ĬP′ik
archetypic
daguerreotypic
electrotypic
hippic
homotypic
idiotypic
monotypic
philippic
phonotypic

prototypic
stereotypic
typic

ĬP′in
pippin

ĬP′ing
griping
hyping
Peiping
piping
sniping
stereotyping
striping
swiping
typing
wiping

ĬP′ing
atripping
chipping
clipping
dipping
dripping
equipping
flipping
gripping
nipping
outstripping
overtripping
quipping
ripping
shipping
sipping
skipping
slipping
snipping
stripping

tipping
transhipping
tripping
whipping

ĬP′ish
grippish
hippish
hyppish
snippish

ĬP′′l
becripple
cripple
grippal
nipple
ripple
sipple
stipple
swiple
tipple
triple

ĬP′lē
cripply
ripply
stipply
triply

ĬP′let
liplet
ripplet
siplet
triplet

ĬP′ling
crippling
Kipling
rippling

stippling
stripling
tippling

ĬP′lur
crippler
tippler

ĬP′ment
equipment
shipment
transhipment

ĪP′nes
dead-ripeness
overripeness
ripeness

ĬP′ō
hippo
gippo

ĬP′res
cypress

ĬP′sē
gypsy
Poughkeepsie
Skipsey
tipsy

ĬP′shun
ascription
circumscription
conniption
conscription
description
Egyptian
inscription
prescription

proscription
rescription
subscription
superscription
transcription

ĬP'sis
ellipsis
tripsis

ĬP'tik
anaglyptic
apocalyptic
cryptic
diptych
ecliptic
elliptic
glyptic
holocryptic
iatraliptic
styptic
triptych

ĬP'tiv
adscriptive
ascriptive
circumscriptive
descriptive
indescriptive
inscriptive
prescriptive
proscriptive
rescriptive
transcriptive

ĬP'tūr
scripture

ĬP'ur

bagpiper
daguerreotyper
electrotyper
griper
linotyper
monotyper
piper
riper
stereotyper
sniper
striper
swiper
typer
viper
wiper

ĬP'ur
Big Dipper
chipper
clipper
day-tripper
dipper
dripper
flipper
fripper
gallinipper
gipper
gripper
Jack the Rip-
per
kipper
lady's slipper
nipper
outstripper
quipper
ripper
shipper
sipper
skipper

slipper
snipper
stripper
swipper
tipper
tripper
whipper
Yom Kippur
zipper

ĬP'urd
kippered
skippered
slippered

Ī'ra
Almira
Elmira
Elvira
Ira
IRA
Lyra
Myra
Palmyra
Thyra

ĬR'ah
sirrah

ĬR'al
gyral
retiral
spiral

ĬR'am
Hiram

ĬR'ant
arch tyrant

aspirant
conspirant
expirant
gyrant
spirant
tyrant
(See also
ĪR'ent.)

ĪR'āt
circumgyrate
dextrogyrate
gyrate
irate
lyrate

ĪR'at
pirate

ĪR'ē
acquiry
dairi
enquiry
inquiry
miry
spiry
squiry
wiry
(See also ĪR'e.)

ĬR'ē
eyrie

ĪR'e
Dies Irae
praemunire
(See also ĪR'ē.)

ĬR'el
squirrel

ōld, ôr, ŏdd, oil, fŏŏt, out; ūse, ûrn, ŭp; THis, thin

Ī′rēm
bireme
trireme

Ī′rēn
Irene
pyrene
squireen

Ī′ren
lepidosiren
siren

ĪR′ent
inquirent
sempervirent
virent
(See also
ĪR′ant.)

ĪR′est
acquirest
admirest
aspirest
attirest
bemirest
conspirest
desirest
direst
enquirest
expirest
firest
hirest
inquirest
inspirest
mirest
perspirest
requirest
respirest

retirest
suspirest
tirest
transpirest
umpirest
wirest

ĪR′eth
acquireth
admireth
aspireth
attireth
bemireth
conspireth
desireth
enquireth
expireth
fireth
hireth
inquireth
inspireth
mireth
perspireth
requireth
respireth
retireth
suspireth
tireth
transpireth
umpireth
wireth

ĪR′flī
firefly

ĪR′ful
direful
ireful

ĪR′id
irid

ĪR′ik
butyric
empiric
lyric
panegyric
Pyrrhic
satiric
satyric

ĪR′il
Cyril
virile

ĪR′ing
acquiring
admiring
aspiring
attiring
bemiring
conspiring
desiring
enquiring
expiring
firing
hiring
inquiring
inspiring
miring
perspiring
requiring
respiring
retiring
squiring
suspiring
tiring
transpiring

unaspiring
undesiring
untiring
wiring

ĪR′is
iris
Osiris

ĪR′ish
Irish

ĪR′ist
irised
lyrist

ĪR′ist
careerist
lyrist
panegyrist

ĪR′it
dispirit
inspirit
master spirit
party-spirit
spirit

ĪR′ling
hireling
squireling

ĪR′man
fireman

ĪR′ment
acquirement
aspirement
bemirement

---

requirement
retirement

ĬR'nes
direness
entireness

ĬR'ō
Cairo
tyro

Ī'rōd
byroad
highroad

ĬR'on
Byron
Chiron
environ
gyron

ĬR'ōs
gyrose
virose

ĬR'sīd
fireside

ĬR'som
iresome
tiresome

ĬR'up
chirrup
stirrup
syrup

ĬR'ur
acquirer
admirer
aspirer

attirer
bemirer
conspirer
desirer
direr
enquirer
expirer
firer
hirer
inquirer
inspirer
mirer
perspirer
requirer
respirer
retirer
suspirer
tirer
wirer

ĬR'us
apyrous
computer virus
Cyrus
desirous
Epirus
gyrus
papyrus
virus

ĬR'wurks
fireworks
wireworks

ĬS'a
Clarissa
Lissa
Melissa
Nerissa

Ī'sāl
skysail
trysail

ĬS'al
paradisal

ĬS'chif
mischief

ĬS'chan
anti-Christian
Christian

ĬS'ē
Datisi
icy
nisi
spicy

ĬS'ē
missy
prissy
sissy

ĬS'ens
license

ĬS'ens
dehiscence
fatiscence
indehiscence
reminiscence
resipiscence
reviviscence

ĬS'ent
dehiscent
indehiscent
reminiscent
reviviscent

ĬS'est
bespicest
concisest
enticest
nicest
precisest
pricest
sacrificest
slicest
spicest
splicest
sufficest

ĬS'est
dismissest
hissest
kissest
missest

ĬS'eth
bespiceth
enticeth
priceth
sacrificeth
sliceth
spiceth
spliceth
sufficeth

ĬS'eth
dismisseth
hisseth
kisseth
misseth

ĬS'ēz
Ulysses

ĬS'ez
abysses

ōld, ôr, ŏdd, oil, fŏŏt, out; ūse, ûrn, ŭp; THis, thin

artifices
benefices
blisses
cockatrices
dismisses
edifices
hisses
kisses
misses
precipices
prejudices
Swisses

ĬS'ful
blissful
remissful
unblissful

ĬSH'a
Elisha

ĬSH'a
Delicia
Letitia
militia

ĬSH'al
accrementitial
artificial
beneficial
comitial
edificial
exitial
extrajudicial
gentilitial
inartificial
initial
interstitial
judicial

natalitial
official
policial
prejudicial
recrementitial
rusticial
sacrificial
solstitial
superficial
tribunitial
veneficial

ĬSH'an
academician
logician
magician
optician
(See also
ĬSH'un.)

ĬSH'ē
fishy
swishy

ĬSH'ens
deficience
efficience
insufficience
maleficience
omniscience
perspicience
proficience
prospicience
self-sufficience

ĬSH'ent
beneficient
calorificient
coefficient

deficient
efficient
indeficient
inefficient
insufficient
maleficient
objicient
omniscient
perficient
proficient
self-sufficient
sufficient
volitient

ĬSH'est
dishest
fishest
swishest
wishest

ĬSH'eth
disheth
fisheth
swisheth
wisheth

ĬSH'ful
dishful
wishful

ĬSH'ing
dishing
fishing
ill-wishing
swishing
well-wishing
wishing

ĬSH'op

bishop

ĬSH'un
abannition
abligurition
abolition
abscission
academician
accrementition
acoustician
acquisition
addition
adhibition
admission
admonition
aesthetician
affinition
agglutition
ambition
ammunition
Apician
apparition
apposition
arithmetician
atomician
attrition
audition
beautician
binary fission
bipartition
circuition
clinician
coalition
cognition
coition
commission
competition
composition
condition

contraposition
contrition
cosmetician
deacquisition
decomposition
dedition
definition
deglutition
demission
demolition
dentition
departition
deperdition
deposition
detrition
diagnostician
dialectician
dietitian
dismission
disposition
disquisition
ebullition
edition
electrician
emission
epinician
epinicion
equipartition
erudition
exhibition
exinanition
expedition
exposition
expromission
extradition
fission
fruition
futurition
Galician

geometrician
geriatrician
glutition
Hebrician
hydrostatician
ignition
illinition
imbibition
immission
imposition
inanition
indisposition
inhibition
inition
inquisition
insition
insubmission
intermission
interposition
intromission
intuition
irremission
juxtaposition
logician
logistician
magician
magnetician
malnutrition
malposition
manumission
mathematician
mechanician
metaphysician
metrician
micturition
mission
monition
mortician
munition

musician
Neoplatonician
nolition
nuclear fission
nutrition
obdormition
obstetrician
omission
opposition
optician
partition
parturition
patrician
Paulician
pediatrician
perdition
permission
perquisition
petition
Phenician
Phoenician
physician
politician
position
practician
precognition
precondition
predisposition
premonition
premunition
preposition
presupposition
preterition
Priscian
prohibition
proposition
punition
pyrotechnician
ratihabition

readmission
recognition
recomposition
recondition
reddition
redhibition
redition
remission
rendition
repartition
repetition
reposition
requisition
resilition
reunition
rhetorician
rubrician
scission
sedition
simplician
sortition
statistician
subaudition
submission
submonition
superaddition
superposition
superstition
supposition
suspicion
tactician
technician
theoretician
Titian
tradition
tralatition
transition
transmission
transposition

ōld, ôr, ŏdd, oil, fŏŏt, out; ūse, ûrn, ŭp; THis, thin

tribunitian
tripartition
tuition
vendition
volition
vomition
vomiturition

ĬSH'und
commissioned
conditioned
ill-conditioned
noncommis-
  sioned
uncommis-
  sioned
(See also
ĬSH'un; add
-ed where
appropriate.)

ĬSH'ur
disher
Fischer
fisher
fissure
ill-wisher
kingfisher
swisher
well-wisher
wisher

ĬSH'us
addititious
adjectitious
adscititious
advectitious
adventitious
ambitious

arreptitious
ascititious
ascriptitious
auspicious
avaricious
capricious
cilicious
deglutitious
delicious
exitious
expeditious
factitious
fictitious
flagitious
gentilitious
inauspicious
injudicious
inofficious
judicious
lateritious
lubricious
malicious
Mauritius
meretricious
multiplicious
natalitious
nutritious
obreptitious
obstetricious
officious
pernicious
piceous
profectitious
propitious
pumiceous
puniceous
repetitious
satellitious
secretitious

seditious
sericeous
silicious
stillatitious
superstitious
supposititious
surreptitious
suspicious
tralatitious
veneficious
vermicious
vicious

ĬS'ik
masticic
silicic

ĬS'il
fissile
missile
scissile

ĪS'id
viscid

ĪS'in
Aureomycin
carbomycin
erythromycin
lysin
neomycin
streptolycin
streptomycin
Terramycin

ĬS'in
datiscin
viscin

ĪS'ing
bespicing
dicing
enticing
icing
pricing
sacrificing
self-sacrificing
self-sufficing
slicing
spicing
splicing
sufficing

ĬS'ing
dehiscing
dismissing
hissing
kissing
missing

ĪS'is
crisis
Isis
phthisis

ĬS'ish
missish

ĬS'it
elicit
explicit
illicit
implicit
licit
solicit

ĪS'iv
cicatrisive

collisive
decisive
derisive
divisive
incisive
indecisive
precisive

ĬS'iv
admissive
commissive
demissive
emissive
intermissive
irremissive
missive
nonsubmissive
omissive
permissive
promissive
remissive
submissive
transmissive

ĬS'ka
Mariska

ĬS'kal
discal
fiscal
obeliscal

ĬS'kāt
confiscate
inviscate

ĬS'kē
frisky
risky

whiskey

ĬS'kest
briskest
friskest
riskest
whiskest

ĬS'ket
brisket
frisket

ĬS'keth
frisketh
risketh
whisketh

ĬSK'ful
friskful
riskful

ĬS'kin
griskin
siskin

ĬS'king
brisking
frisking
risking
whisking

ĬS'kit
biscuit
Triscuit

ĬS'kō
Cisco
Crisco
disco

Francisco
Frisco
Nabisco
San Francisco

ĬS'kur
bewhisker
brisker
frisker
risker
whisker

ĬS'kus
abaciscus
discous
discus
hibiscus
lemniscus
lentiscus
meniscus
trochiscus
viscous

ĬS''l
abyssal
bristle
dismissal
epistle
gristle
missal
scissel
thistle
whistle
(See also
ĬS'il.)

ĬS'lē
Cicely
concisely

nicely
precisely

ĬS'lē
bristly
gristly
thistly

ĬS'les
adviceless
diceless
iceless
miceless
priceless
spiceless
spliceless
viceless
(See also ĬS;
add *-less* where
appropriate.)

ĬS'ling
bristling
whistling

ĬS'ment
enticement
sufficement

ĬS'mus
isthmus
(See also
ĬST'mus.)

ĬS''n
christen
glisten
listen
relisten

ōld, ôr, ŏdd, oil, fŏŏt, out; ūse, ûrn, ŭp; THis, thin

ĬS'nes
conciseness
niceness
overniceness
preciseness

ĬS'nes
remissness
thisness

ĬS'ning
Christening
glistening
listening

ĬS'om
lissome

ĬS'on
bison
Dyson
grison
hyson
Tyson
vison

ĬS'pē
crispy

ĬS'pest
crispest
lispest

ĬS'peth
crispeth
lispeth

ĬS'pin
Crispin
St. Crispin

ĬS'ping
crisping
lisping

ĬS'pur
crisper
lisper
stage whisper
whisper

ĬS'ta
ballista
genista
vista

ĬS'tal, ĬS't'l
crystal
listel
pistol
pocket-pistol

ĬS'tan
Tristan

ĬS'tans
assistance
coexistence
consistence
desistance
distance
equidistance
existence
inconsistence
inexistence
insistence
nonexistence
nonresistance
outdistance
persistence

pre-existence
resistance
subsistence
(See also
ĬS'tant,
ĬS'tent.)

ĬS'tant,
ĬS'tent
assistant
coexistant
consistent
distant
equidistant
existent
inconsistent
inexistent
insistent
nonexistent
nonresistant
persistent
preexistent
resistant
subsistent

ĬST'dom
Christdom

ĬS'ted
assisted
black-listed
close-fisted
consisted
cysted
desisted
encysted
enlisted
entwisted
existed

fisted
hard-fisted
insisted
intertwisted
iron-fisted
limp-wristed
listed
misted
persisted
preexisted
reenlisted
relisted
resisted
subsisted
tightfisted
trysted
twisted
two-fisted
unassisted
unlisted
unresisted
untwisted
white-listed

ĬS'tem
system

ĬS'test
assistest
consistest
desistest
enlistest
existest
insistest
listest
persistest
resistest
subsistest
twistest

āle,   câre,   ădd,   ärm,   ăsk;   mē,   hĕre,   ĕnd;   īce,   ĭll;

ĬS'teth

assisteth
consisteth
desisteth
enlisteth
existeth
insisteth
listeth
misteth
persisteth
relisteth
resisteth
subsisteth
twisteth

ĬST'ful
mistful
wistful

ĬS'tik
absolutistic
adiaphoristic
agonistic
alchemistic
allegoristic
altruistic
anabaptistic
anachronistic
anarchistic
animistic
annalistic
anomalistic
antagonistic
antiphlogistic
aoristic
aphlogistic
aphoristic
artistic

atavistic
atheistic
autistic
ballistic
baptistic
behavioristic
belletristic
bibliopegistic
bibliopolistic
Buddhistic
cabalistic
Calvinistic
cameralistic
cannibalistic
canonistic
capitalistic
casuistic
catechistic
characteristic
chauvinistic
chrematistic
commercialis-
    tic
communalistic
communistic
curialistic
cystic
Dadaistic
deistic
dialogistic
distich
dualistic
dyslogistic
egoistic
egotistic
ekistic
electroballistic
Elohistic
epilogistic

eristic
Eucharistic
eudemonistic
euhemeristic
eulogistic
euphemistic
euphuistic
evangelistic
expressionistic
familistic
fatalistic
fetischistic
feudalistic
feuilletonistic
filiopietistic
fistic
floristic
formalistic
formularistic
futuristic
Hebraistic
hedonistic
Hellenistic
heuristic
holistic
hubristic
humanistic
humoristic
hypnotistic
idealistic
illuministic
imperialistic
Impressionistic
impressionistic
inartistic
individualistic
interimistic
Jehovistic
jingoistic

journalistic
Judaistic
juristic
Lamaistic
Latinistic
liberalistic
linguistic
logistic
masochistic
materialistic
mechanistic
melioristic
mercantilistic
meristic
methodistic
Mithraistic
modernistic
monistic
monopolistic
monotheistic
moralistic
mystic
nationalistic
naturalistic
neologistic
neorealistic
nihilistic
nominalistic
novelistic
optimistic
paleocrystic
pantheistic
papistic
parallelistic
patristic
pessimistic
phenomenalis-
    tic
philanthropistic

philosophistic
phlogistic
pietistic
pistic
polaristic
polytheistic
Populistic
postimpres-
  sionistic
postmod-
  ernistic
pugilistic
puristic
quietistic
rationalistic
realistic
relativistic
ritualistic
Romanistic
romanticistic
royalistic
sadistic
sadomasochis-
  tic
schistic
sciolistic
sensationalistic
sensualistic
Shintoistic
simplistic
socialistic
solecistic
somnambulis-
  tic
sophistic
sphragistic
spiritualistic
statistic
stylistic

Sufistic
surrealistic
syllogistic
symbolistic
synchronistic
synergistic
talmudistic
Taoistic
terroristic
theistic
touristic
tristich
tritheistic
unionistic
universalistic
vitalistic
voluntaristic
voyeuristic

ĬS'tiks
agonistics
mystics
sphragistics
statistics

ĬS'til
pistil

ĬS'tin
amethystine
Philistine
pristine
Sistine

ĬS'ting
assisting
consisting
desisting
enlisting

entwisting
existing
insisting
intertwisting
listing
misting
preexisting
persisting
resisting
subsisting
twisting
unresisting
untwisting

ĬS'tiv
persistive
resistive

ĬST'les
listless
resistless
twistless

ĬST'mus
Christmas

ĬST'ment
agistment
enlistment

ĬS'tral
mistral

ĬS'ram
Tristram

ĬS'tres
mistress

ĬS'tur
agistor
assister
bister
blister
enlister
exister
foster sister
glister
insister
intertwister
lister
magister
mister
passive resister
persister
resister
sister
subsister
twister

ĬS'turn
cistern

ĬS'tus
acathistus
schistous

ĬS'ū
issue
tissue

ĬS'ur
conciser
dicer
enticer
geyser
nicer
preciser

sacrificer
slicer
spicer
splicer

ĬS′ŭr
dehiscer
dismisser
hisser
kisser
misser
remisser

ĬS′us
byssus
Issus
"missus"
narcissus

ĪT′al
cital
detrital
entitle
parasital
recital
requital
title
vital

ĪT′alz
recitals
vitals
(See also ĪT′al;
add -s where
appropriate.)

ĪT′an
Titan

ĬT′an
Britain
Britten
(See also
ĬT′en.)

ĬT′ans
acquittance
admittance
omittance
permittance
pittance
quittance
remittance
transmittance

ĪT′ē
almighty
blighty
flighty
highty-tighty
mighty
mity
whity
(See also ĪT′e.)

ĬT′ē
banditti
city
committee
ditty
flitty
Giovanitti
gritty
kitty
pity
pretty
self-pity
witty

ĪT′e
Amphitrite
Aphrodite
arborvitae
lignum vitae
(See also ĪT′ē.)

ĪT′ed
affrighted
alighted
attrited
bedighted
beknighted
benighted
blighted
cited
clear-sighted
delighted
despited
detrited
dighted
eagle-flighted
eagle-sighted
excited
farsighted
foresighted
frighted
ignited
incited
indicted
indited
invited
knighted
lighted
longsighted
nearsighted
nighted
oversighted
plighted

quick-sighted
recited
requited
reunited
righted
second-sighted
sharp-sighted
shortsighted
sighted
sited
slighted
spited
trothplighted
unaffrighted
unbenighted
undighted
unfrighted
united
unplighted
unrequited
unrighted
unsighted

ĬT′ed
acquitted
admitted
afterwitted
befitted
benefited
bitted
blunt-witted
committed
counterfeited
emitted
fat-witted
fitted
flitted
gritted
half-witted

interknitted	**ĪT'en**	*alightest*	fittest
intermitted	brighten	*beknightest*	*flittest*
knitted	enlighten	*bitest*	hittest
lean-witted	frighten	*blightest*	knittest
mahumitted	heighten	brightest	omittest
nimble-witted	lighten	*citest*	*outwittest*
omitted	tighten	*delightest*	*permittest*
outwitted	Titan	*excitest*	*pittest*
permitted	whiten	*fightest*	*quittest*
pitted	(See also	impolitest	*refittest*
quick-witted	Ī'ton.)	*incitest*	*remittest*
quitted		*inditest*	sittest
ready-witted	**ĬT'en**	*invitest*	*slittest*
recommitted	bitten	*knightest*	*spittest*
refitted	Briton	*lightest*	*splittest*
remitted	conscience-	*mightest*	submittest
sharp-witted	smitten	*plightest*	*twittest*
short-witted	flea-bitten	politest	
slitted	fly-bitten	*recitest*	**ĪT'eth**
spitted	hunger-bitten	*requitest*	*affrighteth*
submitted	kitten	*reunitest*	*alighteth*
subtle-witted	mitten	rightest	*beknighteth*
transmitted	smitten	*sightest*	*biteth*
twitted	sun-smitten	*sleightest*	*blighteth*
unbenefited	terror-smitten	slightest	*citeth*
unbitted	underwritten	*smitest*	*delighteth*
underwitted	unsmitten	*spitest*	*exciteth*
unfitted	unwritten	tightest	*fighteth*
unremitted	weather-bitten	tritest	*igniteth*
witted	written	*unitest*	*inciteth*
writted		uprightest	*inditeth*
	ĬT'ent	whitest	*inviteth*
ĬT'ēd	emittent	*writest*	*plighteth*
citied	intermittent		*reciteth*
pitied	intromittent	**ĬT'est**	*requiteth*
unpitied	remittent	*acquittest*	*righteth*
		admittest	*sighteth*
ĪT'em	**ĪT'est**	*benefitest*	*sleighteth*
item	*affrightest*	*committest*	*smiteth*

āle, câre, ădd, ärm, ăsk; mē, hĕre, ĕnd; īce, ĭll;

spiteth
uniteth
writeth

ĪT′eth
acquitteth
admitteth
befitteth
benefiteth
committeth
fitteth
flitteth
hitteth
knitteth
omitteth
out-witteth
permitteth
pitteth
quitteth
refitteth
remitteth
sitteth
slitteth
spitteth
splitteth
submitteth
twitteth

ĪT′ēz
pyrites
sorites

ĪT′ful
delightful
despiteful
frightful
mightful
rightful
spiteful

sprightful

ĬT′ful
fitful
witful

ĪTH′ē
blithy
lithy

ĬTH′ē
prithee

Ĭth′ē
pithy
smithy
stithy
withy

ĬTH′en
battle-writhen
writhen

ĪTH′est
blithest
lithest
writhest

ĪTH′eth
writheth

ĪTH′ful
blitheful
litheful

Ĭth′ik
eolithic
lithic
megalithic

microlithic
monolithic
mythic
neolithic
ornithic
paleolithic
trilithic

ĪTH′ing
nithing
scything
tithing
trithing
writhing

ĬTH′′m
rhythm

ĬTH′mik
logarithmic
polyrhythmic
rhythmic

ĪTH′nes
blitheness
litheness

Ī′thon
python

ĪTH′som
blithesome
lithesome

ĪTH′ur
blither
either
neither
tither

writher

ĬTH′ur
anywhither
behither
blither
dither
hither
nowhither
slither
somewhither
swither
thither
whither
wither

ĬTH′urd
withered
unwithered

ĬTH′urz
withers

ĬT′ik
aconitic
actinolitic
Adamitic
aerolitic
anaclitic
analytic
anthracitic
anthropomor-
  phitic
anti-Semitic
arthritic
bacteriolytic
biolytic
bronchitic
Cabiritic

catalytic
cenobitic
clitic
conchitic
critic
Cushitic
dendritic
diacritic
dialytic
diphtheritic
dolomitic
dynamitic
electrolytic
enclitic
eophytic
epiphytic
eremitic
erythrocitic
gingitic
granitic
granulitic
graphitic
Hamitic
hematitic
hermaphroditic
heteroclitic
holophytic
hydrolytic
hypercritic
hypocritic
Islamitic
Israelitic
Jacobitic
Jesuitic
laryngitic
lenitic
leukocytic
Levitic
lignitic

lymphocytic
lytic
margaritic
meningitic
mephitic
meteoritic
Nazaritic
Negritic
neophytic
nephritic
neritic
non-Semitic
nonanalytic
nonparasitic
nummulitic
oneirocritic
oolitic
osteoarthritic
palmitic
paralytic
parasitic
phlebitic
phosphoritic
pleuritic
porphyritic
preadamitic
proclitic
protosemitic
psychoanalytic
pyritic
rachitic
sagenitic
Sanskritic
scialytic
selenitic
semiparasitic
Semitic
Shemitic
Shiitic

Sinaitic
Sinitic
spherulitic
stalactitic
stalagmitic
steatitic
strontitic
sybaritic
syenitic
sympatholytic
syphilitic
theodolitic
thermolytic
Titanitic
tonsilitic
toxophilitic
trilobitic
trochitic
trogodytic
tympanitic
unanalytic
unparasitic
uranitic
variolitic
xerophytic
zeolitic
zoophytic

ĬT′iks
analytics
critics
(See also ĬT′ik;
add -s where
appropriate.)

ĬT′in
chitin
(See also ĪT′ĕn,
ĪT′on.)

ĪT′ing
affrighting
alighting
back-biting
beknighting
biting
blighting
citing
copyright-
  ing
delighting
disuniting
dynamiting
exciting
expediting
fighting
frighting
handwriting
igniting
inciting
indicting
inditing
inviting
kiting
knighting
lighting
plighting
reciting
requiting
reuniting
righting
sighting
slighting
smiting
spiting
underwriting
uniting
whiting
writing

āle, câre, ădd, ärm, ăsk; mē, hĕre, ĕnd; īce, ĭll;

ĬT′ing
acquitting
admitting
befitting
benefiting
bitting
committing
counterfeiting
emitting
fitting
flitting
gritting
hair-splitting
hitting
knitting
manumitting
misfitting
omitting
outsitting
outwitting
permitting
pitting
pretermitting
quitting
recommitting
refitting
remitting
sitting
skitting
slitting
spitting
splitting
submitting
transmitting
twitting
unbefitting
unfitting
unremitting
unsubmitting

unwitting
witting

ĬT′is
accidentitis
adenitis
adjectivitis
appendicitis
arteritis
arthritis
baseballitis
big-businessitis
blepharitis
bronchitis
bursitis
carditis
cellulitis
colitis
colonitis
conjunctivitis
cystitis
dermatitis
diverticulitis
duodenitis
educationitis
encephalitis
endocarditis
enteritis
fibrositis
gastritis
gastroenteritis
gingivitis
glossitis
golfitis
hepatitis
hyalitis
ileitis
iritis
jazzitis

keratitis
laryngitis
mastitis
mastoiditis
meningitis
mephitis
metritis
mitis
moneyitis
myelitis
nephritis
neuritis
ophthalmitis
orchitis
osteitis
osteoarthritis
osteomyelitis
otitis
ovaritus
parotitis
pericarditis
peritonitis
pharyngitis
phlebitis
pneumonitis
poliomyelitis
prostatitis
pyelitis
rachitis
retinitis
rhinitis
salpingitis
scleritis
sinusitis
splenitis
spondylitis
synovitis
telephonitis
televisionitis

thyroiditis
tonsillitis
trachitis
typhlitis
urethritis
utriculitis
uveitis
uvulitis
vacationitis
vaginitis
vulvitis
vulvulitis

ĪT′ish
anchoritish
Canaanitish
eremitish
Ishmaelitish
Israelitish
lightish
tightish
whitish

ĬT′ish
British
skittish

ĪT′iv
appetitive
expeditive

ĪT′′l
entitle
title
(See also
ĪT′al.)

ĬT′′l
acquittal

belittle
brittle
committal
knittle
lickspittle
little
noncommittal
remittal
skittle
spital
spittle
tittle
transmittal
victual
whittle

ĬT'lē
brightly
impolitely
Kneightly
knightly
lightly
nightly
politely
rightly
sightly
slightly
sprightly
tightly
tritely
unknightly
unsightly
uprightly
whiteley
whitely

ĬT'lē
fitly
unfitly

ĬT'les
delightless
fightless
frightless
heightless
knightless
lightless
nightless
riteless
sightless
spiteless
sprightless

ĬT'less
witless
(See also ĬT;
add *-less* where
appropriate.)

ĬT'lest
belittlest
brittlest
littlest
(See also ĬT''l;
add *-est* where
appropriate.)

ĬT'leth
belitteth
(See also
ĬT''l; add
-eth where
appropriate.)

ĬT'ling
entitling
titling

ĬT'ling
kitling
titling
witling
whittling

ĬT'lur
brittler
littler
victualler
whittler

ĬT''lz
belittles
skittles
victuals
(See also ĬT''l;
add *-s* where
appropriate.)

ĬT'ment
affrightment
excitement
frightment
incitement
indictment
invitement

ĬT'ment
acquitment
commitment
fitment
refitment
remitment

ĬT'nē
jitney
Mt. Whitney
Whitney

ĬT'nes
brightness
impoliteness
lightness
politeness
rightness
slightness
tightness
triteness
uprightness
whiteness

ĬT'nes
eyewitness
fitness
unfitness
witness

ĬT'ning
brightening
frightening
heightening
lightening
lightning
sheet lightning
tightening
whitening

ĬT'nur
brightener
frightener
heightener
lightener
whitener

ĪT'on
chiton
triton
(See also
ĪT'en.)

ĬT′rāt
nitrate
titrate

ĬT′rē
mitry
nitry

ĬT′rik
nitric

ĬT′rik
citric
vitric

ĬT′ur
alighter
arbeiter
back-biter
bemitre
biter
blighter
brighter
bullfighter
citer
delighter
dynamiter
exciter
fighter
flighter
Gauleiter
ghostwriter
gunfighter
igniter
impoliter
inciter
indicter
inditer
inviter

lamplighter
lighter
miter
moonlighter
niter
plighter
politer
prizefighter
reciter
requiter
righter
scriptwriter
sighter
slighter
smiter
songwriter
tighter
triter
typewriter
underwriter
uniter
unmiter
whiter
writer

ĬT′ur
acquitter
admitter
baby-sitter
befitter
benefitter
bitter
committer
counterfeiter
critter
embitter
emitter
fitter
flitter

fritter
glitter
gritter
hitter
house sitter
intermitter
intromitter
knitter
litter
manumitter
misfitter
omitter
outsitter
outwitter
permitter
pinch hitter
pitter
pretermitter
quitter
rail-splitter
recommitter
refitter
remitter
sitter
slitter
spitter
splitter
submitter
titter
transmitter
twitter
unfitter
Witter

ĬT′urd
frittered
unembittered
(See also
ĬT′ur;

add -ed where
appropriate.)

ĬT′urn
bittern
flittern
gittern

ĬT′urz
bitters
glitters
(See also ĬT′ur;
add -s where
appropriate.)

ĪT′us
St. Vitus
Titus
Vitus

ĪT′wāt
lightweight

ĬT′wit
nitwit

ĬT′zē
Fritzy
itsy-bitsy
Ritzy

Ī′umf
triumph

Ī′un
triune

Ī′ur
amplifier

applier
Bayer
beautifier
Biedermeier
briar
brier
buyer
certifier
clarifier
classifier
codifer
complier
crier
crucifier
cryer
decryer
defier
defyer
deifier
denier
descrier
dignifier
disqualifier
diversifier
drier
dyer
edifier
electrifier
exemplifier
eyer
falsifier
flier
fortifier
friar
frier
fructifier
glorifier
gratifier
hier

higher
horrifier
identifier
implier
indemnifier
intensifier
justifier
kite-flier
lammergeier
liar
lier
liquefier
magnifier
Mayer
Meier
Meyer
modifier
mollifier
mortifier
multiplier
Myer
mystifier
nigher
notifier
nullifier
occupier
pacifier
personifier
petrifier
plyer
prior
prophesier
pryer
purifier
putrifier
qualifier
ramifier
ratifier
rectifier

relier
replier
revivifier
sanctifier
satisfier
scarifier
scorifier
shyer
sigher
signifier
simplifier
skyer
slyer
specifier
speechifier
spryer
spyer
stultifier
stupefier
supplier
sweetbrier
terrifier
testifier
tier
town crier
trier
trior
tyer
typifier
Untermyer
untier
verifier
versifier
vier
vilifier
vivifier
white friar
wryer
(See also ĪR.)

Ī′urn

grappling iron
iron
lofting iron

Ī′urz

briers
Meyers
Myers
pliers
(See also Ī′ur;
add -s where
appropriate.)

Ī′us

bacchius
Darius
nisi prius
pious
Pius
(See also Ī′as.)

ĪV′a

Saiva
saliva
Siva

ĪV′al

adjectival
archival
arrival
conjunctival
estival
imperatival
nominatival
outrival
revival
rival
salival

survival

ĪV'an
Ivan
(See also
ĪV'en.)

ĪV'ans
arrivance
connivance
contrivance
survivance

ĬV'ant
trivant

ĪV'at
private

ĪV'ē
ivy

ĬV'ē
chivvy
divi-divi
divvy
Livy
privy
tantivy
tivy

ĪV'ēd
ivied

ĪV'en
enliven

ĬV'en
driven

forgiven
given
overdriven
riven
scriven
shriven
stormdriven
thriven
undriven
unforgiven
unshriven
weather-driven

ĪV'ent
connivent

ĪV'est
arrivest
connivest
contrivest
deprivest
derivest
divest
drivest
livest
revivest
rivest
shrivest
strivest
survivest
thrivest

ĬV'est
forgivest
givest
livest
misgivest
outlivest

ĬV'et
civet
grivet
privet
rivet
trivet
unrivet

ĪV'eth
arriveth
conniveth
contriveth
depriveth
deriveth
diveth
driveth
reviveth
shriveth
striveth
surviveth
thriveth

ĬV'eth
forgiveth
giveth
liveth
misgiveth
outliveth

ĬV'id
livid
vivid

ĬV'ik
civic

ĬV'il, ĬV'el
civil
drivel
rivel

shrivel
snivel
swivel
uncivil

ĪV'ing
arriving
conniving
contriving
depriving
deriving
diving
driving
hiving
reviving
shriving
striving
surviving
thriving
uncontriving
wiving

ĬV'ing
ever-living
forgiving
giving
lawgiving
life-giving
living
misgiving
outliving
reliving
sieving
thanksgiving
unforgiving
unliving

ĪV'lē
lively

ĬV'lē
appositively
positively
suppositively

ĬV'ling
shrivelling
snivelling

ĬV'ment
deprivement
revivement

ĬV'nes
forgiveness

ĬV'ot
divot
pivot

ĬV'ring
delivering
quivering
shivering
slivering

ĬV'ur
arriver
conniver
contriver
depriver
diver
deriver
driver
fiver
hiver
liver
pearl-diver
reviver

river
screwdriver
scuba diver
shriver
skiver
slave-driver
sliver
stiver
striver
surviver
thriver

ĬV'ur
cantalever
deliver
flivver
forgiver
freeliver
giver
Indian givern
lawgiver
life-giver
liver
misgiver
outliver
quiver
river
shiver
skiver
sliver
Spoon River
stiver
tiver

ĬV'urd
delivered
lily-livered
pigeon-livered
quivered

shivered
slivered
unshivered
white-livered

ĬV'us
acclivous
declivous
proclivous
salivous

ĬV'yal
trivial
(See also
ĬV'ē-al.)

Īwā
byway
highway
skyway

Ī'za
Eliza
Isa

ĪZ'ak
Isaac

ĪZ'al
comprisal
revisal
surprisal

ĬZ'ard
blizzard
gizzard
izard
izzard
lizard

lounge-lizard
scissored
visored
vizard
wizard

ĬZ'dāl
Grisdale

ĬZ'dom
wisdom

ĪZ'ē
sizy

ĬZ'ē
busy
dizzy
frizzy
jizzy
Lizzy
tin-lizzie
tizzy

ĬZ'ēd
busied
dizzied
unbusied

ĪZ'en
bedizen
dizen

ĪZ'en, ĪZ'on
arisen
bedizen
dizen
imprison
mizzen

---

prison
risen
ptisan
wizen

ĪZ'est
advertisest
advisest
agonizest
apologizest
arisest
baptizest
catechizest
chastisest
civilizest
comprisest
compromisest
criticizest
despisest
devisest
disguisest
dramatizest
emphasizest
eulogizest
excisest
exercisest
exorcisest
improvisest
merchandisest
mobilizest
monopolizest
organizest
patronizest
premisest
prizest
realizest
recognizest
revisest
risest

sizest
solemnizest
supervisest
surmisest
surprisest
sympathizest
theorizest
tyrannizest
uprisest
wisest

ĬZ'est
fizzest

ĪZ'eth
advertiseth
adviseth
agonizeth
apologizeth
ariseth
baptizeth
catechizeth
chastiseth
civilizeth
compriseth
compromiseth
criticizeth
despiseth
deviseth
disguiseth
dramatizeth
emphasizeth
eulogizeth
exerciseth
exorciseth
improviseth
merchandiseth
mobilizeth
monopolizeth

organizeth
patronizeth
premiseth
prizeth
realizeth
recognizeth
reviseth
riseth
sizeth
solemnizeth
superviseth
surmiseth
surpriseth
sympathizeth
theorizeth
tyrannizeth
upriseth

ĬZ'eth
fizzeth
(See ĬZ; add
-eth where
appropriate.)

ĬZH'un
abscission
allision
circumcision
collision
concision
decision
derision
division
elision
envision
excision
illision
imprecision
incision

indecision
irrision
misprision
precision
prevision
provision
recision
rescission
revision
scission
stereovision
subdivision
supervision
television
transition
tunnel vision
vision
(See also
ĬZ'ē-an.)

ĬZH'und
provisioned
visioned

ĬZH'ur
scissure

ĪZ'ij
visage

ĬZ'ik
metaphysic
paradisic
phthisic
physic

ĬZ'iks
metaphysics
physics

ĬZ′ing
advertising
advising
aggrandizing
agonizing
analyzing
anglicizing
antagonizing
apologizing
apostatizing
appetizing
apprising
arising
authorizing
baptizing
brutalizing
canonizing
capitalizing
capsizing
catechizing
Catholicizing
cauterizing
centralizing
characterizing
chastising
civilizing
colonizing
comprising
compromising
criticizing
crystallizing
demising
demoralizing
deodorizing
despising
devising
disguising
disorganizing
dramatizing

economizing
emphasizing
enterprising
equalizing
eternalizing
eulogizing
evangelizing
exercising
exorcising
familiarizing
fertilizing
galvanizing
generalizing
gourmandizing
harmonizing
Hebraizing
humanizing
hybridizing
hypnotizing
idealizing
idolizing
immortalizing
improvising
italicizing
jeopardizing
journalizing
localizing
macadamizing
magnetizing
materializing
mesmerizing
methodizing
minimizing
mobilizing
modernizing
monopolizing
moralizing
neutralizing
organizing

paralyzing
patronizing
pauperizing
plagiarizing
premising
prizing
pulverizing
rationalizing
realizing
recognizing
revising
revolutionizing
rising
ruralizing
scandalizing
scrutinizing
secularizing
sermonizing
signalizing
sizing
solemnizing
soliloquizing
specializing
standardizing
sterilizing
stigmatizing
subsidizing
summarizing
supervising
surmising
surprising
symbolizing
sympathizing
systematizing
tantalizing
temporizing
terrorizing
theorizing
totalizing

tranquilizing
tyrannizing
uncompromis-
  ing
underprizing
uprising
utilizing
vaporizing
visualizing
vitalizing
vocalizing
volatilizing
vulgarizing

ĬZ′ing
befrizzing
fizzing
frizzing
phizzing
quizzing
whizzing

ĬZ′it
visit
what-is-it

ĬZ′krak
wisecrack

ĬZ′′l
chisel
crizzle
drizzle
enchisel
fizzle
frizzle
grizzle
mizzle
sizzle

āle,   câre,   ădd,   ärm,   ăsk;   mē,   hĕre,   ĕnd;   īce,   ĭll;

swizzle
twizzle

ĬZ″ld
drizzled
grizzled

ĬZ′lē
chiselly
drizzly
frizzly
grisly
grizzly

ĬZ′ling
chiseling
drizzling
fizzling
frizzling
grizzling
mizzling
sizzling
swizzling

ĬZ″m
izzum-wizzum

ĬZ′mal
abysmal
aneurismal
baptismal
cataclysmal
catechismal
chrismal
dismal
embolismal
paroxysmal
prismal
rheumatismal

strabismal

ĬZ′man
exciseman
prizeman

ĬZ′mē
prismy

ĬZ′ment
aggrandize-
    ment
apprizement
assizement
baptizement

ĬZ′met
kismet

ĬZ′mik
aphorismic
cataclysmic
clysmic
embolismic
paroxysmic

ĬZ′mus
accismus
strabismus
tarantismus
trismus

ĬZ′nes
wiseness

ĬZ′nes
business

ĬZ′om

chrisom

ĬZ′on
horizon
Kyrie eleison

ĬZ′ôrd
visored

ĬZ′ur
advertiser
adviser
aggrandizer
agonizer
alphabetizer
analyzer
apologizer
appetizer
appriser
apprizer
assizer
atomizer
attitudinizer
authorizer
baptizer
Breathalyzer
canonizer
capitalizer
capsizer
catechizer
cauterizer
characterizer
chastiser
civilizer
colonizer
compromiser
criticizer
demagnetizer

demoralizer
deodorizer
despiser
deviser
devisor
dialyzer
disguiser
disorganizer
divisor
dogmatizer
dramatizer
economizer
electrolyzer
elisor
energizer
enterpriser
epitomizer
equalizer
eulogizer
euphemizer
exerciser
exorciser
extemporizer
familiarizer
fertilizer
fraternizer
galvanizer
generalizer
geyser
gourmandizer
guiser
harmonizer
high-riser
humanizer
hybridizer
idealizer
idolizer
immortalizer
improviser

incisor
itemizer
Kaiser
Keyser
Kyser
lionizer
liquidizer
magnetizer
mechanizer
memorializer
memorizer
merchandiser
mesmerizer
methodizer
minimizer
miser
mobilizer
modernizer
moisturizer
monopolizer
moralizer
nationalizer
naturalizer
neutralizer
nonsympa-
   thizer

organizer
ostracizer
oxidizer
oxygenizer
paralyzer
pasteurizer
patronizer
pauperizer
philosophizer
platitudinizer
poetizer
polarizer
popularizer
prizer
proselytizer
pulverizer
rationalizer
realizer
reviser
revolutionizer
riser
satirizer
scandalizer
scrutinizer
secularizer
sermonizer

sizar
sizer
socializer
solemnizer
stabilizer
sterilizer
stigmatizer
subsidizer
supervisor
surmiser
surpriser
symbolizer
sympathizer
synchronizer
synthesizer
systematizer
tantalizer
temporizer
tenderizer
terrorizer
theorizer
totalizer
tranquilizer
tyrannizer
upriser
utilizer

vaporizer
verbalizer
victimizer
visor
visualizer
vitalizer
vocalizer
vulcanizer
vulgarizer
wiser
womanizer

ĬZ'ur
befrizzer
frizzer
quizzer
scissor
visor

ĬZ'urz
scissors
(See also ĬZ'ur;
add -s where
appropriate.)

O

For a discussion of words included under the accented vowels following, see the beginning of O rhymes in Section I.

Ō'a
aloha
anoa
Balboa
balboa
boa
entozoa

epizoa
Genoa
Gilboa
Goa
goa
jerboa
koa

Krakatoa
leipoa
loa
Mauna Loa
Mesozoa
metazoa
Metazoa

moa
Noah
Parazoa
proa
Protozoa
quinoa
Samoa

Shenandoah
spermatozoa
stoa
toatoa

Ō'ab
Joab
Moab

Ō'al
bestowal

Ô'al
withdrawal

Ō'ba
arroba
bona-roba
dagoba

Ô'ba
Cahaba
Catawba

Ō'ball
no-ball
snowball

Ō'bāt
globate
lobate
probate

ŎB'ē
adobe
globy
Gobi
hydrophoby
Kobe

Nairobi
obi

ŎB'ē
bobby
cobby
hobby
knobby
lobby
mobby
nobby
scobby
snobby
squabby

ŌB'est
disrobest
enrobest
probest
robest
unrobest

ŎB'est
daubest
(See also ÔB;
add -*est* where
appropriate.)

ŎB'est
robbest
sobbest
throbbest

ŎB'eth
disrobeth
enrobeth
probeth
robeth
unrobeth

ŎB'et
Cobbett

ÔB'eth
daubeth
(See also ÔB;
add -*eth* where
appropriate.)

ŎB'eth
robbeth
sobbeth
throbbeth

Ō'bī
go by

ŌB'il, ŌB'ēl
automobile
immobile
mobile

ŎB'in
bobbin
dobbin
ragged-robin
robbin
robin
round robin

ŎB'ing
disrobing
enrobing
globing
probing
robing
unrobing

ŎB'ing

---

blobbing
bobbing
cobbing
hobnobbing
jobbing
knobbing
lobbing
mobbing
robbing
snobbing
sobbing
swabbing
throbbing

ŎB'inz
bobbins
Jobbins
Robbins
(See also ŎB'in;
add -*s* where
appropriate.)

ŎB'ish
bobbish
mobbish
nobbish
snobbish
squabbish

ŎB'jekt
object

ŌB''l
ennoble
global
Grenoble
ignoble
mobile
noble

---

unnoble
upwardly
mobile

ŎB''l
bauble

ŎB''l
cobble
coble
gobble
hobble
nobble
squabble
wabble

ŎB'lē
cobbly
squabbly
wabbly
Wobbly

ŎB'lin
goblin

ŎB'ling
cobbling
gobbling
hobbling
nobbling
snobling
squabbling
wabbling

ŎB'lur
cobbler
gobbler
hobbler
knobbler

nobbler
sherry-cobbler
squabbler
wabbler

ŌB'ō
hobo
lobo
oboe
zobo

Ō'boi
doughboy

Ō'bōnz
jawbones
sawbones

ŌB'ra
cobra

Ō'brou
lowbrow

ŌB'son
Jobson
Robeson
Robson

ŌB'son
dobson
Jobson
Robson

ŎB'stur
lobster

ŎB'ūl
globule

lobule

ŌB'ur
disrober
enrober
October
prober
rober
sober

ÔB'ur
bedauber
dauber

ŎB'ur
beslobber
blobber
clobber
cobber
jobber
knobber
lobber
robber
slobber
snobber
sobber
swabber
throbber

ÔB'urn
auburn

ŌB'us
globus
jacobus
obus

ŎB'web
cobweb

ŎCH'ē
blotchy
botchy
notchy
splotchy

ŌCH'est
approachest
broachest
encroachest
poachest
reproachest

ŎCH'est
blotchest
(See also ŎCH;
add -*est* where
appropriate.)

ŎCH'et
crotchet
rotchet

ŌCH'eth
approacheth
broacheth
encroacheth
poacheth
reproacheth

ŎCH'eth
blotcheth
(See also ŎCH;
add -*eth* where
appropriate.)

ŌCH'ez
approaches
broaches

āle,　câre,　ădd,　ärm,　ăsk;　mē,　hĕre,　ĕnd;　īce,　ĭll;

brooches
coaches
encroaches
loaches
poaches
reproaches
roaches
self-reproaches

ŌCH′ful
reproachful

ŌCH′ing
approaching
broaching
coaching
encroaching
poaching
reproaching

ŎCH′ing
blotching
botching
notching
scotching
splotching
watching

ŎCH′man
Scotchman
watchman

ŎCH′ment
approachment
encroachment

ŌCH′ur
approacher
broacher

encroacher
poacher
reproacher
self-reproacher

ŎCH′ur
blotcher
botcher
notcher
splotcher
watcher

ŎCH′wurd
watchword

ŌD′a
coda
pagoda
Rhoda
soda
trinoda

ŌD′al
internodal
modal
nodal
trinodal
yodel

ÔD′al
bicaudal
caudal
caudle
dawdle

ŎD′ard
Goddard
Stoddard

ŌD′ē
toady

ÔD′ē
bawdy
dawdy
gaudy

ŎD′ē
antibody
anybody
body
busy-body
cloddy
disembody
embody
everybody
hoddy
hot toddy
Irrawaddy
nobody
noddy
out-of-body
roddy
shoddy
soddy
somebody
squaddy
toddy
waddy
wadi
(See also
ÄD′ē.)

ŌD′ed
boded
coded
corroded
eroded

exploded
foreboded
goaded
loaded
outmoded
overloaded
unloaded
woaded

ŎD′ed
nodded
plodded
podded
prodded
sodded
wadded

ŌD′el
yodel
(See also
ŌD′al.)

ŌD′en
foreboden
Woden

ÔD′en
broaden

ŎD′en
hodden
sodden
trodden
untrodden
water-sodden
(See also
ÄD′en.)

ŌD′ent
corrodent

ōld, ôr, ŏdd, oil, fŏŏt, out; ūse, ûrn, ŭp; THis, thin

erodent
explodent
rodent

ŎD'es
goddess
(See also
ŎD'is.)

ŌD'est
bodest
corrodest
explodest
forebodest
goadest
loadest
unloadest

ÔD'est
applaudest
belaudest
broadest
defraudest
laudest
maraudest

ŎD'est
immodest
modest
noddest
oddest
ploddest
proddest

ŌD'eth
bodeth
corrodeth
explodeth
forebodeth

goadeth
loadeth
unloadeth

ÔD'eth
applaudeth
belaudeth
defraudeth
laudeth
maraudeth

ŎD'eth
noddeth
(See also ŎD;
add -eth where
appropriate.)

ŎD'ēd
ablebodied
bodied
disembodied
embodied
unbodied
unembodied

ŌD'ik
odic

ŎD'ik
anodic
antispasmodic
episodic
exodic
hellanodic
hydriodic
iodic
kinesodic
melodic
methodic

odic
parodic
periodic
rhapsodic
sarcodic
spasmodic
synodic

ŌD'in
Odin
Wodin

ŌD'ing
boding
corroding
exploding
foreboding
goading
loading
outmoding
overloading
unloading

ÔD'ing
applauding
belauding
defrauding
lauding
marauding

ŎD'ing
codding
nodding
plodding
podding
prodding
wadding

ŎD'is

bodice
(See also
ŎD'es.)

ŎD'ish
cloddish
goddish
oddish

ŌD'ist
codist
modist
palinodist

ÔD'it
audit
plaudit

ÔD'kast
broadcast

ŎD''l
coddle
model
mollycoddle
noddle
remodel
role model
swaddle
toddle
twaddle
waddle

ŎD'lē
godly
twaddly
ungodly
waddly

ÔD'lin
maudlin

ŎD'ling
coddling
codling
godling
modeling
remodeling
swaddling
toddling
twaddling
waddling

ŎD'lur
coddler
modeller
mollycoddler
swaddler
toddler
twaddler
waddler

ŎD'nes
oddness

Ō'dō
dodo
Frodo
quasimodo

ŎD'om
Sodom

ÔD'rē
Audrey
bawdry
tawdry

ŎD'ron
squadron

ŎD'son
Dodson
Hodson

ŌD'stōn
loadstone
lodestone
toadstone

ŌD'stur
goadster
roadster

ŎD'ukt
product

ŎD'ūl
module
nodule

ŌD'ur
corroder
exploder
foreboder
goader
loader
malodor
muzzle-loader
Oder
odor
unloader

ÔD'ur
applauder
belauder
broader

defrauder
lauder
marauder
sawder
soft-sawder

ŎD'ur
codder
dodder
fodder
nodder
odder
plodder
podder
prodder
solder

ŎD'urn
modern

ŌD'us
modus
nodous

Ō'ē
blowy
Bowie
Chloe
doughy
Floey
glowy
Joey
showy
snowy
towy
Zoe

Ô'ē
flawy

jawy
strawy
thawy

Ō'ed
coed

Ō'el
Crowell
Joel
Lowell
Noel

Ō'em
poem
proem

Ō'en
Bowen
Cohen
Owen

Ō'est
bestowest
blowest
crowest
flowest
foregoest
foreknowest
foreshowest
glowest
goest
growest
hoest
knowest
lowest
mowest
outgoest
overflowest

ōld,   ôr,   ŏdd,   oil,   fŏŏt,   out;   ūse,   ûrn,   ŭp;   THis,   thin

overgrowest
overthrowest
owest
rowest
sewest
showest
slowest
snowest
sowest
stowest
throwest
towest
undergoest
undertowest
upthrowest

Ô′est
awest
drawest
overawest
rawest
withdrawest

Ō′et
poet

Ō′eth
bestoweth
bloweth
croweth
floweth
foregoeth
foreknoweth
foreshoweth
gloweth
goeth
groweth
hoeth
knoweth

loweth
moweth
outgoeth
overfloweth
overgroweth
overthroweth
oweth
roweth
seweth
showeth
snoweth
soweth
stoweth
throweth
toweth
undergoeth

Ô′eth
aweth

Ō′fa
sofa

ŌF′ē
Sophie
strophe
trophy

ŎF′ē
coffee
spoffy
toffy

ŎF′er
coffer
cougher
doffer
goffer
golfer

offer
proffer
scoffer

Ō′fet
Tophet

ŎF′et, ŎF′it
archprophet
profit
prophet
soffit
weather
  prophet

ŎF′ik
antistrophic
apostrophic
catastrophic
hypertrophic
philosophic
theosophic
theophilo-
  sophic

ŎF′īl
profile

ŎF′in
coffin
encoffin

ŎF′ing
coughing
doffing
golfing
offing
scoffing

ŎF′is
office

ÔF′ish
crawfish
standoffish

ÔF′ish
offish
spoffish

ŎF′′l
offal
waffle

ŎF′′n
often
soften

ŎF′ted
lofted

ŎF′test
softest

ŎF′tē
lofty
softy

ŎFT′lē
softly

ŎF′tur
crofter
lofter
softer

Ō′ful
woeful

āle, câre, ădd, ärm, ăsk; mē, hĕre, ĕnd; īce, ĭll;

Ô'ful
awful
lawful
unlawful

ÔF'ur
chauffeur
gopher
loafer
Ophir

ŌG'a
Saratoga
snoga
Ticonderoga
toga
yoga

ÔG'a
Chicamauga
Sylacauga

ŌG'al
dogal

ŎG'al
synagogal

ŌG'an
brogan
Hogan
slogan

ŌG'an
toboggan

ŌG'ē
bogey
bogie

dogie
fogey
stogie
yogi

ŎG'ē
boggy
cloggy
doggy
foggy
froggy
groggy
joggy
soggy

ŎG'in
noggin

ŎG'ing
befogging
bogging
clogging
cogging
dogging
flogging
fogging
jogging
nogging
slogging
togging
unclogging

ŎG'ish
doggish
hoggish

ŌG'ish
roguish

ŌG''l
bogle
fogle
ogle

ŎG''l
boondoggle
boggle
coggle
goggle
joggle
toggle

ŎG'ling
boondoggling
boggling
goggling
joggling

ŌG'lur
ogler

ŎG'lʋr
boondoggler
boggler
goggler
joggler

ŎG'mīr
quagmire

ŌG'ram
deprogram
fogram
program

ŌG'res
ogress
progress

ŎG'res
progress

ŎG'trot
dog-trot
jog-trot

ŌG'ur
ogre

ÔG'ūr
auger
augur
inaugur
mauger

ŎG'ur
befogger
cataloger
clogger
cogger
dogger
flogger
hogger
jogger
logger
pettifogger
slogger
togger
wholehogger

ŌG'us
bogus

ÔG'ust
August

ŎG'wood
bog-wood

dogwood
logwood

Ō'hen
Cohen

Ō'hunk
Bohunk

OI'al
chapel-royal
disloyal
loyal
pennyroyal
royal
sur-royal

OI'ans
annoyance
buoyance
clairvoyance
joyance

OI'ant
annoyant
buoyant
chatoyant
clairvoyant
flamboyant
prevoyant

OI'b'l
foible

OID'al
asteroidal
colloidal
conchoidal
conoidal

coralloidal
crinoidal
cycloidal
dendroidal
discoidal
elephantoidal
ellipsoidal
ethnoidal
ganoidal
hemispheroidal
lithoidal
metalloidal
negroidal
ooidal
ovoidal
paraboloidal
planetoidal
prismatoidal
prismoidal
rhomboidal
saccharoidal
sigmoidal
spheroidal
trochoidal
typhoidal

OID'ans
avoidance

OID'ed
avoided
voided

OID'en
hoyden

OID'ur
avoider
broider

embroider
moider
voider

OI'ē
employee

OI'est
annoyest
buoyest
cloyest
convoyest
coyest
decoyest
deployest
destroyest
employest
enjoyest
joyest
toyest

OI'eth
annoyeth
buoyeth
cloyeth
convoyeth
decoyeth
destroyeth
employeth
enjoyeth
joyeth
toyeth

OI'ful
joyful

OI'ij
alloyage
buoyage

voyage

OI'ing
annoying
buoying
cloying
convoying
decoying
deploying
destroying
employing
enjoying
joying
toying

OI'ish
boyish
coyish
toyish

Ō'ij
flowage
stowage
towage

Ō'ik
azoic
benzoic
Cenozoic
dichroic
dyspnoic
Eozoic
heroic
hylozoic
hypozoic
melanochroic
Mesozoic
mock-heroic
Neozoic

āle,   câre,   ădd,   ärm,   ăsk;   mē,   hĕre,   ĕnd;   īce,   ĭll;

Palaeozoic
pleochroic
protozoic
Stoic
Troic
xanthochroic

OIK'a
perestroika
troika

OIL'ē
coyly
doily
oily
roily

OIL'est
boilest
broilest
coilest
despoilest
embroilest
foilest
recoilest
roilest
soilest
spoilest
toilest
uncoilest

OIL'et
oillet
toilet

OIL'eth
boileth
broileth
coileth

despoileth
embroileth
foileth
recoileth
roileth
soileth
spoileth
toileth
uncoileth

OIL'ing
assoiling
boiling
broiling
coiling
despoiling
embroiling
foiling
moiling
oiling
recoiling
soiling
spoiling
toiling
uncoiling

OIL'ment
despoilment
embroilment
recoilment

OIL'ur
boiler
broiler
coiler
despoiler
embroiler
foiler
oiler

recoiler
soiler
spoiler
toiler
uncoiler

OI'man
decoy man
hoyman
toyman

OI'ment
deployment
employment
enjoyment

OIN'dur
rejoinder

OI'nes
coyness

Ō'ing
bestowing
blowing
bowing
churchgoing
cock crowing
concertgoing
crowing
easygoing
flowing
foregoing
foreknowing
foreshowing
glass blowing
glowing
going
growing

helloing
hoeing
inflowing
ingoing
ingrowing
knowing
lowing
moviegoing
mowing
oboeing
ongoing
outflowing
outgoing
outgrowing
overcrowing
overflowing
overgrowing
overthrowing
owing
rowing
seagoing
self-knowing
sewing
showing
slowing
snowing
sowing
stowing
strowing
theatergoing
thoroughgoing
throwing
toeing
towing
undergoing
undertowing
unknowing
unflowing
upgrowing

ōld, ôr, ŏdd, oil, fŏŏt, out; ūse, ûrn, ŭp; THis, thin

Ô'ing
awing
begnawing
cawing
chawing
clawing
drawing
gnawing
guffawing
heehawing
jawing
lawing
outlawing
overawing
overdrawing
pawing
pshawing
sawing
thawing
wiredrawing
withdrawing
yawing

OIN'ij
coinage

OIN'ing
adjoining
coining
conjoining
disjoining
enjoining
groining
joining
purloining
rejoining
subjoining

OIN'ted

anointed
appointed
conjointed
disappointed
disjointed
jointed
pointed
unanointed
unjointed
unpointed

OIN'ting
anointing
appointing
disappointing
disjointing
jointing
pointing

OINT'les
jointless
pointless

OINT'ment
anointment
appointment
disappointment
disjointment
ointment

OINT'tur
anointer
appointer
disappointer
disjointer
jointer
pointer

OIN'ur

coiner
conjoiner
enjoiner
joiner
purloiner
rejoiner

OI'ride
joyride

Ō'is
Lois

Ō'ish
showish
snowish

OIS'ing
rejoicing
voicing
unrejoicing

OIS'les
choiceless
voiceless

OI'som
noisome
toysome

OIS'tē
foisty
moisty

OI'stick
joystick

OIS'ting
foisting

hoisting
joisting

OIS'tral
cloistral
coystrel

OIS'tur
cloister
encloister
foister
hoister
moister
oyster
pearl oyster
royster
uncloister

OIT'ē
dacoity
hoity-toity

OIT'ed
doited
exploited

OIT'ring
loitering
reconnoitring

OIT'ŭr
exploiture
voiture

OIT'ŭr
adroiter
exploiter
gloiter
loiter
reconnoiter

āle, câre, ădd, ärm, ăsk; mē, hĕre, ĕnd; īce, ĭll;

OI′ur
annoyer
Boyar
Boyer
coyer
decoyer
deployer
destroyer
employer
enjoyer
self-destroyer
toyer

OI′us
joyous

OIZ′ē
Boise
noisy

OIZ′ez
boyses
noises
poises

OIZ′ing
noising
poising

OIZ′on
empoison
foison
poison
toison

OIZ′onz
foisons
poisons
(See also

OIZ′on; add
-*s* where
appropriate.)

Ō′jan
Trojan

ŎJ′ez
dodges
Hodges
(See also ŎJ;
add -*s* where
appropriate.)

ŎJ′e
anagoge
apagoge
èpagoge
paragoge

ŎJ′ē
pedagogy
podgy
stodgy

ŎJ′ik
acrologic
aerologic
agogic
agrologic
anagogic
anthropologic
apagogic
archaeologic
astrologic
biologic
catalogic
choplogic
chronologic

cosmologic
curiologic
cytologic
demagogic
demonologic
dialogic
entomologic
epagogic
epilogic
ethnologic
ethologic
etymologic
eulogic
geologic
gnomologic
hierologic
histologic
hogiologic
homologic
horologic
hydrologic
hypnagogic
hypnogogic
hypnologic
ichthyologic
idealogic
isagogic
lexicologic
lithologic
logic
martyrologic
metalogic
meteorologic
micrologic
mineralogic
morphologic
mycologic
myologic
mystagogic

mythologic
necrologic
neologic
ontologic
ophiologic
paragogic
pathologic
pedagogic
philologic
phonologic
photologic
phraseologic
physiologic
phytologic
psychagogic
psychologic
sarcologic
sialagogic
sociologic
tautologic
theologic
toxicologic
tropologic
zoologic
zymologic

ŎJ′iks
pedagogics
(See also ŎJ′ik;
add -*s* where
appropriate.)

ŎJ′ing
dislodging
dodging
lodging

ŎJ′ur
codger

ōld, ôr, ŏdd, oil, fŏŏt, out; ūse, ûrn, ŭp; THis, thin

dislodger
dodger
lodger
Roger

ŎJ'urn
sojourn

Ō'kā
croquet
roquet

ŌK'a
coca
tapioca

ŌK'al
bocal
focal
local
phocal
socle
vocal
yokel

ŎK'ē
choky
cokey
croaky
hokey
joky
Loki
moky
oaky
okeydokey
poky
roky
slowpoky
smoky

soaky
yoky
(See also
ŌK'e.)

ŌK'ē
balky
chalky
gawky
Milwaukee
pawky
squawky
stalky
talkie
talky
walkie

ŎK'ē
cocky
crocky
disc jockey
flocky
hockey
jockey
locky
rocky
stocky
video jockey

ŌK'e
troche
trochee
(See also
ŌK'ē.)

ŌK'en
bespoken
betoken
broken

fair-spoken
fine-spoken
forespoken
foretoken
freespoken
heartbroken
Hoboken
oaken
outspoken
soft-spoken
spoken
token
unbroken
unspoken

ŎK'en
Brocken

ŌK'est
chokest
cloakest
convokest
croakest
evokest
invokest
jokest
provokest
revokest
smokest
soakest
spokest
unyokest
yokest

ÔK'est
balkest
stalkest
talkest
walkest

ŎK'est
bemockest
blockest
dockest
flockest
knockest
lockest
mockest
rockest
sockest
shockest
smockest
stockest
unfrockest
unlockest

ŎK'et
air pocket
brocket
cocket
crocket
Crockett
docket
impocket
locket
Lockett
pickpocket
pocket
rocket
skyrocket
socket
sprocket

ŌK'eth
choketh
cloaketh
convoketh
croaketh
evoketh

invoketh
joketh
poketh
provoketh
revoketh
smoketh
soaketh
spoketh
unyoketh
yoketh

ÔK′eth
balketh
stalketh
talketh
walketh

ŎK′eth
bemocketh
blocketh
docketh
flocketh
knocketh
locketh
mocketh
rocketh
shocketh
smocketh
stocketh
unlocketh

ŎK′hed
blockhead
shock-head

ŎK′īd
cockeyed

ŎK′ij

brokage
cloakage
soakage

ŎK′ij
dockage
lockage
soccage

ŌK′ing
besmoking
choking
cloaking
convoking
croaking
evoking
invoking
joking
poking
provoking
revoking
smoking
soaking
stoking
stroking
troching
uncloaking
yoking

ÔK′ing
balking
calking
hawking
jaywalking
squawking
stalking
talking
walking

ŎK′ing
bemocking
blocking
clocking
cocking
docking
flocking
hocking
interlocking
knocking
locking
mocking
rocking
shocking
smocking
stocking
unlocking

ÔK′inz
Dawkins
Hawkins

ÔK′ish
hawkish
mawkish

ŎK′ish
blockish
cockish
mockish
stockish

ŎK′′l
cockle
hockle
socle
strockle

ÔK′les

cloakless
jokeless
smokeless
yokeless
yolkless

ŎK′ling
cockling
flockling
rockling

ŌK′lôr
folklore

ŎK′man
Brockman
lockman
socman

ŌK′ment
invokement
provokement
revokement

ŎK′nē
cockney

Ō′Kō
baroco
coco
cocoa
koko
loco
locofoco
rococo
troco
Yoko

ŎK′ō
Morocco

sirocco

obnoxious

oxer

evoker
invoker

ŎK'pôrt
Brockport
Lockport
Stockport

ŎK'ra
okra

ŎK'sē
cacodoxy
Coxey
doxy
foxy
heterodoxy
orthodoxy
paradoxy
proxy

**ŎK'sen,
ŎK's'n**
cockswain
oxen

ŎK'shal
equinoctial
trinoctial

ÔK'shun
auction

ŎK'shun
concoction
decoction

ŎK'shus
innoxious
noxious

ŎK'sīd
dioxide
fox-eyed
monoxide
ox-eyed
oxide
peroxide
trioxide

ŎK'sin
aflatoxin
antitoxin
coxswain
toxin
tocsin

ŌK'sing
coaxing
hoaxing

ŎK'sing
boxing
foxing

ŌKS'man
spokesman
strokesman

ŌK'smith
jokesmith

ŌK'sur
coaxer
hoaxer

ŎK'sur
boxer

ŎK'tīl
coctile
trioctile

ŎK'tiv
concoctive
decoctive

ŎK'ton
Blockton
Brockton
Stockton

ŎK'trin
doctrine

ŎK'tur
concocter
doctor
proctor

ŎK'turn
nocturne

Ō'kum
hokum
oakum

Ō'kund
jocund

ŌK'ur
broker
choker
cloaker
convoker
croaker

joker
mediocre
ocher
poker
provoker
revoker
smoker
soaker
stoker
stroker
uncloaker
yoker

ÔK'ur
balker
calker
deerstalker
gawker
hawker
jaywalker
shop-walker
sleepwalker
squawker
stalker
streetwalker
talker
tomahawker
walker

ŎK'ur
blocker
cocker
crocker
docker
Fokker
hougher
Knickerbocker

āle, câre, ădd, ärm, ăsk; mē, hĕre, ĕnd; īce, ĭll;

knocker
locker
mocker
rocker
shocker
soccer
socker
stocker

ŎK′urz
dockers
knickerbockers
(See also
ŎK′ur; add
-s where
appropriate.)

Ō′kus
crocus
focus
hocus
hocus-pocus
Hohokus
locus

ÔK′us
caucus
Daucus
glaucous
raucous

Ō′kust
focussed
locust

ÔK′ward
awkward

Ō′la

Angola
Appalachicola
ayatollah
carambola
Coca-Cola
gola
gondola
Gorgonzola
kola
Leola
Maizola
Pensacola
Ramola
scagliola
stola
viola
Zola

ÔL′a
Eufaula
Guatemala
Paula

ŎL′a
corolla
holla
mollah

ŌL′ak
Polack

ŌL′an
Dolan
Nolan

Ō′land
Boland
Bowland
lowland

Noland
Roland
Rowland

ŌL′ard
bollard
collard
collared
dollared
Lollard
pollard
scollard

ŎL′as
solace

ÔL′chun
falchion

ÔL′da
Alda

ŌL′dē
foldy
moldy

ŌL′ded
blindfolded
enfolded
infolded
manifolded
molded
refolded
scolded
unfolded

ŌL′den
beholden
embolden
golden

holden
misbeholden
olden
withholden

ÔL′den
Alden

ŌL′dest
beholdest
boldest
coldest
enfoldest
foldest
holdest
infoldest
interfoldest
moldest
oldest
refoldest
scoldest
unfoldest
upholdest
withholdest

ÔL′dest
baldest
scaldest

ŌL′deth
beholdeth
enfoldeth
foldeth
holdeth
infoldeth
interfoldeth
moldeth
refoldeth
scoldeth

unfoldeth
upholdeth
withholdeth

ŌL'deth
scaldeth

ŌLD'ham
Oldham

ŌL'ding
beholding
enfolding
folding
holding
infolding
interfolding
molding
refolding
scolding
slaveholding
unfolding
upholding
weather-
  molding
withholding

ÔL'ding
Balding
Paulding
scalding
Spaulding

ŌL'dish
coldish
oldish

ŌLD'lē
boldly

coldly
manifoldly

ŌLD'man
Goldman
Oldman

ŌLD'ment
enfoldment
withholdment

ŌLD'nes
boldness
coldness
oldness

ÔLD'ron
caldron
pauldron

ŌL'drumz
doldrums

ŌLD'smith
Goldsmith

ŌL'dur
beholder
billholder
bolder
bondholder
bottleholder
boulder
candeholder
cold shoulder
cold-shoulder
colder
copyholder
enfolder

folder
freeholder
gasholder
holder
householder
infolder
interfolder
landholder
leaseholder
manifolder
molder
older
pattern-molder
polder
refolder
scolder
shareholder
shoulder
slaveholder
smallholder
smolder
stadtholder
stockholder
unfolder
upholder
withholder

ÔL'dur
alder
balder
Baldur
scalder

ÔL'durd
bouldered
broad-
  shouldered
moldered
shouldered

smoldered

ÔLD'win
Baldwin

ŌL'ē
coaly
holy
lowly
moly
roly-poly
shoaly
slowly
unholy
(See also
ŌL'lē.)

ÔL'ē
Macaulay
Macauley
sprawly
squally
whally

ŎL'ē
Bali
collie
dolly
folly
golly
Holley
holly
jolly
Kali
loblolly
melancholy
Molly
Ollie
Polly

rolley
Trolley
trolley
volley

ŎL'ēg
colleague

ŎL'ej
acknowledge
college
foreknowledge
knowledge
self-knowledge

ŎL'ejd
acknowledged
unacknowl-
　edged

**ŎL'em,
ŎL'um**
column
solemn

ŌL'en
stolen
swollen

ÔL'en
chopfallen
fallen
windfallen

ŎL'ent
equipollent
prepollent

Ô'les

clawless
flawless
jawless
lawless
mawless
sawless

ŌL'est
bowlest
cajolest
condolest
consolest
controllest
dolest
drollest
enrollest
patrollest
pollest
rollest
strollest
tollest
trollest
unrollest
uprollest

ÔL'est
bawlest
bemawlest
brawlest
callest
crawlest
drawlest
enthrallest
forestallest
maulest
scrawlest
smallest
sprawlest
squallest

tallest

ŎL'et
collet
La Follette
walleth

ŌL'eth
bowleth
cajoleth
condoleth
consoleth
controlleth
doleth
enrolleth
patrolleth
polleth
rolleth
strolleth
tolleth
trolleth
unrolleth
uprolleth

ÔL'eth
bawleth
bemawleth
brawleth
calleth
crawleth
drawleth
enthralleth
forestalleth
mauleth
scrawleth
sprawleth
squalleth

ŎL'fin

dolphin

ŎL'fing
golfing

ŌL'ful
bowlful
doleful
soulful

ŎL'fur
golfer

ŎL'fus
Adolphus
Rodolphus
Rudolphus

ŌL'hous
poll house
tollhouse

ŎL'id
olid
solid
squalid
stolid

Ō'līf
lowlife

ÔL'ij
hallage
haulage
stallage

ÔL'ik
aulic
Gallic

ōld, ôr, ŏdd, oil, fŏŏt, out; ūse, ûrn, ŭp; THis, thin

hydraulic
interaulic

ŎL'ik
Aeolic
alcoholic
apostolic
bibliopolic
bucolic
carbolic
colic
diabolic
diastolic
embolic
epipolic
epistolic
frolic
hyperbolic
melancholic
metabolic
parabolic
petrolic
rollick
symbolic
systolic
variolic
vicar-apostolic
vitriolic

ÔL'in
tarpaulin

ŌL'ing
bolling
bowling
cajoling
caracoling
coaling
condoling

consoling
controlling
doling
drolling
enrolling
extolling
foaling
holing
inscrolling
parolling
patrolling
poling
rolling
shoaling
strolling
tolling
trolling
unrolling
uprolling

ÔL'ing
appalling
balling
bawling
befalling
bemawling
blackballing
brawling
calling
caterwauling
crawling
drawling
enthralling
falling
footballing
forestalling
galling
hauling
installing

mauling
miscalling
overhauling
palling
Pawling
recalling
scrawling
snowballing
sprawling
squalling
thralling
trawling
walling

ŎL'ing
caracolling
extolling
lolling

ŎL'inz
Collins
Hollins
Rollins

ŎL'is
Collis
Cornwallis
Hollis
Wallace
Wallis

ŌL'ish
drollish
Polish

ÔL'ish
Gaulish
smallish
squallish

tallish

ŎL'ish
abolish
demolish
polish

ŎL'isht
abolished
demolished
polished
unpolished

ŎL'iv
olive

ŌL'jur
soldier

ŎL'ka
polka

ÔL'kon
falcon
gerfalcon
soar falcon
sorefalcon

ÔLK'nur
falconer

ŌL'lē
drolly
solely
wholly
(See also
ŌL'ē.)

ŌL'man
coal man

āle, câre, ădd, ärm, ăsk; mē, hēre, ĕnd; īce, ĭll;

Coleman
Colman
Holman
tollman

ŌL'ment
cajolement
condolement
controlment
enrollment

ÔL'ment
appallment
disenthrall-
  ment
enthrallment
epaulement
instalment
installment

ÔL'mōst
almost

ŌL'nes
drollness
soleness
wholeness

ÔL'nes
allness
smallness
tallness

Ō'lō
kolo
polo
solo

ŎL'ō

Apollo
follow
hollo
hollow
swallow
wallow

Ō'lok
Moloch
rowlock

ŌL'on
colon
eidolon
semicolon
Solon
stolon
(See also
ŌL'an,
ŌL'en.)

ŎL'op
collop
dollop
escalop
lollop
scallop
trollop
wallop

ŌL'or
dolor

ÔL'sēd
palsied

ÔLS'hŏŏd
falsehood

ÔLS'ness
falseness

ÔL'sō
also

ŌL'som
dolesome
wholesome

ŌL'son
Jolson
Olsen
Olson
Tolson
Toulson

ŌL'stär
polestar

ÔL'stōn
gallstone

ÔL'ston
Alston
Balston
Ralston

ŌL'stur
bolster
holster
upholster

ÔL'tē
faulty
malty
salty
vaulty

ŌL'ted

bolted
jolted
molted
revolted
unbolted

ÔL'ted
assaulted
defaulted
exalted
faulted
halted
malted
salted
vaulted

ŌL'ten
molten

ŌL'test
boltest
(See also ŌLT;
add -*est* where
appropriate.)

ÔL'test
assaultest
defaultest
exaltest
haltest
vaultest

ŌL'teth
bolteth
(See also ŌLT;
add -*eth* where
appropriate.)

ÔL'teth
assaulteth

ōld, ôr, ŏdd, oil, fŏŏt, out; ūse, ûrn, ŭp; THis, thin

defaulteth	**ÔLT'les**	vaulter	stroller
exalteth	faultless	Walter	toller
halteth	maltless		troller
vaulteth	saltless	**ÔL'turn**	unipolar
		saltern	unroller
ŌL'tij	**ŌL'ton**	subaltern	uproller
voltage	Bolton		
	Colton	**ÔLT'sur**	**ÔL'ur**
ÔL'tij	Moulton	waltzer	bawler
maltage			bemawler
vaultage	**ÔL'ton**	**ŌL'ūm**	brawler
	Dalton	colyum	caller
ÔL'tik	Walton	volume	crawler
asphaltic			drawler
Baltic	**ŌL'trē**	**ŌL'um**	enthraller
basaltic	poultry	column	faller
cobaltic		solemn	footballer
peristaltic	**ÔL'tur**		forestaller
	bolter	**ŌL'ur**	hauler
ŌL'ting	colter	bowler	mauler
bolting	jolter	cajoler	scrawler
jolting	revolter	circumpolar	smaller
molting	unbolter	coaler	sprawler
revolting		condoler	squaller
unbolting	**ÔL'tur**	consoler	taller
	altar	controller	trawler
ÔL'ting	alter	doler	
assaulting	assaulter	dolor	**ŎL'ur**
defaulting	defaulter	droller	blue-collar
exalting	exalter	enroller	choler
faulting	falter	molar	collar
halting	Gibraltar	patroller	dollar
malting	halter	polar	Eurodollar
salting	malter	poler	extoller
vaulting	McWalter	poller	loller
	palter	roller	pink-collar
ŌL'tish	psalter	scroller	scholar
coltish	Salter	shoaler	sollar
doltish	unalter	solar	squalor

white-collar

ŌL′us
bolus
holus-bolus
solus

ŎL′usk
mollusk

ŎL′vent
dissolvent
evolvent
insolvent
resolvent
solvent

ŎL′vest
absolvest
devolvest
dissolvest
evolvest
involvest
resolvest
revolvest
solvest

ŎL′veth
absolveth
devolveth
dissolveth
evolveth
involveth
resolveth
revolveth
solveth

ŎL′ving
absolving

devolving
dissolving
evolving
involving
resolving
revolving
solving

ŎLV′ment
devolvement
evolvement
involvement

ŎL′vur
absolver
dissolver
evolver
involver
resolver
revolver
solver

ÔL′wart
stalwart

ÔL′wāz
always
hallways

Ō′ma
aboma
aroma
coma
diploma
Natoma
sarcoma
Roma
Sonoma
Tacoma

theobroma
zygoma

ŎM′a
comma
momma

Ō′mad
nomad
ohmad

Ō′man
bowman
foeman
Roman
showman
snowman
yeoman

ŎM′as
Thomas

ŎM′bat
combat
wombat

ŎM′bē
Abercrombie
Dombey
zombie

ŎM′brus
sombrous

ŎM′bur
hombre
omber
Scomber
somber

ŌM′ē
foamy
homy
loamy

ŎM′ē
mommy
Tommie

ŌM′en,
Ō′men
abdomen
agnomen
bowmen
cognomen
foemen
omen
praenomen
yeomen

ŌM′end
ill-omened
omened

Ō′ment
bestowment
moment

ŎM′et
comet
domett
grommet

ŎM′ij
homage

ŎM′ik
bromic
chromic

ōld, ôr, ŏdd, oil, fŏŏt, out; ūse, ûrn, ŭp; THis,   thin

gnomic
hydrobromic
polychromic

ŌM'ik
agronomic
anatomic
astronomic
atomic
autonomic
cinnamomic
comic
diatomic
dystomic
economic
entomic
gastronomic
heliochromic
isonomic
metronomic
microtomic
monatomic
nomic
orthodromic
palindromic
phantomic
physiognomic
seriocomic
stereochromic
stereotomic
taxonomic
tragicomic
triatomic
vomic

ŎM'iks
economics
phoronomics

ŌM'īn
bromine
theobromine

ŌM'ing
befoaming
coaming
combing
foaming
gloaming
homing
roaming

ŌM'is
promise

ŌM'ish
Romish

ŌM'lē
homely

ŌM'les
combless
foamless
homeless

ŌM'let
homelet
tomelet

ŌM'let
omelet

Ō'mō
chromo
Como
Ecce Homo
major domo

ŎM'on
common

ŎM'pē
Pompey

ŎMP'ish
rompish
swampish

ŎM'plish
accomplish

ŎMP'ted
prompted
unprompted

ŎMP'ton
Brompton
Compton
Lecompton

ŎMP'us
pompous

ŌM'spŭn
homespun

ŌM'sted
homestead

ŌM'ur
beachcomber
comber
gomer
homer
Homer
misnomer
omer

roamer
vomer
wool comber

ŎM'ur
bomber

ŎM'urs
commerce

ŌM'ward
homeward

Ō'na
annona
Arizona
Barcelona
Bellona
Bologna
cinchona
corona
Cremona
Desdemona
Iona
Jonah
mona
Nona
Pomona
Ramona
Rosh Hashanah
Zona

ÔN'a
Mauna

ŎN'a
belladonna
donna
Madonna

---

prima donna

ŌN′al
coronal
hormonal
subumbonal
tonal
zonal

ŎN′ald
Donald
McDonald
Ronald

ŌN′ant
intersonant
sonant
(See also
ŎN′ent.)

ŎN′ark
monarch

ŌN′as
Jonas

ŌN′āt
donate
zonate

ŎN′chō
honcho
poncho

ŎN′da
anaconda

ÔN′dē
arrondi

ŎN′dē
dispondee
spondee

ŎN′ded
absconded
bonded
corresponded
desponded
responded

ŌN′def
stone-deaf
tone-deaf

ŎN′del
rondel

ŎN′dens
correspon-
    dence
despondence
respondence

ŎN′dent
co-respondent
correspondent
despondent
frondent
respondent

ŎN′dest
abscondest
bondest
correspondest
fondest
respondest

ŎN′deth

abscondeth
bondeth
correspondeth
respondeth

ŎN′dij
bondage
frondage
vagabondage

ŎN′ding
absconding
corresponding
desponding
responding

ŎN′d′l
fondle
rondle

ŎND′lē
fondly

ŎND′ling
bondling
fondling

ŎND′nes
blondness
fondness

ŎN′dō
condo
Hondo
mondo
rondeau
rondo
tondo

ŎN′dur
absconder
bonder
corresponder
desponder
fonder
hypochonder
ponder
responder
squander
wander
yonder

ÔN′durz
Saunders

Ō′nē
alimony
aloney
antimony
baloney
bologney
bony
cicerone
Coney
cony
crony
drony
lazzaroni
macaroni
Mahoney
Maloney
matrimony
parsimony
patrimony
phony
pony
sanctimony
stony

testimony
tony

ŌN′ē
brawny
lawny
mulligatawny
orange-tawny
Pawnee
Punxatawnee
sawney
scrawny
Sewanee
Shawnee
Swanee
tawny
yawny

ŎN′ē
bonnie
Bonnie
bonny
Connie
Lonnie
Renee
Ronnie

ŌN′ent
component
deponent
exponent
interponent
opponent
proponent

Ō′nes
lowness
slowness

ŌN′est
atonest
bemoanest
condonest
dethronest
disownest
dronest
enthronest
groanest
intonest
honest
loanest
lonest
moanest
ownest
postponest
stonest
thronest
tonest

ŎN′est
connest
dishonest
donnest
honest
non-est
wannest

ŎN′et
bonnet
sonnet
unbonnet

ŌN′eth
atoneth
begroaneth
bemoaneth
condoneth
dethroneth

disowneth
droneth
enthroneth
groaneth
honeth
intoneth
loaneth
moaneth
owneth
postponeth
stoneth
throneth
toneth

ŎNG′est
longest
strongest

ŎNG′ful
songful
throngful
wrongful

ŎNG′gō
Bongo
Congo

ŎNG′gur
conger
longer

ŎNG′ing
belonging
longing
prolonging
thronging
wronging

ŎNG′ish

longish
prongish
songish
strongish

ŎNG′kē
donkey

ŎNG′kur
conker
conquer

ŎNG′kurz
conquers
Yonkers

ŎNG′lē
longly
strongly
wrongly

ŎNG′nes
longness
wrongness

ŎNG′stur
songster

ŎNG′ur
prolonger
wronger

ŎNG′wāv
long-wave

ŌN′hed
bonehead

ŌN′ik
phonic

zonic

ÔN'ik
Aaronic
aconic
acronyc
Adonic
adonic
agonic
algedonic
ammonic
Amphictyonic
anachronic
anharmonic
anilonic
anticyclonic
antiphonic
aphonic
architectonic
atonic
avilonic
Babylonic
benthonic
bionic
Brythonic
bubonic
Byronic
cacophonic
canonic
carbonic
cataphonic
Chalcedonic
chameleonic
chelidonic
chronic
chthonic
clonic
colophonic

conic
cosmogonic
crotonic
cyclonic
daemonic
demonic
diachronic
diaphonic
diatonic
dodecaphonic
draconic
electronic
electrotonic
embryonic
enharmonic
epitomic
eudaemonic
euphonic
freemasonic
gallionic
ganglionic
geogonic
geoponic
geotectonic
glottoglonic
gnathonic
gnominic
harmonic
hedonic
hegemonic
histrionic
homophonic
Housatonic
hydroponic
hypertonic
hypotonic
iconic
infrasonic
interganglionic

Ionic
ironic
isogonic
isotonic
Japonic
jargonic
laconic
macaronic
masonic
megaphonic
Metonic
microelectronic
microphonic
Miltonic
mnemonic
monochronic
monophonic
monotonic
moronic
Napoleonic
neoplatonic
nonharmonic
nucleonic
obconic
Olympionic
ozonic
paeonic
pantheonic
paratonic
parsonic
pathognomonic
pentatonic
Pharaonic
philharmonic
phonic
photophonic
phototonic
planktonic
Platonic

Plutonic
pneumonic
polyconic
polygonic
polyphonic
polytonic
protonic
pulmonic
Pyrrhonic
pythonic
quadraphonic
radiophonic
sardonic
saxophonic
semitonic
sermonic
siphonic
Slavonic
Solomonic
sonic
stentoronic
stentorophonic
stratonic
subsonic
subtonic
supersonic
supertonic
symphonic
synchronic
syntonic
tectonic
telephonic
Teutonic
theogonic
thermionic
thionic
tonic
transonic
Tychonic

---

typhonic
ultrasonic
unharmonic
xylophonic
yonic
zoonic

ŎN'iks
geoponics
hedonics
histrionics
Megalonyx
mnemonics
onyx
sonics

ŌN'ing
atoning
bemoaning
boning
dethroning
disowning
droning
enthroning
groaning
intoning
moaning
owning
postponing
stoning
throning
toning

ÔN'ing
awning
dawning
fawning
pawning
spawning

undawning
yawning

ŎN'ing
conning
donning

ŌN'is
Adonis
Coronis

ŌN'ish
Babylonish
dronish

ŎN'ish
admonish
astonish
tonnish
wannish

ŎN'jē
congee
pongee

ŌN'lē
lonely
only

ŌN'les
boneless
throneless
toneless
zoneless

ŌN'ment
atonement
condonement
dethronement
disownment

enthronement
postponement

ŌN'nes
knownness
loneness
proneness
unknownness

ŌN'ôr
donor
(See also
ŌN'ur.)

ŎN'rad
Conrad

ŎN'shens
conscience

ŎN'shus
conscious
self-conscious
sub-conscious

ŎN'siv
corresponsive
irresponsive
responsive

ŌN'som
lonesome

ŎN'son
Johnson
Jonson

ŎN'sôr
sponsor

tonsor

ŎN'stant
constant
inconstant

ŎN'ston
Johnston

ŎN'strans
monstrance
remonstrance

ŎN'strāt
demonstrate
remonstrate

ŎN'strous
monstrous

ŎN'stur
monster

ŎN'tal
fontal
frontal
horizontal
peridontal

ŎN'tan
cismontane
tramontane
ultramontane

ÔN'tē
flaunty
jaunty

ÔN'ted
daunted

āle,   câre,   ădd,   ärm,   ăsk;   mē,   hĕre,   ĕnd;   īce,   ĭll;

flaunted	mastodontic	**ÔN'tur**	conner
haunted	pontic	daunter	Connor
taunted	quantic	flaunter	dishonor
undaunted		gaunter	goner
vaunted	**ŎN'tīn**	haunter	honor
wanted	dracontine	saunter	O'Conner
	Hellespontine	taunter	O'Connor
ŎN'ted	pontine	vaunter	wanner
wanted			
	ÔN'ting	**ŌN'ur**	**ŎN'urd**
ÔN'test	daunting	atoner	dishonored
dauntest	flaunting	bemoaner	honored
flauntest	haunting	boner	time-honored
hauntest	jaunting	condoner	unhonored
tauntest	taunting	dethroner	
vauntest	vaunting	droner	**ŎN'urz**
wantest	wanting	groaner	Conners
		honer	Connors
ÔN'teth	**ŎN'ting**	intoner	honors
daunteth	wanting	moaner	O'Connors
flaunteth		owner	
haunteth	**ÔNT'les**	phoner	**Ō'nus**
taunteth	dauntless	postponer	bonus
vaunteth	tauntless	telephoner	onus
wanteth	vauntless	stoner	tonous
		(See also	
ŎN'tif	**ÔNT'let**	ÔN'ôr.)	**ŎN'yard**
pontiff	gantlet		poniard
	gauntlet	**ÔN'ur**	
ÔN'tij		awner	**ŎN'zō**
wantage	**ŎN'ton**	barley-awner	Alonzo
	wanton	brawner	Alphonso
ŎN'tij		fawner	Alphonzo
pontage	**ŎN'trīt**	pawner	
wantage	contrite	spawner	**Ō'on**
	uncontrite	yawner	entozoon
ŎN'tik			epizoon
Anacreontic	**ŎN'tum**	**ŎN'ur**	phytozoon
archontic	quantum	Bonner	zoon

ōld, ôr, ŏdd, oil, fŏŏt, out; ūse, ûrn, ŭp; THis, thin

OŎD'ed
hooded
wooded

OŎD'en
wooden

OŎD'ē
goody
goody-goody
woody

OŎD'ing
gooding
hooding
pudding

OŎD'ish
goodish

OŎD'lē
goodly

OŎD'man
goodman
hoodman
woodman

OŎD'nes
goodness

OŎG'ur
sugar

OŎK'ē
bookie
cookie
hookey
hooky

rooky

OŎK'ed
crooked
(See OŎK;
add -ed where
appropriate.)

OŎK'ing
booking
brooking
cooking
crooking
hooking
ill-looking
looking
overlooking
rooking
unhooking
well-looking

OŎK'let
booklet
brooklet

OŎK'up
hookup

OŎK'ur
cooker
hooker
looker
overlooker
stooker

OŎL'bul
bulbul

OŎL'ē

bully
fully
pulley
woolly

OŎL'ēd
bullied

OŎL'en
woollen

OŎL'et
bullet
pullet

OŎL'ing
bulling
pulling

OŎL'ish
bullish
fullish

OŎL'man
Pullman
Woolman

OŎL'nes
fullness

OŎL'ur
buller
fuller
puller
wire-puller

OŎM'an
anchorwoman
bagwoman

chairwoman
charwoman
forewoman
spokeswoman
woman

OŎ'sē
pussy

OŎT'ed
barefooted
black-footed
catfooted
claw-footed
cloven-footed
clubfooted
duckfooted
flat-footed
fleet-footed
footed
four-footed
hotfooted
left-footed
light-footed
nimble-footed
pussyfooted
right-footed
splayfooted
surefooted
web-footed
wing-footed

OŎT'ing
footing
putting

OŎT'ur
footer
putter

āle, câre, ădd, ärm, ăsk; mē, hĕre, ĕnd; īce, ĭll;

Ō′pa   *elopest*   *loppeth*   electroscopic
Europa   *gropest*   *moppeth*   endotropic
                  hopest   *poppeth*   entopic
Ō′pal, Ō′p'l *interlopest*   *proppeth*   Ethiopic
Adrianople   *mopest*   *·shoppeth*   eurytopic
Bhopal   *ropest*   *stoppeth*   fluoroscopic
Constantinople   *soapest*   *toppeth*   galvanoscopic
nopal   geoscopic
opal   **ŎP′est**   **ŌP′ful**   geotropic
                  choppest   hopeful   gyroscopic
Ō′paz   *droppest*   unhopeful   hagioscopic
topaz   *hoppest*   helioscopic
                  loppest   **ŎP′hed**   heliotropic
ŌP′ē   *moppest*   hophead   heterotopic
dopey   *overtoppest*   horoscopic
mopy   *poppest*   **ŎP′ī**   hydropic
ropy   *proppest*   Popeye   hydroscopic
slopy   *shoppest*   hydrotropic
soapy   *stoppest*   **ŎP′ij**   hygroscopic
                  toppest   proppage   idiotropic
ŎP′ē   stoppage   inotropic
choppy   **ŎP′et**   isentropic
copy   moppet   **ŎP′ik**   isotopic
croppy   poppet   acopic   isotropic
droppy   aerotropic   kaleidoscopic
floppy   **ŌP′eth**   Aesopic   laryngoscopic
hoppy   *copeth*   allotropic   lycanthropic
loppy   *elopeth*   anthropic   lychnoscopic
moppy   *gropeth*   arthroscopic   macroscopic
poppy   *hopeth*   atopic   metopic
shoppy   *interlopeth*   autoscopic   metoscopic
sloppy   *mopeth*   canopic   microscopic
soppy   *ropeth*   Cyclopic   misanthropic
                  soapeth   dexiotropic   monotrophic
Ō′pen   diatropic   myopic
open   **ŎP′eth**   dichroscopic   necroscopic
                  choppeth   dolicho-   neoanthropic
ŌP′est   *droppeth*   prosopic   neurotropic
copest   *hoppeth*   ectopic   nooscopic

nyctalopic
nyctitropic
orthoscopic
orthotopic
paleanthropic
pantascopic
periscopic
philanthropic
phototropic
polyscopic
polytopic
polytropic
poroscopic
presbyopic
prosopic
psilanthropic
radioscopic
scopic
sinopic
spectrosco-
   pic
stenotopic
stenotropic
stereoscopic
stethoscopic
stroboscopic
subtropic
syncopic
syntropic
telescopic
theanthropic
theophilan-
   thropic
therianthropic
thermoscopic
thixotropic
topic
tropic
vagotropic

ŎP'iks
topics
tropics

ŌP'ing
coping
doping
eloping
groping
hoping
interloping
loping
moping
roping
sloping
soaping
stoping
toping

ŎP'ing
bedropping
chopping
clip-clopping
copping
cropping
dropping
eavesdropping
flopping
hopping
lopping
mopping
overtopping
plopping
popping
propping
shopping
slopping
sopping
stopping

stropping
swapping
topping
Wapping
whopping

ŌP'ish
mopish
popish

ŎP'ish
foppish
shoppish

ŎP''l
estoppel
hopple
popple
stopple
topple

ŌP'les
hopeless
popeless
soapless

ŌP'ling
fopling
toppling

ŌP'ment
elopement

Ô'pô
pawpaw

Ō'pōk
slowpoke

ŎP'sē
copsy
dropsy
Mopsy
Topsy

ŎP'shun
adoption
option

ŎP'sis
ampelopsis
lycopsis
synopsis
thanatopsis

ŎP'stur
dopester

ŎP'ted
adopted
co-opted

ŎP'tik
autoptic
Coptic
optic
synoptic

ŎP'trik
catadioptric
catoptric
dioptric

ŌP'ur
coper
doper
eloper
groper

āle,   câre,   ădd,   ärm,   ăsk;   mē,   hĕre,   ĕnd;   īce,   ĭll;

interloper	opus	corax	**Ō'rāt**
moper		storax	chlorate
roper	**Ō'ra**	thorax	deflorate
sloper	Angora		perchlorate
soaper	aurora	**Ō'ral**	
toper	Bora-Bora	auroral	**ÔR'āt**
	Cora	chloral	inaurate
ÔP'ur	Dora	choral	*instaurate*
pauper	dumb Dora	floral	
scauper	Eldora	horal	**ÔR'bē**
	Endora	oral	corbie
ŎP'ur	flora	sororal	orby
chopper	Floradora	thoral	
clodhopper	Leonora	trifloral	**ÔR'bid**
copper	Marmora		morbid
cropper	Masora	**ÔR'al**	
dropper	Mora	aural	**ÔR'bing**
eavesdropper	Nora	binaural	absorbing
finale-hopper	Pandora	coral	orbing
grasshopper	passiflora	immoral	resorbing
hopper	signora	laurel	
improper	Theodora	moral	**ÔR'b'l**
lopper	Torah	quarrel	corbel
mopper		sorrel	warbel
overtopper	**ÔR'a**	(See also	
plopper	aura	Ō'Ral.)	**ÔR'blur**
popper	Chamaesaura		warbler
shopper	Laura	**ŎR'al**	
sopper	Maura	coral	**ÔR'chard,**
stopper		(See also	**ÔR'churd**
swapper	**ŎR'ā**	ÔR'al.)	orchard
tiptopper	foray		tortured
topper		**ŎR'anj**	
whopper	**ŎR'ă**	orange	**ÔR'chur**
	Andorra		scorcher
Ō'pus	Gomorrah	**ÔR'ant**	torcher
Canopus		soarant	
lagopous	**Ō'raks**	vorant	**ÔR'dan**
Lagopus	borax		Jordan

ōld, ôr, ŏdd, oil, fo͞ot, out; ūse, ûrn, ŭp; THis, thin

(See also
ÔR'don.)

ÔR'dans
accordance
concordance
discordance

ÔR'dant
accordant
concordant
disaccordant
discordant
inaccordant
mordant

ŌR'ded
afforded
boarded
forded
hoarded
sworded
unforded
unhoarded
uphoarded

ÔR'ded
accorded
awarded
belorded
chorded
corded
lorded
recorded
rewarded
swarded
unlorded
unrecorded
unrewarded

warded
(See also
ÔR'did.)

ÔR'den
warden
way-warden

ÔR'dest
boardest
fordest
hoardest

ÔR'dest
accordest
awardest
belordest
lordest
recordest
rewardest
wardest

ŌR'deth
boardeth
fordeth
hoardeth

ÔR'deth
accordeth
awardeth
belordeth
cordeth
lordeth
recordeth
rewardeth
wardeth

ÔRD'ful
discordful

rewardful

ÔR'did
sordid
(See also
ÔR'ded.)

ÔR'dij
boardage
bordage

ÔR'dij
cordage

ÔR'ding
affording
boarding
fording
hoarding
unhoarding
uphoarding
weather-
    boarding

ÔR'ding
according
awarding
belording
cording
lording
recording
rewarding
unrecording
unrewarding
warding

ÔRD'lē
lordly
unlordly

ÔR'don
cordon
Gordon

ÔRD'ship
lordship
wardship

ŌR'dur
boarder
forder
hoarder
parlor-boarder

ÔR'dur
accorder
awarder
border
corder
disorder
emborder
money order
order
reorder
rewarder
unorder
videocassette
    recorder
video recorder
videotape
    recorder
warder

ÔR'durd
bordered
disordered
ordered
reordered
well-ordered

āle,   câre,   ădd,   ärm,   ăsk;   mē,   hĕre,   ĕnd;   īce,   ĭll;

ŌRDZ′man
swordsman

Ô′rē
abbreviatory
abjuratory
absolutory
acceleratory
acclamatory
accusatory
additory
adhortatory
adjuratory
admonitory
adulatory
advocatory
affirmatory
a fortiori
aleatory
allegory
alleviatory
Alpha Centauri
amatory
ambagitory
ambulatory
amendatory
amphigory
annotatory
annunciatory
anticipatory
apospory
a posteriori
appellatory
applicatory
appreciatory
approbatory
a priori
aratory
articulatory

aspiratory
asseveratory
assimilatory
auditory
auscultatory
auxiliatory
basement story
bibitory
blindstory
cacciatore
cachinnatory
calculatory
calumniatory
castigatory
category
certificatory
chrismatory
circulatory
circumambula-
  tory
circumgyratory
circumlocutory
circumrotatory
citatory
clerestory
commandatory
commemora-
  tory
commendatory
comminatory
communica-
  tory
compellatory
compensatory
competitory
compulsatory
con amore
conciliatory
condemnatory

condolatory
confabulatory
confirmatory
confiscatory
congratulatory
consecratory
conservatory
consolatory
constellatory
consultatory
contributory
corroboratory
cosignatory
counterflory
crematory
criminatory
culpatory
curatory
damnatory
deambulatory
declamatory
declaratory
decretory
dedicatory
defamatory
dehortatory
delineatory
demonstratory
denunciatory
depilatory
depository
deprecatory
depreciatory
depredatory
derogatory
designatory
desquamatory
desultory
dictatory

dilatory
dimissory
disapprobatory
discriminatory
dispensatory
distillatory
divinatory
donatory
dormitory
dory
edificatory
educatory
ejaculatory
elucidatory
emanatory
emancipatory
emasculatory
emendatory
emigratory
emulatory
enunciatory
exaggeratory
excitatory
exclamatory
excretory
exculpatory
excusatory
execratory
executory
exhibitory
exhortatory
expiatory
expiratory
explanatory
expletory
explicatory
exploratory
expository
expostulatory

expurgatory
extenuatory
exterminatory
extirpatory
feretory
feudatory
flagellatory
flory
frigeratory
fulminatory
fumigatory
fumitory
funambulatory
furore
gesticulatory
gladiatory
glory
gory
gradatory
grallatory
gratulatory
gustatory
gyratory
habilatory
hallucinatory
hoary
hortatory
hunky-dory
immigratory
imperatory
imprecatory
improvisatory
incantatory
incriminatory
incubatory
inculpatory
indicatory
inflammatory
informatory

inhibitory
initiatory
inspiratory
interlocutory
interrogatory
inventory
investigatory
invitatory
invocatory
jaculatory
John Dory
judicatory
juratory
laboratory
lachrymatory
lacrimatory
laudatory
lavatory
libatory
liberatory
libratory
lory
lucubratory
Maggiore
mandatory
manducatory
manipulatory
masticatory
mbori
mediatory
memento mori
migratory
minatory
monitory
Montessori
multistory
mundatory
narratory
natatory

negatory
negotiatory
nugatory
oary
objurgatory
obligatory
observatory
offertory
Old Glory
olitory
oratory
ory
oscillatory
osculatory
pacificatory
palliatory
parlatory
pellitory
perambulatory
peremptory
perfumatory
perspiratory
phantasmagory
phonatory
piscatory
placatory
plauditory
pory
postulatory
potatory
preambulatory
predatory
predicatory
prefatory
premonitory
preparatory
preservatory
probatory
proclamatory

procrastinatory
procuratory
profanatory
prohibitory
promissory
promontory
pronunciatory
propitiatory
pulsatory
punitory
purgatory
purificatory
quarry
radiatory
raspatory
reciprocatory
recognitory
recommenda-
  tory
reconciliatory
recriminatory
reformatory
refrigeratory
refutatory
regeneratory
regulatory
remuneratory
repertory
repository
reprobatory
reptatory
requisitory
respiratory
restoratory
retaliatory
retardatory
retributory
revelatory
reverberatory

āle,   câre,   ădd,   ärm,   ăsk;   mē,   hĕre,   ĕnd;   īce,   ĭll;

revocatory
rogatory
rotatory
sacrificatory
saltatory
salutatory
salvatory
sanatory
sanitory
shory
sibilatory
signatory
significatory
signori
simulatory
snory
sob story
speculatory
statutory
sternutatory
stillatory
story
stridulatory
sublimatory
sudatory
superergatory
suppletory
supplicatory
suppository
sussultatory
terminatory
territory
Tory
tory
transitory
transmigratory
transpiratory
transudatory
undulatory

usurpatory
vacillatory
vainglory
vehiculartory
vesicatory
vibratory
vindicatory
viola d'amore
vomitory
whory
zori

ŎR'ē
Corrie
Florrie
lorry
quarry
sorry

ŌR'ēd
gloried
storied

ŌR'ed
forehead

ŎR'el, ŎR'el
laurel
(See also
ÔR'al, ŎR'al.)

ÔR'en,
ÔR'an
sporran
warren

ÔR'ens
abhorrence
Lawrence

St. Lawrence

ŎR'ens
Dorrance
Florence

ÔR'ent,
ÔR'ant
abhorrent
death warrant
horrent
torrent
warrent

ÔR'est
adorest
borest
deplorest
encorest
explorest
floorest
gorest
hoarest
ignorest
implorest
outsoarest
porest
pourest
restorest
roarest
scorest
snorest
soarest
sorest
storest

ÔR'est
abhorrest
warrest

ŎR'est
afforest
disafforest
enforest
forest

ŌR'eth
adoreth
boreth
deploreth
encoreth
exploreth
flooreth
goreth
ignoreth
imploreth
outsoareth
poreth
poureth
restoreth
roareth
scoreth
snoreth
soareth
storeth

ÔR'eth
abhorreth
warreth

ÔR'fan
orphan

ÔR'fik
allomorphic
anthropomor-
phic
automorphic
dimorphic

ōld, ôr, ŏdd, oil, fŏŏt, out; ūse, ûrn, ŭp; THis, thin

endomorphic
heteromorphic
ichthyomorphic
idiomorphic
isomorphic
mesomorphic
metamorphic
morphic
ophiomorphic
Orphic
pantamorphic
polymorphic
protomorphic
pseudomorphic
theomorphic
trimorphic
zoomorphic

ÔR′fing
dwarfing
wharfing

ÔR′fist
anthropomor-
  phist
metamorphist
wharfist

ÔR′fit
forfeit

ÔR′fiz′m
allomorphism
amorphism
anamorphism
anthropomor-
  phism
automorphism
dimorphism

isodimorphism
isomeromor-
  phism
isomorphism
isotrimorphism
mesomorphism
metamorphism
monomor-
  phism
pleomorphism
polymorphism
trimorphism
zoomorphism

ÔR′fŭs
Morpheus
Orpheus

ÔR′fŭs
amorphous
anthropo-
  morphous
dimorphous
isodimorphous
isomorphous
isotrimorphous
ophiomorphous
paramorphous
polymorphous
trimorphous

ÔR′gan
barrel organ
Dorgan
Morgan
morgen
organ

ÔR′hand

aforehand
beforehand
forehand

ŌR′hous
storehouse
whorehouse

ŌR′id
florid
horrid
torrid

ŎR′ij
shorage
storage

ŎR′ij
borage
forage

Ō′rik
chloric
choric
euchloric
hydrochloric
perchloric
roric

ŎR′ik
allegoric
amphigoric
amphoric
armoric
caloric
camphoric
Doric
elydoric
historic

lithophosphoric
metaphoric
meteoric
paregoric
peloric
phantasmagoric
phosphoric
pictoric
plethoric
prehistoric
prophoric
pyloric
Pythagoric
semaphoric
sophomoric
theoric
zoophoric
zoosporic

Ō′rin
florin

ŌR′ing
adoring
boring
choring
deploring
encoring
exploring
flooring
goring
ignoring
imploring
Loring
outsoaring
poring
pouring
restoring
roaring

āle, câre, ădd, ärm, ăsk;   mē, hĕre, ĕnd; īce, ĭll;

scoring
shoring
snoring
soaring
storing
upsoaring

ŌR'ing
abhorring
warring

ÔR'is
Doris
loris

ÔR'is
Doris

ŌR'is
doch-an-dorris
Doris
Horace
loris
morris
orris

ÔR'ja
Borgia
Georgia

ÔR'jal,
ÔRD'yal
cordial

ÔR'jē
Georgie
orgy
porgy
storge

ÔR'jēz
orgies
porgies

ÔR'jing
forging

ÔR'jiz
Georges
George's

ÔR'jur
forger

ÔR'jus
gorgeous

ÔR'kas
Dorcas

ÔR'kē
corky
forky

ÔR'kid
orchid

ÔR'king
corking
Dorking
forking
uncorking

ŌR'les
coreless
oarless
oreless
shoreless

ÔR'lē
schorly
warly

ŌR'ling
shoreling

ÔR'lok
forelock
oarlock

ÔR'lok
warlock

ÔR'mal
abnormal
anormal
cormal
formal
informal
normal
uniformal

ŌR'man
doorman
floorman
foreman
longshoreman
shoreman

ÔR'man,
ÔR'mon
Gorman
Mormon
Norman
O'Gorman

ÔR'mans
conformance

dormance
performance

ÔR'mant
conformant
dormant
informant

ÔR'mē
dormy
stormy
swarmy

ŌR'ment
adorement
deplorement
explorement
ignorement
implorement
restorement

ÔR'ment
torment

ÔR'mest
conformest
deformest
formest
informest
performest
reformest
stormest
swarmest
transformest
warmest

ÔR'meth
conformeth
deformeth

formeth
informeth
performeth
reformeth
stormeth
swarmeth
transformeth
warmeth

ÔR'ming
bestorming
conforming
deforming
forming
informing
nonconforming
performing
reforming
storming
swarming
transforming
warming

ÔR'mist
conformist
nonconformist
reformist

ÔRM'lē
warmly
uniformly

ÔRM'les
formless
stormless

ÔR'mōst
foremost
head-foremost

ÔR'mur
barnstormer
conformer
deformer
dormer
foot-warmer
former
informer
performer
reformer
stormer
swarmer
transformer
warmer

ÔR'mus
abnormous
cormous
cormus
enormous
multiformous

ÔR'na
cromorna
Lorna
Norna

ÔR'nāt
ornate

ÔR'nē
corny
Hornie
horny
thorny

ÔR'nes
soreness

ŌR'nest
adornest
bescornest
forewarnest
scornest
subornest
warnest

ÔR'net
cornet
hornet

ÔR'neth
adorneth
bescorneth
forewarneth
scorneth
suborneth
warneth

ŌRN'ful
mournful

ÔRN'ful
scornful

ŌR'ning
mourning

ÔR'ning
adorning
bescorning
dehorning
dishorning
forewarning
good morning
horning
morning
scorning

suborning
yester-morning
warning

ÔR'nis
Aepyornis
cornice
Dinornis
Gastornis
Heliornis
Ichthyornis

ÔR'nish
Cornish
hornish

ÔRN'les
hornless
scornless
thornless

ÔRN'ment
adornment

ŌR'nūn
forenoon

ŌR'nur
mourner

ÔR'nur
adorner
bescorner
chimney corner
corner
forewarner
horner
scorner
suborner
warner

Ō′rō
Moro
toro

ŎR′ō
amorrow
borrow
good morrow
morrow
sorrow
tomorrow

ŎR′ōd
borrowed
sorrowed
unsorrowed

ŎR′old
Thorold

ÔR′pid
torpid

ÔR′por
torpor

ŎR′rôr
horror

ÔR′sal
dextrorsal
dorsal
dorsel
morsel
torsel

ŎR′sē
gorsy
horsy

ŌR′sen
coarsen
hoarsen

ŌR′sest
coarsest
coursest
discoursest
divorcest
enforcest
forcest
hoarsest
reinforcest

ÔR′sest
endorsest

ŌR′seth
coarseth
discourseth
divorceth
enforceth
forceth
reinforceth

ÔR′seth
endorseth

ŌRS′ful
forceful
resourceful

ÔRS′ful
remorseful

ŌR′shun
apportion
disproportion
portion

proportion

ÔR′shun
abortion
consortion
contortion
detortion
distortion
extorsion
intorsion
retortion
torsion

ŌR′shund
apportioned
dispropor-
tioned
portioned
proportioned
unportioned

ŌR′sing
coursing
discoursing
divorcing
enforcing
forcing
reinforcing

ŌR′siv
discoursive
divorcive
enforcive

ŌRS′les
forceless
resourceless
sourceless

ÔRS′les
horseless
remorseless

ÔRS′man
horseman
lighthorseman
Norseman

ŌRS′ment
deforcement
divorcement
enforcement
forcement
reinforcement

ÔRS′ment
endorsement

ŌRS′nes
coarseness
hoarseness

ŌR′som
foursome

ÔR′son
Orson

ÔR′song
warsong

ŌR′sur
coarser
courser
discourser
divorcer
enforcer
forcer

hoarser
reinforcer

ÔR'sur
endorser

ŌR'tal
portal
transportal

ÔR'tal
aortal
immortal
mortal
(See also
ÔRT''l.)

ŌR'tans
supportance
transportance

ÔR'tans
importance

ÔR'tant
important

ŌR'ted
courted
disported
exported
imported
reported
sported
supported
transported

ÔR'ted
aborted

assorted
consorted
contorted
detorted
distorted
escorted
exhorted
extorted
resorted
retorted
snorted
sorted
sported
thwarted
unsorted

ŌR'teks
cortex
vortex

ÔR'tem
postmortem

ÔR'ten
shorten

ÔR'tent
portent

ÔR'test
courtest
disportest
exportest
importest
reportest
sportest
supportest
transportest

ÔR'test

assortest
consortest
contortest
detortest
distortest
escortest
exhortest
extortest
resortest
retortest
shortest
snortest
sortest
swartest
thwartest .

ÔR'teth
courteth
disporteth
exporteth
importeth
reporteth
sporteth
supporteth
transporteth

ÔR'teth
assorteth
consorteth
contorteth
detorteth
distorteth
escorteth
exhorteth
extorteth
resorteth
retorteth
snorteth
sorteth

thwarteth

ŌRT'gīd
court-guide
port-guide

ÔR'thē
swarthy

ÔR'tē
forty
pianoforte
snorty
sortie
swarty
warty

ÔR'tij
shortage

ŌR'tīm
aforetime
beforetime

ŌR'ting
courting
deporting
disporting
exporting
importing
reporting
sporting
supporting
transporting

ÔR'ting
aborting
assorting
consorting

āle, câre, ădd, ärm, ăsk; mē, hĕre, ĕnd; īce, ĭll;

contorting
detorting
distorting
escorting
exhorting
extorting
resorting
retorting
snorting
sorting
thwarting

ŌR'tiv
sportive
transportive

ÔR'tiv
abortive
contortive
distortive
ortive
retortive
tortive

ÔRT''l
chortle
whortle
(See also
ÔR'tal.)

ŌRT'land
Courtland
Portland

ŌRT'lē
courtly
portly
uncourtly

ÔRT'lē
shortly

ŌRT'ment
comportment
deportment
disportment
transportment

ŌRT'ment
assortment

ÔRT'nes
swartness
thwartness

ÔRT'nīt
fortnight

ÔR'ton
Horton
Morton
Norton

ŌR'trāt
portrait

ÔR'trés
fortress

ÔRT'ship
courtship

ÔRTS'man
sportsman

ÔR'tūn
befortune
enfortune

fortune
importune
misfortune

ŌR'tur
courter
disporter
exporter
importer
porter
reporter
sporter
supporter
transporter

ÔR'tūr
torture

ÔR'tŭr
assorter
consorter
contorter
detorter
distorter
escorter
exhorter
extorter
mortar
quarter
resorter
retorter
shorter
snorter
sorter
thwarter
weather quar-
  ter
woolsorter

**ÔR'turd,
ÔR'chard**
orchard
tortured

ÔR'turz
assorters
winter quarters
(See also
ŌR'tur; add
-s where
appropriate.)

ÔRT'wāv
shortwave

Ōrum
decorum
forum
indecorum
jorum
quorum
variorum

ŌR'ur
adorer
borer
corer
decorer
deplorer
encorer
explorer
floorer
gorer
ignorer
implorer
outpourer
outsoarer
porer

ōld, ôr, ŏdd, oil, fŏŏt, out; ūse, ûrn, ŭp; THis, thin

pourer
restorer
roarer
scorer
snorer
soarer
sorer
storer

Ō′rus
canorous
chorus
decorous
Horus
imporous
indecorous
porous
pylorus
sonorous
torous
torus

ÔR′us
allosaurus
ankylosaurus
apatosaurus
brachiosaurus
brontosaurus
dolichosaurus
hadrosaurus
ichthyosaurus
kronosaurus
megalosaurus
mosasaurus
nanosaurus
pleiosaurus
plesiosaurus
protosaurus
regnosaurus

stegosaurus
Taurus
teleosaurus
thesaurus
tyrannosaurus

ŌR′ward
foreward
shoreward

ÔR′ward
forward
henceforward
norward
straightforward
thenceforward

ÔR′worn
war-worn

ŌRZ′man
oarsman

Ō′sa
amorosa
Formosa
mimosa

ÔS′chun
exhaustion

ŌS′ē
saucy

ŎS′ē
bossy
drossy
Flossie
flossy

glossy
mossy
posse
tossy

ŎS′est
closest
dosest
grossest

ŎS′est
crossest
embossest
glossest
tossest

ŎS′et
faucet

ŎS′et
bosset
cosset
posset
sack-posset

ŎS′eth
crosseth
embosseih
glosseth
tosseth

Ō′shal
antisocial
intersocial
social

ŎSH′ē
boshy
sloshy

squashy
swashy
toshy
washy
wishy-washy

ŎSH′ing
sloshing
squashing
swashing
washing

ŌSH′ur
gaucher
kosher

ŎSH′ur
cosher
josher
squasher
swasher
washer

Ō′shun
Boeotian
commotion
devotion
emotion
groschen
indevotion
locomotion
lotion
motion
nicotian
notion
ocean
potion
prenotion
promotion

āle,   câre,   ădd,   ärm,   ăsk;   mē,   hĕre,   ĕnd;   īce,   ĭll;

remotion
self-devotion

ÔSH'un
caution
incaution
precaution

ŌSH'us
atrocious
ferocious
nepotious
precocious

ÔSH'us
cautious
incautious
precautious

ÔS'ij
sausage

ŎS'ik
fossick
glossic

ŌS'il
docile
indocile

ŎS'il
docile
dossil
fossil
(See also
ŎS''l.)

ŌS'ing
dosing

engrossing

ŎS'ing
bossing
crossing
dossing
embossing
glossing
railway cross-
ing
tossing

ŎS'ip
gossip

Ō'sis
anadiplosis
anamorphosis
ankylosis
apotheosis
carcinosis
chlorosis
cirrhosis
diagnosis
enantiosis
endosmosis
epanadiplosis
epanorthosis
exosmosis
geognosis
heliosis
heterosis
hypnosis
hypotyposis
ichthyosis
meiosis
metasomatosis
metempsycho-
sis

metemptosis
metensomato-
sis
morosis
morphosis
narcosis
necrosis
neurosis
osmosis
proemptosis
prognosis
psychosis
ptosis
pyrosis
sarcosis
scirrhosis
sorosis
tuberculosis
zygosis
zymosis

ŎS'is
proboscis

ŌS'iv
corrosive
erosive
explosive
inexplosive

ŎS'kar
Oscar

ŎS'kē
bosky

ŎS''l
apostle
colossal

dosel
dossil
fossil
hypoglossal
jostle
throstle
tossel
wassail

ŎS'lē
crossly

ŎS'lur
hostler
jostler
Rossler

ŌS'nes
closeness
grossness
jocoseness
moroseness
verboseness

Ō'sō
amoroso
arioso
doloroso
gracioso
so-so
virtuoso

ŎS'om
blossom
odontoglossum
opossum
orange blossom
possum

ōld, ôr, ŏdd, oil, fŏŏt, out; ūse, ûrn, ŭp; THis, thin

ÔS'on
Dawson
Lawson
Rawson

ŎS'pel
gospel

ŎS'pish
waspish

ŎS'pur
prosper

ŌS'tal
coastal
postal

ŎS'tal
costal
infracostal
intercoastal
Pentecostal
supracostal

ŎS'tāt
apostate
laticostate
quadricostate

ŎS'tē
frosty

ŎS'ted
boasted
coasted
posted
roasted
toasted
unposted

ÔS'ted
exhausted

ŎS'ted
accosted
frosted

ŎS'tel, ŎS''l
hostel

ÔS'ten
Austen

ŌS'tes
hostess

ŌS'test
boastest
coastest
postest
roastest
toastest

ŌS'teth
boasteth
coasteth
posteth
roasteth
toasteth

ŌST'hous
oasthouse
post-house

ŌS'tij
postage

ŎS'tij
hostage

ÔS'tik
catacaustic
caustic
diacaustic
encaustic

ŎS'tik
acrostic
agnostic
diagnostic
eteostic
geognostic
gnostic
paracrostic
pentacostic
prognostic

ŎS'til
hostile

ÔS'tin
Austin

ŌS'ting
boasting
coasting
posting
roasting
toasting

ÔS'ting
exhausting

ŎS'ting
accosting
costing
frosting

ÔS'tiv

exhaustive
inexhaustive

ŎS'tiv
costive

ŌST'lē
ghostly
mostly

ŎST'lē
costly

ŌST'man
postman

ŌST'mark
postmark

ŎS'ton
Boston

Ō'storm
snowstorm

ÔS'tral
austral
claustral

**ŎS'tral,
ŎS'trel**
costrel
lamellirostral
longirostral
rostral

ŎS'trāt
prostrate
rostrate

āle, câre, ădd, ärm, ăsk; mē, hĕre, ĕnd; īce, ĭll;

ŎS′trich
ostrich

ŎS′trum
nostrum
rostrum

ŎS′tūm
costume

ŎS′tur
boaster
coaster
four-poster
poster
roaster
throwster
toaster

ÔS′tur
auster
exhauster

ŎS′tūr
imposture
posture

ŎS′tŭr
accoster
coster
foster
Gloucester
imposter
Paternoster
pentecoster
roster

ŎS′turn
postern

ÔS′tus
Faustus

ŌS′ur
closer
doser
engrosser
grocer
grosser
jocoser
moroser

ÔS′ur
Chaucer
Naw sir
saucer

ŎS′ur
bosser
crosser
dosser
embosser
glosser
josser
tosser

ŎS′us
colossus
molossus

Ō′ta
Dakota
flota
iota
Minnesota
quota
rota

ŌT′al

anecdotal
antidotal
dotal
extradotal
notal
rotal
sacerdotal
sclerotal
teetotal
total

ŌT′ant,
ŌT′ent
flotant
potent
prepotent

ŌT′āt
denotate
notate
rotate

ŎT′ash
potash

ŌT′ē
bloaty
coyote
dhoty
Doty
Doughty
floaty
goaty
throaty

ÔT′ē
haughty
naughty

ŎT′ē
clotty
dotty
knotty
spotty
totty

ŌT′ed
bloated
boated
coated
demoted
denoted
devoted
doted
floated
gloated
misquoted
moated
noted
particoated
petticoated
promoted
quoted
refloated
self-devoted
throated
unnoted
voted

ŎT′ed
allotted
besotted
bespotted
blood-bespot-
    ted
blotted
cheviotted
clotted

---

dotted
garotted
jotted
knotted
lotted
plotted
potted
rotted
shotted
slotted
sotted
spotted
squatted
totted
trotted
unblotted
underplotted
unknotted
unspotted
wainscotted
(See also
ŎT′id.)

ŌT′en
oaten

ŎT′en
begotten
cotton
first-begotten
forgotten
gotten
hard-gotten
ill-gotten
misbegotten
misgotten
rotten
unbegotten
unforgotten

ungotten
(See also
ŎT′on.)

ŌT′est
demotest
denotest
devotest
dotest
floatest
gloatest
misquotest
notest
promotest
quotest
votest

ŎT′est
clottest
(See also ŎT;
add -*est* where
appropriate.)

ŌT′eth
demoteth
denoteth
devoteth
doteth
floateth
gloateth
noteth
misquoteth
promoteth
quoteth
voteth

ŎT′eth
clotteth
(See also ŎT;

add -*eth* where
appropriate.)

ÔT′ful
thoughtful

Ôth′a
quotha

Ôth′al
betrothal

Ôth′am
Gotham
Jotham

Ŏth′am
Gotham

Ŏth′ē
frothy
mothy

ŌTH′est
clothest
loathest

ŌTH′eth
clotheth
loatheth

ŌTH′ful
loathful

Ŏth′ful
slothful

Ôth′ful
wrathful

Ŏth′ik
Gothic
Mesogothic
Ostrogothic
Visigothic

ŌTH′ing
clothing
loathing

Ŏth′ment
betrothment

ŎT′hook
boathook
coathook

Ô′thôrn
Cawthorn
hawthorn

ŌTH′som
loathsome

Ôth′ur
author

ŎTH′ur
bother
fother
pother
(See also
ÄTH′ur,
ĂTH′ur.)

ŎT′id
carotid
parotid
(See also
ŎT′ed.)

ŌT′ij
anecdotage
dotage
floatage
flotage

ŌT′ij
cottage
pottage
wattage

ŌT′ik
otic

ŌT′ik
aeronautic
argonautic
nautic

ŌT′ik
acrotic
agrypnotic
akiotic
amniotic
amphierotic
amphibiotic
anaptotic
anecdotic
ankylotic
antibiotic
antipatriotic
aphotic
aptotic
aquatic
argotic
astronautic
asymptotic
autohypnotic
azotic

binotic
biotic
carotic
catabiotic
catacrotic
cerotic
chaotic
chlorotic
cirrhotic
creosotic
culottic
cyanotic
demotic
despotic
dichotic
dicrotic
diglottic
dizygotic
endosmotic
entotic
enzygotic
epiglottic
epizootic
erotic
escharotic
euphotic
exosmotic
exotic
ezootic
glottic
henotic
hidrotic
homoerotic
hypnotic
ichthyotic
idiotic
indigotic
iscariotic
kenotic

kyphoscoliotic
kyphotic
lordotic
macrobiotic
meiotic
melanotic
microbiotic
monocrotic
morphotic
mycotic
narcotic
necrotic
nepotic
neurohypnotic
neurotic
Nilotic
osmotic
otic
parotic
patriotic
periotic
photic
polycrotic
polyglottic
porotic
posthypnotic
postpsychotic
prepsychotic
psilotic
psychoneurotic
psychotic
pycnotic
pyrotic
quixotic
rhinocerotic
rhizotic
rhotic
robotic
sans-culottic

sarcotic
sclerotic
seismotic
semeiotic
semiotic
stenotic
symbiotic
thalpotic
thrombotic
tricrotic
zoosemiotic
zootic
zygotic
zymotic

ŎT′iks
aeronautics
robotics
(See also
ŎT′ik; add
-s where
appropriate.)

ŌT′ing
bloating
boating
coating
demoting
denoting
devoting
doting
floating
gloating
misquoting
noting
promoting
quoting
throating
voting

ōld, ôr, ŏdd, oil, foŏt, out; ūse, ûrn, ŭp; THis, thin

ŎT'ing
allotting
besotting
blotting
clotting
dotting
garotting
jotting
knotting
plotting
potting
rotting
sotting
spotting
squatting
totting
trotting
underplotting
unknotting
yachting

ŎT'is
epiglottis
glottis

ŌT'ish
dotish
goatish

ŎT'ish
Scottish
sottish

ŎT'ist
anecdotist
noticed
Scotist
unnoticed

ŎT'ist
sans-culottist

ŌT'iv
emotive
locomotive
motive
promotive
votive

ŎT'kins
Otkins
Watkins

ŎT''l
bottle
dottle
glottal
mottle
pottle
throttle
tottle
twattle
wattle

ŎT'lē
hotly
motley

ŌT'les
thoughtless

ŎT'les
blotless
clotless
cotless
dotless
jotless
knotless

lotless
potless
rotless
sotless
spotless
totless
trotless

ŎT'ling
bottling
(See also
ŎT''l; drop
-e and add
-ing where
appropriate.)

ŌT'man
boatman

ŎT'man
Cotman
Ottman

ŌT'ment
demotement
denotement
devotement

ŎT'ment
allotment
besotment

ŎT'nes
hotness
whatness

Ō'tō
De Soto
divoto

ex voto
fagotto
in toto
Kioto
photo

ŎT'ō
blotto
grotto
lotto
motto
otto
ridotto
risotto

ŎT'om
bottom

Ō'ton
Croton
proton

Ô'ton
Lawton

ŎT'on
cotton
Groton
(See also
ŎT'en.)

ŎT'rel
Cottrell
dottrel

ŎT'sē
hotsy-totsy
Nazi
paparazzi

ŎTS'man
Scotsman
yachtsman

ŎT'son
Watson

Ō'tum
quotum
teetotum

ŎT'um
autumn

ŌT'ur
bloater
boater
demoter
denoter
devoter
doter
fagot voter
floater
gloater
locomotor
magnetomotor
motor
noter
promoter
quoter
rotomotor
rotor
scoter
toter
vasomotor
voter

ÔT'ur
backwater

daughter
firewater
fizzwater
giggle water
milk-and-water
slaughter
soda water
water

ŎT'ur
blotter
bogtrotter
clotter
complotter
cotter
dotter
garotter
globetrotter
hotter
jotter
knotter
ottar
otter
plotter
potter
rotter
spotter
squatter
totter
trotter
underplotter
unknotter
yachter

Ō'tus
Gymnotus
lotus
macrotous

OU'al
avowal
disavowal
(See also
OU'el.)

OU'an
gowan
McGowan
rowan
rowen

OU'ans
allowance
avowance
disallowance
disavowance

OU'ard
coward
Howard

OUCH'est
avouchest
(See also
OUCH; add
-*est* where
appropriate.)

OUCH'eth
avoucheth
(See also
OUCH; add
-*eth* where
appropriate.)

OUCH'ing
avouching
couching

crouching
grouching
pouching
slouching
vouching

OUCH'ur
avoucher
coucher
croucher
Goucher
groucher
poucher
sloucher
voucher

OU'da
howdah

OUD'ē
cloudy
crowdy
dowdy
Gowdy
howdie
howdy
pandowdy
proudy
rowdy
shroudy
uncloudy

OUD'ed
beclouded
clouded
crowded
enshrouded
overclouded
overcrowded

ōld, ôr, ŏdd, oil, fŏŏt, out; ūse, ûrn, ŭp; THis, thin

shrouded
unbeclouded
unclouded
unshrouded

OUD'est
becloudest
beshroudest
cloudest
crowdest
enshroudest
loudest
overcloudest
overcrowdest
proudest
shroudest

OUD'eth
becloudeth
beshroudeth
cloudeth
crowdeth
enshroudeth
overcloudeth
overcrowdeth
shroudeth

OUD'ing
beclouding
beshrouding
clouding
crowding
enshrouding
overclouding
overcrowding
shrouding
unshrouding

OUD'ish

loudish
proudish

OUD'lē
loudly
proudly

OUD'nes
loudness
proudness

OUD'ur
baking powder
clam chowder
bepowder
chowder
crowder
louder
powder
prouder
Seidlitz pow-
    der

OU'ē
Dowie
zowie

OU'el
bowel
dowel
embowel
Howell
Powell
Prowell
rowel
towel
trowel
vowel
(See also

OU'al.)

OU'es
prowess

OU'est
allowest
avowest
bowest
cowest
disallowest
endowest
ploughest
vowest

OU'et
Howett
Jowett

OU'eth
alloweth
avoweth
boweth
coweth
disalloweth
endoweth
plougheth
voweth

OU'ing
allowing
avowing
bowing
cowing
disallowing
endowing
ploughing
plowing
rowing

vowing

OU'lē
Cowley
Crowley
Powley
Rowley

OUL'est
foulest
growlest
howlest
prowlest
scowlest

OUL'et
owlet

OUL'eth
growleth
howleth
prowleth
scowleth

OUL'ing
fouling
fowling
growling
howling
prowling
scowling

OUL'ish
foulish
owlish

OUL'ur
fouler
fowler

growler
howler
prowler
scowler
yowler

OU'ment
avowment
endowment

OUN'ded
abounded
astounded
bounded
compounded
confounded
dumfounded
expounded
founded
grounded
hounded
impounded
mounded
pounded
propounded
rebounded
redounded
resounded
rounded
sounded
superabounded
surrounded
unbounded
unfounded
ungrounded
unsounded
well-founded
wounded

OUN'del
roundel

OUN'den
bounden

OUN'dest
aboundest
astoundest
boundest
compoundest
confoundest
expoundest
foundest
groundest
houndest
impoundest
poundest
profoundest
propoundest
reboundest
resoundest
roundest
soundest
superaboundest
surroundest

OUN'deth
aboundeth
astoundeth
boundeth
compoundeth
confoundeth
dumfoundeth
expoundeth
foundeth
groundeth
houndeth
impoundeth

poundeth
propoundeth
reboundeth
redoundeth
resoundeth
roundeth
soundeth
surroundeth

OUN'dij
groundage
poundage
soundage

OUN'ding
abounding
astounding
big-sounding
bounding
compounding
confounding
dumfounding
expounding
founding
grounding
high-sounding
hounding
impounding
pounding
propounding
rebounding
redounding
resounding
rounding
sounding
superabound-
   ing
surrounding
unbounding

wounding

OUND'lē
profoundly
roundly
soundly
unsoundly

OUND'les
boundless
groundless
soundless

OUND'ling
foundling
groundling

OUND'nes
profoundness
roundness
soundness
unsoundness

OUN'drē
foundry

OUN'drel
scoundrel

OUN'dur
bounder
compounder
confounder
dumfounder
expounder
flounder
founder
four-pounder
impounder

ōld, ôr, ŏdd, oil, fŏŏt, out; ūse, ûrn, ŭp; THis, thin

iron-founder
pounder
profounder
propounder
rebounder
resounder
rounder
sounder
surrounder
type-founder

OUN'ē
brownie
browny
downy
frowny
towny

OUN'est
brownest
crownest
drownest
frownest

OUN'eth
browneth
crowneth
drowneth
frowneth

OUN'ing
browning
clowning
crowning
discrowning
downing
drowning
frowning
gowning

intowning
uncrowning

OUN'ish
brownish
clownish
frownish

OUN'jing
lounging

OUN'les
crownless
frownless
gownless

OUN'sest
announcest
(See also
OUNS;
add -*est* where
appropriate.)

OUN'seth
announceth
(See also
OUNS; add
-*eth* where
appropriate.)

OUN'sez
announces
bounces
denounces
flounces
ounces
pounces
pronounces
renounces

trounces

OUN'sing
announcing
bouncing
denouncing
flouncing
pouncing
pronouncing
renouncing
trouncing

OUNS'ment
announcement
denouncement
pronouncement
renouncement

OUN'sur
announcer
bouncer
denouncer
flouncer
pouncer
pronouncer
renouncer
trouncer

OUN'tē
bounty
county
mounty
viscounty

OUN'ted
accounted
amounted
counted
discounted

dismounted
miscounted
mounted
recounted
remounted
surmounted
uncounted
unmounted
unrecounted

OUN'tes
countess

OUN'test
accountest
amountest
countest
discountest
dismountest
miscountest
mountest
recountest
remountest
surmountest

OUN'teth
accounteth
amounteth
counteth
discounteth
dismounteth
miscounteth
mounteth
recounteth
remounteth
surmounteth

OUN'tin
catamountain

āle, câre, ădd, ärm, ăsk; mē, hĕre, ĕnd; īce, ĭll;

fountain
mountain

OUN'ting
accounting
amounting
counting
discounting
dismounting
miscounting
mounting
recounting
remounting
surmounting

OUN'tur
accounter
counter
discounter
encounter
mounter
recounter
reencounter
remounter
surmounter

OUN'ur
browner
crowner
drowner
frowner

OUN'ward
downward
townward

OUN'zman
gownsman
townsman

Ō'ur
bestower
blower
churchgoer
concertgoer
flower
foregoer
foreknower
foreshower
glassblower
glower
goer
grower
hoer
knower
lawn mower
lower
moviegoer
mower
outgoer
overthrower
ower
playgoer
rower
sewer
shower
slower
snowblower
sower
stower
theatergoer
thrower
tower
undergoer
whistle-blower
winegrower

Ô'ur
cawer

clawer
drawer
gnawer
guffawer
"jawer"
overawer
pawer
rawer
sawer
tawer
wiredrawer
withdrawer

Ō'urd, Ō'ard
lowered
toward
untoward

OUR'ē
avowry
cowrie
dowry
floury
houri
(See also
OU'ur-ē.)

OUR'est
bescourest
deflowerest
devourest
scourest
sourest

OUR'eth
bescoureth
def!owereth
devoureth
scoureth

soureth

OUR'ing
bescouring
deflowering
devouring
flouring
off-scouring
scouring
souring
(See also
OU'ur-ing.)

OUR'lē
hourly
sourly

OUR'nes
sourness

OUR'ur
deflowerer
devourer
scourer
sourer

OU'son
Dowson

OUT'ē
doughty
droughty
gouty
grouty
louty
moughty
pouty
snouty
touty

OUT'ed
clouted
doubted
flouted
gouted
grouted
misdoubted
pouted
redoubted
routed
scouted
shouted
spouted
sprouted
undoubted

OUT'est
cloutest
devoutest
doubtest
floutest
poutest
scoutest
shoutest
spoutest
sproudest
stoutest

OUT'eth
clouteth
doubteth
flouteth
pouteth
scouteth
shouteth
spouteth
sprouteth

OUT'ing

beshouting
bespouting
besprouting
clouting
doubting
flouting
grouting
louting
outing
pouting
routing
scouting
shouting
spouting
sprouting
touting
undoubting

OUT'lē
devoutly
stoutly

OUT'let
outlet
troutlet

OUT'nes
devoutness
stoutness

OUT'ur
devouter
doubter
down-and-
    outer
flouter
jowter
out-and-outer
pouter

router
scouter
shouter
spouter
sprouter
stouter
touter

OU'ur
allower
avower
beacon tower
beflower
bower
Brower
candle power
cauliflower
cower
deflower
dower
embower
empower
endower
enflower
flower
glower
horsepower
imbower
lower
overpower
overtower
passionflower
plougher
plower
power
rower
shower
thundershower
tower

vower
waterpower
(See also
OUR.)

OU'urd
bowered
unshowered
untowered
(See also
OU'ard.)

OU'urz
avowers
Powers
(See also
OU'ur; add
-s where
appropriate.)

OU'wou
bowwow
powwow
wow-wow

OU'zal
arousal
carousal
espousal
housel
ousel
spousal
tousle

OU'zand
thousand

OUZ'ē
bowsie

drowzy
frowzy
lousy
mousy

OUZ'est
arousest
(See also OUZ;
add -*est* where
appropriate.)

OUZ'eth
arouseth
(See also OUZ;
add -*eth* where
appropriate.)

OUZ'ez
arouses
blouses
browses
carouses
espouses
houses
rouses
spouses

OUZ'ij
espousage
housage
spousage

OUZ'ing
arousing
blowzing
browzing
carousing
housing
rousing

OUZ'ur
arouser
browser
carouser
espouser
mouser
rouser
Towser
trouser

OUZ'urz
carousers
trousers

Ō'va
bossa nova
Casanova
Jehovah
nova

Ō'val
oval

ŎV'ē
anchovy
covy
grovy

ŎV'el
grovel
hovel
novel

ŎV'en
cloven
hoven
interwoven
inwoven
uncloven

woven

ŌV'īn
bovine
ovine

ŌV'ing
roving
shroving

ŌV'ō
ab ovo
de novo

ŌV'ur
clover
Dover
drover
flopover
half-seas-over
moreover
over
plover
pushover
rollover
rover
searover
stover
takeover
trover
walkover

ŎV'urb
proverb

ŌV'urz
drovers
estovers

Ō'ward
froward

Ō'whâr
nowhere

Ō'yez
oyez

Ō'yur
bowyer
oyer

Ô'yur
lawyer
sawyer
topsawyer

ŌZ'a
Rosa
Spinoza

ŌZ'al
desposal
disposal
interposal
opposal
presupposal
proposal
reposal
rosal
supposal
transposal

ŌZ'bud
rosebud

ŌZ'dīv
nosedive

ōld, ôr, ŏdd, oil, fŏŏt, out; ūse, ûrn, ŭp; THis, thin

ŌZ′ē
cozy
dozy
nosy
posy
prosy
rosy

ÔZ′ē
causey
gauzy

ŌZ′en
chosen
forechosen
frozen
hosen
Posen
rosen
squozen

ŎZ′enj
lozenge

ŎZ′est
closest
composest
decomposest
deposest
disclosest
discomposest
disposest
dozest
enclosest
exposest
imposest
inclosest
interposest
juxtaposest

opposest
posest
presupposest
proposest
recomposest
reimposest
reposest
superimposest
supposest
transposest

ŌZ′eth
closeth
composeth
decomposeth
deposeth
disclosesth
discomposeth
disposeth
dozeth
encloseth
exposeth
imposeth
incloseth
intercloseth
interposeth
juxtaposeth
opposeth
poseth
presupposeth
proposeth
recomposeth
reimposeth
reposeth
superimposeth
supposeth
transposeth

ŌZ′ez

Moses
roses
(See also ŌZ;
add -es where
appropriate.)

ÔZ′ez
causes
clauses
gauzes
pauses
vases

ŌZ′gā
nosegay

Ō′zhan
ambrosian

Ō′zhun
corrosion
erosion
explosion
implosion

ŌZH′ūr
closure
composure
crosier
disclosure
discomposure
disposure
Dozier
exposure
foreclosure
hosier
inclosure
osier
reposure

ŌZ′id
posied
rosied

ŌZ′ing
closing
composing
decomposing
deposing
disclosing
discomposing
disposing
dozing
enclosing
exposing
imposing
inclosing
interposing
juxtaposing
nosing
opposing
posing
predisposing
presupposing
proposing
prosing
recomposing
reposing
supposing
transposing
unclosing
unimposing

ÔZ′ing
causing
pausing

ŎZ′it
closet

ŎZ'it
deposit
interposit
juxtaposit
posit
reposit

ŌZ'iv
applausive
plausive
unapplausive

ŎZ''l
nozzle
schnozzle
sozzle

ŎZ'mik
cosmic
endosmic
macrocosmic
microcosmic

ŌZ'ō
bozo

ŌZ'ōn
ozone

ŌZ'ŭr
bulldozer
closer

composer
deposer
discloser
disposer
dozer
encloser
exposer
forecloser
glozer
imposer
incloser
interposer
juxtaposer
opposer
poser

predisposer
presupposer
proposer
roser
reimposer
reposer
superimposer
supposer
transposer
uncloser

ÔZ'ur
causer
hawser
pauser

U

For a discussion of words included under the accented vowels following, see the beginning of Ŭ rhymes in Section I.

Ū'al
dual
eschewal
pursual
renewal
reviewal
subdual
(See also
Ū'el.)

Ū'an
Chouan
duan
Peguan

Ū'ans
eschewance
pursuance

renewance

Ū'ant
pursuant
truant

Ū'ard
leeward
steward
(See also
Ū'urd.)

Ū'ba
Aruba
Cuba
juba
tuba

ŪB'ē
booby
looby
ruby

ŬB'ē
bubby
chubby
cubby
fubby
grubby
hubby
nubby
rabi
rubby
scrubby
shrubby
stubby

tubby

ŬB'ēd
rubied

Ū'ben
Reuben
Steuben

ŪB'ik
cherubic
cubic
pubic

ŪB'ing
cubing
tubing

ŬB'ing
blubbing

ōld, ôr, ŏdd, oil, fŏŏt, out; ūse, ûrn, ŭp; THis, thin

clubbing
drubbing
dubbing
grubbing
nubbing
rubbing
scrubbing
snubbing
stubbing
subbing
tubbing

ŬB′ish
clubbish
cubbish
grubbish
rubbish
tubbish

ŬB′it
cubit

ŬB′jekt
subject

Ū′b′l
ruble

ŬB′′l
bubble
double
grubble
Hubbell
hubble-bubble
nubble
redouble
rubble
stubble
trouble

ŬB′′ld
bubbled
doubled
redoubled
stubbled
troubled
untroubled

ŬB′lē
bubbly
doubly
knubbly
nubbly
rubbly
stubbly

ŬB′lest
bubblest
(See also
ŬB′′l;
add -*est* where
appropriate.)

ŬB′let
doublet

ŬB′leth
bubbleth
(See also
ŬB′′l;
add -*ly* where
appropriate.)

ŬB′lik
public
republic

ŬB′ling
bubbling

doubling
troubling

ŬB′lish
publish

ŬB′lur
bubbler
doubler
troubler

ŬB′lus
troublous

ŬB′ôrn
stubborn

ŬB′rĭk
lubric
rubric

ŬB′stāk
grubstake

ŬB′stans
substance

ŬB′ur
Buber
goober
Huber
tuber

ŬB′ur
blubber
clubber
drubber
dubber
grubber

india rubber
landlubber
lubber
money-grubber
rubber
scrubber
slubber
stubber
tubber
tub-drubber

ŬB′urd
blubbered
cupboard
Hubbard
mother hubbard
rubbered

ŬB′urt
Hubert

ŬCH′ē
coochy
hoochy-coochy

ŬCH′ē
archduchy
clutchy
duchy
smutchy
touchy

ŬCH′es
archduchess
duchess
Dutchess

ŬCH′est
clutchest

āle,　câre,　ădd,　ärm,　ăsk;　mē,　hĕre,　ĕnd;　īce,　ĭll;

(See also
ŬCH; add
-*est* where
appropriate.)

ŬCH′eth
clutcheth
(See also
ŬCH; add
-*eth* where
appropriate.)

ŬCH′ez
clutches
crutches
hutches
retouches
scutches
smutches
touches

ŬCH′ing
clutching
retouching
scutching
smutching
touching

ŬCH′on
escutcheon

ŬCH′ur
retoucher
scutcher
smutcher
toucher

Ū′da
Barbuda

barracuda
Bermuda
Buddha
Ishkooda
Judah

Ū′dad
doodad

ŪD′al
feudal
paludal
udal

ŪD′ē
broody
moody
nudie
Rudy
scudi
Trudy
Yehudi

ŬD′ē
bloody
buddy
cuddy
muddy
puddy
ruddy
studdy
study

ŪD′ed
alluded
brooded
colluded
concluded
deluded

denuded
detruded
duded
eluded
excluded
extruded
exuded
illuded
included
interluded
intruded
obtruded
occluded
precluded
preluded
protruded
recluded
retruded
secluded
snooded
subtruded
transuded
undeluded

ŬD′ēd
bloodied
muddied
ruddied
studied
unstudied

ŬD′ed
bestudded
blooded
budded
flooded
scudded
spudded
studded

thudded

ŬD′en
sudden

ŪD′ens
jurisprudence
prudence

ŪD′ent
concludent
imprudent
jurisprudent
occludent
prudent
student

ŪD′est
alludest
broodest
concludest
crudest
deludest
denudest
detrudest
eludest
excludest
extrudest
exudest
illudest
includest
intrudest
nudest
obtrudest
precludest
preludest
protrudest
recludest
retrudest

rudest
secludest
shrewdest
subtrudest

ŪD′eth
alludeth
broodeth
colludeth
concludeth
deludeth
denudeth
detrudeth
eludeth
excludeth
extrudeth
exudeth
illudeth
includeth
intrudeth
obtrudeth
occludeth
preludeth
protrudeth
retrudeth
recludeth
secludeth
subtrudeth
transudeth

ŪD′ing
abrooding
alluding
brooding
concluding
deluding
denuding
detruding
eluding

excluding
extruding
exuding
illuding
including
intruding
obtruding
occluding
precluding
preluding
protruding
recluding
retruding
secluding
snooding
subtruding
transuding

ŬD′ing
bestudding
budding
flooding
scudding
spudding
studding

ŪD′ish
prudish
rudish
shrewdish

ŪD′ith
Judith

ŪD″l
boodle
caboodle
canoodle
flapdoodle

kiyoodle
noodle
poodle
Yankee-doodle

ŬD″l
bemuddle
buddle
cuddle
fuddle
huddle
muddle
nuddle
puddle
ruddle
scuddle

ŪD′lē
crudely
lewdly
nudely
rudely
shrewdly

ŪD′lē
Dudley

ŬD′lest
bemuddlest
(See also
ŬD″l; add
-*est* where
appropriate.)

ŬD′leth
bemuddleth
(See also
ŬD″l; add
-*eth* where

appropriate.)

ŬD′ling
bemuddling
cuddling
fuddling
huddling
muddling
puddling
scuddling

ŪD′lum
hoodlum

ŬD′lur
cuddler
fuddler
huddler
muddler
puddler

ŪD′nes
lewdness
nudeness
crudeness
rudeness
shrewdness

ŬD′ok
puddock
ruddock

ŪD′ōs
kudos

ŬD′son
Hudson
Judson

āle, câre, ădd, ärm, ăsk; mē, hĕre, ĕnd; īce, ĭll;

ŪD′ur	sudsy	bedewest	undoest
alluder		beshrewest	unscrewest
brooder	**Ū′ē**	bluest	untruest
concluder	bedewy	brewest	ungluest
cruder	bluey	chewest	viewest
deluder	Bowie	cooest	withdrewest
denuder	buoy	doest	wooest
detruder	chop suey	drewest	
eluder	cooee	enduest	**Ū′et**
excluder	coue	ensuest	cruet
extruder	dewy	eschewest	suet
exuder	fluey	fewest	
illuder	gluey	flewest	**Ū′eth**
includer	Louis	gluest	accrueth
intruder	screwy	grewest	bedeweth
obtruder	thewy	hallooest	beshreweth
occluder	viewy	hewest	breweth
precluder		imbrewest	cheweth
preluder	**Ū′el**	imbuest	cooeth
protruder	bejewel	interviewest	doeth
recluder	crewel	knewest	dreweth
retruder	cruel	mewest	endueth
ruder	duel	newest	ensueth
secluder	fuel	pursuest	escheweth
shrewder	gruel	renewest	glueth
subtruder	Hewell	reviewest	greweth
transuder	jewel	ruest	hallooeth
Tudor	newel	screwest	heweth
	Reuel	shampooest	imbreweth
ŬD′ur	Sewell	shoest	imbueth
dudder	tewel	shooest	intervieweth
flooder	(See also	spuest	kneweth
mudder	Ū′al.)	stewest	meweth
pudder		strewest	pursueth
rudder	**Ū′es**	subduest	reneweth
scudder	Jewess	suest	revieweth
shudder		tattooest	rueth
udder	**Ū′est**	threwest	screweth
ŬD′zē	accruest	truest	shampooeth

---

shoeth
shooeth
speweth
steweth
subdueth
sueth
streweth
tabooeth
tattooeth
threweth
undoeth
unglueth
unscreweth
vieweth
withdreweth
wooeth

Ū'fa
chufa
stufa
tufa
Ufa

ŬF'ē
goofy
roofy
spoofy
Sufi
woofy

ŬF'ē
bluffy
buffy
chuffy
fluffy
huffy
pluffy
puffy
sloughy

snuffy
stuffy

Ū'fēld
Bluefield
Newfield

ŬF'en
roughen
toughen

ŬF'est
bepuffest
bluffest
cuffest
gruffest
luffest
muffest
puffest
rebuffest
roughest
sloughest
snuffest
stuffest
toughest

ŬF'et
buffet

ŬF'eth
bluffeth
(See also ŬF;
add -*eth* where
appropriate.)

ŬF'hous
roughhouse

ŬF'in

muffin
puffin
ragamuffin

ŬF'ing
roofing
waterproofing
woofing

ŬF'ing
bluffing
cuffing
fluffing
huffing
luffing
puffing
roughing
sloughing
stuffing

ŬF'ish
gruffish
huffish
roughish
toughish

ŬF''l
bemuffle
buffle
double-shuffle
duffel
muffle
ruffle
scuffle
shuffle
snuffle
truffle
unmuffle
unruffle

ŬF''ld
bemuffled
(See also
ŬF''l; add
-*d* where
appropriate.)

ŬF'lē
bluffly
gruffly
muffly
roughly
ruffly
scuffly
sluffly
snuffly
toughly
truffly

ŬF'lest
bemufflest
(See also
ŬF''l; add
-*st* where
appropriate.)

ŬF'leth
bemuffleth
(See also
ŬF''l; add
-*th* where
appropriate.)

ŬF'ling
bemuffling
muffling
ruffling
scuffling
shuffling

āle, câre, ădd, ärm, ăsk; mē, hĕre, ĕnd; īce, ĭll;

snuffling
unmuffling
unruffling

ŬF′lur
muffler
ruffler
scuffler
shuffler
snuffler
unmuffler

ŬF′nes
bluffness
gruffness
roughness
toughness

ŬF′tē
mufti
tufty

ŬF′ted
tufted

ŪF′ur
aloofer
hoofer
roofer
spoofer

ŬF′ur
bluffer
buffer
cuffer
duffer
gruffer
huffer
luffer
puffer

rougher
snuffer
stuffer
suffer
tougher

Ū′fus
goofus
rufous
Rufus

ŬG′a
meshuggah

Ū′gar
cougar

ŬG′ard
sluggard

ŬG′ē
buggy
muggy
puggi
puggy
sluggy

ŬG′ed
rugged
(See also ŬG;
add -ed or
-ged where
appropriate.)

ŬG′est
druggest
huggest
juggest
luggest
muggest

pluggest
shruggest
sluggest
smuggest
snuggest
tuggest
(See also
ŬG′ist.)

ŬG′et
drugget
nugget

ŬG′eth
druggeth
huggeth
juggeth
luggeth
muggeth
pluggeth
shruggeth
sluggeth
tuggeth

ŬG′hous
bughouse

ŬG′ij
luggage

ŬG′ing
drugging
hugging
jugging
lugging
mugging
plugging
shrugging
slugging
tugging

ŬG′ish
muggish
sluggish
smuggish
snuggish

ŬG′ist
druggist

ŬG′′l
bugle
febrifugal
frugal
fugal
infrugal
jugal
McDougall
vermifugal

ŬG′′l
death struggle
guggle
juggle
smuggle
snuggle
struggle

ŬG′lē
guggly
juggly
plug-ugly
smugly
snuggly
struggly
ugly

ŬG′lest
jugglest

(See also
ŬG''l; add
-*st* where
appropriate.)

ŬG'leth
juggleth
(See also
ŬG''l; add
-*th* where
appropriate.)

ŬG'ling
guggling
juggling
smuggling
struggling

ŬG'lur
bugler
fugler

ŬG'lur
juggler
smuggler
snuggler
struggler

ŬG'nes
smugness
snugness

Ū'gō
Hugo

ŬG'ur
drugger
hugger
hugger-mugger

lugger
mugger
plugger
rugger
shrugger
snugger
tugger

ŬG'wump
mugwump

Ū'īd
blue-eyed
true-eyed

Ū'ĭd
druid
fluid

Ū'ij
brewage
sewage

Ū'ik
catechuic
toluic

Ū'in
blue-ruin
bruin
ruin
sewen

Ū'ing
accruing
barbecuing
bedewing
bestrewing
blueing

brewing
canoeing
chewing
clewing
cooing
cueing
doing
enduing
ensuing
eschewing
eweing
gluing
hallooing
hewing
imbruing
imbuing
interviewing
mewing
mildewing
misconstruing
misdoing
mooing
outdoing
overdoing
poohpoohing
pursuing
renewing
reviewing
screwing
shampooing
shoeing
spewing
stewing
strewing
subduing
suing
tattooing
undoing
unscrewing

viewing
well-doing
wooing
wrong-doing

Ū'ingz
doings
misdoings
(See also
Ū'ing; add
-*s* where
appropriate.)

Ū'is
Lewis
Louis
(See also Ū'es.)

Ū'ish
blueish
glueish
Jewish
newish
shrewish
truish

ŬJ'ē
pudgy
sludgy
smudgy

ŬJ'el
cudgel

ŬJ'est
begrudgest
(See also ŬJ;
add -*st* where
appropriate.)

āle, câre, ădd, ärm, ăsk; mē, hĕre, ĕnd; īce, ĭll;

ŬJ'et
budget

ŬJ'eth
begrudgeth
(See also ŬJ;
add -*th* where
appropriate.)

ŬJ'ez
adjudges
begrudges
budges
drudges
forejudges
fudges
grudges
judges
misjudges
nudges
prejudges
rejudges
sludges
smudges
trudges

ŬJ'ing
adjudging
regrudging
budging
drudging
forejudging
fudging
grudging
judging
misjudging
nudging
prejudging
rejudging

sludging
trudging
ungrudging

ŬJ'ment
judgment

ŬJ'on
bludgeon
curmudgeon
dudgeon
gudgeon

ŬJ'ur
adjudger
begrudger
budger
drudger
forejudger
fudger
grudger
judger
misjudger
nudger
prejudger
rejudger
sludger
smudger
trudger

Ū'ka
bucca
felucca
festuca
fistuca
garookuh
palooka
sambouka
yucca

Ū'kal
archducal
ducal
noctilucal
nuchal
Pentateuchal

Ū'kan
antelucan
Lukan
Moluccan
toucan

Ū'kas
ukase

ŪK'ăs
Clucas
Lucas

ŪK'ē
fluky
snooky
spooky

ŬK'ē
ducky
Kentucky
lucky
mucky
plucky
unlucky

ŪK'est
rebukest
(See also ŪK;
add -*est* where
appropriate.)

ŬK'est
pluckest
(See also ŬK;
add -*est* where
appropriate.)

ŬK'et
bucket
Luckett
Nantucket
Pawtucket
Puckett
sucket
tucket

ŪK'eth
rebuketh
(See also ŪK;
add -*eth* where
appropriate.)

ŬK'eth
plucketh
(See also ŬK;
add -*eth* where
appropriate.)

ŪK'ing
puking
rebuking

ŬK'ing
bucking
chucking
clucking
ducking
mucking
plucking
shucking

sucking
trucking
tucking

ŬK'ish
buckish
muckish
puckish

ŬK''l
bruckle
buckle
chuckle
honeysuckle
huckle
knuckle
muckle
parbuckle
suckle
truckle
unbuckle

ŬK''ld
buckled
chuckled
knuckled
suckled
truckled
unbuckled

ŬK'les
luckless

ŬK'lest
bucklest
(See also
ŬK''l; add
-*est* where
appropriate.)

ŬK'leth
buckleth
(See also
ŬK''l; add
-*eth* where
appropriate.)

ŬK'ling
buckling
chuckling
duckling
knuckling
suckling
truckling
unbuckling

ŬK'lur
buckler
chuckler
knuckler
swashbuckler
truckler

Ū'kō
Duco
Pernambuco

ŬK'old
cuckold

ŬK'rāk
muckrake

ŬK'shot
buckshot
duck-shot

ŬK'siv
influxive

ŬK'som
buxom
lucksome

ŬK'stur
huckster

ŬK'shun
abduction
adduction
affluxion
conduction
construction
deconstruction
deduction
defluxion
destruction
diduction
duction
eduction
effluxion
fluxion
induction
influxion
instruction
introduction
manuduction
misconstruction
nonconduction
obduction
obstruction
overproduction
production
reduction
reproduction
ruction
seduction
self-destruction
subduction

substruction
suction
superinduction
superstruction
traduction

ŬK'tans
reluctance

ŬK'tant
reluctant

ŬK'ted
abducted
conducted
constructed
deducted
fructed
inducted
instructed
misconstructed
obstructed
superstructed
unobstructed

ŬK'test
abductest
conductest
constructest
deductest
inductest
instructest
misconstructest
obstructest

ŬK'teth
abducteth
conducteth
constructeth

āle, câre, ădd, ärm, ăsk; mē, hĕre, ĕnd; īce, ĭll;

deducteth
inducteth
instructeth
misconstructeth
obstructeth

ŬK′til
ductile
inductile
productile

ŬK′ting
abducting
conducting
constructing
deducting
inducting
instructing
misconducting
nonconducting
nonobstructing
obstructing

ŬK′tiv
adductive
conductive
constructive
deductive
destructive
inductive
instructive
introductive
obstructive
productive
reconductive
reconstructive
reductive
reproductive
seductive

self-destructive
superinductive
superstructive
traductive

ŬK′tres
conductress
instructress
introductress
seductress

ŬK′tūr
structure
substructure
superstructure

ŬK′tŭr
abductor
adductor
conductor
constructor
destructor
ductor
eductor
inductor
instructor
introductor
manuductor
non-conductor
obstructor

ŬK′ū, OŌ′kū
cuckoo

Ū′kur
euchre
fluker
lucre
puker

rebuker

ŬK′ur
bucker
chucker
chukker
clucker
ducker
mucker
pucker
sap-sucker
seer-sucker
shucker
succor
sucker
trucker
tucker

Ū′kus
caducous
fucus
leucous
mucous
noctilucous
rukus

Ū′la
Ashtabula
Beulah
Boola Boola
Eula
hula-hula
Loula
Missoula
pula
Wallula

ŬL′a
ampulla

medulla
mullah
nullah

ŬL′da
Hulda

Ū′lē
bluely
Cooley
coolie
coolly
Dooley
duly
Gilhooley
Gillooley
Gilluley
guly
newly
patchouli
Thule
truly
tule
Ultima Thule
unduly
unruly

ŬL′ē
cully
dully
gully
hully
sully

ŬL′ēd
gullied
sullied
unsullied

ōld, ôr, ŏdd, oil, fŏŏt, out; ūse, ûrn, ŭp; THis, thin

ŬL'en
Cullen
sullen
(See also
ŬL'in.)

Ū'lep
julep
(See also
Ū'lip.)

Ū'les
clueless
cueless
dewless
Jewless
mewless
pewless
screwless
viewless

ŪL'est
befoolest
coolest
foolest
pulest
rulest

ŬL'est
annullest
cullest
dullest
lullest
scullest

ŬL'et
cullet
gullet
mullet

ŬL'eth
befooleth
(See also ŪL;
add -eth where
appropriate.)

ŬL'eth
annulleth
gulleth
lulleth
sculleth

ŬL'fur
sulfur

ŬL'gar
vulgar

ŬL'gāt
promulgate
vulgate

ŬL'ij
Coolidge

ŬL'ij
gullage
sullage
ullage

ŬL'in
McMullin
medullin
mullein

ŪL'ing
befooling
cooling
drooling

fooling
mewling
misruling
overruling
puling
ruling
schooling
spooling
tooling

ŬL'ing
annulling
culling
dulling
gulling
hulling
lulling
mulling
sculling

ŬL'inz
Mullins

Ū'lip
tulip
(See also
Ū'lep.)

ŬL'is
portcullis

ŬL'ish
coolish
foolish
mulish
pound-foolish
tom-foolish

ŬL'ish

dullish
gullish

Ū'liks
spondulix

ŬL'jens
effulgence
indulgence
refulgence
self-indulgence

ŬL'jent
circumfulgent
effulgent
emulgent
fulgent
indulgent
interfulgent
profulgent
refulgent
self-indulgent

ŬL'jest
indulgest
(See also ŬLJ;
add -st where
appropriate.)

ŬL'jeth
indulgeth
(See also ŬLJ;
add -th where
appropriate.)

ŬL'jez
bulges
divulges
effulges
indulges

ŬL'jing
bulging
divulging
effulging
indulging
promulging

ŬLJ'ment
divulgement
indulgement

ŬL'jur
divulger
indulger
promulger

ŬL'kāt
inculcate
sulcate
trisulcate

ŬLK'ē
bulky
hulky
sulky

ŬLK'ing
bulking
hulking
skulking
sulking

ŬLK'ur
bulker
skulker
sulker

ŬL'man
Ullman

ŬL'nes
coolness

ŬL'nes
dullness

ŬL'ok
hullock
rowlock

ŬL'pāt
disculpate
exculpate
inculpate

ŬL'pē
gulpy
pulpy

ŬL'pest
gulpest

ŬL'peth
gulpeth

ŬL'pīn
vulpine

ŬL'prit
culprit

ŬLP'tôr
sculptor

ŬLP'tūr
sculpture

ŬL'sest
repulsest

ŬL'set
dulcet

ŬL'seth
repulseth
(See also ŬLS;
add -th where
appropriate.)

ŬL'shun
appulsion
avulsion
compulsion
convulsion
demulsion
divulsion
emulsion
evulsion
expulsion
impulsion
propulsion
pulsion
repulsion
revulsion

ŬL'sing
convulsing
pulsing
repulsing

ŬL'siv
appulsive
compulsive
convulsive
divulsive
emulsive
expulsive
impulsive
propulsive

pulsive
repulsive
revulsive

ŬL'sur
repulser
ulcer

ŬL'tan
sultan

ŬL'tans
exultance
resultance

ŬL'tant
exultant
resultant

ŬL'ted
consulted
exulted
insulted
occulted
resulted

ŬL'test
consultest
(See also ŬLT;
add -est where
appropriate.)

ŬL'teth
consulteth
(See also ŬLT;
add -eth where
appropriate.)

ōld, ôr, ŏdd, oil, fŏŏt, out; ūse, ûrn, ŭp; THis, thin

ŬL'ting
consulting
exulting
insulting
occulting
resulting

ŬL'tiv
consultive
resultive

ŬLT'nes
adultness
occultness

ŬL'trē
sultry

ŬL'tūr
agriculture
apiculture
arboriculture
aviculture
culture
floriculture
horticulture
inculture
multure
pisciculture
self-culture
sylviculture
terra-culture
viticulture
vulture

ŬL'tur
consulter
exulter
insulter

resulter

Ū'lū
Honolulu
Lulu
Zulu

Ū'lur
cooler
drooler
mewler
puler
ridiculer
ruler
spooler
wine cooler

ŬL'ur
annuller
color
cruller
culler
discolor
duller
guller
huller
luller
meduller
miscolor
Muller
multicolor
rose-color
sculler
technicolor
tricolor
watercolor

ŬL'urd
colored

discolored
dullard
high-colored
over-colored
party-colored
peach-colored
rosy-colored
sky-colored
wine-colored

Ū'lūs
screw-loose

ŬL'yar
peculiar

ŬL'yun
cullion
mullion
scullion

Ū'ma
duma
mazuma
Montezuma
puma
Yuma

Ū'man
human
inhuman
Newman
superhuman
Truman

ŪM'at
despumate
exhumate
inhumate

ŬM'at
consummate

ŬM'ba,
ŪM'ba
rumba

ŬM'bat
combat
(See also
ŎM'bat.)

ŬM'bel
dumbbell

ŬM'bent
accumbent
decumbent
incumbent
procumbent
recumbent
superincumbent

ŬM'bik
columbic
plumbic

ŬM'b'l
bejumble
bumble
crumble
fumble
grumble
humble
jumble
mumble
rumble
scumble
stumble

tumble
umbel

ŬM'b'ld
crumbled
unhumbled
(See also
ŬM'b'l; add
-ed where
appropriate.)

ŬM'blē
crumbly
humbly
stumbly
tumbly

ŬM'blest
crumblest
fumblest
grumblest
humblest
jumblest
mumblest
rumblest
stumblest
tumblest

ŬM'bleth
crumbleth
fumbleth
grumbleth
humbleth
jumbleth
mumbleth
rumbleth
stumbleth
tumbleth

ŬM'bling
crumbling
fumbling
grumbling
humbling
jumbling
mumbling
rumbling
stumbling
tumbling

ŬM'blur
crumbler
drumbler
fumbler
grumbler
humbler
jumbler
mumbler
rumbler
stumbler
tumbler

ŬM'bō
Dumbo
gumbo
Jumbo
mumbo jumbo

ŬM'brāt
adumbrate
inumbrate
obumbrate

ŬM'brij
umbrage

ŬM'bril
tumbril

ŬM'brus
cumbrous
penumbrous
slumbrous
unslumbrous

ŬM'bug
humbug

ŬM'bul
Trumbull

ŬM'bur
cumber
disencumber
encumber
Humber
lumbar
lumber
number
outnumber
slumber
number

ŬM'burd
cumbered
unnnumbered
(See also
ŬM'bur; add
-ed where
appropriate.)

ŬM'drum
humdrum

ŪM'ē
bloomy
broomy
Fiume
fumy

gloomy
plumy
rheumy
roomy
spumy

ŬM'ē
crumby
crummie
dummy
gummy
lummy
mummy
plummy
rummy
scrummy
scummy
thrummy
tummy
yummy

ŬM'el
bepummel
hummel
pommel

Ū'men
acumen
albumen
bitumen
catechumen
legumen
rumen
(See also
ŪM'in.)

Ū'ment
accrument
eschewment

imbruement
imbuement
induement
subduement

ŪM'est
assumest
bloomest
boomest
consumest
costumest
doomest
entombest
exhumest
fumest
groomest
illumest
perfumest
plumest
presumest
resumest

ŬM'est
becomest
comest
drummest
dumbest
glummest
gummest
hummest
numbest
rummest
strummest
succumbest

ŬM'et
grummet
plummet
(See also

ŬM'it.)

ŪM'eth
assumeth
bloometh
boometh
consumeth
costumeth
doometh
entombeth
exhumeth
fumeth
groometh
illumeth
perfumeth
plumeth
presumeth
resumeth

ŬM'eth
becometh
cometh
drummeth
gummeth
hummeth
strummeth
succumbeth

ŬM'fal
triumphal

ŬM'fant
triumphant

ŬM'fit
comfit

ŬM'fort
comfort

ŬM'frē
Humphrey

ŬM'frēz
Humphreys

ŪM'ful
bloomful
doomful

ŪM'id
humid
tumid

ŪM'ij
fumage
plumage

ŬM'ij
chummage
rummage
scrummage

ŪM'in
illumine
relumine
(See also
Ū'-men.)

ŪM'ing
assuming
blooming
booming
consuming
disentombing
dooming
entombing
exhuming
fuming

glooming
grooming
illuming
looming
perfuming
pluming
predooming
presuming
resuming
unassuming
unpresuming

ŬM'ing
becoming
benumbing
chumming
coming
drumming
forthcoming
gumming
humming
mumming
numbing
overcoming
plumbing
plumming
scrumming
shortcoming
slumming
strumming
succumbing
summing
thumbing
unbecoming

ŬM'is
pumice

ŬM'it
summit
(See also
ŬM'et.)

ŪM'les
bloomless
broomless
doomless
fumeless
groomless
loomless
plumeless
roomless
tombless

ŪM'let
boomlet
groomlet
plumelet

ŬM'lē
Chumley
comely
cumbersomely
dumbly
frolicsomely
glumly
humorsomely
numbly
rumly
troublesomely
(See also ŬM;
add -ly where
appropriate.)

ŬM'nal
autumnal
columnal

ŬM'nes
dumbness
glumness
numbness

ŬM'nur
Sumner

ŬM'ok
hummock
stomach

ŬM'oks
lummox

ŬM'on
come-on
summon

ŬM'ond
Drummond

ŬM'pas
compass
encompass
rumpus

ŬM'pē
bumpy
chumpy
clumpy
crumpy
dumpy
frumpy
grumpy
humpy
jumpy
lumpy
mumpy

plumpy
slumpy
stumpy
thumpy

ŬM'pest
bethumpest
bumpest
dumpest
humpest
jumpest
lumpest
plumpest
pumpest
stumpest
thumpest
trumpest

ŬM'pet
crumpet
strumpet
trumpet

ŬM'peth
bethumpeth
bumpeth
dumpeth
humpeth
jumpeth
lumpeth
pumpeth
stumpeth
thumpeth
trumpeth

ŬMP'ing
bethumping
bumping
dumping

jumping
lumping
mumping
plumping
pumping
slumping
stumping
thumping
trumping

ŬMP'īr
umpire

ŬMP'ish
bumpish
dumpish
frumpish
grumpish
humpish
jumpish
lumpish
mumpish
plumpish
slumpish

ŬMP'kin
bumpkin
pumpkin

ŬM'p'l
crumple
rumple
unrumple

ŬM'plest
crumplest
(See also
ŬM'p'l; add
-est where
appropriate.)

ōld, ôr, ŏdd, oil, foͦot, out; ūse, ûrn, ŭp; THis, thin

ŬM'pleth
crumpleth
(See also
ŬM'p'l; add
-*eth* where
appropriate.)

ŬM'pling
crumpling
dumpling
rumpling

ŬMP'nes
plumpness

ŬM'pō
Bumpo

ŬMP'shun
assumption
consumption
gumption
presumption
resumption
subsumption

ŬMP'shus
bumptious
scrumptious

ŬMP'tiv
assumptive
consumptive
presumptive
resumptive
subsumptive

ŬM'pur
bethumper

bumper
counterjumper
dumper
jumper
lumper
mumper
plumper
pumper
stumper
thumper
trumper
tub-trumper

ŬM'pus
rumpus
(See also
ŬM'pas.)

ŪM'stōn
tombstone

ŬM'tur
Sumter

ŪM'ur
assumer
baby boomer
bloomer
boomer
consumer
doomer
entomber
fumer
humor
ill-humor
illumer
late bloomer
perfumer
plumer

presumer
resumer
roomer
rumor
tumor

ŬM'ur
comer
Cummer
drummer
dumber
glummer
grummer
gummer
hummer
incomer
midsummer
mummer
newcomer
number
plumber
rummer
scrummer
scummer
strummer
summer

ŪM'urd
good-humored
humored
ill-humored
rumored

ŪM'urz
bloomers
rumors
(See also
ŪM'ur; add
-*s* where

appropriate.)

ŬM'urz
Somers

ŪM'us
brumous
dumous
fumous
grumous
humous
humus
implumous
plumous
spumous

ŪMZ'dā
doomsday

ŬM'zē
clumsy
mumsie

ŪMZ'man
doomsman
groomsman

Ū'na
Acuna
fortuna
lacuna
luna
Peruna
tuna
Una
Varuna
vicuna

āle, câre, ădd, ärm, àsk; mē, hĕre, ĕnd; īce, ĭll;

Ū'nal
lacunal
tribunal

ŬN'chē
bunchy
crunchy
hunchy
punchy

ŬN'chest
bunchest
(See also
ŬNCH; add
-*est* where
appropriate.)

ŬN'cheth
buncheth
(See also
ŬNCH; add
-*eth* where
appropriate.)

ŬN'chez
brunches
bunches
crunches
hunches
lunches
munches
punches
scrunches

ŬN'ching
bunching
crunching
hunching
lunching

munching
number-
  crunching
punching
scrunching

ŬN'chun
bruncheon
luncheon
nuncheon
puncheon
scuncheon
truncheon

ŬN'chur
bruncher
buncher
cruncher
huncher
luncher
muncher
number-
  cruncher
puncher
scruncher

ŬN'dān
antemundane
extramundane
infra-mundane
intermundane
intramundane
mundane
supermundane
supramundane
ultramundane

ŬN'dans
abundance

redundance
sun dance
superabundance

ŬN'dant
abundant
redundant
superabundant

ŬN'dāt
fecundate
secundate

ŬN'dē
Bundy
fundi
Fundy
Grundy
Lundy
Monday
salmagundi
Sunday

ŪN'ded
unwounded
wounded

ŬN'ded
funded
refunded
retunded

ŪN'dest
woundest
(See also
ŪND; add
-*est* where
appropriate.)

ŬN'dest
fundest
(See also ŬND;
add -*est* where
appropriate.)

ŪN'deth
woundeth
(See also ŪND;
add -*eth* where
appropriate.)

ŬN'deth
fundeth
(See also ŬND;
add -*eth* where
appropriate.)

ŬN'din
hirundine

ŬN'ding
funding
refunding

ŬN'd'l
bundle
trundle
unbundle

ŬN'dlest
bundlest
(See also
ŬN'd'l; add
-*est* where
appropriate.)

ŬN'dleth
bundleth

ōld, ôr, ŏdd, oil, fŏŏt, out; ūse, ûrn, ŭp; THis, thin

(See also
ŬN'd'l; add
-th where
appropriate.)

ŬND'ling
bundling
trundling
(See also
ŬN'd'l; drop
-e and add
-ing where
appropriate.)

ŬN'don
London

ŬN'drē
sundry
thund'ry

ŬN'dred
hundred

ŬN'drus
wondrous

ŬN'dur
asunder
blunder
dissunder
dunder
down-under
enthunder
Gunder
plunder
refunder
rotunder
sunder

thereunder
thunder
under
wonder

ŬN'ē
Cluny
Dooney
loony
Mooney
Moonie
moony
Mulrooney
Muni
puisne
puny
spoony
uni

ŬN'ē
acrimony
agrimony
alimony
antimony
bunny
funny
gunny
honey
matrimony
money
parsimony
patrimony
sanctimony
sonny
Sunni
sunny
Tunney
tunny
unsunny

ŬN'el
funnel
gunwale
runnel
trunnel
tunnel

ŬN'et
punnet
runnet

Ū'nes
blueness
fewness
newness
trueness

ŪN'est
attunest
communest
croonest
entunest
harpoonest
importunest
impugnest
moonest
oppugnest
prunest
soonest
spoonest
swoonest
tunest

ŬN'est
runnest
(See also ŬN;
add -nest or
-est where
appropriate.)

ŪN'eth
attuneth
communeth
crooneth
entuneth
harpooneth
impugneth
mooneth
oppugneth
pruneth
spooneth
swooneth
tuneth

ŬN'eth
runneth
(See also ŬN;
add -eth where
appropriate.)

ŪN'ful
tuneful
runeful
spoonful

UNG'g'l
bungle
jungle

UNG'gling
bungling

UNG'gur
balladmonger
boroughmonger
costermonger
enhunger
fishmonger
hunger

---

ironmonger
monger
Munger
warmonger
younger

ŬNG'gus
fungus
humongous
mundungus
smellfungus

ŬNGK'al
carbuncle
caruncle
peduncle
truncal
uncle

ŬNGK'āt
averruncate
detruncate
truncate

ŬNGK'ē
chunky
flunkey
funky
hunky
monkey
powder mon-
    key
punkie
spunky

ŬNGK'en
drunken
shrunken
sunken

ŬNGK'et
junket
Plunkett

ŬNG'kin
punkin
(See also
ŬN'kan.)

ŬNGK'ish
funkish
monkish
skunkish

ŬNGK'ō
bunco
junco

ŬNGK'shun
adjunction
compunction
conjunction
defunction
disjunction
expunction
function
injunction
interjunction
interpunction
inunction
junction
punction
sejunction
subjunction
unction

ŬNGK'shus
compunctious
rambunctious

unctious

ŬNGK'tiv
abjunctive
adjunctive
compunctive
conjunctive
disjunctive
subjunctive

ŬNGK'tur
acupuncture
conjuncture
juncture
puncture

ŬNGK'um
Buncombe
bunkum

ŬNGK'ur
bunker
drunker
dunker
flunker
funker
hunker
junker
punker
tunker

ŬNGK'urd
bunkered
drunkard
Dunkard

ŬNGK'us
aduncous
dohunkus

juncous

ŬNG'ling
youngling

ŬN'grē
hungry

ŬNG'stur
tonguester
youngster

ŬNG'ur
lunger

ŬN'ij
dunnage
gunnage
tonnage

ŪN'ik
Munich
Punic
runic
tunic

ŬN'in
run-in

ŪN'ing
ballooning
communing
crooning
expugning
harpooning
impugning
mooning
nooning
oppugning

pruning
spooning
swooning
tuning

ŬN'ing
cunning
dunning
funning
gunning
outrunning
overrunning
punning
running
shunning
stunning
sunning

Ū'nis
Eunice
Tunis

ŪN'-ish
buffoonish
poltroonish

ŬN'ish
Hunnish
punish
punnish

ŪN'ist
balloonist
bassoonist
contrabassoon-
ist
harpoonist
opportunist

Ū'nit
unit

ŪN'iz'm
buffoonism
opportunism
poltroonism

ŬN'jē
plungy
spongy

ŬN'jent
pungent

ŬN'jest
expungest
(See also ŬNJ;
add -*st* where
appropriate.)

ŬN'jeth
expungeth
(See also ŬNJ;
add -*eth* where
appropriate.)

ŬN'jez
expunges
lunges
plunges
sponges

ŬN'jing
expunging
lunging
plunging
sponging

ŬN'jun
dungeon
plungeon

ŬN'jur
blunger
expunger
lunger
plunger
sponger

ŬN'kan
Duncan
(See also
ŬNG'kin.)

ŪN'les
moonless
runeless
tuneless

ŬN'les
punless
runless
sonless
sunless

ŪN'līt
moonlight
noonlight

ŬN'man
gunman

ŪN'nes
inopportune-
ness
jejuneness
opportuneness

Ū'nō
Bruno
Juno

ŪN'rīz
moonrise

ŬN'sē
Munsey

**ŬN'stan,
ŬN'ston**
Dunstan
Funston

ŬN'stur
gunster
munster
punster

ŬN'tal
contrapuntal
frontal
gruntle

ŬN'tē
punty
runty
stunty

ŬN'ted
affronted
blunted
bunted
confronted
fronted
grunted
hunted
punted

āle, câre, ădd, ärm, ăsk; mē, hẹre, ĕnd; īce, ĭll;

shunted
stunted
unblunted
unwonted
wonted

ŬN'test
affrontest
bluntest
buntest
confrontest
gruntest
huntest
puntest
shuntest
stuntest

ŬN'teth
affronteth
blunteth
bunteth
confronteth
grunteth
hunteth
punteth
shunteth
stunteth

ŬN'ting
affronting
bunting
confronting
fronting
grunting
headhunting
hunting
punting
reed-bunting
shunting

stunting
yellow-bunting

ŬNT'les
frontless
wontless

ŬNT'nes
bluntness
stuntness

ŬN'tō
junto

ŬN'trē
country

ŬN'tū
unto

ŬN'tur
affronter
blunter
bunter
confronter
fortune hunter
grunter
Gunter
headhunter
hunter
legacy hunter
punter
shunter
stunter

ŬNTS'vil
Blountsville
Huntsville

Ū'nuk
eunuch

ŪN'ur
attuner
ballooner
communer
crooner
dragooner
harpooner
importuner
impugner
interlunar
lacunar
lampooner
lunar
mooner
novilunar
oppugner
piano tuner
plenilunar
pruner
schooner
semilunar
sooner
spooner
sublunar
swooner
translunar
tuner

ŬN'ur
dunner
forerunner
gunner
overrunner
punner
runner
stunner

ŬN'yon
communion
disunion
excommunion
intercommu-
nion
reunion
trades union
union

ŬN'yon
bunion
munnion
onion
ronyon
trunnion

ŪN'yôr
junior

Ū'pa
pupa
supa

ŬP'ans
comeuppance
thruppence

ŪP'ē
croupy
droopy
groupie
loopy
rupee
snoopy
soupy
whoopee

ōld, ôr, ŏdd, oil, fŏŏt, out; ūse, ûrn, ŭp; THis, thin

ŬP'ē
cuppy
guppy
puppy
yuppie

ŬP'est
coopest
droopest
dupest
groupest
loopest
recoupest
scoopest
stoopest
swoopest
troopest
whoopest

ŬP'est
suppest

ŬP'et
puppet

ŪP'eth
coopeth
droopeth
dupeth
groupeth
loopeth
recoupeth
scoopeth
stoopeth
swoopeth
troopeth
whoopeth

ŬP'eth

suppeth

Ū'pid
Cupid
stupid

Ū'pil
pupil

ŪP'ing
cooping
drooping
duping
grouping
hooping
looping
recouping
scooping
stooping
swooping
trooping
whooping

ŬP'ing
cupping
supping
tupping

ŬP'ish
puppish
uppish

ŬP''l
octuple
quadruple
quintuple
septuple
sextuple
scruple

subduple

ŬP''l
couple
supple

ŬP'lest
scruplest

ŬP'lest
couplest

ŬP'let
octuplet
quintuplet

ŪP'leth
scrupleth

ŬP'leth
coupleth

ŬP'lur
coupler
suppler

ŬP'ment
aggroupment
recoupment

Ū'pon
coupon
jupon

ŪP'ôr
stupor
(See also
ŪP'ur.)

ŬP'shal
antenuptial
nuptial
postnuptial
prenuptial

ŬP'shun
abruption
corruption
disruption
eruption
incorruption
interruption
irruption
ruption

ŬP'ted
abrupted
corrupted
disrupted
interrupted
irrupted

ŬP'test
abruptest
corruptest
interruptest

ŬP'teth
corrupteth
(See also ŬPT;
add -*eth* where
appropriate.)

ŬP'ting
corrupting
erupting
interrupting

ĬP'tiv
corruptive
disruptive
eruptive
incorruptive
interruptive
irruptive

ĬPT'lē
abruptly
corruptly

ĬPT'nes
abruptness
corruptness
incorruptness

ŪP'ur
cooper
drooper
duper
grouper
hooper
looper
recouper
scooper
snooper
stooper
stupor
super
super-duper
swooper
trooper
whooper

ĬP'ur
crupper
cupper
scupper

supper
upper

ĬP'urt
Rupert

ĬP'ward
upward

Ū'ra
Angostura
appoggiatura
bravura
caesura
coloratura
Cuticura
datura
fissura
flexura
Keturah
pietra-dura
pleura
purpura
sura
velatura
vettura

Ū'ral
antemural
caesural
commissural
crural
extramural
intermural
interneural
intramural
jural
mural
neural

pleural
plural
rural
sinecural
sural
tellural
Ural

ÛR'ans
allurance
assurance
durance
endurance
insurance
perdurance
reassurance

ŪR'āt
curate

ŪR'ăt
jurat
obdurate

ÛR'bal
herbal
verbal

ÛR'ban
interurban
suburban
turban
urban

ÛR'bans
disturbance

ÛR'bar
durbur

ÛR'bāt
acerbate
masturbate
perturbate

ŬR'best
blurbest
curbest
disturbest
perturbest

ÛR'bet
sherbet

ÛR'beth
blurbeth
curbeth
disturbeth
perturbeth

ÛR'bē
derby
herby
Iturbi
kirby
Roller Derby

ÛR'bid
herbid
turbid

ÛR'bīn
turbine

ÛR'bing
curbing
disturbing
perturbing

ÛR′bot
burbot
turbot

ÛR′bur
Berber
blurber
curber
disturber
Ferber
Gerber
perturber
superber

ÛR′burt
Herbert

ÛR′chant
merchant
perchant

ÛR′chas
purchase

ÛR′chast
purchased

ÛR′chen
birchen

ÛR′chest
birchest
lurchest
perchest
searchest
smirchest
(See also
ÛR′-chast.)

ÛR′cheth
bircheth
lurcheth
percheth
searcheth
smircheth

ÛR′chez
besmirches
birches
churches
lurches
perches
researches
searches
smirches

ÛR′chif
kerchief

ÛR′ching
besmirching
birching
churching
lurching
perching
searching
smirching

ÛRCH′les
churchless
smirchless

ÛR′chur
besmircher
bircher
lurcher
percher
researcher

searcher
smircher
(See also
ÛR′tŭr.)

ÛRD′book
herdbook
wordbook

ÛR′dē
birdie
birdy
curdy
hurdy-gurdy
sturdy
wordy

ÛR′ded
begirded
curded
engirded
girded
herded
sherded
worded

ÛR′den
burden
disburden
overburden
unburden
(See also
ÛR′don.)

ÛR′dest
absurdest
begirdest
engirdest
girdest

heardest

ÛR′deth
begirdeth
(See also ÛRD;
add -*eth* as
appropriate.)

ÛR′dikt
verdict

ÛR′ding
begirding
engirding
girding
herding
ungirding
wording

ÛR′d′l
begirdle
curdle
engirdle
girdle
hurdle

ÛR′don
Burdon
guerdon
(See also
ÛR′den.)

ÛR′dūr
verdure
(See also
ÛR′jūr.)

ÛR′dŭr
absurder

āle, câre, ădd, ärm, ăsk; mē, hĕre, ĕnd; īce, ĭll;

Burder
engirder
girder
herder
murder
self-murder
thirder

ÛRDZ'man
herdsman
wordsman

ÛR'ē
de jure
Drury
ewry
fury
houri
Jewry
jury
Missouri

ÛR'ē
burry
curry
firry
flurry
furry
hurry
hurry-scurry
lurry
Murray
scurry
Surrey
slurry
whirry
worry

ÛR'ēd

curried
flurried
hurried
scurried
worried

ÛR'el
Burrell
squirrel

ÛR'ens
concurrence
deterrence
incurrence
intercurrence
occurrence
recurrence
reoccurrence
transference

ÛR'ent,
ÛR'ant
concurrent
currant
current
decurrent
deterrent
intercurrent
recurrent
susurrant
undercurrent

ÛR'est
abjurest
adjurest
allurest
assurest
conjurest
curest

demurest
endurest
ensurest
immurest
impurest
insurest
lurest
maturest
moorest
obscurest
poorest
procurest
purest
reassurest
securest
surest
tourest
unmoorest

ÛR'est
bestirrest
blurrest
concurrest
conferrest
deferrest
demurrest
errest
incurrest
inferrest
interrest
preferrest
purrest
referrest
spurrest
stirrest
transferrest

ÛR'et
turret

ÛR'eth
abjureth
adjureth
allureth
conjureth
cureth
endureth
immureth
lureth
matureth
obscureth
procureth
secureth
assureth
ensureth
insureth
mooreth
reassureth
toureth
unmooreth

ÛR'eth
bestirreth
blurreth
concurreth
conferreth
deferreth
erreth
demurreth
incurreth
inferreth
interreth
occurreth
preferreth
purreth
recurreth
referreth
spurreth
stirreth

transferreth	a tergo	**ÛR'in**	deferring
	ergo	burin	demurring
ÛR'ēz	Virgo	daturin	erring
curries		neurin	incurring
flurries	**ÛR'gur**	neurine	inferring
hurries	burgher		interring
scurries	*jerguer*	**ÛR'ing**	nonconcurring
worries		abjuring	occurring
	ÛR'gus	adjuring	preferring
ÛR'fē	demiurgus	alluring	purring
Durfey	Mergus	assuring	recurring
Murphy	thaumaturgus	conjuring	referring
scurfy		curing	shirring
surfy	**ÛR'id**	during	slurring
turfy	lurid	enduring	spurring
		ensuring	stirring
ÛR'fekt	**ÛR'ij**	everduring	transferring
perfect	moorage	immuring	unerring
	murage	insuring	whirring
ÛR'fit		inuring	
surfeit	**ÛR'ij**	juring	**ÛR'ish**
	courage	luring	amateurish
ÛR'fūm	demurrage	manuring	boorish
perfume	discourage	maturing	Moorish
	encourage	mooring	poorish
ÛR'gāt		nonjuring	
expurgate	**ÛR'ik**	obscuring	**ÛR'ish**
objurgate	hydrosulfuric	procuring	burrish
virgate	hydrotelluric	reassuring	currish
	purpuric	securing	flourish
ÛR'g'l	sulfuric	touring	nourish
burgle	telluric	unmooring	
gurgle			**ÛR'ist**
	ÛR'ik	**ÛR'ing**	caricaturist
ÛR'glar	myrrhic	astirring	jurist
burglar		bestirring	purist
gurgler	**ÛR'im**	blurring	tourist
	purim	concurring	
ÛR'gō	urim	conferring	**ÛR'iz'm**

---

purism
tourism

ÛR′jē
aciurgy
clergy
dirgie
dramaturgy
metallurgy
periergy
surgy
thaumaturgy

ÛR′jens
convergence
deturgence
divergence
emergence
resurgence
submergence

ÛR′jent
abstergent
assurgent
convergent
detergent
divergent
emergent
insurgent
resurgent
splurgent
turgent
urgent
vergent

ÛR′jest
convergest
dirgest
divergest

emergest
mergest
purgest
scourgest
splurgest
submergest
surgest
urgest

ÛR′jeth
convergeth
dirgeth
divergeth
emergeth
mergeth
purgeth
scourgeth
splurgeth
submergeth
surgeth
urgeth

ÛR′jez
asperges
Boanerges
converges
dirges
diverges
emerges
merges
purges
scourges
serges
submerges
surges
urges
verges

ÛR′jid

turgid

ÛR′jik
chirurgic
demiurgic
dramaturgic
energic
liturgic
metallurgic
thaumaturgic
theurgic

ÛR′jin
virgin

ÛR′jing
converging
dirging
diverging
emerging
immerging
merging
purging
scourging
splurging
submerging
surging
urging
verging

ÛR′jist
dramaturgist
metallurgist
thaumaturgist

ÛR′jun
burgeon
Spurgeon
sturgeon

surgeon

ÛR′jŭr
perjure
(See also
ÛR′dŭr.)

ÛR′jŭr
converger
dirger
diverger
emerger
merger
purger
scourger
submerger
urger
verger

ÛR′jus
verjuice

ÛR′kal
Lupercal
novercal
(See also
ÛR′k'l.)

ÛR′kē
jerky
lurky
mirky
murky
perky
quirky
shirky
smirky
talk turkey
turkey

ÛR′kest
clerkest
(See also
ÛRK; add
-*est* where
appropriate.)

ÛR′keth
clerketh
(See also
ÛRK; add
-*eth* where
appropriate.)

ÛR′kin
firkin
gherkin
jerkin
merkin

ÛR′king
aworking
clerking
hard-working
jerking
lurking
perking
shirking
smirking
working

ÛR′kish
quirkish
Turkish

ÛR′kins
Firkins
Perkins
gherkins

(See also
ÛR′kin; add
-*s* where
appropriate.)

ÛR′kit
circuit

ÛR′k'l
circle
encircle
Merkle
semicircle
turkle

ÛR′klet
circlet

ÛR′klē
circly
clerkly

ÛR′kling
circling

ÛRK′man
Turkman
workman

ÛRK′som
irksome
mirksome

ÛR′kur
burker
jerker
jerquer
lurker
shirker

smirker
tearjerker
wonder-worker
worker

ÛR′kus
bifurcous
circus
Quercus

ÛR′kwoiz
turquoise

ÛRLD′lē
worldly

ÛRLD′ling
worldling

ÛR′lest
curlest
furlest
hurlest
swirlest
twirlest
unfurlest
whirlest

ÛR′leth
curleth
furleth
hurleth
purleth
swirleth
twirleth
unfurleth
whirleth

ÛRL′hood

girlhood

ÛR′lē
demurely
maturely
obscurely
poorly
purely
securely

ÛR′lē
burly
churly
curly
early
girlie
girly
hurly-burly
knurly
pearly
Shirley
surly
swirly
whirly

ÛR′lin
merlin
pearlin

ÛR′ling
curling
furling
herling
hurling
pearling
purling
Sperling
sterling
Stirling

swirling
twirling
uncurling
unfurling
upcurling
upwhirling

ÛR′lish
churlish
girlish
pearlish

ÛR′loin
purloin
sirloin

ÛR′lū
curlew
purlieu

ÛR′lur
burler
curler
furler
hurler
pearler
purler
skirler
twirler
whirler

ÛR′ma
Burma
derma
Irma
syrma

ÛR′mād
mermaid

ÛR′mal
dermal
diathermal
epidermal
geothermal
hydrothermal
hypodermal
isogeothermal
isothermal
pachydermal
synthermal
taxidermal
thermal

ÛR′man
cousin-german
firman
German
merman
(See also
ER′mon.)

ÛR′mans
affirmance
confirmance
disaffirmance

ÛR′mē
germy
taxidermy
wormy

ÛR′ment
abjurement
allurement
conjurement
immurement
obscurement
procurement

ÛR′ment,
ÛR′mant
affirmant
averment
deferment
determent
disinterment
ferment
interment
preferment
referment

ÛR′mest
confirmest
firmest
infirmest
squirmest
termest
wormest

ÛR′meth
confirmeth

ÛR′mēz
Hermes
kermes

ÛR′mik
adiathermic
dermic
diathermic
endermic
endodermic
epidermic
esodermic
exodermic
geothermic
hydrodermic
hypodermic

isogeothermic
mesodermic
pachydermic
sclerodermic
taxidermic
thermic

ÛR′min
determine
ermine
vermin

ÛR′mind
determined
ermined
undetermined

ÛR′ming
affirming
confirming
squirming
worming

ÛR′mis
dermis
endodermis
epidermis
exodermis

ÛR′mish
skirmish

ÛR′mīt
termite

ÛR′mĭt
hermit
permit

ÛRM′lē
firmly
termly

ÛR′moil
turmoil

ÛR′mur
affirmer
bemurmur
confirmer
firmer
infirmer
murmur
squirmer
termer
termor
wormer

ÛR′na
Myrna
Verna

ÛR′nal
cavernal
coeternal
colonel
diurnal
diuternal
eternal
external
fraternal
hesternal
hibernal
hodiernal
infernal
internal
journal
kernel

lucernal
maternal
nocturnal
paraphernal
paternal
semidiurnal
sempiternal
sternal
supernal
urnal
vernal

ÛR′nant,
ÛR′nent
alternant
secernent
vernant

ÛR′nard
Bernard

ÛR′nas
furnace

ÛR′nāt
alternate
cothurnate
subalternate
ternate

ÛR′nē
attorney
Berney
Birney
burny-burny
ferny
Gurney
journey
Turney

tourney

ÛR′ned
learned
(See also
ÙRN; add
-ed where
appropriate.)

ÛR′nes
demureness
immatureness
impureness
insecureness
matureness
obscureness
poorness
pureness
secureness
sureness

ÛR′nes
Furness
(See also
ÙR′nas.)

ÛR′nest
adjournest
burnest
churnest
concernest
discernest
earnest
Ernest
learnest
overearnest
overturnest
returnest
sojournest

spurnest
sternest

ÛR′nest
turnest
yearnest

ÛR′neth
adjourneth
burneth
churneth
concerneth
discerneth
learneth
overturneth
returneth
sojourneth
spurneth
turneth
yearneth

ŬR′ning
adjourning
booklearning
burning
churning
concerning
discerning
earning
heartburning
learning
overburning
overturning
returning
sojourning
spurning
table-turning
turning
undiscerning
unlearning
upturning

āle,   câre,   ădd,   ärm,   ăsk;   mē,   hĕre,   ĕnd;   īce,   ĭll;

urning
yearning

ÛR′nish
burnish
furnish

ÛR′nisht
burnished
furnished
unburnished
unfurnished

ÛRN′ment
adjournment
attornment
concernment
discernment
secernment
sojournment

ÛRN′nes
sternness

ÛR′nō
inferno
Sterno

ÛR′num
laburnum

ÛR′nur
adjourner
burner
discerner
earner
learner
overturner
returner

sojourner
spurner
sterner
turner
yearner

ÛR′nus
cothurnus

ÛR′ō
bureau
chiaroscuro
maduro

ÛR′ō
borough
burrow
furrow
thorough

ÛR′od
burrowed
furrowed
unfurrowed

ÛR′or
furor
juror
(See also
ÛR′ur.)

ÛR′pent
serpent

ÛR′pest
chirpest
(See also ÛRP;
add -*est* where
appropriate.)

ÛR′peth
chirpeth
turpeth
usurpeth

ÛR′ping
burping
chirping
usurping

ÛR′p'l
empurple
purple

ÛR′pos
purpose

ÛR′pur
burper
chirper
usurper

ÛR′sa
ursa
vice versa

ÛR′sal
controversal
rehearsal
reversal
tercel
transversal
universal
ursal
versal

ÛR′sant
aversant
recursant

versant

ÛR′sē
Circe
controversy
gramercy
mercy
Mersey
Percy
pursy
Searcy

ÛR′sed
accursed
(See also ŬRS;
add -*ed* where
appropriate.)

ÛR′sest
accurest
becursest
coercest
conversest
cursest
disbursest
dispersest
immersest
interspersest
nursest
rehearsest
reimbursest
reversest
traversest

ÛR′set
tercet

ÛR′seth
accurseth

becurseth
coerceth
converseth
curseth
disburseth
disperseth
immerseth
intersperseth
nurseth
rehearseth
reimburseth
reverseth
traverseth

ÛR′sez
accurses
amerces
becurses
coerces
converses
curses
disburses
disperses
hearses
immerses
intersperses
nurses
purses
rehearses
reimburses
reverses
submerses
traverses
verses

ÛR′shal
commercial
controversial
tertial

uncommercial

ÛR′ship
worship

ÛR′shum
nasturtium

ÛR′shun
abstersion
animadversion
apertion
aspersion
assertion
aversion
circumversion
Cistercian
coercion
concertion
contraversion
controversion
conversion
demersion
desertion
disconcertion
discursion
dispersion
diversion
emersion
eversion
excursion
exertion
extension
immersion
incursion
insertion
inspersion
intersertion
interspersion

introversion
inversion
lacertian
mersion
nasturtion
obversion
perversion
recursion
retroversion
reversion
self-assertion
submersion
subversion
tertian
version

ÛR′sing
accursing
becursing
coercing
conversing
cursing
disbursing
dispersing
immersing
nursing
rehearsing
reimbursing
reversing
transversing
traversing
versing

ÛR′siv
abstersive
animadversive
aspersive
aversive
coercive

conversive
cursive
decursive
detersive
discursive
dispersive
eversive
excursive
incursive
perversive
precursive
subversive

ŬRS′ment
amercement
disbursement
imbursement
reimbursement

ŬRS′nes
adverseness
averseness
perverseness
terseness

ÛR′son
anchorperson
chairperson
Gerson
McPherson
newsperson
nonperson
person
salesperson
spokesperson
unperson
waitperson

ÛR′stē

thirsty

ÛR'sted
bursted
thirsted
worsted

ÛR'stest
burstest
(See also
ÛRST; add
-est where
appropriate.)

ÛR'steth
bursteth
(See also
ÛRST; add
-eth where
appropriate.)

ÛR'sting
bursting
thirsting
worsting

ÛR'stur
burster
thirster

ÛR'sur
accurser
amercer
ante-cursor
bursar
coercer
commercer
converser
curser

cursor
disburser
disperser
hearser
immerser
mercer
nurser
perverser
precursor
purser
rehearser
reimburser
reverser
traverser
verser
worser

ÛR'sus
excursus
thyrsus
ursus
versus

ÛR'ta
Alberta
Elberta

ÛR'tan
certain
curtain
encurtain
incertain
uncertain

ÛR'ted
adverted
asserted
averted
blurted

concerted
converted
deserted
disconcerted
diverted
exerted
flirted
inserted
interserted
inverted
perverted
preconcerted
reverted
spurted
squirted
subverted
undiverted
unperverted

ÛR'tēn
thirteen

ÛR'tens
advertence
inadvertence
misadvertence

ÛR'test
advertest
assertest
avertest
blurtest
concertest
controvertest
covertest
curtest
disconcertest
divertest
exertest

hurtest
insertest
invertest
pertest
pervertest
revertest
skirtest
spurtest
subvertest

ÛR'teth
adverteth
asserteth
averteth
blurteth
concerteth
controverteth
converteth
disconcerteth
diverteth
exerteth
hurteth
inserteth
inverteth
perverteth
reverteth
skirketh
spurteth
subverteth

ÛR'tha
Bertha
Hertha

ÛR'THen
burthen
disburthen
unburthen

ōld, ôr, ŏdd, oil, fŏŏt, out; ūse, ûrn, ŭp; THis, thin

ÛR'then
earthen

ÛR'THur
further

ÛR'THest
furthest

ÛRth'ful
mirthful
worthful

ÛRth'les
birthless
mirthless
worthless

ÛR'THē
noteworthy
seaworthy
trustworthy
worthy
unworthy

ÛR'thē
earthy

ÛR'tē
cherty
dirty
flirty
Gertie
thirty

ÛR'ting
adverting
asserting
averting

blurting
concerting
controverting
converting
deserting
disconcerting
diverting
exerting
flirting
hurting
inserting
interserting
interverting
inverting
perverting
preconcerting
retroverting
reverting
self-asserting
shirting
skirting
spurting
squirting
subverting

ÛR'tiv
assertive
divertive
exertive
furtive
revertive
self-assertive

ÛR'tis
Curtis

ÛR't'l
fertile
hurtle

kirtle
myrtle
spurtle
turtle
whortle

ÛRT'lē
alertly
curtly
expertly
inertly
inexpertly
pertly

ÛRT'les
shirtless
skirtless

ÛRT'nes
alertness
curtness
expertness
inertness
inexpertness
pertness

ÛR'ton
Berton
(See also
ÛR'tan.)

ÛR'trūd
Gertrude

ÛRT'sē
curtsey

ÛR'tū
virtue

ÛR'tūr
nurture
(See also
ÛR'chur.)

ÛR'tŭr
adverter
animadverter
asserter
averter
converter
curter
disconcerter
diverter
exerter
hurter
inserter
inverter
perter
perverter
preconcerter
spurter
squirter
subverter

ÛR'up
stirrup
(See also
ĬR'up.)

ÛR'ur
abjurer
adjurer
allurer
assurer
conjurer
curer
demurer
endurer

āle, câre, ădd, ärm, ăsk; mē, hĕre, ĕnd; īce, ĭll;

ensurer
immurer
impurer
insurer
inurer
juror
lurer
manurer
maturer
moorer
nonjuror
obscurer
poorer
procurer
purer
reassurer
securer
surer
tourer
unmoorer
(See also
ŬR'or.)

ŪR'ur
averrer
bestirrer
blurrer
concurrer
conferrer
deferrer
demurrer
incurrer
inferrer
interrer
preferrer
spurrer
stirrer
transferrer

ŪR'us
anurous
Arcturus
dolichurus
Eurus
urus

ÛR'us
susurrous
wurrus

ÛR'uz
Burroughs
Burrows
(See also
ŬR'ō; add
-s where
appropriate.)

ÛR'va
Minerva

ÛR'val
acerval
curval

ÛR'vans,
ÛR'vens
fervence
inobservance
observance
unobservance

ÛR'vant,
ÛR'vent
conservant
curvant
fervent
inobservant

observant
recurvant
servant
unobservant

ÛR'vāt
acervate
curvate
enervate
incurvate
recurvate
trinervate

ÛR'vē
nervy
scurvy
topsy-turvy

ÛR'ven
nervine

ÛR'vest
conservest
curvest
deservest
observest
preservest
reservest
servest
swervest
unnervest

ÛR'veth
conserveth
curveth
deserveth
observeth
preserveth
reserveth

serveth
swerveth
unnerveth

ÛR'vid
fervid
perfervid

ÛR'vīl
servile

ÛR'vĭl
chervil
servile

ÛR'vim
cervine
nervine

ÛR'ving
conserving
curving
deserving
Irving
nerving
observing
preserving
reserving
serving
swerving
time-serving
undeserving
unnerving
unobserving
unswerving

ÛR'vis
lip service
merchant
　service

Purvis
sea service
service
unservice

ÛRV'les
nerveless

ÛR'vur
conserver
deserver
fervor
game-preserver
life-preserver
nerver
observer
preserver
reserver
server
swerver
time-server
unnerver

ÛR'vus
nervous
recurvous

ÛR'win
Erwin
Irwin
Merwin

ÛRZ'dā
Thursday

ÛR'zē
furzy
jersey
kersey

ÛR'zha
Persia

ÛR'zhun
animadversion
aspersion
aversion
bioconversion
coercion
conversion
demersion
discursion
dispersion
diversion
emersion
eversion
excursion
extroversion
incursion
interspersion
introversion
inversion
obversion
Persian
perversion
recursion
retroversion
reversion
submersion
subversion
version

Ū'sa
Arethusa
Coosa
Medusa
Sousa
Susa
Tallapoosa

Tuscaloosa

ŪS'al
hypotenusal

ŪS'chun
adustion
combustion
fustian

ŪS'ē
goosy
juicy
Lucy
sluicy

ŬS'ē
fussy
hussy
mussy

ŪS'ed
deuced
(See also ŪS;
add *-ed* where
appropriate.)

ŪS'en
loosen
unloosen

ŪS'ens
translucence

ŪS'ent
abducent
adducent
conducent
interlucent

lucent
producent
reducent
relucent
traducent
tralucent
translucent
unlucent

ŪS'est
abstrusest
adducest
conducest
deducest
inducest
introducest
loosest
producest
profusest
reducest
reproducest
seducest
sprucest
traducest
unloosest

ŬS'est
fussest
(See also ŬS;
add *-est* where
appropriate.)

ŬS'et
gusset
russet

ŪS'eth
adduceth
conduceth

deduceth
educeth
induceth
introduceth
looseth
produceth
reduceth
reproduceth
seduceth
spruceth
traduceth
unlooseth

ŬS′eth
fusseth
(See also ŬS;
add -*eth* where
appropriate.)

ŪS′ez
abuses
adduces
burnooses
cabooses
conduces
deduces
Druses
excuses
induces
introduces
juices
looses
nooses
produces
reduces
reproduces
seduces
sluices
spruces

traduces
truces
unlooses
uses

ŬS′ez
buses
busses
cusses
discusses
fusses
Gus's
musses
trusses

ŬS′ful
juiceful
useful

ŪSH′a
Jerusha

ŬSH′a
Prussia
Russia

ŪSH′al
crucial
fiducial

ŬSH′an
Prussian
Russian

ŪSH′ē
blushy
brushy
gushy
lushy

rushy
slushy

ŬSH′est
blushest
brushest
crushest
flushest
gushest
hushest
rushest

ŬSH′eth
blusheth
brusheth
crusheth
flusheth
gusheth
husheth
rusheth

ŬSH′ez
blushes
brushes
crushes
flushes
gushes
hushes
lushes
mushes
onrushes
plushes
rushes
thrushes
tushes
uprushes

ŬSH′ing
douching

ruching

ŬSH′ing
blushing
brushing
crushing
flushing
gushing
hushing
lushing
rushing
unblushing

Ū′shun
ablution
absolution
Aleutian
allocution
attribution
caducean
circumlocution
circumvolution
collocution
comminution
Confucian
consecution
constitution
contribution
convolution
counter-
　revolution
crucian
destitution
devolution
dilution
diminution
dissolution
distribution
electrocution

ōld, ôr, ŏdd, oil, fŏŏt, out; ūse, ûrn, ŭp; THis, thin

elocution
evolution
execution
illocution
imminution
insecution
institution
interlocution
involution
irresolution
Lilliputian
locution
obvolution
overcontribu-
 tion
overdilution
perlocution
persecution
pollution
postrevolution
prerevolution
prosecution
prostitution
reattribution
reconstitution
redargution
redissolution
redistribution
reinstitution
resolution
restitution
retribution
revolution
Rosicrucian
solution
substitution
ventrilocution
volution

ŬSH'un
concussion
discussion
incussion
percussion
Prussian
recussion
repercussion
Russian
succussion

ŬSH'ur
blusher
brusher
crusher
flusher
gusher
husher
plusher
rusher
usher

ŪSH'us
Confucius
Lucius

ŬSH'us
luscious

ŪS'id
lucid
mucid
pellucid
translucid

ŪS'ij
abusage
usage

ŪS'il
protrusile

ŪS'ing
adducing
conducing
deducing
educing
inducing
introducing
loosing
producing
reducing
reproducing
seducing
sprucing
traducing
unloosing

ŬS'ing
bussing
cussing
discussing
fussing
mussing
trussing

ŪS'iv
abusive
allusive
collusive
conclusive
conducive
confusive
contusive
deducive
delusive
diffusive
effusive

elusive
exclusive
illusive
inclusive
inconclusive
infusive
inobtrusive
intrusive
obtrusive
perfusive
reclusive
seclusive
seducive
transfusive

ŬS'iv
concussive
discussive
percussive
repercussive
successive

ŬS'kan
Della-Cruscan
dusken
Etruscan
molluscan
Tuscan

ŬS'kāt
coruscate
infuscate
obfuscate

ŬS'kē
dusky
husky
musky
tusky

āle, câre, ădd, ärm, ăsk; mē, hĕre, ĕnd; īce, ĭll;

ǓS′kest
duskest
(See also ǓSK;
add *-est* where
appropriate.)

ǓS′ket
busket
musket

ǓS′keth
dusketh
(See also ǓSK;
add *-eth* where
appropriate.)

ǓS′kin
buskin
Ruskin

ǓS′king
dusking
husking
tusking

ǓS′kŭl
crepuscule
majuscule
minuscule
opuscule

ǓS′kur
husker
tusker

ǓS′′l
bustle
corpuscle
hustle

justle
muscle
mussel
opuscle
rustle
tussle

ǓS′les
juiceless
useless

ǓS′lest
bustlest
(See also
ǓS′′l; add
-st where
appropriate.)

ǓS′leth
bustleth
(See also
ǓS′′l; add
-th where
appropriate.)

ǓS′ling
bustling
hustling
muscling
rustling
tussling

ǓS′lur
bustler
hustler
rustler
tussler

ǓS′′lz

Brussels
bustles
(See also
ǓS′′l; add
-s where
appropriate.)

ǓS′ment
conducement
deducement
inducement
reducement
seducement
superinduce-
ment
traducement

ǓS′nes
abstruseness
diffuseness
looseness
obtuseness
profuseness
recluseness
spruceness

Ū′sō
Crusoe
trousseau
whoso

Ū′som
gruesome
twosome

ǓS′ta
Augusta

ǓS′tas

Eustace

ǓS′tāt
incrustate

ǓS′tē
crusty
dusty
fustie
fusty
gusty
lusty
musty
rusty
trusty

ǓS′ted
adjusted
bedusted
betrusted
busted
combusted
crusted
disgusted
distrusted
dusted
encrusted
entrusted
fusted
lusted
mistrusted
rusted
trusted

ǓS′test
adjustest
disgustest
distrustest
dustest

ōld,   ôr,   ŏdd,   oil,   fŏŏt,   out;   ūse,   ûrn,   ŭp;   THis,   thin

encrustest
entrustest
justest
lustest
mistrustest
robustest
rustest
thrustest
trustest

ŬS′teth
adjusteth
disgusteth
distrusteth
dusteth
encrusteth
entrusteth
lusteth
mistrusteth
thrusteth
trusteth

ŬST′ful
distrustful
lustful
mistrustful
overtrustful
trustful
untrustful

ŬS′tik
fustic
rustic

ŬS′tin
Dustin
Justin

ŬS′ting

adjusting
bedusting
betrusting
busting
coadjusting
crusting
disgusting
distrusting
dusting
encrusting
entrusting
lusting
mistrusting
overtrusting
rusting
self-adjusting
thrusting
trusting
unmistrusting

ŬS′tingz
dustings
hustings
thrustings

ŬS′tis
Custis
justice

ŬS′tiv
adjustive
combustive

ŬST′lē
augustly
justly
robustly

ŬST′ment

adjustment
encrustment
maladjustment

ŬST′nes
augustness
justness
robustness

ŬS′tō
gusto

ŬS′tom
custom

ŬS′tral
lacustral
lustral
palustral

ŬS′trāt
frustrate
illustrate

ŬS′trin
lacustrine
palustrine

ŬS′trum
flustrum
lustrum

ŬS′trus
blustrous
lustrous

ŬS′tur
booster
brewster

Fewster
jouster
rooster
Worcester

ŬS′tur
adjuster
bluster
buster
coadjuster
cluster
Custer
distruster
duster
filibuster
fluster
juster
knuckle-duster
lackluster
luster
muster
readjuster
robuster
thruster
trustbuster
truster

ŬS′turd
blustered
bustard
clustered
custard
flustered
lustered
mustard
mustered

ŬS′tus
Augustus

āle, câre, ădd, ärm, ăsk; mē, hĕre, ĕnd; īce, ĭll;

Justus

ŪS'ur
abstruser
adducer
conducer
deducer
inducer
introducer
looser
producer
reducer
reproducer
seducer
sprucer
traducer

ŬS'ur
cusser
discusser
fusser
musser
trusser

ŪT'al
brutal
footle
tootle
(See also
ŪT'il.)

ŪT'āt
circumnutate
immutate
scutate

ŪT'ē
agouti
booty

beauty
cootie
cutie
Djibouti
duty
fluty
freebooty
fruity
Jibuti
looty
rooty
snooty
sooty
tutti-frutti

ŬT'ē
butty
gutty
jutty
nutty
putty
rutty
smutty
tutty

ŪT'ed
allocuted
bebooted
booted
bruited
comminuted
commuted
computed
confuted
constituted
convoluted
cornuted
deputed
diluted

disputed
elocuted
electrocuted
executed
fluted
fruited
hooted
immuted
imputed
instituted
involuted
looted
mooted
muted
permuted
persecuted
polluted
prosecuted
prostituted
putid
recruited
refuted
reputed
revoluted
rooted
saluted
self-constituted
substituted
suited
tooted
transmuted
unbooted
unconfuted
undisputed
unpersecuted
unpolluted
unrooted
unsuited
uprooted

voluted

ŬT'ed
butted
rutted
(See also ŬT;
add -ed or
-ted where
appropriate.)

ŪT'est
acutest
astutest
commutest
confutest
constitutest
cutest
deputest
dilutest
disputest
executest
imputest
institutest
lootest
minutest
mutest
persecutest
recruitest
refutest
resolutest
salutest
shootest
substitutest
suitest
transmutest
uprootest

ŬT'est
buttest

ruttest

ŪT′eth
commuteth
confuteth
constituteth
deputeth
diluteth
disputeth
executeth
hooteth
imputeth
instituteth
looteth
overshooteth
persecuteth
polluteth
prosecuteth
recruiteth
refuteth
rooteth
saluteth
shooteth
suiteth
transmuteth
unbooteth
uprooteth

ŬT′eth
butteth
rutteth
(See also ŬT;
add -*eth* where
appropriate.)

ŪT′ful
fruitful

ŪTH′est

smoothest
soothest

Ūth′ful
ruthful
toothful
truthful
untruthful
youthful

ŪTH′ing
smoothing
soothing

Ūth′ing
toothing

Ŭth′ing
doth-ing
nothing

Ūth′les
ruthless
toothless
truthless

ŪTH′nes
smoothness

Ŭth′nes
uncouthness

Ūth′som
toothsome
youthsome

ŪTH′ur
smoother
soother

Ūth′ur
Luther
uncouther

Ūth′ful

Ūth′ur
another
brother
Charter
brother
foremother
foster brother
foster mother
half-brother
mother
other
smother
t'other

ŬTH′urn
Sothern
southern

ŪT′ij
fruitage
mutage
scutage

ŪT′ik
diazeutic
emphyteutic
hermeneutic
maieutic
pharmaceutic
propaedeutic
scorbutic
therapeutic
toreutic

ŪT′il

futile
inutile
rutile
sutile
(See also
ŪT′al.)

ŪT′ing
booting
comminuting
commuting
computing
confuting
constituting
darned tooting
deputing
diluting
disputing
executing
fluting
fruiting
high-faluting
hooting
imputing
instituting
looting
mooting
offshooting
outshooting
overshooting
permuting
persecuting
polluting
prosecuting
prostituting
reconstituting
recruiting
refuting
rooting

---

saluting
scooting
shooting
substituting
suiting
tooting
transmuting
unbooting
unrooting
uprooting

ŬT'ing
abutting
butting
crosscutting
cutting
glass-cutting
glutting
gutting
jutting
nutting
putting
rebutting
rutting
shutting
strutting

ŬT'ish
brutish
sootish

ŬT'ish
ruttish
sluttish

ŪT'ist
flutist
hermeneutist
lutist

pharmaceutist
therapeutist

ŪT'iv
coadjutive
constitutive
indutive
persecutive
resolutive

ŪT'iz'm
brutism
mutism

ŬT''l
abuttal
cuttle
guttle
rebuttal
ruttle
scuttle
shuttle
space shuttle
subtle
suttle
Tuttle

ŬT'las
cutlass

ŬT'lē
absolutely
posilutely

ŪT'les
bootless
fruitless

ŬT'lest

scuttlest
(See also
ŬT''l; add
-*st* where
appropriate.)

ŬT'let
cutlet

ŬT'leth
scuttleth
(See also
ŬT''l; add
-*th* where
appropriate.)

ŪT'ling
footling
tootling

ŬT'ling
gutling
scuttling
sutling

ŬT'lur
butler
cutler
scuttler
subtler
sutler

ŪT'ment
confutement
imbrutement
recruitment

ŪT'nes
absoluteness

acuteness
astuteness
cuteness
hirsuteness
minuteness
muteness

Ū'tō
Bluto
Pluto

Ū'ton
Brewton
Newton
Teuton

ŬT'on
bachelor's
  button
button
Dutton
glutton
Hutton
mutton
Sutton

ŪT'or
suitor
tutor
(See also
ŪT'ŭr.)

ŪT'ral
neutral

ŬT'res
buttress

ŪT'rid
putrid

ŪT'riks
persecutrix
tutrix

ŪT'ron
neutron

ŪT'sē
tootsie-wootsie
tootsy

ŪT'ūr
future
puture
suture

ŪT'ŭr
accouter
acuter
astuter
beanshooter
booter
bruiter
chuter
coadjutor
collocuter
comminutor
commuter
computer
confuter
constitutor
cooter
crapshooter
cuter
deputer

digital
  computer
diluter
disputer
executor
fluter
fouter
freebooter
fruiter
hooter
imputer
institutor
looter
luter
microcomputer
minicomputer
minuter
mooter
muter
neuter
parachuter
peashooter
permuter
persecutor
personal
  computer
pewter
polluter
prosecutor
prostitutor
protutor
recruiter
refuter
restitutor
ringtailed
  tooter
rooter
router
saluter

scooter
sharpshooter
shooter
souter
substitutor
suitor
tooter
transmuter
troubleshooter
tutor
uprooter

ŬT'ur
abutter
apple butter
bread-and-
  butter
butter
clutter
cutter
daisy-cutter
flutter
glass cutter
glutter
grasscutter
gutter
leaf cutter
meatcutter
mutter
nutter
peanut butter
pilot-cutter
putter
rebutter
rutter
scutter
shutter
splutter
sputter

stonecutter
strutter
stutter
surrebutter
swartrutter
utter
woodcutter

ŬT'urd
fluttered
unuttered

Ū'ur
barbecuer
bedewer
bestrewer
bluer
brewer
canoer
chewer
construer
cooer
derring-doer
doer
enduer
eschewer
evildoer
ewer
fewer
gluer
hallooer
hewer
imbuer
interviewer
mewer
misconstruer
misdoer
newer
outdoer
overdoer

āle, câre, ădd, ärm, ăsk; mē, hĕre, ĕnd; īce, ĭll;

pooh-pooher
pursuer
queuer
renewer
revenuer
reviewer
ruer
screwer
sewer
shampooer
shoer
skewer
spewer
stewer
strewer
subduer
suer
tattooer
truer
undoer
unscrewer
viewer
well-doer
wooer
wrongdoer

Ū'urd
sewered
skewered
steward

ŪV'al
approval
disapproval
disproval
removal
reproval

ŪV'ē

groovy
movie
stag movie

ŬV'ē
covey
dovey
lovey

ŬV'ed
beloved

ŬL'el
scovel
shovel

ŬV'en
hooven
proven

ŬV'en
coven
oven
sloven

ŪV'est
approvest
disapprovest
disprovest
improvest
movest
provest
removest
reprovest

ŪV'eth
approveth
disapproveth
disproveth

improveth
moveth
proveth
removeth
reproveth

ŪV'ing
approving
disapproving
disproving
grooving
improving
moving
proving
removing
reproving
unmoving

ŬV'ing
gloving
loving
self-loving
shoving
ungloving
unloving

ŬV'les
gloveless
loveless

ŬV'ment
approvement
improvement
movement

ŬV'ur
approver
disapprover
disprover

groover
Hoover
improver
louver
maneuver
mover
outmaneuver
prover
remover
reprover
Vancouver

ŬV'ur
cover
discover
glover
hover
lover
plover
recover
rediscover
shover
table cover
uncover
undercover
windhover

ŬV'urn
govern

Ū'ya
alleluia

Ū'yans
buoyance

Ū'yant
buoyant

ŪZ'a
lallapalooza

ŪZ'al
musal
refusal

ŪZ'an
Susan

ŪZ'ard
buzzard

ŪZ'band
househusband
husband

ŪZ'dē, ŪZ'dā
Tuesday

ŪZ'ē
boozy
fluzie
oozy
woozy

ŬZ'ē
fuzzy
hussy

ŪZ'est
abusest
accusest
amusest
boozest
bruisest
choosest
confusest
cruisest

diffusest
excusest
fusest
infusest
losest
musest
oozest
perusest
refusest
snoozest
suffusest
transfusest
usest

ŬZ'est
buzzest
(See also ŬZ;
add -*est* where
appropriate.)

ŪZ'eth
abuseth
accuseth
amuseth
boozeth
bruiseth
chooseth
confuseth
cruiseth
diffuseth
excuseth
fuseth
infuseth
loseth
museth
oozeth
peruseth
refuseth
snoozeth

suffuseth
transfuseth
useth

ŬZ'eth
buzzeth
(See also ŬZ;
add -*eth* where
appropriate.)

ŪZ'ez
abuses
accuses
amuses
bemuses
bruises
chooses
circumfuses
confuses
contuses
cruises
diffuses
disabuses
disuses
druses
excuses
fuses
infuses
interfuses
loses
misuses
muses
nooses
oozes
peruses
refuses
snoozes
suffuses
transfuses

uses

ŬZ'ez
buzzes
fuzzes

Ū'zhun
abstrusion
abusion
affusion
allusion
circumfusion
collusion
conclusion
confusion
contusion
delusion
detrusion
diffusion
disillusion
effusion
elusion
exclusion
extrusion
fusion
illusion
inclusion
infusion
interclusion
interfusion
intrusion
malocclusion
Malthusian
obtrusion
occlusion
perfusion
pertusion
preclusion
profusion

āle, câre, ădd, ärm, ăsk; mē, hĕre, ĕnd; īce, ĭll;

prolusion
protrusion
reclusion
refusion
retrusion
seclusion
self-delusion
suffusion
transfusion
trusion
(See also
ŪZ′ē-an.)

ŪZ′ik
music

ŬZ′in
cousin
cozen
dozen

Ū′ing
abusing
accusing
amusing
boozing
bruising
choosing
confusing
contusing
cruising
diffusing
disusing
excusing
fusing
infusing
interfusing
losing
musing

oozing
perusing
refusing
self-accusing
snoozing
suffusing
transfusing
using

ŬZ′ing
buzzing
fuzzing

ŬZ′inz
cousins
cozens
couzens
dozens

ŪZ′iv
amusive
unamusive

ŪZ″l, ŪZ′al
bamboozle
foozle
gumfoozle
perusal
refusal

ŬZ″l
bemuzzle
fuzzle
guzzle
muzzle
nuzzle
puzzle
unmuzzle

ŬZ′lest
bemuzzlest
(See also
ŬZ″l; add
-*est* where
appropriate.)

ŬZ′leth
bemuzzleth
(See also
ŬZ″l; add
-*eth* where
appropriate.)

ŬZ′lin
muslin

ŬZ′ling
bemuzzling
guzzling
muzzling
nuzzling
puzzling

ŬZ′lur
bamboozler
foozler

ŬZ′lur
guzzler
muzzler
puzzler

ŬZ′m
izzum-wuzzum

ŪZ′man
newsman
trewsman

ŪZ′ment
amusement
bemusement

ŬZ′om
bosom

ŪZ′rēl
newsreel

ŪZ′ur
abuser
accuser
amuser
boozer
bruiser
chooser
confuser
cruiser
diffuser
excuser
fuser
infuser
interfuser
lallapaloozer
loser
misuser
muser
nonuser
oozer
palouser
peruser
reabuser
refuser
snoozer
suffuser
transfuser
user

ōld, ôr, ŏdd, oil, fŏŏt, out; ūse, ûrn, ŭp; THis, thin

■ Section III ■

WORDS ACCENTED ON THE THIRD SYLLABLE FROM THE END: ANTEPENULTS; TRIPLE RHYMES

A

For a discussion of words included under the accented vowels following, see the beginning of A rhymes in Section I.

(Note on Archaic Verb Forms Among Triple Rhymes — The archaic verb forms ending in -est and -eth have not as a rule been listed among the triple rhymes, to avoid needlessly expanding the book. When desired, they can be found by locating the present participles of triple-rhymed verbs, the -ing form: such forms as laboring, bracketing, fracturing, dallying, hampering, clamoring, meandering, and the rest. These can be turned without difficulty into the desired archaic forms: as, laborest, laboreth; bracketest, bracketeth; and so with all of them.)

Ā′a-b'l
conveyable
defrayable
impayable
playable
portrayable
prepayable
repayable
sayable
slayable
surveyable

unpayable
unplayable
unprayable
unsayable
unsurveyable
unswayable
unweighable
weighable

ĂB′a-sis
anabasis

catabasis
metabasis

ĀB′ē-a
Arabia
Bessarabia
labia
Swabia

ĀB′ē-an
Arabian

Bessarabian
Fabian
gabion
Sabian
Sorabian
Swabian

ĂB′ē-est
flabbiest
shabbiest

āle, câre, ădd, ärm, ăsk; mē, hĕre, ĕnd; īce, ĭll;

ĀB′el-ur
gabeler
labeler

ĂB′ē-nes
flabbiness
shabbiness
scabbiness
slabbiness

ĂB′ē-ur
flabbier
gabbier
shabbier

ĂB′id-nes
rabidness
tabidness

AB′i-fī
dissyllabify
labefy
syllabify
tabefy

ĂB′i-kal
Arabical
monosyllabical
polysyllabical
syllabical

AB′i-lē
crabbily
flabbily
scabbily
shabbily

ĂB′i-net
cabinet
tabinet

ĂB′i-tūd
habitude
tabitude

ĂB′la-tiv
ablative
bablative

ĂB″′l-ment
babblement
brabblement
dabblement
gabblement
rabblement

ĀB″′l-ness
ableness
sableness
stableness
unstableness

ĂB′o-la
Metabola
parabola
sporabola

ĀB′rē-el
Gabriel

ĂB′ū-lar
acetabular
confabular
cunabular
fabular
incunabular
pabular
tabular
tintinnabular

ĂB′ū-lāt
confabulate
tabulate

ĂB′ū-list
fabulist
incunabulist
vocabulist

ĂB′ū-lum
acetabulum
incunabulum
pabulum
tintinnabulum

ĂB′ū-lus
fabulous
fantabulous
pabulous
sabulous
tintinnabulous

ĀB′ur-ing
belaboring
laboring
neighboring
taboring
unlaboring

ĀB′ur-ur
laborer
taborer

ĂCH′a-b'l
attachable
catchable
detachable
immatchable
matchable

scratchable
unmatchable

**ĀD′a-b'l,
ĀD′i-b'l**
biodegradable
blockadable
braidable
degradable
dissuadable
evadable
gradable
invadable
nondegradable
persuadable
raidable
retradable
shadable
tradable
upbraidable
wadable

ĀD′ē-an
Acadian
Arcadian
Barbadian
Canadian
nomadian
Orcadian
Palladian

ĀD′ē-ant
irradiant
radiant

ĀD′ed-nes
bejadedness
degradedness
fadedness

---

jadedness
persuadedness
shadedness

ĀD′ē-ent
gradient

ĀD′ē-um
palladium
radium
stadium
vanadium

ĂD′ē-us
Thaddeus

ĂD′i-tiv
additive
traditive

ĂD′ō-ing
foreshadowing
overshadowing
shadowing

ĂF′a-nus
diaphanous

ĂF′i-kal
autobiographi-
   cal
autographical
bibliographical
biographical
calligraphical
cartographical
cosmographi-
   cal
diagraphical

ethnographical
geographical
glossographical
graphical
lexicographical
lexigraphical
orthographical
paleontograph-
   ical
photographical
physiographi-
   cal
phytographical
pterylographi-
   cal
seraphical
topographical
typographical

ĂF′ti-lē
craftily
draughtily

ĂG′ed-lē
jaggedly
raggedly

ĂG′ed-nes
craggedness
jaggedness
raggedness

ĂG′ē-nes
bagginess
cragginess
knagginess
scragginess
shagginess

ĂG′on-ist
agonist
antagonist
protagonist

ĂG′on-īz
agonize
antagonize

ĂG′on-iz′m
agonism
antagonism

ĂG′ran-sē
flagrancy
fragrancy
vagrancy

ĂG′ur-ē
faggery
jaggery
raggery
waggery
zigzaggery

ĂG′ur-ing
staggering
swaggering

ĂG′ur-ur
staggerer
swaggerer

Ā′ik-al
algebraical
archaical
Hebraical
laical
paradisaical

pharisaical

Ā′it-ē
gaiety
laity

ĀJ′a-b′l
assuageable
gaugeable

ĀJ′ē-an
Brobdingnagian
magian
pelagian

ĂJ′i-kal
magical
tragical

ĂJ′īl-nes
agileness
fragileness

ĂJ′in-al
imaginal
paginal
vaginal

ĂJ′in-us
cartilaginous
farraginous
lumbaginous
mucilaginous
oleaginous
voraginous

ĀJ′us-nes
advantageous-
   ness

āle,   câre,   ădd,   ärm,   ăsk;   mē,   hĕre,   ĕnd;   īce,   ĭll;

courageousness
disadvanta-
  geousness
outrageousness
rampageousness
umbrageousness

ĂK′a-b'l
breakable
impacable
implacable
mistakable
pacable
placable
undertakable
unshakeable

ĂK′ē-an
batrachian
eustachian
Noachian

ĂK′ē-nes
flakiness
quakiness
shakiness
snakiness

ĂK′et-ed
bracketed
jacketed
racketed

ĂK′et-ing
bracketing
jacketing
racketing

ĂK′ish-nes

brackishness
knackishness
slackishness

ĂK′ri-tē
acrity
alacrity

ĂK′ron-iz'm
anachronism
metachronism

ĂK′sa-b'l
faxable
relaxable
taxable
untaxable

ĂK′shun-al
factional
fractional
pactional
redactional

ĂK′shus-nes
factiousness
fractiousness

**ĂK′ta-b'l,
ĂK′ti-b'l**
attractable
compactible
contractible
detractible
distractible
extractible
infractible
intactable
intractable

refractable
retractable
tactable
tractable

ĂK′ted-nes
abstractedness
contractedness
distractedness
protractedness

ĂK′ti-kal
didactical
practical

ĂK′ti-lus
didactylous
hexadactylous
leptodactylous
pachydactylous
pterodactylous

ĂK′tiv-nes
abstractiveness
activeness
attractiveness
contractiveness
detractiveness
distractiveness
protractiveness
putrefactiveness
refractiveness

ĂK′to-rē
detractory
dissatisfactory
factory
lactary
manufactory

olfactory
phylactery
refractory
satisfactory
tractory

ĂK′tū-al
actual
factual
tactual

ĂK′tur-ing
fracturing
manufacturing

ĂK′ū-lar
oracular
piacular
spectacular
supernacular
tabernacular
tentacular
vernacular

ĂK′ū-lat
bimaculate
ejaculate
immaculate
jaculate
maculate

ĂK′ū-lus
abaculus
miraculous
oraculous
piaculous
vernaculous

ĀK′ur-ē

bakery
fakery
fakiry
rakery

ĂK'ur-ē
hackery•
hijackery
knick-knackery
quackery
Thackeray
Zachary

ĀK'ur-iz'm
fakirism
Quakerism
Shakerism

ĀK'wē-us
aqueous
subaqueous
terraqueous

ĂL'a-b'l
assailable
available
bailable
exhalable
mailable
retailable
sailable
saleable
unassailable
unavailable
unsailable

Ā'lē-a
Adalia
Attalia

Australia
azalea
Centralia
echolalia
Eulalia
Fidelia
regalia
Rosalia
Sedalia
Thalia

**ĂL'ē-āt,
ĂL'i-āt**
malleate
palliate

ĂL'ē-ing
dallying
rallying
sallying
tallying

ĂL'ē-nes
dailiness
scaliness

ĂL'en-tīn
Ballantine
Valentine

ĂL'ē-um
pallium
thallium

ĂL'ē-ur
dallier
rallier
sallier
tallier

ĂL'i-bur
caliber
Excalibur

ĂL'id-nes
impallidness
invalidness
pallidness
validness

ĂL'i-fī
alkalify
calefy
salify

ĂL'i-sis
analysis
catalysis
dialysis
paralysis
psychoanalysis
urinalysis

ĂL'i-son
Alison
Allison
Callison

ĂL'i-tē
abnormality
accidentality
actuality
alamodality
amorality
animality
artificiality
atonality
banality
bestiality

biblicality
bipedality
bisexuality
bitonality
brutality
carnality
causality
centrality
circumstantial-
  ity
classicality
clericality
coevality
collaterality
collegiality
colloquiality
comicality
commensality
commerciality
commonality
conditionality
confidentiality
congeniality
conjecturality
conjugality
connubiality
conseptuality
consequentiality
constitutionality
consubstantial-
  ity
conventionality
conviviality
cordiality
corporality
corporeality
cosmicality
criminality
curiality

devotionality
dextrality
duality
effectuality
egality
elementality
ephemerality
essentiality
ethereality
eventuality
exceptionality
externality
exterritoriality
extraterritorial-
   ity
fantasticality
farciality
fatality
feminality
feudality
filiality
finality
finicality
formality
frugality
fundamentality
generality
geniality
graduality
gutturality
heterosexuality
homosexuality
horizontality
horozontality
hospitality
hypersexuality
hyposexuality
ideality
illegality

illogicality
immateriality
immorality
immortality
impartiality
imperiality
impersonality
impracticality
inconsequen-
   tiality
individuality
ineffectuality
informality
inhospitality
inimicality
instrumental-
   ity
integrality
intellectuality
intentionality
internality
intrinsicality
irrationality
joviality
laicality
laterality
legality
lethality
liberality
lineality
literality
locality
logicality
magistrality
materiality
mentality
meridionality
mesnality
modality

molality
morality
mortality
municipality
mutuality
nasality
natality
nationality
naturality
neutrality
nonsensicality
normality
notionality
occidentality
officiality
orientality
originality
orthodoxality
parochiality
partiality
pastorality ·
pedality
penality
perenniality
personality
plurality
polytonality
potentiality
practicality
pragmaticality
preternatural-
   ity
primordiality
principality
prodigality
proportionality
provinciality
prudentiality
punctuality

quadrupedality
radicality
rascality
rationality
reality
reciprocality
regality
rivality
rurality
sectionality
sensuality
sentimentality
septentrional-
   ity
sequentiality
seriality
sesquipedality
severality
sexuality
signality
sociality
sodality
speciality
spectrality
spiality
spirality
spirituality
subnormality
substantiality
superficiality
supernaturality
technicality
temporality
territoriality
theatricality
tonality
topicality
totality
traditionality

ōld, ôr, ŏdd, oil, fŏŏt, out; ūse, ûrn, ŭp; THis, thin

transcendental-
  ity
triality
triviality
unconvention-
  ality
universality
unreality
unusuality
vegetality
venality
veniality
verbality
verticality
virtuality
visuality
vitality
vocality
whimsicality
zonality

ĂL'jē-a
neuralgia
nostalgia

ĂL'ō-est
callowest
fallowest
hallowest
sallowest
shallowest

ĂL'ō-ish
sallowish
shallowish
tallowish

ĂL'ō-jē
analogy

crustalogy
genealogy
genethlialogy
mammalogy
mineralogy
paralogy
petralogy
pyroballogy
tetralogy

ĂL'ō-jist
analogist
decalogist
dialogist
genealogist
mammalogist
mineralogist
penalogist

ĂL'ō-jīz
analógize
dialogize
genealogize
paralogize

ĂL'ō-jiz'm
analogism
dialogism
paralogism

ĂL'ō-nes
callowness
fallowness
sallowness
shallowness

ĂL'ō-ur
callower
hallower

sallower
shallower
tallower

ĀL'ur-ē
nailery
raillery

ĀL'ur-ē
gallery
raillery
salary

**ĀL'yen-iz'm,
ĀL'yan-iz'm**
alienism
bacchanalian-
  ism
episcopalianism
saturnalianism
sesquipedalian-
  ism
universalianism

ĂM'a-b'l
blamable
claimable
framable
irreclaimable
namable
reclaimable
tamable
unblamable
untamable

ĂM'a-rē
gramarye
mammary

ĂM'a-tist
dramatist
epigrammatist
grammatist
hierogrammatist
lipogrammatist
melodramatist

ĂM'a-tiv
amative
exclamative

ĂM'a-tīz
anagrammatize
diagrammatize
dramatize
epigrammatize

ĂM'bū-lāt
ambulate
deambulate
funambulate
perambulate
somnambulate

ĂM'bū-list
funambulist
noctambulist
somnambulist

ĂM'bu-liz'm
funambulism
noctambulism
nectambulism
somnambulism

Ā'mē-a
lamia
Mesopotamia

āle, câre, ădd, ärm, ăsk; mē, hĕre, ĕnd; īce, ĭll;

ĂM'et-er
diameter
dynameter
hexameter
octameter
parameter
pentameter
peirameter
pluviameter
tetrameter
viameter
voltameter

ĂM'ful-nes
blamefulness
shamefulness

ĂM'i-kal
amical
balsamical
dynamical

ĂM'in-a
lamina
stamina

ĂM'i-nāt
contaminate
laminate

ĂM'is-trē
palmistry
psalmistry

ĂM'i-tē
amity
calamity

ĂM'les-nes

aimlessness
blamelessness
damelessness
famelessness
namelessness
shamelessness
tamelessness

ĂM'on-īt
Ammonite
Mammonite

ĂM'on-iz'm
Mammonism
Shamanism

ĂM'ôr-us
amorous
clamorous
glamorous

ĂM'pē-on
campion
champion
tampion

ĂM'pur-ing
hampering
pampering
scampering
tampering

ĂM'pur-ur
hamperer
pamperer
scamperer
tamperer

ĂM'ūl-us

famulus
hamulus
ramulous

ĂM'ur-ing
clamoring
hammering
stammering
yammering

ĂM'ur-on
Decameron
Heptameron

ĂM'ur-ur
clamorer
hammerer
stammerer

ĀN'a-b'l
ascertainable
attainable
chainable
constrainable
containable
detainable
distrainable
drainable
explainable
gainable
maintainable
obtainable
ordainable
overstrainable
restrainable
retainable
sprainable
strainable
sustainable

trainable
unattainable

ĂN'a-b'l
insanable
sanable
tannable
(See also
ĂN'i-bal.)

ĀN'ar-ē
chicanery
lanary
planary

ĂN'a-rē
granary
panary
(See also
ĂN'ur-ē.)

ĂN'ches-tur
Granchester
Manchester

ĂND'a-b'l
commandable
countermand-
   able
demandable
reprimandable
sandable
understandable

ĂN'dē-nes
dandiness
handiness
sandiness

ōld, · ôr, ŏdd, oil, fŏŏt, out; ūse, ûrn, ŭp; THis, thin

ĂN'di-fī
candify
dandify

ĂN'drē-an
Alexandrian
meandrian
Menandrian

ĂN'dur-ing
meandering
pandering
philandering
slandering

ĀN'dur-ing
wandering
(See also ŎN-
dur-ing.)

ĂN'dur-son
Anderson
Sanderson

ĂN'dur-ur
meanderer
panderer
philanderer
slanderer

ĀN'dur-ur
launderer
wanderer
(See also
ŎN'dur-ur.)

ĂN'dur-us
panderous
slanderous

Ā'-nē-a
Albania
Anglomania
Aquitania
bibliomania
bruxomania
castanea
choreomania
collectanea
decalcomania
demonomania
dipsomania
dromania
egomania
eleutheromania
empleomania
erotomania
Francomania
Gallomania
kleptomania
Lithuania
logomania
Lusitania
mania
Mauretania
megalomania
melomania
metromania
miscellanea
monomania
mythomania
nymphomania
onomatomania
Pennsylvania
phaneromania
potickomania
potomania
pyromania
Rumania

Ruritania
succedanea
Tasmania
thanatomania
theomania
Titania
Transylvania
trichotillomania
Tripolitania
Ukrainia
Urania
xenomania

Ā'nē-ak
bibliomaniac
dipsomaniac
eleutheroma-
  niac
kleptomaniac
maniac
megalomaniac
monomaniac
nymphomaniac

Ā'nē-al
cranial
domanial
subterraneal

Ā'-nē-an
Albanian
Alcmanian
Aquitanian
circumforanean
cyanean
extemporanean
Iranian
Lithuanian
Mauretanian

Mediterranean
Pennsylvanian
Rumanian
Sandemanian
subterranean
Tasmanian
Transylvanian
Tripolitanian
Turanian
Ukrainian
Uranian
volcanian

ĂN'el-ing
channelling
panelling

Ā'nē-um
cranium
geranium
pericranium
succedaneum
titanium
uranium

ĀN'ē-us
antecedaneous
araneous
circumforaneous
coetaneous
contemporane-
  ous
cutaneous
dissentaneous
extemporaneous
exterraneous
extraneous
instantaneous
mediterraneous

āle, câre, ădd, ärm, ăsk; mē, hĕre, ĕnd; īce, ĭll;

membraneous
miscellaneous
momentaneous
porcelaneous
simultaneous
spontaneous
subcutaneous
subterraneous
succedaneous
temporaneous
terraneous

ĀN′ful′ē
banefully
disdainfully
painfully

ĀN′ful-nes
disdainfulness
gainfulness
painfulness

ĂNGK′ur-ing,
ĂNGK′ôr-ing
anchoring
cankering
encankering
hankering

ĂNGK′-ur-us
cankerous
cantankerous

ĂNG′′l-som
anglesome
tanglesome
wranglesome

ĂNG′ū-lar

angular
octangular
pentangular
quadrangular
rectangular
slangular
trianglar

ĂN′ē-el
Daniel
Nathaniel

ĂN′i-bal
cannibal
Hannibal

ĂN′i-fī
humanify
insanify
sanify

ĂN′i-gan
Brannigan
Flannigan
Mullanigan

ĂN′i-kal
botanical
Brahmanical
charlatanical
galvanical
mechanical
panicle
tyrannical

ĂN′i-kin
manikin
pannikin

ĂN′i-mus
animus
magnanimous
multanimous
pusillanimous
unanimous

ĂN′i-shing
banishing
planishing
vanishing

ĂN′ish-ment
banishment
evanishment
vanishment

ĂN′is-tur
banister
canister
ganister

ĂN′i-tē
aldermanity
Christianity
gigmanity
humanity
immanity
inanity
inhumanity
inorganity
insanity
inurbanity
mundanity
paganity
profanity
sanity
subterranity
urbanity

vanity
volcanity

ĂN′jen-sē
plangency
tangency

ĂN′ji-b′l
frangible
infrangible
intangible
refrangible
tangible

ĂN′ō-graf
galvanograph
pianograph

ĂN′ō-skōp
diaphanoscope
galvanoscope

ĂN′shē-an
Byzantian
(See also
ĂN′shun.)

ĂN′shē-āt
circumstantiate
substantiate
transubstantiate

ĂN′siv-nes
advanciveness
expansiveness

ĂN′som-est
handsomest
ransomest

ĂN′som-ur
handsomer
ransomer

ĂNT′a-b'l
grantable
plantable

ĂN′tur-ing
bantering
cantering

ĂNT′ur-ur
banterer
canterer

ĂN′thrō-pē
apanthropy
aphilanthropy
lycanthropy
misanthropy
philanthropy
physianthropy
psilanthropy
theanthropy
theophilan-
thropy
zoanthropy

ĂN′thrō-pist
misanthropist
philanthropist
psilanthropist
theophilan-
thropist

ĂN′thro-
piz'm
psilanthropism

theanthropism
theophilan-
thropism

ĂN′ti-sīd
giganticide
infanticide

ĂN′tik-nes
franticness
giganticness
romanticness

ĂN′ū-al
annual
manual

ĂN′ū-la
cannula
granula

ĂN′ū-lar
annular
cannular
penannular

ĂN′ū-lāt
annulate
campanulate
granulate

ĂN′ur-ē
cannery
charlatanery
granary
panary
stannary
tannery

ĂN′ur-et
banneret
lanneret

ĂP′a-b'l
capable
drapable
escapable
incapable
inescapable
papable
shapeable

ĂP′ē-est
happiest
sappiest
snappiest

ĂP′ē-nes
happiness
sappiness
snappiness

ĂP′ē-ur
happier
sappier
snappier

ĂP′id-lē
rapidly
sapidly
vapidly

ĂP′id-nes
rapidness
sapidness
vapidness

ĂP′i-lē

happily
snappily

ĀP′o-lis
Annapolis
Indianapolis
Minneapolis

ĀP′ur-ē
apery
drapery
grapery
napery
papery
vapory

ĀP′ur-ing
capering
papering
tapering
vaporing

ĀP′ur-ur
caperer
paperer
vaporer

ÂR′a-b'l
airable
bearable
dareable
declarable
pairable
repairable
swearable
tearable
unbearable
unwearable
wearable

āle, câre, ădd, ärm, ăsk; mē, hĕre, ĕnd; īce, ĭll;

ĂR′a-b'l	Bulgaria	aquarian	millenarian
arable	caballeria	Arian	miscellanarian
parable	Calceolaria	Aryan	necessarian
	Cineraria	atrabilarian	necessitarian
ĂR′a-dĭs	dataria	attitudinarian	nectarian
imparadise	digitaria	aularian	nonagenarian
paradise	Hilaria	authoritarian	nonsectarian
	malaria	barbarian	octagenarian
ĂR′as-ing	wistaria	Bavarian	ovarian
embarrassing		Briarean	Parian
harrassing	**ÂR′ē-al**	Bulgarian	parliamentarian
	actuarial	Caesarian	planarion
ĂR′as-ment	areal	centenarian	platitudinarian
embarrassment	calendarial	cnidarian	plenitudinarian
harassment	commissarial	communitarian	predestinarian
	diarial	Darien	proletarian
ĂR′a-tiv	glossarial	diarian	quadragenarian
comparative	malarial	dietarian	quinquagenarian
declarative	nectarial	disciplinarian	Rastafarian
narrative	notarial	doctrinarian	riparian
preparative	ovarial	egalitarian	rosarian
reparative	puparial	equalitarian	Rotarian
	secretarial	estuarian	sabbatarian
ĂR′bur-ing	vicarial	experimentarian	sacramentarian
barbering		fruitarian	sanitarian
harboring	**ÂR′ē-an**	futilitarian	sectarian
	abecedarian	grammarian	seminarian
ĂR′dē-an	Adessenarian	humanitarian	sententiarian
guardian	agrarian	Hungarian	septimanarian
pericardian	alphabetarian	Icarian	septuagenarian
	altitudinarian	infralapsarian	sertularian
ĂR′dē-nes	anecdotarian	Janizarian	sexagenarian
fool-hardiness	antidisestablish-	lapidarian	societarian
hardiness	mentarian	latitudinarian	stipendarian
tardiness	antiquarian	libertarian	sublapsarian
	antisabbatarian	librarian	suburbicarian
Â′rē-a	antitrinitarian	limitarian	supralapsarian
adversaria	apiarian	lunarian	Tartarean
area	Apollinarian	Megarian	totalitarian

ōld, ôr, ŏdd, oil, fŏŏt, out; ūse, ûrn, ŭp; THis, thin

tractarian
trinitarian
ubiquarian
ubiquitarian
unitarian
utilitarian
valetudinarian
vegetarian
veterinarian
vulgarian

ÂR′ē-ant
cóntrariant
omniparient
variant

ÂR′ē-āt
variate
vicariate

ÂR′ē-at
commissariat
lariat
proletariat
prothonotariat
secretariat

ÂR′ē-est
chariest
variest
wariest

ĂR′ē-et,
ĂR′ē-ot
Harriet
Iscariot
Marryatt
Marriott

ĂR′ē-ing
carrying
harrying
marrying
tarrying

ÂR′ē-nes
airiness
arbitrariness
chariness
contrariness
glariness
hairiness
salutariness
sanguinariness
sedentariness
solitariness
temporariness
tumultuariness
ubiquitariness
voluntariness
wariness

ĂR′ē-nes
starriness
tarriness

ĂR′ē-ō
impresario

ĂR′ē-on
clarion
Marion
(See also
ĂR′ē-an.)

ÂR′ē-um
aquarium
aqua-vivarium

barium
columbarium
glaciarium
honorarium
sacrarium
sanitarium
tepidarium
termitarium
vivarium

ÂR′ē-ur
charier
warier

ĂR′ē-ur
barrier
carrier
farrier
harrier
marrier
tarrier

ÂR′ē-us
arbitrarious
arenarious
Aquarius
atrabilarious
calcareous
contrarious
denarius
frumentarious
gregarious
hilarious
horarious
malarious
multifarious
nectareous
nefarious
omnifarious

precarious
quadragenarious
Sagittarius
tartareous
temerarious
testudinarious
vagarious
valetudinarious
various
vicarious
viparious

ÂR′ful-ē
carefully
prayerfully
uncarefully

ÂR′ful-nes
carefulness
prayerfulness
sparefulness
uncarefulness
warefulness

ĂR′i-fī
clarify
saccharify
scarify

ÂR′i-form
peariform
scalariform

ĂR′i-gan
Garrigan
Harrigan

ÂR′ing-lē
blaringly

āle,   câre,   ădd,   ärm;   ăsk;   mē;   hĕre,   ĕnd;   īce,   ĭll;

daringly
flaringly
glaringly
sparingly
tearingly

ĂR′ing-ton
Barrington
Carrington
Farrington
Harrington

ĂR′i-son
garrison
Harrison

ÂR′i-tē
debonairity
rarity

ĂR′i-tē
angularity
barbarity
capillarity
charity
circularity
clarity
curvilinearity
disparity
dissimilarity
exemplarity
familiarity
fissiparity
gemmiparity
globularity
granularity
hilarity
imparity
insularity

irregularity
jocularity
modularity
molarity
molecularity
multiparity
muscularity
omniparity
orbicularity
oviparity
parity
particularity
peculiarity
perpendicular-
   ity
piacularity
polarity
popularity
pupilarity
rectangularity
rectilinearity
regularity
secularity
similarity
singularity
solidarity
Solidarity
titularity
triangularity
uncharity
unfamiliarity
unpopularity
vascularity
vernacularity
viviparity
vulgarity

ĂR′i-tūd
amaritude

claritude

ĂR′ki-kal
archical
hierarchical
hylarchical
monarchical
tetrarchical

ĂR′la-tan
charlatan
tarlatan

ĂR′ming-lē
alarmingly
charmingly
farmingly
harmingly

ĂR′nish-ing
garnishing
tarnishing
varnishing

ĂR′nish-ur
garnisher
tarnisher
varnisher

ĂR′ō-ē
arrowy
marrowy
sparrowy
yarrowy

ĂR′ō-est
harrowest
narrowest

ĂR′ō-ing
harrowing
narrowing

Â′ron-īt
Aaronite
Maronite

ĂR′ō-ur
harrower
narrower

ĂR′sen-ē
coparceny
larceny

ĂR′sen-ur
coparcener
larcener
parcener

ĂR′shal-iz′m
martialism
partialism

ĂR′ted-nes
departedness
falseheartedness
frankhearted-
   ness
freeheartedness
hardheartedness
kindheartedness
lightheartedness
openheartedness
softheartedness
tenderhearted-
   ness
trueheartedness

ōld, ôr, ŏdd, oil, fŏŏt, out; ūse, ûrn, ŭp; THis, thin

warmhearted-
   ness

ĂR′ti-k'l
article
particle

ĂR′ti-zan
artisan
bartizan
bipartisan
partisan

ÄRT′les-lē
artlessly
heartlessly

ÄRT′les-nes
artlessness
heartlessness

ÄRT′ur-ing
bartering
chartering
martyring

ÄRT′ur-ur
barterer
charterer

ĂS′a-b'l
chasable
effaceable
erasible
evasible
ineffaceable
retraceable
traceable

ĂS′en-sē
adjacency
complacency
interjacency

Ā′sē-ul
basial

ĂS′ē-nes
laciness
raciness

ĂS′ē-nes
brassiness
classiness
glassiness
grassiness
massiness
sassiness

ĂS′ful-nes
disgracefulness
gracefulness
ungracefulness

A′shē-a
acacia
Asia
Aspasia

ĂSH′ē-a
cassia
Parnassia
quassia

Ā′shē-an
Alsatian
Asian
Athanasian

Australasian
Galatian
Haytian
Hieracian
Horatian
Latian
Pancratian
Thracian
(See also
  Ā′shun,
  Ā′zhun.)

ĂSH′ē-an
Circassian
Parnassian
(See also
  ĂSH′un.)

Ā′shē-āt
emaciate
expatiate
glaciate
ingratiate
insatiate
satiate

Ā′shē-ent
calefacient
delirefacient
facient
liquefacient
parturifacient
rubefacient
sensifacient
sorbefacient
stupefacient
tumefacient
(See also
  Ā′shent.)

ĂSH′ē-nes
ashiness
flashiness
trashiness

Ā′shun-al
associational
coeducational
combinational
commemora-
  tional
compensational
condensational
congregational
conjugational
conservational
conversational
convocational
creational
denominational
deputational
derivational
dissertational
educational
emigrational
equational
gestational
gradational
gravitational
gyrational
ideational
imitational
immigrational
inclinational
incubational
informational
inspirational
interrogational
irrigational

āle, câre, ădd, ärm, ăsk; mē, hēre, ĕnd; īce, ĭll;

motivational
navigational
observational
occupational
operational
presentational
probational
progestational
quotational
radiational
recreational
relational
representational
respirational
revelational
rotational
salutational
sensational
stational
terminational
translational
variational
vibrational
vocational

ĂSH′un-al
international
irrational
national
rational

ĂSH′un-at
compassionate
dispassionate
impassionate
incompassion-
  ate
passionate

ĂSH′un-ing
compassioning
fashioning
passioning

Ā′shun-ist
annexationist
annihilationist
annotationist
causationist
colonizationist
conversationist
convocationist
creationist
cremationist
deflationist
degenerationist
educationist
emancipationist
emigrationist
imitationist
inflationist
innovationist
inspirationist
isolationist
moderationist
neo-isolationist
neocoloniza-
  tionist
populationist
recreationist
repudiationist
restorationist
salvationist
tolerationist
transmutation-
  ist
vacationist

Ā′shun-les
conversationless
educationless
emigrationless
foundationless
immigrationless
imitationless
inspirationless
temptationless

Ā′shun-ur
foundationer
oblationer
probationer
reprobationer
restorationer
stationer

ĂSH′ur-ē
fashery
haberdashery
sashery

Ā′shus-nes
audaciousness
capaciousness
contumacious-
  ness
disputatious-
  ness
edaciousness
efficaciousness
fallaciousness
fugaciousness
graciousness
incapaciousness
ineffaciousness
loquaciousness
mendaciousness

ostentatiousness
perspicacious-
  ness
pertinaciousness
pugnaciousness
rapaciousness
sagaciousness
salaciousness
sequaciousness
spaciousness
tenaciousness
ungraciousness
veraciousness
vexatiousness
vivaciousness
voraciousness

ĂS′i-b'l
impassible
irascible
passable
passible
renascible
surpassable

ĂS′i-nāt
abbacinate
assassinate
deracinate
exacinate
fascinate

ĂS′i-tē
audacity
bellacity
bibacity
capacity
contumacity
dicacity

ōld, ôr, ŏdd, oil, fŏŏt, out; ūse, ûrn, ŭp; THis, thin

edacity
feracity
fugacity
incapacity
loquacity
mendacity
minacity
mordacity
opacity
perspicacity
pertinacity
pervicacity
procacity
pugnacity
rapacity
sagacity
salacity
saponacity
sequacity
tenacity
veracity
vivacity
voracity

ĂS'ĭv-lē
impassively
massively
passively

Ă'sĭv'nes
dissuasiveness
evasiveness
persuasiveness
pervasiveness
suasiveness

ĂS'ĭv-nes
impassiveness
massiveness

passiveness

ĂSP'ing-lē
gaspingly
raspingly

ĂS'tar-dē
bastardy
dastardy

ĀST'ful-ē
tastefully
wastefully
distastefully

ĂS'ti-kal
ecclesiastical
elastical
encomiastical
enthusiastical
fantastical
gymnastical

ĂS'ti-lē
hastily
pastily
tastily

ĂS'ti-siz'm
ecclesiasticism
fantasticism
monasticism
scholasticism

ĂS'trē-an
alabastrian
Lancastrian
Zoroastrian

ĂS'trō-fē
catastrophe
epanastrophe

ĂS'tur-ship
mastership
pastorship

ĂS'tur-ē
dicastery
mastery
plastery
self-mastery

ĂS'tur-ing
beplastering
mastering
overmastering
plastering

ĂS'ur-āt
emacerate
lacerate
macerate

ĂS'ur-ē
bracery
embracery
tracery

ĀT'a-b'l
abatable
beratable
collatable
creatable
debatable
dilatable
gratable
hatable

matable
ratable
regulatable
statable
translatable
untranslatable

ĂT'a-b'l
combatable
(See also
ĂT'ĭ-b'l.)

ĂT'e-līt
patellite
satellite

Ā'ten-sē
latency
patency

ĀT'ful-ē
fatefully
gratefully
hatefully

ĀT'ful-nes
fatefulness
gratefulness
hatefulness

Ā'thē-an
Carpathian
Sabbathian

Ăth'e-sis
diathesis
parathesis

Ăth'ĭ-kal

anthropopathi-
cal
chrestomathical

ĂTH'ur-ing
blathering
foregathering
gathering
lathering
upgathering
wool-gathering

ĂTH'ur-ur
foregatherer
gatherer
latherer
tax-gatherer
toll-gatherer
upgatherer

ĂT'i-b'l
combatable
come-atable
compatible
impatible
incompatible
patible

ĂT'i-fī
beatify
gratify
ratify
stratify

ĂT'ik-a
Attica
dalmatica
hepatica
sciatica

ĂT'ik-al
abbatical
acroamatical
acrobatical
aerostatical
anagrammatical
anathematical
anidiomatical
apophthegmati-
cal
apostatical
aquatical
aristocratical
asthmatical
autocratical
automatical
axiomatical
bureaucratical
climatical
democratical
diplomatical
dogmatical
dramatical
ecstatical
emblematical
emphatical
enigmatical
epigrammatical
erratical
fanatical
grammatical
hebdomatical
hieratical
hydrostatical
hypostatical
idiomatical
leviratical
mathematical
numismatical

operatical
phantasmatical
piratical
pragmatical
primatical
prismatical
problematical
sabbatical
schismatical
sciatical
separatical
Socratical
spasmatical
statical
symptomatical
systematical
ungrammatical
unsystematical
vatical

ĂT'in-āt
gelatinate
Palatinate

ĀT'ē-nes
slatiness
weightiness

ĂT'ē-nes
chattiness
fattiness
nattiness

ĂT'in-īz
gelatinize
Latinize
platinize

ĂT'i-nus

gelatinous
platinous

ĂT'i-sīz
emblematicize
fanaticize
grammaticize

ĂT'i-siz'm
Asiaticism
fanaticism
grammaticism

ĂT'i-tūd
attitude
beatitude
gratitude
ingratitude
latitude
platitude

Ā'tiv-nes
alliterativeness
imitativeness
nativeness
penetrativeness

ĂT''l-ment
battlement
embattlement
prattlement
tattlement

ĂT'ōm-ē
anatomy
atomy

ĂT'om-ist
anatomist

ōld, ôr, ŏdd, oil, fŏŏt, out; ūse, ûrn, ŭp; THis, thin

atomist

ĂT′om-īz
anatomize
atomize

ĂT′om-iz′m
anatomism
atomism

ĂT′om-us
diatomous
paratomous

ĂT′ôr-ē
obsecratory
ratiocinatory
recapitulatory

ĂT′ri-kal
idolatrical
theatrical

ĂT′ri-sīd
fratricide
matricide
patricide

Ā′tron-al
matronal
patronal

Ā′tron-ij
matronage
patronage

Ā′tron-īz
matronize
patronize

ĂT′ū-lāt
congratulate
gratulate
spatulate

ĂT′ūr-al
natural
preternatural
supernatural

ĂT′ŭr-al
bilateral
collateral
equilateral
lateral
quadrilateral
unilateral

ĂT′ur-an
cateran
Lateran

ĂT′ur-āt
maturate
saturate
supersaturate

ĂT′ur-ē
battery
flattery
shattery
slattery
tattery

ĂT′ur-ing
battering
beflattering
bepattering
bescattering

bespattering
blattering
chattering
clattering
flattering
pattering
scattering
shattering
smattering
spattering
splattering

ĂT′ur-ur
batterer
blatterer
chatterer
clatterer
flatterer
patterer
scatterer
shatterer
smatterer
splatterer

Ā′ur-ē
aëry
faërie

ĂV′an-ēz
Havanese
Javanese

Ā′vē-a
Batavia
Belgravia
Moravia
Octavia
Pavia
Scandinavia

Ā′vē-an
avian
Batavian
Belgravian
Moravian
Scandinavian
Shavian

ĂV′el-ing
graveling
raveling
traveling
unraveling

ĂV′el-ur
raveler
traveler
unraveler

ĂV′en-dur
chavender
lavender

ĂV′ij-ing
ravaging
scavaging

ĂV′ij-ur
ravager
savager
scavager

ĂV′ish-ing
enravishing
lavishing
ravishing

ĂV′ish-ment
enravishment

āle, câre, ădd, ärm, ăsk; mē, hĕre, ĕnd; īce, ĭll;

lavishment
ravishment

ĂV'ish-nes
knavishness
slavishness

ĂV'ish-ur
lavisher
ravisher

ĂV'i-tē
cavity
concavity
depravity
gravity
pravity
suavity

ĀV'ur-ē
bravery
gravery
savory
slavery
unsavory

ĀV'ur-ing
favoring
flavoring
quavering
savoring
unwavering
wavering

ĀV'ur-ur
favorer
flavorer
quaverer

waverer

ĀV'ur-us
flavorous
savorous

ĂV'ur-us
cadaverous
papaverous

Ā'zē-a
Aspasia
athanasia
aphasia
euthanasia
paronomasia

Ā'zē-an
Asian

Athanasian
Australasian
Caucasian
Eurasian
Rabelaisian
(See also
Ā'zhun.)

ĀZ'ē-nes
craziness
haziness
laziness
maziness

ĀZ'i-b'l
persuasible
praisable
raisable
suasible

E

For a discussion of words included under the accented vowels following, see the beginning of E rhymes in Section I.

Ē'a-b'l
agreeable
creable
decreeable
disagreeable
feeable
irremeable

Ē'al'ist
idealist
neorealist
realist
surrealist

Ē'al-īz
idealize
realize

Ē'al-iz'm
idealism
neorealism
realism
surrealism

Ē'al-tē
fealty
realty

Ē'an-iz'm
epicureanism
Laodiceanism
peanism
plebeianism
Pythagoreanism
Sabaeanism

ĒB'rē-us
ebrious
funebrious
inebrious
tenebrious

ĔCH'a-b'l
bleachable
impeachable
reachable
teachable
unimpeachable
unteachable

ĔCH'ē-nes
sketchiness
tetchiness

ĔCH'ur-ē

lechery
treachery

ĔCH′ur-us
lecherous
treacherous

ĔD′a-b'l
exceedable
impedible
obedible
pleadable
readable

ĔD′a-b'l
dreadable
spreadable
threadable
(See also
ĔD′i-b'l.)

Ē′dē-al
bimedial
intermedial
medial
pedial
remedial

Ē′dē-an
comedian
encyclopedian
median
tragedian

Ē′dē-at
immediate
intermediate
mediate

Ē′dē-ens
disobedience
expedience
inexpedience
obedience

Ē′dē-ent
disobedient
expedient
inexpedient
ingredient
obedient

ĒD′ē-est
beadiest
greediest
neediest
reediest
seediest
speediest
weediest

ĔD′ē-est
headiest
readiest
steadiest
unsteadiest

ĒD′ē-nes
greediness
neediness
seediness
speediness
weediness

ĔD′ē-nes
headiness
readiness
steadiness

threadiness
unreadiness
unsteadiness

Ē′dē-um
medium
tedium

ĒD′ē-ur
beadier
greedier
needier
reedier
seedier
speedier
weedier

ĔD′ē-ur
headier
readier
steadier
unsteadier

Ē′dē-us
intermedious
tedious

ĔD′ful-nes
heedfulness
needfulness
unheedfulness
unneedfulness

ĔD′i-b'l
credible
dreadable
edible
incredible

ĔD′i-kal
medical
pedicle

ĔD′i-kant
medicant
predicant

ĔD′i-kāt
dedicate
medicate
predicate

ĔD′i-lē
greedily
needily
speedily

ĔD′i-lē
headily
readily
steadily
unsteadily

ĔD′i-ment
impediment
pediment
sediment

ĔD′i-nus
mucedinous
putredinous
rubedinous

ĔD′i-ted
accredited
credited
discredited
edited

āle, câre, ădd, ärm, ăsk; mē, hĕre, ĕnd; īce, ĭll;

miscredited
unaccredited

ĔD′i-ting
accrediting
crediting
discrediting
editing
miscrediting

ĔD′i-tiv
redditive
sedative

ĔD′i-tor
creditor
editor

ĒD′les-lē
heedlessly
needlessly

ĒD′les-nes
heedlessness
needlessness

ĔD′ū-lus
credulous
incredulous
sedulous

ĔD′ur-al
federal
hederal

ĒD′ur-ship
leadership
readership

ĔF′ē-nes
beefiness
leafiness

ĔF′i-sens
beneficence
maleficence

ĔF′i-sent
beneficent
maleficent

ĔF′ur-ens
cross-reference
deference
preference
reference

ĔF′ur-ent
deferent
efferent

ĔG′a-b'l
beggable
legable

Ē′gal-iz'm
legalism
regalism

Ē′gal-nes
illegalness
legalness
regalness

ĔG′ē-nes
dregginess
legginess

ĔG′nan-sē
pregnancy
regnancy

ĔG′ur-ē
beggary
eggery

Ē′gur-lē
eagerly
meagrely
overeagerly

Ē′gur-nes
eagerness
meagreness
overeagerness

Ē′i-tē
aseity
contemporane-
   ity
corporeity
deity
diathermaneity
erogeneity
extraneity
femineity
gaseity
haecceity
hermaphrodeity
heterogeneity
homogeneity
incorporeity
instantaneity
ipseity
multeity
omneity
perseity

personeity
plebeity
seity
simultaneity
spontaneity
terreity
velleity

Ē′jē-an
collegian
Fuegian
Norwegian
(See also
ĒJ′un.)

ĒJ′i-b'l
allegeable
dredgeable
illegible
legible
pledgeable
wedgeable

Ē′jus-nes
egregiousness
sacrilegiousness

ĒK′a-b'l
speakable
unspeakable

ĔK′a-b'l
impeccable
insecable
peccable

ĒK′i-lē
cheekily
creakily

---

leakily
sleekily
sneakily
squeakily
treacly

ĒK′ē-nes
cheekiness
creakiness
leakiness
sneakiness
squeakiness

ĔK′ish-nes
cliquishness
freakishness
sneakishness

ĔK′on-ing
beckoning
dead-reckoning
reckoning

ĔK′re-ment
decrement
recrement

ĔK′shun-al
affectional
bisectional
complexional
connectional
convectional
correctional
directional
flectional
flexional
inflectional
insurrectional

interjectional
intersectional
objectional
projectional
protectional
reflectional
resectional
resurrectional
sectional
vivisectional

ĔK′shun-ist
insurrectionist
perfectionist
protectionist
resurrectionist

ĔK′shun-īz
resurrectionize
sectionize

ĔK′si-b'l
flexible
inflexible
nexible
reflexible

ĔK′si-tē
complexity
convexity
intercomplexity
perplexity
reflexity

ĔK′siv-nes
perplexiveness
reflexiveness

ĔK′ta-b'l

affectable
correctable
deflectable
delectable
detectable
erectable
expectable
rejectable
respectable
subjectable
suspectable
unaffectable
uncorrectable
undelectable
undetectable
unerectable
unrejectable
unrespectable
unsuspectable

ĔK′tar-ē
nectary
(See also
ĔK′tō-rē.)

ĔK′ted-nes
abjectedness
affectedness
dejectedness
disaffectedness
infectedness
suspectedness
unsuspected-
    ness

ĔK′ti-b'l
collectible
connectible
defectible

dissectible
effectible
indefectible
ineffectible
unconnectible
unperfectible

ĔK′ti-fī
objectify
rectify

ĔK′ti-kal
apoplectical
dialectical

ĔK′ti-tūd
rectitude
senectitude

ĔK′tiv-lē
collectively
defectively
effectively
(See also
ĔK′tiv; add
-ly where
appropriate.)

ĔK′tiv-nes
collectiveness
defectiveness
effectiveness
ineffectiveness
objectiveness
prospectiveness
protectiveness
reflectiveness
subjectiveness

āle, câre, ădd, ärm, ăsk; mē, hĕre, ĕnd; īce, ĭll;

ĔK′tō-mē
appendectomy
hysterectomy
lipectomy
lumpectomy
mastectomy
orchidectomy
tonsillectomy
vasectomy

ĔK′tō-ral
electoral
pectoral
protectoral
rectoral
sectoral

ĔK′tō-rāt
directorate
electorate
expectorate
protectorate
rectorate

ĔK′tō-rē
correctory
directory
nectary
rectory
refectory
sectary

ĔK′tū-al
effectual
ineffectual
intellectual
lectual

ĔK′tur-al

architectural
conjectural

ĔK′tur-ur
conjecturer
lecturer

ĔK′ū-lar
molecular
secular
specular

ĔK′ū-lāt
peculate
speculate

ĔK′ū-tiv
consecutive
executive
subsecutive

ĔL′a-b'l
annealable
appealable
concealable
congealable
dealable
healable
inconcealable
peelable
repealable
revealable
sealable
uncongealable
undealable
unhealable
unpeelable
unrepealable
unsealable

ĔL′a-tiv
compellative
correlative
relative

Ē′lē-a, ĔL′ya
Amelia
Aurelia
Bedelia
Cecelia
Celia
Cordelia
Cornelia
Fidelia
Lelia
Ophelia

Ē′lē-an
Aristotelian
carnelian
Delian
Hegelian
Ismaelian
Machiavellian
Mephistophe-
  lian
Mingrelian

ĔL′ē-an
Boswellian
Cromwellian
evangelian
selion

ĔL′e-gāt
delegate
relegate

Ē′lē-on

anthelion
aphelion
chameleon

**Ē′lē-us,
ĔL′yus**
Aurelius
Cornelius

ĔL′fish-nes
elfishness
selfishness

**ĔL′i-b'l,
ĔL′a-b'l**
compellable
delible
expellable
fellable
foretellable
gelable
indelible
ingelable
jellable
quellable
sellable
smellable
spellable
tellable
unforetellable
unjellable
unquellable
unsellable
unsmellable
unspellable
untellable

ĔL′i-kal
angelical

---

bellical
evangelical
helical
pellicle

ĔL'ish-ing
embellishing
relishing

ĔL'ish-ment
embellishment
relishment

ĔL'ō-est
bellowest
mellowest
yellowest

ĔL'ō-ing
bellowing
mellowing
yellowing

ĔL'on-ē
felony
melony

ĔL'ō-ur
bellower
mellower
yellower

ĔL'thē-est
healthiest
stealthiest
wealthiest

ĔL'thē-ur
healthier

stealthier
wealthier

ĔL'thi-lē
healthily
stealthily
wealthily

ĔL'tur-ē
sheltery
smeltery

ĔL'tur-ing
sheltering
weltering

ĔL'tur-ur
shelterer
welterer

ĔL'ū-lar
cellular
intercellular
stellular
unicellular

ĔL'ur-ē
celery
stellary

ĔL'us-lē
jealously
overzealously
zealously

ĒM'a-b'l
esteemable
redeemable

Ē'ma-tist
schematist
thematist

ĒM'a-tist
emblematist
theorematist

ĒM'bur-ing
Decembering
dismembering
membering
Novembering
remembering
unremembering

Ē'mē-a
Bohemia
Euphemia

Ē'mē-al
academial
endemial
gremial
vindemial

Ē'mē-an
academian
Bohemian

ĒM'ē-nes
creaminess
dreaminess
steaminess

Ē'mē-on
anthemion
procemion

ĒM'ē-ur
beamier
creamier
dreamier
premier

ĔM'i-kal
academical
alchemical
chemical
electro-chemical
endemical
epidemical
polemical

ĒM'i-lē
beamily
creamily
dreamily
steamily

ĔM'i-nal
feminal
geminal
seminal

ĔM'i-nāt
effeminate
geminate
ingeminate

ĔM'ni-tē
indemnity
solemnity

ĔM'on-ē
Agapemone
anemone

āle,   câre,   ădd,   ärm,   ăsk;   mē,   hĕre,   ĕnd;   īce,   ĭll;

ĔM'or-al
femoral
nemoral

ĔM'o-rē
Emery
Emory
memory

ĔM'por-ur,
ĔM'pur-ur
emperor
temperer

ĔM'ū-lent
temulent
tremulent

ĔM'ū-lus
emulous
tremulous

Ĕm'ur-ald
emerald
ephemeralled

ĒM'ur-ē
creamery
dreamery

ĔM'ur-ē
gemmery
(See also
ĔM'o-rē.)

ĔM'ur-ist
ephemerist
euhemerist

Ē'na-b'l
amenable
convenable

ĔN'a-rē
centenary
denary
decennary
hennery

ĔN'a-tôr
senator
progenitor

ĔND'i-b'l
accendible
amendable
appendable
ascendable
bendable
commendable
comprehendible
defendable
dependable
descendable
emendable
endable
extendible
lendable
mendable
recommendable
rendable
rendible
suspendable
unamendable
unascendable
unbendable

uncommend-
able
undefendable
unemendable
unlendable
unmendable
unvendible
vendible

ĔN'den-sē
ambitendency
appendancy
ascendancy
attendancy
dependency
equipendency
impendency
independency
intendancy
interdepen-
dency
pendancy
resplendency
superinten-
dency
tendency
transcendency
transplendency

ĔN'dē-us
compendious
incendious

ĔND'les-lē
endlessly
friendlessly

ĔND'les-nes
endlessness
friendlessness

ĔN'dur-est
engenderest
renderest
slenderest
surrenderest
tenderest

ĔN'dur-ing
engendering
gendering
rendering
surrendering
tendering

ĔN'dur-lē
slenderly
tenderly

ĔN'dur-nes
slenderness
tenderness

ĔN'dur-ur
engenderer
renderer
slenderer
surrenderer
tenderer

ĔN'dus-lē
stupendously
tremendously

Ē'nē-a
Armenia
asthenia
catamenia
Eugenia
gardenia

ōld, ôr, ŏdd, oil, fŏŏt, out; ūse, ûrn, ŭp; THis, thin

hebephrenia
hypoadrenia
leukopenia
myasthenia
neomenia
neurasthenia
oligophrenia
Parthenia
phonasthenia
presbyophrenia
psychasthenia
Ruthenia
sarracenia
schizophrenia
taenia
Xenia
xenia

Ē′nē-al
congenial
demesnial
genial
homogeneal
menial
primigenial
primogenial
splenial
uncongenial
venial
xenial
(See also
ĒN′yal.)

ĔN′ē-al
bicentennial
biennial
centennial
decennial
duodecennial

millennial
novennial
octennial
perennial
quadrennial
quadricenten-
   nial
quincentennial
quinquennial
septennial
septicentennial
sexennial
tercentennial
tricentennial
triennial
vicennial

Ē′nē-an
Armenian
Athenian
Cyrenian
Estremenian
Fenian
Hellenian
Madrilenian
Ruthenian

Ē′nē-ens
convenience
inconvenience
lenience
(See also
ĒN′yens.)

ĔN′ē-ent
advenient
convenient
inconvenient
intervenient

introvenient
lenient
supervenient
(See also
ĔN′yent.)

ĔN′e-sis
abiogenesis
agenesis
anthropogenesis
biogenesis
catagenesis
ectogenesis
epigenesis
eugenesis
genesis
hematogenesis
heterogenesis
histogenesis
homogenesis
metagenesis
monogenesis
morphogenesis
neogenesis
ontogenesis
oogenesis
organogenesis
osteogenesis
palingenesis
pangenesis
paragenesis
parenesis
parthenogenesis
pathogenesis
phylogenesis
phytogenesis
polygenesis
psychogenesis
pyrogenesis

regenesis
spermatogenesis
sporogenesis
thermogenesis
xenogenesis

ĔN′et-ing
jenneting
renneting

Ē′nē-um
proscenium
selenium
xenium

Ē′nē-us
arsenious
extrageneous
genius
heterogeneous
homogeneous
ingenious
nitrogeneous
pergameneous
primigenious
selenious

ĔN′i-fôrm
antenniform
penniform

ĔN′i-kal
arsenical
cathechumenical
ecumenical
scenical
sirenical

ĔN′i-tē

āle, câre, ădd, ärm, ăsk; mē, hĕre, ĕnd; īce, ĭll;

amenity
lenity
obscenity
serenity
terrenity

ĔN′i-tiv
genitive
lenitive
primogenitive
splenitive

ĔN′i-tūd
lenitude
plenitude
serenitude

ĔN′i-zon
benison
denizen
endenizen
venison

ĔN′sa-b'l
condensable
(See also
ĔN′si-b'l.)

ĔN′sa-rē
dispensary
(See also
ĔN′so-rē.)

ĔN′sa-tiv
compensative
condensative
defensative
dispensative
insensitive

intensitive
pensative
sensitive

ĔN′sha-rē
penitentiary
residentiary

ĔN′shē-āt
essentiate
licentiate
potentiate

ĔN′shē-ent
assentient
consentient
dissentient
insentient
presentient
sentient

ĔN′shun-al
ascensional
attentional
contentional
conventional
descensional
dimensional
extensional
intentional
preventional
unintentional
unconventional

ĔN′shun-ist
ascentionist
extensionist
recensionist

ĔN′shus-nes
conscientious-
  ness
contentious-
  ness
licentiousness
pretentiousness

ĔN′si-b'l
apprehensible
comprehensible
condensable
defensible
deprehensible
dispensable
distensible
extensible
incomprehensi-
  ble
incondensable
indefensible
indispensable
insensible
irreprensible
ostensible
reprehensible
sensible
subsensible
suspensible
tensible

ĔN′si-kal
forensical
nonsensical

ĔN′si-tē
condensity
density
immensity

intensity
propensity
tensity

ĔN′siv-nes
comprehensive-
  ness
expensiveness
extensiveness
inoffensiveness
intensiveness
offensiveness
pensiveness

ĔNS′les-lē
defenselessly
senselessly

ĔNS′les-nes
defenselessness
senselessness

ĔN′so-rē
defensory
dispensary
extrasensory
incensory
ostensory
prehensory
reprehensory
sensory
suspensory

ĔN′ta-b'l
contentable
fermentable
frequentable
inventible
lamentable

ōld, ôr, ŏdd, oil, fŏŏt, out; ūse, ûrn, ŭp; THis, thin

presentable
preventable
rentable
representable
unpresentable
unpreventable
unrepresentable

ĔN′ta-k'l
pentacle
tentacle

ĔN′tal-ē
accidentally
complimentally
continentally
departmentally
detrimentally
developmentally
elementally
environmentally
experimentally
fragmentally
fundamentally
governmentally
incidentally
instrumentally
mentally
monumentally
occidentally
orientally
ornamentally
parentally
pigmentally
regimentally
segmentally
sentimentally
supplementally

temperamentally
transcendentally

ĔN′tal-ist
continentalist
environmentalist
experimentalist
fundamentalist
instrumentalist
mentalist
Occidentalist
Orientalist
sacramentalist
sentimentalist
transcendentalist

ĔN′tal-īz
compartmentalize
continentalize
departmentalize
experimentalize
Orientalize
sentimentalize

ĔN′tal-iz'm
accidentalism
continentalism
departmentalism
elementalism
environmentalism
experimentalism
fundamentalism

instrumentalism
Orientalism
sacramentalism
sentimentalism
transcendentalism

ĔN′tal-nes
accidentalness
fundamentalness
gentleness
incidentalness
instrumentalness
sentimentalness
ungentleness

ĔN′ta-rē
accidentary
alimentary
complementary
complimentary
dentary
elementary
filamentary
instrumentary
integumentary
parliamentary
pigmentary
placentary
rudimentary
sacramentary
sedimentary
tegumentary
tenementary
testamentary

unparliamentary

ĔN′ta-tiv
alimentative
argumentative
augmentative
commentative
complimentative
experimentative
fermentative
frequentative
misrepresentative
presentative
pretentative
preventative
representative
tentative

ĔN′ti-kal
authentical
conventical
conventicle
denticle
identical

ĔN′ti-kūl
denticule
lenticule

ĔN′ti-ment
presentiment
sentiment

ĔN′ti-nal
dentinal
sentinel

ĔN′ti-tē

āle,　câre,　ădd,　ärm,　ăsk;　mē,　hĕre,　ĕnd;　īce,　ĭll;

entity
identity
nonentity

ĔN'tiv-nes
alimentiveness
attentiveness
inattentiveness
inventiveness
retentiveness

ĔN'tū-al
accentual
advental
conventual
eventual

ĔN'tū-āt
accentuate
eventuate

ĔN'tus-lē
momentously
portentously

ĔN'tus-nes
momentous-
  ness
portentousness

ĔN'ū-ant
attenuant
genuant

ĔN'ū-āt
attenuate
extenuate
tenuate

ĔN'ur-āt
degenerate
generate
ingenerate
intenerate
progenerate
regenerate
venerate

ĒN'ur-ē
deanery
greenery
machinery
plenary
scenery

ĔN'ū-rē
penury

ĔN'ur-ē
denary
decennary
hennery
senary
venery

ĔN'ū-us
disingenuous
ingenuous
strenuous
tenuous

ĔN'yen-sē
conveniency
inconveniency
leniency

ĔP'i-lē
creepily
sleepily

ĔP'ē-nes
creepiness
sleepiness
steepiness
weepiness

ĔP'ta-b'l
acceptable
deceptible
imperceptible
insusceptible
perceptible
receptible
susceptible

ĔP'ti-kal
antiseptical
protreptical
receptacle
sceptical

ĔP'tiv-nes
deceptiveness
receptiveness
susceptiveness

ĔP'ur-us
leperous
obstreperous
perstreperous
streperous

ĔR'an-sē
aberrancy
errancy
inerrancy

ĔR'a-pē
balneotherapy

hydrotherapy
kinesitherapy
phototherapy
radiotherapy

ĒR'ē-a, Ē'rē-a
Algeria
diphtheria
Egeria
eleutheria
Etheria
hesperia
hysteria
icteria
Liberia
Nigeria
Valkyria

**ĒR'ē-al,
Ē'rē-al**
aerial
arterial
cereal
ethereal
ferial
funereal
immaterial
imperial
magisterial
managerial
manerial
material
ministerial
monasterial
presbyterial
rhinocerial
serial
siderial
vizierial

ẼR′ē-an
Abderian
aerian
Algerian
Celtiberian
Cimmerian
Hanoverian
Hesperian
Iberian
Keplerian
Luciferian
phalansterian
Pierian
Presbyterian
Shakespearean
Shakesperian
Siberian
Spenserian
Valerian
Valkyrian
Wertherian
(See also
ẼR′ē-on and
IR′ē-an.)

ẼR′ē-est
beeriest
bleariest
cheeriest
dreariest
eeriest
weariest

ĔR′ē-est
buriest
ferriest
merriest

ẼR′ē-ez

congeries
series

ĔR′ē-ing
berrying
burying
ferrying
wherrying

ĔR′ē-man
ferryman
Merriman
wherryman

ĔR′ē-ment
merriment
(See also
ŨR′ē-ment.)

ẼR′ē-nes
beeriness
bleariness
cheeriness
dreariness
eeriness
weariness

ẼR′ē-on
allerion
criterion
Hyperion
(See also
ẼR′ē-an.)

ẼR′ē-or
anterior
exterior
inferior
interior

posterior
superior
ulterior
(See also
ẼR′ē-ur.)

Ē′rē-um
acroterium
apodyterium
dinotherium
megatherium
palaeotherium
titanotherium

ẼR′ē-ur
beerier
blearier
bleerier
cheerier
drearier
eerier
wearier
(See also
ẼR′ē-or.)

ĔR′ē-ur
burier
merrier
terrier

Ē′rē-us,
ẼR′ē-us
cereous
cereus
deleterious
ethereous
imperious
mysterious
serious

siderous

ẼR′ful-ē
cheerfully
fearfully
tearfully

ẼR′ful-nes
cheerfulness
fearfulness
tearfulness

ĔR′i-dēz
Anterides
Hesperides
Pierides

ĔR′i-kal
alexiterical
atmospherical
chimerical
clerical
climacterical
esoterical
exoterical
heliospherical
helispherical
hysterical
numerical
phylacterical
rhinocerical
spherical
sphericle

ẼR′i-lē
cheerily
drearily
eerily
wearily

ĔR'i-lē
merrily
verily

ĔR'ish-ing
cherishing
perishing
unperishing

ĔR'i-ted
disherited
disinherited
emerited
ferreted
inherited
merited

ĔR'i-tē
ambidexterity
asperity
austerity
celerity
dexterity
indexterity
insincerity
legerity
posterity
procerity
prosperity
severity
sincerity
temerity
verity

ĔR'it-ing
ferreting
inheriting
meriting

ĔR'les-nes
cheerlessness
fearlessness
peerlessness

ĔR'ō-gāt
interrogate
(See also
ÛR'o-gat.)

ĔR'yal-ist
immaterialist
imperialist
materialist

ĔR'yal-iz'm
immaterialism
imperialism
materialism

ĒS'a-b'l
creasable
releasable

ĔS'a-rē
confessary
intercessory
pessary
professory
successary

Ē'sen-sē
decency
indecency
recency

ĔS'en-sē
acescency
acquiescency

adolescency
alkalescency
convalescency
defervescency
delitescency
effervescency
efflorescency
erubescency
excrescency
incalescency
incandescency
liquescency
pubescency
quiescency
recrudescency
rejuvenescency
turgescency

Ē'sent-lē
decently
indecently
recently

Ē'shē-an
Capetian
Epictetian
geodesian
Grecian
gynaecian
Megalesian
Melanesian
Peloponnesian
Silesian
Venetian
(See also
ĔSH'an,
ĔSH'un.)

ĔSH'ē-ens

nescience
prescience

ĔSH'ē-nes
fleshiness
meshiness

ĔSH'lē-nes
fleshliness
freshliness
unfleshliness

ĔSH'un-al
accessional
confessional
congressional
digressional
discretional
expressional
intercessional
possessional
processional
professional
progressional
recessional
retrocessional
sessional
successional
transgressional

ĔSH'un-ist
expressionist
impressionist
neo-expression-
ist
neo-impression-
ist
postimpression-
ist

ōld, ôr, ŏdd, oil, fŏŏt, out; ūse, ûrn, ŭp; THis, thin

progressionist
secessionist
successionist

ĔSH′un-ur
possessioner
processioner
secessioner

Ē′shus-nes
facetiousness
speciousness

ĔS′i-b'l
accessible
compressible
concessible
concrescible
effervescible
expressible
fermentescible
impressible
imputrescible
inaccessible
incessable
imcompressible
ineffervescible
inexpressible
insuppressible
irrepressible
marcescible
putrescible
redressible
repressible
suppressible
transgressible
vitrescible

ĔS′i-mal

centesimal
decimal
infinitesimal
millesimal
nonagesimal
quadragesimal
septuagesimal
sexagesimal

ĔS′i-tē
obesity

ĔS′i-tē
necessity
obesity

ĔS′iv-nes
aggressiveness
depressiveness
excessiveness
expressiveness
impressiveness
inexpressiveness
oppressiveness
progressiveness

ĔS′tē-al
agrestial
bestial
celestial
supercelestial

ĔS′tē-nes
reastiness
yeastiness

ĔS′tē-nes
restiness
testiness

ĔS′ti-b'l
comestible
congestible
contestable
detestable
digestible
divestible
incontestable
indigestible
intestable
testable

ĔS′tin-al
destinal
intestinal

ĔS′tin-āt
destinate
festinate
predestinate

ĔS′tiv-nes
festiveness
restiveness
suggestiveness

ĒST′lē-nes
beastliness
priestliness

ĔS′trē-al
extraterrestrial
pedestrial
superterrestrial
terrestrial
trimestrial

ĔS′trē-an
campestrian

equestrian
palestrian
pedestrian
sylvestrian

ĔS′trē-us
pedestrious
terestrious

ĔS′tū-ral
gestural
vestural

ĔS′tur-ing
festering
pestering
westering

ĔS′tū-us
incestuous
tempestuous

ĒT′a-b'l
cheatable
eatable
entreatable
escheatable
uneatable

ĔT′a-b'l
forgettable
gettable
regrettable
settable
unforgettable

ĔT′al-ēn
acetylene

āle, câre, ădd, ärm, ăsk; mē, hĕre, ĕnd; īce, ĭll;

ĚT′a-līn
metalline
petaline

ĚT′al-iz′m
bimetallism
monometallism
petalism

ĚT′ē-nes
meatiness
peatiness
sleetiness

ĚT′ē-nes
jettiness
pettiness
sweatiness

ĚT′ful-ē
forgetfully
fretfully
regretfully

ĚT′ful-nes
forgetfulness
fretfulness
regretfulness

Ěth′les-lē
breathlessly
deathlessly

Ěth′les-nes
breathlessness
deathlessness

ĚTH′ur-ē
feathery
heathery

leathery
weathery

ĚTH′ur-ing
feathering
leathering
tethering
weathering

ĚT′i-kal
aesthetical
aloetical
alphabetical
anchoretical
antipathetical
antithetical
apathetical
apologetical
arithmetical
catechetical
cosmetical
dietetical
emporetical
energetical
epithetical
exegetical
heretical
hermetical
homiletical
hypothetical
noetical
planetical
poetical
theoretical

ĚT′i-kūl
poeticule
reticule

ĚT′in-ū

detinue
retinue

ĚT′ish-lē
coquettishly
pettishly

ĚT′ish′nes
coquettishness
pettishness

ĚT′i-siz′m
aestheticism
asceticism
athleticism
peripateticism

ĒT′o-rē
completory
depletory
repletory
secretory

ĚT′ri-kal
alkalimetrical
asymmetrical
barometrical
craniometrical
diametrical
geometrical
gnomiometrical
graphometrical
horometrical
isoperimetrical
metrical
obstetrical
perimetrical
planimetrical
pluviometrical

stichometrical
symmetrical
trigonometrical

ĚT′ri-ment
detriment
retriment

ĚT′ur-ing
bettering
fettering
lettering

ĒV′a-b′l
achievable
believable
cleavable
conceivable
deceivable
grievable
imperceivable
inconceivable
irretrievable
perceivable
receivable
relievable
retrievable
unbelievable
undeceivable

Ē′vē-āt
abbreviate
alleviate
deviate

ĚV′el-est
bevellest
dishevellest
levelest

ōld, ôr, ŏdd, oil, fŏŏt, out; ūse, ûrn, ŭp; THis, thin

revellest

ĔV′el-ing
bedeviling
beveling
disheveling
leveling
reveling

ĔV′el-iz'm
devilism
levelism

ĔV′el-ur
beveler
bedeviler
disheveler
leveler
reveler

Ē′vĕ-us
devious
previous

ĔV′il-ment
bedevilment
devilment
revelment

ĔV′il-rē
devilry
revelry

Ē′vish-lē
peevishly
thievishly

Ē′vish-nes
peevishness
thievishness

ĔV′i-tē
brevity
levity
longevity

ĔV′ōl-ens
benevolence
malevolence

ĔV′ōl-ent
benevolent
malevolent

ĔV′ōl-us
benevolous
malevolous

ĔV′ōl-ūt
evolute
revolute

ĔV′ur-est
cleverest
endeavorest
Everest
severest

ĔV′ur-môr
evermore
nevermore

ĔV′ur-ur
cleverer
endeavorer
severer

Ē′za-b'l
appeasable
cohesible
defeasible

feasible
freezable
inappeasable
indefeasible
infeasible
seizable
squeezable
unappeasable

ĔZ′an-trē
peasantry
pheasantry
pleasantry

Ē′zē-an
artesian
cartesian
ecclesian
Ephesian
etesian
magnesian
Milesian
Polynesian
trapezian

ĔZ′ē-nes
breeziness
cheesiness
easiness
greasiness
queasiness
sleaziness
uneasiness
wheeziness

Ē′zhē-a, Ē′zē-a
amnesia
anaesthesia
ecclesia

esthesia
magnesia
parrhesia
Rhodesia
Silesia
Zambesia

ĔZ′i-dent
president
resident
vice president

ĒZ′i-lē
breezily
easily
greasily
uneasily
wheezily

ĔZ′ing-lē
appeasingly
freezingly
pleasingly
teasingly
wheezingly

Ē′zon-ing
reasoning
seasoning
unreasoning

ĔZ′ur-ing
measuring
pleasuring
treasuring

ĔZ′ur-ur
measurer
pleasurer
treasurer

I

For a discussion of words included under the accented vowels following, see the beginning of I rhymes in Section I.

Ī′a-b'l
acidifiable
appliable
classifiable
compliable
deniable
diversifiable
electrifiable
exemplifiable
falsifiable
fortifiable
friable
impliable
justifiable
liable
liquefiable
magnifiable
modifiable
pacifiable
petrifiable
pliable
qualifiable
rarefiable
rectifiable
reliable
saponifiable
satisfiable
solidifiable
triable
undeniable
verifiable
viable
vitrifiable

Ī′a-blē
deniably
justifiably
reliably
undeniably
(See also
Ī′a-b'l; change
-e to -y where
appropriate.)

Ī′a-dēz
hamadryades
Hyades
Pleiades

Ī′a-kal
bibliomaniacal
cardiacal
demoniacal
elegiacal
encyclopediacal
heliacal
hypochondria-
    cal
maniacal
monomaniacal
paradisiacal
prosodiacal
simoniacal
zodiacal

**Ī′an-sē,
Ī′en-sē**
cliency

compliancy
pliancy
riancy

Ī′ant-lē
compliantly
defiantly
pliantly
reliantly

Ī′ar-ē
diary
friary
(See also
Ī′ur-ē.)

Ī′ar-ist
diarist
Piarist

Ī′ar-kē
diarchy
triarchy

Ī′a-sis
elephantiasis
hypochondriasis
psoriasis

Ī′a-siz'm
demoniacism
hypochon-
    driacism

Ī′a-tur
psychiater

ĬB′a-b'l
bribable
describable
indescribable
inscribable
scribable
subscribable
undescribable

ĬB′ē-a
amphibia
Libya
tibia

ĬB′ē-al
amphibial
stibial
tibial

ĬB′ē-an
amphibian
Libyan

ĬB′ē-us
amphibious
bathybius
stibious

ĬB′i-tĭv
exhibitive
prohibitive

ōld, ôr, ŏdd, oil, fŏŏt, out; ūse, ûrn, ŭp; THis, thin

ĬB′ū-lar
fibular
infundibular
mandibular
vestibular

ĬCH′ē-nes
bitchiness
itchiness
pitchiness

ĬCH′ur-ē
bewitchery
michery
stitchery
witchery

ĪD′a-b'l
bestridable
decidable
dividable
ridable
(See also ĪD;
add -*able*
where
appropriate.)

ĬD′ē-al
noctidial
presidial

ĬD′ē-an
antemeridian
Gideon
Lydian
meridian
Midian
nullifidian
Numidian
obsidian
ophidian
Ovidian
postmeridian
quotidian
rachidian

ĬD′ē-āt
dimidiate
insidiate

ĬD′en-nes
forbiddenness
hiddenness

**ĬD′ē-om,
ĬD′ē-um**
idiom
iridium
peridium

ĬD′ē-us
avidious
fastidious
hideous
insidious
invidious
lapideous
ophidious
parricidious
perfidious
Phidias
splendidious
stillicidious

ĬD′i-fī
acidify
lapidify
solidify

ĬD′i-kal
druidical
juridical
pyramidical
veridical

ĬD′i-nus
libidinous

ĬD′i-tē
acidity
acridity
aridity
avidity
cupidity
frigidity
insipidity
insolidity
intrepidity
invalidity
gelidity
gravidity
hispidity
humidity
hybridity
limpidity
liquidity
lividity
lucidity
marcidity
morbidity
pallidity
pavidity
pellucidity
putidity
putridity
quiddity
rabidity
rancidity
rapidity
rigidity
sapidity
solidity
squalidity
stolidity
stupidity
timidity
torpidity
torridity
trepidity
tumidity
turbidity
turgidity
validity
vapidity
viridity
viscidity
vividity

ĬD′ū-al
individual
residual

ĬD′ū-āt
assiduate
individuate

ĬD′ū-lāt
acidulate
stridulate

ĬD′ū-lus
acidulous
stridulous

ĬD′ū-us
assiduous
deciduous

āle, câre, ădd, ärm, ăsk; mē, hĕre, ĕnd; īce, ĭll;

prociduous
residuous
succiduous
viduous

Ī'en-sē
cliency
(See also
Ī'an-sē.)

Ī'et-al
dietal
hyetal
parietal
varietal

Ī'et-ē
anxiety
contrariety
dubiety
ebriety
filiety
impiety
impropriety
inebriety
insobriety
luxuriety
mediety
nimiety
notoriety
nullibiety
omniety
piety
propriety
satiety
sobriety
society
ubiety
variety

Ī'et-ed
dieted
disquieted
quieted
rioted

Ī'et-est
dietest
quietest
riotest

Ī'et-ing
dieting
disquieting
quieting
rioting

Ī'et-ist
anxietist
dietist
pietist
proprietist
quietist
varietiest

Ī'et-iz'm
pietism
quietism
varietism

Ī'et-ur, Ī'et-ôr
dieter
proprietor
quieter
rioter

ĬF'i-kal
beatifical
dolorifical
lanifical
pontifical
specifical

ĬF'i-kant
insignificant
mundificant
sacrificant
significant

ĬF'i-kāt
certificate
pontificate
significate

ĬF'i-sens
magnificence
munificence

ĬF'i-sent
magnificent
mirificent
munificent

ĪF'ī-sur
artificer
opificer

ĬF'lū-us
dulcifluous
fellifluous
ignifluous
mellifluous
sanguifluous

ĬF'on-ē
antiphony
oxyphony
polyphony

ĬF'ra-gus
fedrifragous
ossifragous
saxifragous

ĬF'ta-b'l
liftable
shiftable

ĬF'tē-ness
shiftiness
thriftiness

ĬF'ti-lē
shiftily
thriftily

ĬFT'les-nes
shiftlessness
thriftlessness

ĬF'ū-gal
centrifugal
febrifugal
vermifugal

ĬF'ur-us
acidiferous
aliferous
aluminiferous
ammonitiferous
antenniferous
aquiferous
argentiferous
armiferous
astriferous
auriferous
bacciferous

ōld, ôr, ŏdd, oil, fŏŏt, out; ūse, ûrn, ŭp; THis, thin

balániferous
balsámiferous
bránchiferous
búlbiferous
calcáriferous
calcíferous
carbóniferous
célliferous
chéliferous
círriferous
cónchiferous
cóniferous
corálliferous
crúciferous
cúpriferous
diamántiferous
diamóndiferous
dolóriferous
ensíferous
fatíferous
férriferous
fíliferous
flámmiferous
flóriferous
flúctiferous
fóliferous
foráminiferous
fóssiliferous
fróndiferous
frúctiferous
frúgiferous
fúmiferous
fúrciferous
gémmiferous
geódiferous
glándiferous
glandúliferous
grániferous
granúliferous

gúttiferous
gýpsiferous
hedériferous
hérbiferous
ígniferous
láctiferous
lamélliferous
lamíniferous
lánciferous
lániferous
latíciferous
láuriferous
léthiferous
lígniferous
lignítiferous
límbiferous
lúciferous
lucríferous
lúctiferous
lúminiferous
magnétiferous
máliferous
mammáliferous
mámmiferous
margarítiferous
mélliferous
membrániferous
metálliferous
mónstriferous
mórtiferous
múciferous
múltiferous
nectáriferous
níckeliferous
nímbiferous
nítriferous
nóctiferous
núbiferous
núciferous

odóriferous
óleiferous
ómniferous
oólitiferous
óssiferous
óstriferous
ozóniferous
pálmiferous
papílliferous
papúliferous
péstiferous
petróliferous
píliferous
pistílliferous
platíniferous
plúmbiferous
polýpiferous
póriferous
próliferous
prúniferous
pulmóniferous
quartíziferous
racémiferous
ramúliferous
resíniferous
róriferous
saccháriferous
sácciferous
sáliferous
salíniferous
salútiferous
sanguíferous
scópiferous
scútiferous
sébiferous
sénsiferous
sétiferous
silíciferous
sobóliferous

sómniferous
sóniferous
sopóriferous
spíciferous
spíniferous
spléndiferous
spúmiferous
staméniferous
stánniferous
stélliferous
stolóniferous
súcciferous
sudóriferous
tentáculiferous
térgiferous
thúriferous
tubériferous
umbélliferous
umbráculiferous
úmbriferous
válviferous
vapóriferous
vásculiferous
venéniferous
vocíferous
zínciferous

ĬG′am-ē
bígamy
dígamy
polýgamy
trígamy

ĬG′am-ist
bígamist
polýgamist
trígamist

ĬG′am-us

bigamous
digamous
polygamous
trigamous

ĬG′ma-tist
enigmatist
stigmatist

ĬG′ma-tīz
enigmatize
paradigmatize
stigmatize

ĬG′nan-sē
indignancy
malignancy

ĬG′nē-us
igneous
ligneous

ĬG′ni-fī
dignify
ignify
lignify
malignify
signify
undignify

ĬG′ni-tē
benignity
dignity
indignity
malignity

ĬG′ôr-us
rigorous
vigorous

ĬG′ra-fē
calligraphy
epigraphy
lexigraphy
pasigraphy
poligraphy
pseudepigrahy
stratigraphy
tachygraphy

ĬG′ū-lāt
figulate
ligulate

ĬG′ur-ē
piggery
Whiggery
wiggery

ĬG′ū-us
ambiguous
contiguous
exiguous
irriguous

ĬJ′ē-an
Cantabrigian
Phrygian
Stygian

ĬJ′en-us
alkaligenous
coralligenous
epigenous
fuliginous
gelatigenous
ignigenous
indigenous
marigenous

melligenous
montigenous
nubigenous
omnigenous
oxygenous
polygenous
pruriginous
sanguigenous
terrigenous
uliginous
unigenous
vertiginous
vortiginous

ĬJ′id-lē
frigidly
rigidly

ĬJ′id-nes
frigidness
rigidness

ĬJ′i-tē
digity
fidgety

ĬJ′ur-āt
belligerate
frigerate
refrigerate

ĬJ′ur-ent
belligerent
refrigerant

ĬJ′ur-us
aligerous
armigerous
belligerous

cirrigerous
coralligerous
cornigerous
crucigerous
dentigerous
immorigerous
lanigerous
linigerous
morigerous
navigerous
ovigerous
palpigerous
pedigerous
pennigerous
piligerous
plumigerous
proligerous
setigerous
spinigerous

ĬJ′us-nes
litigiousness
prodigiousness
religiousness

ĬK′a-ment
medicament
predicament

ĬK′a-tiv
abdicative
desiccative
exsiccative
fricative
indicative
predicative
siccative

ĬK′ē-nes

stickiness
trickiness

ĬK'en-ing
quickening
sickening
thickening

ĬK'et-ē
pernicketty
rickety
thicketty

ĬK'et-ing
cricketing
picketing
ticketing

ĬK'et-ur
cricketer
picketer

ĬK'i-lē
stickily
trickily

ĬK'lē-nes
prickliness
sickliness

ĬK'ō-list
agricolist
ignicolist
plebicolist

ĬK'ō-lus
agricolous
Nicholas
sepicolous

terricolous

ĬK'ō-mus
auricomous
flavicomous

ĬK'sa-b'l
fixable
mixable

ĬK'shun-al
contradictional
fictional
frictional
jurisdictional

ĬK'si-tē
fixity
prolixity
siccity

ĬK'tiv-lē
restrictively
vindictively

ĬK'tiv-nes
restrictiveness
vindictiveness

ĬK'to-rē
benedictory
contradictory
interdictory
valedictory
victory

ĬK'ū-la
Canicula
fidicula

reticula
zeticula

ĬK'ū-lar
acicular
adminicular
articular
auricular
calycular
canicular
clavicular
cubicular
cuticular
fascicular
follicular
funicular
lenticular
navicular
orbicular
ovicular
particular
pellicular
perpendicular
quinquarticular
radicular
reticular
spicular
subcuticular
vehicular
ventricular
vermicular
versicular
vesicular

ĬK'ū-lāt
articulate
canaliculate
denticulate
fasciculate

funiculate
geniculate
gesticulate
matriculate
monticulate
paniculate
particulate
reticulate
spiculate
vehiculate
vermiculate
vesiculate

ĬK'ū-lum
curriculum
geniculum

ĬK'ū-lus
dendiculous
denticulus
fasciculus
folliculous
meticulous
ridiculous
urbiculous
ventriculous
vermiculous
vesiculous

ĬK'wi-tē
antiquity
iniquity
obliquity
ubiquity

ĬK'wi-tus
iniquitous
ubiquitous

āle, câre, ădd, ärm, ăsk; mē, hĕre, ĕnd; īce, ĭll;

ĬL′a-b′l
distillable
fillable
refillable
syllable
tillable
unrefillable

Ī′lan-dur
highlander
islander

ĬL′a-rē
Hilary
(See also
ĬL′ur-ē.)

ĬL′ē-a
memorabilia
notabilia
sedilia

ĬL′ē-ad
chiliad
Iliad

ĬL′ē-an
Brazilian
Castilian
Cecilian
crocodilian
Kurilian
lacertilian
Lilian
Maximilian
perfectibilian
reptilian
Virgilian
(See also

ĬL′yun.)

ĬL′ē-ar
atrabiliar
auxiliar
conciliar
domiciliar
(See also
ĬL′yar.)

ĬL′ē-at
affiliate
conciliate
domiciliate
filiate
humiliate

ĬL′ē-ens
consilience
dissilience
resilience
transilience
(See also
ĬL′yans.)

ĬL′ē-ent
dissilient
resilient
transilient
(See also
ĬL′yant.)

ĬL′ē-est
chilliest
hilliest
silliest
stilliest

ĬL′ē-nes

chilliness
hilliness
silliness

ĬL′ē-ō
pulvillio
punctilio

ĬL′et-ed
billeted
filleted
unfilleted

ĬL′et-ing
billeting
filleting

ĬL′ē-us
atrabilious
bilious
punctilious
supercilious
(See also
ĬL′yus.)

ĬL′ful-ē
guilefully
wilefully

ĬL′ful-ē
skilfully
wilfully
unskilfully

ĬL′ful-nes
guilefulness
wilefulness

ĬL′ful-nes

skilfulness
wilfulness
unskilfulness

ĬL′i-fī
fossilify
nobilify
stabilify
vilify

ĬL′i-fôrm
filiform
plumiliform

ĬL′i-gan
Gilligan
McMilligan

ĬL′ij-ur
pillager
villager

ĬL′i-ka
basilica
silica

ĬL′i-kal
basilical
filical
silicle
umbilical

ĬL′ing-lē
killingly
thrillingly
trillingly
willingly

ĬL′i-tāt

---

abilitate
debilitate
facilitate
habilitate
impossibilitate
militate
nobilitate
rehabilitate
stabilitate

ÌL'i-tē
ability
absorbability
accendibility
acceptability
accessibility
accountability
acquirability
adaptability
addibility
adjustability
admirability
admissibility
adoptability
adorability
advisability
affability
affectibility
agility
agreeability
alienability
alterability
amability
amenability
amiability
amicability
amissibility
anility

answerability
appetibility
applicability
approachability
assimilability
associability
attainability
attemptability
attractability
audibility
availability
bribability
calculability
capability
censurability
changeability
chargeability
civility
coagulability
cognoscibility
cohesibility
collapsibility
combustibility
commen-
    surability
communicabil-
    ity
commutability
comparability
compatibility
comprehensi-
    bility
compressibility
computability
conceivability
condensability
conducibility
conductability
conformability

confusability
contemptibility
contractibility
contractility
convincibility
convertibility
corrigibility
corrodibility
corrosibility
corruptibility
credibility
creditability
crocodility
culpability
curability
damnability
debility
deceptibility
deducibility
defectibility
defensibility
delectability
demisability
demonstrabil-
    ity
deplorability
descendibility
describability
desirability
despicability
destructibility
determinability
detestability
diffusibility
digestibility
dilatability
dirigibility
disability
dispensability

disputability
dissolubility
dissolvability
distensibility
divisibility
docibility
docility
ductility
durability
edibility
educability
eligibility
enunciability
equability
errability
exchangeability
excitability
exhaustibility
exility
expansibility
extensibility
facility
fallibility
feasibility
febrility
fermentability
fertility
fictility
flammability
flexibility
fluctuability
fluxibility
formidability
fossility
fragility
frangibility
friability
fusibility
futility

āle, câre, ădd, ärm, ăsk; mē, hĕre, ĕnd; īce, ĭll;

generability
gentility
governability
gracility
gullibility
habitability
hereditability
hostility
humility
ignobility
illability
illegibility
illimitability
imbecility
imitability
immeability
immeasurabil-
ity
immiscibility
immobility
immovability
immutability
impalpability
impartibility
impassibility
impeccability
impenetrability
imperceptibility
imperdibility
imperfectibility
imperishability
impermeability
imperturbabil-
ity
imperviability
implacability
imponderability
impossibility
impracticability

impregnability
imprescriptibil-
ity
impressibility
impressionabil-
ity
improbability
improvability
imputability
inability
inaccessibility
inadmissibility
inaudibility
incalculability
incapability
incivility
incogitability
incognoscibility
incombustibil-
ity
incommen-
surability
incommuni-
cability
incommutabil-
ity
incomparability
incompatibility
incomprehensi-
bility
incompressibil-
ity
inconceivability
incondensabil-
ity
incontestability
incontroverti-
bility
inconvertibility

incorrigibility
incorruptibility
incredibility
incurability
indefatigability
indefeasibility
indefectibility
indefensibility
indelibility
indemonstra-
bility
indescribability
indestructibility
indigestibility
indiscernibility
indiscerptibility
indispensability
indisputability
indissolubility
indivisibility
indocibility
indocility
inductility
ineffability
ineffervescibil-
ity
ineligibility
inerrability
inevitability
inexcusability
inexhaustibility
inexorability
inexplicability
inexpressibility
infallibility
infantility
infeasibility
infertility
inflammability

inflexibility
influenceability
infrangibility
infusibility
inhability
inhabitability
inheritability
inimitability
innumerability
inoperability
insanability
insatiability
inscrutability
insensibility
inseparability
insociability
insolubility
instability
insuperability
insurability
insurmount-
ability
insusceptibility
intangibility
intelligibility
interchange-
ability
intractability
inutility
invariability
invendibility
invincibility
inviolability
invisibility
invulnerability
irascibility
irreconcilability
irredeemability
irreducibility

irrefragability
irrefutability
irremissibility
irremovability
irreparability
irrepressibility
irreproachabil-
   ity
irresistibility
irresistibility
irresolvability
irresponsibility
irretrievability
irreversibility
irrevocability
irritability
justifiability
juvenility
knowability
lability
laminability
laudability
legibility
liability
malleability
manageability
manipulability
marketability
measurability
memorability
mensurability
miscibility
mobility
modifiability
modificability
motility
movability
mutability
nameability

navigability
negotiability
neurility
nihility
nobility
notability
nubility
opposability
organizability
ostensibility
palpability
partibility
passibility
peccability
penetrability
pensility
perceptibility
perceptibility
perdurability
perfectibility
perishability
permeability
permissibility
persuasibility
perturbability
placability
plausibility
pliability
ponderability
portablity
possibility
potability
practicability
precipitability
predictability
preferability
prehensility
prescriptibility
preventability

probability
producibility
provability
puerility
punishability
questionability
quotability
ratability
readability
receivability
receptibility
recognizability
reconcilability
redeemability
reducibility
reductibility
reflectibility
reflexibility
reformability
refragability
refrangibility
refutability
relatability
reliability
remissibility
removability
remunerability
renewability
reparability
repealability
resistibility
resolvability
respectability
responsibility
retractability
retractility
retrievability
reversibility
revocability

risibility
saleability
salvability
sanability
satiability
scurrility
senility
sensibility
separability
servility
sociability
solubility
solvability
sportability
squeezability
stability
sterility
suability
subtility
suggestibility
suitability
susceptibility
suspensibility
tactility
tamability
tangibility
taxability
temptability
tenability
tensibility
tensility
tolerability
torsibility
tortility
traceability
tractability
tractility
tranquillity
transferability

āle,   câre,   ădd,   ärm,   ăsk;   mē,   hĕre,   ĕnd;   īce,   ĭll;

translatability
transmissibility
transmutability
transportability
unaccountabil-
    ity
unbelievability
undesirability
unreliability
unsuitability
untranslatabil-
    ity
unutterability
utility
vaporability
variability
vegetability
vendibility
venerability
verisimility
vernility
versability
versatility
viability
vibratility
vincibility
vindicability
violability
virility
visibility
volatility
volubility
vulnerability
wearability
workability
writability

ĬL′kē-est

milkiest
silkiest

ĬL′kē-ur
milkier
silkier

Ī′lō-bāt
stylobate
trilobate

ĬL′ō-ē
billowy
pillowy
willowy

ĬL′ō-ing
billowing
pillowing

ĬL′ō-jē
antilogy
brachylogy
dilogy
fossilogy
palilogy
trilogy

ĬL′ō-jīz
epilogize
syllogize

ĬL′ō-jiz′m
epilogism
episyllogism
syllogism

ĬL′ō-rē
pillory

(See also
ĬL′ur-ē.)

ĬL′ō-kwens
blandiloquence
breviloquence
grandiloquence
magniloquence
somniloquence
stultiloquence

ĬL′ō-kwent
flexiloquent
grandiloquent
magniloquent
melliloquent
pauciloquent
sanctiloquent
stultiloquent
sauviloquent
veriloquent

ĬL′ō-kwē
dentiloquy
gastriloquy
pauciloquy
pectoriloquy
soliloquy
somniloquy
stultiloquy
suaviloquy
ventriloquy

ĬL′ō-kwist
dentiloquist
gastriloquist
somniloquist
ventriloquist

ĬL′ō-kwīz
soliloquize
ventriloquize

ĬL′ō-kwiz′m
gastriloquism
pectoriloquism
somniloquism
ventriloquism

ĬL′ō-kwus
grandiloquous
magniloquous
pectoriloquous
somniloquous
ventriloquous

ĬL′ur-ē
artillery
capillary
cilery
codicillary
distillery
Hilăry
phyllary
pillory
Sillery

ĬL′yan-sē
brilliancy
resiliency
transiliency

ĬL′yar-ē
atrabiliary
auxiliary

ĬM′a-nus
longimanous

ōld, ôr, ŏdd, oil, fŏŏt, out; ūse, ûrn, ŭp; THis, thin

pedimanous

ĬM′a-tūr
climature
limature

ĬM′bri-kāt
fimbricate
imbricate

ĬM′ē-an,
ĬM′ē-on
Endymion
simian
Simeon

ĬM′ē-nes
griminess
sliminess

Ī′mer-ē
primary
rhymery

ĬM′et-rē
alkalimetry
asymmetry
bathymetry
calorimetry
isoperimetry
longimetry
planimetry
polarimetry
saccharimetry
symmetry

ĬM′et-ur
alkalimeter
altimeter

calorimeter
dasymeter
dimeter
focimeter
gravimeter
limiter
lucimeter
pelvimeter
perimeter
planimeter
polarimeter
pulsimeter
rhysimeter
saccharimeter
salimeter
scimiter
tasimeter
trimeter
velocimeter
zymosimeter

ĬM′i-kal
alchymical
homonymical
inimical
metonymical
mimical

ĬM′i-nal
criminal
regiminal
subliminal
viminal

ĬM′i-nāt
accriminate
criminate
discriminate
eliminate

incriminate
indiscriminate
recriminate

ĬM′i-nē
Bimini
jiminy
nimini-pimini
postliminy

ĬM′i-nus
criminous
moliminous

ĬM′i-tē
anonymity
dimity
equanimity
magnanimity
parvanimity
proximity
pseudonymity
pusillanimity
sanctanimity
sublimity
unanimity

ĬM′pur-ing
simpering
whimpering

ĬM′pur-ur
simperer
whimperer

ĬM′ū-lāt
assimulate
dissimulate
simulate
stimulate

ĬM′ū-lus
limulus
stimulus

ĬM′ur-us
dimerous
polymerous

ĬN′a-b'l
assignable
combinable
declinable
definable
designable
finable
inclinable
indeclinable
indefinable
signable

ĬN′ar-ē
binary
(See also
ĬN′ur-ē.)

ĬN′a-tiv
combinative
finative

ĬN′di-kāt
indicate
syndicate
vindicate

ĬN′dur-ē
bindery
grindery

ĬN′dur-ē
cindery

āle,   câre,   ădd,   ärm,   ăsk;   mē,   hĕre,   ĕnd;   īce,   ĭll;

tindery

IN'ē-a
Abyssinia
Lavinia
Sardinia
Virginia
Zinnia

ĬN'ē-al
consanguineal
finial
gramineal
interlineal
lineal
pectineal
pineal
stamineal

ĬN'ē-an
Abyssinian
anthro-
   pophaginian
Arminian
Augustinian
Carolinian
Carthaginian
czarinian
Darwinian
Delphinian
Eleusinian
Hercynian
Justinian
Palestinean
Sardinian
serpentinian
Socinian
viraginian
Virginian

(See also
ĬN'yon.)

ĬN'ē-āt
delineate
laciniate
lineate
miniate

ĬN'ē-est
briniest
shiniest
spiniest
tiniest

ĬN'e-ma
cinema
kinema

ĬN'ē-ur
brinier
shinier
spinier
tinier

ĬN'ē-us
cartilagineous
consan-
   guineous
flamineous
fulmineous
gramineous
ignominious
sanguineous
stamineous
stramineous
testudineous
vimineous

ĬNG'gur-ing
fingering
lingering
malingering

ĬNG'gur-ur
fingerer
lingerer
malingerer

ĬNG'ē-nes
ringiness
springiness
stringiness

ĬNGK'a-b'l
drinkable
shrinkable
thinkable
undrinkable
unshrinkable
unsinkable
unthinkable

ĬNGK'ē-nes
inkiness
kinkiness
pinkiness
slinkiness

ĬNGK'wi-tē
longinquity
propinquity

ĬN'i-fôrm
actiniform
aluminiform
laciniform

ĬN'i-kin
finikin
minikin

ĬN'i-k'l
adminicle
binnacle
binocle
Brahminical
clinical
cynical
dominical
finical
flaminical
pinnacle
Sinical
synclinical

ĬN'i-ment
liniment
miniment

ĬN'ish-ing
diminishing
finishing

ĬN'is-tral
ministral
sinistral

ĬN'is-tur
administer
minister
sinister

ĬN'i-tē
affinity
alkalinity
asininity

consanguinity
divinity
felinity
femininity
infinity
Latinity
masculinity
patavinity
peregrinity
salinity
sanguinity
satinity
trinity
vicinity
viraginity
virginity

ĬN'i-tiv
combinative
finitive
infinitive

ĬN'jen-sē
astringency
contingency
refringency
stringency

ĬN'jē-an
Carlovingian
Merovingian
Thuringian

ĬN'ji-lē
dingily
stingily

ĬN'jē-nes
dinginess

stinginess

ĬN'lan-dur
Finlander
inlander

ĬN'ō-lin
crinoline
quinoline

ĬN'thē-an
absinthian
Corinthian
hyacinthian
labyrinthian

ĬN'tur-est
interest
splinterest
winterest

ĬN'tur-ē
printery
splintery
wintery

ĬN'ur-ē
alpinery
binary
finary
finery
pinery
quinary
refinery
swinery
vinery

ĬN'ū-āt
continuate

insinuate
sinuate

ĬN'ū-us
continuous
sinuous

Ī'ōl-a
variola
viola

Ī'ō-let
triolet
violet

Ī'ō-list
sciolist
violist

Ī'ō-lus
gladiolus
sciolous
variolous

Ī'ō-pē
Calliope
myopy
presbyopy

Ī'ō-tur
rioter
(See also
Ī'et-ur.)

Ī'ō-sēn
Miocene
Pliocene
post-Pliocene

ĬP'ar-us
biparous
criniparous
deiparous
fissiparous
floriparous
foliiparous
frondiparous
fructiparous
gemelliparous
gemmiparous
larviparous
multiparous
omniparous
opiparous
oviparous
ovoviviparous
polyparous
polypiparous
sebiparous
sudoriparous
tomiparous
uniparous
vermiparous
viviparous

ĬP'a-thē
antipathy
kinesipathy
somnipathy

ĬP'a-thist
antipathist
somnipathist

ĬP'ed-al
equipedal
solipedal
(See also

ĒD'al.)

ĬP'li-kāt
sesquiplicate
triplicate

ĬP'ō-lē
Gallipoli
Tripoli

ĬP'ō-tens
armipotence
ignipotence
omnipotence
plenipotence

ĬP'ō-tent
armipotent
bellipotent
ignipotent
multipotent
omnipotent
plenipotent

ĬP'ti-kal
apocalyptical
cryptical
elliptical

ĬP'tur-us
dipterous
peripterous
tripterous

ĬP'ū-lāt
astipulate
manipulate
stipulate

ĬP'ur-ē
frippery
slippery

ĪR'a-b'l
acquirable
desirable
expirable
perspirable
requirable
respirable
transpirable
untirable

ĪR'as-ē
piracy
retiracy

ĪR'as-ē
conspiracy
deliracy

ĪR'ful-nes
direfulness
irefulness

ĪR'ē-an
Assyrian
Styrian
Syrian
Tyrian
(See also
ĘR'i-an.)

ĪR'i-kal
empirical
lyrical
miracle
panegyrical

satirical

ĬR'i-siz'm
empiricism
lyricism

ĬR'ē-us
delirious
Sirius
(See also
ĘR'i-us.)

ĪR'on-ē
gyronny
irony

ĪS'ē-est
iciest
spiciest

ĪS'ē-nes
iciness
spiciness

ĬS'en-ing
christening
glistening
listening
unlistening

ĬS'en-sē
reminiscency
reviviscency

ĬS'en-ur
christener
listener

Ī'sē-us

Dionysius

ĬSH'al-ē
judicially
officially
prejudicially
superficially

ĬSH'al-iz'm
judicialism
officialism

ĬSH'ē-a
Alicia
Delicia
Felicia
Luticia

ĬSH'ē-āt
initiate
maleficiate
novitiate
officiate
patriciate
propitiate
vitiate

ĬSH'ē-ens
omniscience
(See also
ĬSH'ens.)

ĬSH'ē-ent
omniscient
(See also
ĬSH'ent.)

ĬSH'en-sē
alliciency

ōld, ôr, ŏdd, oil, fŏŏt, out; ūse, ûrn, ŭp; THis, thin

beneficiency
deficiency
efficiency
inefficiency
insitiency
insufficiency
proficiency
self-sufficiency
sufficiency

ĬSH′on-al
additional
commissional
conditional
definitional
dispositional
disquisitional
inquisitional
intuitional
positional
prepositional
propositional
repetitional
suppositional
traditional
transitional
transpositional
volitional

ĬSH′on-ist
abolitionist
coalitionist
exhibitionist
expeditionist
oppositionist
prohibitionist
requisitionist
traditionist

ĬSH′on-ur
admonitioner
coalitioner
commissioner
exhibitioner
missioner
practitioner
traditioner

ĬSH′us-nes
adventitiousness
auspiciousness
avariciousness
capriciousness
deliciousness
expeditiousness
fictitiousness
flagitiousness
inauspicious-
    ness
judiciousness
maliciousness
meretricious-
    ness
perniciousness
propitiousness
seditiousness
superstitious-
    ness
supposititious-
    ness
suspiciousness
viciousness

ĬS′i-b'l
admissible
amissible
dismissible
immiscible

incommiscible
irremissable
miscible
omissible
permiscible
permissible
remissible
scissible
transmissible

Ĭ′si-k'l
bicycle
icicle
tricycle

ĬS′i-lē
icily
spicily

ĬS′i-mō
bravissimo
fortissimo
generalissimo
pianissimo
prestissimo

ĬS′i-nal
fidicinal
medicinal
officinal
vaticinal
vicinal

ĬS′i-tē
accomplicity
achromaticity
authenticity
benedicite
caloricity

canonicity
catholicity
causticity
centricity
clericity
complicity
conicity
domesticity
duplicity
eccentricity
elasticity
electricity
electrotonicity
ellipticity
endemicity
evangelicity
felicity
historicity
hygroscopicity
immundicity
impudicity
inelasticity
infelicity
lubricity
mendicity
multiplicity
pepticity
periodicity
plasticity
publicity
pudicity
rubricity
rusticity
simplicity
spasticity
sphericity
spheroidicity
stoicity
stypticity

āle,   câre,   ădd,   ärm,   ăsk;   mē,   hĕre,   ĕnd;   īce,   ĭll;

tonicity
triplicity
unicity
verticity
volcanicity
vulcanicity

ĬS′it-nes
explicitness
illicitness
implicitness
licitness

ĬS′i-tūd
solicitude
spissitude
vicissitude

ĬS′iv-lē
decisively
derisively
incisively
indecisively

ĬS′iv-nes
decisiveness
derisiveness
incisiveness
indecisivenes

ĬS′kē-est
friskiest
riskiest

ĬS′on-us
fluctisonous
unisonous

ĬS′ôr-ē, ĬS′ur-ē

decisory
derisory
incisory
spicery

ĬS′ôr-ē
admissory
dismissory
emissory
remisory
rescissory

ĬS′ten-sē
consistency
distancy
existency
inconsistency
persistency
pre-existency
subsistency

ĬS′ti-kal
agonistical
alchemistical
anarchistical
anomalistical
antagonistical
antarchistical
aoristical
apathistical
aphoristical
artistical
atheistical
cabalistical
Calvanistical
casuistical
cathechistical
characteristical
chemistical

deistical
dialogistical
egostical
egotistical
eucharistical
eulogistical
euphemistical
hemistichal
linguistical
methodistical
mystical
paragraphistical
pietistical
puristical
sophistical
statistical
theistical
theosophistical

ĬS′ti-kāt
dephlogisticate
sophisticate

ĬST′les-nes
listlessness
resistlessness

ĬS′to-rē
consistory
history
mystery

ĪT′a-b'l
citable
excitable
ignitible
incitable
indictable
lightable

requitable
unitable
writable

ĪT′a-b'l
admittable
fittable
irremittable
knittable
quittable
transmittible

ĪT′an-ē
dittany
kitteny
litany

ĪT′a-tiv
excitative
incitative
writative

ĪT′ē-nes
almightiness
flightiness
mightiness

ĪT′ē-nes
flittiness
grittiness
prettiness
wittiness

ĪT′ful-ē
delightfully
frightfully
rightfully
spitefully

Ĭth′e-sis
antithesis
epithesis

ĬTH′som-lē
blithesomely
lithesomely

ĬTH′som-nes
blithesomeness
lithesomeness

ĬTH′ur-ward
hitherward
thitherward
whitherward

ĬT′i-gant
litigant
mitigant

ĬT′i-gāt
litigate
mitigate

ĬT′i-kal
Abrahamitical
acritical
analytical
anchoritical
cosmopolitical
critical
diacritical
electrolytical
hermitical
hypercritical
hypocritical
Jesuitical
Levitical

political
pulpitical
soritical
thersitical

ĬT′i-lē
grittily
prettily
wittily

ĬT′i-siz′m
Britticism
witticism

ĬT′lē-nes
knightliness
spriteliness
unsightliness

ĬT′′l-nes
brittleness
littleness

ĬT′ū-al
habitual
obitual
ritual

ĬT′ū-āt
habituate
situate

ĬT′ū-lar
capitular
titular

ĬT′ur-āt
iterate
obliterate

reiterate
transliterate

ĬT′ur-at
illiterate
literate

ĬT′ur-est
bitterest
embitterest
fritterest
glitterest

ĬT′ur-ing
bittering
embittering
frittering
glittering
tittering
twittering

Ī′ur-ē
briery
diary
fiery
friary

ĪV′a-b′l
contrivable
deprivable
derivable
revivable

ĬV′a-b′l
forgivable
givable
livable
unforgivable

ĬV′a-lent
equivalent
multivalent
omnivalent
quinquivalent
trivalent
univalent

ĪV′an-sē
connivancy
survivancy

ĪV′a-tiv
derivative
privative

ĬV′ē-a
Bolivia
Livia
Olivia
trivia

ĬV′ē-al
convivial
lixivial
oblivial
quadrivial
trivial

ĬV′ē-an
Bolivian
Vivian

ĬV′el-ur,
ĬV′il-ur
civiller
driveller
sniveller

ĬV′ē-us
bivious
lascivious
lixivious
multivious
oblivious

ĬV′id-nes
lividness
vividness

ĬV′i-tē
absorptivity
acclivity
activity
captivity
causativity
cogitativity
collectivity
conductivity
declivity
festivity
impassivity
incogitativity
instinctivity
motivity
nativity
negativity
objectivity
passivity
perceptivity
positivity
privity
proclivity
productivity
receptivity
relativity
sensitivity
subjectivity

ĬV′ō-kal
equivocal
univocal

ĬV′ō-lē
Rivoli
Tivoli

ĪV′o-rē,
ĪV′ar-ē
ivory
vivary

ĬV′or-us
carnivorous
equivorous
frugivorous
fucivorous
graminivorous
granivorous
herbivorous
insectivorous
omnivorous
ossivorous
panivorous
phytivorous
piscivorous
sanguinivorous
vermivorous

ĬV′ur-ē
delivery
gaol-delivery
jail-delivery
livery
rivery
shivery

ĬV′ur-ing

delivering
quivering
shivering

ĬV′ur-ur
deliverer
quiverer
shiverer

ĬZ′a-b'l
advisable
analyzable
crystallizable
demisable
despisable
devisable
electrolyzable
excisable
exercisable
magnetizable
organizable
oxidizable
prizable
realizable
recognizable
sizable
vaporizable

ĬZ′a-b'l
acquisible
devisible
indivisible
invisible
risible
visible

ĬZ′ē-an
Elysian
Frisian

Paradisean
Parisian
precisian
(See also
ĬZH′un.)

ĬZ′ē-est
busiest
dizziest

ĬZ′ē-ur
busier
dizzier
frizzier

ĬZH′on-al
divisional
provisional
revisional
transitional
visional

ĬZ′i-kal
metaphysical
paradisical
phthisical
physical
psychophysical

ĬZ′i-lē
busily
dizzily

ĬZ′i-tor
acquisitor
inquisitor
requisitor
visitor

ōld, ôr, ŏdd, oil, fŏŏt, out; ūse, ûrn, ŭp; THis, thin

ĪZ'ôr-ē   irrisory   revisory
advisory   provisory   supervisory

O

For a discussion of words included under the accented vowels
following, see the beginning of O rhymes in Section 1.

Ō'bē-a	bibliophobia	eosophobia	hyalophobia
acarophobia	bromidosiphobia	eremophobia	hydrophobia
acrophobia	brontophobia	ereuthophobia	hygrophobia
acousticophobia	cancerophobia	ergasiophobia	hylephobia
acrophobia	carcinophobia	ergophobia	hypengyophobia
aerophobia	cardiophobia	erotophobia	hypnophobia
agoraphobia	cenophobia	erythrophobia	ichthyophobia
agyiophobia	chromatophobia	Francophobia	ideophobia
aichmophobia	chromophobia	gamophobia	iophobia
ailurophobia	chronophobia	gephyrophobia	Japanophobia
alcoholophobia	cibophobia	Germanophobia	kenophobia
algophobia	claustrophobia	graphophobia	keraunophobia
amathophobia	climacophobia	gymnophobia	kleptophobia
amaxophobia	clithrophobia	gynephobia	kopophobia
androphobia	cobia	hadephobia	laliophobia
anemophobia	coitophobia	hamartophobia	levophobia
Anglophobia	coprophobia	hamaxophobia	lyssophobia
anthropophobia	cremnophobia	haphephobia	maieusiophobia
apiphobia	crystallophobia	harmatophobia	maniaphobia
aquaphobia	cynophobia	harpaxophobia	mechanophobia
arachnephobia	cypridophobia	hedonophobia	melissophobia
astrapophobia	dermatophobia	heliophobia	merinthophobia
ataxiophobia	dextrophobia	helminthopho-	metallophobia
automysophobia	doraphobia	bia	meteorophobia
autophobia	dysmorpho-	hematophobia	microphobia
ballistophobia	phobia	hemophobia	molysmophobia
basiphobia	ecophobia	hierophobia	monophobia
bathophobia	electrophobia	hodophobia	mysophobia
batrachophobia	emetophobia	homilophobia	necrophobia
belonephobia	entomophobia	homophobia	Negrophobia

āle,   câre,   ădd,   ärm,   ăsk;   mē,   hĕre,   ĕnd;   īce,   ĭll;

neophobia
nomatophobia
nosophobia
nostophobia
nyctophobia
obeah
phobia
ochlophobia
odontophobia
ombrophobia
onomatophobia
ophidiophobia
osmophobia
osphresio-
  phobia
panphobia
paraliphobia
parasitophobia
pathophobia
pecattiphobia
pediculophobia
pediophobia
phagophobia
pharmacophobia
phasmophobia
phengophobia
phobia
phobophobia
phonophobia
photophobia
pnigophobia
polyphobia
ponophobia
potamophobia
proctophobia
psychophobia
pyrexiophobia
pyrophobia
rectophobia

rhabdophobia
rhypophobia
Russophobia
scopophobia
scotophobia
selaphobia
siderodromo-
  phobia
Sinophobia
sitophobia
spectrophobia
stasibasiphobia
stasiphobia
stygiophobia
taphophobia
teratophobia
thalassophobia
thanatophobia
theophobia
thermophobia
tocophobia
tonitrophobia
topophobia
toxicophobia
traumatophobia
tremophobia
trichopatho-
  phobia
trichophobia
triskaidekapho-
  bia
vaccinophobia
venereophobia
xenophobia
zelophobia
Zenobia
zoophobia

ŎB'i-net

bobbinet
robinet

ŎB'ū-lar
globular
lobular

ÔB'ur-ē
daubery

ŎB'ur-ē
bobbery
jobbery
robbery
slobbery
snobbery
stockjobbery

ŎB'ur-ing
clobbering
slobbering

ŌD'ē-al
allodial
custodial
episodial
palinodial
prosodial
threnodial

ŌD'ē-an
custodian
Herodian
prosodian
Rhodian

ŎD'el-ur
modeler
(See also

ŎD'lur.)

ÔD'ē-nes
bawdiness
gaudiness

ŌD'ē-um
odium
rhodium
sodium

ŌD'ē-us
commodious
incommodious
melodious
odious

ŎD'i-fī
codify
modify

ŎD'i-kal
codical
episcodial
methodical
monodical
nodical
periodical
prosodical
rhapsodical
spasmodical
synodical

ŎD'i-tē
commodity
incommodity
oddity

ÔD'rē-nes

---

bawdriness
tawdriness

ŎD′ū-lar
modular
nodular

ŎD′ur-ik
Roderick
Theoderic

ŎD′ur-ing
doddering
foddering

ÔF′a-gan
saprophagan
sarcophagan
theophagan
zoophagan

ŎF′a-gē
androphagi
anthropophagi
cardophagi
heterophagi
hippophagi
lithophagi
Lotophagi
sarcophagi

ŎF′a-gus
androphagous
batracho-
   phagous
esophagus
galactophagous
geophagous
hippophagous

hylophagous
lithophagous
necrophagous
ophiophagous
pantophagous
phytophagous
saprophagous
sarcophagus
theophagous
xylophagous
zoophagous

ŎF′a-jē
anthropophagy
chthonophagy
hippiphagy
ichthyophagy
pantophagy
phytophagy
theophagy
xerophagy

ŎF′a-jist
galactophagist
geophagist
hippophagist
ichthyophagist
pantophagist

ŎF′i-kal
philosophical
theosophical
trophical

ŎF′i-list
bibliophilist
Russophilist
zoophilist

ŎF′i-liz'm
bibliophilism
necrophilism
Russophilism

ŎF′il-us
acidophilus
anemophilous
Theophilus
xylophilous

ŎF′o-nē
cacophony
homophony
laryngophony
microphony
orthophony
photophony
Satanophany
tautophony
theophany

ŎF′on-us
cacophonous
homophonous
hydrophanous
hygrophanous
megalophonous
monophanous
pyrophanous

ŎF′or-us
actinophorous
adenophorous
electrophorous
galactophorous
isophorus
mastigophorous
phyllophorous

pyrophorous
zoophorous

Ô′ful-ē
awfully
lawfully
unlawfully

Ô′ful-nes
awfulness
lawfulness
unlawfulness

ÔF′ur-ing
coffering
offering
peace-offering
proffering

ŎG′am-ē
coenogamy
deuterogamy
endogamy
exogamy
misogamy
monogamy

ŎG′am-ist
deuterogamist
misogamist
monogamist
neogamist

ŎG′am-us
endogamus
exogamous
heterogamous
monogamous
phaenogamous

---

phanerogamous

ŎG′a-tiv
derogative
interrogative
prerogative

Ō′gē-is′m
bogeyism
fogeyism

ŎG′nō-mē
craniognomy
pathognomy
physiognomy

ŎG′ra-fē
anthography
anthropography
areography
astrophotography
autobiography
autography
balneography
bibliography
biogeography
biography
cacography
calcography
cardiography
cartography
cerography
chalcography
chartography
chirography
choreography
Christianography

chromatography
chromolithography
chromophotography
chromotypography
chromoxylography
chronography
cinematography
climatography
cosmography
cryptography
crystalography
dactyliography
dactylography
demography
dendrography
discography
dittography
doxography
electrocardiography
encephalography
epistolography
ethnography
filmography
galvanography
geography
glossography
glyphography
glyptography
gypsography
hagiography
haliography
haplography
heliography

heliotypography
hematography
heresiography
heterography
hierography
histography
historiography
holography
homography
horography
horologiography
hyalography
hydrography
hyetography
hymnography
hypsography
ichnography
ichthyography
iconography
ideography
isography
lexicography
lichenography
lipography
lithography
logography
macrography
mammography
mechanography
metallography
microcosmography
micrography
mimography
monography
morphography
myography
mythography
neography

neurography
nomography
nosography
numismatography
oceanography
odontography
ophiography
oreography
organography
orography
orthography
osteography
otemography
paleography
paleontography
paneiconography
pantography
perspectography
petrography
phantasmatography
pharmacography
phonography
photography
photolithography
phototypography
phycography
physiography
phythogeography
phytography
planography
plastography
pneumatography
pneumography
pornography
potamography

ōld,   ôr,   ŏdd,   oil,   fŏŏt,   out;   ūse,   ûrn,   ŭp;   THis,   thin

prosopography
psalmography
pseudography
psychography
pterography
pterylography
pyelography
pyrography
radiography
reprography
rhyparography
scenography
sciography
seismography
selenography
semeiography
siderography
sigillography
sphenography
steganography
stelography
stenography
stereography
stereotypogra-
    phy
stratography
stylography
symboleography
tacheography
technography
telephotography
thalassography
thermography
tomography
topography
toreumatogra-
    phy
typography
uranography

xerography
xylography
xylopyrography
zincography
zoogeography
zoography

ŎG′ra-fist
chirographist
lichenographist
mechano-
    graphist
metallographist
monographist
museographist
organographist
orthographist
paleographist
phonographist
photographist
psalmographist
selenographist
siderographist
sphenographist
steganographist
stenographist
topographist
uranographist
zoographist

ŎG′ra-fur
autobiographer
bibliographer
biographer
calcographer
cardiographer
cartographer
chalcographer
chartographer

chirographer
choreographer
chorographer
chronographer
cinematographer
cosmographer
cryptographer
crystallographer
dactylographer
demographer
discographer
doxographer
ethnographer
geographer
glossographer
glyphographer
glyptographer
haliographer
heresiographer
hierographer
historiographer
holographer
horologiogra-
    pher
hydrographer
hymnographer
iambographer
lexicographer
lichenographer
lithographer
logographer
minographer
monographer
mythographer
nomographer
oceanographer
orthographer
osteographer
paleographer

petrographer
phonographer
photographer
photolithogra-
    pher
phythogeogra-
    pher
pornographer
psalmographer
pterographer
pyrographer
selenographer
sphenographer
stenographer
telephotographer
thalassographer
topographer
typographer
xylographer
zincographer
zoogeographer
zoographer

OI′a-b'l
employable
enjoyable

OI′al-ē
loyally
royally

OI′al-ist
loyalist
royalist

OI′al-iz′m
loyalism
royalism

OI′al-tē

loyalty
royalty
viceroyalty

Ō'i-kal
egoical
heroical
stoical

OIN'ted-lē
disjointedly
pointedly

OIS'tur-ing
cloistering
roistering

Ō'jē-an
archaeologian
astrologian
gambogian
geologian
mythologian
neologian
philologian
theologian

ŎJ'en-ē
abiogeny
anthropogeny
biogeny
embryogeny
ethnogeny
geogeny
heterogeny
histogeny
homogeny
hymenogeny
misogyny

monogeny
odontogeny
ontogeny
osteogeny
pathogeny
philogyny
photogeny
phylogeny
progeny
protogyny
zoogeny

ŎJ'en-ist
abiogenist
biogenist
heterogenist
misogynist
monogenist
philogynist

ŎJ'en-us
endogenous
exogenous
hydrogenous
hyopgynous
lithogenous
nitrogenous
pyrogenous
thermogenous

ŎJ'i-kal
aerological
amphibiological
amphibological
analogical
anthological
anthropological
archaeological
astrological

bibliological
biological
bryological
chronological
climatological
conchological
cosmological
craniological
demagogical
demonological
deontological
dialogical
doxological
Egyptological
etiological
etymological
genealogical
geological
glossological
glottological
homological
hydrological
ichnological
ideological
illogical
lithological
logical
mazological
metalogical
meteorological
mythological
necrological
neological
neurological
nosological
odontological
organological
ornithological
orological

osteological
paleontological
pantological
paralogical
penological
perissological
petrological
philological
phraseological
phrenological
physiological
phytological
pneumatological
pomological
psychological
selenological
semeiological
Sinological
sociological
spectrological
symbological
synagogical
tautological
technicological
technological
teleological
teratological
terminological
theological
toxicological
tropological
universological
zoological
zoophytological
zymological

ŎJ'on-ē
autogony
cosmogony

ōld, ôr, ŏdd, oil, fŏŏt, out; ūse, ûrn, ûp; THis, thin

geogony
pathogony
physiogony
theogony
zoogony

ŎJ'o-nist
cosmogonist
theogonist

ŌK'a-līz
focalize
localize
vocalize

ŌK'al-iz'm
localism
vocalism

ŎK'a-tiv
locative
invocative
provocative
vocative

ŌK'en-lē
brokenly
outspokenly

ÔK'i-lē
chalkily
gawkily
pawkily

ÔK'ē-nes
chalkiness
gawkiness
pawkiness
squawkiness

talkiness

ŎK'ē-nes
cockiness
rockiness
stockiness

ŎK'ra-sē
aristocracy
arithmocracy
autocracy
cottonocracy
democracy
demonocracy
despotocracy
gerontocracy
gynecocracy
hagiocracy
hierocracy
hypocrisy
idiocrasy
logocracy
mobocracy
monocracy
neocracy
nomocracy
ochlocracy
pantisocracy
pedantocracy
plantocracy
plousiocracy
plutocracy
shopocracy
slavocracy
snobocracy
stratocracy
theocracy
theocrasy
timocracy

ŎK'ra-tiz'm
democratism
Socratism

ŎK'rō-mē
heliochromy
metallochromy
monochromy
stereochromy

ŎK'ron-us
isochronous
tautochronous

ŎK'si-kal
orthodoxical
paradoxical
toxical

ŎK'tor-ship
doctorship
proctorship

ŎK'ū-lar
binocular
jocular
locular
monocular
ocular
vocular

ŎK'ur-ē
crockery
mockery
rockery

ŌL'a-b'l
consolable
controllable

rollable
tollable

ÔL'a-b'l
enthrallable
recallable

ŌL'a-rē
bolary
cajolery
polary
solary
volary

ŌL'ar-īz
polarize
solarize

ŎL'a-trē
anthropolatry
astrolatry
bibliolatry
cosmolatry
demonolatry
geolatry
gyneolatry
heliolatry
hierolatry
ichthyolatry
idiolatry
idolatry
litholatry
lordolatry
Mariolatry
necrolatry
ophiolatry
physiolatry
pyrolatry
symbolatry

āle, câre, ădd, ärm, ăsk; mē, hĕre, ĕnd; īce, ĭll;

thaumatolatry
topolatry
zoolatry

ŎL′a-trus
idolatrous
symbolatrous

ŎL′a-tur
bibliolater
heliolater
iconolater
idolater
Mariolater
pyrolater

Ō′lē-a
Aetolia
magnolia
melancholia
Mongolia

Ō′lē-an
Aeolian
capitolian
Creolean
melancholian
metabolian
Mongolian
Napoleon
Pactolian

ŎL′ē-āt
foliate
infoliate
spoliate

Ō′lē-est
holiest

lowliest

Ō′lē-nes
holiness
lowliness
shoaliness
unholiness

Ō′lē-ō
folio
olio
portfolio
Sapolio

ŌL′ē-um
linoleum
petroleum
scholium
trifolium

Ō′lē-ur
Grolier
holier
lowlier
olier
unholier

ŌL′ful-nes
dolefulness
soulfulness

ŎL′id-lē
solidly
squalidly
stolidly

ŎL′id-nes
solidness
squalidness

stolidness

ŎL′i-fī
idolify
mollify
qualify

ŎL′i-fīd
mollified
qualified
unqualified

ŎL′i-kal
apostolical
bibliopolical
catholical
diabolical
hyperbolical
parabolical
symbolical

ŎL′ik-som
frolicsome
rollicksome

ŎL′ish-ing
abolishing
demolishing
polishing

ŎL′ish-ur
abolisher
demolisher
polisher

ŎL′i-tē
equality
frivolity
inequality

interpolity
isopolity
jollity
polity
quality

ŎL′i-vur
Oliver
Tolliver

ŎL′o-gus
heterologous
homologous
isologous
tautologous

ŎL′ō-ing
following
holloing
hollowing
swallowing
wallowing

ŎL′ō-jē
acarology
acology
actinology
adenochirapsol-
    ogy
aerology
aesthiology
agathology
agmatology
agriology
agrobiology
agrology
agrostology
alethiology
algology

amphibiology
amphibology
anemology
anesthesiology
angelology
anthology
anthropology
aphnology
apology
arachnology
archaeology
archology
areology
aretology
aristology
arteriology
asthenology
astrogeology
astrology
astrometeorol-
ogy
astrotheology
atheology
atomology
audiology
autecology
axiology
bacteriology
balneology
barology
battology
bibliology
biocenology
biology
botanology
bromatology
brontology
bryology
bugology

cacology
campanology
carcinology
cardiology
carpology
cephalology
cetology
chartology
chorology
Christology
chromatology
chronology
chrysology
climatology
conchology
conchyliology
coprology
cosmology
craniology
criminology
cryobiology
cryptology
ctetology
cynology
cytology
dactyliology
dactylology
deltiology
demonology
dendrochronol-
ogy
dendrology
deontology
dermatology
desmology
diabology
diabolology
dialectology
dicaeology

dittology
dosology
doxology
dysteleology
ecclesiology
eccrinology
ecology
edaphology
Egyptology
electrobiology
electrology
electrophysiol-
ogy
embryology
emetology
emmonology
endemiology
endocrinology
enigmatology
enteradenology
enterology
entomology
entozoology
environmentol-
ogy
enzymology
epidemiology
epistemology
eschatology
esthematology
esthesiology
esthesiophysi-
ology
ethnology
ethology
etiology
etymology
euchology
exobiology

exocrinology
filicology
fossilology
fungology
galvanology
gastroenterology
gastrology
gemology
genesiology
genology
geochronology
geology
geomorphology
geratology
gerontology
gigantology
glaciology
glossology
glottology
gnomology
gnomonology
graphology
gynecology
gypsology
hagiology
hamartiology
haplology
helminthology
hematology
heresiology
herpetology
heterology
hierology
hippology
histology
historiology
homology
horology
hydrology

hyetology
hygiology
hygrology
hylology
hymenology
hymnology
hypnology
hysterology
iatrology
ichnolithnology
ichnology
ichorology
ichthyology
iconology
ideology
immunology
insectology
kinology
koniology
laryngology
leptology
lexicology
lichenology
limnology
lithology
liturgiology
macrology
malacology
mantology
Mariology
martyrology
mastology
mazology
melittology
membranology
menology
metamorphol-
ogy
metapsychology

meteorology
methodology
metrology
miasmology
microbiology
microclimatol-
ogy
microgeology
micrology
micropaleon-
tology
misology
monadology
monology
morphology
muscology
museology
musicology
mycology
myology
myrmecology
mythology
naology
necrology
neology
neontology
neos-sology
nephology
nephrology
neurology
neuropathology
neurypnology
nomology
noology
nosology
numerology
numismatology
oceanology
odontology

oenology
olfactology
ology
ombrology
oncology
oneirology
onology
onomatology
ontology
oology
ophiology
ophthalmology
orchidology
organology
orismology
ornithichnology
ornithology
orology
orthology
oryctology
osmonosology
osteology
otology
otolaryngology
ovology
paleanthropol-
ogy
paleoethnology
paleogeology
paleology
paleontology
paleophytology
paleopsychology
paleozoology
paletiology
palynology
pantheology
pantology
papyrology

paradoxology
parapsychology
parasitology
parisology
paroemiology
paromology
parthenology
pathology
patrology
patronomatology
pedology
pelology
penology
periodology
perissology
pestology
petrology
pharmacology
pharology
pharyngology
phenology
phenomenology
philology
phlebology
phonology
photology
phraseology
phrenology
phycology
physiology
phytolithology
phytology
phytopathology
phytopathology
phytophysiology
phytosociology
pistology
planktology
plutology

ŏld, ôr, ŏdd, oil, fŏŏt, out; ūse, ûrn, ŭp; THis, thin

pneumatology
pneumology
podology
pogonology
pomology
ponerology
posology
potamology
praxiology
primatology
proctology
protophytology
protozoology
psephology
pseudology
psilology
psychobiology
psychology
psychonosology
psychopathol-
ogy
psychotechnol-
ogy
pteridology
punnology
pyretology
pyritology
pyrology
quinology
radiobiology
radiology
rheology
rheumatology
rhinology
roentgenology
runology
sarcolory
scatology
scientology

seismology
selenology
semasiology
sematology
semeiology
semiology
serology
sexology
sinology
sitology
skeletology
sociobiology
sociology
somatology
sophiology
soteriology
Sovietology
spasmology
speciology
spectrology
speleology
spermatology
spermology
splanchnology
splenology
spongology
statistology
stoichiology
stomatology
stromatology
symbology
symptomatol-
ogy
synchronology
syndesmology
synecology
syphilology
systematology
tautology

taxology
technology
teleology
teratology
terminology
termonology
testaceology
thanatology
thaumatology
theology
thereology
thermology
therology
thremmatology
threpsology
tidology
tocology
tonology
topology
toreumatology
toxicology
trichology
trophology
tropology
typhlology
typology
typtology
universology
uranology
urinology
urology
uronology
venereology
virology
volcanology
vulcanology
xylology
zoology
zoophytology

zymology

ŎL'ō-jist
acarologist
aerologist
agriologist
agrobiologist
agrologist
agrostologist
anesthesiologist
anthropologist
apologist
archaeologist
Assyriologist
astrogeologist
audiologist
autecologist
axiologist
bacteriologist
battologist
biologist
campanologist
carcinologist
cardiologist
chronologist
conchologist
cosmologist
craniologist
criminologist
crustaceologist
cryobiologist
cynologist
cytologist
deltiologist
demonologist
dendrochronol-
ogist
dendrologist
deontologist

---

dermatologist
diabologist
ecclesiologist
ecologist
Egyptologist
electrobiologist
embryologist
entomologist
environmentol-
ogist
enzymologist
ethnologist
ethologist
etymologist
exobiologist
galvanologist
gastroenterolo-
gist
gemmologist
geochronologist
geologist
geomorpholo-
gist
gerontologist
glaciologist
glossologist
glottologist
graphologist
gynecologist
gypsologist
hagiologist
helminthologist
hematologist
heresiologist
herpetologist
hierologist
histologist
horologist
hydrologist

hymnologist
hypnologist
ichthyologist
ideologist
immunologist
lexicologist
limnologist
lithologist
mantologist
Mariologist
martyrologist
mazologist
melittologist
metapsycholo-
gist
meteorologist
microbiologist
microclimatol-
ogist
micropaleon-
tologist
monologist
morphologist
museologist
musicologist
mycologist
myologist
myrmecologist
mythologist
necrologist
neologist
neontologist
neurologist
noologist
nosologist
numerologist
numismatolo-
gist
oenologist

oncologist
oneirologist
onomatologist
ontologist
oologist
ophiologist
ophthalomolo-
gist
orchidologist
ornithologist
orologist
oryctologist
osteologist
otolaryngologist
paleanthropol-
ogist
paleoethnolo-
gist
paleologist
paleontologist
paletiologist
pantheologist
pantologist
papyrologist
parapsycholo-
gist
paroemiologist
pathologist
patrologist
pedologist
penologist
petrologist
pharmacologist
phenologist
philologist
phonologist
photologist
phraseologist
phrenologist

physiologist
phytolithologist
phytologist
phytopathologist
pneumatologist
pomologist
primatologist
proctologist
protozoologist
pseudologist
psychobiologist
psychologist
psychopatholo-
gist
pteridologist
pyrologist
quinologist
radiobiologist
radiologist
rheologist
rheumatologist
rhinologist
roentgenologist
runologist
saintologist
sarcologist
scientologist
seismologist
semasiologist
serologist
sexologist
Sinologist
sociobiologist
sociologist
Sovietologist
speleologist
stomatologist
symbologist
synecologist

ōld, · ôr, ŏdd, oil, f͝o͝ot, out; ūse, ûrn, ŭp; THis, thin

syphilologist
tautologist
technologist
teleologist
teratologist
theologist
thereologist
therologist
toxicologist
trichologist
typologist
universologist
urinologist
venereologist
virologist
vulcanologist
zoologist
zymologist
(See also
ŎL'ō-jē;
change -y to
-ist where
appropriate.)

ŎL'ō-jīz
apologize
astrologize
battologize
doxologize
entomologize
etymologize
geologize
mythologize
neologize
philologize
sociologize
tautologize
theologize
zoologize

ŎL'o-jur
acknowledger
astrologer
botanologer
etymologer
geologer
horologer
mythologer
osteologer
philologer
phonologer
phrenologer
physiologer
sockdolager
theologer

ŎL'ō-ur
follower
hollower
swallower
wallower

ÔL'tē-est
faultiest
saltiest

ÔL'tē-nes
faultiness
maltiness
saltiness

ÔL'tur-ing
altering
faltering
paltering
unaltering
unfaltering

ÔL'tur-ur

alterer
falterer
palterer

ŎL'ū-b'l
insoluble
soluble
voluble

ŎL'ū-tiv
solutive
supervolutive

ŎL'va-b'l
absolvable
dissolvable
indissolvable
insolvable
resolvable
solvable

ŎL'ven-sē
insolvency
revolvency
solvency

ŎM'ak-ē
alectryomachy
gigantomachy
iconomachy
logomachy
monomachy
psychomachy
sciomachy
theomachy

ŎM'ath-ē
chrestomathy
philomathy

Ō'ma-tiz'm
achromatism
chromatism
diplomatism

ŎM'en-a
antilegomena
paralipomena
phenomena
prolegomena

ŎM'en-on
phenomenon
prolegomenon

ŎM'e-trē
allometry
anemometry
anthropomome-
  try
barometry
biometry
chronometry
colometry
craniometry
dynamometry
eudiometry
galvanometry
gasometry
geometry
goniometry
helicometry
horometry
hydrometry
hygrometry
hypsometry
iodometry
Mahometry
micrometry

āle,   câre,   ădd,   ärm,   ăsk;   mē,   hĕre,   ĕnd;   īce,   ĭll;

morphometry
odometry
optometry
orthometry
osteometry
ozonometry
pathometry
photometry
planometry
pneumometry
polygonometry
psychometry
pyrometry
rheometry
saccharometry
seismometry
sociometry
stereometry
stichometry
stoichiometry
tachometry
trigonometry
uranometry

ŎM′e-tur

absorptiometer
accelerometer
actinometer
aerometer
alcoholometer
algometer
altometer
anemometer
areometer
arithmometer
astrometer
atmometer
audiometer
barometer

bathometer
biometer
bolometer
cardiometer
cephalometer
chartometer
chromatometer
chromometer
chronometer
climatometer
clinometer
coulometer
craniometer
cryometer
cyclometer
cyrtometer
declinometer
dendrometer
diaphanometer
drosometer
dynamometer
echometer
electrometer
endosmometer
ergometer
eudiometer
fluorometer
fluviometer
galvanometer
gasometer
geometer
geothermometer
goniometer
graphometer
haptometer
hectometer
heliometer
horometer
hydrometer

hygrometer
hypsometer
inclinometer
interferometer
kilometer
lactometer
logometer
macrometer
magnetometer
manometer
micrometer
micronometer
monometer
nauropometer
nitrometer
odometer
oleometer
olfactometer
ombrometer
oncometer
oometer
opisometer
optometer
orometer
oscillometer
osmometer
ozonometer
pantometer
passometer
pedometer
phonometer
photometer
piezometer
planometer
platometer
pluviometer
pneumatometer
potentiometer
psychometer

psychrometer
pulmometer
pulsometer
pycrometer
pyrometer
radiometer
refractometer
respirometer
rheometer
saccharometer
salinometer
sclerometer
seismometer
sensitometer
sonometer
spectrometer
speedometer
spherometer
sphygmo-
     manometer
sphygmometer
spirometer
stactometer
stalagmometer
stereometer
stethometer
strabismometer
stratometer
tachometer
tannometer
tellurometer
tensiometer
thalassometer
thermometer
tonometer
tribometer
trigonometer
trochometer
tromometer

tropometer
udometer
variometer
vibrometer
vinometer
viscometer
volumenometer
volumeter
zymometer

ŎM′ik-al
anatomical
agronomical
astronomical
atomical
comical
coxcombical
domical
economical
iconomachal
tragicomical
zootomical

ŎM′in-al
abdominal
cognominal
nominal
prenominal
surnominal

ŎM′in-ans
dominance
predominance
prominence

ŎM′in-ant
dominant
predominant

prominent
subdominant
superdominant

ŎM′i-nāt
abominate
agnominate
comminate
denominate
dominate
nominate
ominate
predominate
prenominate

ŎM′in-ē
Chickahominy
dominie
hominy

ŎM′in-us
abdominous
dominous
ominous
prolegomenous

ŎM′ur-us
glomerous
isomerous

ŎN′a-b′l
loanable
tonable
unatonable

ŎN′dur-ing
pondering
squandering
unwandering
wandering

ŎN′dur-ur
ponderer
squanderer
wanderer

Ō′nē-a
Adonia
ammonia
Ansonia
Antonia
aphonia
begonia
bryonia
Donia
Fredonia
Ionia
Laconia
Latonia
Patagonia
pneumonia
Slavonia
Sonia
Sophronia
Usonia
valonia

Ō′nē-ak
demoniac
simoniac

Ō′nē-al
baronial
ceremonial
colonial
demonial
intercolonial
matrimonial
monial
oxygonial

patrimonial
sanctimonial
testimonial

Ō′nē-an
Aberdonian
Amazonian
Ammonian
Aonian
Ausonion
Babylonian
Baconian
bezonian
Caledonian
Cameronian
Catonian
Chelonian
Chthonian
Ciceronian
colophonian
Cottonian
Daltonian
demonian
Devonian
Draconian
Etonian
Favonian
Gorgonean
Grandisonian
halcyonian
Heliconian
Ionian
Johnsonian
Laconian
Lapponian
Livonian
Macedonian
Miltonian
Myrmidonian

Neronian
Newtonian
Oxonian
Patagonian
Plutonian
Pyrrhonian
Sardonian
Serbonian
Simonian
Slavonian
Thessalonian
Usonian

ÔN′ē-est
brawniest
tawniest

ŎN′el-ē
Connolly
Donnelly

Ō′nē-um
harmonium
pandemonium
pelargonium
stramonium
zirconium

Ō′nē-us
acrimonious
alimonious
Antonius
ceremonious
erroneous
euphonious
felonious
harmonious
inharmonious
matrimonious

parsimonious
querimonious
sanctimonious
simonious
symphonious
Trebonius
ultroneous

ŎN′i-fī
personify
saponify

ŎN′i-ka
harmonica
Monica
veronica

ŎN′i-kal
acronycal
antichronical
antiphonical
architectonical
Babylonical
canonical
chronicle
conical
diaphonical
euphonical
geophonical
harmonical
iconical
ironical
Sorbonical
synchronical
tautophonical
thrasonical
tonical
uncanonical

ŎN′i-kon
chronicon
harmonicon

ŎN′i-mē
homonymy
metonymy
paronymy
polyonymy
synonymy

ŎN′i-mus
anonymous
autonomous
eponymous
heteronymous
homonymous
paronymous
polyonymous
pseudonymous
synonymous

ŎN′ish-ing
admonishing
astonishing
monishing

ŎN′ish-ment
admonishment
astonishment
premonishment

ŎN′i-siz′m
histrionicism
Taconicism
Teutonicism

ŎN′ō-graf
chronograph

monograph

ŎN′ō-me
agronomy
astronomy
autonomy
dactylonomy
Deuteronomy
economy
gastronomy
heteronomy
isonomy
morphonomy
taxonomy

ŎN′ō-mist
agronomist
autonomist
economist
eponymist
gastronomist
synonymist

ŎN′ō-mīz
astronomize
economize
gastronomize

ŎN′ō-mur
astronomer
gastronomer

ŎOD′ē-nes
woodiness

ŎOK′ur-ē
bookery
cookery
rookery

Ō′ō-līt
oolite
zoolite

ŎŎM′an-lē
womanly

ŎP′ath-ē
allopathy
enantiopathy
heteropathy
homoeopathy
hydropathy
ideopathy
isopathy
neuropathy
psychopathy
somnopathy
theopathy

ŎP′ath-ist
allopathist
homeopathist
hydropathist
hylopathist
osteopathist
somnopathist

Ō′pē-a
Ethiopia
myopia
presbyopia
Utopia

**Ō′pē-an,
Ō′pe-an**
Aesopian
Esopian
Ethiopian

Fallopian
Utopian

ŌP′ē-nes
dopiness
ropiness
slopiness
soapiness

ŎP′ē-nes
choppiness
sloppiness
soppiness

ŎP′i-kal
allotropical
metoposcopi-
  cal
microscopical
misanthropical
subtropical
topical
tropical

ŌP′ish-nes
dopishness
mopishness
popishness

ŎP′ō-lis
acropolis
cosmopolis
Heliopolis
megalopolis
metropolis
necropolis

ŎP′ō-list
bibliopolist

monopolist
pharmacopolist

ŎP′ō-līt
cosmopolite
metropolite

ŎP′si-kal
dropsical
mopsical
Popsicle

ŎP′ti-kal
autoptical
optical

ŎP′tur-us
lepidopterous
macropterous
orthopterous

ŎP′ū-lāt
copulate
populate

ŌP′ur-ē
dopery
popery
ropery

ŎP′ur-ē
coppery
foppery

ŌR′a-b'l
adorable
deplorable
explorable
restorable

ŌR′a-tiv
explorative
restorative

ÔR′dē-al
cordial
exordial
primordial

**ÔR′dē-on,
ÔR′dē-an**
accordion
Gordian

ÔR′di-nāt
coordinate
foreordinate
insubordinate
ordinate
subordinate

ÔR′dur-ing
bordering
ordering

Ō′rē-a
aporia
Astoria
Castoria
dysphoria
euphoria
Gloria
Honoria
infusoria
littoria
Peoria
phantasmagoria
Pretoria
scoria
victoria

āle,   câre,   ădd,   ärm,   ăsk;   mē,   hĕre,   ĕnd;   īce,   ĭll;

Ō′rē-al
accessorial
accusatorial
adaptorial
admonitorial
amatorial
ambassadorial
ancestorial
arboreal
armorial
assertorial
auctorial
auditorial
authorial
boreal
cantorial
censorial
clamatorial
commentatorial
compromisso-
  rial
compurgatorial
consistorial
conspiratorial
corporeal
correal
curatorial
cursorial
dedicatorial
dictatorial
directorial
disquisitorial
doctorial
editorial
electorial
emporial
enchorial
equatoreal
Escorial

escritorial
executorial
expurgatorial
exterritorial
extraterritorial
factorial
fossorial
gladiatorial
grallatorial
gressorial
gubernatorial
historial
immemorial
imperatorial
improvisatorial
incorporeal
infusorial
inquisitorial
insessorial
intercessorial
inventorial
legislatorial
manorial
marmoreal
mediatorial
memorial
mentorial
monitorial
motorial
multifactorial
noctatorial
observatorial
oratorial
oriel
phantasmago-
  rial
phosphoreal
pictorial
piscatorial

praetorial
preceptorial
prefatorial
prefectorial
proctorial
procuratorial
professorial
proprietorial
protectorial
purgatorial
raptorial
rasorial
rectorial
repertorial
reportorial
reptatorial
responsorial
risorial
rosorial
sartorial
scansorial
scriptorial
sectorial
seigniorial
seignorial
senatorial
sensorial
spectatorial
speculatorial
sponsorial
subboreal
suctorial
territorial
textorial
tinctorial
tonsorial
tutorial
uxorial
vectorial

victorial
visitatorial
(See also Ō′rē-
  ol, ÔR′ē-ol.)

Ō′rē-an
amatorian
Bosphorian
censorian
consistorian
dictatorian
Dorian
gladiatorian
Gregorian
Hectorean
historian
hyperborean
marmorean
mid-Victorian
Nestorian
oratorian
praetorian
purgatorian
salutatorian
senatorian
stentorian
valedictorian
Victorian

Ō′rē-āt
excoriate
professoriate

ÔR′ē-at
aureat
baccalaureate
laureate
poet laureate

ŌR'ē-nes
desultoriness
dilatoriness
goriness
hoariness
peremptoriness

Ō'rē-ol
gloriole
gloryhole
oriole

ÔR'ē-ol
aureole
laureole

Ō'rē-um
aspersorium
auditorium
ciborium
corium
crematorium
digitorium
emporium
fumatorium
haustorium
inclinatorium
moratorium
praetorium
prospectorium
sanitorium
scriptorium
sensorium
sudatorium
suspensorium
thorium
triforium

Ō'rē-us

amatorious
arboreous
censorious
circulatorious
desultorious
expiatorious
expurgatorious
glorious
hippicanorious
inglorious
inquisitorious
laborious
lusorious
meritorious
notorious
oratorious
purgatorious
raptorious
saltatorious
scorious
senatorious
stentorious
stertorious
suctorious
uproarious
ustorious
uxorious
vainglorious
victorious

ÔR'gon-īz,
ÔR'gan-īz
gorgonize
organize

ŎR'id-lē
floridly
horridly
torridly

Ō'ri-fī
glorify
scorify

ŎR'i-fī
historify
horrify
torrefy

ŎR'i-kal
allegorical
categorical
coracle
historical
metaphorical
oracle
oratorical
pictorical
rhetorical
tautegorical

ŎR'i-tē
anteriority
authority
deteriority
exteriority
inferiority
interiority
juniority
majority
meliority
minority
posteriority
priority
seniority
sorority
superiority

ÔR'ma-tiv

afformative
dormitive
formative
informative
reformative
transformative

ÔR'mi-tē
abnormity
conformity
deformity
enormity
inconformity
multiformity
noncomformity
uniformity

ŎR'ō-ing
borrowing
sorrowing

ŎR'ō-ur
borrower
sorrower

ŌRS'a-b'l,
ŌRS'i-b'l
divorceable
enforceable
forcible

ÔR'ti-fī
fortify
mortify

ÔRT'i-kal
cortical
vortical

āle, câre, ădd, ärm, ăsk; mē, hĕre, ĕnd; īce, ĭll;

ÔRT′ē-nes
swartiness
wartiness

ÔRT′lē-nes
courtliness
portliness
uncourtliness

ÔR′tu-nat
fortunate
importunate

Ō′rus-lē
decorously
porously
sonorously

ÔR′yus-lē
gloriously
ingloriously
laboriously
meritoriously
notoriously
stentoriously
uproariously
uxoriously
vaingloriously
victoriously

ŎS′ē-nes
drossiness
glossiness
mossiness

ŎS′fôr-us
Bosphorus
phosphorus

Ō′shē-an
Boeotian
Nicotian

Ō′shun-al
devotional
emotional
notional

Ō′shus-nus
atrociousness
ferociousness
precociousness

ŎS′i-nāt
patrocinate
ratiocinate

ÔS′i-tē
paucity
raucity

ŎS′i-tē
actuosity
anfractuosity
angulosity
animosity
anonymosity
aquosity
atrocity
caliginosity
callosity
carnosity
curiosity
docity
dubiosity
ebriosity
fabulosity
ferocity

foliosity
fuliginosity
fumosity
fungosity
furiosity
gemmosity
generosity
gibbosity
glandulosity
glebosity
globosity
glutinosity
grandiosity
gulosity
gummosity
hideosity
impecuniosity
impetuosity
ingeniosity
inunctuosity
libidinosity
litigiosity
lugubriosity
luminosity
monstrosity
muscosity
musculosity
nebulosity
negotiosity
nervosity
nodosity
oleosity
otiosity
pilosity
plumosity
pomposity
ponderosity
porosity
preciosity

precocity
pretiosity
reciprocity
religiosity
ridiculosity
rimosity
rugosity
sabulosity
saporosity
scirrhosity
scrupulosity
sensuosity
serosity
sinuosity
speciosity
spicosity
spinosity
tenebrosity
torosity
tortuosity
tuberosity
tumulosity
unctuosity
varicosity
velocity
verbosity
viciosity
villosity
vinosity
virtuosity
viscosity
vitiosity
vociferosity

Ō′siv-nes
corrosiveness
explosiveness

ŎS′kō-pē

ōld, ôr, ŏdd, oil, fŏŏt, out; ūse, ûrn, ŭp; THis, thin

autoscopy
bioscopy
colonoscopy
cranioscopy
cryoscopy
dactyloscopy
deuteroscopy
endoscopy
fluoroscopy
gastroscopy
geloscopy
geoscopy
hieroscopy
horoscopy
meteoroscopy
metoposcopy
microscopy
necroscopy
omoplatoscopy
oneiroscopy
ophthal-
  moscopy
organoscopy
ornithoscopy
proctoscopy
retinoscopy
rhinoscopy
sigmoidoscopy
spectroscopy
stereoscopy
stethoscopy
uranoscopy
uroscopy

ŎS′kō-pist
endoscopist
fluoroscopist
gastroscopist
metoposcopist

microscopist
oneiroscopist
opthalmos-
  copist
ornithoscopist
proctoscopist
sigmoidoscopist
spectroscopist
stereoscopist
stethoscopist
uroscopist

ŎS′of-ē
gymnosophy
philosophy
psilosophy
theosophy

ŎS′o-fist
chirosophist
deipnosophist
gymnosophist
philosophist
theosophist

ŎS′o-fīz
philosophize
theosophize

ŎS′o-fur
philosopher
psilosopher
theosopher

Ō′ta-b'l
floatable
notable
potable
quotable
votable

Ō′tal-iz'm
sacerdotalism
teetotalism

ŎT′an-ē
botany
botonee
cottony
monotony

Ō′ta-rē
notary
rotary
votary

Ō′ta-tiv
connotative
denotative
rotative

ŌT′ed-lē
bloatedly
devotedly
notedly

ÔT′ē-est
haughtiest
naughtiest

ÔT′ē-ness
haughtiness
naughtiness

ŎT′ē-nes
dottiness
knottiness
spottiness

ÔT′ē-ur

haughtier
naughtier

ŎT′i-kal
anecdotical
bigotical
despotical
erotical
exotical
zealotical

ÔT′i-lē
haughtily
naughtily

ŎT′om-ē
apotome
autotomy
bottomy
bronchotomy
cardiotomy
colotomy
craniotomy
crystotomy
cyclotomy
dermotomy
dichotomy
encephalotomy
episiotomy
gastrotomy
herniotomy
hysterotomy
ichthyotomy
laparotomy
laryngotomy
leucotomy
lithotomy
lobotomy

microtomy
necrotomy
nephrotomy
neurotomy
osteotomy
ovariotomy
phlebotomy
phytotomy
pogonotomy
sclerotomy
scotomy
stereotomy
tenotomy
thoracotomy
tonsillotomy
tracheotomy
trichotomy
varicotomy
zootomy

ŎT'o-mist
ichthyotomist
phlebotomist
phytotomist
zootomist

ÔT'ur-ē
cautery
watery

ŎT'ur-ē
lottery
pottery
tottery
trottery

ÔT'ur-ing
slaughtering
watering

ÔT'ur-ur
slaughterer
waterer

OU'a-b'l
allowable
avowable
endowable

OUD'ed-nes
cloudedness
crowdedness
overcrowded-
  ness
uncloudedness

OUD'ē-iz'm
dowdyism
rowdyism

OUD'ē-nes
cloudiness
dowdiness
rowdiness

OUL'ur-ē
owlery
prowlery

OUND'a-b'l
compoundable
soundable
unsoundable

OUND'ed-nes
astoundedness
confoundedness
dumfoundedness
unboundedness

ungroundedness

OUND'les-lē
boundlessly
groundlessly
soundlessly

OUND'les-nes
boundlessness
groundlessness
soundlessness

OUNT'a-b'l
accountable
countable
discountable
insurmountable
mountable
surmountable
unaccountable

OUT'ē-nes
doughtiness
droughtiness
goutiness

OU'ur-ē
bowery
dowery
flowery
glowery
lowery
showery
towery

OU'ur-ing
cowering
dowering
empowering

flowering
glowering
lowering
overpowering
overtowering
showering
towering
(See also
OUR'ing.)

OUZ'ē-nes
drowsiness
frowziness

Ō'vē-al
jovial
synovial

Ō'vē-an
Cracovian
Jovian

ŎV'el-ing
grovelling
hovelling

Ō'zē-est
coziest
nosiest
prosiest
rosiest

Ō'zē-nes
coziness
doziness
nosiness
prosiness
rosiness

ōld, ôr, ŏdd, oil, fŏŏt, out; ūse, ûrn, ŭp; THis, thin

Ō′zē-ur	Ō′zhē-a,	O′zhē-an,	prosily
cozier	Ō′zē-a	Ō′zē-an	rosily
crosier	ambrosia	ambrosian	
Dozier	symposia	(See also	Ō′zur-ē
hosier		Ō′zhun.)	composery
nosier	Ō′zhē-al,		dozery
osier	Ō′zē-al	Ō′zi-lē	rosary
prosier	ambrosial	cozily	
rosier	roseal	nosily	

U

For a discussion of words included under the accented vowels following, see the beginning of U rhymes in Section I.

Ū′a-b'l	Ū′brē-us	tuberous	ŪD′i-b'l
doable	insalubrious		eludible
pursuable	lugubrious	ŪD′a-b'l	includible
renewable	salubrious	alludable	
reviewable		deludable	ŬD′i-lē
suable	Ū′bi-kal	includable	bloodily
subduable	cubical	protrudable	muddily
	cherubical		ruddily
Ū′bē-an		ŪD′ē-nes	
Danubian	Ū′bi-lāt	moodiness	Ū′di-nal
Nubian	enubilate		aptitudinal
rubian	jubilate	ŬD′ē-nes	attitudinal
	nubilate	bloodiness	consuetudinal
ŬB′ē-nes	obnubilate	muddiness	longitudinal
chubbiness	*volubilate*	ruddiness	testudinal
grubbiness			
scrubbiness	Ū′bri-kāt	ŪD′en-sē	Ū′di-nīz
shrubbiness	lubricate	concludency	attitudinize
stubbiness	rubricate	pudency	platitudinize
		recrudency	
			Ū′di-nus
Ū′bē-us	Ū′bur-us	ŪD′dē-us	fortitudinous
dubious	protuberous	preludious	latitudinous
rubious	suberous	studious	multitudinous

āle, câre, ădd, ärm, ăsk; mē, hĕre, ĕnd; īce, ĭll;

paludinous
platitudinous
solicitudinous
vicissitudinous

Ū′di-tē
crudity
nudity
rudity

ŬD′ur-ē
duddery
shuddery
studdery

Ū′el-ing
bejeweling
duelling
fueling
grueling

Ū′el-ur
crueler
dueler
fueler
jeweler

Ū′ē-nes
dewiness
glueyness

ŬF′ē-nes
fluffiness
huffiness
puffiness
stuffiness

ŬG′ur-ē
pugaree

snuggery
thuggery

Ū′in-us
pruinous
ruinous

Ū′ish-nes
Jewishness
shrewishness

Ū′i-tē
acuity
ambiguity
annuity
assiduity
circuity
conspicuity
contiguity
continuity
discontinuity
exiguity
fatuity
gratuity
ingenuity
innocuity
perpetuity
perspicuity
promiscuity
strenuity
suety
superfluity
tenuity
vacuity

Ū′i-tus
circuitous
fatuitous
fortuitous

gratuitous
pituitous

ŪJ′i-nus
aeruginous
ferruginous
lanuginous
salsuginous

ŬK′i-lē
luckily
pluckily

ŬK′shun-al
constructional
fluxional
inductional
instructional

ŬK′shun-ist
constructionist
deconstruction-
  ist
destructionist
fluxionist
reconstruction-
  ist

ŬK′ti-b'l
conductible
destructible
indestructible
instructible

ŬK′tiv-lē
constructively
destructively
instructively
productively

ŬK′tiv-nes
constructive-
  ness
destructiveness
instructiveness
productiveness

ŬK′to-rē
conductory
introductory
reproductory

Ū′kū-lent
luculent
muculent

ŬK′ur-ing
puckering
succoring

Ū′lē-an
cerulean
herculean
Julian

ŬL′ish-nes
foolishness
mulishness

Ū′li-tē
credulity
garrulity
incredulity
sedulity

ŬL′kē-nes
bulkiness
sulkiness

ōld, ôr, ŏdd, oil, fŏŏt, out; ūse, ûrn, ŭp; THis, thin

ŬL'mi-nant
culminant
fulminant

ŬL'mi-nāt
culminate
fulminate

ŬL'siv-lē
convulsively
impulsively
repulsively

ŬL'siv-nes
compulsiveness
convulsiveness
impulsiveness
repulsiveness
revulsiveness

ŬL'tur-ē
adultery
consultary

ŬL'tūr-is'm
agriculturism
vulturism
(See also
ŬL'tūr; drop
-e and add
-ism where
appropriate.)

ŬL'ur-ē
gullery
medullary
scullery

ŬL'vur-in
culverin
pulverin

ŪM'a-b'l
assumable
consumable
presumable
resumable

Ū'man-lē
humanly

ŬM'bur-ē
slumbery
umbery

ŬM'bur-ing
cumbering
encumbering
lumbering
numbering
outnumbering
slumbering
unslumbering

ŬM'bur-ur
cumberer
encumberer
lumberer
numberer
slumberer

Ū'mi-nant
illuminant
luminant
ruminant

Ū'mi-nāt
acuminate

catechumenate
ferruminate
illuminate
luminate
ruminate

ŬM'ē-nes
gloominess
roominess
spuminess

ŬM'ing-lē
becomingly
benumbingly
hummingly
numbingly
unbecomingly

Ū'mi-nus
aluminous
bituminous
fluminous
leguminous
luminous
voluminous

ŬM'pish-nes
dumpishness
frumpishness
grumpishness
lumpishness
mumpishness

ŬMP'shus-lē
bumptiously
scrumptiously

ŬMP'tū-us
presumptuous
sumptuous

Ū'mū-lāt
accumulate
tumulate

Ū'mū-lus
altocumulus
cirrocumulus
cumulus
mammato-
cumulus
stratocumulus
tumulous

Ū'mur-al
humeral
numeral

ŬM'ur-ē
perfumery
plumery
rumory

ŬM'ur-ē
flummery
mummery
nummary
plumbery
summary
summery

Ū'mur-us
humerus
humorous
numerous
rumorous

ŪN'a-b'l
expugnable
tunable

āle, câre, ădd, ärm, ăsk; mē, hĕre, ĕnd; īce, ĭll;

Ū′na-rē
lunary
(See also
Ū′nur-ē.)

ŬN′di-tē
fecundity
jocundity
jucundity
moribundity
profundity
rotundity
rubicundity

ŬN′dur-ing
blundering
plundering
sundering
thundering
wondering

ŬN′dur-song
undersong
wonder song

ŬN′dur-ur
blunderer
plunderer
sunderer
thunderer
wonderer

ŬN′dur-us
blunderous
thunderous
wonderous

ŬN′dur-wurld
underworld

wonder world

ŬNG′gur-ing
hungering
mongering

ŬNGK′shun-al
conjunctional
functional

ŬNGK′ū-lar
avuncular
carbuncular
caruncular
peduncular
uncular

Ū′ni-kāt
communicate
excommunicate
tunicate

Ū′ni-form
cuniform
luniform
uniform

ŬN′i-lē
funnily
sunnily

Ū′ni-tē
community
immunity
importunity
impunity
inopportunity
intercommu-
nity
jejunity

opportunity
triunity
unity

Ū′ni-tiv
punitive
unitive

ŬNT′ed-lē
affrontedly
stuntedly
unwontedly
wontedly

ŬN′ur-ē
buffoonery
cocoonery
pantaloonery
poltroonery

ŬN′ur-ē
gunnery
nunnery

Ū′pur-āt
recuperate
vituperate

Ū′ra-b'l
assurable
curable
durable
endurable
incurable
insurable
procurable
securable

ÛR′a-b'l

conferrable
demurrable
inferable
referable
transferable

Ū′ral-ist
pluralist
ruralist

Ū′ral-is'm
pluralism
ruralism

Ū′ra-tiv
curative
depurative
indurative
maturative

ÛR′bal-ist
herbalist
verbalist

ÛR′bal-iz'm
herbalism
verbalism

ÛRB′ē-al
adverbial
proverbial
suburbial

ÛR′bū-lent
herbulent
turbulent

ÛR′di-lē
sturdily
wordily

ÛRD′ur-ur
murderer
verderer

Û′rē-a
Lemuria
Manchuria

Û′rē-al
augurial
figural
mercurial
purpureal
seigneurial

ÛR′ē-an,
Û′rē-an
centurian
Etrurian
Missourian
scripturian
Silurian

Û′rē-ans
luxuriance

Û′rē-ant
luxuriant

Û′rē-āt
infuriate
luxuriate
muriate
parturiate

Û′rē-ens
prurience

Û′rē-ent

esurient
parturient
prurient
scripturient

ÛR′ē-ist
furriest
hurriest
worriest

ÛR′ē-ing
currying
flurrying
hurrying
scurrying
worrying

ÛR′ē-ment
worriment
(See also
ĔR′ē-ment.)

ÛR′en-sē
concurrency
currency
recurrency

ÛR′et-ed
turreted
(See also
ĔR′i-ted.)

ÛR′ē-ur
currier
flurrier
furrier
hurrier
scurrier
worrier

Û′rē-us
curious
furious
incurious
injurious
luxurious
penurious
perjurious
spurious
strangurious
sulphureous
usurious

ÛR′flū-us
subterfluous
superfluous

Û′ri-fī
purify
thurify

ÛR′ish-ing
flourishing
nourishing

Û′ri-tē
demurity
immaturity
impurity
insecurity
maturity
obscurity
prematurity
purity
security

ÛR′jen-sē
assurgency
convergency

counterinsur-
    gency
detergency
divergency
emergency
insurgency
urgency
vergency

ÛR′ji-kal
chirurgical
clergical
demiurgical
energical
liturgical
surgical
thaumaturgical
theurgical

ÛR′jur-ē
chirurgery
perjury
purgery
surgery

ÛR′kū-lar
circular
furcular
tubercular

ÛR′kū-lāt
circulate
recirculate
tuberculate

ÛR′kū-lus
surculus
surculous
tuberculous

āle, câre, ădd, ärm, ăsk; mē, hĕre, ĕnd; īce, ĭll;

ÛR′lē-est
burliest
churliest
curliest
earliest
pearliest
surliest
unburliest

ÛR′lē-nes
burliness
curliness
earliness
pearliness
surliness

ÛR′lish-lē
churlishly
girlishly

ÛR′lish-nes
churlishness
girlishness

ÛR′mi-nal
germinal
terminal

ÛR′mi-nant
determinant
germinant
terminant

ÛR′mi-nāt
determinate
exterminate
germinate
indeterminate
interminate

terminate

ÛR′mi-nus
coterminous
terminus
verminous

ÛR′na-b'l
burnable
discernible
indiscernible
learnable
overturnable
returnable

ÛR′nal-ist
eternalist
journalist

ÛR′nal-īz
eternalize
externalize
journalize

ÛR′nal-iz'm
externalism
infernalism
journalism

ÛR′nē-an
Avernian
Falernian
Hibernian
Saturnian

ÛR′nish-ing
burnishing
furnishing

ÛR′nish-ur
burnisher
furnisher

ÛR′ni-tē
alternity
diuternity
eternity
fraternity
maternity
modernity
paternity
sempiternity
taciturnity

ÛR′nur-ē
fernery
turnery

ÛR′ō-gat
surrogate
(See also
ĔR′ō-gat.)

ÛR′pen-tīn
serpentine
turpentine

ÛR′sa-rē
anniversary
aspersory
bursary
controversary
cursory
nursery
precursory

ÛR′sē-al
controversial

ÛR′shē-an
Cistercian
lacertian
Persian

**ÛR′si-b'l,
ÛR′sa-b'l**
amerceable
conversable
conversible
coercible
immersible
incoercible
irreversible
reimbursable
reversible

ÛR′si-fôrm
diversiform
ursiform
versiform

ÛR′siv-nes
coerciveness
detersiveness
discursiveness
excursiveness

ĔRth′les-nes
mirthlessness
worthlessness

ÛR′ti-tūd
certitude
incertitude
inertitude

ÛR′van-sē
conservancy

---

fervency

ÛR′va-tiv
conservative
curvative
enervative
observative
preservative
reservative

ÛR′zhun-ist
excursionist
immersionist
versionist

**Ū′sē-an,
Ū′si-an**
caducean
Confucian
Rosicrucian

Ū′sed′lē
deucedly
lucidly
mucidly
pellucidly

Ū′sen-sē
lucency
tralucency
translucency

Ū′shē-al
crucial
fiducial

Ū′shun-al
circumlocu-
tional

constitutional
elocutional
evolutional
institutional
substitutional

Ū′shun-ist
circumlocution-
ist
constitutionist
elocutionist
evolutionist
resolutionist
revolutionist

Ū′shun-ur
ablutioner
executioner
resolutioner
revolutioner

Ū′si-b′l
adducible
conducible
crucible
deducible
educible
inducible
irreducible
producible
reducible
seducible
traducible

Ū′siv-nes
abusiveness
allusiveness
conclusiveness
conduciveness

delusiveness
diffusiveness
effusiveness
exclusiveness
illusiveness
inconclusive-
ness
inobtrusiveness
intrusiveness
obtrusiveness

ŬS′ki-lē
duskily
huskily
muskily

ŬS′kū-lar
bimuscular
corpuscular
crepuscular
muscular

ŬS′kū-lus
corpusculous
crepusculous
musculous

Ū′so-rē
collusory
conclusory
delusory
elusory
exclusory
extrusory
illusory
lusory
prelusory
reclusory

ŬST′ful-ē
distrustfully
lustfully
mistrustfully
trustfully

ŬST′i-b′l
adjustible
combustible
dustible
incombustible

ŬS′tē-est
crustiest
dustiest
fustiest
gustiest
lustiest
mustiest
rustiest
trustiest

ŬS′tē-nes
crustiness
dustiness
fustiness
gustiness
lustiness
mustiness
rustiness
trustiness

ŬS′trē-us
illustrious
industrious

ŬS′ti-lē
crustily
dustily

āle, câre, ădd, ärm, ăsk; mē, hĕre, ĕnd; īce, ĭll;

fustily
gustily
lustily
mustily
rustily
thrustily

ŬS'tur-ing
blustering
clustering
flustering
mustering

Ū'ta-b'l
commutable
computable
confutable
disputable
executable
immutable
imputable
incommutable
inscrutable
mootable
mutable
permutable
refutable
scrutable
suitable
transmutable

Ū'ta-tiv
commutative
confutative
disputative
imputative
putative
sputative
sternutative

Ū'tē-us
beauteous
duteous
luteous

Ūth'ful-ē
ruthfully
truthfully
youthfully

Ūth'ful-nes
truthfulness
youthfulness

Ūth'les-lē
ruthlessly
truthlessly
youthlessly

ŬTH'ur-hood
brotherhood
motherhood

ŬTH'ur-ē
brothery
mothery
smothery

ŬTH'ur-ing
brothering
mothering
smothering

ŬTH'ur-lē
brotherly
motherly
southerly
unbrotherly
unmotherly

ŬTH'ur-līk
brotherlike
motherlike

Ū'ti-fī
beautify
brutify

Ū'ti-ful
beautiful
dutiful

Ū'ti-k'l,
Ū'ti-kal
cuticle
latreutical
pharmaceutical
scorbutical
therapeutical

Ū'ti-nẽr
mutineer
scrutineer

Ū'ti-nē
mutiny
scrutiny

Ū'ti-nus
glutinous
mutinous
velutinous
scrutinous

ŬT'lur-ē
cutlery
sutlery

ŬT'on-ē

buttony
gluttony
muttony

Ū'tur-ē
freebootery
fruitery
pewtery
rootery

ŬT'ur-ing
buttering
fluttering
guttering
muttering
spluttering
sputtering
stuttering
uttering

ŬT'ur-ur
butterer
flutterer
mutterer
splutterer
sputterer
stutterer
utterer

ŪV'a-b'l
approvable
immovable
improvable
irremovable
movable
provable
removable
reprovable

ōld, ôr, ŏdd, oil, fŏŏt, out; ūse, ûrn, ŭp; THis, thin

Ū'vē-al
alluvial
antediluvial
diluvial
effluvial
exuvial
fluvial
postdiluvial
pluvial

Ū'vē-an
antediluvian

diluvian
Peruvian
postdiluvian
Vesuvian

Ū'vē-us
Jupiter Pluvius
Vesuvius

Ū'za-b'l
amusable
confusable

diffusible
excusable
fusible
inexcusable
infusible
losable
transfusible
usable

Ū'zē-an
Carthusian
(See also

Ū'zhun.)

ŬZ'ē-nes
fuzziness
muzziness
wuzziness

SOURCES

Unabridged Dictionaries
Webster's Third New International Dictionary, G & C Merriam, 1976.
The Random House Dictionary of the English Language, 2nd ed., Random House, 1987.

College-Level Dictionaries
Webster's Ninth New Collegiate Dictionary, Merriam-Webster, 1984.
The American Heritage Dictionary, 2nd college ed., Houghton-Mifflin, 1982.
Webster's New World Dictionary, 3rd college ed., Simon & Schuster, 1988.

Rhyming Dictionaries
Capricorn Rhyming Dictionary, Bessie G. Redfield, Perigee Books/Putnam 1938, 1986.
The Penguin Rhyming Dictionary, Rosalind Fergusson, Penguin Books, 1985.
Words to Rhyme With, Willard R. Espy, Facts-on-File Publications, 1986.

"New-Word" Books
The Barnhart Dictionary of New English Since 1963, Clarence L. Barnhart, Sol Steinetz, Robert K. Barnhart, Barnhart/Harper & Row, 1973.
12,000 Words, A Supplement to Webster's Third New International Dictionary, Merriam-Webster Inc., 1986.